Sunil Kumar Parameswaran

Fixed Income Securities

Sunil Kumar Parameswaran

Fixed Income Securities

Concepts and Applications

PRESS

ISBN 978-1-5474-1673-8
e-ISBN (PDF) 978-1-5474-0066-9
e-ISBN (EPUB) 978-1-5474-0068-3

Library of Congress Control Number: 2019948232

Bibliographic information published by the Deutsche Nationalbibliothek
The Deutsche Nationalbibliothek lists this publication in the Deutsche Nationalbibliografie; detailed bibliographic data are available on the Internet at http://dnb.dnb.de.

Published by Walter de Gruyter Inc., Boston/Berlin
Cover image: Freestocker/iStock/Getty Images Plus
Typesetting: VTeX UAB, Lithuania
Printing and binding: CPI books GmbH, Leck

www.degruyter.com

Advance Praise for *Fixed Income Securities*

This book is a very concise work which collects the major themes of fixed income. For example, you treat mortgages and their mathematics which are very useful, but which surprisingly aren't addressed anywhere else in an accessible way. The abundance of examples in this book makes it very useful for university professors as a base to teach fixed income and I will certainly consider adopting this as a book in my university and recommend it to others.

Prof. Yaacov Kopeliovich, University of Connecticut

Dr. Parameswaran's new book, *Fixed Income Securities: Concepts and Applications*, achieves something that is truly hard—an introduction to the world of fixed income markets that is both comprehensive and lucid. Each chapter introduces a new concept, and explains the theory through detailed examples. The underlying mathematics is demystified by working out each step explicitly. The simplicity of the exposition makes the book suitable not only for a graduate class, but also for an advanced undergraduate class. The accessibility of the book also makes it suitable for self-study.

Prof. Nikunj Kapadia, University of Massachusetts

This book provides comprehensive learning material for fixed income securities and the related markets. The author does a great job covering both the fundamental concepts and the more advanced applications of fixed income securities. The scope of the book is broad, yet it also provides the right amount of depth on each topic.

What makes this book stand out is the author's review of related key finance concepts before diving into the world of fixed income securities.

This book thus can be used as a comprehensive textbook for an undergraduate course on fixed income securities, an easy-to-absorb self-learning guide for someone who is new to fixed income securities, and a reference book for more experienced readers who are looking to refresh their knowledge on a specific topic.

Prof. Lingling Wang, University of Connecticut

https://doi.org/10.1515/9781547400669-201

Foreword

I was pleased and honored when Sunil asked me to write a foreword for his upcoming book, *Fixed Income Securities: Concepts and Applications*. Sunil and I were graduate students at Duke University's Fuqua School of Business in the mid-1980s, completing our relevant classwork and working for the same professor. While Sunil subsequently went on to complete his PhD, I left after earning my MBA, and joined Smith Breeden Associates where I worked for 30 years in the institutional fixed income asset management business primarily as a lead port- folio manager. At Smith Breeden, I started in the research department building complex models to value mortgage backed securities. After a few years, I was promoted to the portfolio management side. In that role I managed a billion dollar fixed income portfolio comprised of the same fixed income securities so well covered in this book by Sunil. Needless to say, I would have been an avid consumer of this book, if it had been made available a few years earlier. Sunil's book covers in adequate detail the theoretical intricacies and formulas that I used regularly to build models, and focuses on the tools which enabled me to manage highly complex institutional bond portfolios. Novel investment strategies can blossom from the most rudimentary concepts in finance with a bit of creativity. An example would be the S&P 500 plus portfolios I managed which garnered attention in the form of featured articles from *Money* magazine, *Fortune* magazine and other well-read periodicals. I was often asked, "What is a fixed income geek doing managing an equity product?" The simple answer is that the two product classes are not mutually exclusive. Utilizing the detailed knowledge of various debt financial instruments covered in this book, Sunil provides the tools and knowledge that professionals like me need to port or transfer our fixed income expertise over to the equity markets. An in-depth understanding of the assets and hedging tools covered in this book is the lynchpin to construct any fixed income portfolio. At Smith Breeden we built portfolios of longer duration spread assets where we had specific expertise (often Agency MBS) and then immunized or hedged the portfolio duration to near zero utilizing futures contracts or interest rate swaps. The remaining negative convexity was hedged utilizing swaptions, futures options, or dynamically hedged using futures contracts. The end result was the creation of a cash like portfolio in terms of duration and convexity risk, but which retained the asset spread (and risk) of the underlying assets which we desired. Fixed income geeks like me could now use their expertise in one market to add value to another market. This opened up a whole new market for us and generated significant marketing buzz as well. I am of the opinion that the theoretical precision, and expositional clarity of this book would have been an invaluable asset for me and my colleagues. This is just one example of how the topics covered in such great detail here can be utilized by a serious finance student or investment professional. Sunil's book covers all these topics and more in the concise and easy to locate manner of a reference book. I wish I had this book as a resource for all the relevant fixed income

https://doi.org/10.1515/9781547400669-202

formulas and Excel commands while I was building high powered fixed income tools and models. This book is comprehensive, concise, and embellished with the required expositional clarity. It has the required rigor without being too mathematically heavy to be out of reach for a reader. Current students and practitioners are lucky to have it all here.

John Sprow, Chapel Hill, NC, USA
Former Senior Portfolio Manager, Chief Risk Officer, Executive Committee,
Board of Directors at Smith Breeden Associates. Currently retired.

Preface

This book is the end result of 25 years of teaching at business schools across the globe, and about 15 years of corporate training for some of the leading information technology, and financial services companies. The feedback from my students and clients, has been extremely valuable and I am indebted to them for the inputs and constructive criticism. Nothing is more valuable for teachers and authors, than feedback, both positive as well as critical.

As a student I was deeply influenced by various books on fixed income products, in particular, the works of Frank Fabozzi. Later on in the course of my professional career, I have benefited from the books of various authors such as Kenneth Garbade, Moorad Choudhary, and Suresh Sundaresan. I owe a tremendous intellectual debt to these and other authors who have influenced me.

I have over the years made extensive use of Excel while teaching courses and programs on fixed income products. I am of the opinion that Excel facilitates the exposition, and aids the comprehension of concepts. In particular, Excel functions make the computation of complex mathematical expressions extremely easy. This book therefore illustrates various Excel functions which are essential for the study of fixed income markets. Each function, and the parameters required to be specified, is discussed in detail. Goal Seek and Solver, are two tools in Excel that facilitate computation of solutions for complex non-linear expressions. I have made extensive use of these and there is an appendix at the end of the book, which explains how to use them.

This course starts and builds from first principles. All that I expect is that the reader have a basic knowledge of finance, and an interest in fixed income markets. The first chapter is on time value of money, which is the fundamental building block for any study of finance theory. The chapter is detailed, and demonstrates the use of Excel in elaborate detail to solve problems. There is a detailed discussion of futures and forwards, options, and swaps toward the end of the book. To help the reader I have provided a comprehensive primer on derivatives. There are two reasons for this. The first is to ensure that a reader need not refer to another textbook, if he or she were to have any queries pertaining to theoretical issues on derivatives. Second, I wanted to ensure that the material on derivatives is written in my style, so that it seamlessly blends into my presentations on fixed income products.

This book should be a valuable reference for practitioners and professionals in financial markets in the English speaking world. Students in MBA programs, and possibly adventurous students in BBA programs, should also find this book to be an extremely useful resource. The book has a global focus and perspective, and hence should cater to readers across geographies.

https://doi.org/10.1515/9781547400669-203

I invite feedback and criticism from readers. Any comments are welcome and I do not consider anything to be trivial. I hope you get as much pleasure in reading the book, as I did in writing it.

Sunil Kumar Parameswaran
Director & CEO
Tarheel Consultancy Services

Acknowledgments

I wish to thank the participants who have taken this course at various stages of their MBA programs, and the executives who have been a part of my corporate training programs. Their endorsement and criticism of the material, has gone a long way in making this book acquire its final form. I also owe a deep gratitude to the academics and practitioners, whose books on fixed income markets have served as invaluable resources in facilitating my study and understanding of this subject.

I am extremely grateful to Jeff Pepper and Jaya Dalal of De Gruyter for their constant support and encouragement and for ensuring that I stuck to the submission deadlines set by them. A very special thanks to Nick Wallwork of De Gruyter. I did two books when Nick was with John Wiley in Singapore. Over the years he has given me enormous support, and his faith and confidence in me have gone a long way in motivating me to write more for a global audience. Chris Nelson, the editor, has contributed enormously to make the final product user friendly. He went through the manuscript with a tooth comb, and his incisive comments and observations have been of immense help.

I am indebted to Tom Smith, Lingling Wang, Yaacov Kopeliovich, Nikunj Kapadia, and Jocelyn Evans for their comments and thoughts. Sankarshan Basu, with whom I have taught this course on a number of occasions, has been of a lot of help, as has Shrikant Ramamurthy, off whom I have bounced a lot of ideas over the years.

Finally my mother has put up with my moods and tantrums over the past year that this book has been in progress, and I cannot thank her enough for that.

https://doi.org/10.1515/9781547400669-204

Acknowledgments

Contents

Chapter 1
A Primer on the Time Value of Money

All of us have either paid and/or received interest at some point in our lives. Those of us who have taken educational, housing, or automobile loans have paid interest to the lending institution. On the other hand, those of us who have deposited funds with a bank in the form of a savings account or a time deposit have received interest. The same holds true for people who have bought bonds or debentures.

Interest may be defined as the compensation paid by the borrower of capital to the lender, for permitting him to use his funds. An economist would define interest as the *rent* paid by the borrower of capital to the lender, to compensate him for the loss of the opportunity to use the funds when it is on loan. After all when we decide not to live in an apartment or house owned by us, we typically let it out to a tenant. The tenant will pay us a monthly rental because as long as he is occupying our property, we are deprived of an opportunity to use it ourselves. The same principle is involved when it comes to a loan of funds. The difference is that the compensation in the case of property is termed as *rent*, whereas when it comes to capital, we term it as *interest*.

Nominal and Effective Rates of Interest

The quoted rate of interest per period is called the *nominal rate of interest*. The nominal rate is usually quoted on a per annum basis. The *effective rate of interest* may be defined as the interest that a unit of currency invested at the beginning of a year would have earned by the end of the year. Quite obviously the effective rate will be equal to the quoted or nominal rate if interest is compounded once per annum. However, if the interest is compounded more frequently, then the effective rate will exceed the nominal rate of interest. The term *"effective"* connotes that compounding at the stated frequency using the quoted nominal rate, is equivalent to compounding once a year at the effective rate of interest.

Variables and Terms to Be Used and the Corresponding Symbols

$P \equiv$ amount of principal that is invested at the outset
$N \equiv$ number of periods for which the investment is being made. It may be in terms of years, or in terms of smaller intervals of time, such as a half-year or a quarter.
$r \equiv$ nominal rate of interest per annum
$i \equiv$ effective rate of interest per annum
$m \equiv$ number of times interest is compounded per annum
$P.V. \equiv$ present value of a stream of cash flows
$F.V. \equiv$ future value of a stream of cash flows

https://doi.org/10.1515/9781547400669-001

The Concept of Simple Interest

Consider the case of an investment of \$$P$ that has been made for N years. According to the principle of simple interest, the interest that will be earned every period is a constant. In other words, interest is computed every period and credited only on the original principal, and no interest is payable on any interest that has been accumulated at an intermediate stage.

If r is the quoted rate of interest per year, then an investment of \$$P$ will become dollars $P(1 + r)$ after one year. In the second year, interest will be paid only on P and not on $P(1 + r)$. Consequently the accumulated value after two years will be $P(1 + 2r)$. Extending the logic, the terminal balance will be $P(1 + rN)$. N need not be an integer: that is, investments may be made for a fraction of a year.

Example 1.1. Maureen Chen deposited $10,000 with First National Bank for a period of three years. If the deposit earns simple interest at the rate of 10% per annum, how much will she have at the end?

An investment of $10,000 will become

$$10{,}000 \times 1.10 = \$11{,}000$$

after one year. During the second year, only the original principal of $10,000 will earn interest and not the accumulated value of $11,000. Consequently the accumulated value after two years will be

$$10{,}000 \times 1.10 + 1{,}000 = \$12{,}000$$

By the same logic the terminal balance after three years will be $13,000.

$$13{,}000 = 10{,}000 \times (1 + 0.10 \times 3) \equiv P(1 + rN)$$

Example 1.2. Andrew Gordon deposited $10,000 with ABC Bank five years and six months ago, and wants to withdraw the balance now. If the bank pays 8% interest per annum on a simple interest basis, how much is he eligible to withdraw?

$$P(1 + rN) = 10{,}000 \times (1 + 0.08 \times 5.5) = \$14{,}400$$

Thus Andrew can withdraw $14,400.

The Concept of Compound Interest

Consider the case of an investment of \$$P$ that has been made for N years. Assume that the interest is compounded once per annum: that is, the quoted rate is equal to the effective rate.

According to the principle of compound interest, every time interest is earned it is automatically reinvested at the same rate for the next period. Thus, the interest earned every year will not be a constant like in the case of simple interest, but will steadily increase. In this case an original investment of $\$P$ will become $P(1+r)$ dollars after one year. The difference is that during the second year the entire amount will earn interest and consequently the balance at the end of two years will be $P(1+r)^2$. Extending the logic, the balance after N years will be $P(1+r)^N$. Once again N need not be an integer.

Example 1.3. Assume that Maureen Chen has deposited $10,000 with First National Bank for three years, and that the bank pays 10% interest per annum compounded annually. How much will she have at the end?

The investment of $10,000 will become

$$10{,}000 \times 1.10 = \$11{,}000$$

after one year. The difference in this case as opposed to the earlier example where simple interest was considered, is that the entire accumulated value of $11,000 will earn interest during the second year. Thus, the accumulated value after two years will be

$$11{,}000 \times 1.10 = \$12{,}100$$

By the same logic the balance after three years will be $13,310:

$$12{,}100 \times 1.10 = \$13{,}310 = 10{,}000 \times (1.10)^3 \equiv P(1+r)^N$$

Example 1.4. Assume that Andrew Gordon deposited $10,000 with ABC Bank five years and six months ago and that the bank has been paying interest at the rate of 8% per annum on a compound interest basis. The question is, how much can he withdraw?

$$P(1+r)^N = 10{,}000 \times (1.08)^{5.5} = \$15{,}269.71$$

As can be seen from the examples, for a given time period, compounding can yield substantially more than the return given by simple interest. And since the rate of interest is taken to the power of N, the larger the value of N, the greater will be the impact of compounding. In other words, the earlier that one starts investing, the greater will be the return.

Example 1.5. Jesus was born 2019 years ago. Assume that an investment of $1 was made in that year in a bank which has been paying 1% interest per annum since then, compounded annually. What will be the accumulated balance at the end of 2019?

$$1 \times (1.01)^{2019} = \$530{,}705{,}596$$

Thus the terminal amount will be in excess of 530 million.

Properties of Simple and Compound Interest

1. If $N = 1$ (that is, an investment is made for one year) then both the simple and the compound interest techniques will give the same accumulated value.
2. If $N < 1$ (that is, the investment is made for less than a year), the accumulated value using simple interest will be higher. That is

   $$(1 + rN) > (1 + r)^N \quad \text{if } N < 1$$

   A lot of people are not aware of this. Thus, if a bank were to quote an interest rate of r% per annum compounded annually, and you were to deposit for nine months, the payoff would be greater if the bank were to compute the interest on a simple interest basis. Using similar logic, if a bank were to quote a rate of r% per annum with semiannual compounding, and you were to deposit for three months, the payoff would be greater if the bank were to use simple interest.
3. If $N > 1$ (that is, the investment is made for more than a year), the accumulated value using compound interest will always be greater. That is

   $$(1 + rN) < (1 + r)^N \quad \text{if } N > 1$$

Simple interest is usually used for short-term transactions, that is, for investments for a period of one year or less. Consequently, simple interest is the norm for money market calculations.[1] However, in the case of capital market securities, that is, medium to long-term debt securities and equities, we use the compound interest principle. Simple interest is at times used as an approximation for compound interest over fractional periods.

Example 1.6. Take the case of Andrew Gordon who has deposited $10,000 with ABC Bank for five years and six months. Assume that the bank pays compound interest at the rate of 8% per annum for the first five years and simple interest for the last six months. How much will he be eligible to withdraw?

The balance at the end of five years will be

$$10{,}000 \times (1.08)^5 = 14{,}693.28$$

The terminal balance will be

$$14{,}693.28 \times (1 + 0.08 \times 0.5) = \$15{,}281.01$$

In the earlier example when interest was compounded for five years and six months, the accumulated value was $15,269.71. The reason why we get a higher value in the second case is that for a fractional period, which is the last six months in this case, simple interest will give a greater return than compound interest.

---

1 The money market is the market for debt securities with a time to maturity at the time of issue of one year or less.

Effective Versus Nominal Rates of Interest

We will first illustrate the difference between nominal rates and effective rates using a numerical illustration and then derive a relationship between the two symbolically.

Example 1.7. ABC Bank is quoting a rate of 9% per annum compounded annually on deposits placed with it, whereas XYZ Bank is quoting 8.75% per annum compounded quarterly on funds deposited with it. From the definitions given at the beginning of the chapter, we can see that the nominal rate of interest being offered by ABC Bank is 9% per annum, and the nominal rate being offered by XYZ Bank is 8.75% per annum. In the case of ABC Bank the effective rate of interest is also 9% per annum because interest is being compounded annually. However, the effective rate of interest being offered by XYZ Bank will obviously be higher than the rate being quoted by it, since it is compounding on a quarterly basis. The question is, what is the effective rate being offered by XYZ Bank?

8.75% per annum corresponds to $\frac{8.75}{4} = 2.1875\%$ per quarter. Consequently, a deposit of $1 for one year, or four quarters, would accumulate to

$$1 \times (1.021875)^4 = 1.090413$$

Thus, a rate of 8.75% per annum compounded quarterly is equivalent to a rate of 9.0413% with annual compounding. And so, the effective rate of interest being offered by XYZ Bank is 9.0413%. So, when the frequencies of compounding are different, comparisons between alternative investments ought to be based on the effective rates of interest and not on the nominal rates. In this case, although ABC Bank is offering a higher nominal rate, the investor would obviously be better off by investing with XYZ Bank.

It must be remembered that the distinction between nominal and effective rates is of relevance only when compound interest is being paid. The concept is of no consequence if simple interest is being paid.

A Symbolic Derivation of the Relationship Between Effective and Nominal Rates of Interest

Assume that a borrower is offering a nominal rate of $r\%$ per annum, and that interest is being compounded m times per annum. The effective rate of interest i is therefore given by

$$(1 + i) = \left(1 + \frac{r}{m}\right)^m \tag{1.1}$$

We can also derive the equivalent nominal rate if the effective rate is given:

$$r = m[(1 + i)^{\frac{1}{m}} - 1] \tag{1.2}$$

Example 1.8. ABC Bank is offering 10% per annum compounded quarterly. If an investor deposits $10,000 with the bank, how much will he have after one year?

The terminal value will be

$$10{,}000 \times \left(1 + \frac{0.10}{4}\right)^4 = \$11{,}038.13$$

The effective annual rate is therefore

$$\frac{(11{,}038.13 - 10{,}000)}{10{,}000} \equiv 10.3813\%$$

Now assume that ABC Bank wants to offer an effective annual rate of 10% per annum with quarterly compounding. The question is, what nominal rate of interest should it quote?

We know that $r = m[(1+i)^{\frac{1}{m}} - 1]$. Therefore,

$$r = 4[(1.10)^{0.25} - 1] = 0.096455 \equiv 9.6455\%$$

Thus ABC Bank should quote a rate of 9.6455% per annum if it wants to offer an effective annual rate of 10% per annum.

Computing Effective and Nominal Rates in Excel

Let's revisit Example 1.8. The nominal annual rate is 10% per annum, and the frequency of compounding is four times per annum. To calculate the effective annual rate, we use an Excel function called EFFECT. The parameters are:

- Nominal_rate: This is the nominal rate of interest per annum.
- Npery: This is the frequency of compounding per annum.

The nominal rate is 10% or 0.10 in this case. The frequency of compounding per annum is four. Using the function, we get the effective annual rate of 10.3813%:

$$\text{EFFECT}(0.10, 4) = 10.3813\%.$$

If we are given the effective rate, we can compute the equivalent nominal rate using the NOMINAL function in Excel. The parameters are

- Effect_rate: This is the effective rate of interest per annum.
- Npery: This is the frequency of compounding per annum.

In this case the effective rate is 10%, and the frequency of compounding is four. Thus,

$$\text{NOMINAL}(0.10, 4) = 9.6455\%$$

Principle of Equivalency of Interest Rates

Two nominal rates of interest compounded at different intervals of time are said to be equivalent if a given principal invested for the same total length of time at each of the two rates, produces the same accumulated value at the end. In other words, two nominal rates compounded at different intervals of time may be said to be equivalent if they yield the same effective interest rate.

Assume that ABC Bank is offering 9% per annum with semiannual compounding. What should be the equivalent rate offered by XYZ Bank if it intends to compound interest quarterly?

The first step is to calculate the effective annual rate being offered by ABC Bank:

$$(1 + i) = \left(1 + \frac{0.09}{2}\right)^2 = 1.092025$$

The next step is to calculate the nominal annual rate that gives the same effective annual rate with quarterly compounding:

$$r = 4[(1.092025)^{0.25} - 1] = 0.0890 \equiv 8.90\%$$

Thus 9% per annum with semiannual compounding is equivalent to 8.90% per annum with quarterly compounding. That is, given a choice between a deposit yielding 9% per annum with semiannual compounding, and an alternate deposit yielding 8.90% with quarterly compounding, an investor will be indifferent.

Continuous Compounding of Interest

Consider an amount of $\$P$ that is invested for N years at a nominal annual rate of $r\%$ per period. If interest is compounded m times per year, we know that the accumulated value after N years will be

$$P\left(1 + \frac{r}{m}\right)^{mN}$$

In the limit as $m \to \infty$

$$P\left(1 + \frac{r}{m}\right)^{mN} \to Pe^{rN}$$

where $e = 2.71828$. This is called the case of *continuous compounding*. If r is the nominal annual rate, then the effective annual rate with continuous compounding is $e^r - 1$.

Example 1.9. Norah Roberts has deposited $10,000 with COZY Bank for a period of five years at 10% per annum compounded continuously. What will be the final balance in the account?

$$10{,}000 \times e^{0.10\times5} = 10{,}000 \times 1.6487 = \$16{,}487$$

Example 1.10. COZY Bank is quoting an interest rate of 10% per annum with quarterly compounding. What is the equivalent rate with continuous compounding?

We know that two nominal rates are equivalent if they give the same effective annual rate. Let r be the nominal rate with continuous compounding and k the equivalent nominal rate with quarterly compounding. We require that

$$e^r = \left(1 + \frac{k}{m}\right)^m$$

$$\Rightarrow r = m \times \ln\left(1 + \frac{k}{m}\right) \tag{1.3}$$

where ln is the natural logarithm of the expression in parentheses.

$$\Rightarrow \left(1 + \frac{k}{m}\right) = e^{\frac{r}{m}}$$

$$\Rightarrow k = m[e^{\frac{r}{m}} - 1] \tag{1.4}$$

In this case,

$$r = 4 \times \ln\left(1 + \frac{0.10}{4}\right) = 0.09877 \equiv 9.877\%$$

Using Excel to Compute the Effective Rate with Continuous Compounding

Let's first revisit Example 1.9. To compute the terminal value using continuous compounding, we can use the EXP function in Excel. In this case,

$$10{,}000 \times \text{EXP}(0.10 \times 5) = 16{,}487$$

An alternative, using Excel, is to compute the effective annual rate, by specifying a high compounding frequency of, say, 500,000. Compounding 500,000 per annum, in a year that is assumed to consist of 360 days, is equivalent to compounding 58 times per hour, which is essentially the same as continuous compounding.

EFFECT(0.1,500,000) = 10.5171%

$$10{,}000 \times (1.105171)^5 = \$16{,}487$$

Now turn to Example 1.10. Given a rate of 10% per annum with quarterly compounding, we seek to find the equivalent rate with continuous compounding.

First let's find the effective annual rate:

$$\text{EFFECT}(0.1, 4) = 10.3813\%$$

Let's then convert this effective rate to an equivalent nominal rate with continuous compounding:

$$\text{NOMINAL}(0.103813, 500\,000) = 9.877\%$$

Thus 10% per annum with quarterly compounding, is equivalent to a rate of 9.877% per annum with continuous compounding.

Future Value of Cash Flows

We have already encountered the concept of future value in this chapter although we did not term it as such. When an amount is deposited for a certain time period at a given rate of interest, the amount that is accrued at the end of the designated period of time is called the *future value* of the original investment. So if $\$P$ is invested for N periods at a periodic interest rate of $r\%$, then the future value of the investment after N periods is given by

$$F.V. = P(1 + r)^N \tag{1.5}$$

The expression $(1 + r)^N$ is the amount to which an investment of \$1 will grow at the end of N periods, if it is invested at a rate r. It is called the *FVIF* (future value interest factor). It is a function of r and N. The advantage of knowing the *FVIF* is that we can find the future value of any principal amount, for given values of the interest rate and the time period, by simply multiplying the principal by the factor. The process of finding the future value given an initial investment is called *compounding*.

Example 1.11. Sonia Smith has deposited \$10,000 for five years in an account that pays interest at the rate of 10% per annum compounded annually. What is the future value of her investment?

$$FVIF(10, 5) = (1.10)^5 = 1.6105$$

Thus,

$$F.V. = \$10{,}000 \times 1.6105 = \$16{,}105$$

Computing the Future Value Using Excel

To compute the future value using Excel, we need to use the FV function.[2] The parameters are

- Rate: Rate is the periodic interest rate, which in this case is 10% or 0.10.
- Nper: Nper is the number of periods which is 5 in this case.
- Pmt: Pmt stands for the periodic payment, and is not applicable in this case, because there are no periodic cash flows. Thus, we can either put a zero, or else an extra comma in lieu.

---

2 We are using F.V. to denote the future value of a stream of cash flows, and FV to denote the Future Value function in Excel. Similarly, we are using P.V. to denote the present value of a stream of cash flows, while PV is being used to denote the Present Value function in Excel.

- Pv: Pv stands for the present value, or the initial investment, which in this case is \$10,000. We input it as −10,000 in order to ensure that the answer is positive. In many Excel functions, cash flows in one direction are positive, while those in the opposite direction are negative. Thus if the investment is positive, the subsequent inflow is negative and vice versa. In this case, if we specify a negative number for the present value, we get the future value with a positive sign. If, however, the present value were to be given with a positive sign, the future value, although it would have the same magnitude, would have a negative sign.
- Type: This is a binary variable which is either 0 or 1. It is not required at this stage, and we can just leave it blank.[3]

We will invoke the function as, FV(0.1, 5, , −10,000), and the answer is \$16,105. In this function we are inputting an extra comma lieu of the value for Pmt. As an alternative we could have given the value as zero.

Example 1.12. Sharon Peters has deposited \$10,000 for four years in an account that pays a nominal annual interest of 10% per annum with semiannual compounding. What is the future value of her investment?

10% per annum for four years, with semiannual compounding, is equivalent to 5% per half-year for eight half-yearly periods.

$$FVIF(5,8) = (1.05)^8 = 1.4775$$

Thus,

$$F.V. = \$10{,}000 \times 1.4775 = \$14{,}775$$

In Excel, the parameters would be: Rate = 0.05, Nper = 8, and Pv = −10, 000.

$$\text{FV}(0.05, 8, , -10{,}000) = \$14{,}775$$

Example 1.13. Let's assume that Sonia deposits \$10,000 for five years and six months at a nominal annual rate of 10% with annual compounding. What will be the future value?

$$F.V. = 10{,}000 \times (1.10)^{5.5}$$
$$\Rightarrow \ln(F.V.) = \ln(10{,}000) + 5.5 \times \ln(1.10) = 9.2103 + 0.5242 = 9.7345$$
$$\Rightarrow F.V. = e^{9.7345} = \$16{,}891$$

Once again ln stands for the natural logarithm. In Excel, of course, it is simple:

$$\text{FV}(0.10{,}5.5, , -10{,}000) = \$16{,}891.$$

---

3 We will use it later while dealing with annuities and annuities due.

Present Value of Cash Flows

When calculating the future value of an investment, we seek to determine the terminal value that will be earned, given a rate of interest for a specified period. Now let's look at an investment from another angle. Suppose we want our investment to yield a given terminal value. How much should we invest at the outset, if the applicable rate of interest is $r\%$ and the number of periods is N. That is, instead of computing the terminal value of a given principal, we seek to compute the principal that corresponds to a given terminal value. The principal amount that is obtained is called the *present value* of the terminal amount.

Assume that an investment pays an interest rate of $r\%$ per period on a compound interest basis. If we want to have $\$F$ after N periods, how much should we deposit today? Quite obviously

$$P.V. = \frac{F}{(1+r)^N} \tag{1.6}$$

Example 1.14. Paula wants to deposit an amount of $\$P$ with her bank in order to ensure that she has \$15,000 at the end of three years. If the bank pays 10% interest per annum compounded annually, how much does she have to deposit today?

$$P = \frac{15{,}000}{(1.10)^3} = \$11{,}269.7220$$

The expression $\frac{1}{(1+r)^N}$ is the amount that must be invested today if we are to have \$1 at the end of N periods, in the case of an investment that pays interest at the rate of $r\%$ per period. It is called the *PVIF* (present value interest factor). It is a function of r and N. The advantage of knowing the *PVIF* is that we can find the present value of any terminal amount, for given values of the interest rate and time period, by simply multiplying the future amount by the factor. The process of finding the principal corresponding to a given future amount is called *discounting* and the interest rate that is used is called the *discount rate.*

There is a relationship between the *PVIF* and the *FVIF* for given values of r and N. One is simply a reciprocal of the other.

Computing Present Values of Cash Flows Using Excel

The required function in Excel is PV. The parameters are:

- Rate
- Nper
- Pmt
- Fv
- Type

Fv stands for the future value. The other parameters have the same meaning as specified for the FV function. Let's revisit Example 1.14.

$$PV(0.10, 3, , -15{,}000) = \$11{,}269.72.$$

As before, the extra comma is in lieu of the input for Pmt.

The Internal Rate of Return of an Investment

Suppose we are told that an initial investment of $18,000 will entitle us to receive the cash flows depicted in Table 1.1. The question is, what is the rate of return that we are being offered?[4]

Table 1.1: Vector of cash flows.

Year	Cash Flow
0	(18,000)
1	2,500
2	4,000
3	5,000
4	7,500
5	10,000

The rate of return r is obviously the solution to the following equation:

$$18{,}000 = \frac{2{,}500}{(1+r)} + \frac{4{,}000}{(1+r)^2} + \frac{5{,}000}{(1+r)^3} + \frac{7{,}500}{(1+r)^4} + \frac{10{,}000}{(1+r)^5}$$

The solution to this equation is termed as the internal rate of return (IRR). It can be obtained using the IRR function in Excel.[5] The parameters are Values and Guess, though Guess is usually not required for cash flow streams like this with a single sign change. We will have more to say about this shortly. If we assume that the data in Table 1.1 is given in columns A and B of the Excel sheet, we would specify the values as B1:B6, and invoke the function as IRR(B1:B6). In this case the solution is 14.5189%.

4 Numbers in parentheses denote cash outflows. Thus the parentheses are the equivalent of a negative sign.

5 We are using the acronym IRR to denote both the internal rate of return and its corresponding function in Excel.

Pure and Mixed Cash Flows

A vector of cash flows with one sign change is referred to as a *pure* cash flow, whereas a vector with more than one sign change is referred to as a *mixed* cash flow. Table 1.2 provides an illustration of pure and mixed cash flows.

Table 1.2: Pure and mixed cash flows.

Year	Pure Cash Flow	Mixed Cash Flow
0	(20,000)	(20,000)
1	2,500	2,500
2	5,000	5,000
3	8,000	(8,000)
4	8,000	12,500
5	6,000	6,000

Column two in Table 1.2 represents a pure cash flow, for the sign changes only once, that is, between Year 0 and Year 1. However in the third column the sign changes three times. It first changes between Year 0 and Year 1, then between Year 2 and Year 3, and finally between Year 3 and Year 4. Thus column three of Table 1.2 represents a mixed cash flow.

Descartes' Rule of Signs and the IRR

The IRR is a solution to a polynomial of degree N and consequently has N roots. Descartes' rule of signs states that the number of real positive roots is either equal to the number of sign changes, or less than it by an even number. Multiple roots of the same value are counted separately. The reason why the number of real positive roots is less than the maximum number by a multiple of two, is because imaginary roots always come in conjugate pairs.

Thus in Table 1.2, the pure cash flow can have only one real positive IRR. However, the mixed cash flow may have a maximum of three real positive IRRs.

A Point About Effective Rates of Interest

Suppose that we are asked to calculate the present value or future value of a series of cash flows arising every six months, and are given a rate of interest in annual terms, without specifying the frequency of compounding. The normal practice is to divide the annual rate by two to determine the periodic interest rate for discounting or compounding. That is, the quoted rate is treated as the nominal annual rate and not as the effective annual rate. In general, if we are given an annual rate of interest and the cash flows arise at intervals of time equal to n years, then the periodic rate is taken as $\frac{r}{\frac{1}{n}}$. For instance, if the cash flows arise on a quarterly basis, then $n = 0.25$ years, and the periodic rate will be $\frac{r}{4}$.

Example 1.15. Consider the series of cash flows depicted in Table 1.3. Assume that the annual rate of interest is given to be 10%.

Table 1.3: Vector of cash flows.

Period	Cash Flow
6 Months	1,000
12 Months	2,000
18 Months	3,000
24 Months	4,000

The present value will be calculated as

$$P.V. = \frac{1{,}000}{(1.05)} + \frac{2{,}000}{(1.05)^2} + \frac{3{,}000}{(1.05)^3} + \frac{4{,}000}{(1.05)^4} = \$8{,}648.7627$$

Similarly the future value will be

$$F.V. = 1{,}000 \times (1.05)^3 + 2{,}000 \times (1.05)^2 + 3{,}000 \times 1.05 + 4{,}000 = \$10{,}512.625$$

However, if it were to be explicitly stated that the effective annual rate is 10%, then the calculations would change. The present value will then be given by

$$P.V. = \frac{1{,}000}{(1.10)^{0.5}} + \frac{2{,}000}{(1.10)} + \frac{3{,}000}{(1.10)^{1.5}} + \frac{4{,}000}{(1.10)^2} = \$8{,}677.782$$

Similarly the future value will then be given by

$$\begin{aligned} F.V. &= 1{,}000 \times (1.10)^{1.5} + 2{,}000 \times (1.10) + 3{,}000 \times (1.10)^{0.5} + 4{,}000 \\ &= \$10{,}500.1162 \end{aligned}$$

The present value is higher when we use an effective annual rate of 10% for discounting. This is because the lower the discount rate, the higher the present value, and an effective rate of 10% per annum is obviously lower than a nominal annual rate of 10% with half-yearly compounding. By the same logic the future value is lower when we use an effective annual rate of 10% to compound.

Similarly, if we were to calculate the IRR for this cash flow stream, we would get a semiannual rate of return. We would then multiply it by two to get the annual rate of return.

Level Annuities

A level annuity is a series of identical payments made at equally spaced intervals of time. Examples include house rent (until the rent is revised), monthly salary (until the salary is revised), insurance premiums, and monthly installments on housing loans and automobile loans.

In the case of an ordinary annuity, the first payment will be made one period from now. The interval between successive payments is called the *payment period.* We assume that the payment period is the same as the time period over which interest is compounded. That is, if the annuity pays annually, we assume annual compounding, whereas if it pays semiannually, we assume half-yearly compounding and so on.[6]

An annuity which makes periodic payments of $\$A$ for N periods is depicted in Figure 1.1, where today is depicted as time 0.

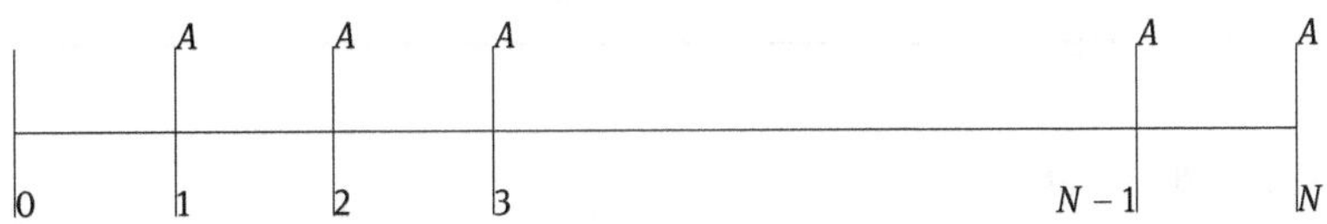

Figure 1.1: A level annuity.

If the applicable rate of interest is $r\%$, then we can calculate the present and future values as explained in the following two sections.

Present Value of a Level Annuity

The present value of a level annuity is given by the following equation:

$$P.V. = \frac{A}{(1+r)} + \frac{A}{(1+r)^2} + \frac{A}{(1+r)^3} + - - - - + \frac{A}{(1+r)^N}$$

$$\text{Therefore, } P.V.(1+r) = A + \frac{A}{(1+r)} + \frac{A}{(1+r)^2} + - - - - + \frac{A}{(1+r)^{N-1}}$$

$$\Rightarrow P.V.[(1+r)-1] = A - \frac{A}{(1+r)^N}$$

$$\Rightarrow P.V. = \frac{A}{r}\left[1 - \frac{1}{(1+r)^N}\right] \tag{1.7}$$

$\frac{1}{r}[1 - \frac{1}{(1+r)^N}]$ is called the *present value interest factor annuity (PVIFA). PVIFA*(r, N) is the present value of an annuity that pays \$1 at periodic intervals for N periods, computed using a discount rate of $r\%$. The present value of any annuity that pays $\$A$ per period can therefore be computed by multiplying A by the appropriate value of *PVIFA*.

6 We can handle more complex cases. That is, payments may come annually and interest may be compounded quarterly, or else payments may come quarterly and interest may be compounded annually.

Example 1.16. Apex Corporation is offering an instrument that promises to pay \$1,000 per year for 20 years, beginning one year from now. If the annual rate of interest is 5%, what is the present value of the annuity?

The present value of the annuity using a discount rate of 5% is

$$1{,}000 \times PVIFA(5, 20) = 1{,}000 \times 12.4622 = \$12{,}462.20$$

The same can be computed using Excel. The parameters are: Rate = 0.05, Nper = 20, Pmt = −1,000. There is no need to input parameters for Fv and Type. This is because there is no lump sum terminal cash flow, and so there is no need to input a value for the future value. Type needs to be input only for annuities due, as we shall demonstrate shortly.

$$\text{PV}(0.05, 20, -1000) = \$12{,}462.21$$

Future Value of a Level Annuity

The future value of a level annuity is given by the following equation:

$$F.V. = A(1+r)^{N-1} + A(1+r)^{N-2} + A(1+r)^{N-3} + - - - - + A$$

$$\text{Therefore, F.V.}(1+r) = A(1+r)^{N} + A(1+r)^{N-1}$$

$$+ A(1+r)^{N-2} + - - - - + A(1+r)$$

$$\Rightarrow F.V.[(1+r) - 1] = A(1+r)^{N} - A$$

$$\Rightarrow F.V. = \frac{A}{r}[(1+r)^{N} - 1] \tag{1.8}$$

$\frac{1}{r}[(1+r)^N - 1]$ is called the *future value interest factor annuity (FVIFA).* It is the future value of an annuity that pays \$1 per period for N periods, where interest is compounded at the rate of r% per period. Once again, if we know the factor, we can calculate the future value of any annuity that pays \$$A$ per period.

Example 1.17. Patricia Beck expects to receive \$10,000 per year for the next five years, starting one year from now. If the cash flows can be invested at 10% per annum, how much will she have after five years?

$$F.V. = 10{,}000 \times FVIFA(10, 5) = 10{,}000 \times 6.1051 = \$61{,}051$$

In Excel FV(0.10, 5, −10,000) = \$61,051.

Relationship Between PVIFA and FVIFA for a Level Annuity

There is a relationship between the present value interest factor and the future value interest factor for an annuity.

$$PVIFA = \frac{1}{r}\left[1 - \frac{1}{(1+r)^N}\right] = \frac{(1+r)^N - 1}{r(1+r)^N}$$

$$= \frac{(1+r)^N - 1}{r} \times \frac{1}{(1+r)^N}$$
$$= FVIFA \times PVIF \tag{1.9}$$

Conversely

$$FVIFA = \frac{PVIFA}{PVIF} = PVIFA \times FVIF \tag{1.10}$$

Level Annuities Due

The difference between an annuity and an *annuity due* is that in the case of an annuity due the cash flows occur at the beginning of the period. An N period annuity due that makes periodic payments of $\$A$ may be depicted as shown in Figure 1.2. The first cash flow occurs at time 0, and the last cash flow occurs at time $N - 1$.

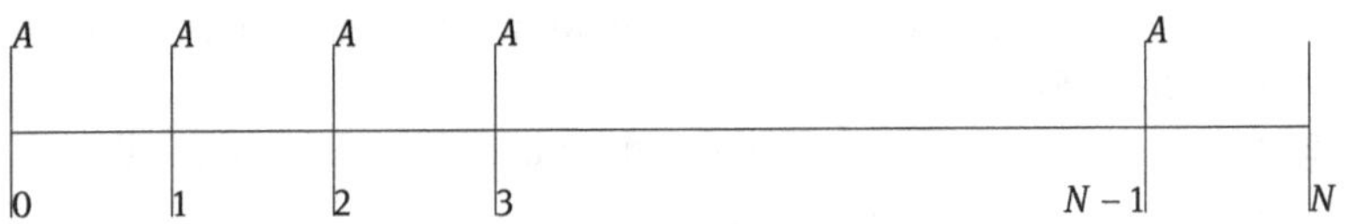

Figure 1.2: A level annuity due.

Present Value of a Level Annuity Due

The present value of a level annuity due is given by the following equation:

$$P.V. = A + \frac{A}{(1+r)} + \frac{A}{(1+r)^2} + - - - - - + \frac{A}{(1+r)^{N-1}}$$
$$\text{Therefore, P.V.}(1+r) = A(1+r) + A + \frac{A}{(1+r)} + - - - - - + \frac{A}{(1+r)^{N-2}}$$
$$\Rightarrow P.V.[(1+r) - 1] = A(1+r) - \frac{A}{(1+r)^{N-1}}$$
$$\Rightarrow P.V. = \frac{A}{r}\left[1 - \frac{1}{(1+r)^N}\right](1+r)$$
$$\text{Hence } PVIFA_{AD}(r,N) = PVIFA(r,N) \times (1+r) \tag{1.11}$$

The present value of an annuity due that makes N payments is obviously greater than that of a corresponding annuity that makes N payments, because in the case of the annuity due, each of the cash flows has to be discounted for one period less.

An obvious example of an annuity due is an insurance policy, because the first premium is due as soon as the policy is purchased.

Example 1.18. David Mathew has just bought an insurance policy. The annual premium is $12,000, and he is required to make 25 payments. What is the present value of this annuity due if the discount rate is 10% per annum:

$$P.V. = \frac{12{,}000}{0.10}\left[1 - \frac{1}{(1.10)^{25}}\right] \times 1.10$$
$$= \$119{,}816.93$$

Computation in Excel of the Present Value of an Annuity Due

The present value of the annuity due considered in Example 1.18 can be computed using Excel as follows: Rate = 0.10, Nper = 25, Pmt = –12,000, Type = 1

$$\text{PV}(0.10, 25, -12{,}000, , 1) = \$119{,}816.93.$$

The extra comma is to account for the fact that there is no terminal lump sum cash flow, and consequently no FV.

Alternately, we can find the present value of an ordinary annuity that makes 24 payments and add the initial cash flow. That is:

$$\text{PV}(0.10, 24, -12{,}000) + 12{,}000 = \$119{,}816.93$$

The third approach is to find the value of an ordinary annuity that makes 25 payments and then multiply the result by one plus the interest rate:

$$\text{PV}(0.10, 25, -12{,}000) \times 1.10 = \$119{,}816.93$$

Future Value of an Annuity Due

The future value of a level annuity due is given by the following equation.

$$F.V. = A(1+r)^N + A(1+r)^{N-1} + A(1+r)^{N-2} + - - - - + A(1+r).$$
$$\text{Therefore, } F.V(1+r) = A(1+r)^{N+1} + A(1+r)^N + A(1+r)^{N-1}$$
$$+ - - - - + A(1+r)^2$$
$$\Rightarrow F.V.[(1+r) - 1] = A(1+r)^{N+1} - A(1+r)$$
$$\Rightarrow F.V. = \frac{A}{r}[(1+r)^N - 1](1+r)$$
$$\text{Hence } FVIFA_{AD}(r, N) = FVIFA(r, N) \times (1+r) \tag{1.12}$$

The future value of an annuity due that makes N payments is higher than that of a corresponding annuity that makes N payments if the future values in both cases are computed at the end of N periods. This is because, in the first case, each cash flow has to be compounded for one period more.

Example 1.19. In the case of Mathew's insurance policy, the cash value at the end of 25 years can be calculated as follows:

$$\begin{aligned} F.V. &= 12{,}000 \times \left[\frac{(1.10)^{25} - 1}{.10}\right] \times 1.10 \\ &= \$1{,}298{,}181.19 \end{aligned}$$

Computation of the Future Value of an Annuity Due in Excel

Consider the data given in Example 1.19.

$$\begin{aligned} &\text{Rate} = 0.10, \quad \text{Nper} = 25, \quad \text{Pmt} = -12{,}000, \quad \text{Type} = 1 \\ &\text{FV}(0.10, 25, -12{,}000, , 1) = \$1{,}298{,}181.19. \end{aligned}$$

The second approach is to find the future value of an ordinary annuity that makes 25 payments and then multiply the result by one plus the interest rate:

$$\text{FV}(0.10, 25, -12000) \times 1.10 = \$1{,}298{,}181.19$$

Relationship Between PVIFA and FVIFA for Annuity Dues

Like in the case of an annuity, there is a relationship between the present value interest factor and the future value interest factor for an annuity due.

$$\begin{aligned} PVIFA_{AD}(r, N) &= PVIFA(r, N) \times (1 + r) = FVIFA(r, N) \times PVIF \times (1 + r) \\ &= FVIFA_{AD}(r, N) \times PVIF \qquad (1.13) \end{aligned}$$

$$\begin{aligned} \text{Conversely, } FVIFA_{AD}(r, N) &= FVIFA(r, N) \times (1 + r) = PVIFA(r, N) \times FVIF \times (1 + r) \\ &= PVIFA_{AD}(r, N) \times FVIF \qquad (1.14) \end{aligned}$$

Perpetuities

An annuity that pays forever is called a *perpetuity*. The future value of a perpetuity is obviously infinite. But it turns out that a perpetuity has a finite present value.

The present value of an annuity that pays for N periods is

$$P.V = \frac{A}{r}\left[1 - \frac{1}{(1 + r)^N}\right]$$

The present value of the perpetuity can be found by letting N tend to infinity. As $N \to \infty$, $\frac{1}{(1+r)^N} \to 0$. The present value of a perpetuity is therefore $\frac{A}{r}$.

Example 1.20. Consider a financial instrument that promises to pay $1,000 per year forever. If you require a 20% rate of return, how much should you be willing to pay for it?

$$P.V. = \frac{1{,}000}{0.20} = \$5{,}000$$

A perpetuity due pays an additional cash flow of $\$A$ at time 0, that is, right at the outset. Thus, its present value is

$$\frac{A}{r} + A = \frac{A(1+r)}{r} \tag{1.15}$$

Thus the present value of a perpetuity due is equal to the present value of a perpetuity multiplied by one plus the rate of interest. This is not surprising since a perpetuity is a special case of an annuity.

The Amortization Method of Loan Repayment

The amortization process refers to the process of repaying a loan by means of equal installment payments at periodic intervals. It is obvious that the installment payments form an annuity whose present value is equal to the original loan amount. Each installment will consist of a partial repayment of principal, and payment of interest on the outstanding loan balance. An *amortization schedule* is a table that shows the division of each payment into a principal component and interest component, together with the outstanding loan balance after each payment is made.

Consider a loan which is repaid in N installments of $\$A$ each. We will denote the original loan amount by L and the periodic interest rate by r.

$$L = A \times \text{PVIFA(r,N)} = \frac{A}{r}\left[1 - \frac{1}{(1+r)^N}\right] \tag{1.16}$$

The interest component of the first installment:

$$\begin{aligned} &= r \times \frac{A}{r}\left[1 - \frac{1}{(1+r)^N}\right] \\ &= A\left[1 - \frac{1}{(1+r)^N}\right] \end{aligned} \tag{1.17}$$

The principal component:

$$\begin{aligned} &= A - A\left[1 - \frac{1}{(1+r)^N}\right] \\ &= \frac{A}{(1+r)^N} \end{aligned} \tag{1.18}$$

The outstanding balance at the end of the first payment

$$
\begin{aligned}
&= \frac{A}{r}\left[1 - \frac{1}{(1+r)^N}\right] - \frac{A}{(1+r)^N} \\
&= \frac{A}{r}\left[1 - \frac{1}{(1+r)^{(N-1)}}\right]
\end{aligned}
\tag{1.19}
$$

In general, the interest component of an installment is

$$A\left[1 - \frac{1}{(1+r)^{N-t+1}}\right]$$

where t represents the number of time periods from time zero; the principal component of an installment is

$$\frac{A}{(1+r)^{N-t+1}};$$

and the outstanding balance after making the principal payment is

$$\frac{A}{r}\left[1 - \frac{1}{(1+r)^{N-t}}\right]$$

Example 1.21. Sharon has borrowed \$10,000 from Royal Syndicate Bank and has to pay it back in five equal annual installments. If the interest rate is 10% per annum on the outstanding balance, what is the installment amount? Draw up an amortization schedule.

Let's denote the unknown installment amount by A. We know that

$$
\begin{aligned}
10{,}000 &= \frac{A}{0.10} \times \left[1 - \frac{1}{(1.10)^5}\right] \\
&= A \times 3.7908 \Rightarrow A = 2{,}637.97
\end{aligned}
$$

We will analyze the first few entries in Table 1.4 in order to clarify the principles involved. At time 0, the outstanding principal is \$10,000. After one period, a payment of \$2,637.97 is made. The interest due for the first period is 10% of \$10,000, which is \$1,000. So obviously, the excess payment of

Table 1.4: Amortization schedule.

Year	Payment	Interest	Principal Repayment	Outstanding Principal
0	–	–	–	10000.00
1	2637.97	1000.00	1637.97	8362.03
2	2637.97	836.20	1801.77	6560.25
3	2637.97	656.03	1981.95	4578.30
4	2637.97	457.83	2180.14	2398.16
5	2637.97	239.82	2398.16	0.00

$1,637.97 represents a partial repayment of principal. Once this amount is adjusted, the outstanding balance at the end of the first period becomes $8,362.03. At the end of the second period, another installment of $2,637.97 is paid. The interest due for this period is 10% of $8,362.03, which is $836.20. The balance, which is $1,801.77, constitutes a partial repayment of principal.

The value of the outstanding principal at the end is zero. As can be seen, the outstanding principal declines after each payment. Since the payments are constant, the interest component steadily declines while the principal component steadily increases. Thus, if a loan is repaid in this fashion, the initial periodic payments will largely consist of interest payments, and the payments towards the end will largely consist of principal repayments.

Obtaining the Amortization Schedule Using Excel

Consider, once again, the loan of $10,000, which has to be paid back in five equal periodic installments. The periodic interest rate is 10%.

The periodic installment can be computed using the PMT function in Excel. The parameters are:

- Rate
- Nper
- Pv
- FV
- Type

There are two ways in which the PMT function can be invoked for periods other than the first. For the first period, PMT(0.10, 5, −10,000) = $2,637.97. Now consider the second period. We can specify the Nper as 4, and the PV as the outstanding principal, which is 8,362.03. Thus,

$$\text{PMT}(0.10, 5, -10{,}000) = \text{PMT}(0.10, 4, -8{,}362.03) = \$2{,}637.97$$

Similarly,

$$\text{PMT}(0.10, 5, -10{,}000) = \text{PMT}(0.10, 3, -6{,}560.25) = \$2{,}637.97$$

Now consider the interest and principal components of each installment. We can use a function in Excel called IPMT to compute the interest component of an installment and another function called PPMT to compute the principal component of the installment. The parameters, for both, are

- Rate: This is the periodic interest rate.
- Per: This stands for period and will be explained shortly.
- Nper: This represents the total number of periods.
- Pv: This is the present value.
- Fv: This is the future value.
- Type: This has the usual meaning.

Consider the interest and principal components of the first installment.

IPMT(0.10, 1, 5, −10,000) = $1,000. While computing the interest component of the second installment, we can invoke IPMT as IPMT(0.10, 2, 5, −10,000) or as IPMT(0.10, 1, 4, −8,362.03). Both will return a value of $836.20. Similarly, the principal component of the first installment is PPMT(0.10, 1, 5, −10,000) = $1,637.97. For the second period, PPMT(0.10, 2, 5, −10,000) = PPMT(0.10, 1, 4, −8,362.03) = $1,801.77.

The Rationale for Why IPMT and PPMT Can Be Used with Two Different Sets of Parameters

IPMT and PPMT can be used with two sets of parameters. We can keep the total number of periods at the initial value, specify the present value as the initial loan amount and keep changing Per to compute the interest and principal components. For the first installment, Per = 1, and for the nth installment, it is equal to n. The alternative is to re-amortize the outstanding at the beginning of each period over the remaining number of periods. Remember that each time we re-amortize, we are back to the first period. Thus, IPMT(0.10, 2, 5, −10,000) = IPMT(0.10, 1, 4, −8,362.03). After every payment, we are back to the first period of a loan whose life is equal to the remaining time to maturity, and whose principal amount is equal to the remaining outstanding balance.

Amortization with a Balloon Payment

Victoria Tolkin has taken a loan of $100,000 from ABC Bank. The loan requires her to pay in five equal annual installments along with a terminal payment of $25,000. This terminal payment, that, has to be made over and above the scheduled installment in year five, is called a *balloon payment*. The interest rate is 10% per annum on the outstanding principal. The annual installment may be calculated as follows:

$$100{,}000 = \frac{A}{0.10} \times \left[1 - \frac{1}{(1.10)^5}\right] + \frac{25{,}000}{(1.10)^5}$$

$$\Rightarrow A = 22{,}284.81$$

Obviously, the larger the balloon, the smaller the periodic installment payment is for a given loan amount. The amortization schedule may be depicted as shown in Table 1.5.

Handling the Balloon Using Excel

The only difference is that in the functions PMT, IPMT, and PPMT, we specify the FV as 25,000, which represents the balloon. Remember that PV and FV must have opposite signs. In the end, instead of going to zero, the outstanding balance will go to 25,000.

Table 1.5: Amortization schedule with a balloon payment.

Year	Payment	Interest	Principal Repayment	Outstanding Principal
0	–	–	–	100,000.00
1	22,284.81	10,000.00	12,284.81	87,715.19
2	22,284.81	8,771.52	13,513.29	74,201.90
3	22,284.81	7,420.19	14,864.62	59,337.28
4	22,284.81	5,933.73	16,351.08	42,986.20
5	47,284.81	4,298.62	42,986.19	0.01

When this is paid out in the form of a lump sum, the outstanding balance will be zero. Once again,

$$\text{IPMT}(0.10, 2, 5, -100{,}000, 25{,}000) = \text{IPMT}(0.10, 1, 4, -87715.19, 25000) = \$8{,}771.52$$

A Growing Annuity

In a *growing annuity*, the cash flows are not constant, but increase over time. Thus every period they grow at $i\%$. The periodic discount rate is $r\%$.

Consider an annuity that makes a payment of $A(1+i)$ after one period, and whose cash flows grow at a rate of $i\%$ every period. The discount rate is $r\%$. The cash flows are as shown in Figure 1.3, where today is depicted as time 0.

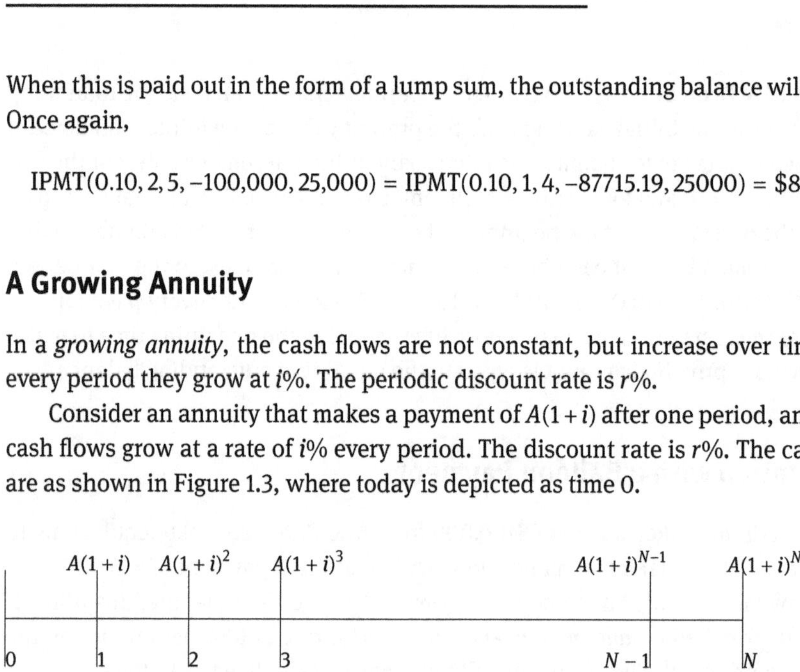

Figure 1.3: A growing annuity.

Present Value of a Growing Annuity

The present value of a growing annuity is given by the following equation:

$$P.V. = \frac{A(1+i)}{(1+r)} + \frac{A(1+i)^2}{(1+r)^2} + \frac{A(1+i)^3}{(1+r)^3} + - - - - + \frac{A(1+i)^N}{(1+r)^N}$$

$$\text{Therefore, } P.V.\frac{(1+r)}{(1+i)} = A + \frac{A(1+i)}{(1+r)} + \frac{A(1+i)^2}{(1+r)^2} + - - - - + \frac{A(1+i)^{N-1}}{(1+r)^{N-1}}$$

$$\Rightarrow P.V.\left[\frac{(1+r)}{(1+i)} - 1\right] = A - \frac{A(1+i)^N}{(1+r)^N}$$

$$\Rightarrow P.V. = \frac{A(1+i)}{(r-i)}\left[1 - \frac{(1+i)^N}{(1+r)^N}\right] \tag{1.20}$$

Example 1.22. Alpha Corporation is offering an instrument that promises to pay $ 1,000 × 1.05 after one year. The payments will increase by 5% every year, and the annuity will in all make 20 payments. If the annual discount rate is 8%, what is the present value of the annuity?

The present value of the annuity using a discount rate of 8% is

$$\frac{1{,}000 \times 1.05}{0.08 - 0.05}\left[1 - \frac{(1.05)^{20}}{(1.08)^{20}}\right] = \$15{,}075.89$$

The same can be computed using Excel. The effective discount rate is

$$\frac{(1+r)}{(1+i)} - 1 = \frac{(0.08-0.05)}{1.05} = 2.8571\%$$

$$\text{PV}(0.028571, 20, -1{,}000) = \$15{,}075.89.$$

In the preceding illustration, the growth rate was less than the discount rate. This need not necessarily be the case, and the former may be higher than the latter. The PV function can be used in Excel even in this case. However, the effective discount rate will be negative.

Future Value of a Growing Annuity

The future value of a growing annuity is given by the following equation:

$$F.V. = A(1+i)(1+r)^{N-1} + A(1+i)^2(1+r)^{N-2} + A(1+i)^3(1+r)^{N-3}$$
$$+ - - - - + A(1+i)^N$$

$$\text{Therefore, } F.V.\frac{(1+r)}{(1+i)} = A(1+r)^N + A(1+i)(1+r)^{N-1}$$
$$+ A(1+i)^2(1+r)^{N-2} + - - - - + A(1+i)^{N-1}(1+r)$$

$$\Rightarrow F.V.[\frac{(1+r)}{(1+i)} - 1] = A(1+r)^N - A(1+i)^N$$

$$\Rightarrow F.V. = \frac{A(1+i)}{(r-i)}[(1+r)^N - (1+i)^N] \tag{1.21}$$

As can be seen, the future value is equal to the present value multiplied by $(1+r)^N$.

Example 1.23. Beta Corporation is offering an annuity that promises to pay $ 2,500 × 1.05 after one year. The payments will increase by 5% every year, and the annuity will in all make 20 payments. If the annual rate of interest is 8%, what is the future value of the annuity?

The future value of the annuity using an interest rate of 8% is

$$\frac{2{,}500 \times 1.05}{0.08 - 0.05}\left[(1.08)^{20} - (1.05)^{20}\right] = \$175{,}670.20$$

Growing Perpetuity

We can calculate the present value of a *growing perpetuity* only if the discount rate is greater than the growth rate of the cash flows. If it isn't the series will not converge. The present value as $N \to \infty$ is given by $\frac{A(1+i)}{r-i}$.

Example 1.24. Assume that the annuity in Example 1.23 is a perpetuity. The present value will be:

$$\frac{2{,}500 \times (1.05)}{0.03} = \$87{,}500$$

Growing Annuity Due

Consider an annuity that makes a payment of A immediately. The cash flows grow at a rate of $i\%$ every period. The periodic interest rate is $r\%$. The last cash flow is received after $N - 1$ periods. The cash flows can be depicted as shown in Figure 1.4, where today is depicted as time 0.

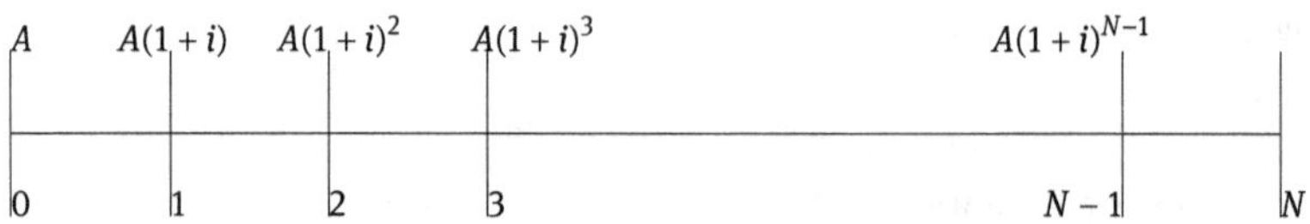

Figure 1.4: A growing annuity due.

Present Value of a Growing Annuity Due

The equation for the present value of a growing annuity due is the following.

$$P.V. = A + \frac{A(1+i)}{(1+r)} + \frac{A(1+i)^2}{(1+r)^2} + \frac{A(1+i)^3}{(1+r)^3} + - - - - + \frac{A(1+i)^{N-1}}{(1+r)^{N-1}}$$

$$\text{Therefore, } P.V.\frac{(1+r)}{(1+i)} = A\frac{(1+r)}{(1+i)} + A + \frac{A(1+i)}{(1+r)} + \frac{A(1+i)^2}{(1+r)^2} + - - - - + \frac{A(1+i)^{N-2}}{(1+r)^{N-2}}$$

$$\Rightarrow P.V.[\frac{(1+r)}{(1+i)} - 1] = A\frac{(1+r)}{(1+i)} - \frac{A(1+i)^{N-1}}{(1+r)^{N-1}}$$

$$\Rightarrow P.V. = \frac{A}{(r-i)}\left[(1+r) - \frac{(1+i)^N}{(1+r)^{N-1}}\right]$$

$$= \frac{A}{(r-i)}\left[1 - \frac{(1+i)^N}{(1+r)^N}\right](1+r) \qquad (1.22)$$

Thus the present value of the growing annuity due is equal to the present value of the growing annuity multiplied by $\frac{(1+r)}{(1+i)}$. If the discount rate is greater than the growth rate, the annuity due will have a higher present value than a corresponding annuity. However, if the discount rate is less than the growth rate, the annuity due will have a lower present value. The rationale is as follows: As compared to a growing annuity, in the case of a growing annuity due, every cash flow grows for one period less, and is discounted for one period less. Consequently, if the discount rate is greater than the growth rate, the annuity due will have a higher present value as compared to the annuity. But if the discount rate were to be lower, then it would have a lower present value.

Example 1.25. Consider a growing annuity, with a value of \$1,000 for A, that makes a total of 20 payments. The growth rate is 5%, and the discount rate is 8%. The present value, as computed in Example 1.22, is \$15,075.89. Had it been a 20 period annuity due, the present value would be

$$15{,}075.89 \times \frac{1.08}{1.05} = \$15{,}506.63$$

Now consider another annuity with the same cash flows, but with a discount rate of 5%, and a growth rate of 8%. The present value of the annuity would be:

$$\frac{1{,}000 \times 1.08}{0.05 - 0.08}\left[1 - \frac{(1.08)^{20}}{(1.05)^{20}}\right] = \$27{,}239.97$$

Were it an annuity due, the present value would be:

$$27{,}239.97 \times \frac{1.05}{1.08} = \$26{,}483.30$$

The results can be verified using Excel. The effective discount rate in the first case is:

$$\frac{(1+r)}{(1+i)} - 1 = \frac{(0.08 - 0.05)}{1.05} = 2.8571\%$$

$$\text{PV}(0.028571, 20, -1{,}000) = \$15{,}075.89$$

For the annuity due, we need to make the Type 1:

$$\text{PV}(0.028571, 20, -1{,}000,, 1) = \$15{,}506.63$$

The effective discount rate in the second case is:

$$\frac{(0.05 - 0.08)}{1.08} = -2.7778\%$$

$$\text{PV}(-0.027778, 20, -1{,}000) = \$27{,}239.97$$

Had it been an annuity due,

$$\text{PV}(-0.027778, 20, -1{,}000,, 1) = \$26{,}483.30.$$

Future Value of a Growing Annuity Due

The future value of a growing annuity due is given by the following equation.

$$F.V. = A(1+r)^N + A(1+i)(1+r)^{N-1} + A(1+i)^2(1+r)^{N-2} + ----$$
$$+ A(1+i)^{N-1}(1+r)$$
$$\text{Therefore, } F.V.\frac{(1+r)}{(1+i)} = A\frac{(1+r)^{N+1}}{(1+i)} + A(1+r)^N$$
$$+ A(1+i)(1+r)^{N-1} + ---- + A(1+i)^{N-2}(1+r)^2$$
$$\Rightarrow F.V.[\frac{(1+r)}{(1+i)} - 1] = A\frac{(1+r)^{N+1}}{(1+i)} - A(1+i)^{N-1}(1+r)$$
$$\Rightarrow F.V. = \frac{A}{(r-i)}[(1+r)^N - (1+i)^N](1+r) \tag{1.23}$$

As can be seen, the future value is equal to the present value multiplied by $(1+r)^N$.

Example 1.26. Beta Corporation is offering an annuity that promises to pay \$1, 000 immediately. The payments will increase by 5% every year, and the annuity will in all make 20 payments. If the annual rate of interest is 8%, what is the future value of the annuity?

The future value of the annuity using an interest rate of 8% is

$$\frac{1{,}000}{0.08-0.05}\left[(1.08)^{20} - (1.05)^{20}\right] \times 1.08 = \$72{,}275.74$$

The present value is \$15,506.63:

$$15{,}506.63 \times (1.08)^{20} = \$72{,}275.74$$

Growing Perpetuity Due

We can calculate the present value of a growing perpetuity due only if the discount rate is greater than the growth rate of the cash flows. The present value as $N \to \infty$ is given by $\frac{A(1+r)}{r-i}$.

Example 1.27. Assume that the annuity in Example 1.25 is a perpetuity. The present value is:

$$\frac{1{,}000 \times (1.08)}{0.03} = \$36{,}000$$

The present value of a perpetuity due is equal to the present value of a perpetuity, which was derived earlier, multiplied by $\frac{(1+r)}{(1+i)}$.

The present value, had it been a perpetuity, would have been:

$$\frac{1{,}000 \times (1.05)}{0.03} = \$35{,}000$$

$$36{,}000 = 35{,}000 \times \frac{1.08}{1.05}$$

Chapter Summary

In this chapter, we studied the fundamentals of the time value of money, such as the present and future values of a cash flow stream. We introduced the concepts of simple and compound interest. We also examined the difference between the nominal rate of interest and the effective rate of interest, and the importance of the latter when interest is compounded more than once per annum. We studied level annuities and annuities due, and the corresponding perpetuities. We saw that although the future value of a perpetuity cannot be computed, it will have a finite present value. We discussed the internal rate of return, the related issues of pure and mixed cash flows, and Descartes rule of signs. We studied the structure of amortized loans, which are commonly used in the context of real estate transactions. Finally, we studied growing annuities and annuities due, and the corresponding perpetuities. Whenever possible, we used Excel to illustrate the concepts applicable.

In the next chapter, we study the fundamentals of bonds and bond markets.

Chapter 2
An Introduction to Bonds

Bonds are a source of funds for corporations and governments. For companies, they represent a supplementary source of funds, in addition to equity shares. For a government, however, they represent the sole means of raising funds, by way of issuance of securities. For neither a federal, state, nor local government, can issue equity shares. Companies must necessarily issue equity shares. They have the option of issuing bonds to augment this source of funds if they so desire. Of course a government has alternative means of fundraising such as levy of taxes, and the printing of currency.

There exists a related type of security termed as a *debenture*. In some markets the words bond and debenture are used interchangeably. But in markets like the United States, a bond is a secured debt security, whereas a debenture represents an unsecured debt security. The word "secured" means that the issue is backed by specified collateral. So in the event of the borrower being unable to repay, the debt holders can have the collateral liquidated in order to receive what is due to them. Unsecured bonds are not backed by specified collateral. Holders can only hope that the issuer will have adequate resources when the time comes for repayment. Government debt, in all countries, is always referred to as bonds.

Bonds and debentures are referred to as fixed income securities. The reason is that once the rate of interest is set at the onset of the period for which it is due to be paid, it is not a function of the profitability of the firm. If a firm issues bonds with an interest rate of 5% per annum, it cannot subsequently ask holders to accept a lesser amount on account of poor performance. The flip side is that in the event of extra-ordinary performance, the bond holders cannot demand more than 5%. This is unlike the case of equity shares, where the percentage of dividends declared by the company can fluctuate from year to year. Interest payments are therefore contractual obligations, and failure to pay what was promised at the start of an interest computation period is tantamount to default. In contrast a firm is under no obligation to declare a dividend in a given year. The decision to pay a dividend is taken by the board of directors, which also decides the magnitude of the dividend. Dissident shareholders, if they are in a majority, may be able to force a company to overturn its dividend decision.

Why do firms issue bonds? It is because bonds allow the firm to raise additional capital without diluting the stake of the shareholders. Unlike a shareholder, a bond holder is a stake holder in a business but is not a part owner of the business. A bond holder is entitled only to the interest that was promised and to the repayment of principal at the time of maturity of the security, and does not partake in the profits of the firm. Bonds have two other important properties, namely they give the firm a tax shield and provide leverage.

https://doi.org/10.1515/9781547400669-002

The Leverage Effect

Bonds provide equity shareholders with leverage. Table 2.1 provides a detailed illustration. Company XEON is entirely equity financed and has issued shares worth \$5,000,000. Company BORA has raised the same amount of capital, half in the form of debt and the other half in the form of equity. The debt carries interest at the rate of 8% per annum. Let's consider two situations: in the first, both companies make a profit of \$500,000 from operations, and in the second, they both take a loss of \$500,000. To keep matters simple, we will assume that the firms do not have to pay tax.

Table 2.1: Illustration of leverage.

	Case-A		Case-B	
	Firms Make a Profit		Firms Take a Loss	
	XEON	BORA	XEON	BORA
Profits from Operations	500,000	500,000	(500,000)	(500,000)
Less Interest	0	(200,000)	0	(200,000)
PAT	500,000	300,000	(500,000)	(700,000)
ROI	10%	12%	−10%	−28%

PAT stands for profit after tax and represents what the shareholders are entitled to.
ROI is the return on investment for shareholders.

As we can see from Table 2.1, the presence of debt in the capital structure creates leverage. The profit for the shareholders is magnified from 10% to 12%, when a firm is financed 50% with debt. On the other hand, a loss is also magnified, in this case, from −10% to −28%. As they say, leverage is a double edged sword. It magnifies returns, irrespective of whether the returns are positive or negative.[1] We can also see, from the case of BORA, that incurring a loss does not give the flexibility to the firm to avoid or postpone the interest due to bond holders. Interest on bonds is indeed a contractual obligation.

Tax Shield Due to Interest Payments

Unlike dividends, which are paid out of post-tax profits, the interest paid on bonds and debentures is deductible as an expense when computing the net income. Thus the effective interest cost for the issuer is lower than the stated rate. We say that interest provides a tax shield. By allowing the firm to deduct the interest as an expense, the

1 In finance, we are concerned with profits and losses in relation to the investment made, and not in absolute terms. Thus a loss of \$25,000 on an investment of \$50,000 is considered more serious than an identical loss on an investment of \$1,000,000.

government collects a lower amount by way of taxes. In a sense, therefore, it is offering a subsidy to the issuing entity.

Consider the illustration in Table 2.2. Both firms are assumed to have a profit of $250,000, and the applicable tax rate is assumed to be 30%.

Table 2.2: Illustration of a tax shield.

Company	XEON	BORA
Profit from Operations	250,000	250,000
Interest	NIL	30,000
PBT	250,000	220,000
Tax	(75,000)	(66,000)
PAT	175,000	154,000

PBT stands for profits before tax
PAT stands for profits after tax

Let's analyze the last row of Table 2.2. If company BORA had been a zero debt company like XEON, its shareholders would have been entitled to a cash flow of $175,000. However, because it has paid interest, the shareholders are entitled to only $154,000, which is $21,000 less. Thus, from the standpoint of the shareholders of BORA, they have effectively paid interest of $21,000. So what explains the missing $9,000, for after all, we know that BORA did pay $30,000 to its bond holders? The answer is that by allowing the firm to deduct the interest paid as an expense, prior to the computation of tax, the government has foregone taxes to the extent of $9,000. The tax shield, as we term it, is equal to the product of the tax rate and the interest paid. In this case it is $0.30 \times 30{,}000 = \$9{,}000$.

If the rules were to be amended and interest on debt were no longer to be tax deductible, BORA would have to pay tax on $250,000, and the profit after tax, which is what belongs to the shareholders, would be only $145,000. In this situation, the shareholders will feel the full burden of the interest paid by the firm.

Debt securities may be negotiable or non-negotiable. A negotiable security is one that can be traded in the secondary market, whereas a non-negotiable security cannot be signed over by the holder in favor of another investor. Bank accounts are classic examples of non-negotiable investments, for if an investor were to open a term deposit with a commercial bank, although he can always withdraw the investment and pay a third party, he cannot transfer the ownership of the deposit. Most corporate and government bonds can be traded prior to maturity, either directly on an organized exchange, or via a dealer in an over-the-counter (OTC) trade.

The most basic form of a debt security is referred to as a plain vanilla bond. Bonds are referred to as IOUs, an acronym which stands for "*I owe you.*" A plain vanilla bond is an IOU that promises to pay a fixed rate of interest every period, which is usually every six months, and to repay the principal at maturity. Any bond with additional features, is said to have *bells and whistles* attached. For instance, in the case of floating rate bonds, the interest rate does not remain constant from period to period, but fluctuates with changes in the benchmark to which it is linked.

There are also bonds with embedded options. For example, *Convertible bonds* can be converted to shares of stock by the investor. *Callable bonds* can be prematurely retired by the issuing company, and *putable bonds* can be prematurely surrendered by the bond holders in return for the repayment of the principal.

Variables Influencing the Bond Price

There are four variables that influence the price of a plain vanilla bond. These are:
- Face value
- Term to maturity
- Coupon
- Yield to maturity

Face Value

The face value—also known as par value, redemption value, maturity value, or principal value—is the principal amount underlying the bond. It is the amount raised by the issuer from the first holder[2] and the amount repayable by the issuer to the last holder. We denote it by the symbol M.

Term to Maturity

Term to maturity is the time remaining in the life of the bond as measured at the point of valuation. You can understand it as the length of time after which the debt ceases to exist and the borrower redeems the issue by repaying the holder. Equivalently, you can understand it as the length of time for which the borrower has to service the debt in the form of periodic interest payments. The words *maturity, term, tenor, tenure,* and *term to maturity* are used interchangeably. We will assume that we are at time zero and denote the point of maturity by T. Thus the number of periods until maturity is T, which is normally measured in years.

In the debt market, we make a distinction between the original term to maturity of a security, and its actual term to maturity. The original term to maturity is the term

2 In most cases, bonds are issued at the face value, although there are instances where they are issued at higher or lower values, as you will see later.

to expiration as measured at the time of issue. However, the actual term to maturity is the term to maturity as computed at the current point in time. As time elapses, the actual term to maturity (*ATM*) continues declining, whereas the original term to maturity (*OTM*) remains constant.

Coupon

The contractual interest payment made by the issuer is called a *coupon* payment. The name came about because in earlier days bonds were issued with a booklet of postdated coupons. On an interest payment date, the holder was expected to detach the relevant coupon and claim his payment. Even today, bearer bonds come with a booklet of coupons. These are bonds where no record of ownership is maintained, unlike in the case of conventional or registered bonds. Thus the holder of a bearer bond needs to produce the coupon to claim the interest that is due.

The coupon may be denoted as a rate or as a dollar value. We will denote the coupon rate by c. The dollar value, C, is therefore given by $c \times M$. Most bonds pay interest on a semiannual basis, and consequently the semiannual cash flow is $c \times M/2$. Semiannual coupons are the norm in the UK, US, Japan, and Australia. However, in certain regions like the European Union, bonds typically pay annual coupons.

Consider a bond with a face value of $1,000 that pays a coupon of 8% per annum on a semiannual basis. The annual coupon rate is 0.08. The semiannual coupon payment is $0.08 \times 1{,}000/2 = \$40$.

Yield to Maturity

The yield to maturity, like the coupon rate, is also an interest rate. The difference is that whereas the coupon rate is the rate of interest paid by the issuer, the yield to maturity, commonly referred to as the YTM, is the rate of return required by the market. At a given point in time, the yield may be greater than, equal to, or less than the coupon rate. The YTM is denoted by y and is the rate of return that a buyer gets when acquiring the bond at the prevailing price and holding it to maturity.

Valuation of a Bond

To value a bond, we first assume that we are standing on a coupon payment date. That is, we assume that a coupon has just been received, and consequently the next coupon is exactly six months or one period away. If T is the term to maturity in years, we have N coupons remaining where $N = 2T$. We receive N coupon payments during the life of the bond, where each payment or cash flow is equal to $C/2$. This payment stream obviously constitutes an annuity. The present value of this annuity is

$$\frac{\frac{c \times M}{2}}{\frac{y}{2}}\left[1-\frac{1}{(1+\frac{y}{2})^N}\right]$$

The terminal payment of the face value is a lump sum payment. Because we are discounting the cash flows from the annuity on a semiannual basis, this payment needs to be discounted on a similar basis. Thus the present value of this cash flow is:

$$\frac{M}{(1+\frac{y}{2})^N}$$

Hence the price of the bond is given by:

$$\frac{\frac{c \times M}{2}}{\frac{y}{2}}\left[1-\frac{1}{(1+\frac{y}{2})^N}\right]+\frac{M}{(1+\frac{y}{2})^N}$$

As you can be see, the YTM is that discount rate that makes the present value of the cash flows from the bond equal to its price. The price of a bond is like the initial investment in a project. The remaining cash flows are similar to the inflows from the project. Consequently the YTM is exactly analogous to the IRR, or internal rate of return, a concept used in capital budgeting.

Example 2.1. Omega has issued bonds with 10 years to maturity and a face value of $1,000. The coupon rate is 8% per annum payable on a semiannual basis. If the required yield in the market is equal to 10%, what should be the price of the bond? The periodic cash flow is $0.08 \times 1{,}000/2 = \$40$. Thus the present value of all the coupons is:

$$\frac{\frac{0.08 \times 1{,}000}{2}}{\frac{0.10}{2}}\left[1-\frac{1}{(1.05)^{20}}\right] = \$498.4884$$

The present value of the face value is

$$\frac{1{,}000}{(1.05)^{20}} = \$376.8895$$

Thus the price of the bond is $498.4884 + 376.8895 = \$875.3779$

Par, Premium, and Discount Bonds

In Example 2.1, the price of the bond is less than its face value. Such a bond is said to be trading at a discount to the par value and is therefore referred to as a *discount bond*. If the price of the bond is greater than its face value, then it is said to be trading at a premium to its face value and consequently is referred to as a *premium bond.* If the price is equal to the face value, then the bond is said to be trading at *par.* As you see from the pricing equation, price and yield are inversely related. If the rate of return offered by the issuer is equal to that demanded by the market, then the bond obviously trades at par. However, if the market demands a higher rate of return, it then brings the price down until the desired yield is obtained. On the other hand, if the desired yield is lower than the coupon, then traders will be willing to pay a price that is higher than the face value of the bond.

Influence of Variables on the Bond Price

Let's first differentiate the price with respect to the face value, keeping other variables constant:

$$\frac{\partial P}{\partial M} = \frac{\frac{c}{2}}{\frac{y}{2}}\left[1 - \frac{1}{(1+\frac{y}{2})^N}\right] + \frac{1}{(1+\frac{y}{2})^N} > 0 \tag{2.1}$$

Thus the partial derivative of the price with respect to the face value is positive. That is, keeping other variables constant, the higher the face value, the higher the bond price.

Now consider the derivative with respect to the coupon rate:

$$\frac{\partial P}{\partial c} = \frac{\frac{M}{2}}{\frac{y}{2}}\left[1 - \frac{1}{(1+\frac{y}{2})^N}\right] > 0 \tag{2.2}$$

Thus the partial derivative with respect to the coupon rate is positive. That is, keeping other variables constant, the higher the coupon rate is, the higher the bond price.

Let's now consider the derivative of the price with respect to the time to maturity. Unlike other variables, the number of coupons can only increase in increments of 1. When there are N coupons remaining until maturity, the price is given by:

$$P_0 = \frac{Mc}{y} \times \left[1 - \frac{1}{(1+\frac{y}{2})^N}\right] + \frac{M}{(1+\frac{y}{2})^N} \tag{2.3}$$

When there are $N+1$ coupons remaining until maturity, the price is given by:

$$P_1 = \frac{Mc}{y} \times \left[1 - \frac{1}{(1+\frac{y}{2})^{(N+1)}}\right] + \frac{M}{(1+\frac{y}{2})^{(N+1)}} \tag{2.4}$$

$$\Rightarrow P_1 - P_0 = \Delta P = \frac{M}{(1+\frac{y}{2})^{N+1}} \times \left[\frac{c}{2} - \frac{y}{2}\right] \tag{2.5}$$

For a par bond, the price change is zero. Thus as we go from one coupon date to the next, the price of a par bond continues to be equal to its face value. For a premium bond the price change is positive. Thus, holding other parameters constant, as the time to maturity of a premium bond increases, its price also increases. Finally, for a discount bond, the price change is negative. Thus if the time to maturity increases, a discount bond declines in price.

Finally, let's consider the derivative of the price with respect to the yield to maturity:

$$\frac{\partial P}{\partial y} = \frac{-cM}{y^2}\left[1 - \frac{1 + \{\frac{y}{2} \times (N+1)\}}{(1+\frac{y}{2})^{N+1}}\right] - \frac{NM}{2} \times \frac{1}{(1+\frac{y}{2})^{N+1}} \tag{2.6}$$

Let's define $\frac{y}{2}$ as r . From the expression for a Maclaurin series we know that:[3]

$$(1+r)^{N+1} = 1 + r(N+1) + \frac{N(N+1)r^2}{2} + \text{h.o.t.} \tag{2.7}$$

Thus

$$\begin{aligned} & 1 + r(N+1) < (1+r)^{N+1} \\ \Rightarrow & 1 + \left\{\frac{y}{2} \times (N+1)\right\} < \left(1 + \frac{y}{2}\right)^{N+1} \\ \Rightarrow & \frac{1 + \{\frac{y}{2} \times (N+1)\}}{(1+\frac{y}{2})^{N+1}} < 1 \\ & \text{Thus } \frac{\partial P}{\partial y} < 0 \end{aligned}$$

Thus, as the YTM increases, the price of the bond declines.

The Pull to Par Effect

The price of a premium bond is greater than the face value, whereas that of a discount bond is less than the face value. At maturity all bonds trade at par. As we have demonstrated, when the number of coupons is increased, the price change, is zero for a par bond. Thus a par bond continues to trade at par on every successive coupon date if the YTM remains constant. However, for premium bonds, the price increases with an increasing time to maturity, keeping the YTM constant. Thus as we approach maturity, the price of a premium bond steadily declines and approaches par. Finally, for a discount bond, the price change is negative if the time until maturity increases. Hence as we approach maturity, the price of a discount bond steadily increases and approaches par.

3 h.o.t stands for higher order terms.

This phenomenon is known as the *pull to par* effect. The rationale is as follows: When we move from one coupon date to the next coupon date, we have one coupon less. Thus the contribution of coupons to the price goes down, leading to a decline in the price. However, the present value of the face value increases because the face value is discounted for one period less. This therefore leads to an increase in the bond price. For premium bonds, the first effect dominates, and the price steadily declines as we go from one coupon date to the next. In the case of discount bonds, the second effect is more significant, and the bond price steadily increases. For par bonds, the two effects neutralize each other, and there is no change in the bond price, which continues to remain at par.

Example 2.2. Consider two bonds with three years to maturity and a face value of $1,000. Assume that the coupon for the first bond is 8% per annum and the YTM is 10% per annum. The bond will obviously sell at a discount. In the case of the second bond, let's assume that the coupon is 10% per annum and the YTM is 8% per annum. This bond will obviously trade at a premium. Let's trace the evolution of the price for these bonds as we approach maturity. The results are summarized in Table 2.3.

Table 2.3: The pull to par effect.

Time to Maturity in Periods	Price of Discount Bond	Price of Premium Bond
6	949.24	1,052.42
5	956.71	1,044.52
4	964.54	1,036.30
3	972.77	1,027.75
2	981.41	1,018.86
1	990.48	1,009.62
0	1,000.00	1,000.00

An Interesting Result about Bond Prices

Let's consider a situation where the coupon and the YTM are both changed by the same percentage. Thus the new coupon is equal to *ac*, where *c* is the original coupon rate, and *a* is the scaling factor. Similarly, the new YTM is *ay*, where a may be greater than one or less than one. The original price is given by

$$P = \frac{\frac{c \times M}{2}}{\frac{y}{2}}\left[1 - \frac{1}{(1+\frac{y}{2})^N}\right] + \frac{M}{(1+\frac{y}{2})^N}$$

The new price P^* is given by

$$\frac{\frac{ac \times M}{2}}{\frac{ay}{2}}\left[1 - \frac{1}{(1+\frac{ay}{2})^N}\right] + \frac{M}{(1+\frac{ay}{2})^N}$$

$$= \frac{\frac{c\times M}{2}}{\frac{y}{2}}\left[1-\frac{1}{(1+\frac{ay}{2})^N}\right]+\frac{M}{(1+\frac{ay}{2})^N}$$

$$\Rightarrow P^* - P = M\times\left[\frac{1}{(1+\frac{ay}{2})^N}-\frac{1}{(1+\frac{y}{2})^N}\right]\times\left[1-\frac{c}{y}\right] \tag{2.8}$$

$$\text{If } a>1, \frac{1}{(1+\frac{ay}{2})^N}<\frac{1}{(1+\frac{y}{2})^N}$$

$$\Rightarrow M\times\left[\frac{1}{(1+\frac{ay}{2})^N}-\frac{1}{(1+\frac{y}{2})^N}\right]<0$$

$$\text{If } c>y, 1-\frac{c}{y}<0$$

Thus for a premium bond, $\triangle P > 0$. Hence if we increase the coupon and the YTM of a bond by the same percentage, a premium bond will increase in price.

For a discount bond:

$$1-\frac{c}{y}>0 \quad \text{and hence} \quad \triangle P<0$$

Thus, for a discount bond, if we increase the yield and the coupon by the same percentage, the price will decline.

Now let's consider the case where $a < 1$. That is, the yield and coupon are decreased by the same percentage.

$$\frac{1}{(1+\frac{ay}{2})^N}>\frac{1}{(1+\frac{y}{2})^N}$$

$$\Rightarrow M\times\left[\frac{1}{(1+\frac{ay}{2})^N}-\frac{1}{(1+\frac{y}{2})^N}\right]>0$$

In this case, for a premium bond, $\triangle P < 0$. Hence if we decrease the coupon and the YTM of a bond by the same percentage, a premium bond will decline in price. For a discount bond, $\triangle P > 0$. Thus, for a discount bond, if we decrease the yield and the coupon by the same percentage, the price will increase.

Example 2.3. Consider two bonds, both with a face value of \$1,000 and five years to maturity. Bond A pays a coupon of 8% per annum on a semiannual basis, whereas Bond B pays a coupon of 10% per annum, also on a semiannual basis. Bond A has a YTM of 10% per annum, and Bond B has a YTM of 8% per annum. Thus Bond A is a discount bond, and, Bond B is a premium bond.

The initial price of Bond A is \$922.7827, whereas the initial price of Bond B is \$1,081.1090. Let's increase both the coupons and yields by 25%. For Bond A, the new coupon is 10% per annum, and the YTM is 12.50% per annum. For Bond B, the new coupon is 12.50% per annum, and the new YTM is 10% per annum. The new price of Bond A is \$909.0789, and the price of Bond B is \$1,096.5217. Thus the premium bond has increased in price, whereas the discount bond has declined in price.

Now let's instead reduce both the coupon and the yield of both the bonds by 25%. For Bond A the new coupon is 6% per annum, and the new YTM is 7.50% per annum. For Bond B the new coupon is

7.50% per annum, and the YTM is 6% per annum. The new price of Bond A is $938.4041, and that of Bond B is $1,063.9765. In this case, the discount bond has increased in price, whereas the premium bond has decreased in price.

Eurobonds and Foreign Bonds

There are three categories of bonds depending on the currency of issue, and the nationality of the issuer. If the currency in which a bond is denominated is different from the currency of the country of issue we term it a *Eurobond*. This is not related to the location of issue. That is, Eurobonds can be issued outside Europe. Thus bonds denominated in U.S. dollars that are sold in Europe are classified as Eurobonds. The nationality of the issuing entity is irrelevant. Thus if Microsoft were to issue U.S. dollar-denominated bonds in Europe, we would term them Eurobonds. The same would be the case if Mercedes were to issue dollar-denominated bonds in Europe.

If a bond is denominated in the currency of the country in which the issue is taking place, but the issuer is from a different country, then we classify the debt security as a *foreign bond*. Thus if Microsoft were to issue bonds denominated in euros in Frankfurt, then it would constitute a foreign bond issue. Foreign bonds are known by nicknames. Bonds sold in the U.S. are called Yankee bonds; those sold in Japan are called Samurai bonds; and those sold in the U.K. are called Bulldog bonds.

Finally if the issuing entity belongs to the country of issue and the currency is also local, then the bond is categorized as a *domestic bond*. Thus if Mercedes were to issue bonds denominated in euros in Germany, then we would term it a domestic bond.

Thus if the issuer and the currency are both local, then it is a domestic bond. If the currency is local but the issuer is not, then it is a foreign bond. And finally if the currency is not local, it is a Eurobond, irrespective of the nationality of the issuer.

The Eurobond market has grown much more rapidly than the foreign bond market. This is due to several reasons. Eurobond issues are not subject to the regulations of the country in whose currency they are denominated. Consequently, they can be brought to the market quickly and with less disclosure. This gives the issuer of the bonds greater flexibility to take advantage of favorable market conditions. On the other hand, domestic securities issues are regulated by the market regulator of the country, like the SEC in the U.S.

The origin of the Eurobond market was fueled by the imposition of a cess[4] called the Interest Equalization Tax, which was imposed by the U.S. government in 1963, on the interest received by American investors from Yankee bonds. What had happened was that, due to the low interest rate ceiling in the U.S., domestic institutions were unable to pay a high rate of interest to investors. Foreigners sought to take advantage of this situation by issuing Yankee bonds with relatively higher rates of return.

---

4 It is a form of tax.

The objective of the Interest Equalization Tax was to ensure that American investors did not perceive Yankee bonds to be attractive, despite their higher interest rates. The motivation for this measure was to arrest the perceived flight of capital from the U.S. As a consequence, foreigners were forced to relocate their dollar borrowings outside the U.S.

Eurobonds offer favorable tax status, for they are usually issued in bearer form. That is, the name and address of the owner are not mentioned on the bond certificate. Thus, in the case of bearer securities, physical possession is the sole evidence of ownership. Such securities are easier to transfer and offer investors the potential freedom to avoid and evade taxes. Thus, holders who desire anonymity can receive interest payments from such securities without revealing their identities. Also, interest on Eurobonds is generally not subject to withholding taxes, or tax deduction at source. Because of their unique features, investors are willing to accept a lower yield from Eurobonds than from other securities of comparable risk that lack the favorable tax status.

Eurobonds are not usually registered with any particular regulatory agency, but may be listed on a stock exchange, typically London or Luxembourg. Listing is done not just for the purpose of facilitating trading, but to circumvent restrictions imposed on certain institutional investors like pension funds that are prohibited from purchasing unlisted securities. Most of the trading in Eurobonds takes place over the counter or OTC, which refers to a market that is a network of broker-dealers.

Coupon Dates and Coupon Frequencies

Bonds in the U.S., U.K., Japan, and Australia typically pay coupons on a semiannual basis. However, Eurobonds, and bonds issued in the EU generally, pay coupons on an annual basis. In the case of bonds paying semiannual coupons, there are six monthly combinations possible—January/July, February/August, March/September, April/October, May/November, and June/December. In each case, the coupon date is usually the 1st or the 15th of the month. Thus the bond dealers' quote sheets usually state the following codes:

- JJ-01 or JJ-15
- FA-01 or FA-15
- MS-01 or MS-15
- AO-01 or AO-15
- MN-01 or MN-15
- JD-01 or JD-15

It should also be noted that in practice we are highly unlikely to find a bond with the last day of February as the coupon date because this creates practical complications, due to the fact that February has an extra day once in four years.

Zero Coupon Bonds

Unlike a plain vanilla bond that pays coupons at periodic intervals, zero coupon bonds, also known as *deep discount bonds* do not pay any interest. Such instruments are always traded at a discount to the face value, and at maturity, the holder receives the face value. For instance, consider a zero coupon bond with a face value of \$1,000 and 10 years to maturity. Assume that the required yield is 8% per annum. The price may be computed as follows:

$$P = \frac{1{,}000}{(1.04)^{20}} = \$456.39$$

Notice that we have chosen to discount at a rate of 4% for 20 half-year periods, and not at 8% for 10 annual periods. The reason is that in practice a potential investor has a choice between plain vanilla bonds and zero coupon bonds. Comparisons between bonds, are made on the basis of yields, and to draw meaningful inferences it is imperative that the discounting technique be common across bond types. Because the cash flows from plain vanilla bonds are usually discounted on a semiannual basis, we choose to do the same for zero coupon bonds.

A zero coupon bond never sells at a premium. It always trades at a discount except at the time of maturity when it trades at the face value. That does not mean that a buyer of such a bond always experiences a capital gain. A buyer who purchases, and holds it to maturity obviously will have a capital gain. But if a buyer chooses to sell it prior to maturity, the result may well end up being a capital loss as we shall demonstrate.

Example 2.4. Alex bought a zero coupon bond when there were 10 years to maturity. The prevailing yield was 8% per annum. Today, a year later, the YTM is 10% per annum. The purchase price was \$456.39. The price at the time of sale is \$415.52. Thus in this case the investor has a capital loss of \$40.87.

Creating a Synthetic Zero Coupon Bond

A zero coupon bond can be synthesized using two plain vanilla bonds each of which pays a coupon at a different rate. Consider two bonds, both with a face value of M and with N coupons remaining till maturity. The first bond has a coupon of c_1, and the second has a coupon rate of c_2. Assume we buy w units of the first bond and $(1 - w)$ units of the second.

The payment every semiannual period will be

$$w \times M \times \frac{c_1}{2} + (1 - w) \times M \times \frac{c_2}{2}$$

Let's choose w, such that the cash flow from the portfolio is zero

$$w\left(\frac{c_1}{2}-\frac{c_2}{2}\right)=-\frac{c_2}{2}$$
$$\Rightarrow w=-\frac{c_2}{c_1-c_2}$$

The cash flow at maturity will be

$$w\times M\times\left(1+\frac{c_1}{2}\right)+(1-w)\times M\times\left(1+\frac{c_2}{2}\right)=M$$

Hence we have created a zero coupon bond with a face value of M, and N semiannual periods to maturity. Here is a numerical example.

Example 2.5. Consider a bond with a coupon of 8% per annum, paid semiannually, and another with a coupon of 10% per annum, payable half-yearly. Both the bonds have N half-year periods until expiration and a face value of $1,000.

$$w=-\frac{0.10}{0.08-0.10}=-\frac{0.10}{-0.02}=5.\quad\text{Thus }(1-w)=-4$$

Hence we need to go long in five units of the first bond and short in four units of the second. The periodic cash flow is

$$5\times40-4\times50=0$$

The terminal cash flow is:

$$5\times1{,}040-4\times1{,}050=\$1{,}000$$

The No-arbitrage Price of the Zero Coupon Bond

As we have seen a zero coupon bond can be synthesized using two coupon paying bonds. To rule out arbitrage, the price of the zero should be a weighted average of the prices of the coupon paying bonds. Consider the data in Example 2.5. Assume the two bonds have a time to maturity of five years, and that the bond with an 8% coupon has a YTM of 10% per annum, while the bond with a coupon of 10% has a YTM of 11% per annum. Thus the prices of the two bonds will be $922.7827 and $962.3119. To create the synthetic zero we need to go long in five units of the former, and short in four units of the latter. Thus the price of the synthetic zero should be $5\times922.7827-4\times962.3119=$ $764.6659. Thus

$$\frac{1{,}000}{(1+\frac{y}{2})^{10}}=764.6659$$
$$\Rightarrow y=5.4390\%$$

Price Quotes for Bonds

Bond prices are always quoted as a percentage of par, or per 100 currency units of face value. The reason is the following. Consider two bonds, one with a face value of $1,000 and another with a par value of $2,000. Assume that both securities are quoting at $1,500. The first is obviously a premium bond and the second a discount bond. However this cannot be discerned from the observed prices unless the corresponding face values are also specified. On the other hand if the price were to be expressed for a par value of $100, any value less than 100 would signify a discount bond while a value more than 100 would connote a premium bond. In the US market prices are quoted as a percentage of par plus 32nds. In other words the bond market is not decimalized and prices vary in increments of $\frac{1}{32}$. For instance consider a quote of 97-08. This does not mean a price of 97 dollars and 8 cents per dollar 100 of face value. What it means is that the price per dollar 100 of face value is 97 + 8/32 or $97.25. So if we were to buy bonds with a face value of $1MM, the amount payable will be $1{,}000{,}000 \times 97.25/100 =$ $972,500. In some cases the price will have a trailing + sign. This indicates that a $\frac{1}{64}$ needs to be added. For instance a quote of 97-08+ would connote a price of $97 + 8/32 +$ $1/64$ or 97.265625 per 100 dollars of face value.

Computation of the Bond Price Using Excel

If we are on a coupon date, the PV function in Excel may be used to determine the price of a bond. The required parameters for the function are:

- Rate: This is the periodic yield to maturity. Thus if a bond pays coupons semiannually, the rate is half the applicable YTM.
- Nper: This is the is the number of coupon periods remaining till maturity. Thus, for a bond paying semiannual coupons, it will be twice the number of years left.
- Pmt: This is the periodic coupon payment. Thus if a bond with a face value of $1,000 were to pay a coupon of 8% per annum on a semiannual basis, Pmt will be $40.
- Fv: This is the face value of the bond, which is typically $1,000.

In the PV Excel function, cash flows in one direction are positive while those in the other direction are negative. Thus if we want the price, which represents our investment, to be positive, then the cash flows received from the bond must be negative. Thus Pmt in the above case will be stated as –40, and Fv as –1,000.

Example 2.6. Consider a bond with a face value of $1,000 and five years to maturity. The coupon is 7.5% per annum and the YTM is 10% per annum. Thus the inputs to the PV function will be (0.05, 10, –37.50, –1,000). The answer is $903.48.

If we know the price, we can compute the YTM using the RATE function in Excel. The required parameters are Nper, Pmt, Pv, and Fv. For obvious reasons, if Pmt and Fv are entered with positive signs, then Pv must be entered with a negative sign. The answer will be in terms of the rate per period. Thus if the bond pays semiannual coupons, the rate that is obtained must be multiplied by two to annualize it. Here is an illustration.

Example 2.7. Consider a bond with a face value of $1,000 and five years to maturity. The coupon is 7.5% per annum and the price is $925. What is the YTM? The inputs to the RATE function are (10, −37.50, 925, −1,000). The answer is 4.7075%. This is a semiannual rate. Thus the annual YTM is 9.4151%.

Different Bond Types

We have already discussed some alternatives to plain vanilla bonds, what we have termed as bonds with bells and whistles. These include zero coupon bonds and bonds with built-in options such as callable, putable, and convertible bonds. We will discuss these bonds in more detail subsequently. For the moment, let's analyze certain other types of bonds with bells and whistles.

Amortizing Bonds

A plain vanilla bond is also known as a *bullet bond*, because the entire principal is repaid in one installment at the time of maturity. In the case of an amortizing bond, however, the principal is repaid in installments. Let's consider a three-year amortizing bond with a face value of $1,000 and coupon of 8% per annum payable semiannually. The face value is repaid in four equal installments starting with the time of payment of the third coupon. Thus the cash flows from the bond are as depicted in Table 2.4.

The first two cash flows represent coupon payments of $40 each. The third consists of a principal payment of $250 and a coupon payment that is 4% of 1,000. The fourth cash flow consists of a principal payment of $250 and a coupon of 4% on a

Table 2.4: Cash flows from an amortizing bond.

Time Period	Cash Flow
1	40
2	40
3	290
4	280
5	270
6	260

principal of $750. The penultimate cash flow consists of a principal payment of $250 and interest at a rate of 4% on a principal of $500. The final cash flow consists of a principal of $250 and interest at the rate of 4% on a principal of the same amount.

Some issuers issue such bonds because their asset base also has a similar cash flow profile. These bonds generally can be issued with a lower coupon as compared to plain vanilla bonds that are similar in all other respects. This is because in the case of the latter, the entire principal repayment is concentrated at the end. Consequently there is a greater risk of default for the holder, as opposed to an investor in an amortized bond, who recovers a percentage of the face value prior to maturity. Table 2.5 compares the cash flows from a plain vanilla bond, with those from an amortizing bond.

Comparison of a Plain Vanilla Bond with an Amortizing Bond

Table 2.5: YTM of a plain vanilla bond versus that of an amortizing bond.

Time	Cash Flow	Cash Flow	Cash Flow	Cash Flow	Cash Flow	Cash Flow
0	−1,000	−1,000	−925	−925	−1,025	−1,025
1	40	40	40	40	40	40
2	40	40	40	40	40	40
3	40	290	40	290	40	290
4	40	280	40	280	40	280
5	40	270	40	270	40	270
6	1,040	260	1,040	260	1,040	260
YTM	8.0000%	8.0000%	11.0028%	11.9620%	7.0608%	6.7780%

As can be seen in the table, if a plain vanilla bond and an amortizing bond, with the same coupon rate, time to maturity, and face value, are trading at par, then both of them will have the same YTM, which is obviously equal to the coupon rate. However, if the two are trading at a discount, with the same price, the amortizing bond will have a higher YTM. On the other hand, if the two are trading at a premium, once again with the same price, the amortizing bond will have a lower YTM. We will see a similar result when we analyze mortgage-backed securities later in the book.

The rationale is as follows. Compared to an amortizing bond, a plain vanilla bond has a concentrated cash flow at the end. The impact of a given yield change, is more on long-term cash flows than on shorter-term cash flows. If the yield is more than the coupon, a plain vanilla bond will trade at a discount. If an amortizing bond were to have the same yield, it would trade at a higher price. Consequently, if they are trading at the same price, the amortized bond must have a higher YTM. On the other hand, if the yield is less than the coupon, the plain vanilla bond will trade at a premium. If an amortizing bond were to have the same yield, it would trade at a lower price.

Consequently, if they are trading at the same price, the amortized bond must have a lower YTM.

Bonds with Step-Up Coupons and Step-Down Coupons

Take the case of a newly established company, or a company with a relatively virgin product or service. The market may expect such entities to offer a higher coupon. However, such firms are unlikely to have a high level of earnings, because revenues are likely to peak only after the product or service has acquired sufficient market share. As these companies cannot afford to pay a high coupon at the outset, they may go in for a step-up coupon bond, where the coupon increases as the bond becomes more seasoned. For instance, take a company that is in a position to issue a five-year bond with a coupon of 8% per annum. It may instead decide to issue a bond with a coupon of 6% per annum for the first three years, and 10% per annum for the last two years. Such a bond gives the issuer elbow room in the earlier years.

In practice these bonds are usually callable on each coupon date. These bonds may be of the one-step type or the multi-step variety. In the case of the former, the coupon resets once during the life of the bond, whereas in the case of the latter it resets more than once. As the coupon rate on such bonds rises over comparable rates, the bond is likely to be called. Thus in practice the investors may not receive the higher payments due after the coupon is scheduled to reset. As compensation for the right to redeem early, the issuers are required to offer a higher coupon. It may also be the case that the scheduled coupon increases do not keep pace with the market rates. Thus, despite the step-up feature, the enhancement in coupon may not be adequate.

In the case of step-down coupon bonds, the security initially offers a high coupon, and the coupon rate reduces with the passage of time. These may also be callable. A company which is required to pay a high coupon because of the perceived risk level, but is confident that its image will improve over a period of time, may issue such bonds with a higher coupon in the initial years, and lower coupons in subsequent years.

Payment-In-Kind (PIK) Bonds

Payment-in-kind bonds do not pay coupons in the form of cash. Such bonds require the issuer to offer additional securities to the investors, without any monetary consideration, when the coupon falls due. Again, like in the case of step-up coupons, this offers the issuer time to prepare for enhanced cash outlays. The security used to pay interest is usually identical to the underlying bond, but in principle may be different. Compared to investors in plain vanilla bonds, investors in PIK bonds take more risk but are likely to get higher returns.

Treasury Securities

Government securities in the U.S. are termed *Treasury securities*. The Department of the Treasury issues three categories of marketable debt securities: T-bills, T-notes, and T-bonds. T-bills are zero coupon securities with a maximum time to maturity of 52 weeks. T-notes have maturities ranging from 1–10 years, and T-bonds have maturities in excess of 10 years, going up to 30 years in practice. Both T-notes and T-bonds pay coupons. For a given maturity, a Treasury security is considered to be the safest type of debt security from the perspective of default risk. This is because the federal government of a country has two powers that other institutions do not. It can print more currency whenever it wants, and it also can increase the rates of taxes as and when it deems fit. Consequently, for a given maturity, the YTM of a Treasury security is usually lower than the yields of all other securities with the same maturity. In practice there are other factors at work. For instance, Municipal bonds provide holders with exemption from paying Federal income tax, as a consequence of which, holders may be prepared to accept a lower yield.

Whereas corporations have a choice between equity and debt, for raising funds, governments as discussed earlier, can issue only debt securities. There are many reasons why a government might choose to issue debt. It may have a deficit in the current financial year because expenses are in excess of projected revenues. Or it may have issued debt in the past, and needs funds to pay interest on the same. Finally, there could be a situation where debt issued earlier is maturing, and funds are required to make the redemption payment. The U.S. Treasuries market is the largest bond market in the world, as well as the most liquid market.

Sometimes the Treasury may follow up an issue with a subsequent issue with the same remaining term to maturity and coupon rate. The issuance of such a tranche is termed as a *reopening* of an existing issue. For instance, assume that six months ago, the Treasury issued a 10-year note with a coupon of 4% per annum. If it were to now issue additional 9 1/2-year notes with a coupon of 4%, we would term it as a reopening, for we are deepening the pool of securities that are already trading in the market.

Treasury Auctions

The interest rate of a Treasury security is determined by the market, and is not set by the government. The Treasury sells bills, notes, and bonds, by way of an auction process. There are two types of bids–competitive and non-competitive. The auctions may be price based or yield based. Auctions for new securities are yield based. Competitive bidders indicate the minimum yield they require as well as the quantity sought. Re-openings of existing securities are price based. Competitive bidders indicate the maximum price that they are prepared to pay as well as the quantity sought. In either price-based or yield-based auctions, non-competitive bidders indicate only the quantity sought. The implicit statement is that they are prepared to accept any price/yield that is determined at the auction.

Smaller investors generally submit non-competitive bids. There is an upper limit of $5 million for such bidders in the U.S. In some countries there is a separate quota for such investors. In a price-based auction, bids are arranged in descending order of price, for priority is given to a party willing to pay more. In a yield-based auction, the bids are arranged in ascending order of yield, for a party willing to accept a lower rate is given preference.[5] In the U.S. all non-competitive bids are accepted in toto. The total amount of such bids is subtracted from the amount being offered, and the balance is offered to the competitive bidders. A competitive bidder is also subject to a restriction in the U.S. that it cannot be allotted more than 35% of the amount being auctioned, no matter how aggressively it bids.

There are two ways in which securities can be allotted, the multiple price/yield auction known as a *French auction*, and the uniform price/yield auction known as a *Dutch auction*. We will illustrate both methods by way of an example.

Illustration of a Treasury Auction

The Treasury is offering $35 billion worth of T-bonds. $5 billion worth of non-competitive bids have been received. These are fully accepted, and therefore the amount available for competitive bidders is $30 billion. There are eight competitive bids which have been arranged in ascending order of yield. Had it been a price-based auction, we would have arranged in descending order of price.

Table 2.6: A Treasury auction.

Bidder	Bid Yield	Bid Amount	Aggregate Demand
Dealer-1	2.372	3 bn	3 bn
Dealer-2	2.375	7 bn	10 bn
Dealer-3	2.380	5 bn	15 bn
Dealer-4	2.385	10 bn	25 bn
Dealer-5	2.388	10 bn	35 bn
Dealer-6	2.388	15 bn	50 bn
Dealer-7	2.400	5 bn	55 bn
Dealer-8	2.405	15 bn	70 bn

5 Price and yield are inversely related.

Dealers 1–4 will have their bids accepted in full. This is because the total quantity sought by the four of them is $25 billion, which is less than the available amount of $30 billion. After this $5 billion is left to be allocated, but the total demand at the next yield level is $25 billion. Both Dealer-5 and Dealer-6 have bid 2.388. Because only $5 billion is left at this stage, there is pro-rata allocation. Their total demand is $25 billion, of which Dealer-5 has asked for $10 billion which is 40% of the amount, and Dealer-6 has asked for $15 billion which is 60%. Thus 40% of the remaining amount of $5 billion, which is $2 billion will be given to Dealer-5, and the balance $3 billion to Dealer-6. Dealers 7 and 8 are not allocated any securities and are said to be *shut out* of the auction. However a party who is shut out can always go to the secondary market and acquire securities after the issue process.

In the U.S. the market clearing yield, also known as the *stop-yield* or *high-yield*, which in this case is 2.388%, is rounded down to the nearest multiple of 0.125 to determine the coupon. In this illustration, the coupon is set equal to 2.375%. In a Dutch auction, Dealers 1–6 pay a price corresponding to a YTM of 2.388%. Obviously parties who are prepared to accept a lower yield will have no objection to accepting a higher yield. Because the coupon is the nearest lower multiple of 0.125%, the securities are issued at par or at a discount. In a French auction, however, successful bidders pay a price corresponding to their bid. Thus the price paid steadily decreases as we go from Dealer-1 to Dealer-6. In either case, there is pro-rata allocation at the *high-yield*, and bidders bidding higher than the market clearing yield are shut out.

The ratio of bids received, the total of competitive as well as non-competitive bids, to the amount awarded is termed the *bid-to-cover* ratio. The higher the ratio, the more the perceived success of the auction. Assume that the Treasury is issuing $25 billion of bonds. If $150 billion worth of bids are received, the bid to cover ratio is 6:1. However if $200 billion worth of bids are received, the ratio is 8:1, and the auction is deemed to be more successful.

Security Identification

In the U.S. and Canada, securities are identified on the basis of a CUSIP number. CUSIP stands for Committee on Uniform Securities Identification Procedures and is a 9-character alpha-numeric code. Most countries use ISIN, which stands for International Securities Identification Number. An ISIN is a 12-character alpha-numeric code. To convert a CUSIP to a corresponding ISIN, a 2-character country code is added at the beginning and a check digit is added at the end. For U.S. securities the code is US, whereas for Canadian securities it is CA.

While specifying the details of a bond prior to a trade, it is essential to state the issuer, the coupon, and the year and month of issue. In certain cases the currency of issue also needs to be specified. In contrast, a stock usually can be identified by just the name of the issuer. This is because most companies issue only one category of shares.[6] However if we take an issuer like IBM, a bond maturing in 2030 may mature in January or in October. If it were to mature in October the coupon may be 4% or 5%. Thus merely stating that the issue is an IBM bond maturing in 2030 is not adequate. Both the month of expiration and the coupon rate have to be specified. Some issuers have securities identical in terms of year and month of expiration as well as the coupon, but differ with respect to the currency of issue. In such cases the currency of issue also needs to be spelled out.

Coupon Strips

Coupon stripping is a technique for deriving zero-coupon bonds based on the underlying coupon-paying bonds. What used to happen in the 1980s was the following: An investment bank would buy a large lot of a Treasury bond and transfer it to a special purpose vehicle (SPV). The SPV would then issue synthetic zero-coupon securities, backed by the underlying coupon-paying T-bonds. The SPV was a single-purpose dedicated trust.[7] The SPV was empowered to hold the mother bonds, but it could not sell them or lend them, pledge them as collateral, or write options on them. It was entitled to issue zeroes, where each type of security represented the entitlement to a single cash flow from the mother bond. This process of creating synthetic zeroes from a conventional mother bond is coupon stripping. If the mother bond has N years to maturity, we can create $2N + 1$ types of zeroes because the mother bond will pay $2N$ coupons, and there will be a terminal face value payment at the end. Thus the essence of coupon stripping is that the entitlement to each cash flow from the underlying bond, is sold separately. Thus while one investor may buy a security corresponding to the first coupon, another may buy a security entitling him to a subsequent coupon or face value. Assume that a T-bond with a face value of $100 million, annual coupon of 10% paid semiannually, and 10 years to maturity, is acquired by an investment bank. There will be 21 cash flows, that is, 20 coupons and one face value. Thus 21 types of securities can be issued. Each coupon payment would be for $5 million. If we assume that the synthetic securities have a face value of $1,000, 5,000 securities corresponding to each of the coupons can be issued. 100,000 zeroes corresponding to the principal cash flow can also be issued. The motivation to issue these securities is that if the sum of the prices of the baby bonds differs from that of the mother bond, then there is an arbitrage opportunity. Coupon stripping is a type of financial engineering, whereby securities that do not otherwise exist, are created.

The investment banks came up with exotic names for the synthetic zeroes. Merrill Lynch, which was the pioneer, offered what it called TIGRS (Treasury Investment

6 Sometimes there could be multiple categories due to non-voting shares, or shares with differential voting rights (DVR).

7 See Smith [56].

Growth Receipts). Salomon came up with CATS (Certificates of Accrual on Treasury Securities), and Lehman came up with LIONS (Lehman Investment Opportunity Notes). Consequently these securities came to be known as *"Animal Products,"* and this segment of the capital market was known as the *"Zoo."*

Trademarks are no longer being issued, because in 1985 the Treasury itself got into the act to facilitate coupon stripping. An investor cannot buy a coupon or principal strip directly from the Treasury. What happens is that a dealer who owns a T-bond can ask the regional Federal Reserve Bank (FRB) where it is held, to replace it with an equivalent set of STRIPS, or Separate Trading of Registered Interest and Principal of Securities. There are two categories of STRIPS: C-STRIPS, which come from coupon payments, and P-STRIPS, which come from principal payments. In 1987 the Treasury started to allow the reverse process known as a *Reconstitution*. That is, a trader who owns all the C-STRIPS and the P-STRIP corresponding to a T-bond, can request that the FRB replace it with the mother bond. Every C-STRIP and P-STRIP emanating from a mother bond is assigned a CUSIP. The mother bond is also assigned a CUSIP.

A C-STRIP maturing on a given date, say 15 May 2022, will have the same CUSIP as another C-STRIP maturing on that day, although the two may have been generated from different mother bonds. Thus the supply of C-STRIPS scheduled to mature on a given date increases over time. For instance, take a 20-year T-bond issued on 15 May 2015 with a coupon of 4%. It will pay a coupon on 15 May 2022. Another 20-year T-bond issued on 15 May 2018 with a coupon of 3%, will also pay a coupon on 15 May 2022. The C-STRIPS corresponding to the two mother bonds will have the same CUSIP. We say that they are fungible. However, P-STRIPS are not fungible. Every P-STRIP corresponding to a mother bond has a unique CUSIP. Thus unlike C-STRIPS whose supply increases over time, the supply of P-STRIPS is fixed at the time of issuance of the mother bond.[8] In practice, a C-STRIP and a P-STRIP maturing on the same day usually do not have the same price. One reason is that the P-STRIPS are more liquid due to greater availability. For instance, a T-bond with a face value of $100 million and a coupon of 10% and 10 years to maturity, will generate 5,000 C-STRIPS corresponding to each coupon date, and it will generate 100,000 P-STRIPS. There is yet another reason for the popularity of P-STRIPS. Possession of them facilitates reconstitution.[9] Assume that the sum of the STRIPS is cheaper than the mother bond. If a dealer has the P-STRIP, he only has to acquire the C-STRIPS, which are relatively easier to obtain because of fungibility. However, if he were to possess only some of the C-STRIPS, he would have to buy the P-STRIP and the remaining C-STRIPS. Thus P-STRIPS carry a higher price, or a lower yield, than C-STRIPS maturing on the same date. There is however a category of investors termed as buy-and-hold investors, who as the name suggests will buy and not trade prior to maturity. Such investors are likely to prefer

8 See Smith [56].

9 See Smith [56].

C-STRIPS, as they offer a higher YTM. Long-term investors, like pension funds and insurance companies, prefer such strategies because their liabilities are long term in nature. Consequently, by investing in such securities, they can lock in a rate of return without worrying about issues such as the reinvestment of intermediate cash flows.

STRIPS are primarily acquired by institutional investors. However they are accessible to individuals, as well. Many mutual funds invest in these securities and offer an alternative avenue of investment to retail investors.

When Issued (WI) Trading

WI stands for when, as, and if issued.[10] It is a market for forward trading in bonds. That is, although the issue of these bonds has been announced, they are yet to be issued. Trades commence on the date of announcement from the Treasury, and end on the actual issue date. The WI market helps investors to gauge the market's interest in a security prior to the actual auction. Traders can take both long and short positions, which will settle on the scheduled issue date. The activity in the WI market has a bearing on the outcome of a Treasury auction. Bidders who take long positions in the WI market enter the auction with long positions, whereas those who are short in the WI market do so with short positions. Thus the strategy employed by a trader is influenced by activities in the WI market. The presence of the WI market facilitates price discovery. On or before the date of the auction, securities trade on a yield basis in the WI market. This is because the coupon has not been set, and consequently the price cannot be determined. From the day after the auction, securities can be traded on a price basis because the coupon has been established.

Coupon Rolls

In a coupon roll, a dealer acquires the most recently issued security for a maturity from a client and simultaneously sells the same amount of the recently announced security. Thus a roll has two legs. The first leg settles on a $T + 1$ basis, whereas the second leg is essentially a forward contract. There also exists what is called a *reverse roll*. In this case, the dealer sells the most recently issued security to a client and simultaneously buys the same amount of the newly announced security. The forward leg in rolls and the reverse rolls is a when issued (WI) trade.

The issue of interest is the spread between the yield on the new security and that on the outstanding security. If a dealer "gives" 10 basis points (bp) in a roll, it means that the WI security has a YTM that is higher by 10 bp compared to the existing security.

---

10 See Liaw [43].

On the contrary, if a dealer “takes” 10 bp in a roll, it means that the WI security has a YTM that is lower by 10 bp compared to the outstanding issue.

Accounting for Bonds

Bonds are typically issued at par, but may be issued at a premium or at a discount. Accounting for a par bond issue is fairly simple. Assume Alpha Corporation issues 1,000 JD-15 bonds on 15 June 2018. The face value is $1,000, the coupon is 10% per annum paid semiannually, and the time to maturity is three years. When the bonds are issued, there is an inflow of cash. Thus cash, which is an asset, is debited with $1,000,000, and bonds payable, a liability is credited with $1,000,000. On the first coupon date which is 15 December 2018, the total interest payable is $50,000. Bond interest expenses is debited with $50,000. If the payout is immediate, cash is credited with $50,000. Otherwise, interest payable is credited with $50,000.

Issue of Discount Bonds

Now assume that while the coupon continues to remain at 10% per annum, the YTM at the time of issue is 12%. The bond will obviously trade at a discount. The price will be $950.8268. If 1,000 bonds are issued, the cash inflow will be $950,827. Thus cash will be debited with this amount. Bonds payable will be credited with $1,000,000. Unamortized bond discount will be debited with the difference, which is $49,173. This discount has to be amortized, or written off, during the life of the bond. Thus the discount will steadily decline, and the carrying value, which is the difference between the face value and the unamortized discount, will steadily increase. At the time of maturity of the bond, the unamortized discount will be zero, and the carrying value will be equal to the face value. When a company issues a bond at a discount, the effective interest paid is greater than the coupon rate. This is because at the outset, the issuer receives an amount less than the face value, whereas at maturity it has to pay the entire face value. Thus the discount must be added to the total coupon paid, in order to arrive at the effective interest. In our illustration, the total coupon paid over three years is $300,000. The discount is $49,173. Thus the total interest cost is $349,173. The discount is allocated over the life of the security. Thus every period, the interest expense will be equal to the coupon interest paid, plus the amortized discount. This procedure is called *amortization of bond discount*. There are two approaches, the *straight line method (SLM)* and the *effective interest method (EIM)*. We discuss both in the following sections.[11]

11 See Needles and Powers [50].

The Straight Line Method for Amortizing the Bond Discount

SLM equalizes the amortized discount for every period. In our case $50,000 interest is paid out twice a year for three years. As per the SLM, the interest expense per period is $\frac{349{,}173}{6}$ = $58,195.50. Thus, while the cash interest paid is $50,000, the interest expense is higher by $8,195.50. In the books of accounts, we debit bond interest expense with $58,195.50, and credit cash with $50,000. Unamortized bond discount is credited with the difference, which is $8,195.50. At maturity, the unamortized bond discount will be zero.

This method is simple, but has an inherent weakness. Every period the carrying value increases, whereas the interest expense remains constant. Thus the rate of interest declines over time.

The Effective Interest Method for Amortizing the Bond Discount

In this method, the YTM prevailing at the time of issue is multiplied by the carrying value of the bond at the beginning of the period. The amount amortized each period is the difference between the interest computed using the YTM and the actual interest paid. In our case the original YTM is 12%, or 6% per half-yearly period. The discount is $49,173, and the initial carrying value is $950,827.

The interest expense for the first half-year is 0.06 × 950,827 = $57,050. The actual interest paid is $50,000. Thus the amortized discount is $7,050. The unamortized discount at the end of the first half-yearly period is 49,173 – 7,050 = $42,123. This will decline at the end of every period. Thus the carrying value will steadily increase. In accounting terms, we would do the following. Debit interest expense with $57,050. Credit cash with $50,000 and credit unamortized bond discount with $7,050. Similarly the interest expense for the next semiannual period is 0.06 × (950,827 + 7,050) = $57,473. The actual interest paid is $50,000, and the amortized discount is $7,473. The unamortized discount is 42,123 – 7,473 = $34,650. The carrying value at the end of the second half-yearly period is $965,349. The sequence of entries over the life of the bond is summarized in Table 2.7.

Table 2.7: Accounting for a discount bond.

Period	Beginning Carrying Value	Interest Expense	Coupon	Amortized Discount	Unamortized Discount	Ending Carrying Value
0					49,173	950,827
1	950,827	57,050	50,000	7,050	42,123	957,877
2	957,877	57,473	50,000	7,473	34,651	965,349
3	965,349	57,921	50,000	7,921	26,730	973,270
4	973,270	58,396	50,000	8,396	18,334	981,666
5	981,666	58,900	50,000	8,900	9,434	990,566
6	990,566	59,434	50,000	9,434	0	1,000,000

As can be seen, the carrying value gradually increases and approaches the face value at maturity. The interest expense is a fixed percentage of the carrying value, and therefore it too increases every period. Because the coupon payments are constant, the amortized discount steadily increases.

Issue of Premium Bonds

Let's consider the same data for the issue of premium bonds. 1,000 bonds are issued with a face value of $1,000 each and three years to maturity. The coupon is 10% per annum payable semiannually, and the YTM is 8% per annum, not 12%, as assumed earlier.

The initial cash inflow from the bonds is $1,052,421. Thus there is an unamortized bond premium of $52,421. This too needs to be amortized over the life of the securities. The premium represents an amount that need not be paid by the issuer at maturity. Thus it may be considered an advance reduction of the total interest paid over the life of the bond. The total interest over three years is $300,000. As the premium is $52,421, the total interest cost is $247,579. Once again this may be amortized using the SLM or the EIM.

Straight Line Method for Amortizing the Bond Premium

SLM equalizes the amortized premium for every period. In our case $50,000 interest is paid out twice a year for three years. As per the SLM the interest expense per period is $\frac{247{,}579}{6} = \$41{,}263$. Thus, while the cash interest paid is $50,000, the interest expense is lower by $8,737. In the books of accounts, we debit bond interest expense with $41,263. Cash is credited with $50,000. Unamortized bond premium is debited with the difference, which is $8,737. At maturity, the unamortized bond premium will be zero.

This method is simple, but has the same inherent weakness, as the SLM for bond discounts. Every period the carrying value decreases, whereas the interest expense remains constant. Thus the rate of interest increases over time.

The Effective Interest Method for Amortizing the Bond Premium

In this method, the YTM prevailing at the time of issue is multiplied by the carrying value of the bond at the beginning of the period. The amount amortized each period is the difference between the interest computed using the YTM and the actual interest paid. In our case, the premium is $52,421, and the initial carrying value is $1,052,421.

The interest expense for the first half-year is $0.04 \times 1{,}052{,}421 = \$42{,}097$. The actual interest paid is $50,000. Thus the amortized premium is $7,903. The unamortized premium at the end of the first half-yearly period is $52{,}421 - 7{,}903 = \$44{,}518$. This declines at the end of every period. Thus the carrying value steadily declines. In accounting terms we would do the following: Debit interest expense with $42,097, credit cash with $50,000, and debit unamortized bond premium with $7,903. Similarly the interest expense for the next semiannual period is $0.04 \times (1{,}052{,}421 - 7{,}903) = \$41{,}781$. The actual interest paid is $50,000, and the amortized premium is $8,219. The unamortized premium is $44{,}518 - 8{,}219 = \$36{,}299$. The carrying value at the end of the second half-yearly period is $1,036,299. The sequence of entries over the life of the bond is summarized in Table 2.8.

Table 2.8: Accounting for a premium bond.

Period	Beginning Carrying Value	Interest Expense	Coupon	Amortized Premium	Unamortized Premium	Ending Carrying Value
0					52,421	1,052,421
1	1,052,421	42,097	50,000	7,903	44,518	1,044,518
2	1,044,518	41,781	50,000	8,219	36,299	1,036,299
3	1,036,299	41,452	50,000	8,548	27,751	1,027,751
4	1,027,751	41,110	50,000	8,890	18,861	1,018,861
5	1,018,861	40,754	50,000	9,246	9,615	1,009,615
6	1,009,615	40,385	50,000	9,615	0	1,000,000

Risks Inherent in Bonds

Before we go on to study the various types of risks that impact a bond holder, let's first define risk. The term *risk* refers to the possibility of loss arising due to uncertainty regarding the outcome of a transaction. Thus there are two conditions, for a transaction to be classified as risky. First, there must be more than one possible outcome. And second, at least one of the probable outcomes should lead to a loss. All bonds expose bond holders to multiple sources of risk.

Credit Risk

Credit risk, also known as default risk, refers to the probability of default by the borrower. That is, it is the risk that coupon payments and/or principal payments may not be made as promised. Treasury securities or federal government securities are backed by the full faith and credit of the federal government. Consequently they are virtually devoid of default risk.

At the time of a bond issue, the issuer provides an offer document or prospectus that gives information about its financial soundness and credit-worthiness. But every potential investor cannot be expected to decipher the intricacies of such a document.

Thus in practice, we have credit rating agencies. Rating agencies, such Standard & Poor's Corporation (S&P), Moody's Investors Service, and Fitch Ratings, specialize in evaluating the credit quality of an issue at the time of issue. Subsequently they constantly monitor the financial health of the issue and re-rate or modify their recommendations if it found to be necessary.

Top quality issues are classified as investment grade, whereas issues of a lower quality are termed as speculative grade, or junk bonds.

Moody's Ratings Scale

Moody's uses the following rating scale for long-term instruments:
- Aaa: The issue is of the highest quality and carries minimal risk.
- Aa: The issue is of high quality and has very low credit risk.
- A: The security is of upper medium grade and has low credit risk.
- Baa: The security is of medium grade with moderate credit risk.
- Ba: The security has a speculative element and has substantial credit risk.
- B: The security is speculative and has high credit risk.
- Caa: The security is of poor quality and has very high credit risk.
- Ca: The security is highly speculative and is likely to default. However, there is some possibility of recovery of principal and interest.
- C: This is the lowest rating; such bonds are typically in default. There is very little possibility of recovery of principal and interest.

Moody's appends modifiers of 1, 2, and 3 to grades Aa to Caa. A modifier of 1 indicates that the security is at the higher end of the category. On the other hand, a modifier of 2 indicates that the security is at the middle of the category. Finally a modifier of 3 indicates that the security is at the lower end of the category. Aaa to Baa are considered to be of investment grade, whereas the rest are of speculative grade.

S&P's Rating Scale

Standard and Poor's rates issues on a scale from AAA to D. Country risk and currency of repayment are factored into the credit analysis and reflected in the issue rating.
- AAA: These securities are of the highest quality. The issuer's capacity to meet its financial commitments is extremely strong.
- AA: These securities are slightly below those rated AAA. The issuer's capacity to meet its financial commitments is very strong.
- A: These are somewhat more vulnerable to adverse changes in economic conditions. The issuer's capacity to meet its financial commitments is still strong.

- BBB: These securities display adequate protection parameters. But adverse economic conditions are more likely to weaken the issuer's capacity to meet its financial commitments.
- BB: These are speculative grade securities. However, they are less risky compared to other securities which are in this category. They are vulnerable to adverse economic conditions, which could seriously impact the issuers' capacity to meet its financial commitments.
- B: These are more vulnerable to non-payment compared to BB rated securities. But the issuer currently has the capacity to meet its financial commitments.
- CCC: These securities are currently vulnerable to non-payment. Favourable market conditions are required, if the issuer is to meet its commitment. If economic conditions become adverse, the issuer is unlikely to have the capacity to meet its financial commitments.
- CC: These securities are highly vulnerable to non-payment. Default has not yet occurred, but is considered to be a virtual certainty.
- C: These are extremely vulnerable to nonpayment and the chance of recovery is lower compared to higher rated securities.
- D: These securities are in default or the issuer has filed for bankruptcy.

Grades from AA to CCC may be modified by a + or a – sign, to indicate relative standing. Bonds rated AAA to BBB are considered to be of investment grade, while those with lower rankings are categorized as speculative.

Fitch's Rating Scale

Fitch assigns ratings ranging from AAA at one end to D at the other extreme. Grades AAA to BBB are investment grade. The rest are speculative grade.

- AAA: Lowest expectation of default risk. It indicates that the issuer is exceptionally strong from the standpoint of meeting financial commitments.
- AA: Very high credit quality. It indicates an expectation of very low default risk. It indicates that the issuer is very strong from the standpoint of meeting financial commitments.
- A: High credit quality. It indicates an expectation of low default risk. It indicates that the issuer is strong from the standpoint of meeting financial commitments.
- BBB: Good credit quality. It indicates that the expectation of default risk is currently low. The issuer's capacity to meet financial commitments is adequate.
- BB: Speculative. There is a greater risk of default. However, the issuer has financial flexibility that could facilitate the fulfillment of financial obligations.
- B: Highly speculative. There is material default risk, but also a limited margin of safety. Although financial obligations are currently being met, the future is uncertain.

- CCC: Substantial credit risk. Default is a real possibility.
- CC: Very high level of credit risk. Default appears probable.
- C: Near default. A default or default-like process has begun.
- RD: Restricted default. There has been a default but the issuer has not filed for bankruptcy, and continues to operate.
- D: Default. The issuer has ceased business and entered into bankruptcy filing or liquidation.

Non-investment grade bonds are also known as *junk* bonds, or *high-yield bonds*. There are two types of junk bonds. *Original issue junk bonds* carry a lower rating from the time of issue. *Fallen angels* on the other hand were originally classified as investment grade, but have been subsequently downgraded to junk status. Thus bond ratings can change over time. If a rating agency is planning to change its rating, it will signal its intention. S&P places the security on *Credit Watch*. Moody's places it on a list termed as *Under Review*, whereas Fitch places it on a list termed as *Rating Watch*. The appearance of a security on one or more of these lists is a signal that a change in ratings is on the way.

Rating agencies take various facts and factors into account when assigning a rating. The primary task is to evaluate the ability of issuers to meet their commitments on time. Factors considered include the issuer's financial condition and quality of management; the features of the security being issued; and the nature of revenue sources backing the issue. The last issue is very important for bonds used to generate funds for projects that are projected to yield revenues directly. For instance, a municipality may be planning the construction of an airport with a projected footfall of five million passengers a year. The rating agency will recalculate the projections using a lower figure of say three million passengers per annum. The standard policy is to scale down the projected revenue and scale up the projected expenses, and see whether the project is still financially viable.

In case you are wondering about the accuracy of these ratings, here are some statistics.[12] Moody's did a survey using data for an 81-year period from 1920 to 2001. They found that not a single Aaa-rated bond defaulted in the first year following issue, during this 81-year period. However, about 7% of B-rated bonds defaulted in the first year. When they considered a 10-year period following issue, they found that fewer than 1% of Aaa bonds defaulted, whereas about 44% of B-rated bonds did default.

Bond Insurance

A potential bond issuer can approach an insurance company to insure its bonds to enhance the credit quality. The rating assigned to the bond depends on the rating of the insurance company. Thus the issuer needs to obtain insurance from a company

12 See Liaw [43].

whose rating is superior to its own. The insurer charges a premium, but this can be passed on to the bond investors in the form of a lower coupon. In the case of such bonds the insurance company guarantees the timely payment of the principal and interest. Rating agencies evaluate the issue based on the insurer's capital adequacy and claims paying ability.

In the U.S. an investor can have his personal bond portfolio insured by an insurance company. However, this feature is not available in all countries. In the case of insured bonds, the guarantee provided is unconditional and irrevocable. This means that if the rating agencies subsequently downgrade the issue, the insurance will not be revoked. From the standpoint of an investor, an insured bond carries the assurance of extensive credit analysis and due diligence by two parties, namely the rating agency and the insurance company.

Liquidity Risk

A market is said to be illiquid or thin when there is an insufficient number of buyers and sellers. In a liquid market, trades take place at prices close to the true or fair value of the asset. In an illiquid market, buyers may have to pay a large premium to buy, or sellers may have to accept a significant discount to sell. Illiquid markets are characterized by large bid-ask spreads because trades will be few and far between. In other words, if the volume of activity is low, the margin for the dealer must be high, and consequently the spread will be higher. The impact cost of a trade is another measure of the liquidity of a market. Consider the limit order book for a security, as depicted in Table 2.9.

Table 2.9: Illustration of a limit order book.

Quantity	Price	Price	Quantity
100	99.00	100.00	200
200	98.75	100.50	300
300	98.00	101.00	500
500	97.50	102.00	250
1000	97.00	102.50	500

The best bid is \$99 and the best ask is \$100. Thus no buyer is willing to pay more than \$99, while no seller is willing to accept less than \$100. The truth is obviously in between, and our best guess would be a simple average. Consequently we define the fair price (*FP*) as the average of the two prices, which in this case is \$99.50. Consider a buy order for 400 shares; 200 shares would be bought at a price of \$100, and another 200 at \$100.50. Thus the weighted average price (*WAP*) is \$100.25. We define the impact cost of the trade as

$$\frac{\text{WAP} - \text{FP}}{\text{FP}}$$

In this case it is $\frac{100.25-99.50}{99.50}$ = 0.7538%. For a sell order we would define the cost as

$$\frac{\text{FP} - \text{WAP}}{\text{FP}}$$

For buy orders the weighted average price is greater than the fair price. However, for sell orders, the weighted average price is less than the fair price. Thus by definition the impact cost is always positive. The impact cost depends on the size of the trade as well as the direction. That is, a buy order for N shares does not usually have the same impact cost as a sell order for the same quantity. For an order of a given size, the lower the impact cost, the greater the perceived liquidity.

Interest Rate Risk

Interest rates or yields are the key variable of interest in debt markets. The term *interest rate risk* refers to the possibility of rates moving in an adverse direction from the standpoint of the bond holder. Unlike other sources of risk, interest rate risk affects bonds in not one, but in two ways. The first source of risk is what is termed as *reinvestment risk*. All bonds, other than zero-coupon bonds, make payments periodically in the form of coupon payments. These inflows have to be reinvested. Reinvestment risk refers to the possibility that rates may decline by the time the coupon is received. If so, the cash inflow has to be invested at a lower than expected rate. This risk impacts all bonds that make payments prior to maturity. Thus zero-coupon bonds are not subject to this risk, and that explains their popularity among certain classes of investors.

The second source of interest rate risk is what is termed as *market risk* or *price risk*. An investor who holds the bond until maturity gets the face value. However, if the bond is sold prior to maturity, the trader receives the market price prevailing at that point in time, which would be inversely related to the prevailing yield. If interest rates increase, the bonds have to be sold at a lower price. This is termed market risk or price risk. The two risks work in opposite directions. Reinvestment risk affects the investor if rates decline, whereas price risk impacts him if rates increase.

Inflation Risk

Inflation refers to the erosion of the purchasing power of money. Most bonds, including Treasury bonds, promise cash flows in dollar terms. There is no assurance about the basket of goods and services that can be purchased with the cash received. Inflation risk is the risk that the actual inflation may be higher than the expected inflation. When a buyer acquires a bond, the market has a perceived rate of inflation, on the basis of which the nominal or dollar rate of interest is set. However, the actual inflation at the time the coupon is received may be higher, which means that the investor has to settle for a smaller basket of goods and services. The rate of return, as measured by the ability to buy goods and services, is termed as the *real* rate of return. Thus, if the ex-post rate of inflation is higher than the ex-ante rate, the ex-post real rate of return will be lower than the ex-ante rate.[13] This risk is termed as inflation risk.

There exists a category of bonds known as indexed bonds. In the case of such bonds the coupon is linked to a price index. The higher the inflation is, the higher the value of the price index and the larger the coupon. Thus these bonds offer higher cash flows when the inflation rate is high and lower cash flows when it is low, thereby ensuring that the real return is kept at a virtually constant level.[14]

Timing Risk

In the case of a plain vanilla bond, there is no uncertainty about when the cash flows will be received, unless of course there is a default. But consider a callable bond. The investor has no idea when this bond may be recalled in the future. That is, he is unsure about the number of coupons he will receive and the point of receipt of the face value. This is termed as *timing risk.*

Foreign Exchange Risk

The rate of conversion of one currency into another is known as the *exchange rate*. Like stock prices and interest rates, exchange rates are also random variables. Take the case of an American investor who buys a bond whose cash flows are denominated in euros. The bond is scheduled to pay a coupon of 10 euros every six months. Assume the rate at the beginning is 1.2000 U.S. dollars per euro. However, the dollar appreciates, and the rate after six months is 1.0500 U.S. dollars per euro. Thus while the anticipated cash inflow is $12, the actual inflow will be only $10.50. This is called *foreign exchange risk.*

Chapter Summary

This chapter began by illustrating the benefits of a bond issue to the issuer, due to issues such as leverage and tax shields. The variables influencing the price of a plain

13 Ex-ante means before the event and ex-post means after the event.

14 We examine such bonds in Chapter 7.

vanilla bond were analyzed in detail, and the fundamental bond valuation equation was derived. In this context the pull to par effect and its inherent reasons were studied in detail. The topics of Eurobonds and foreign bonds were elaborated upon. We then looked at zero-coupon bonds and the synthesis of such bonds using two plain vanilla bonds. Subsequently we studied certain bond types with bells and whistles, such as amortizing bonds, bonds with step-up and step-down coupons, and payment-in-kind bonds. The Treasury securities market was the next focus of attention, and we analyzed a hypothetical Treasury auction in detail. The related issue of coupon stripping was presented in depth. In this context we looked at trademarks, as well as their successors, namely STRIPS. While bonds are often issued at par, they may at times be issued at a discount or at a premium. We looked at the accounting implications for such issues. The chapter concluded by studying the various types of risks inherent in bonds. In this context we presented the rating scales of Moody's, Fitch, and S&P in detail.

In the next chapter, we examine the valuation of bonds between coupon dates, and the related concepts of day-count conventions and accrued interest. We examine various yield measures, such as the yield to maturity, the realized compound yield, and the horizon yield. We also introduce the real-life issue of income tax and examine its implication for the realized compound yield, as well as for the yield to maturity. At the end of the chapter, we examine the case of bonds with sinking fund provisions and introduce the concepts of the yield to average life and the yield to equivalent life.

Chapter 3
Bonds: Advanced Concepts

Let us now examine the process of valuing a bond between coupon dates. While valuing a bond between coupon dates, the difference is that the next coupon is not exactly one period away, but is k periods away where $k < 1$. Assume that we have a bond with a face value of M, paying a coupon of $C/2$ every six months, and with N coupons left prior to maturity. The semiannual yield to maturity is $y/2$.

Required Symbols for the Variables

- $y \equiv$ Yield to maturity.
- $N \equiv$ Number of coupons left in the life of the bond.
- $k \equiv$ Time until the receipt of the first coupon expressed as a fraction of six months. If we are standing on a coupon date, then $k = 1$ else $k < 1$.
- $P_{i,t} \equiv$ Clean price of bond i in the spot market at time t.
- $P_d \equiv$ Dirty price.
- $AI_{i,t_1,t} \equiv$ Accrued interest on bond i from t_1 (the last coupon date) till t (the settlement date).

We first value the bond at time 1, or the next coupon date, and then discount the value so obtained, back to time 0, or the actual settlement date.

At time 1 we receive a coupon of $\frac{C}{2}$. There are $N - 1$ coupons left subsequently, whose value is

$$\frac{\frac{C}{2}}{\frac{y}{2}}\left[1 - \frac{1}{(1+\frac{y}{2})^{N-1}}\right]$$

The present value of the face value is $\frac{M}{(1+\frac{y}{2})^{N-1}}$ Thus the value of the bond at time 1 is

$$\begin{aligned}
&\frac{C}{2} + \frac{\frac{C}{2}}{\frac{y}{2}}\left[1 - \frac{1}{(1+\frac{y}{2})^{N-1}}\right] + \frac{M}{(1+\frac{y}{2})^{N-1}} \\
&= \frac{\frac{C}{2}}{\frac{y}{2}}\left[\frac{(1+\frac{y}{2})^{N} - 1}{(1+\frac{y}{2})^{N-1}}\right] + \frac{M}{(1+\frac{y}{2})^{N-1}}
\end{aligned}$$

Discounting back to time 0, we get a value of

$$\left[\frac{\frac{c \times M}{2}}{(1+\frac{y}{2})^{k}} \times \frac{\left[(1+\frac{y}{2})^{N} - 1\right]}{(\frac{y}{2})(1+\frac{y}{2})^{N-1}}\right] + \frac{M}{(1+\frac{y}{2})^{N-1+k}}$$

https://doi.org/10.1515/9781547400669-003

Day-Count Conventions

To value the bond using the preceding approach, we need to estimate k, that is, the length of the fractional first period. Unfortunately, there is no universal approach for computing k. Different markets use different approaches, and at times, even within a market, the convention varies from product to product. Consequently, we need to be familiar with various conventions known as *day-count conventions*. We will first look at the *Actual/Actual* method which is used for Treasury bonds in the U.S.

The Actual/Actual Approach

Assume that we are standing on 25 July 2018. There is a T-bond maturing on 15 November 2035 that pays a coupon of 10% per annum on 15 May and 15 November every year. The face value is $1,000 and the YTM is 12.50% per annum. In the Actual/Actual method, we need to calculate the actual number of days between the settlement date and the date of the next coupon. Let's call this period as N_1. In our case, the next coupon date is 113 days away as can be determined from Table 3.1.

We have to then compute the number of days between the last coupon date and the next coupon date. We denote the period as N_2. In our example, the number of days between the last coupon date and the next coupon date is 184 days as can be determined from Table 3.2.

Table 3.1: Number of days between the settlement date and the next coupon date.

Month	No. of Days
July	6
August	31
September	30
October	31
November	15
Total	113

Table 3.2: Number of days between the two coupon dates.

Month	No. of Days
May	16
June	30
July	31
August	31
September	30
October	31
November	15
Total	184

Hence the next coupon is $k = \frac{N_1}{N_2} = \frac{113}{184} = 0.6141$ semiannual periods away.

The Actual/Actual method, often denoted by ACT/ACT and pronounced ack/ack by Wall Street traders, is one of many day-count conventions that are used in the world of finance. We will discuss other methods shortly. The denominator under this convention varies from 181 to 184 days, depending on the coupon payment dates of the bond that is under consideration. Note that while calculating the numerator and denominator for computing the fractional period, we can either include the starting date or the ending date, but not both. We have chosen to include the ending date.

Having determined the value of k, the price of the Treasury bond may be determined in one of two ways: the market method or the Treasury method.

The Market Method for Bond Valuation

Wall Street traders compute T-bond prices using the expression derived earlier in this chapter.

$$P_d = \left[\frac{\frac{c \times M}{2}}{\left(1+\frac{y}{2}\right)^k} \times \frac{\left[\left(1+\frac{y}{2}\right)^N - 1\right]}{\left(\frac{y}{2}\right)\left(1+\frac{y}{2}\right)^{N-1}} \right] + \frac{M}{\left(1+\frac{y}{2}\right)^{N-1+k}} \tag{3.1}$$

Using the example from the preceding section, the price as determined by this method is

$$\frac{\frac{0.10 \times 1{,}000}{2}}{\left(1+\frac{0.125}{2}\right)^{0.6141}} \times \frac{\left[\left(1+\frac{0.125}{2}\right)^{35} - 1\right]}{\left(\frac{0.125}{2}\right)\left(1+\frac{0.125}{2}\right)^{35-1}} + \frac{1{,}000}{\left(1+\frac{0.125}{2}\right)^{35-1+0.6141}}$$
$$= \$843.4655$$

In Excel, we would use the PRICE function, in conjunction with the ACCRINT function, to compute the dirty price using the market method, as we shall shortly demonstrate. However, the price can be computed even without invoking the PRICE function. We can use the PV function to first compute the bond's price on the next coupon date. We can then add that day's coupon to it, and discount the whole expression back to time 0, using the fractional period that we have computed.

In our case, the present value = PV(0.125/2, 34, –50, –1000) = \$825.4593. To that we add the coupon of 50, which adds up to \$875.4593. This can be discounted for 0.6141 periods to get the final answer of \$843.4655.

The Treasury Method for Bond Valuation

The difference between the market's approach and that of the Treasury is that the Treasury uses simple interest to discount for the fractional first period. Hence, the Treasury calculates the bond price as follows:[1]

$$P_d = \left[\frac{\frac{c\times M}{2}}{(1+k\times\frac{y}{2})}\times\frac{\left[(1+\frac{y}{2})^N-1\right]}{(\frac{y}{2})(1+\frac{y}{2})^{N-1}}\right]+\frac{M}{(1+k\times\frac{y}{2})(1+\frac{y}{2})^{N-1}} \tag{3.2}$$

Using the same example, the price as determined by this method is

$$\begin{aligned}&\frac{\frac{0.10\times1{,}000}{2}}{\left(1+\frac{0.6141\times0.125}{2}\right)}\times\frac{\left[(1+\frac{0.125}{2})^{35}-1\right]}{(\frac{0.125}{2})(1+\frac{0.125}{2})^{35-1}}\\&+\frac{1{,}000}{\left(1+\frac{0.6141\times0.125}{2}\right)(1+\frac{0.125}{2})^{35-1}}\\&=\$843.1000\end{aligned}$$

This can be easily computed using the PV function. From earlier, we know that the value on the next coupon date, is $875.4593.

$$\frac{875.4593}{\left(1+\frac{0.125\times0.6141}{2}\right)}=\$843.1000$$

For a given value of k, the Treasury's approach always gives a lower price, because when a fractional period is involved, the discount factor using simple interest is higher than the factor obtained with compound interest. Consequently the present value, which is nothing but the bond price, is lower.

Accrued Interest

Consider the period between two coupon dates t_1 and t_2. Let's denote the ex-dividend date for the bond by t_d, where $t_1 < t_d < t_2$. Between t_1 and t_d, the bond trades *cum dividend*, which means that the person who buys the bond at any point in time during this period is entitled to the coupon that is paid on t_2.[2] This facet is captured by the bond pricing equation (3.1), because the price includes the present value of the next coupon.

The price that is obtained as the present value of all the remaining cash flows is termed as the *dirty price*. It includes the compensation due to the seller for parting with the entire next coupon payment, although he has held the bond for a part of the

1 See Garbade [33].

2 The term ex-dividend is a misnomer, for bonds pay coupons and not dividends, unlike stocks. However the implication is the same as that for a stock.

current coupon period. This compensation is called *accrued interest* and is calculated as follows:

$$\text{Accrued interest} = AI = \frac{c \times M}{2} \times \frac{(t - t_1)}{(t_2 - t_1)} \tag{3.3}$$

where t is the settlement date. Using the previous example, the accrued interest as of 25 July, 2018 is

$$\frac{0.10 \times 1000}{2} \times \frac{71}{184} = \$19.2935$$

However the bond prices that are quoted in practice are called *clean prices* and are computed by subtracting the accrued interest from the dirty price. Therefore

$$P_{i,t} = P_d - AI_{i,t1,t} \tag{3.4}$$

The rationale for computing clean prices is the following. Consider the bond price after three days, that is, on 28 July. The dirty price on this day is \$844.2995. The passage of three days time leads to an increase of \$0.8340 in the dirty price, even though the YTM has remained unchanged. We know that the price will change if the YTM changes. However, even if the YTM remains constant, the dirty price will change with the sheer passage of time. But the clean price will stay relatively constant for short periods, unless there is a change in the YTM. In this example, the clean price on 25 July is \$824.1721, whereas on 28 July it is \$824.1908. The difference in the two prices is \$0.0187.

For a bond market analyst, it is important to monitor the changes in the yields prevalent in the market. If the price data were to consist of dirty prices, it would be difficult to separate the effect of yield changes from the impact of the accrued interest. However if clean prices were used for the analysis, any price changes in the short run, would be induced primarily by yield changes. It is for this reason that the reported bond prices are invariably clean prices.

One question that may strike you is, whether the accrued interest can be negative. That is, can there be cases where the seller of the bond has to pay accrued interest to the buyer? The answer is *yes*. In some bond markets, the bonds begin to trade ex-dividend after a certain date. That is, from this date onwards, the sale of a bond results in the next coupon going to the seller rather than to the buyer. On the ex-dividend date, the dirty price falls by the present value of the next coupon, and the dirty price is less than the clean price. We can illustrate this with the help of Example 3.1.

Example 3.1. Consider the bond that matures on 15 November 2035. We will assume that we are standing on 10 November 2018, which happens to be the ex-dividend date.

The cum-dividend price of the bond is

$$\frac{\frac{0.10\times1{,}000}{2}}{\left(1+\frac{0.125}{2}\right)^{0.0272}} \times \frac{\left[\left(1+\frac{0.125}{2}\right)^{35}-1\right]}{\left(\frac{0.125}{2}\right)\left(1+\frac{0.125}{2}\right)^{35-1}} + \frac{1{,}000}{\left(1+\frac{0.125}{2}\right)^{35-1+0.0272}}$$

$$= \$874.0168$$

The moment the bond goes ex-dividend, the dirty price falls by the present value of the forthcoming coupon, because the buyer is no longer be entitled to it. Thus, the ex-dividend dirty price is

$$874.0168 - \frac{\frac{0.10\times 1{,}000}{2}}{\left(1+\frac{0.125}{2}\right)^{0.0272}}$$
$$= \$824.0992$$

This is the amount payable by the person who buys the bond an instant after it goes ex-dividend.

The accrued interest an instant before the bond goes ex-dividend is

$$\frac{0.10\times 1{,}000}{2}\times\frac{179}{184} = \$48.6413$$

Thus the clean price at the time of the bond going ex-dividend is

$$874.0168 - 48.6413 = \$825.3755$$

As you can see the clean price is greater than the ex-dividend dirty price. This negative accrued interest represents the fact that the seller of the bond has to compensate the buyer because although the buyer is entitled to receive his share of the next coupon, the entire amount is received by the seller. The fraction of the next coupon that is payable to the buyer is

$$\frac{0.10\times 1{,}000}{2}\times\frac{5}{184} = \$1.3587$$

Hence the buyer has to pay 825.3755 − 1.3587 = $824.0168, which is close to the ex-dividend dirty price.

All bonds do not exhibit the ex-dividend phenomenon. Some trade cum-dividend till the coupon date. Consequently the accrued interest in such cases is always positive.

The Impact of Time on the Dirty Price

To understand the impact of time on the price, let us derive the partial derivative of the dirty price of the bond, with respect to time.

$$P_d = \frac{1}{\left(1+\frac{y}{2}\right)^k}\times\left\{\frac{c\times M}{2}\times\frac{\left[\left(1+\frac{y}{2}\right)^N-1\right]}{\left(\frac{y}{2}\right)\left(1+\frac{y}{2}\right)^{N-1}}+\frac{M}{\left(1+\frac{y}{2}\right)^{N-1}}\right\}$$

$$\frac{\partial P_d}{\partial k} = -P_d\times\ln\left(1+\frac{y}{2}\right)$$

As k decreases, the price increases. Hence, the dirty price steadily increases as we go from one coupon date to the next, keeping the other parameters constant.

Computation of Price and Accrued Interest Using Excel

When we price a bond on a coupon date, we can use the PV function in Excel to compute the clean price. This is the same as the dirty price on that day, since the accrued interest is zero.[3] However, when we value a bond between coupon dates, we need to use the Excel function called PRICE to compute the clean price. The accrued interest has to be separately computed using the ACCRINT function. The two can then be added together determine the dirty price.

Consider the PRICE function. The parameters are

- *Settlement* is the settlement date, and has to be entered using the DATE function in a YYYY,MM,DD format.
- *Maturity* refers to the maturity date that has to be entered in a similar fashion using the DATE function.
- *Rate* is the annual coupon rate.
- *Yld* is the annual YTM.
- *Redemption* represents the percentage of par that is payable when the bond matures and in most cases is 100 or 100%. It is not the face value, which in most cases is $1,000.
- *Frequency* is the frequency of coupon payments. For bonds paying coupons on a semiannual basis, the frequency is 2.
- *Basis* denotes the day-count convention. For the PRICE function, we need to specify one of the values given in Table 3.3.

Table 3.3: Basis values in Excel for different day-count conventions.

Basis	Day-Count Convention
0	30/360 NASD
1	Actual/Actual
2	Actual/360
3	Actual/365
4	Actual/360 E

In our case we invoke the PRICE function using the following parameters: DATE(2018,07,25),DATE(2035,11,15),0.10,0.125,100,2,1. Since the face value is $1,000, the price has to be multiplied by 10. The value obtained is $824.1705.

To compute the accrued interest, we need to invoke the ACCRINT function.

3 Obviously, on a coupon date, the accrued interest is zero.

The parameters are

- Issue: The issue date of the bond, to be input using the DATE function.
- First_interest: The next coupon date, to be input using the DATE function.
- Settlement: The settlement date, to be input using the DATE function.
- Rate: The annual coupon rate in decimals.
- Par: We can give the full par value, whatever it may be. Thus if the bond has a face value of $1,000, we will give the par as 1,000.
- Frequency: The frequency of coupon payments in a year, which is usually 2.
- Basis: The day-count convention.
- Calc_method: This is required when we specify the actual issue date for the Issue parameter. If however we were to input the previous coupon date as the date of issue, this variable is not required. A more detailed explanation is given in the paragraph that follows.

If we happen to know the issue date, we can specify it using the DATE function. However, if we do not know when the bond was issued, the issue date should be entered as the previous coupon date. In our case, we specify it as DATE(2018,05,15). The First_interest date is the next coupon date. In our case it is DATE(2018,11,15). Settlement is the settlement date, which for us is DATE(2018,07,25). Rate is the annual coupon rate, that is, 0.10. Par is the actual par value which is 1,000. Frequency is 2 because the bond pays semiannual coupons. Basis is 1 because it is a Treasury bond, for which the Actual/Actual convention is applicable. Calc method enters the picture when the actual issue date is specified and not the previous coupon date. If calc method is given as 0 (or omitted), the accrued interest is calculated from the previous coupon date to the settlement date. However, if the calc method is given as 1, the cumulative coupon is computed from the issue date till the settlement date. If we choose to enter the issue date as the previous coupon date, as we have done, the calc method can either be omitted, which is tantamount to a value of 0, or it can be entered as 1.

Accrued interest

$$= \text{ACCRINT}(\text{DATE}(2018{,}05{,}15), \text{DATE}(2018{,}11{,}15), \text{DATE}(2018{,}07{,}25), 0.10, 1000, 2, 1)$$
$$= \$19.2935$$

The dirty price is 824.1705 + 19.2925 = $843.4640.

If we had given the issue date as 15 May, 2017 keeping other parameters the same, and input a value of 1 for the calc method, we would have gotten a value of $119.2935, which is essentially one year's coupon (May 2017 to May 2018), plus the accrued interest from 15 May 2018 until 25 July 2018.

Accrued interest

$$= \text{ACCRINT}(\text{DATE}(2017{,}05{,}15), \text{DATE}(2018{,}11{,}15), \text{DATE}(2018{,}07{,}25), 0.10, 1000, 2, 1)$$
$$= \$119.2935$$

Computation of the YTM Between Coupon Dates

As mentioned earlier, the RATE function can be used to compute the YTM when we are on a coupon date. However, when we are between coupon dates, since a fractional first period is involved, we need to use the YIELD function. Assume that we are standing on 25 August 2018 and have a bond which is maturing on 15 November 2035. The coupon is 10% per annum paid semiannually. The day-count convention is Actual/Actual. The quoted price is 98-12 which translates to $98.375 per $100 of face value.

The parameters are

- Settlement or the settlement date: In this case it is DATE(2018,08,25).
- Maturity or the maturity date: In this case it is DATE(2035,11,15).
- Rate or the annual coupon rate: In this case it is 0.10.
- Pr or the Clean Price per $100 of face value: In this case it is $98.375. If we have the dirty price, we need to compute and subtract the accrued interest, before invoking this function.
- Redemption or redemption value: This is invariably 100.
- Frequency: In this case it is 2 because the bond pays coupons semiannually.
- Basis or the day-count convention: In this case it is 1 because we are following an Actual/Actual convention.

The YTM = YIELD(DATE(2018,08,25),DATE(2035,11,15),0.10,98.375,100,2,1) = 10.1984%

Because we are giving a frequency of 2 in the function, it automatically returns the annual YTM. Thus there is no need to multiply the answer by 2.

Other Day-Count Conventions

The Actual/Actual day-count convention is one of the many conventions used in bond markets. For products other than Treasury bonds, the convention may be different, even in the U.S. We discuss other conventions in the following sections.

The 30/360 NASD Approach

30/360 NASD is the method used for corporate bonds in the U.S. In this method, the denominator is taken to be 180. That is, the length between successive coupon dates is always taken to be 180. Each month is therefore considered to consist of 30 days. The numerator is then calculated by defining the start and end dates, D_1 and D_2 as follows:

$$D_1 = (year_1, month_1, day_1)$$
$$D_2 = (year_2, month_2, day_2)$$

The numerator is then calculated as follows:

$$360(year_2 - year_1) + 30(month_2 - month_1) + (day_2 - day_1)$$

The following additional rules are involved:

1. If $day_1 = 31$, then set $day_1 = 30$.
2. If day_1 is the last day of February, then set $day_1 = 30$.
3. If $day_1 = 30$ or has been set equal to 30, on the basis of Rule 1, then if $day_2 = 31$, set $day_2 = 30$.

The following illustrations calculate the number of days, using the 30/360 NASD approach, for various start dates and end dates:

- Illustration 1
  Fractional period from 15 August 2018 to 15 November 2018:
  $N_1 = 360 \times (2018 - 2018) + 30 \times (11 - 08) + (15 - 15) = 90$
- Illustration 2
  Fractional period from 31 August 2018 to 15 November 2018:
  $N_1 = 360 \times (2018 - 2018) + 30 \times (11 - 08) + (15 - 30) = 75$
- Illustration 3
  Fractional period from 31 August 2018 to 31 December 2018:
  $N_1 = 360 \times (2018 - 2018) + 30 \times (12 - 08) + (30 - 30) = 120$
- Illustration 4
  Fractional period from 30 August 2018 to 30 December 2018:
  $N_1 = 360 \times (2018 - 2018) + 30 \times (12 - 08) + (30 - 30) = 120$
- Illustration 5
  Fractional period from 30 August 2018 to 31 December 2018:
  $N_1 = 360 \times (2018 - 2018) + 30 \times (12 - 08) + (30 - 30) = 120$
- Illustration 6
  Fractional period from 29 August 2018 to 30 December 2018:
  $N_1 = 360 \times (2018 - 2018) + 30 \times (12 - 08) + (30 - 29) = 121$
- Illustration 7
  Fractional period from 29 August 2018 to 31 December 2018:
  $N_1 = 360 \times (2018 - 2018) + 30 \times (12 - 08) + (31 - 29) = 122$
- Illustration 8
  Fractional period from 28 February 2018 to 29 July 2018:
  $N_1 = 360 \times (2018 - 2018) + 30 \times (07 - 02) + (29 - 30) = 149$
- Illustration 9
  Fractional period from 28 February 2018 to 31 July 2018:
  $N_1 = 360 \times (2018 - 2018) + 30 \times (07 - 02) + (31 - 30) = 151$

Valuation of a Corporate Bond Between Coupon Dates

Consider the case of a corporate bond that pays interest on 15 May and 15 November every year. The coupon is 8% per annum, and the YTM is 10% per annum. Assume that we are standing on 15 July of 2018 and the bond matures on 15 November 2037. What is the dirty price?

$$k = \frac{120}{180} = 0.6667$$

$$P = \left[\frac{\frac{80}{2}}{\left(1+\frac{0.10}{2}\right)^{0.6667}} \times \frac{\left[\left(1+\frac{0.10}{2}\right)^{39} - 1\right]}{\left(\frac{0.10}{2}\right)\left(1+\frac{0.10}{2}\right)^{39-1}} \right] + \frac{1{,}000}{\left(1+\frac{0.10}{2}\right)^{39-1+0.6667}}$$
$$= \$843.4344$$

30/360 European Convention

In the 30/360 European (E) convention, if the settlement date, day_2, is equal to 31, then it is always set equal to 30. The additional rules may therefore be stated as follows:

1. If $day_1 = 31$, set $day_1 = 30$
2. If $day_2 = 31$, set $day_2 = 30$

The second rule effectively means that if $day_2 = 31$, then set it equal to 30, no matter what the value of day_1 is. However, in the case of the 30/360 NASD rule, the condition is that if $day_1 = 30$, or has been set equal to 30, then if $day_2 = 31$, set it equal to 30.

Example 3.2. Consider the fractional period from 29 March 2018 to 31 July 2018.

If we use the 30/360 NASD convention, we compute the numerator as

$$N_1 = 360 \times (2018 - 2018) + 30 \times (07 - 03) + (31 - 29) = 122$$

However, as per the 30/360 E convention:

$$N_1 = 360 \times (2018 - 2018) + 30 \times (07 - 03) + (30 - 29) = 121$$

Actual/365 Convention

The difference between the Actual/365 and the Actual/Actual methods is that the denominator consists of 365 days even in leap years. For instance, consider a 10% coupon paying bond that pays interest on 15 November and 15 May every year. Assume that we are standing on 25 July 2018. The accrued interest can be calculated as follows:

$$AI = 1{,}000 \times 0.10 \times \frac{71}{365} = 19.4521$$

Notice that while calculating the accrued interest we multiply M by c and not by $\frac{c}{2}$. This is because the denominator of the day count fraction represents the number of days in an entire year and not in a coupon period.

An Actual/365 bond that pays periodic interest usually accrues interest at a rate such that the interest accrued over a full coupon period does not equal the periodic coupon payment. Thus, for an Actual/365 issue, day count functions and interest accruals over a full coupon period need not generate the actual coupon payment for the period. Example 3.3 is an illustration from Stigum and Robinson [59].

Example 3.3. Consider the period 15 November 1991 to 15 May 1992. The number of days is 182. The day count fraction for the full coupon period is

$$\frac{182}{365} = .499$$

and not .500. Because the semiannual coupon payment must equal exactly half the coupon, the interest accrued on a given Actual/365 security over a full coupon period need not equal the exact coupon payment at the end of the period. This anomalous result cannot occur for an Actual/Actual security.

Actual/360 Convention

Actual/360 is a simple variant of Actual/365. This is the interest payment convention used for money market instruments in many countries, including the U.S.

Comparison of Day-Count Conventions

Consider a bond with a face value of $1,000 paying a coupon of 8% per annum on 25 July and 25 January every year. Assume we are on 31 August of a year. Calculate the accrued interest using the following day-count conventions:

a) Actual/Actual
b) 30/360 NASD
c) 30/360 European
d) Actual/360
e) Actual/365

Actual/Actual:

$$AI = 40 \times \frac{37}{184} = 8.0435$$

ACCRINT(DATE(2018,07,25),DATE(2019,01,25),DATE(2018,08,31),0.08,1000,2,1) = 8.0435

30/360 NASD:

$$AI = 40 \times \frac{36}{180} = 8.0000$$

ACCRINT(DATE(2018,07,25),DATE(2019,01,25),DATE(2018,08,31),0.08,1000,2,0) = 8.0

30/360 E:

$$AI = 40 \times \frac{35}{180} = 7.7778$$

ACCRINT(DATE(2018,07,25),DATE(2019,01,25),DATE(2018,08,31),0.08,1000,2,4) = 7.7778

Actual/360:

$$AI = 80 \times \frac{37}{360} = 8.2222$$

ACCRINT(DATE(2018,07,25),DATE(2019,01,25),DATE(2018,08,31),0.08,1000,2,2) = 8.2222

Actual/365:

$$AI = 80 \times \frac{37}{365} = 8.1096$$

ACCRINT(DATE(2018,07,25),DATE(2019,01,25),DATE(2018,08,31),0.08,1000,2,3) = 8.1096

Additional Coupon-Related Excel Functions

The functions that we describe below compute various statistics pertaining to a coupon period.

- COUPDAYBS: Returns the number of days between the previous coupon date and the settlement date.
- COUPDAYS: Returns the number of days in the coupon period.
- COUPDAYSNC: Returns the number of days between the settlement date and the next coupon date.
- COUPNUM: Returns the number of coupons between the settlement date and the maturity date.

The common parameters for all these functions are:

- Settlement
- Maturity
- Frequency
- Basis

Example 3.4. Consider a bond paying semiannual coupons. The day-count convention is 30/360 NASD. The settlement date is 10 June 2018 and the maturity date is 15 August 2030.

- COUPDAYBS(DATE(2018,06,10),DATE(2030,08,15),2) = 115
  $360(2018 - 2018) + 30(06 - 02) + (10 - 15) = 115$
  This function computes the number of days between the previous coupon date and the settlement date.
- COUPDAYS(DATE(2018,06,10),DATE(2030,08,15),2) = 180
  $360(2018 - 2018) + 30(08 - 02) + (15 - 15) = 180$
  This function computes the number of days in the coupon period.
- COUPDAYSNC(DATE(2018,06,10),DATE(2030,08,15),2) = 65
  $360(2018 - 2018) + 30(08 - 06) + (15 - 10) = 65$
  This function computes the number of days between the settlement date and the next coupon date.
- COUPNUM(DATE(2018,06,10),DATE(2030,08,15),2) = 25
  This function computes the number of coupon periods in a time interval. In this case, one coupon on 15 August 2018 and two coupons every year for the next 12 years.

Valuing a Bond in the Final Coupon Period

A plain vanilla bond, with one coupon left, is effectively a zero coupon bond. Because the time to maturity is less than six months, it is usually treated as a short-term debt security or a money market security. Thus the cash flow is discounted using simple interest.

Example 3.5. A bond has a face value of $1,000 and a coupon of 10% per annum payable semiannually. Today is 25 August 2018 and the maturity date is 15 November 2018. The quoted price is 99-12. The day-count convention is Actual/Actual.

The number of days until maturity is 82, and the number of days in the coupon period is 184. Thus the fractional period remaining is 0.4457. The accrued interest is $50 \times (1 - 0.4457) = \$27.715$. Thus the dirty price is:

$$99.375 \times 10 + 27.715 = \$1{,}021.465$$

Using the dirty price, we compute the YTM as follows:

$$1{,}021.465 = \frac{1{,}050}{(1 + i \times 0.4457)}$$
$$\Rightarrow i = 0.0627 \equiv 6.27\%$$

The annual YTM is 12.54%.

Had we used the compound interest principle for discounting, we would have gotten a value of 12.75%. This is because for a given yield, the discount factor is greater when the simple interest principle is adopted. Thus the simple interest approach would give us a lower present value for a given interest rate. Hence, if the present value is to be the same, the yield should be lower in the case of simple interest.

Yield Measures: An Introduction

Once we know the market's required rate of return from a bond, we can calculate its price by calculating the present values of the cash flows generated by it. On the other hand, if we are given information about the price of a bond, we can find the rate of return that equates the present value of the cash flows to the price. This is nothing but the *internal rate of return* (IRR) of the bond. The IRR of a bond is termed as its *yield to maturity* (YTM) or its *redemption yield*. For a bond that pays N coupons, the YTM is a solution to a polynomial of degree N. The easiest way to compute the YTM of a bond, on a coupon date, is by using the RATE function in Excel. Alternately, one can use the approximate yield to maturity demonstrated later on in this chapter as a starting point and obtain a more precise value using linear interpolation. If we are between coupon dates, we need to use the YIELD function in Excel to compute the YTM.

In practice an investor has a choice between a wide variety of bonds with different coupons and terms to maturity. Besides, the creditworthiness of the issuer varies from bond to bond. Consequently, although data about bonds may be provided in the form of prices, it is the yield measure that facilitates comparison between different instruments. The yield to maturity is one of the key measures of the yield from a bond. However, in practice other measures of yield are computed, as well. Let's now examine the various yield measures that are used in the market.

Current Yield of a Bond

The current yield measure is perhaps the most unsatisfactory measure. But, it is reported in practice, and you should be acquainted with it. It is also called the *flat yield*, *interest yield*, *income yield*, or *running yield*.

The current yield relates the annual coupon payment to the current market price:

$$CY = \frac{\text{Annual Coupon Interest}}{\text{Price}} \tag{3.5}$$

One of the issues is, whether the price should be the clean price or the dirty price. The advantage of using the clean price is that the current yield stays constant unless the yield changes. If the dirty price is used then the current yield will be higher in the period between the ex-dividend date and the coupon date, because the dirty price will be lower than the clean price, due to the negative accrued interest phenomenon. However, the current yield will be lower in the interval between the coupon date and the ex-dividend date, because the dirty price will be higher than the clean price.[4] This gives rise to a sawtooth pattern. The current yield is more than the coupon rate if the

4 This issue is irrelevant in markets where the bond trades cum-dividend till the coupon date.

bond is trading at a discount, and less than the coupon rate if it is trading at a premium.

The current yield suffers from two major technical deficiencies. First, it ignores any capital gain or loss experienced by the bond holder. Second, it fails to consider the time value of money. Nevertheless, it is used to estimate the cost of, or profit from, holding a bond. The difference between the current yield and the cost of funding the bond is known as the *net carry*. If the short-term funding rate in the market is higher than the current yield, the bond is said to involve a running cost. This is also known as *negative carry* or *negative funding*.

The current yield computes the interest yield for an investor with a one-year horizon. However, an investor with a one-year horizon experiences a capital gain or loss, when he sells the bond after one year. Consequently the current yield measure, does not fully capture all the facets of the return, even for such an investor.

Example 3.6. A bond which pays a coupon of 8% per annum is currently trading at $95. A bond holder buys the bond by borrowing at the rate of 8.25% per annum. What is the current yield and what is the net carry?

$$\text{CY} = \frac{8}{95} = 0.0842 \equiv 8.42\%$$

The cost of funding is 8.25%. So the net carry or return is 0.17%.

Simple Yield to Maturity

The simple yield to maturity measure attempts to rectify the shortcomings of the current yield by taking into account capital gains and losses. The assumption made is that capital gains and losses accrue evenly over the life of the bond, or in other words on a straight line basis.

The formula is:

$$\text{Simple YTM of a Bond} = \frac{C}{P} + \frac{M - P}{\frac{N}{2} \times P} \tag{3.6}$$

The problem with the simple yield to maturity is that it does not account for the fact that an investor in a bond can earn compound interest. As coupons are paid, they can be reinvested and hence can earn interest. This increases the overall return from holding the bond. Besides the assumption that capital gains and losses arise evenly over the life of the bond is an over simplification.

The simple yield to maturity (SYTM) is also known as the *Japanese yield*, for it is the main yield measure that is used in the Japanese Government Bond (JGB) market. If a bond is selling at a discount, the SYTM is higher than the current yield. However, if it is trading at a premium, then the SYTM is lower than the current yield.

Example 3.7. Assume that a bond with 10 years to maturity and a coupon of 8% per annum is trading at \$95. The face value is \$100.

$$\begin{aligned}\text{SYTM} &= \frac{8}{95} + \frac{(100-95)}{10 \times 95} \\ &= 0.0842 + 0.0053 = 0.0895 \equiv 8.95\%\end{aligned}$$

Yield to Maturity of a Bond

The YTM is the interest rate that equates the present value of the cash flows from the bond(assuming that the bond is held to maturity) to the price of the bond. Consider a bond that makes an annual coupon payment of C on a semiannual basis. The face value is M, the price is P, and the number of coupons remaining is N. The YTM is the value of y, that satisfies the following equation:

$$P = \sum_{t=1}^{N} \left[\frac{\frac{C}{2}}{(1+\frac{y}{2})^t} \right] + \frac{M}{(1+\frac{y}{2})^N} \tag{3.7}$$

The value of y that we compute in this fashion is the nominal annual yield, which is also called the *bond equivalent yield* (BEY). From the principles of time value of money, you can understand that the effective annual yield is $(1+\frac{y}{2})^2 - 1$.

The Approximate Yield to Maturity Approach

The bond valuation equation is a non-linear equation. The issue is how to calculate the YTM given other variables. One way, of course, is to use the IRR function, or the RATE function in Excel. We will now demonstrate an alternative procedure, using the *approximate yield to maturity* or AYM.

$$\text{AYM} = \frac{C + \frac{M-P}{N/2}}{\frac{M+P}{2}} \tag{3.8}$$

The Rationale for the AYM Approach

The annual coupon interest income is C. The capital gain/loss if the bond is held to maturity ($N/2$ years) on a straight line basis, is $\frac{M-P}{N/2}$. If the bond is a discount bond, there is a capital gain if it is held to maturity otherwise, there is a capital loss. Thus, the annual income is $C + \frac{M-P}{N/2}$. The initial investment is P. An instant before redemption, the money that is locked up in the bond is M. Thus the average investment is $\frac{M+P}{2}$. The approximate YTM is the annual income divided by the average investment and is equal to

$$\frac{C + \frac{M-P}{N/2}}{\frac{M+P}{2}}$$

The AYM gives us a starting point. We choose a higher value and a lower value, such that the higher yield gives a price that is lower than the actual price, and the lower yield gives a price that is higher than the actual price. Using these prices, we can compute the yield to maturity using linear interpolation.

Example 3.8. Consider a 10% coupon bond with a face value of \$1,000, a price of \$860, and 10 years to maturity. Assume that the bond pays interest on a semiannual basis. What is the yield to maturity?

$$\begin{aligned} \text{AYM} &= \frac{100 + \frac{1{,}000-860}{10}}{\frac{1{,}000+860}{2}} \\ &= \frac{100 + 14}{930} \equiv 12.2581\% \end{aligned}$$

Consider two rates, 12% and 13%

Price at 12% = \$885.3008

This price is above \$860

Price at 13% = \$834.7224

This price is below \$860.

Now let's interpolate. 12%–13% corresponds to a price difference of 885.3008 – 834.7224. Thus 12% – y^* should correspond to a price difference of 885.3008 – 860, where y^* is the true YTM.

Take the ratio of the two, and solve for y^*:

$$\frac{-0.01}{0.12 - y^*} = \frac{50.5784}{25.3008}$$

$$\Rightarrow y^* = 0.12 + 0.01 \times \frac{25.3008}{50.5784} = 12.5002\%$$

We can verify the accuracy of our approximation using Excel. PV(0.125002/2, 20, −50, −1000) = \$859.48. Thus the approximation is excellent.

As we have discussed, we generally require a computer program to calculate the YTM. A less precise, but very often an effective method, is the use of the AYM with interpolation. The calculation is fairly simple for a coupon bond with two periods left to maturity, and for zero coupon bonds. The former has only two cash flows, which implies a quadratic equation for computing the YTM, whereas the latter has a single cash flow.

Example 3.9. A Reliance bond with a face value of \$1,000 and a coupon rate of 10% per annum, payable semiannually, has one year left to maturity. It is currently selling at \$900. What is the YTM?

$$\begin{aligned} 900 &= \frac{50}{(1+\frac{y}{2})} + \frac{50}{(1+\frac{y}{2})^2} + \frac{1{,}000}{(1+\frac{y}{2})^2} \\ &\equiv \frac{50}{(1+i)} + \frac{1{,}050}{(1+i)^2} \end{aligned}$$

where, we have denoted $\frac{y}{2}$ by i.

Therefore

$$900(1+i)^2 = 50(1+i) + 1{,}050$$
$$\Rightarrow 900(1+i)^2 - 50(1+i) - 1{,}050 = 0$$

This is a quadratic equation of the form

$$ax^2 + bx + c = 0,$$

where x in this case is $(1+i)$.

The equation has two roots:

$$x = \frac{-b \pm \sqrt{(b^2 - 4ac)}}{2a}$$

Therefore

$$(1+i) = \frac{50 \pm \sqrt{[(-50)^2 - 4 \times (900) \times (-1{,}050)]}}{1{,}800}$$
$$= \frac{50 \pm 1{,}944.87}{1{,}800} = 1.1083 \text{ or } -1.0527$$

Therefore

$$i = \frac{y}{2} = 0.1083 \text{ or } -2.0527$$

We discard the negative root since the yield is inevitably positive.

Thus, the nominal annual YTM = 0.1083 × 2 = 0.2166 ≡ 21.66 %

Example 3.10. Consider a zero coupon bond with a face value of \$1,000, maturing five years from now. The current price is \$500. What is the YTM?

The first question is, whether we use

$$500 = \frac{1{,}000}{(1+y)^5},$$

or

$$500 = \frac{1{,}000}{\left(1+\frac{y}{2}\right)^{10}}$$

The second approach is preferred, as mentioned earlier, because we may like to compare our results with coupon paying bonds, which typically pay interest on a semi annual basis.

Therefore,

$$\left(1+\frac{y}{2}\right)^{10} = \frac{1{,}000}{500} = 2$$

That is,

$$\frac{y}{2} = (2)^{0.1} - 1 = 1.0718 - 1 = 0.0718$$

Thus $y = 0.1436 \equiv 14.36\%$

The YTM calculation takes into account the coupon payments, as well as any capital gains/losses that accrue to an investor who buys and holds a bond to maturity. Before we analyze the YTM in detail, let's consider the various sources that contribute to the returns received by a bond holder.[5]

A bond holder can expect to receive income from the following sources:

- Coupon payments, which are typically paid every six months.
- A capital gain/loss that is obtained when the bond matures, is called before maturity, or is sold before maturity. From the YTM equation, you can see that we are assuming that the bond is held to maturity.
- Reinvestment of coupon payments, from the time each coupon is paid until the time the bond matures, is sold, or is called. Once again, the YTM calculation assumes that the bond is held to maturity. The reinvestment income is the *interest on interest* income.

A satisfactory measure of the yield should take into account all three sources of income. The YTM does take all three sources of income into account. However, it makes two key assumptions:

- The bond is held until maturity.
- The intermediate coupon payments are reinvested at the YTM itself.

The second assumption is in built into the mathematics of the YTM calculation, as we shall shortly demonstrate.

The YTM is called a *promised yield*. Why do we use the word *promised*? It is a promise because, in order to realize it, the bond holder has to satisfy the preceding two conditions. If either of them is violated, the bond holder may not get the promised yield.[6]

The assumption that the bond is held to maturity is fairly easy to comprehend. Let's now focus on the reinvestment assumption.

Consider a bond with a face value of M, annual coupon of C, and number of coupons left N. Let the bond pay interest on a semiannual basis, i.e. it pays $C/2$ every six months. Let r be the rate at which one can reinvest the coupon payments until maturity. r would depend on the prevailing rate of interest when the coupon is received, and need not be equal to y, the initial YTM, or c, the coupon rate. For ease of exposition, we can assume that r is a constant for the life of the bond. In practice, the rate is likely to vary from period to period.

Thus each coupon payment is reinvested at $\frac{r}{2}$ (for six monthly periods). The coupon stream is obviously an annuity. The final payoff from reinvesting the coupons is therefore given by the future value of this annuity, using a rate of $\frac{r}{2}$ for every six monthly period.

5 See Fabozzi [26].

6 Remember, the IRR calculation also assumes that intermediate cash flows are reinvested at the IRR itself.

The future value is

$$\frac{\frac{C}{2}}{\frac{r}{2}}\left[\left(1+\frac{r}{2}\right)^N-1\right]$$

Note that this amount represents the sum of all coupons that are reinvested (which in this case is the principal), plus interest earned on reinvesting the coupons.

The total value of the coupons $= \frac{C}{2} \times N = \frac{NC}{2}$

Thus, interest on interest is equal to

$$\frac{\frac{C}{2}}{\frac{r}{2}}\left[\left(1+\frac{r}{2}\right)^N-1\right]-\frac{NC}{2}$$

The YTM calculation assumes that $\frac{r}{2} = \frac{y}{2}$

In Example 3.11 we demonstrate that an investor gets a rate of return equal to the YTM, only if he manages to reinvest all the coupons at the YTM.

Example 3.11. Consider an ABC bond that has 10 years to maturity. The face value is $1,000. It pays a semiannual coupon at the rate of 10% per annum. The YTM is 12% per annum.

Let's first calculate the price

$$\begin{aligned} P &= 50 \times \text{PVIFA}(6,20) + 1{,}000 \times \text{PVIF}(6,20) \\ &= 50 \times 11.4699 + 1{,}000 \times .3118 = 885.295 \end{aligned}$$

We assume that the semiannual interest payments can be reinvested at a six-month rate of 6%, which corresponds to a nominal annual rate of 12%.

Let's analyze the sources of income for a bond holder, assuming that he holds the bond to maturity.

1. Total coupon received = 50 × 20 = $1,000.
2. Interest on interest got by reinvesting the coupons:

$$\begin{aligned} &= \frac{50[(1.06)^{20}-1]}{0.06} - 1{,}000 \\ &= 50 \times 36.786 - 1{,}000 = \$839.3 \end{aligned}$$

   Notice that, if we do not deduct 1,000 (or $\frac{NC}{2}$) in the preceding equation, we can calculate the income from both sources together. We have separated them for expositional clarity.
3. Finally, in the end, the bond holder gets back the face value of $1,000.

Thus, the terminal cash flow for the bond holder is 1,000 + 839.3 + 1,000 = $2,839.3.

To get this income the bond holder has to pay $885.295 at the outset, which is the investment. So what is the rate of return? It is the value of *i* that satisfies the following equation:

$$\begin{aligned} &885.295(1+i)^{20} = 2{,}839.3 \\ \Rightarrow (1+i) &= \left[\frac{2{,}839.3}{885.295}\right]^{0.05} = 1.0600 \end{aligned}$$

$\Rightarrow i = 0.06 \equiv 6\%$ on a semiannual basis, or 12% on a nominal annual basis, which is exactly the same as the YTM.

So, how did the bond holder realize the YTM? Only by being able to reinvest the coupons at a nominal annual rate of 12%, compounded on a semiannual basis. Notice that the reinvestment rate affects only the interest on interest income. The other two sources are unaffected. If $r > y$, the interest on interest would have been higher, and i would have been greater than y. On the contrary, if $r < y$, the interest on interest would have been lower, and i would have been less than y.

So, if an investor buys a bond by paying a price that corresponds to a given YTM, he realizes that YTM only if both the following are true:

1. He holds the bond to maturity.
2. He is able to reinvest the coupons at the YTM.

In the preceding scenario, the risk that the investor faces is that future reinvestment rates may be less than the YTM that was in effect at the time he purchased the bond. This risk is called *reinvestment risk*. The degree of reinvestment risk depends critically on two factors, namely, the time to maturity, and the quantum of the coupon. For a bond with a given YTM and coupon rate, the greater the time to maturity, the more dependent is the bond's total return on the reinvestment income. Thus, everything else remaining constant, the longer the time to maturity, the greater is the reinvestment risk.[7] Secondly, for a bond with a given maturity and YTM, the greater the quantum of the coupon, or in other words, the higher the coupon rate, the more dependent is the bond's total return on income from reinvestment. Hence, everything else remaining constant, the larger the coupon rate is, the greater the reinvestment risk. For bonds selling at a premium, i.e. $c > y$, vulnerability to reinvestment risk is higher than that for a bond selling at par. Correspondingly, discount bonds are less vulnerable than bonds selling at par.

The important thing to note is that for a zero coupon bond, if it is held to maturity, there is absolutely no reinvestment risk because there are no intermediate coupon payments. Hence, if a ZCB is held to maturity, the yield actually earned equals the promised YTM. Thus, in order to earn the YTM of a zero coupon bond, only one condition needs to be satisfied. The bond has to be held to maturity. This explains the popularity of such securities among long-term investors such as pension funds and insurance companies. If they buy and hold the security to maturity, they are assured of earning the YTM without having to take any additional steps.

Reinvestment Assumption Behind the YTM Calculation

We can claim that we have received a YTM of y% per annum, if the compounded semiannual return on our initial investment is $\frac{y}{2}$.

7 See Fabozzi [26].

The initial investment is

$$P = \frac{\frac{C}{2}}{\frac{y}{2}}\left[1 - \frac{1}{(1+\frac{y}{2})^N}\right] + \frac{M}{(1+\frac{y}{2})^N}$$

The compounded value of the investment is

$$P \times \left(1 + \frac{y}{2}\right)^N$$
$$= \frac{\frac{C}{2}}{\frac{y}{2}}\left[\left(1 + \frac{y}{2}\right)^N - 1\right] + M$$

The terminal cash flow from holding the bond, assuming that each coupon is reinvested at $\frac{r}{2}$ per semiannual period, is

$$= \frac{\frac{C}{2}}{\frac{r}{2}}\left[\left(1 + \frac{r}{2}\right)^N - 1\right] + M$$

Equating the two, we get

$$\frac{r}{2} = \frac{y}{2}$$

Thus in order to get an annual YTM of y%, every intermediate cash flow must be reinvested at $\frac{y}{2}$% per six-month period.

The Realized Compound Yield

To calculate the realized compound yield (RCY), we once again assume that the bond is held until maturity. But we make an explicit assumption about the rate at which the coupons can be reinvested. That is, unlike in the case of the YTM, we no longer take it for granted that intermediate cash flows can be reinvested at the YTM.

Example 3.12. Consider the ABC bond. Assume that intermediate coupons can be reinvested at 7% for six months, or at a nominal annual rate of 14%.

Compared to the earlier example, the coupon income and the final face value payment remain the same, but, the reinvestment income changes.

$$\text{Interest on Interest} = \frac{50}{0.07}[(1.07)^{20} - 1] - 1{,}000$$
$$= 50 \times 40.995 - 1{,}000 = 1{,}049.75$$

So, the final amount received = 1,000 + 1,049.75 + 1,000 = \$3,049.75.
The initial investment is \$885.295.

Therefore, the rate of return is given by,

$$885.295(1+i)^{20} = 3{,}049.75$$

$$\Rightarrow (1+i) = \left[\frac{3049.75}{885.295}\right]^{0.05} = 1.0638$$

$$\Rightarrow i = 6.38\%$$

This is the return for six months. The nominal annual return is 6.38×2 = 12.76%. 12.76% is greater than the YTM of 12%.

Thus, the realized compound yield is greater than the YTM if the reinvestment rate is greater than the YTM. If the reinvestment rate were less than the YTM, the RCY would be less than the YTM.

The RCY can be an ex-ante measure if one makes an assumption about the reinvestment rate. It can also be an ex-post measure, if one uses the rate at which the investor is actually able to reinvest.

The Horizon or Holding Period Return

Now we can relax both the assumptions that we made to calculate the YTM. First, the investor may not hold the bond to maturity, and, second, may not be able to reinvest the coupons at the YTM.

Let's suppose that the investor has an investment horizon that is less than the time to maturity. The return depends on three sources, namely, the coupons received, the reinvestment income, and the price at which the investor expects to sell the bond.[8]

Example 3.13. An investor has a seven year investment horizon, and wants to buy the ABC bond discussed in Example 3.12. The current price is $885.295. He gets coupons for seven years or 14 periods. The total coupon income = 50 × 14 = $700.

The investor believes that coupons can be reinvested at 7% per six-month period. He also believes that when he is ready to sell the bond, the YTM will be 12% per annum on a nominal annual basis. The first step is to calculate the expected price at the time of sale. Remember that the bond will have three years to maturity.

$$\begin{aligned} P(\text{after 7 years}) &= 50PVIFA(6,6) + 1{,}000PVIF(6,6) \\ &= 50 \times 4.9173 + 1{,}000 \times .705 = \$950.83 \end{aligned}$$

$$\begin{aligned} \text{Interest on Interest} &= \frac{50[(1.07)^{14} - 1]}{.07} - 700 \\ &= 50 \times 22.55 - 700 = 427.5 \end{aligned}$$

The terminal value = 700 + 427.5 + 950.865 = $2,078.35.

8 The selling price may not be equal to the face value and depends on the YTM at the time of sale.

The rate of return is given by

$$885.295(1+i)^{14} = 2{,}078.35$$
$$\Rightarrow (1+i) = \left[\frac{2078.35}{885.295}\right]^{\frac{1}{14}} = 1.0629$$
$$\Rightarrow i = 6.29\%$$

The nominal annual return = 6.29 × 2 = 12.58%.
This is the *horizon yield.* Again, can be calculated on either an ex-ante or ex-post basis.

The Realized Compound Yield with Taxes

In most countries, both the coupon income from a bond, and the capital gain, if any, is taxed.[9] In practice the rate of tax levied on capital gains may or may not be the same as the rate applicable for income from coupons. The incidence of tax on coupon income has certain negative consequences for the bond holder. First, the amount of cash received at the end of every coupon period is reduced. For instance, if the coupon due is \$50, and the tax rate is 30%, the post-tax coupon is only \$35. Thus the total coupon income over the life of the bond is reduced. If we assume that the bond under consideration has 20 periods until maturity, the post-tax coupon will be \$700, as compared to the \$1,000 that would have been received in the absence of the tax. The other consequence of the tax on coupons is that it brings down the reinvestment income. This is because, as a consequence of the tax, there is less to reinvest every period. Finally, the interest earned by reinvesting coupon interest, also comes down because of the tax rate.

Consider a bond with a face value of $\$M$, and N coupons remaining. The semiannual coupon rate is c, and the semiannual reinvestment rate is r. In the absence of taxes, the terminal value of reinvested coupons would be

$$M \times \frac{c/2}{r/2}\left[\left(1+\frac{r}{2}\right)^N - 1\right]$$

In the presence of taxes, the periodic coupon rate is $\frac{c(1-T)}{2}$. The effective semiannual reinvestment rate is $\frac{r(1-T)}{2}$. Thus the post-tax value of re-invested coupons is

$$M \times \frac{c(1-T)/2}{r(1-T)/2}\left[\left(1+\frac{r\{1-T\}}{2}\right)^N - 1\right]$$
$$= M \times \frac{c}{r}\left[\left(1+\frac{r\{1-T\}}{2}\right)^N - 1\right]$$

9 See Smith [56].

The post-tax terminal cash flow, when the face value is repaid, is

$$M - (M - P) \times \text{Capital Gains Tax}$$

Example 3.14 illustrates this.

Example 3.14. Consider the bond with a coupon of 10% per annum and a face value of $1,000, maturing after 10 years. The price is $885.30, and we assume that coupons, paid semiannually, can be reinvested at 8% per annum. Coupon income is taxed at 30%, and capital gains at 25%. We assume that the bond is held to maturity.

The cash flow from the coupons as computed at the time of expiration is:

$$1{,}000 \times \frac{0.05}{0.04}\left[(1 + .04 \times 0.7)^{20} - 1\right]$$
$$= \$921.5625$$

The capital gain is 1,000 − 885.30 = $114.70. The post tax cash flow from the face value at the end is 1,000−114.70×0.25 = $971.325. Thus an investment of 885.30 yields an inflow of 921.5625+971.325 = $1,892.8875 after 20 periods. The realized compound yield is 7.7455% on a per annum basis.

Computing the YTM with Taxes

Let's revisit Example 3.14. Assume that the price of the bond is $975.50. What is the post-tax YTM? The post-tax periodic cash flow is 50 × 0.7 = $35. The post-tax cash flow from the face value is 1,000 − (1,000 − 975.50) × 0.25 = $993.875. We now invoke the RATE function in Excel.

RATE(20, −35,975.50, −993.875) = 3.6535% ≡ 7.3069% per annum.

The Portfolio Yield for Bonds

Suppose you hold a collection of bonds. A simple way to calculate the yield is as a weighted average of the yields of the individual bonds in the portfolio. But from a technically more accurate stand-point, you should first compute the cash flows for the portfolio, and then find the interest rate that makes the present value of the cash flows equal to the sum of the prices of the components of the portfolio. This is nothing but the computation of the portfolio IRR. We illustrate both the techniques in the following sections.

Peter Burns buys a Raccoon bond and a YKK bond. The Raccoon bond has a time to maturity of five years, a face value of $1,000, and pays coupons semiannually at the rate of 10% per annum. The YTM is 12% per annum. The YKK bond has a face value of $1,000, time to maturity of four years, and pays a coupon of 10% per annum, every six months. The YTM is 16% per annum. If he buys one of each bond, what is the yield on his portfolio?

The first step is to calculate the two prices

$$
\begin{aligned}
P(\text{Raccoon}) &= 50PVIFA(6,10) + 1{,}000PVIF(6,10)\\
&= 50 \times 7.3601 + 1{,}000 \times .5584 = 926.405\\
P(\text{YKK}) &= 50PVIFA(8,8) + 1{,}000PVIF(8,8)\\
&= 50 \times 5.7466 + 1{,}000 \times .5403 = 827.63
\end{aligned}
$$

The initial investment = 926.405 + 827.63 = \$1,754.035

The Weighted Average Approach

The weighted average portfolio yield, is an average of the yields of the component bonds, where the prices of the bonds serve as the weights.

$$
\begin{aligned}
y_p &= 0.12 \times \frac{926.405}{1{,}754.035} + 0.16 \times \frac{827.63}{1{,}754.035}\\
&= 0.0634 + 0.0755 = 0.1389 \equiv 13.89\%
\end{aligned}
$$

The IRR Approach

Let's set up the cash flow table, as shown in Table 3.4. The first seven cash flows are \$100 because the two bonds pay a coupon of \$50 each. In the eighth period, one bond pays a coupon of \$50, whereas the other, which is maturing, pays \$1,050. In the ninth period, the remaining bond pays a coupon of \$50, and in the tenth period, it too matures after paying out \$1,050.

Calculate the IRR using Excel. The answer comes out to be 13.76% on a nominal annual basis.

Table 3.4: Cash flows from the bond portfolio.

Period	Cash Flow from Raccoon	Cash Flow from YKK	Total Cash Flow
0	(926.405)	(827.63)	(1,754.035)
1	50	50	100
2	50	50	100
3	50	50	100
4	50	50	100
5	50	50	100
6	50	50	100
7	50	50	100
8	50	1050	1,100
9	50		50
10	1050		1,050

The Taxable Equivalent Yield (TEY)

Certain bonds, like municipal bonds, are tax exempt. In the U.S., unlike in many other countries, both the federal and state governments can levy income tax. Often, an investor would like to compare the yield of a bond whose income is taxable, with the yield of another bond whose income is tax free. For this purpose it becomes essential to compute the *taxable equivalent yield*, or TEY, of the tax-free bond.

Governments in the U.S. follow the guideline of mutual reciprocity. That is, federal government bonds are exempt from state income taxes, and state and local government bonds are exempt from federal income tax. There are certain securities that are exempt from all taxes or in other words, are totally tax-free.

The method of computation of the TEY depends on the applicable tax rate. Consider a municipal bond yielding 6% per annum. Assume that it is exempt from federal income tax, but is subject to state tax. On the other hand, there is a bond whose income is subject to both forms of tax. Assume that the federal tax rate is 25%. The taxable equivalent yield of the bond is given by

$$\text{TEY} = \frac{6.00}{(1 - 0.25)} = 8\%$$

There is no need to adjust for state income tax because it is applicable for both bonds. Thus if a taxable bond were to yield more than 8% per annum, if would be preferred to the municipal bond. Otherwise the municipal bond would be more attractive.

Sometimes a bond may be totally tax free, that is, it is exempt from federal as well as state taxes. In this case, we compute the TEY as follows. First we need to calculate the effective tax rate. This, contrary to what the reader may think, is not the sum of the two rates because the state tax that is paid is a deductible expense when computing the federal tax.

Assume the federal tax rate is 25% and the state tax rate is 8%. On \$100 income, \$8 are payable by way of state tax. The net income, \$92, attracts federal tax at the rate of 25%, which amounts to \$23. Thus the post-tax income is \$69, and the effective tax rate is 31%. Consider a municipal bond with a YTM of 6.0375%. The TEY is

$$\frac{6.0375}{(1 - 0.31)} = 8.75\%$$

Sinking Fund Provisions

At times, a bond issue may carry a sinking fund provision in its indenture, which requires the issuer to set aside money periodically in order to redeem a percentage of the bonds at regular intervals. In practice the issuer sets up an account with a custodian, into which the periodic payments are directed. This account is meant to be used for the sole purpose of retiring the debt. The periodic payments made by the issuer may be fixed or variable, depending on the terms of the bond indenture.

Sinking funds have several positive features from the standpoint of a bond investor. First, because bonds are being periodically redeemed, there is less risk of default for bond holders compared to a situation where the entire issue has to be redeemed on a single future date. Second, the redemption in the case of sinking funds takes place at the sinking fund call price. If yields have gone up after issue, and the current market price is lower, then this offers a benefit for holders whose bonds are being redeemed. Third, the act of periodic purchase of bonds, leads to demand, which has the effect of increasing the liquidity. In an environment where yields are increasing and prices are falling, the buying pressure due to the sinking fund provision may help prop up the bond price.

However, there are drawbacks to a sinking fund. In a market with declining yields, a bond holder may not benefit because his bond may be redeemed at the price specified at the outset. Related to this is the risk that cash flows in a declining rate environment may have to be reinvested at lower rates of interest. In the case of a plain vanilla bond, the risk for the holder is that coupons may have to be reinvested at lower rates. However, in the case of a bond with a sinking fund provision, the risk is that the principal itself may be returned prematurely, and consequently may have to be reinvested at a lower rate.

Despite the pros and cons, bonds with a sinking fund provision usually have a lower YTM than bonds that do not have this feature, but are otherwise similar. This is first because there is lower default risk and second because there is downside protection in a falling price environment.

Serial Bonds

In the case of plain vanilla bonds, all the issued bonds mature on the same future date. However, in the case of a serial bond issue, a fraction of the outstanding bonds mature at regular intervals until the entire issue is redeemed. For an investor, such bonds pose less risk of default as compared to a plain vanilla bullet bond, where it is necessary to ensure that the issuer has adequate funds on the pre-specified maturity date to be able to redeem the entire issue. Serial bonds, as well as bonds with sinking funds, are considered less risky than plain vanilla bonds issued by the same issuer.

In the case, of serial bonds and bonds with a sinking fund, a portion of the issue is redeemed at periodic intervals, but the mechanics are different. With sinking funds, the issuer makes periodic payments into a custodial account. The trustee uses these funds to buy bonds in the secondary market and retire them. The trustee either buys bonds from whoever is willing to sell in the secondary market, or else selects randomly drawn serial numbers to retire the corresponding bonds. In the case of a serial bond, however, it is specified right at the outset when a particular bond will be retired.

Yield to Average Life

The yield to average life measure is applicable for bonds with a sinking fund provision, where a percentage of outstanding bonds is redeemed every year at a specified price.[10] Assume that a company has issued bonds with a face value of $100 million and four years to maturity. Coupon is paid at the rate of 10% per annum, on an annual basis. At the end of the first year, 20% of the bonds is redeemed; at the end of the second year, another 25% is redeemed; and finally at the end of three years, 30% of the issue is redeemed. The residual 25% is redeemed at maturity. The redemption price varies from year to year as depicted in Table 3.5.

Table 3.5: Redemption schedule for a bond with a sinking fund.

Year	Fraction Redeemed	Redemption Price
1	0.20	102.50
2	0.25	101.75
3	0.30	101.00
4	0.25	100.00

The average life is defined as:

$$\sum_{i=1}^{4}(t_i w_i P_i) \div \sum_{i=1}^{4}(w_i P_i)$$

The numerator is:

$$1 \times 0.20 \times 102.50 + 2 \times 0.25 \times 101.75 + 3 \times 0.30 \times 101 + 4 \times 0.25 \times 100 = 262.275$$

The denominator is:

$$0.20 \times 102.50 + 0.25 \times 101.75 + 0.30 \times 101 + 0.25 \times 100 = 101.2375$$

Thus the average life is = 262.275 ÷ 101.2375 = 2.5907 years.

The yield to average life is based on three assumptions:

1. The bond matures at the time corresponding to the average life.
2. The cash flow at the time of maturity is the average redemption price plus coupon for one period.

10 See Blake [4].

3. The bond pays coupons at regular intervals prior to the time corresponding to the average life.

$$P = \sum_{i=1}^{N} \frac{C}{(1+y)^i} + \frac{M+C}{(1+y)^{N^*}} \tag{3.9}$$

In this equation, M is the average redemption price; N^* is the time corresponding to the average life; N is the number of periodic coupons received before the time corresponding to the average life; and y is the yield to average life. In our example: M = 101.2375; N^* = 2.5907; N = 2; and C = 10. If we assume that the bond price is 99-12, the yield to average life is 12.2162%, as computed using Excel.

Yield to Equivalent Life

The mechanics of computing the yield to equivalent life are similar to the method adopted for the computation of the yield to average life, except that we consider the present value of the redemption price and not the price itself. This is done to account for the fact that redemption prices are received at different points in time.

$$\sum_{i=1}^{4}[t_i w_i PV(P_i)] \div \sum_{i=1}^{4}[w_i PV(P_i)]$$

It must be noted that the present values are computed using the yield to equivalent life as the discount rate. Hence, unlike the case of yield to average life, we need to compute the yield to equivalent life before we can calculate the equivalent life.

The yield to equivalent life is defined as:

$$P = \sum_{i=1}^{N} \frac{C + w_i P_i}{(1+y)^i} \tag{3.10}$$

where N is the number of remaining coupon periods; w_i is the redemption fraction at time i; P_i is the redemption price corresponding to time i; and y is the yield to equivalent life.

In our illustration: N = 4; C = 10; P = 99.375. The yield to equivalent life using Excel is 15.2176%. The equivalent life is

$$\begin{aligned}&[0.2 \times 1 \times 88.96 + 0.25 \times 2 \times 76.65 + 0.30 \times 3 \times 66.03 + 0.25 \times 4 \times 56.74]\\ &\div [0.20 \times 88.96 + 0.25 \times 76.65 + 0.30 \times 66.03 + 0.25 \times 56.74]\\ &= 172.2909 \div 70.9505 = 2.4283\end{aligned}$$

years.

Chapter Summary

In this chapter, we first relaxed the assumption, that the bond is being valued on a coupon date. In order to measure fractional time periods, we introduced the concept of day-count conventions. We studied the concepts of clean and dirty prices, and the related issue of accrued interest, and explained why quoted bond prices are clean prices. We illustrated the computation of clean prices, accrued interest, and the yield to maturity, using Excel, and compared the results of different day-count conventions for a given set of data. We then went on to look at yield measures. First we studied the current yield and the simple yield to maturity, and then went on to look at the more technically precise yield to maturity. We examined the assumptions behind the yield to maturity and gradually relaxed them, to compute the realized compound yield and the horizon yield. Coupons and capital gains from bonds may be taxable. We studied the implications of taxes for the realized compound yield, as well as the YTM. We then looked at the technique for computing a precise yield for a portfolio of bonds. In real life, an investor may have a choice between taxable and tax-free bonds. To make a comparison, we need to compute the taxable equivalent yield of a tax-free bond, and we looked at related issues. Finally we introduced the concept of a sinking fund provision and looked at two related yield measures, namely the yield to average life and the yield to equivalent life.

In the next chapter, we study the various theories of the *term structure* of interest rates, and pay close attention to the concepts of the *spot rate* and the *forward rate*.

Chapter 4
Yield Curves and the Term Structure

At any point in time, while taking a decision to invest in debt securities, an investor typically has access to a large number of bonds with different yields and varying times to maturity. Consequently, it is a common practice for investors and traders to examine the relationship between the yields on bonds belonging to a particular risk class. A plot of the yields of bonds that differ only with respect to their time to maturity, versus their respective times to maturity, is called a *yield curve*. The curve is an important indicator of the state of the bond market, and provides valuable information, to traders and analysts.

While constructing the yield curve, it is very important to ensure that the data pertain to bonds of the same risk class, having comparable degrees of liquidity. For example, a curve may be constructed for government securities or AAA-rated corporate bonds, but not for a mixture of both. The primary yield curve in any domestic capital market is the government bond yield curve, for these instruments are free of default risk. In the U.S. debt market for instance, the primary yield curve is the U.S. Treasury yield curve.

Analyzing the Yield Curve

The yield curve is an indicator of where the bond market is trading currently. It also has implications for what the market thinks will happen in the future.

The yield curve sets the yield for all debt market instruments. First it fixes the price of money over the maturity structure. In practice, the yields of government bonds from the shortest maturity instrument to the longest set the benchmark for yields on all other debt instruments. This means that if a five-year government security is trading at a yield of 5%, all other five-year bonds, irrespective of the issuer, will be trading at yields over 5%. The excess over the yield on the corresponding government security is called the *credit spread*.

The yield curve also acts as an indicator of future yield levels. It assumes certain shapes in response to market expectations of future interest rates. Market participants therefore analyze the current shape of the curve to determine the direction of future interest rates. The curve is scrutinized to divine information, not just by bond traders and fund managers, but also by corporate finance personnel. Traders and fund managers want to identify securities they believe are under-valued or over-valued so that they can take suitable investment decisions. Investment bankers handling new debt issues for their clients want to know the rate of return required by the market for debt securities of the risk class represented by a client. This enables them to set the coupon on the to-be-issued security. Central banks and government treasury departments also

https://doi.org/10.1515/9781547400669-004

analyze the curve for its information content about future interest levels. This information is then used to set rates for the economy as a whole.

Spot Rates of Interest

The spot rate of interest for a particular time period is the discount rate that is applicable for a zero coupon instrument maturing at the end of the period. Unless otherwise stated, we take one period as six months.

For instance, assume that the price of a six-month zero coupon bond with a face value of $1,000 is $975. The one-period spot rate is given by

$$975 = \frac{1{,}000}{(1 + \frac{s_1}{2})} \Rightarrow s_1 = 0.051282 \equiv 5.1282\%$$

Similarly, if a one-year or a two-period zero coupon bond has a price of $910, then the two-period spot rate is given by

$$910 = \frac{1{,}000}{(1 + \frac{s_2}{2})^2} \Rightarrow s_2 = 0.096569 \equiv 9.6569\%$$

The Relationship Between Spot Rates and the YTM

A plain vanilla bond consists of a series of cash flows arising at six-month intervals. Thus such a bond is equivalent to a portfolio of zero coupon bonds, where each cash flow represents the face value of a zero coupon bond maturing at that particular instant. The correct way to price a bond is by discounting each cash flow at the spot rate for the corresponding period. The yield to maturity, is that single rate that makes the present value of all future cash flows from the bond equal to its dirty price. Thus the yield to maturity is a complex non-linear average of spot rates.

Let's take the case of a bond with a face value of $1,000 and one year to maturity. Assume that it pays a coupon of 7% per annum on a semiannual basis. Using the spot rates derived in the previous section, we can calculate the price of the bond to be

$$P = \frac{35}{(1.025641)} + \frac{1{,}035}{(1.048285)^2} = \$975.9747$$

The yield to maturity of this bond is given by

$$975.9747 = \frac{35}{(1 + \frac{y}{2})} + \frac{1{,}035}{(1 + \frac{y}{2})^2}$$

$$\Rightarrow y = 9.5764\%$$

The fact that the YTM is a complex average of spot rates need not pose any problems per se. The problem with the yield to maturity is that it is a function of the coupon rate for bonds with identical terms to maturity but with different coupons.[1]

For instance, let's take a 15% coupon bond with a face value of \$1,000 and one year to maturity. Its price is given by

$$P = \frac{75}{(1.025641)} + \frac{1{,}075}{(1.048285)^2} = \$1{,}051.3746$$

The yield to maturity of this bond is given by

$$1{,}051.3746 = \frac{75}{\left(1 + \frac{y}{2}\right)} + \frac{1{,}075}{\left(1 + \frac{y}{2}\right)^2}$$

$$\Rightarrow y = 9.4939\%$$

Why is there a difference in the yields to maturity of the two bonds? After all they both have one year to maturity. Let's take the 7% bond first. It has

$$\frac{\frac{35}{(1.025641)}}{975.9747} = 0.034965 \equiv 3.4965\%$$

of its value tied up in one-period money and the balance 96.5035% tied up in two-period money.

However, in the case of the 15% bond,

$$\frac{\frac{75}{(1.025641)}}{1{,}051.3746} = 0.069552 \equiv 6.9552\%$$

of its value is tied up in one-period money, whereas the balance 93.0448% is tied up in two-period money.

The one-period spot rate is less than the two-period spot rate, which implies that one-period money is cheaper than two-period money. Because the second bond has a greater percentage of its value tied up in one-period money, its yield to maturity is lower. This is a manifestation of what is termed the *coupon effect*. In other words, because the yield to maturity is a complex average of spot rates, it tends to vary with the coupon rate on the bond, when we compare bonds with different coupons, but with the same time to maturity.

Yield Curve versus the Term Structure

Technically speaking, a "yield curve" is a graph depicting the relationship between the yield to maturity, which is plotted along the Y-axis, and the time to maturity, which

1 See Fabozzi [28].

is plotted along the X-axis. For the purpose of constructing the yield curve, it is imperative that the bonds being compared belong to the same credit risk class. This is the most commonly used version of the yield curve for the simple reason that the YTM is the most commonly used measure of the yield from a bond.

The expression *"term structure of interest rates,"* on the other hand, refers to a graph depicting the relationship between spot rates of interest, as shown along the Y-axis, and the corresponding times to maturity, which are plotted along the X-axis. Once again, to facilitate meaningful inferences, the data used to construct the graph should be applicable to bonds of the same risk class. The "term structure of interest rates" is also referred to as the *"zero coupon yield curve"* because the YTM of a zero coupon bond is nothing but the spot rate. The zero coupon yield curve is considered to be the true term structure of interest rates because there is no reinvestment risk. This is because such bonds do not give rise to any cash flows prior to maturity, and consequently there is no risk that cash flows may have to be reinvested at a lower than anticipated rate.

The yield curve is equivalent to the term structure if the term structure is flat, or in other words, the spot rates are the same for all maturities. This is because, when the term structure is flat, the YTM, which is a complex average of spot rates, is equal to the observed spot rate. However, when the term structure is not flat, as is usually the case, the YTM is somewhere between the lowest spot rate, and the highest spot rate.

Required Symbols

We will use the following symbols in connection with our analysis of yield curves and the term structure:

- $y_i \equiv$ the yield to maturity for an i period bond.
- $s_i \equiv$ the i period spot rate, or equivalently the yield to maturity of an i period zero coupon bond.
- $f_n^{m-n} \equiv$ the $m-n$ period implied forward rate for a loan to be made after n periods.
- $E_0[{}_nS_{m-n}] \equiv$ the current expectation of the $m-n$ period spot rate that is expected to prevail n periods from now.

Bootstrapping to Obtain Spot Rates

In practice, we are unlikely to have data for the prices of zero coupon bonds conveniently maturing at regularly spaced intervals of time. *Bootstrapping* is a technique for determining the term structure of interest rates, given price data for a series of coupon paying bonds. It works as illustrated in Example 4.1.

Example 4.1. Assume that we have the following data for four bonds, each of which matures at the end of the stated period of time. For ease of exposition, we also assume that the bonds pay coupons on an annual basis. The face value is $1,000 for all the bonds.

Table 4.1: Inputs for determining the zero coupon yield curve.

Time to Maturity	Price in Dollars	Coupon
1 Year	980	6%
2 Years	960	8%
3 Years	940	9%
4 Years	925	10%

The one-year spot rate is given by:

$$980 = \frac{1{,}060}{(1 + s_1)}$$
$$\Rightarrow s_1 = 8.1633\%$$

Using this information, the two-year spot rate can be determined as follows:

$$960 = \frac{80}{(1.081633)} + \frac{1{,}080}{(1 + s_2)^2}$$
$$\Rightarrow s_2 = 10.4042\%$$

Similarly, the three-year spot rate can be determined as follows:

$$940 = \frac{90}{(1.081633)} + \frac{90}{(1.104042)^2} + \frac{1{,}090}{(1 + s_3)^3}$$
$$\Rightarrow s_3 = 11.6597\%$$

And, finally, using the same logic,

$$925 = \frac{100}{(1.081633)} + \frac{100}{(1.104042)^2} + \frac{100}{(1.116597)^3} + \frac{1{,}100}{(1 + s_4)^4}$$
$$\Rightarrow s_4 = 12.8321\%$$

Practical Difficulties with Bootstrapping

In Example 4.1 we used the prices of four bonds, maturing after one, two, three, and four years, respectively. In some cases, there may be several bonds of the same risk class, maturing at a given point in time. Usually each has its own coupon. When estimating spot rates for a given maturity, obviously the coupon rates of the bonds being used are a factor. One of the other major issues, when estimating the term structure using bootstrapping, is that a bond may not exist or may not actively trade for a particular maturity. And it is not necessary that we always have access to a set of bonds whose maturity dates are conveniently spaced exactly one period apart.

Finally, all traded bonds may not be plain vanilla in nature. Institutions like the U.S. Treasury have issued bonds that can be recalled after a point in time. This too has implications for the bootstrapping procedure, for we cannot compare apples with oranges.

Coupon Yield Curves and Par Bond Yield Curves

One of the other problems with bootstrapping is that in practice we receive data in the form of prices of bonds with different coupons. One way of getting over this estimation-related problem is by using data for bonds that all have the same coupon. The "yield curve" that is so obtained is called the *"coupon yield curve."* If we construct such a curve, we can see that in general higher coupon bonds trade at a discount (have higher yields) relative to lower coupon bonds. This is due to reinvestment risk.

The *"par bond yield curve"* on the other hand, is an estimate of the yield curve obtained from data for bonds that have different coupons, but all of which trade at par. In this case, the coupon for each of these bonds is nothing but its yield to maturity. Bootstrapping can then be applied to such a data set to derive the vector of spot rates as before. Example 4.2 is a numerical illustration of this procedure. We are using the data given in Table 4.1 but assuming that all the bonds are trading at par.

Example 4.2. The one-year spot rate is obviously 6%. Using this information, the two-year spot rate can be determined as follows:

$$1{,}000 = \frac{80}{(1.06)} + \frac{1{,}080}{(1+s_2)^2}$$

$$\Rightarrow s_2 = 8.08\%$$

Similarly, the three year spot rate can be determined as follows:

$$1{,}000 = \frac{90}{(1.06)} + \frac{90}{(1.0808)^2} + \frac{1{,}090}{(1+s_3)^3}$$

$$\Rightarrow s_3 = 9.16\%$$

Table 4.2: The par-bond approach to bootstrapping.

Time to Maturity	Price in dollars	YTM = Coupon
1 Year	1,000	6%
2 Years	1,000	8%
3 Years	1,000	9%
4 Years	1,000	10%

And, finally, using the same logic,

$$1{,}000 = \frac{100}{(1.06)} + \frac{100}{(1.0808)^2} + \frac{100}{(1.0916)^3} + \frac{1{,}100}{(1+s_4)^4}$$

$$\Rightarrow s_4 = 10.30\%$$

The par bond yield curve is not commonly encountered in secondary market trading. However it is often constructed and used by people in *corporate finance* departments and others who are involved with issues in the primary market. Investment bankers use par bond yield curves to determine the required coupon for a new bond that is to be issued at par. This is because new issues are typically issued at par and consequently the banker needs to know the coupon that needs to be offered to ensure that the bonds can be issued at par. In practice, the market uses data from non-par plain vanilla bonds to first derive the zero coupon yield curve. This information is then used to deduce the hypothetical par yields that would be observed if traded par bonds were to be available.

Deducing a Par Bond Yield Curve

The par bond yield curve can be derived using a vector of spot rates. Let us consider the spot rates that we derived in Example 4.1.

Example 4.3. The yield for a one-year par bond is obviously 8.1633%. The yields for the other bonds are summarized in Table 4.3.

The yield, or equivalently, the coupon for the two-year par bond can be deduced as follows:

$$1{,}000 = \frac{C}{(1.081633)} + \frac{1{,}000 + C}{(1.104042)^2}$$

$$\Rightarrow C = \$102.9235 \Rightarrow c = 10.2924\%$$

Similarly,

$$1{,}000 = \frac{C}{(1.081633)} + \frac{C}{(1.104042)^2} + \frac{1{,}000 + C}{(1.116597)^3}$$

$$\Rightarrow C = \$114.3581 \Rightarrow c = 11.4358\%$$

Table 4.3: Inputs for inferring a par bond yield curve.

Time to Maturity	Spot Rate
1 Year	8.1633%
2 Years	10.4042%
3 Years	11.6597%
4 Years	12.8321%

and

$$1{,}000 = \frac{C}{(1.081633)} + \frac{C}{(1.104042)^2} + \frac{C}{(1.116597)^3} + \frac{1{,}000 + C}{(1.128321)^4}$$
$$\Rightarrow C = \$124.3489 \Rightarrow c = 12.4349\%$$

Thus a two-year bond of this risk class ought to be issued with a coupon of 10.2924% if it is to be sold at par. Similarly, three-year and four-year bonds should carry coupons of 11.4358% and 12.4349%, respectively.

Implied Forward Rates of Interest

Consider an investor who is contemplating investing for two periods. He has the option of investing in a two-period zero coupon bond yielding s_2. Or he can invest in a one-period bond yielding a rate of s_1, and buy a forward contract to lock in a roll over rate f_1^1. The two options are equivalent to the investor if

$$(1 + s_2)^2 = (1 + s_1)(1 + f_1^1) \tag{4.1}$$

f_1^1 is the one-period forward rate, or the rate as of today, for a forward contract to make a one-period loan one period from today. It is the implied forward rate that is contained in the term structure. In general, if we have an n period spot rate and an m period spot rate, where $m > n$, then

$$(1 + s_m)^m = (1 + s_n)^n (1 + f_n^{m-n})^{m-n} \tag{4.2}$$

where f_n^{m-n} is the $m-n$ period implied forward rate for a loan to be made after n periods.

Forward rates are believed to convey information about the expected future interest rate structure. In fact, one theory called the *unbiased expectations hypothesis* holds that such rates are nothing but current expectations of future interest rates.

Example 4.4. The one-year spot rate is 5%, the two-year spot rate is 6%, the three-year spot rate is 8%, and the four-year spot rate is 10%. Using this information what can we deduce about implied forward rates?

$$(1 + s_2)^2 = (1 + s_1)(1 + f_1^1) \Rightarrow f_1^1 = 0.07$$

The rate for a forward contract to make a one-period loan after one period is 7% per annum.

$$(1 + s_3)^3 = (1 + s_1)(1 + f_1^2)^2 \Rightarrow f_1^2 = 0.0953$$

The rate for a forward contract to make a two-period loan after one-period is 9.53% per annum.

$$(1 + s_3)^3 = (1 + s_1)(1 + f_1^1)(1 + f_2^1) \Rightarrow f_2^1 = 0.1212$$

That is, the rate for a forward contract to make a one-period loan after two periods is 12.12%.

$$(1+s_4)^4 = (1+s_1)(1+f_1^3)^3 \Rightarrow f_1^3 = 0.1172$$

The rate for a forward contract to make a three-period loan after one period is 11.72%.

$$(1+s_4)^4 = (1+s_2)^2(1+f_2^2)^2 \Rightarrow f_2^2 = 0.1415$$

The rate for a forward contract to make a two-period loan after two periods is 14.15%. Finally,

$$(1+s_4)^4 = (1+s_3)^3(1+f_3^1) \Rightarrow f_3^1 = 0.1622$$

That is, the rate for a forward contract to make a one-period loan after three periods is 16.22%.

Fitting the Yield Curve

When plotting a yield curve, we fit a series of discrete points of yield against the corresponding maturities. Similarly, for the term structure of interest rates, we plot spot rates for a fixed time period against the time period. The yield curve itself, however, is a smooth curve drawn through these discrete points. We require a method that allows us to fit the curve as accurately as possible. This aspect of yield curve analysis is known as *yield curve modeling* or *estimating the term structure.*

The yield curve is derived from coupon bond prices and yields. In attempting to model the curve from bond yield data, we need to be aware of two fundamental issues. First, there is the problem of gaps in the maturity spectrum because in the real world bonds do not mature at regular intervals of time. Second, the term structure is defined in terms of spot rates or zero-coupon interest rates. But in many markets there is no zero coupon bond market.

With all this on mind, we now can study four methods for modeling the yield curve.[2]

Interpolation

The simplest method that can be used to fit the yield curve is *linear interpolation.* For example, assume that we are given the following data:

$$s_5 = 8\% \quad \text{and} \quad s_{10} = 9\%$$

We can then calculate the eight-year spot rate as

$$s_8 = 8.00 + \frac{(8-5)}{(10-5)} \times (9.00 - 8.00) = 8.60\%$$

2 See Choudhry [11].

Polynomial Models of the Yield Curve

A *polynomial* of degree k can be expressed as

$$y_i = \alpha + \beta_1 t + \beta_2 t^2 + \cdots + \beta_k t^k + u_i \tag{4.3}$$

where y_i is the YTM of bond i, t is its term to maturity, and u_i is the residual error. To determine the coefficients of the polynomial, we minimize the sum of the squared residual errors given by

$$\sum_{i=1}^{N} u_i^2$$

where N is the number of bonds used.

Regression Models of the Yield Curve

Regression is a variation of the polynomial approach. This method uses bond prices as the dependent variable and the coupons and face values of the bonds as the independent variables. The standard format is

$$P_i = \beta_1 C_{1i} + \beta_2 C_{2i} + \cdots + \beta_N (C_{Ni} + M) + u_i \tag{4.4}$$

In this expression, P_i is the dirty price of bond i, C_{ji} is the coupon of bond i in period j, and u_i is the residual error. The spot rates can be derived from the estimated relationships using the expression

$$\beta_n = \frac{1}{(1 + s_n)^n}$$

The Nelson-Siegel Model of the Yield Curve

Before we describe the Nelson-Siegel technique, we need to familiarize ourselves with bond pricing in a continuous time framework.

Take a zero coupon bond that pays \$1 after n periods. In a discrete time setting, we would express the bond price as:

$$P(0, n) = \frac{1}{(1 + s_n)^n} \tag{4.5}$$

where s_n is the n-period spot rate at time 0. If we were to compound interest 'm' times per period where $m > 1$, then we would express the bond price as:

$$P(0, n) = \frac{1}{(1 + \frac{s_n}{m})^{mn}} \tag{4.6}$$

For instance, if we were to compound four times every period, then m would be equal to 4. In the limit $m \to \infty$, we get the case of continuous compounding. In the limit, we can express the price of the bond as:

$$P(0,n) = e^{-s_n \times n} \tag{4.7}$$

We know that in the discrete time framework the n-period spot rate can be expressed as

$$(1+s_n)^n = (1+s_1)(1+f_1^1)(1+f_2^1)\ldots(1+f_{n-1}^1) \tag{4.8}$$

In the case of continuous compounding, the equivalent representation is:

$$s_n \times n = \int_0^n f_s ds \tag{4.9}$$

where f_s is the instantaneous forward rate.

Nelson-Siegel proposed the following representation for the instantaneous forward rate:

$$f_s = \beta_0 + \beta_1 e^{-s/\theta} + \beta_2 \times \frac{s}{\theta} e^{-s/\theta} \tag{4.10}$$

Integrating this function we get the following expression for the n-period spot rate:

$$s_n = \beta_0 + \beta_1 \times \left[\frac{1-e^{-n/\theta}}{n/\theta}\right] + \beta_2 \times \left[\frac{1-e^{-n/\theta}}{n/\theta} - e^{-n/\theta}\right] \tag{4.11}$$

The four parameters $\beta_0, \beta_1, \beta_2$, and θ have to be empirically estimated.

Interpretation of the Nelson-Siegel Model

We can interpret the parameters that must be estimated, as follows:

Using L' Hôpital's rule, we find that

$$\lim_{n\to\infty} f(n) = \beta_0$$

$$\lim_{n\to zero} f(n) = \beta_0 + \beta_1$$

$$\lim_{n\to\infty} \left[\frac{1-e^{\frac{-n}{\theta}}}{\frac{n}{\theta}}\right] = 0$$

$$\lim_{n\to\infty} \left[\frac{1-e^{\frac{-n}{\theta}}}{\frac{n}{\theta}} - e^{\frac{-n}{\theta}}\right] = 0$$

Thus,

$$\lim_{n \to \infty} s_n = \beta_0$$

$$\lim_{n \to zero} \left[\frac{1 - e^{\frac{-n}{\theta}}}{\frac{n}{\theta}} \right] = 1$$

$$\lim_{n \to zero} \left[\frac{1 - e^{\frac{-n}{\theta}}}{\frac{n}{\theta}} - e^{\frac{-n}{\theta}} \right] = 0$$

And,

$$\lim_{n \to zero} s_n = \beta_0 + \beta_1$$

An Economic Interpretation

β_0 is a constant that represents the long-term interest rate level.[3] β_1 captures the slope of the curve. If it is positive, the curve slopes downward, whereas if it is negative, the curve slopes upward. β_2 captures the hump or the trough in the curve. If it is positive, there is a hump, but if it is negative, there is a trough. The higher the absolute value of β_2 the more pronounced the hump or the trough. θ is the shape parameter. It determines the steepness of the slope and the location of the hump or trough.

When the time to maturity tends to infinity, the slope and curvature components vanish, and both the long-term spot rate and the forward rate converge to β_0. From an economic standpoint, we would assume β_0 to be close to the empirical long-term spot rate and positive in sign. When the time to maturity tends to zero, only the curvature component vanishes, and the forward and spot rates converge to $\beta_0 + \beta_1$. $\beta 1$ measures the slope of the term structure. The degree of curvature is controlled by β_2. Finally, θ determines the maximum or minimum as the case may be, depending on whether there is a hump or a trough.

Svensson extended the model by adding two additional variables, to create what has been termed as the Nelson-Siegel-Svensson model. This model can be stated as:

$$s_n = \beta_0 + \beta_1 \times \left[\frac{1 - e^{\frac{-n}{\theta_1}}}{\frac{n}{\theta_1}} \right] + \beta_2 \times \left[\frac{1 - e^{\frac{-n}{\theta_1}}}{\frac{n}{\theta_1}} - e^{\frac{-n}{\theta_1}} \right] + \beta_3 \times \left[\frac{1 - e^{\frac{-n}{\theta_2}}}{\frac{n}{\theta_2}} - e^{\frac{-n}{\theta_2}} \right] \tag{4.12}$$

In this case we need to estimate six parameters, the two additional parameters being β_3 and θ_2. β_3 and θ_2 have an interpretation similar to β_2 and θ_1. Thus by including β_3, Svensson incorporates an additional hump or trough.

The Nelson-Siegel method for estimating the term structure has a number of advantages. First, its functional form can handle a variety of shapes of the term structure

3 See Annaert et al. [1].

that are observed in the market. Second, the model avoids the need to introduce other assumptions for interpolation between intermediate points. For instance, the bootstrapping approach gives us a vector of spot rates spaced six months apart. To value a bond whose life is not an integer multiple of semiannual periods, we obviously need to interpolate. On the contrary, using the Nelson-Siegel approach, we can derive the spot rate at any point in time and not just at certain discrete points.

Theories of the Term Structure

From observing yield curves in different markets at various points in time, an individual who studies the bond market notices that the yield curve tends to adopt one of the four basic shapes:

- *Upward sloping*: In the case of a yield curve with a positive slope, also termed as a rising yield curve, short term yields are lower than long term yields.
- *Downward sloping*: In the case of a yield curve with a negative slope, also termed as an inverted yield curve, long term rates are substantially lower than short term rates.
- *Humped*: A humped yield curve is characterized by lower rates at the short end of the spectrum. The curve then rises, reaching a peak at the middle of the maturity spectrum, and then gradually slopes downward at longer maturities.
- *U-shaped*: A U-shaped yield curve is characterized by higher rates at the short end of the spectrum. The curve then falls, reaching a minimum at the middle of the maturity spectrum, and then gradually slopes upward at longer maturities.

A great deal of effort is expended by analysts and economists in analyzing and interpreting the yield curve, for there is often substantial information that is associated with the curve at any point in time. Various theories have been advanced that purport to explain the observed shapes of the curve. However, no theory by itself is able to explain all aspects of the curves that are observed in practice. So often analysts seek to explain specific shapes of the curve using a combination of the accepted theories.[4]

The Pure or Unbiased Expectations Hypothesis

The unbiased expectations hypothesis states that the current implied forward rates are unbiased estimators of future spot rates. Per this theory, long-term rates are geometric averages of expected future short-term rates. Thus a positively sloped yield curve would be consistent with the argument that the market expects spot interest rates to

4 See Choudhry [11] and Taggart [64].

rise. If rates are expected to rise, then investors in long-term bonds become perturbed for they face the specter of a capital loss. This is because rising interest rates lead to declining bond prices, and long-term bonds are more sensitive to rising interest rates than short-term bonds. In such situations investors start selling long-dated securities and buying short-dated securities. This leads to an increase in yields on long-term bonds and a decline in yields on short-term bonds. The overall result is an upward sloping yield curve. On the contrary, an inverted yield curve indicates that the market expects future spot rates to fall.

The hypothesis can be used to explain any shape of the yield curve. For instance, a humped yield curve is consistent with the explanation that investors expect short-term rates to rise and long-term rates to fall. Expectations or views on the future direction of the market are a function mainly of the expected rate of inflation. If the market expects inflationary pressures in the future, the yield curve slopes positively, whereas, if inflation is expected to decline, then the yield curve slopes negatively.

The Liquidity Preference Theory (LPT)

Intuitively, most of us feel that longer maturity instruments are riskier than shorter maturity ones. An investor lending money for five years usually demands a higher rate of interest than when lending money to the same entity for a year. This is because the borrower may not be able to repay the loan over a longer term period. For this reason, long-dated yields should be higher than short dated yields.

Take the case where the market expects inflation to remain fairly stable over time. The expectations hypothesis postulates that this scenario would be characterized by a flat yield curve. However, the *liquidity preference theory* (LPT) predicts a positively sloping yield curve. The argument is as follows. Generally a borrower would like to borrow over a long period, whereas a lender would like to lend over a short period. Thus lenders have to be suitably rewarded if they are to be induced to lend for longer periods of time. This compensation can be considered a premium for the loss of liquidity from the standpoint of the lender. The premium can be expected to increase the farther the investor lends across the term structure. So that the longest dated instruments, all else being equal, have the highest yield.

Per this hypothesis, the yield curve should almost always be upward sloping, reflecting the bond holders' preference for liquidity. However, the theory can explain inverted yield curves by postulating that interest rates are likely to decline in the future, and a consequence of this, despite the liquidity premium, is that long-term rates may be lower than short-term rates.

The Expectations Hypothesis versus the LPT: A Mathematical Analysis

Per the expectations hypothesis, forward rates are unbiased expectations of future spot rates. Thus

$$f_n^{m-n} = E_0[{}_nS_{m-n}] \tag{4.13}$$

In other words, the rate for a forward contract to make an $m - n$ period loan, n periods from today, is the current expectation of the $m - n$ period spot rate that is expected to prevail n periods from now. The expectations hypothesis can explain any shape of the term structure. For instance, an expectation that future short-term interest rates will be above the current level leads to an upward sloping term structure.

Example 4.5. Assume that $s_1 = 5.50\%$; $E[{}_1s_1] = 6.0\%$; $E[{}_2s_1] = 7.5\%$, and $E[{}_3s_1] = 8.5\%$. If so, then

$$s_2 = [(1.055)(1.06)]^{0.5} - 1 = 5.75\%$$
$$s_3 = [(1.055)(1.06)(1.075)]^{0.3333} - 1 = 6.33\%$$
$$s_4 = [(1.055)(1.06)(1.075)(1.085)]^{0.25} - 1 = 6.87\%$$

According to the expectations hypothesis, investors care only about expected returns and not about risk. Let's take the case of an investor who chooses to invest for two periods. He can buy a two-period bond yielding a rate of s_2. Or he can buy a one-period bond that yields s_1 and then roll over into another one-period bond at maturity. Per this hypothesis, the investor will be indifferent between the two strategies if the expected returns in both cases are equal.

In other words, the hypothesis predicts that the market will be in equilibrium if

$$(1 + s_2)^2 = E[(1 + s_1)(1 + {}_1s_1)] = (1 + s_1)E[(1 + {}_1s_1)] \tag{4.14}$$

But we know that if arbitrage is to be ruled out, then

$$(1 + s_2)^2 = (1 + s_1)(1 + f_1^1) \tag{4.15}$$

Thus, per the expectations hypothesis

$$f_1^1 = E({}_1s_1)$$

Now let's focus on the liquidity preference theory. Take the case of an investor who has a one-period investment horizon. He can buy a one-period bond and lock in a rate of s_1. Or he can buy a two-period bond and sell it after one year. In the second case, the rate of return is uncertain at the outset, for it depends on the one-period rate that prevails one period from now.

Consider a two-period zero coupon bond with a face value of $1,000. Its current price is

$$\frac{1{,}000}{(1+s_2)^2} = \frac{1{,}000}{(1+s_1)(1+f_1^1)}$$

The expected price of the bond after one period is

$$E\left[\frac{1{,}000}{(1+{}_1s_1)}\right] \geq \frac{1{,}000}{1+E({}_1s_1)}$$

How do we know that the expected price after one year will be greater than or equal to the face value discounted by the expected one-period spot rate one period from now. This deduction arises from a result called *Jensen's Inequality*. It states that for a convex function

$$E[f(X)] \geq f[E(X)]$$

That is, the expectation of the function is greater than or equal to the function of the expectation. In our case, $\frac{1{,}000}{1+{}_1s_1}$ is a convex function because the second derivative is positive.

The expected rate of return from the two-period bond over the first year is:

$$\begin{aligned}
&\frac{E\left[\frac{1{,}000}{(1+{}_1s_1)}\right] - \frac{1{,}000}{(1+s_1)(1+f_1^1)}}{\frac{1{,}000}{(1+s_1)(1+f_1^1)}} \\
&\geq \frac{\frac{1{,}000}{1+E({}_1s_1)} - \frac{1{,}000}{(1+s_1)(1+f_1^1)}}{\frac{1{,}000}{(1+s_1)(1+f_1^1)}} \\
\Rightarrow\ &\frac{E\left[\frac{1{,}000}{(1+{}_1s_1)}\right] - \frac{1{,}000}{(1+s_1)(1+f_1^1)}}{\frac{1{,}000}{(1+s_1)(1+f_1^1)}} \\
&\geq \frac{(1+s_1)(1+f_1^1)}{1+E({}_1s_1)} - 1
\end{aligned}$$

A sufficient condition for the expected one-period return from the two-period bond to be greater than the one-period spot rate, s_1, is $f_1^1 > E({}_1s_1)$. Thus the expected one-period return from a two-period bond is greater than the current one-period spot rate if the implied forward rate is greater than the current expectation of next period's one-period spot rate.

Now an investor with a one-period investment horizon will obviously choose to hold a two-period bond only if its expected return is greater than the assured return on a one-period bond. This is because if the investor chooses to hold the two-period bond, he will have to sell it after one period at a price that is unknown at the outset. From the previous analysis this implies that the forward rate must be higher than the expected one-period spot rate. Thus if investors are risk averse, which is the normal assumption made in finance theory, the forward rate will exceed the expected spot rate by an amount equal to the risk premium or what may be termed as the *liquidity* premium.[5]

We know that

$$(1 + s_2)(1 + s_2) = (1 + s_1)(1 + f_1^1)$$

as per the LPT,

$$(1 + s_1)(1 + f_1^1) > (1 + s_1)[1 + E(_1s_1)]$$

Therefore,

$$(1 + s_2)(1 + s_2) > (1 + s_1)[1 + E(_1s_1)]$$

Consider a downward sloping yield curve. That implies that $s_1 > s_2$. Therefore, it must be the case that $E(_1s_1)$ is substantially less than s_1. In other words, the market expects spot rates to decline substantially. For instance, if $s_1 = 7\%$ and $s_2 = 6\%$, then $f_1^1 = 5.01\%$. Per the expectations hypothesis, $E(_1s_1) = 5.01\%$. However, per the LPT, $E(_1s_1) < 5.01\%$. If we assume that the liquidity premium is 0.50%, then $E(_1s_1) = 4.51\%$.

Now let's take the case of a flat term structure. Per the expectations hypothesis,

$$s_1 = s_2 = f_1^1 = E(_1s_1)$$

However, according to the LPT, $E(_1s_1) < s_1 = s_2$. Thus, although the expectations hypothesis implies that the market expects spot rates to remain unchanged, the prediction according to the liquidity preference theory is that the market expects spot rates to decline. For instance, if $s_1 = s_2 = 7\%$, then according to the expectations hypothesis, $E(_1s_1) = 7\%$. However, according to the LPT, $E(_1s_1) = 7 - 0.50 = 6.50\%$.

Finally let's take the case of an upward sloping yield curve. If $s_1 < s_2$, then for a slightly upward sloping yield curve, the LPT would predict that rates are going to marginally decline. However, if the curve slopes steeply upward, then the LPT implies that short term rates are going to rise. For instance, assume that $s_1 = 7\%$ and $s_2 = 7.1\%$. If so,

$$f_1^1 = 7.2\% \Rightarrow E(_1s_1) = 7.20 - 0.50 = 6.70\%$$

However, if $s_2 = 7.3\%$, then

$$f_1^1 = 7.6\% \Rightarrow E(_1s_1) = 7.60 - 0.50 = 7.10\%$$

In both these cases, however, the expectations hypothesis predicts that spot rates are likely to rise. In the first scenario, per the expectations hypothesis, $E(_1s_1) = 7.20\%$, whereas in the second case $E(_1s_1) = 7.60\%$.

5 See Bodie et al. [5].

The Money Substitute Hypothesis

According to the money substitute hypothesis, short-term bonds are substitutes for holding cash. Investors hold only short-dated bonds because they are viewed as having low or negligible risk. As a result the yields on short-dated bonds are depressed due to increased demand, and consequently long-term yields are greater than short-term yields. Borrowers, on the other hand, prefer to issue debt for long maturities and on as few occasions as possible to minimize costs. Thus the yields on long-term securities are driven upward due to increased supply and consequently lower prices.[6]

The Market Segmentation Hypothesis

The market segmentation hypothesis states that the capital market is made up of a wide variety of issuers, each with different requirements. Certain classes of investors prefer short-dated bonds, and others prefer long-dated bonds. The theory argues that activity is concentrated in certain specific areas of the market, and that there are no interrelationships between these segments of the market. The relative amount of funds invested in each market segment causes differentials in supply and demand that lead to humps in the yield curve.

Thus, per this theory, the observed shape of the yield curve is determined by the supply and demand for specific maturity investments, and the dynamics in a particular market segment have no relevance for any other part of the curve. For example, banks concentrate a large part of their activity at the short-end of the curve as a part of daily cash management known as *asset-liability management*, and for regulatory purposes known as *liquidity requirements*. On the other hand, fund managers such as pension funds and insurance companies are active at the long-end of the market.[7] Few institutions, however, have a preference for medium-dated bonds. This behavior leads to high prices and low yields at both the short and long ends of the maturity spectrum and to high yields in the middle of the term structure.

The theory argues that financial institutions like banks, pension funds, and mutual funds often act as risk minimizers and not as profit maximizers as a theory such as the unbiased expectations hypothesis would have us believe. In their quest for minimizing risk, they hedge the risk of fluctuations in prices and yields by balancing the maturity of their assets with that of their liabilities. For instance, the treasurer or CFO of a company who has surplus funds for a short period invests only in short-term money market securities such as commercial paper. On the contrary a pension fund, whose liabilities are long term, invests only in long-term bonds.

6 See Choudhry [11].

7 See Choudhry [11].

Thus, this theory argues that risk aversion precludes agents from switching from one market segment to another. This is true no matter how attractive rates may be in another segment of the market. Thus the yield curve is a collection of sub markets. Each of these has its own supply and demand dynamics and consequently its own equilibrium rate of interest. Thus the implied forward rate is unrelated to expected future spot rates.

One policy implication of this hypothesis is that if the submarkets are isolated, the central bank can alter the shape of the curve by influencing the supply and demand dynamics in one or more market segments. For instance, if the objective is to have an upward sloping yield curve, the central bank can flood the market with long-term bonds and acquire short-term bonds. This causes long-term bond prices to fall or, equivalently, long-term yields to rise. At the same time the induced demand for short-term bonds, pushes up prices in this market segment, causing short-term yields to fall. The net consequence is an upward sloping yield curve.

While the expectations hypothesis argues that securities are perfect substitutes for each other, this theory goes to the other extreme, by arguing that investors and issuers are so risk averse that they buy and sell bonds only for maturities matching their desired time horizons.

The Preferred Habitat Theory

The preferred habitat theory is a slightly modified version of the segmentation hypothesis. This suggests that different market participants have an interest in specified areas of the yield curve but can be persuaded to hold bonds from other parts of the maturity spectrum if they are provided with sufficient incentives. Hence, banks, which typically operate at the short-end of the spectrum, may at times hold long-dated bonds when the price of these bonds falls to a certain level, thereby ensuring that the returns from holding such bonds is commensurate with the attendant risk. Similar considerations may persuade long-term investors to hold short-term debt. So the incentive for an investor to shift out of his preferred habitat is the inducement offered by way of a higher rate of interest.

Features of the Debt Market and Theories of the Term Structure

In practice we find that the yield curve is generally upward sloping, and yields tend to taper off at longer maturities.[8] The liquidity preference theory postulates the investors require a higher rate of return from long-term bonds because they subject the

8 See Smith [56] for a detailed exposition.

holders to greater risk. The market segmentation theory argues that demand for long-term funds is strong relative to short-term funds while supply of short-term funds is strong relative to long-term funds. This is consistent with the observation that whereas borrowers want to lock in rates for longer periods, lenders prefer the flexibility of short-term investments. Thus the long-term debt capital market is characterized by high demand for funds and lower supply, which translates into a high supply of bonds and low demand. This means that long-term rates will be high. However, the short-term debt capital market is characterized by lower demand for funds and higher supply, which would manifest itself as a low supply of bonds and a high demand for the same. This implies that short-term rates would be lower. This could explain the fact that the yield curve is typically upward sloping.

In practice we find that short-term yields are more volatile than longer-term yields. In other words, the term structure of volatility is downward sloping. Both the expectations theory and the liquidity preference theory explain this by arguing that because long-term rates are an average of future short term rates, they are less volatile. This is because averages are always less volatile. The market segmentation theory says that there is a lot of activity in the money market, whereas the long-term debt market is relatively more stable. One reason could be that long maturity bonds attract buy and hold investors like life insurance companies and pension funds. These entities are in the game for the long run and consequently long-term bonds are less actively traded. Investors with a shorter time horizon frequently engage in asset reallocation. While doing so, the tendency is typically to park funds in the money market until a suitable alternate investment is identified. This could explain the volatility of the money market.

Yet another real-life observation is that both short-term and long-term yields usually change in the same direction. Thus shifts in the yield curve are usually parallel. This could be explained as follows. Macroeconomic factors such as inflation, monetary policy, balance of trade, foreign exchange rates, and fiscal policy usually tend to influence both short-term and long-term rates in a similar fashion. This argument is consistent with all the postulated theories.

The liquidity premium hypothesis predicts that long-term yields will be higher than a geometric average of expected short-term rates. This is because most investors have a short-term horizon and therefore need an inducement, to hold longer-term securities. In other words, such investors confront the specter of market risk or price risk. On the other hand, consider a scenario where most traders have a long-term horizon. Such participants need an inducement to hold short-term securities, for such investment strategies expose them to reinvestment risk. So whether the long-term rates are higher or lower than a geometric average of expected short-term rates depends on how investors are distributed across maturities.

In practice, speculative bond traders as well as dealers usually have a short-term horizon. Speculative traders, taking a view on short-term rates,prefer short-term bonds as vehicles of speculation. Bond dealers too typically seek to rotate their inventory frequently and therefore are short-term holders. Hence they tend to demand higher yields from long-term bonds because the latter expose them to greater risk. Both speculators and dealers prefer to hold short-term bonds, and the high demand for these is consistent with a low yield. These observations perhaps explain why the yield curve is generally upward sloping.

Chapter Summary

In this chapter, we introduced the concept of the yield curve and the closely related issue of the term structure. The former refers to the relationship between the yield to maturity and the term to maturity, whereas the latter describes the relationship between spot rates of interest and the term to maturity. We analyzed the coupon effect in detail, which explains why otherwise identical bonds with different coupons, may have different yields to maturity. The bootstrapping technique for estimating spot rates was studied in detail, and its practical difficulties were elaborated upon. We introduced the issue of forward rates of interest, and looked at different interpretations of the forward rate, such as the expectations hypothesis and the liquidity premium hypothesis. Finally, we attempted to explain real-life observations about yields, using different theories of the yield curve.

In the next chapter, we examine the issues of duration, convexity, and dispersion of bonds, and study the application to bond immunization strategies.

Chapter 5
Duration, Convexity, and Immunization

The duration of a plain vanilla bond can be defined as its average life. It is very easy to define duration in the case of securities that yield a single cash flow, like a zero coupon bond. In such cases there is no difference between the average time to maturity and the actual time to maturity, for we need concern ourselves only with the terminal payment. Consequently, in such cases, the duration of the security is nothing but its stated term to maturity.

However the definition is not so clearcut in the case of a conventional coupon paying debt security. In such cases, the asset gives rise to a series of cash flows, usually on a semiannual basis, as well as a relatively large cash flow at the end that constitutes the principal repayment. The average life of such a security can be obtained only by taking cognizance of the times to maturity of the component cash flows. Because the cash flows occur at different points in time, we also need to factor in the issue of the time value of money.

Convexity of a bond accounts for the fact that the price-yield relationship of a bond is convex and not linear. Whereas, duration accounts for a first order approximation to the price-yield relationship, convexity factors into the fact that the relationship is indeed convex. Immunization strategies protect a bond or a bond portfolio against interest rate risk. As discussed earlier, interest rate changes impact bonds in two ways. The higher the interest rate, the more the income from the re-investment of coupons. However the higher the rate, the lower the sale price of the bond at the end of the investment horizon. See Figure 5.1. An immunization strategy helps ensure that the terminal cash flow from a bond portfolio at the end of the investment horizon is adequate to meet the liability of the holder.

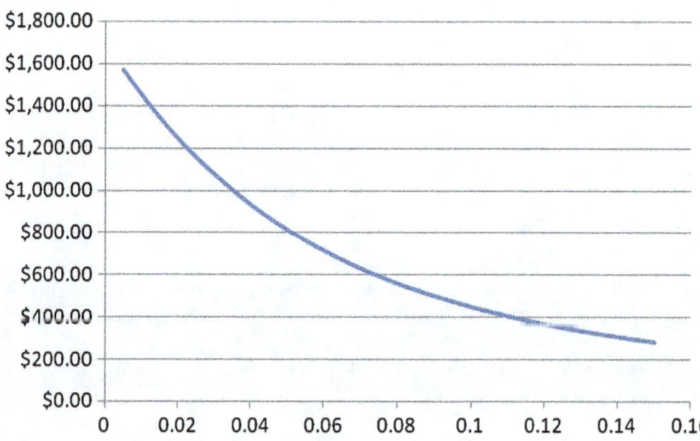

Figure 5.1: The price of the bond and its rate are inversely related.

https://doi.org/10.1515/9781547400669-005

Frederick Macaulay came up with the concept of what he called *duration*. Per his definition, duration is *the weighted average maturity of the bond's cash flows, where the present values of the cash flows serve as the weights*. This definition is comprehensive, for it accounts for all the cash flows emanating from the instrument and factors in the critical concept of the time value of money.

A Mathematical Definition of Duration

Macaulay's duration may be stated using the following formula:

$$\sum_{t=1}^{N} \frac{CF_t \times t}{P \times (1 + \frac{y}{2})^t}$$

Let's define the symbols used in the preceding expression:

- $CF_t \equiv$ the cash flow arising at time t. If the bond pays a coupon of $\frac{C}{2}$ at semiannual intervals, all the cash flows from the first to the penultimate are equal to $\frac{C}{2}$, and the terminal cash flow is equal to $\frac{C}{2}+M$, where M is the maturity value of the bond.
- $y \equiv$ the yield to maturity of the bond expressed in annual terms. At times, it means the semiannual YTM.
- $P \equiv$ the dirty price of the bond.

Since t represents the corresponding semiannual period, the final value arrived at is in half-years and consequently has to be divided by two in order to annualize it.

Example 5.1. Consider a T-note with exactly five years to maturity. The face value is \$1,000, and the coupon is 6% per annum paid on a semiannual basis. The yield to maturity is 6.50%. The dirty price is given by

$$P = 30 \times \text{PVIFA}(3.25, 10) + 1{,}000 \times \text{PVIF}(3.25, 10) = \$978.9440$$

The duration calculation is depicted in Table 5.1.

Table 5.1: Computation of the duration on a coupon date.

Time	Cash Flow	$PVCF_t$	w_t	$w_t \times t$
1	30	29.0557	0.029681	0.029681
2	30	28.1411	0.028746	0.057493
3	30	27.2553	0.027842	0.083525
4	30	26.3974	0.026965	0.107861
5	30	25.5665	0.026116	0.130582
6	30	24.7617	0.025294	0.151766
7	30	23.9823	0.024498	0.171487
8	30	23.2274	0.023727	0.189816
9	30	22.4963	0.022980	0.206821
10	1,030	748.0603	0.764150	7.641503

PVCF stands for present value of the cash flow.
The symbol w_t stands for the weight.

The duration is 8.7705 semiannual periods or 4.3853 years.

A Useful Excel Function

When we want to multiply two vectors of data in Excel and add, a useful function is SUMPRODUCT. Consider the data in Table 5.1. To compute the duration we need to multiply the time vector with the weight vector. Assume that the time vector runs from cells A1 to A10, and the weight vector runs from cells D1 to D10. We invoke the function as sum total = SUMPRODUCT(A1:A10,D1:D10). The answer is 8.7705.

Duration of a Bond When the Settlement Date Is Between Two Coupon Dates

Assume that the first coupon is k periods away, where k is calculated using the prescribed day-count convention. The duration formula may be expressed as

$$\sum_{t=0}^{N-1} \frac{CF_{t+k} \times (t+k)}{P \times (1 + \frac{y}{2})^{t+k}}$$

Example 5.2. Consider the bond that we discussed in Example 5.1. Assume that there are 4.875 years to maturity, or that the first coupon is 0.75 periods away. The duration can be calculated as illustrated in Table 5.2.

Table 5.2: Computation of the duration between coupon dates.

Time	Cash Flow	$PVCF_t$	w_t	$w_t \times t$
0.75	30	29.28894	0.029681	0.022260
1.75	30	28.36702	0.028746	0.050306
2.75	30	27.47411	0.027842	0.076564
3.75	30	26.60930	0.026965	0.101119
4.75	30	25.77172	0.026116	0.124053
5.75	30	24.96051	0.025294	0.145442
6.75	30	24.17483	0.024498	0.165362
7.75	30	23.41387	0.023727	0.183884
8.75	30	22.67688	0.022980	0.201076
9.75	1,030	754.06560	0.764150	7.450465

PVCF stands for present value of the cash flow.
The symbol w_t stands for the weight.

The dirty price is $986.8028, and the duration is 8.5205 semiannual periods or 4.2603 years.

A Concise Formula for the Duration on a Coupon Date

Let's redefine the following variables:

$y \equiv \frac{y}{2} \equiv$ the semiannual YTM

$c \equiv \frac{c}{2} \equiv$ the semiannual coupon rate

The duration of a plain vanilla bond, on a coupon date, can be stated as[1]

$$\text{Duration} = \frac{(1+y)}{y} - \frac{(1+y) + N(c-y)}{c\left[(1+y)^N - 1\right] + y}$$

The Case of a Par Bond

For a par bond, $c = y$. So,

$$\begin{aligned}\text{Duration} &= \frac{(1+y)}{y} - \frac{(1+y)}{y(1+y)^N} \\ &= \frac{(1+y)}{y} \times \left[1 - \frac{1}{(1+y)^N}\right]\end{aligned}$$

Example 5.3. Consider the five-year T-note with a face value of $1,000. c is 3% and y is 3.25%. Thus,

$$\begin{aligned}D &= \frac{1.0325}{.0325} - \frac{(1.0325) + 10(.03 - .0325)}{.03\left[(1.0325)^{10} - 1\right] + .0325} \\ &= 31.7692 - 22.9987 = 8.7705 \text{ semiannual periods}\end{aligned}$$

Duration of a Level Annuity

The duration of an annuity that pays a cash flow of $A every period for N periods is given by[2]

$$\frac{(1+y)}{y} - \frac{N}{[(1+y)^N - 1]}$$

Example 5.4. Consider an annuity that pays $50 per half-year period for five years. The YTM is 6.50% per annum. The duration is given by

$$\begin{aligned}D &= \frac{(1.0325)}{.0325} - \frac{10}{[(1.0325)^{10} - 1]} \\ &= 31.7692 - 26.5326 = 5.2366 \text{ semiannual periods}\end{aligned}$$

---

1 See Appendix 5.1.

2 See Appendix 5.2 for a derivation.

Duration of a Perpetuity

The duration of a perpetuity is given by $\frac{(1+y)}{y}$. The derivation is given in Appendix 5.2.

Example 5.5. Consider a perpetuity that pays $50 per half-year forever. Assume that the semiannual yield is 3.25%. The duration is given by

$$\frac{1.0325}{0.0325} = 31.7692 \text{ semiannual periods}$$

The Rationale Behind Duration

It was observed many years ago that long-term bonds are more sensitive to changes in the YTM, compared to relatively shorter-term bonds. This was explained by arguing that because long-term cash flows are more impacted by a given change in yield, long-term bonds are more sensitive to such changes, as they have more cash flows coming later. The reason why a long-term cash flow is more impacted by a yield change is the following: The present value of a cash flow is $\frac{CF_t}{(1+\frac{y}{2})^t}$. In the denominator 1 plus the discount rate is raised to the power of time. The larger the value of time, the greater is the impact of a given yield change, $\triangle y$.

However, it was also observed that an N year zero coupon bond is more price sensitive than an N year coupon paying bond. This was initially perplexing because both have a time to maturity of N years. In the case of a zero coupon bond, there is a single cash flow, and the stated time to maturity is no different from the effective time to maturity. However, in the case of a coupon paying bond, when we say that the maturity is N years, we are essentially saying that the last cash flow has a maturity of N years. The first cash flow, however, has a maturity of only six months. Thus Macaulay argued that the effective term to maturity, or the weighted average of the terms to maturity of the component cash flows, is less than the term to maturity of a coupon paying bond. This weighted average time to maturity, which we now understand as duration, is the appropriate measure of price sensitivity. In the case of a zero coupon bond, there is no difference between the stated term to maturity and the effective term to maturity or duration. However, in the case of coupon paying plain vanilla bonds, the effective term to maturity is always shorter than the stated term to maturity.

Example 5.6. Consider 5-year and 10-year plain vanilla bonds, both with a face value of $1,000; a coupon of 8% per annum paid semiannually; and a YTM of 8% per annum. Obviously both the bonds trade at par. Now assume that the YTM of both the bonds changes to 10% per annum. The price of the 5-year bond declines to $922.7827, which corresponds to a percentage change of −7.7217%. On the other hand, the price of the 10-year bond, declines to $875.3779, which corresponds to a percentage change of −12.4622%. As can be seen, the 10-year bond is indeed more sensitive to a change in yield.

Now let's consider 5-year and 10-year zero coupon bonds, both with a face value of $1,000. When the YTM is 8% per annum, the respective prices are $675.5642 and $456.3869. When the

YTM increases to 10% per annum, the corresponding prices are \$613.9133 and \$376.8895. Thus the 5-year zero coupon bond declines in price by 9.1258%, and the 10-year zero coupon bond declines by 17.4189% in price.

Thus we see that the 10-year plain vanilla bond is more sensitive than the 5-year plain vanilla bond, and the 10-year zero coupon bond is more sensitive than the 5-year zero coupon bond. However, the 5-year zero is more sensitive than the 5-year plain vanilla bond, and the 10-year zero is more sensitive than the 10-year plain vanilla bond. The inference, therefore, is that although the price sensitivity of a bond is related to its time to maturity, the maturity of the bond is not the sole influencing variable.

Factors Influencing Duration

There are five primary influences on the duration of a plain vanilla bond. These are:
- Term to maturity
- Coupon
- Yield to maturity
- Accrued interest
- Coupon frequency

Term to Maturity

Holding the coupon rate constant, the duration of a bond generally increases with its time to maturity. For par and premium bonds, duration always increases with the term to maturity. In the case of bonds trading at a discount, the duration generally increases with the term to maturity. However, there could be bonds trading at a substantial discount from par, for which the duration can actually decrease with an increase in the time to maturity.

Proof of the Relationship Between Duration and Time to Maturity

When there are N coupons remaining until maturity, the price of a bond is given by:

$$P_0 = \frac{Mc}{y} \times \left[1 - \frac{1}{(1 + \frac{y}{2})^N}\right] + \frac{M}{(1 + \frac{y}{2})^N} \tag{5.1}$$

When there are $N + 1$ coupons remaining until maturity, the price is given by:

$$P_1 = \frac{Mc}{y} \times \left[1 - \frac{1}{(1 + \frac{y}{2})^{(N+1)}}\right] + \frac{M}{(1 + \frac{y}{2})^{(N+1)}} \tag{5.2}$$

$$\Rightarrow P_1 - P_0 = \triangle P = \frac{M}{(1 + \frac{y}{2})^{N+1}} \times \left[\frac{c}{2} - \frac{y}{2}\right] \tag{5.3}$$

The formula for the duration of a bond when there are N semiannual periods to maturity is

$$D_0 = \frac{[Mc/2] \times 1}{P_0(1+\frac{y}{2})} + \frac{[Mc/2] \times 2}{P_0(1+\frac{y}{2})^2} + - - - - - - - \frac{[Mc/2] \times N}{P_0(1+\frac{y}{2})^N} + \frac{M \times N}{P_0(1+\frac{y}{2})^N} \tag{5.4}$$

If we increase the number of coupon periods by one, the duration is given by:

$$D_1 = D_0 \times \frac{P_0}{P_1} + \frac{MN\,[\frac{c}{2} - \frac{y}{2}] + M\,(1+\frac{c}{2})}{P_1(1+\frac{y}{2})^{N+1}} \tag{5.5}$$

Substituting for P_0 from Equation (5.1), we get

$$D_1 = D_0 + \frac{(N - D_0)M}{P_1(1+\frac{y}{2})^{(N+1)}} \times \left[\frac{c}{2} - \frac{y}{2}\right] + \frac{M\,(1+\frac{c}{2})}{P_1(1+\frac{y}{2})^{(N+1)}} \tag{5.6}$$

Consider Equation (5.6). The first and the third terms are positive. For a plain vanilla bond, the duration is positive and less than the term to maturity. That is, $D_0 > 0$ and $D_0 < N$. For a par bond the middle term is zero. Thus the duration increases with the term to maturity. For premium bonds the middle term is positive. Hence the duration once again increases as the time to maturity increases. For discount bonds the middle term is negative. If the coupon rate is much lower than the yield to maturity, or in other words the bond is trading at a substantial discount, this component may result in a declining duration as the term to maturity increases.

The implication of this result is the following. A plain vanilla bond with an infinite time to maturity is a perpetuity. A perpetuity has a duration of $\frac{(1+y)}{y}$, where y is the periodic YTM. Thus for par and premium bonds, the duration steadily increases and approaches this limit. In the case of discount bonds, if the duration declines with an increase in the time to maturity, it has to subsequently reverse the direction of change in order to reach the limiting value.

We have seen, that duration is generally related positively to a bond's remaining time to maturity. However, duration increases at a decreasing rate. For zero coupon bonds, duration increases at a constant rate with respect to the time to maturity. This is because for a zero coupon bond

$$D = N \Rightarrow \frac{\partial D}{\partial N} = 1$$

Duration and term to maturity are generally related positively for two key reasons. One is that the principal repayment is a large contributor to the bond price and is a major influence on the duration. If this cash flow is postponed, then it pulls the duration along with it. Second, the additional long-term coupons assist this process. Because, long maturity bonds receive a considerable number of cash flows after a corresponding shorter duration bond has matured.[3]

3 See Douglas [22].

Example 5.7. Consider three bonds with 5, 10, and 30 years, respectively, to maturity. Assume that the coupon = yield = 10% per annum. Consider the 10-year bond first. It generates a total cash flow of 20 × 50 + 1,000 = $2,000. Of this amount, $1,500 is received after 5 years. This is 75% of the total cash flow. The 30-year bond generates a total cash flow of 60 × 50 + 1,000 = $4,000. Of this amount, $3,500 is received after 5 years. This is 87.50% of $4,000. $3,000 is received after 10 years, which is 75% of the total cash flow.

Due to these factors, long maturity bonds tend to have a higher duration. However, duration increases at a decreasing rate. This is because long-term cash flows of a fixed nominal amount are assigned progressively lower present values.

Coupon

If we keep the maturity and the yield constant, the higher the coupon rate is, the lower the duration. Consider a bond with a face value of $1,000, 10 years to maturity, and a YTM of 7%.

Table 5.3: Impact of higher coupons on the duration.

Coupon Rate	Duration
1%	9.341265
2%	8.827750
3%	8.416202
5%	7.797649
8%	7.177614
10%	6.885319
15%	6.386328
20%	6.071655

As you can be see, duration declines as the coupon increases, keeping the maturity and yield constant. There are two reasons for this. First, higher coupon bonds have a greater percentage of total cash flows occurring before the maturity date. This reduces the relative influence of the principal repayment. Take the 10-year 10% coupon bond. It generates a total cash flow of $2,000, of which 50% arises in the form of coupon payments. On the other hand, a 10-year bond with a coupon of 15% per annum generates a total cash flow of $2,500 of which 60% is received in the form of coupon payments. The second factor is that the discounting process has less effect on the earlier cash flows, which consist exclusively of coupons, than on the later cash flows, which are a combination of coupons plus principal. Thus larger earlier cash flows in the form of coupons are assigned greater weights in present value terms.

Yield to Maturity

The duration of a bond is inversely related to its yield to maturity. High-yield environments lead to low duration, whereas low-yield environments create high durations. Let's consider a bond with a face value of $1,000 and 30 years to maturity. The coupon is 7% per annum paid semiannually. As you can see from Table 5.4, duration decreases as the yield to maturity increases.

Table 5.4: Impact of higher yields on the duration.

Yield to Maturity	Duration
1%	19.00552
2%	17.97389
3%	16.92821
5%	14.85735
8%	12.00854
10%	10.38785
15%	7.409989
20%	5.630574

There are two reasons why duration and YTM are inversely related. First, duration is based on the present value weights of the cash flows. As the discount rate increases the impact is higher on later cash flows. Thus we are assigning relatively lower weights to long-term cash flows and higher weights to short-term cash flows. The consequence is a decline in the duration. The second factor is that as the discount rate increases the present value of the terminal principal amount declines disproportionately, which drives down its relative contribution to the price of the bond.

Also newly issued bonds have a coupon that is close to the prevailing YTM. That is, high yield environments lead to the issue of high coupon bonds, while low yield environments result in the issue of low coupon bonds. Thus in a high yield environment the coupon component of a newly issued bond's market value is even higher, which makes it very sensitive to changes in the yield.

Accrued Interest

A bond's duration is inversely related to the amount of accrued interest present in the dirty price.[4] The duration computation is based on dirty prices and not clean prices. Thus accrued interest has an impact on duration. Accrued interest is an investment with a duration of zero. The forthcoming coupon payment reimburses the bond holder

4 See Douglas [22].

for the accrued interest he pays up front. Thus a bond with a higher accrued interest has a shorter duration than a similar bond with a lower accrued interest. That is, the accrued interest component of a bond's dirty price pulls down the duration. On a coupon date, the accrued interest reverts to zero. Consequently there is a jump in the duration because the dirty price no longer includes the accrued interest which is a zero duration component.

Example 5.8. Consider a T-bond with a face value of \$1,000, a coupon and yield of 7% per annum, and 20 years to maturity. Let's assume that the bond has been issued on 15 July 2018 and that we are on 14 January 2019. The duration is 10.5540 years. The next day, 15 January 2019, after the coupon has been paid, the duration jumps to 10.9205.

Coupon Frequency

As we have seen, duration is inversely related to accrued interest. The impact of accrued interest is more pronounced in the case of bonds which pay coupons less frequently. For instance, a bond that pays coupons annually has a greater buildup of accrued interest than a bond that pays semiannual coupons. This is because in the case of the former, a full year's coupon has to be accrued, whereas in the case of the latter a maximum of half the annual coupon is accrued.

Example 5.9. Let's reconsider the T-bond with a coupon and yield of 7%, and 30 years to maturity. Assume that the bond has been issued on 15 July 2018 and that we are on 14 July 2019. If we also assume semiannual coupons, the duration is 12.3460 years, whereas if we assume annual coupons, the duration is 12.2805 years. On the next day, 15 July 2019, the semiannual coupon-paying bond has a duration of 12.7752 years, and the bond with annual coupons has a duration of 13.1371 years.

As we can see, the jump in duration on the coupon date is significantly higher for the bond paying annual coupons. Also it has a higher duration on the coupon date than the bond with semiannual coupons. This is because in the case of the annual coupon-paying bond, the entire year's coupon is received at the end of the year, whereas in the case of the bond paying half yearly coupons, half the coupon is received six months prior.

Percentage Price Change and Duration

Consider a coupon bond that pays coupons m times per year, and assume that it has T years to maturity. Let the annual YTM be y, the annual coupon be C, and the face value be M.[5]

5 We are using the symbol y to denote the periodic, usually semiannual, YTM in certain cases, and the annual YTM in other instances. To avoid confusion, we are explicitly restating the meaning, every time we redefine the variable.

$$P = \sum_{t=1}^{mT} \frac{\frac{C}{m}}{(1 + \frac{y}{m})^t} + \frac{M}{(1 + \frac{y}{m})^{mT}} \tag{5.7}$$

Therefore,[6]

$$\frac{dP}{dy} \times \frac{1}{P} = -\frac{1}{m} \times \frac{1}{(1 + \frac{y}{m})} \times D \tag{5.8}$$

Thus, for a bond that pays semiannual coupons

$$\frac{dP}{dy} \times \frac{1}{P} = -\frac{1}{2} \times \frac{1}{(1 + \frac{y}{2})} \times D \tag{5.9}$$

And

$$\frac{dP}{P} = -\frac{1}{2} \times \left[\frac{1}{(1 + \frac{y}{2})} \times D \right] \times dY \tag{5.10}$$

Because duration is expressed in semiannual terms, $\frac{1}{2} \times D$ is the duration in annual terms. The annual duration divided by one plus the periodic yield is referred to as the modified duration. Thus

$$D_m = \frac{1}{2} \times \left[\frac{1}{(1 + \frac{y}{2})} \times D \right]$$

$$\Rightarrow \frac{dP}{P} = -D_m \times dY \tag{5.11}$$

The percentage change in the price of a bond is directly proportional to its modified duration. $\frac{dP}{P}$ is the limiting value of the percentage change in price. For a finite yield change, the percentage change in price is $\frac{\Delta P}{P}$. As $\Delta y \to 0, \frac{\Delta P}{P} \to \frac{dP}{P}$.

Duration of Annuities Due and Perpetuities Due

For an annuity due,

$$\text{Duration} = \frac{1}{r} - \frac{N}{[(1 + r)^N - 1]} \tag{5.12}$$

For a perpetuity due,

$$\text{Duration} = \frac{1}{r} \tag{5.13}$$

One may think that a perpetuity due has the same duration as an identical perpetuity because the first cash flow occurs at time 0. However, because of the additional cash flow at the outset, a perpetuity due has a higher price, and consequently a lower duration.

6 See Appendix 5.3.

Dollar Duration

The product of the modified duration and the price of the bond is referred to as the *dollar duration* of the bond. In Example 5.1, the duration was 4.3853 years, the semiannual yield was 3.25%, and the price was $978.9440. Thus the dollar duration is

$$\frac{4.3853}{1.0325} \times 978.9440 = 4{,}157.8335$$

Computing Duration and Modified Duration with Excel

Assume we are on 15 May 2018. There is a five-year bond with a face value of $1,000, which pays a coupon of 6% per annum semiannually, and the YTM is 6.50% per annum. To calculate the duration, we use the DURATION function in Excel. The required parameters are

- Settlement: We need to give it using the DATE function with the YYYY,MM,DD format. In this example it is DATE(2018,05,15).
- Maturity: We need to give it using the DATE function. We know that it is a five-year bond, so we give the same date five years later. Thus in our case it is DATE(2023,05,15).
- Coupon: We need to give the annual coupon. In this case it is 0.06.
- Yield: We need to give the annual YTM. In this case it is 0.065.
- Frequency: Because the bond pays coupons on a semiannual basis, the frequency is 2.
- Basis: This captures the day-count convention. This bond has an integer number of years to maturity. Thus the basis can be specified as any value. We give it as 0.

The duration = DURATION(Date(2018,05,15),Date(2023,05,15),0.06,.065,2,0) = 4.3853

Note that since we are giving the frequency of coupons as a variable, both the coupon rate and the YTM should be stated in annual terms. As a consequence, the duration is directly derived in terms of the number of years.

Modified Duration

The required function is MDURATION. The parameters are identical. The answer is 4.2472. We can verify it manually:

$$\frac{4.3853}{1.0325} = 4.2472$$

Approximating Duration

The modified duration of a bond can be approximated using the prices obtained by changing the annual YTM by Δy in both directions. Before we proceed, let's define the required symbols:

- $P_0 \equiv$ the current dirty price
- $P_- \equiv$ the dirty price when the YTM declines by Δy
- $P_+ \equiv$ the dirty price when the YTM increases by Δy

The percentage price change when the YTM declines by Δy is $\frac{P_- - P_0}{P_0}$.

Thus $\frac{P_- - P_0}{(P_0 \times \Delta y)}$ gives us an approximation for the rate of percentage change in price with respect to yield.

We obtain a similar expression when we increase the YTM by Δy. That is $\frac{P_0 - P_+}{(P_0 \times \Delta y)}$.

The two expressions are not identical because the impact of a yield decline of x basis points is not the same as that of a yield increase of the same magnitude. So the best option is to take a simple arithmetic average:

$$\frac{1}{2} \times \left[\frac{P_- - P_0}{(P_0 \times \Delta y)} + \frac{P_0 - P_+}{(P_0 \times \Delta y)} \right] = \frac{P_- - P_+}{(2P_0 \, \Delta y)}$$

$\frac{\Delta P}{P \Delta y}$ is an estimate of the modified duration.

Example 5.10. Consider a bond with a face value of $1,000 and five years to maturity. The coupon is 8% per annum and the yield is 10% per annum. The coupon is paid on a semiannual basis.

If we use the MDURATION function in Excel, we get a value of 3.9808. Let's compare it with the approximate value. Assume the change in the annual YTM is 25 basis points and P_0 = \$922.7827, P_- = \$932.0228, P_+ = \$913.6554:

$$\frac{932.0228 - 913.6554}{(2 \times 922.7827 \times 0.0025)}$$
$$= 3.9809$$

The approximation is excellent.

The Concept of Effective Duration

In the case of a plain vanilla bond, the occurrence of a yield change has no impact on the cash flows from the bond. But there exist other fixed income securities, such as bonds with built-in call or put options, and mortgage-backed securities, where a change in yield may have consequences for the cash flows from the security. The approximate duration formula that we have derived can be used in these situations and is termed as the *effective duration*.

Duration as a Center of Gravity

The duration of a plain vanilla bond may be interpreted as its center of gravity, as the following argument demonstrates:[7]

$$\text{Duration} = \frac{1}{P}\left[\sum_{t=1}^{N} \frac{M\frac{c}{2} \times t}{\left(1+\frac{y}{2}\right)^t} + \frac{MN}{\left(1+\frac{y}{2}\right)^N}\right]$$

$$\Rightarrow DP = \left[\sum_{t=1}^{N} \frac{M\frac{c}{2} \times t}{\left(1+\frac{y}{2}\right)^t} + \frac{MN}{\left(1+\frac{y}{2}\right)^N}\right] \tag{5.14}$$

$$P = \left[\sum_{t=1}^{N} \frac{M\frac{c}{2}}{\left(1+\frac{y}{2}\right)^t} + \frac{M}{\left(1+\frac{y}{2}\right)^N}\right]$$

$$\Rightarrow DP = \left[\sum_{t=1}^{N} \frac{M\frac{c}{2} \times D}{\left(1+\frac{y}{2}\right)^t} + \frac{M \times D}{\left(1+\frac{y}{2}\right)^N}\right] \tag{5.15}$$

If we subtract Equation (5.15) from Equation (5.14), we get

$$0 = \left[\sum_{t=1}^{N} \frac{M\frac{c}{2} \times (t-D)}{\left(1+\frac{y}{2}\right)^t} + \frac{M(N-D)}{\left(1+\frac{y}{2}\right)^N}\right]$$

Portfolio Duration

Consider a portfolio of N bonds. To compute the portfolio IRR, we need to project all the cash flows until the maturity of the bond with the longest time until maturity. The initial investment is equal to the sum of the prices of the components of the portfolio. Using the vector of cash flows, we can compute the IRR and consequently the duration.

The portfolio duration can be approximated in the following way. First we can find the weights of the bonds, where the weight of bond i is $P_i \div \sum_{i=1}^{N} P_i$. We can compute the durations of the component bonds using the respective YTMs, and compute a weighted average duration. However, if we want to get the precise portfolio duration in the form of a weighted average, we need to do the following. We need to recompute the prices of all the components using the portfolio IRR. Let's term these the portfolio prices. The weight attached to a bond is $P^*{}_i \div \sum_{i=1}^{N} P^*{}_i$, where P^* is the portfolio price. Using these weights we can compute a weighted average of the duration of the components of the portfolio, where the discount rate is the portfolio IRR. In this case, we get the same duration, as calculated using the portfolio cash flows and the corresponding IRR. Note that although the portfolio price of a bond is different from its actual price,

7 See Taggart [64].

the sum of the portfolio prices for all the components of the portfolio is equal to the sum of the actual prices, which is obviously the initial investment. The portfolio IRR is a non-linear average of the individual YTMs. When we use the portfolio IRR to reprice a component of the portfolio, its price increases if its YTM is higher than the portfolio IRR. However the recomputed price is lower if the YTM of the bond is lower than the portfolio IRR.

Here is an example.

Example 5.11. Consider three bonds, Alpha, Beta, and Gamma. Alpha has a term to maturity of three years; Beta has a maturity of four years; and Gamma has five years till maturity. All three bonds have a face value of $1,000 and pay coupons on a semiannual basis. Alpha carries a coupon of 6% per annum and a YTM of 10% per annum; Beta carries a coupon of 8% per annum and a YTM of 12% per annum; and Gamma carries a coupon of 10% per annum and a YTM of 8% per annum. Their respective prices are $898.4862, $875.8041, and $1,081.1090. The durations of the bonds, using their respective YTMs, as computed using the DURATION function in Excel, are 2.7761 years, 3.4605 years, and 4.0954 years. The weighted average using the bond prices is 3.4855 years or 6.9711 semiannual periods.

Now let's compute the portfolio duration directly. The portfolio IRR is 9.77% per annum. Using this IRR and the vector of cash flows for the portfolio, the duration is 6.9260 half-years. The data is depicted in Table 5.5. The approximation using the weighted average of the individual durations is therefore reasonably close.

Table 5.5: Computing portfolio duration.

Time	Portfolio Cash Flow	PVCF	Weight
0	(2,855.3992)	(2,855.3992)	
1	120	114.4108	0.0401
2	120	109.082	0.0382
3	120	104.0013	0.0364
4	120	99.1573	0.0347
5	120	94.5389	0.0331
6	1120	841.2657	0.2946
7	90	64.4531	0.0226
8	1090	744.2406	0.2606
9	50	32.5494	0.0114
10	1050	651.7003	0.2282

PVCF stands for present value of the cash flow

Now let's recompute the prices of the three bonds, using the portfolio IRR as the yield for each. Bond Alpha has a price of $903.9615; Bond Beta has a price of $942.5222; and Bond Gamma has a price of $1,008.9155. Let's call these the portfolio prices. As expected, the two bonds with a YTM greater than the portfolio IRR have increased in price. However, the third bond, whose YTM was lower than the portfolio IRR, has declined in price. It can be verified that the sum of the original prices is equal to the sum of the portfolio prices, which in this case is equal to \$2,855.3992. The durations of the three bonds, as computed using the portfolio IRR as the discount rate, are 2.7769, 3.4833, and 4.0587. We know that as the YTM increases, the duration declines. In the case of Bonds Alpha and Beta, the YTMs are higher than the portfolio IRR. Consequently the durations computed using the respective YTMs are lower than the values obtained using the portfolio IRR as the discount rate. However, in the case of the third bond, the original YTM is lower than the portfolio IRR. Consequently, the duration computed using the original YTM is greater than the duration obtained by using the portfolio IRR as the discount rate.

$$\frac{903.9615}{2{,}855.3992} \times 2.7769 + \frac{942.5222}{2{,}855.3992} \times 3.4833 + \frac{1{,}008.9155}{2{,}855.3992} \times 4.0587$$
$$= 3.4630 \text{ years or } 6.9260 \text{ half-years}$$

Thus, the weighted average of the durations computed, using the portfolio IRR as the discount rate and the portfolio prices as the weights, is exactly the value obtained by discounting the portfolio cash flows using the portfolio IRR.

Bond Convexity

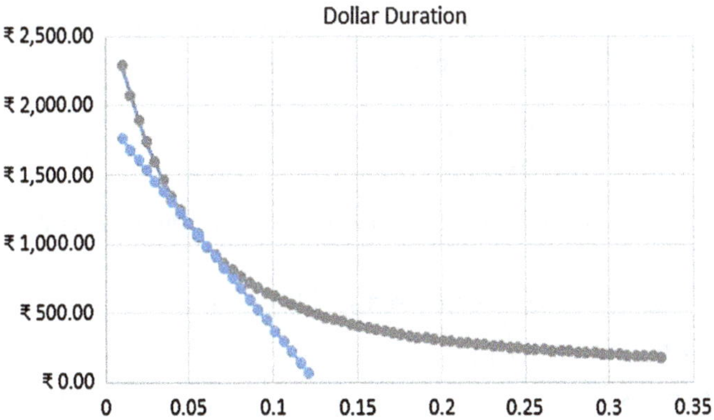

Figure 5.2: The slope of the price-yield curve is the dollar duration.

Dollar duration is the first derivative of the price-yield function. Convexity is the derivative of the dollar duration with respect to the yield, divided by the dirty price of the bond. Dollar duration is the slope of the price yield curve at a specified point (see Figure 5.2). Convexity, in approximate terms, measures the gap between the tangent line and the price-yield curve. Convexity can be viewed as an approximate measure of the difference between the actual bond price and the price predicted by the tangent line. Convexity enhances a bond's performance in both bull and bear markets, but not in a uniform fashion. For plain vanilla bonds, the convexity is always positive.

That is, the price-yield curve always lies above the dollar duration tangent line. The convexity effect becomes greater with larger changes in yield. That is, the gap between the tangent line and the price yield curve increases with an increase in the magnitude of the yield. Dollar duration is a good estimate for small yield changes, but loses its predictive power when yield changes are large. A bond's duration increases in a bull market as yields fall. This enhances the price gain. The duration reduces in a bear market, as yields rise, which mitigates the price decline.

For a plain vanilla bond, we know that the price is given by:

$$P = \frac{Mc}{y}\left[1 - \frac{1}{(1+y)^N}\right] + \frac{M}{(1+y)^N} \tag{5.16}$$

$$\frac{dP}{dY} = -\frac{Mc}{y^2} + \frac{Mc}{y^2(1+y)^N} + \frac{McN}{y(1+y)^{N+1}} - \frac{NM}{(1+y)^{N+1}}$$

$$\begin{aligned}\frac{d^2P}{dy^2} &= \frac{2Mc}{y^3} - \frac{2Mc}{y^3(1+y)^N} - \frac{NMc}{y^2(1+y)^{N+1}} \\ &\quad - \frac{McN}{y^2(1+y)^{N+1}} - \frac{McN(N+1)}{y(1+y)^{N+2}} + \frac{MN(N+1)}{(1+y)^{N+2}} \\ &= \frac{2Mc}{y^3}\left[1 - \frac{1}{(1+y)^N}\right] - \frac{2NMc}{y^2(1+y)^{N+1}} + \frac{N(N+1)}{(1+y)^{N+2}}\left[M - \frac{Mc}{y}\right]\end{aligned} \tag{5.17}$$

where y represents the semiannual YTM and c is the semiannual coupon. N is the number of coupons remaining. The convexity of a bond is defined as

$$\frac{d^2P}{dy^2} \times \frac{1}{P}$$

The convexity in terms of the number of years for a bond that pays m coupons per year is given by $\frac{\text{Periodic Convexity}}{m^2}$.

duration of a bond in periodic terms is expressed as $\sum_{t=1}^{N} \frac{CF_t \times t}{P\times(1+y)^t}$.

modified duration is expressed as $\sum_{t=1}^{N} \frac{CF_t \times t}{P\times(1+y)^{t+1}}$.

dollar duration is stated as $\sum_{t=1}^{N} \frac{CF_t \times t}{(1+y)^{t+1}}$.

If we differentiate the dollar duration with respect to the yield, and divide by the dirty price, we get the convexity. Thus convexity is given by

$$\sum_{t=1}^{N} \frac{CF_t \times t \times (t+1)}{P \times (1+y)^{t+2}}$$

Example 5.12. Let's consider the five-year T-note with a price of 978.9440. The coupon is 6% per annum, and the YTM is 6.50% per annum.

We need to compute:

$$\sum_{t=1}^{N} \frac{CF_t \times t \times (t+1)}{P \times (1+y)^{t+2}}$$

Table 5.6: Computation of convexity.

Time	Cash Flow	w_t	$t(t+1)$	$t(t+1) \times w_t$
1	30	0.029681	2	0.059361
2	30	0.028746	6	0.172478
3	30	0.027842	12	0.334098
4	30	0.026965	20	0.539303
5	30	0.026116	30	0.783492
6	30	0.025294	42	1.062362
7	30	0.024498	56	1.371895
8	30	0.023727	72	1.708344
9	30	0.02298	90	2.068213
10	1,030	0.76415	110	84.05653
			Sum	92.15608

The symbol w_t stands for the weight.

The convexity in semiannual terms is $\frac{92.15608}{(1.0325)^2} = 86.4458$. The convexity in annual terms is therefore 21.6115.

Approximating the Price Change of a Bond for a Given Change in Yield

The change in the price of a bond may be expressed as[8]

$$dP = \frac{\partial P}{\partial y} \times dY + \frac{1}{2}\frac{\partial^2 P}{\partial y^2} \times (dY)^2 + h.o.t \tag{5.18}$$

Thus,

$$\frac{dP}{P} = \frac{\partial P}{\partial y} \times \frac{dY}{P} + \frac{1}{2}\frac{\partial^2 P}{\partial y^2} \times \frac{(dY)^2}{P} + \frac{h.o.t}{P} \tag{5.19}$$

The first term of Equation 5.19 captures the approximate percentage price change due to duration. The second term of Equation 5.19 captures the contribution of convexity to the price change. This may be measured as

$$\frac{1}{2} \times \text{Convexity} \times (dY)^2$$

Example 5.13. Consider a 50 basis points increase in the annual YTM of the five-year T-note,with a coupon of 6% per annum and a YTM of 6.50% per annum. The face value is $1,000, and coupons are

8 h. o. t. stands for *higher order terms*.

paid semiannually. The current price, as we have seen, is \$978.9440. The new price will be \$958.4170. The exact price change is

$$958.4170 - 978.9440 = -20.5270$$

The price change due to duration is

$$-4.2473 \times 978.9440 \times 0.005 = -20.7892$$

The price change due to convexity is

$$0.5 \times 21.6115 \times 978.9440 \times (0.005)^2 = 0.2645$$

Thus the approximate price change due to both duration and convexity is:

$$-20.7892 + 0.2645 = -20.5247$$

As you can see, the combination of duration and convexity does a much better job of predicting the price change, compared to duration alone. One may wonder why we do not use third and higher order terms. The rationale is that if we have a third-order term, it would be multiplied by $(\Delta Y)^3$. Thus if the change in yield is 50 basis points, we multiply by 1.25×10^{-7}. This obviously is trivial from the standpoint of attaining precision.

Dispersion of a Bond

The dispersion of a bond is defined as[9]

$$\text{Dispersion} = \frac{1}{P} \times \sum_{t=1}^{N} \frac{CF_t \times t^2}{(1+y)^t} - (\text{Duration})^2 \tag{5.20}$$

The dispersion of a zero coupon bond is equal to zero. This is because it gives rise to a single cash flow.

We know that convexity is defined as

$$\text{Convexity} = \frac{1}{P(1+y)^2}\left[\sum_{t=1}^{N} \frac{CF_t \times t(t+1)}{(1+y)^t}\right] \tag{5.21}$$

$$\Rightarrow \text{Convexity} = \frac{1}{P(1+y)^2} \times \left[\sum_{t=1}^{N} \frac{CF_t \times (t^2+t)}{(1+y)^t}\right]$$

$$= \frac{1}{P(1+y)^2}\left[\sum_{t=1}^{N} \frac{CF_t \times t}{(1+y)^t} + \frac{CF_t \times t^2}{(1+y)^t}\right]$$

---

9 We are using the symbol y to denote the semiannual YTM.

$$\Rightarrow \text{Convexity} = \frac{1}{(1+y)^2}[\text{Dispersion} + (\text{Duration})^2 + \text{Duration}] \tag{5.22}$$

Thus, for a given level of duration, the lower the dispersion is, the lower the convexity. Hence for a given level of duration, zero coupon bonds have the lowest convexity. For a given level of dispersion, the higher the duration, the greater the convexity.

Example 5.14. Consider a bond with a coupon of 6% per annum, paid semiannually, and a YTM of 6.50% per annum. Assume that there are five years to maturity. The dispersion may be calculated as illustrated in Table 5.7.

Table 5.7: Computation of dispersion.

Time	Cash Flow	$PVCF_t$	t^2	w_t	$w_t \times t^2$
1	30	29.28894	1	0.029681	0.029681
2	30	28.36702	4	0.028746	0.114986
3	30	27.47411	9	0.027842	0.250574
4	30	26.60930	16	0.026965	0.431443
5	30	25.77172	25	0.026116	0.65291
6	30	24.96051	36	0.025294	0.910596
7	30	24.17483	49	0.024498	1.200408
8	30	23.41387	64	0.023727	1.518528
9	30	22.67688	81	0.022980	1.861392
10	1,030	754.06560	100	0.764150	76.41503

PVCF stands for present value of the cash flow.
The symbol w_t stands for the weight.

The sum of the last column is 83.38554. If we subtract the square of the duration, in semiannual terms, we get a value of 6.4633.

Dispersion + Duration^2 + Duration = 6.4633 + 76.9217 + 8.7705 = 92.1561.

$$\frac{92.1561}{(1.0325)^2} = 86.4458$$

which is the convexity in periodic terms.

Convexity of a Zero Coupon Bond

A zero coupon bond has a duration of N, in periodic terms, and a dispersion of zero. Thus the convexity of a zero coupon bond in semiannual terms is:

$$\frac{N(N+1)}{(1+\frac{y}{2})^2} \quad \text{where } y \text{ is the annual YTM}$$

Example 5.15. Consider a zero coupon bond with five years to maturity. The YTM is 8% per annum. The convexity in periodic terms is

$$\frac{10 \times 11}{(1.04)^2} = 101.7012$$

The convexity in annual terms is

$$\frac{101.7012}{4} = 25.4253$$

Dispersion as an Expected Value

A bond's dispersion is the variance of the times to receipt of all of its cash flows, whereas its duration is the mean of the times to receipt of all the cash flows. For a variable X, the mean is $E(X)$, while the variance is $E[X^2] - [E(X)]^2$. Thus duration is a measure of the mean, whereas dispersion is a measure of the variance.

The dispersion of a plain vanilla bond measures how spread out in time the payments are relative to the duration. The more spread out the cash flows are relative to the mean time to payment (the duration), the greater the dispersion. For a given duration, the higher the dispersion is the greater the convexity. For plain vanilla bonds, the duration and the dispersion are non negative. Consequently the convexity is positive.

Portfolio Convexity and Dispersion

Let's consider the three-bond portfolio that we examined in Example 5.11. In periodic terms, the portfolio convexity is 55.4231 and the dispersion is 6.0747. We have used the portfolio IRR to compute these statistics. Using the portfolio IRR as the discount rate, Bond Alpha has a price of \$903.9616, a convexity of 34.4230, and a dispersion of 1.4694; Bond Beta has a price of \$942.5222, a convexity of 54.3085, and a dispersion of 4.2431; and Bond Gamma has a price of \$1008.9155, a convexity of 75.2801 and a dispersion of 8.8040.

The weighted average convexity is

$$\frac{903.9616}{2855.3992} \times 34.4230 + \frac{942.5222}{2855.3992} \times 54.3085 + \frac{1{,}008.9150}{2855.3992} \times 75.2801 = 55.4231$$

The weighted average dispersion is

$$\frac{903.9616}{2855.3992} \times 1.4694 + \frac{942.5222}{2855.3992} \times 4.2431 + \frac{1{,}008.9150}{2855.3992} \times 8.8040 = 4.9765$$

As we can see, the portfolio convexity is equal to a weighted average of the convexities of the component bonds. However, unlike duration and convexity, portfolio dispersion is not a weighted average of the dispersions of the component bonds. This is consistent with the statistical result that although the mean of a sum of variables is equal to the sum of the individual means, the variance is not a sum of the individual variances.

Properties of Convexity

From Equation (5.22) we can see that the primary factors that influence a bond's convexity are the duration and the dispersion of the cash flows. Thus, keeping duration constant, the greater the dispersion is, the higher the convexity.

The Impact of Duration

Convexity is positively related to the duration of the bond. Long duration bonds carry higher convexities than bonds with a shorter duration. The convexity of a bond is not only positively related to its duration, it is also an increasing function of the duration. That is, a bond with twice the duration of another has more than double the convexity.

$$\text{Convexity} = \frac{1}{(1+y)^2}[\text{Dispersion} + (\text{Duration})^2 + \text{Duration}]$$

$$\frac{\partial \text{Convexity}}{\partial \text{Duration}} = \frac{1}{(1+y)^2}[2 \times \text{Duration} + 1]$$

As the YTM of a bond increases, its duration decreases. Because duration and convexity are positively related, the convexity of the bond decreases. Thus plain vanilla bonds are said to exhibit positive convexity. Similarly, as the coupon increases, the duration decreases and so does the convexity. And, the higher the accrued interest, the lower the duration and consequently the lower the convexity. The duration of a bond generally increases with its time to maturity, with the exception of certain bonds trading at a deep discount. Hence the convexity of a bond also generally increases with its time to maturity.

The Irrelevance of the Face Value

The duration, convexity, and dispersion of a bond are independent of the face value. This is because the face value appears in every term of the numerator of these three measures, and it also appears in the denominator in the form of the bond price. For the same reason, the durations of annuities and perpetuities, are also independent of the size of the periodic cash flow.

Dollar Convexity

A bond's convexity multiplied by its dirty price is termed its *dollar convexity*. We know that the price change attributable to convexity is given by

$$\frac{1}{2} \times \text{Convexity} \times P \times (dY)^2$$

$$= \frac{1}{2} \times \text{Dollar Convexity} \times (dY)^2$$

Thus dollar convexity is a measure of the second derivative of the price-yield relationship.

Approximate Convexity

We know that convexity may be expressed as $\frac{1}{P} \times \frac{\partial^2 P}{\partial y^2}$

$$\frac{\Delta P_-}{\Delta y} = \frac{P_- - P_0}{\Delta y} \quad \text{and} \quad \frac{\Delta P_+}{\Delta y} = \frac{P_0 - P_+}{\Delta y}$$

Thus the rate of change of $\frac{\Delta P}{\Delta y}$ with respect to the yield is given by $\frac{P_- + P_+ - 2P_0}{\Delta y^2}$.

If we divide this by P_0, we get the expression for the approximate convexity:

$$\text{Convexity} = \frac{P_- + P_+ - 2P_0}{P_0 \,\Delta\, y^2} \tag{5.23}$$

Example 5.16. Consider a bond with five years to maturity and a face value of \$1,000, paying semiannual coupons. The annual coupon rate is 8% per annum and the YTM is 10% per annum. For a 25-basis point change in the annual YTM

$$P_0 = \$\,922.7827; P_- = \$\,932.0228; P_+ = \$913.6554$$

$$P_- + P_+ - 2P_0 = 0.1128; P_0 \,\Delta\, y^2 = 0.0057673$$

Thus the approximate convexity is 19.5585. The exact value is 19.5736.

Convexity of Annuities and Perpetuities

Let r be the periodic (usually semiannual) yield, and A the periodic cash flow. The convexity of an annuity is

$$\frac{2}{r^2} - \frac{2N}{r(1+r)\left[(1+r)^N - 1\right]} - \frac{N(N+1)}{(1+r)^2\left[(1+r)^N - 1\right]}$$

and that of an annuity due is[10]

$$\frac{2}{r^2(1+r)} - \frac{2N}{r(1+r)^2\left[(1+r)^N - 1\right]} - \frac{N(N+1)}{(1+r)^2\left[(1+r)^N - 1\right]}$$

In Example 5.17 we compute the convexity using the discounted cash flow approach as well as the concise formulas.

---

10 See Appendix 5.3 for both derivations.

Example 5.17. Consider an annuity and an annuity due, both of which pay a cash flow of \$50 for four periods. The periodic discount rate is 4%. From the concise formulas, the convexity of the annuity is

$$\frac{2}{0.04 \times 0.04} - \frac{2 \times 4}{0.04 \times 1.04[(1.04)^4 - 1]} - \frac{4 \times 5}{(1.04)^2[(1.04)^4 - 1]}$$
$$= 1{,}250.0000 - 1{,}132.1643 - 108.8620 = 8.9744$$

The convexity of the annuity due is

$$= \frac{2}{0.04 \times 0.04 \times 1.04} - \frac{8}{0.04 \times (1.04)^2[(1.04)^4 - 1]}$$
$$- \frac{4 \times 5}{(1.04)^2[(1.04)^4 - 1]}$$
$$= 1{,}201.9231 - 1{,}088.6189 - 108.8620 = 4.4423$$

The calculations, cash flow by cash flow, are demonstrated in Tables 5.8 and 5.9.

Table 5.8: Computation of convexity for an annuity.

Time	C. Flow	PVCF	Weight	$w_t \times t \times (t+1)$
1	50	48.0769	0.2649	0.5298
2	50	46.2278	0.2547	1.5282
3	50	44.4498	0.2449	2.9389
4	50	42.7402	0.2355	4.7098
	SUM	181.4948	SUM	9.7067

C. Flow stands for cash flow
PVCF stands for present value of the cash flow
w_t stands for the weight

Convexity = $\frac{9.7067}{(1.04)^2} = 8.9744$

Now let's consider the annuity due.

Table 5.9: Computation of convexity for an annuity due.

Time	C. Flow	PVCF	Weight	$w_t \times t \times (t+1)$
0	50	50.0000	0.2649	0.0000
1	50	48.0769	0.2547	0.5094
2	50	46.2278	0.2449	1.4695
3	50	44.4498	0.2355	2.8259
	SUM	188.7546	SUM	4.8048

C. Flow stands for cash flow
PVCF stands for present value of the cash flow
w_t stands for the weight

Convexity = $\frac{4.8048}{(1.04)^2} = 4.4423$

Perpetuities

The convexity of a perpetuity is

$$\frac{2}{r^2} = \frac{2}{0.04 \times 0.04} = 1{,}250$$

The convexity of a perpetuity due is

$$\frac{2}{(r^2)(1+r)} = \frac{2}{0.04 \times 0.04 \times 1.04} = 1{,}201.923$$

Thus a perpetuity due has a lower convexity than a perpetuity.

Immunization of a Bond Portfolio

A pension fund has promised to pay a return of 8.40% per annum compounded annually on an initial investment of $5 million, eight years from the date of investment. If it were to deposit the corpus in a fixed income security, it is exposed to two types of risk. The first is reinvestment risk, or the risk that cash flows received at intermediate stages may have to be invested at lower rates of interest. The second risk, which is termed price risk or market risk, is the risk that rates could increase, causing the price of the bond to decline at the end of the investment horizon.

The two risks obviously work in opposite directions. The issue is therefore, can we find a security that ensures that the terminal cash flow is adequate to satisfy the liability, irrespective of whether rates decline or increase. The process of protecting a bond portfolio against a change in the interest rate is termed *bond immunization*. Let's consider a simple immunization strategy where we have to immunize a portfolio that is held in order to satisfy a single liability. It turns out that there are four conditions that need to be satisfied in such cases. The first is that the present value of the liability should be equal to the amount invested in the fixed income security at the outset. Second, the duration of the security should be equal to the investment horizon.[11] Third, there should be a parallel shift in the yield curve. Finally, if there is a yield change, then it should be a one-time change, at the very outset.

Example 5.18. Consider a bond with a face value of $1,000 and 12 years to maturity. Assume that the coupon, paid on an annual basis, is equal to the market yield of 8.40% per annum. The bond obviously trades at par and can be shown to have a duration of 8 years. Consider the impact of a one-time change in the interest rate right at the outset. Also consider increments and decrements in multiples of 20 basis points from the prevailing rate of interest. Because the liability is $5 million, and the price of the

11 See Appendix 5.4 for a derivation.

bond is $1,000, we need to invest in 5,000 bonds. The terminal cash flow after 8 years, corresponding to each of the assumed interest rates, is summarized in Table 5.10.

Table 5.10: Illustration of single-period immunization.

Interest Rate	Future Value of Coupons	Selling Price	Total Cash Flow	CF for 5,000 Bonds	Amount Due	Deviation
0.094	939.92	967.89	1,907.81	9,539,032.94	9,532,444	6,588.95
0.092	933.13	974.20	1,907.33	9,536,629.29	9,532,444	4,185.30
0.090	926.39	980.56	1,906.95	9,534,767.40	9,532,444	2,323.41
0.088	919.71	986.98	1,906.69	9,533,448.42	9,532,444	1,004.43
0.086	913.07	993.46	1,906.53	9,532,673.53	9,532,444	229.54
0.084	906.49	1,000	1,906.49	9,532,444.00	9,532,444	0.00
0.082	899.96	1,006.59	1,906.55	9,532,761.07	9,532,444	317.09
0.080	893.48	1,013.25	1,906.73	9,533,626.14	9,532,444	1,182.16
0.078	887.05	1,019.96	1,907.01	9,535,040.58	9,532,444	2,596.60
0.076	880.67	1,026.73	1,907.40	9,537,005.85	9,532,444	4,561.86
0.074	874.34	1,033.57	1,907.90	9,539,523.44	9,532,444	7,079.45

As you can be see, the income from reinvested coupons steadily increases with the interest rate whereas the sale price steadily decreases with the interest rate. When the rate does not change, the terminal cash flow is exactly adequate to meet the liability. In all other cases, there is a surplus. In other words, the terminal cash flow from the bond is adequate to meet the liability, irrespective of the change in the interest rate. Thus if the pension fund invests in an asset whose duration is equal to the time to maturity of the liability, then the terminal inflow is always adequate to meet the contractual outflow.

To immunize the portfolio as we have just demonstrated, the following conditions need to be satisfied:

1. The amount invested in the bond must be equal to the present value of the liability.
2. The duration of the bond must be equal to the maturity of the liability.
3. There must be a one-time change in interest rates, right at the outset.
4. There must be a parallel shift in the yield curve.

A Point on Long-Dated Treasury Bonds

Treasury bonds are issued with a maturity of up to 30 years. These bonds have high durations and high convexities. Consequently, they are sought after by traders in search of convexity. Pension fund managers, who have long term liabilities, need bonds with high durations to construct immunized portfolios. Therefore, long-dated treasuries are popular with such market participants.

Chapter Summary

In this chapter, we introduced the concept of duration, and showed that the price change of a bond due to a change in its YTM is proportional to its duration. Thus duration, and not the time to maturity, is an appropriate measure of interest rate sensitivity. We showed how to compute the duration by discounting each cash flow, by using a concise formula, and by using the DURATION function in Excel. We derived the duration of annuities, annuities due, perpetuities, and perpetuities due. We studied the properties of duration and examined the impact of the variables that influence the price of a bond on its duration. We also demonstrated the computation of the approximate or effective duration of a bond. We then looked at the concepts of convexity and dispersion. We studied the properties of convexity, and examined the impact of the variables that influence the price of a bond on its convexity. Then, we derived closed-form expressions for the convexities of annuities, annnuities due, perpetuities, and perpetuities due. We also examined the duration, convexity, and dispersion of a portfolio of bonds. Finally, we examined the the immunization of a bond portfolio. In this context, we stated the required conditions to be satisfied for single-period immunization to be a success.

In the next chapter, we study the market for short-term debt securities, which are termed *money market securities.*

Appendix 5.1: Derivation of a Concise Formula for Duration

The price of a bond on a coupon date can be expressed as

$$P = \frac{\frac{C}{2}}{\frac{y}{2}}\left[1 - \frac{1}{(1+\frac{y}{2})^N}\right] + \frac{M}{(1+\frac{y}{2})^N}$$

Let's redefine the following variables:

$y \equiv \frac{y}{2} \equiv$ the semiannual YTM

$c \equiv \frac{c}{2} \equiv$ the semiannual coupon rate

The preceding expression for the price can then be written as

$$\begin{aligned} P &= \frac{Mc}{y}\left[1 - \frac{1}{(1+y)^N}\right] + \frac{M}{(1+y)^N} \\ &= \frac{Mc}{y} - \frac{Mc}{y(1+y)^N} + \frac{M}{(1+y)^N} \\ &= \frac{M[c\{(1+y)^N - 1\} + y]}{y(1+y)^N} \end{aligned}$$

We know that duration is defined as

$$\sum_{t=1}^{N} \frac{CF_t \times t}{P \times (1+\frac{y}{2})^t}$$

In terms of our redefined variables, it can be expressed as

$$\sum_{t=1}^{N} \frac{CF_t \times t}{P \times (1+y)^t}$$

We already have an expression for the price. Let's now derive an expression for

$$\sum_{t=1}^{N} \frac{CF_t \times t}{(1+y)^t} = \frac{Mc}{(1+y)} + \frac{2Mc}{(1+y)^2} + \frac{3Mc}{(1+y)^3} + \cdots + \frac{NMc}{(1+y)^N} + \frac{NM}{(1+y)^N}$$

$$= Mc\left[\frac{1}{(1+y)} + \frac{2}{(1+y)^2} + \cdots + \frac{N}{(1+y)^N}\right] + \frac{NM}{(1+y)^N}$$

Let's define:

$$S = \left[\frac{1}{(1+y)} + \frac{2}{(1+y)^2} + \cdots + \frac{N}{(1+y)^N}\right]$$

$$S(1+y) = \left[1 + \frac{2}{(1+y)} + \cdots + \frac{N}{(1+y)^{N-1}}\right]$$

$$S(1+y) - S = yS = \left[1 + \frac{1}{(1+y)} + \frac{1}{(1+y)^2} + \cdots + \frac{1}{(1+y)^{N-1}}\right] - \frac{N}{(1+y)^N}$$

$$\Rightarrow S = \frac{1}{y}\left[1 + \frac{1}{(1+y)} + \frac{1}{(1+y)^2} + \cdots + \frac{1}{(1+y)^{N-1}}\right] - \frac{N}{y(1+y)^N}$$

Let's define:

$$Z = \left[1 + \frac{1}{(1+y)} + \frac{1}{(1+y)^2} + \cdots + \frac{1}{(1+y)^{N-1}}\right]$$

$$Z(1+y) = \left[1 + y + 1 + \frac{1}{(1+y)} + \cdots + \frac{1}{(1+y)^{N-2}}\right]$$

$$\Rightarrow Z = \frac{(1+y)}{y} - \frac{1}{y(1+y)^{N-1}}$$

Thus,

$$S = \frac{1}{y}\left[\frac{(1+y)}{y} - \frac{1}{y(1+y)^{N-1}}\right] - \frac{N}{y(1+y)^N}$$

Therefore,

$$\sum_{t=1}^{N} \frac{CF_t \times t}{(1+y)^t} = Mc\left\{\frac{(1+y)}{y^2} - \frac{1}{y^2(1+y)^{N-1}} - \frac{N}{y(1+y)^N}\right\} + \frac{NM}{(1+y)^N}$$

Thus,

$$\sum_{t=1}^{N} \frac{CF_t \times t}{P \times (1+y)^t}$$

$$= \frac{\frac{c(1+y)\left[(1+y)^N-1\right]-Ny(c-y)}{y^2(1+y)^N}}{\frac{c\left[(1+y)^N-1\right]+y}{y(1+y)^N}}$$

$$= \frac{(1+y)}{y} - \frac{(1+y)+N(c-y)}{c\left[(1+y)^N-1\right]+y}$$

Appendix 5.2: Duration of Annuities and Perpetuities

The price of an annuity that pays $\$A$ every period is

$$\frac{A}{r}\left[1-\frac{1}{(1+r)^N}\right]$$

where r is the periodic interest rate.

The duration of an annuity is given by

$$\frac{1}{P}\left[\sum_{t=1}^{N} \frac{CF_t \times t}{(1+r)^t}\right]$$

$$= \frac{1}{P}\left[\frac{A}{(1+r)} + \frac{2A}{(1+r)^2} + \frac{3A}{(1+r)^3} + \cdots + \frac{NA}{(1+r)^N}\right]$$

$$= \frac{A}{P}\left[\frac{1}{(1+r)} + \frac{2}{(1+r)^2} + \cdots + \frac{N}{(1+r)^N}\right]$$

From the result derived in the previous appendix, this may be expressed as:

$$\frac{A}{P}\left\{\frac{(1+r)}{r^2} - \frac{1}{r^2(1+r)^{N-1}} - \frac{N}{r(1+r)^N}\right\}$$

If we substitute for P, the cash flow A drops out.

$$\text{Duration} = \frac{\left\{\frac{(1+r)}{r^2} - \frac{1}{r^2(1+r)^{N-1}} - \frac{N}{r(1+r)^N}\right\}}{\left[\frac{1}{r} - \frac{1}{r(1+r)^N}\right]}$$

$$= \left\{\frac{(1+r)}{r^2} - \frac{1}{r^2(1+r)^{N-1}} - \frac{N}{r(1+r)^N}\right\} \times \frac{r(1+r)^N}{[(1+r)^N-1]}$$

$$= \frac{[(1+r)^{N+1} - (1+r) - Nr]}{r[(1+r)^N-1]}$$

$$= \frac{(1+r)}{r} - \frac{N}{[(1+r)^N-1]}$$

Consider the expression:

$$D = \frac{(1+r)}{r} - \frac{N}{[(1+r)^N - 1]}$$

Define $f(N) = N$ and $g(N) = [(1+y)^N - 1]$. As $N \to \infty$, both $f(N)$ and $g(N) \to \infty$. From L'Hôpital's rule

$$\text{Limit}_{N\to\infty}\frac{f(N)}{g(N)} = \text{Limit}_{N\to\infty}\frac{\frac{df}{dN}}{\frac{dg}{dN}}$$

In this case

$$\frac{df}{dN} = 1$$

and

$$\frac{dG}{dN} = (1+y)^N \ln(1+y)$$

Thus,

$$\text{Limit}_{N\to\infty}\frac{\frac{df}{dN}}{\frac{dg}{dN}} = 0$$

Thus for a perpetuity, the duration is given by $\frac{(1+r)}{r}$.

An alternative derivation:

price of perpetuity is given by

$$P = \frac{A}{r}$$

$$\frac{dP}{dr} = -\frac{A}{r^2}$$

$$\frac{dP}{Pdr} = -\frac{1}{r}$$

$$-\frac{dP}{Pdr} \times (1+r) = \frac{(1+r)}{r}$$

The price of an annuity due that pays \$$A$ every period is:

$$P = \frac{A}{r}\left[1 - \frac{1}{(1+r)^N}\right](1+r)$$

$$= \frac{A}{r}\left[1 - \frac{1}{(1+r)^N}\right] + A \times \left[1 - \frac{1}{(1+r)^N}\right]$$

$$\frac{dP}{dr} = -\frac{A}{r^2}\left[1 - \frac{1}{(1+r)^N}\right] + \frac{AN}{r(1+r)^{N+1}} + \frac{AN}{(1+r)^{N+1}}$$

$$= -\frac{A}{r^2}\left[1 - \frac{1}{(1+r)^N}\right] + \frac{AN}{r(1+r)^{N+1}} \times (1+r)$$

$$\frac{dP}{Pdr} = \frac{-1}{r(1+r)} + \frac{N}{(1+r)[(1+r)^N - 1]}$$

$$-\frac{dP}{Pdr} \times (1+r) = \frac{1}{r} - \frac{N}{[(1+r)^N - 1]}$$

So the duration of an annuity due is $\frac{1}{r} - \frac{N}{[(1+r)^N-1]}$. As $N \to \infty$, the second term tends to zero. Hence, the duration of a perpetuity due is $\frac{1}{r}$.

Appendix 5.3: Duration and Interest Rate Sensitivity

Let's state the expression for the dirty price of a plain vanilla bond, that pays coupons m times per year.

$$P = \frac{\frac{C}{m}}{(1+\frac{y}{m})} + \frac{\frac{C}{m}}{(1+\frac{y}{m})^2} + - - - - - - - - - - - + \frac{\frac{C}{m}}{(1+\frac{y}{m})^{mT}} + \frac{M}{(1+\frac{y}{m})^{mT}}$$

Let's differentiate P with respect to y:

$$\frac{dP}{dy} = -\frac{1}{m} \times \frac{\frac{C}{m}}{(1+\frac{y}{m})^2} - \frac{1}{m} \times 2 \times \frac{\frac{C}{m}}{(1+\frac{y}{m})^3} - - - - - - - - -$$

$$-\frac{1}{m} \times mT \times \frac{\frac{C}{m}}{(1+\frac{y}{m})^{mT+1}} - \frac{1}{m} \times mT \times \frac{M}{(1+\frac{y}{m})^{mT+1}}$$

$$= -\frac{1}{m} \times \frac{1}{(1+\frac{y}{m})}\left[\frac{1 \times \frac{C}{m}}{(1+\frac{y}{m})} + \frac{2 \times \frac{C}{m}}{(1+\frac{y}{m})^2} + - - - - - - -\right.$$

$$\left. + \frac{mT \times \frac{C}{m}}{(1+\frac{y}{m})^{mT}} + \frac{mT \times M}{(1+\frac{y}{m})^{mT}}\right]$$

Therefore

$$\frac{dP}{dy} \times \frac{1}{P} = -\frac{1}{m} \times \frac{1}{(1+\frac{y}{m})}\left\{\left[\frac{1 \times \frac{C}{m}}{(1+\frac{y}{m})} + \frac{2 \times \frac{C}{m}}{(1+\frac{y}{m})^2} + - - - - - - -\right.\right.$$

$$\left.\left. + \frac{mT \times \frac{C}{m}}{(1+\frac{y}{m})^{mT}} + \frac{mT \times M}{(1+\frac{y}{m})^{mT}}\right]\frac{1}{P}\right\}$$

The term in parentheses is nothing but the duration of the bond. Therefore,

$$\frac{dP}{dy} \times \frac{1}{P} = -\frac{1}{m} \times \frac{1}{(1+\frac{y}{m})} \times D$$

Appendix 5.4: Convexity of Annuities and Perpetuities

The price of an annuity that pays $A every period is

$$P = \frac{A}{r}\left[1 - \frac{1}{(1+r)^N}\right]$$

$$\frac{dP}{dr} = -\frac{A}{r^2}\left[1 - \frac{1}{(1+r)^N}\right] + \frac{AN}{r(1+r)^{N+1}}$$

$$\frac{d^2P}{dr^2} = \frac{2A}{r^3}\left[1 - \frac{1}{(1+r)^N}\right] - \frac{2AN}{r^2(1+r)^{N+1}} - \frac{AN(N+1)}{r(1+r)^{N+2}}$$

$$\frac{d^2P}{Pdr^2} = \frac{2}{r^2} - \frac{2N}{r(1+r)\left[(1+r)^N - 1\right]} - \frac{N(N+1)}{(1+r)^2\left[(1+r)^N - 1\right]}$$

Using L' Hôpital's rule, as

$$N \to \infty \text{ Convexity} \to \frac{2}{r^2}$$

The convexity of a perpetuity is $\frac{2}{r^2}$.

The price of an annuity due is

$$\begin{aligned} P &= \frac{A}{r}\left[1 - \frac{1}{(1+r)^N}\right](1+r) \\ &= \frac{A}{r}\left[1 - \frac{1}{(1+r)^N}\right] + A\left[1 - \frac{1}{(1+r)^N}\right] \\ \frac{dP}{dr} &= \frac{AN}{(1+r)^{N+1}} - \frac{A}{r^2}\left[1 - \frac{1}{(1+r)^N}\right] + \frac{AN}{r(1+r)^{N+1}} \\ \frac{d^2P}{dr^2} &= -\frac{AN(N+1)}{(1+r)^{N+2}} + \frac{2A}{r^3}\left[1 - \frac{1}{(1+r)^N}\right] - \frac{2AN}{r^2(1+r)^{N+1}} - \frac{AN(N+1)}{r(1+r)^{N+2}} \\ \frac{d^2P}{Pdr^2} &= \frac{2}{r^2(1+r)} - \frac{2N}{r(1+r)^2\left[(1+r)^N - 1\right]} - \frac{N(N+1)}{(1+r)^2\left[(1+r)^N - 1\right]} \end{aligned}$$

Using L' Hôpital's rule, as

$$N \to \infty \text{ Convexity} \to \frac{2}{r^2(1+r)}$$

Thus the convexity of a perpetuity due is $\frac{2}{r^2(1+r)}$.

Appendix 5.5: Proof of Single-Period Immunization

We now demonstrate that if the duration of the asset is equal to the investment horizon, then the reinvestment risk balances the price risk.[12]

12 See Taggart [64] for a similar proof.

Assume that an investor has an investment horizon of H years. The bond has N annual coupons remaining, where each coupon is for \$$C$. The face value of the bond is \$$M$. Let's assume that out of the N coupons, M are received before the investment horizon and $N - M$ coupons are received after that. The final wealth can be divided into two components. The first is the future value of the M coupons received before the horizon date. The second is the liquidation value of the un-matured bond at the horizon date. Both these components depend on the level of interest rates following the purchase of the bond. If rates increase, the first component increases while the second declines. The bond as a whole is an immunized or risk-less investment if a change in one component is exactly offset by an opposite change in the other. Let's assume that rates change only once, and that the change occurs immediately after the acquisition of the bond.

Assume that each coupon can be reinvested at a rate R. The total proceeds from the re-invested coupons is given by

$$I = C(1+R)^{H-1} + C(1+R)^{H-2} + \cdots + C(1+R)^{H-M}$$

$$\frac{\partial I}{\partial R} > 0$$

Thus the higher the reinvestment rate is, the greater the future value of reinvested coupons.

The liquidation value of the bond at a YTM of R is

$$L = \frac{C}{(1+R)^{M+1-H}} + \frac{C}{(1+R)^{M+2-H}} + \cdots + \frac{C}{(1+R)^{N-1-H}} + \frac{C+M}{(1+R)^{N-H}}$$

$$\frac{\partial L}{\partial R} < 0$$

Thus the higher the YTM is, the lower the sale price.

The investor's final wealth is $W = I + L$. We need a condition such that $\frac{\partial W}{\partial R} = 0$; that is, the final wealth is invariant to changes in the interest rate.

$$W = C(1+R)^{H-1} + C(1+R)^{H-2} + \cdots + C(1+R)^{H-M} + \frac{C}{(1+R)^{M+1-H}}$$
$$+ \frac{C}{(1+R)^{M+2-H}} + \cdots + \frac{C}{(1+R)^{N-1-H}} + \frac{C+M}{(1+R)^{N-H}}$$

Divide both sides of the equation by $(1+R)^H$:

$$\frac{W}{(1+R)^H} = \frac{C}{(1+R)} + \frac{C}{(1+R)^2} + \cdots + \frac{C}{(1+R)^M}$$
$$+ \frac{C}{(1+R)^{M+1}} + \frac{C}{(1+R)^{M+2}} + \frac{C}{(1+R)^{N-1}} + \frac{C+M}{(1+R)^N}$$

The RHS is nothing but the bond price at the outset. Thus,

$$
\begin{aligned}
&\frac{W}{(1+R)^H} = P \\
\Rightarrow\ & W = P(1+R)^H \\
&\frac{\partial W}{\partial R} = HP(1+R)^{H-1} + (1+R)^H \frac{\partial P}{\partial R} \\
&= (1+R)^H \left[\frac{\partial P}{\partial R} + \frac{HP}{(1+R)}\right] \\
&\frac{\partial P}{\partial R} = -\frac{DP}{(1+R)} \\
\Rightarrow\ & \frac{\partial W}{\partial R} = (1+R)^H \left[-\frac{DP}{(1+R)} + \frac{HP}{(1+R)}\right] \\
&= (1+R)^{H-1} \times P[H-D]
\end{aligned}
$$

Thus $\Rightarrow \frac{\partial W}{\partial R} = 0$, if $H = D$.

Chapter 6
The Money Market

The market for capital is divided into the money market and the capital market. Medium-term and long-term bonds and equity securities are issued in the capital market. This market is an arena where parties raise funds to make long-term investments. Thus if a manufacturing company wishes to set up a new factory, or a company seeks to borrow to construct a new building for its headquarters, it usually approaches the capital market. However, in practice, funds may also be required for managing liquidity imbalances. Take the case of the federal government. It gets its revenues primarily by way of taxes. However, tax receipts tend to be lumpy, and inflows do not occur throughout the year on a uniform basis. On the other hand, expenditures are usually incurred on a daily basis. Consequently, even if the federal government has a surplus budget for the year as a whole, which is usually not the case, during most of the year it will have a deficit. In such a situation, it has no choice but to borrow for short periods and hence approaches the money market. Similarly, take the case of a company that needs short-term capital for meeting revenue expenditure. Such a company may be profitable for the year, but may often have a cash deficit and require short-term capital for meeting expenditures. In such cases, it too approaches the money market. Thus, both government and business entities will approach the money market when they are in need of short-term funds.

What motivates lenders to lend in such markets? For most business and government entities, cash inflows and outflows are not perfectly synchronized, and consequently there is a short-term deficit or surplus. While entities with a deficit have no option but to borrow, parties with a surplus seek to lend because money is a perishable asset.

If cash is kept idle, there is an opportunity cost in terms of interest foregone. When large amounts of funds are involved, the lost income can be substantial. Take for instance the case of an institution that has \$100 million available. If we assume that the interest rate is 3% per annum and the year consists of 360 days, which is the assumption in the U.S. money market, the loss if the funds are kept idle for six days is

$$100{,}000{,}000 \times 0.03 \times \frac{6}{360} = \$50{,}000$$

This lost income cannot be recovered subsequently. One can argue that we might be able to invest at double the rate in the following week. However, even assuming that were to be the case, if we invest for two weeks, we get two weeks worth of interest, whereas if we invest only for the second week, we get only a week's worth of interest. Thus we say that money is perishable. *Use it or lose it.* Similar analogies can be given from the hotel and airline industries. If the Boston Marriott has 10 unoccupied rooms on a given day, then the revenue that is lost is lost forever. For, obviously, the hotel

https://doi.org/10.1515/9781547400669-006

cannot accommodate two guests in a room on a subsequent day. Similarly, if Emirates flies from New York to Dubai with 10 empty seats then the income that is lost is lost forever, because on the next flight two passengers cannot be assigned the same seat.

Because fund inflows and outflows are not predictable, no entity is usually a permanent borrower or lender in the money market. A business may suddenly require money to pay income tax and approach the money market to borrow on a short-term basis. However, two weeks hence, a customer who had been supplied on credit may make a large payment that would result in an inward surge of cash. In this situation, it is likely that the business will approach the market once again, this time as a lender. Also, there are institutions that simultaneously operate on both sides of the market. Take the case of a large commercial bank such as Citibank. As a bank it needs money to accommodate the needs of its clients who seek to borrow from it. Consequently, it issues negotiable certificates of deposit and borrows federal funds, activities which warrant its classification as a borrower. However, at the same time, it is likely that the bank is making short-term loans to satisfy the needs of its corporate clients. So the answer to the question, as to whether Citibank is a borrower or a lender in a money market, is that it is both. In some transactions it takes the role of a borrower, and in others, it plays the part of a lender.

Risk Factors in the Money Market

Investors in the money market seek to keep their temporary surpluses gainfully invested, without compromising on credit risk or liquidity. Liquidity needs cannot be anticipated, and parties seek the freedom to enter as borrowers and/or as lenders at short notice. Thus it is imperative from the standpoint of such parties that the market be characterized by the presence of plenty of active buyers and issuers of securities who can facilitate transactions without a major price impact. In developed nations, the money markets are extremely liquid and can absorb large volumes of transactions with only a relatively small impact on security prices and interest rates. Consequently, it is possible for borrowers to issue large quantities of securities at short notice, often in a matter of minutes. Safety is also critical because investments are made for short periods and may need to be liquidated at any time. For this reason money market investors are especially sensitive to default risk. Even the slightest perception of a decline in credit quality can bring the market to a grinding halt.

Money market securities, like other debt securities, are in principle vulnerable to interest rate risk. However, the prices of such securities are relatively more stable over time. Thus, although such securities do not offer prospects for significant capital gains, they do not raise the specter of significant capital losses either. There are essentially two reasons for this. First, interest rate movements over relatively short periods of time tend to be moderate. Second, the price impact due to a given interest rate change is greater, the longer the term to maturity of the cash flow being impacted. In this case, the maximum term to maturity of a security is one year. Similarly, default risk is minimal in the money market. This is because the ability to borrow in such markets is restricted to well-established institutions with impeccable credit ratings, usually from multiple rating agencies. That is, it is usually not adequate for an issuer to obtain a rating from, say, S&P; it also needs a second rating from Moody's or Fitch.

Supervision of the Money Market

The money market is an over-the-counter market made up of dealers and brokers. Consequently there is no money market exchange. The money markets are overseen by the respective central banks of the countries in which they operate. The major central banks in the world are listed in Table 6.1.

Table 6.1: Major central banks.

The United States Federal Reserve
The European Central Bank
The Bank of England
The Bank of Japan
The Swiss National Bank
The Bank of Canada
The Reserve Bank of Australia
The Reserve Bank of New Zealand

The U.S. Federal Reserve system consists of 12 district Federal Reserve Banks. These are identified by the cities in which they are located. The 12 banks are listed in Table 6.2.

Table 6.2: The District Federal Reserve Banks.

Federal Reserve Bank of Boston
Federal Reserve Bank of New York
Federal Reserve Bank of Philadelphia
Federal Reserve Bank of Cleveland
Federal Reserve Bank of Richmond
Federal Reserve Bank of Atlanta
Federal Reserve Bank of Chicago
Federal Reserve Bank of St. Louis
Federal Reserve Bank of Minneapolis
Federal Reserve Bank of Kansas City
Federal Reserve Bank of Dallas
Federal Reserve Bank of San Francisco

Key Dates in Money Market Transactions

There are three key dates in the lives of money market instruments:
- Transaction date
- Value date
- Maturity date

The transaction date is the date on which the terms and conditions of a financial instrument, such as the term to maturity, transaction amount, and price, are agreed upon. In other words, it is the date on which the two counter-parties enter into a contract with each other.

The value date is the date on which the instrument starts to earn or accrue a return. The value date may or may not be the same as the transaction date. If the two dates are the same, then the transaction is said to be for *same day value* or *value today*. In other cases, the value date is the following business day. Transactions with such a feature are said to be for *next-day value* or *value tomorrow*. Finally, there are markets and transactions where the value date is two business days after the transaction date. A transaction with such a feature is referred to as a *spot transaction* and is said to be for *spot value*.

The maturity date is the date on which the instrument ceases to accrue a return. The maturities of money market instruments are often fixed not by agreeing to a specific date of maturity, but by agreeing to a term to maturity, which is a specified number of weeks or months after the value date.

Roll Conventions in the Event of Market Holidays

If the maturity date of a transaction is a market holiday, then it needs to be rolled forward, or at times backward, to a regular working day. The market may follow one of three possible conventions for the roll-over. These are
- The following business day convention
- The modified following business day convention
- The preceding business day convention

Irrespective of the roll convention, there is one common rule. That is maturity is set for the same date as the value date. For instance, if the value date is 21 June, the maturity date for a three-month deposit is 21 September, and for a six month deposit, it is 21 December.

Now let's consider the modified following business day convention. Per this convention, if the maturity date happens to be a holiday, then it moves to the following business day. Take the case of a three-month deposit with a value date of 21 June. Under normal circumstances the maturity date is 21 September. However, if 21 September falls on a Saturday, for instance, then the maturity date becomes Monday, the 23rd of September, assuming of course that this day is not a market holiday. However, in the process of rolling forward, one cannot select a date in the subsequent calendar month. In such a situation, the maturity date moves back to the last business day of the maturity month. Consider a one-month deposit made on 31 July. The scheduled maturity date is normally, 31 August, but assume that 31 August is a Sunday. In this case however, the following business day falls in September which is the next calendar month. Consequently, the maturity date moves back to the last business day of August, which is 29 August.

The following business day convention differs slightly, for it says that in the event of rolling forward, it is acceptable to cross over to the next calendar month. Thus, if the maturity date is 31 August, which is a market holiday, then it is modified to 1 September.

The preceding business day convention says that if the scheduled maturity date is a holiday, it is rolled backward to the previous working day. So if 21 June, the scheduled maturity date, is a Saturday, then it is rescheduled to Friday 20 June.

The End/End Rule

This rule states that if the value date is the last business day of a calendar month, then the maturity date is the last business day of the corresponding calendar month. For example, take a one-month deposit with a value date of 31 May. It matures on 30 June, assuming it is a business day. Similarly, a one-month deposit with a value date of 30 June matures on 31 July, assuming once again that it is a business day.

A one-month deposit with a value date of 31 January matures on 28 or 29 February depending on whether it is a leap year. A one-month deposit with a value date of 28 or 29 February matures on 31 March. However, if the maturity date per this rule is a holiday, then the prescribed roll convention applies.

The Interbank Market

The interbank market is a market for large or wholesale loans and deposits. It is an arena for borrowing and lending deals between commercial banks, with tenors less than or equal to one year. Why do economies require an interbank market? On any given day, certain commercial banks have a surplus of funds while others are confronted with the specter of a deficit. For a bank whose inflow on account of deposits exceeds the outflow on account of loans and investments, there is a surge in its reserves. On the contrary, banks whose demand for funds on account of loan requests by their clients exceeds the availability of funds by way of deposits, face a depletion of *reserves*. The term reserves refers to the balance that a commercial bank has on deposit with the regional Federal Reserve Bank. Because money is perishable, it is prudent for banks with surpluses to lend them to those with a deficit, despite the fact that interest rates for such transactions tend to be relatively low. Although the loan of funds is a manifestation of the desire of lending institutions to keep idle resources productively invested, on the part of the borrowers, it reflects the fact that they have to bridge the shortfall. Loans made in the inter-bank market are unsecured.

Types of Loans in the Inter-bank Market

Overnight money refers to money that is borrowed/lent on a given banking day and scheduled to be repaid on the next banking day. *Weekend money* is the term used to describe loans that are made on Friday with repayment being scheduled for the following Monday. Interest on weekend money is payable for a period of three days.

Call money refers to deposits for an unspecified term. The lender can call back the funds at any time and will be repaid on the same day.

Notice money is money that is lent with a short notice of withdrawal, for example with seven days' notice.

Term money is money that is lent or deposited for a fixed period, such as a week or a month.

Intra-day money refers to money that is lent and repaid on the same day. Borrowing takes place in the morning of the business day, and repayment is scheduled for the same afternoon. Although many consider an overnight loan to have the shortest maturity among money market transactions, technically intra-day loans have the shortest maturity.

LIBOR

LIBOR is an acronym for London Interbank Offer Rate. It is defined as the rate at which a top-rated bank in London is prepared to lend to a similar bank. It is the main benchmark rate in the London interbank market. In practice, LIBOR is quoted for a number of tenors: 1 month, 2 months, 3 months, 6 months, and 12 months. Thus there are several LIBOR rates quoted at any point in time, and any quotation must be prefixed by its term to maturity. Every bank in London quotes its own LIBOR rate for each tenor. But usually the rates quoted by competing banks are identical, with some minor differences being observed occasionally.

Although LIBOR is the globally recognized benchmark for loans granted by a top-rated depository institution to parties with a high credit rating, highly rated banks and companies can often borrow short-term at a rate below the prevailing LIBOR. On the other hand, institutions with a lower credit rating may have no option but to borrow at a rate above LIBOR. Indicative LIBOR rates for the London market as a whole are released daily by the Intercontinental Exchange (ICE).

ICE LIBOR

ICE LIBOR is the most widely used benchmark or reference rate for short-term interest rates. It is compiled by ICE and released shortly after 11:00 a. m. London time each day. ICE maintains a reference panel of contributor banks. The objective is to provide a reference panel that reflects the balance of the market, by country and by type of institution. Individual banks are selected on the basis of reputation, scale of market activity, and perceived expertise in the currency concerned. ICE publishes the quotes of the panel on the screen. The top quartile and bottom quartile of the quotes are disregarded, for they may constitute outliers, and the middle two quartiles are averaged to arrive at a trimmed arithmetic mean known as the ICE LIBOR rate. ICE provides the LIBOR for five currencies: the US Dollar, British pound; euro; Swiss franc; and Japanese yen.

LIBID

LIBID is the acronym for the *London Inter-bank Bid Rate*. It is the rate that a bank in London with a good credit rating is prepared to pay for funds deposited with it by another highly rated London bank. LIBID, just like LIBOR, is quoted for a number of tenors. However, whereas LIBOR represents the rate that a bank seeking to borrow in the interbank market has to pay on a loan availed by it, LIBID is the rate that a bank with surplus funds has to accept on funds it deposits with another bank. LIBID is lower than LIBOR. Although the size of the spread between the two rates can vary, the difference is usually just a few basis points for the same tenor.

In an interbank transaction, the rate agreed upon is often somewhere between LIBID and LIBOR, frequently the average of the two rates. Some depository institutions, therefore, use LIMEAN, which is an arithmetic average of the LIBID and the LIBOR, as the reference rate for their interbank transactions.

Interest Computation Methods

For some money market instruments, interest is payable on the principal value of the instrument. That is, interest is paid at the end of the loan period, along with the repayment of principal to the investor. This is termed as the *add-on approach*. On the other hand, other securities like Treasury bills are what we term as *discount securities*. That is, they are issued at a discount to their principal value and repay the principal at maturity. Quite obviously they are analogous to zero coupon bonds. The difference may be illustrated by way of a numerical example.

Example 6.1. Consider a security with a par value of \$100 and a quoted yield of 8%. The maturity is 90 days, and let's assume that the market convention is that the year consists of 360 days.

If the yield is quoted on an add-on basis, the implication is that an investment of \$100 is to be repaid as \$102 after 90 days. The quoted rate is 8% per annum, and the actual annualized return is also 8% per annum.

$$100\left[1+\frac{0.08\times 90}{360}\right]=102$$
$$\frac{(102-100)}{100}\times\frac{360}{90}=0.08\equiv 8\%$$

If, however, the yield is quoted on a discount basis, the investor has to invest \$98 in return for \$100 after three months. Whereas the quoted rate is 8% per annum, the actual annualized return is 8.1632%.

$$100\left[1-\frac{0.08\times 90}{360}\right]=98$$
$$\frac{2}{98}\times\frac{360}{90}=8.1632\%$$

Thus, in the case of add-on securities, the quoted yield and the actual return are identical, but in the case of a discount security, the actual rate of return is always higher than the quoted yield.

Money Market Forward Rates

Assume that s_1 is the quoted rate for an A-day loan and s_2 is the rate for a B-day loan, where $B > A$. If the rate is quoted on an add-on basis, then we can state that

$$\left[1+\frac{s_1\times A}{360}\right]\times\left[1+\frac{f\times(B-A)}{360}\right]=\left[1+\frac{s_2\times B}{360}\right] \tag{6.1}$$

where f is the forward rate for a $(B-A)$-day loan, as fixed at time 0.

Example 6.2. Assume that the 72-day rate is 4% and the 180-day rate is 5.25%. The implied forward rate is given by

$$\left[1+\frac{0.04\times 72}{360}\right]\times\left[1+\frac{f\times 108}{360}\right]=\left[1+\frac{0.0525\times 180}{360}\right]$$
$$\Rightarrow f=6.0350\%$$

If the rate is quoted on a discount basis, the relationship can be stated as

$$\left[1-\frac{s_1\times A}{360}\right]\times\left[1-\frac{f\times(B-A)}{360}\right]=\left[1-\frac{s_2\times B}{360}\right] \tag{6.2}$$

Example 6.3. Assume that the 72-day rate is 4% and the 180-day rate is 5.25%. The implied forward rate is given by

$$\left[1-\frac{0.04\times 72}{360}\right]\times\left[1-\frac{f\times 108}{360}\right]=\left[1-\frac{0.0525\times 180}{360}\right]$$
$$\Rightarrow f=6.1324\%$$

For interbank loans, interest is computed and paid along with the principal. The method of calculating the interest differs according to the currency under consideration. Interest on most currencies, including the U.S. dollar and the euro, is calculated on the assumption that the year has 360 days and is based on the ACT/360 day-count convention. This means that the interest payable on a loan for T days with a principal of P and carrying an interest rate of r is

$$P \times \frac{r}{100} \times \frac{T}{360}$$

For certain currencies, however, like the British pound, interest is calculated on the assumption of a 365-day year and is based on an ACT/365 day-count convention. Consequently the formula for computing interest is

$$P \times \frac{r}{100} \times \frac{T}{365}$$

Example 6.4. A bank in New York makes a loan of $25 million from 15 July until 15 October at an interest rate of 6.00% per annum. The number of days is: 16 + 31 + 30 + 15 = 92. Notice that although the loan is for three months we consider the actual number of days in the period and do not automatically take the period as consisting of 90 days. This is because the numerator of ACT/360 is the actual number of days in the period. The interest is given by:

$$25{,}000{,}000 \times 0.06 \times \frac{92}{360} = \$383{,}333.32$$

Example 6.5. A bank in Atlanta makes a loan of $75 million for a period of one year (365) days at an interest rate of 6.25% per annum. The interest is given by

$$75{,}000{,}000 \times 0.0625 \times \frac{365}{360} = \$4{,}752{,}604.17$$

Notice that although the actual number of days exceeds 360, we still compute on a simple interest basis. This is a feature of money markets.

Term Money Market Deposits

A term money market deposit is a short-term deposit, with a maximum maturity of one year, that is placed with a bank or a security house. Such deposits carry a fixed rate of interest, and the rate is linked to the prevailing LIBOR for the same term. Interest is usually on an add-on basis and paid along with the principal when the deposit matures. These deposits are non-negotiable, that is, they cannot be sold to another party prior to maturity by the depositor. Depositors can usually break or terminate the deposit prematurely, that is, they have the option to withdraw their money prior to expiration. However, this feature at times carries an attached penalty. These days due to the competitive pressures in the banking industry, it may be possible to place a deposit with no penalty in the event of premature withdrawal.

Federal Funds

Federal funds are the principal means of making payments in the money market in the U.S. By definition, the term "federal funds" refers to money that can be immediately transferred from the buyer of securities to the seller, or from the lending institution to the borrower. This term is used because the principal way of effecting an immediate fund transfer is by debiting the reserve account held by the buyer's bank or the lending bank at the regional Federal Reserve Bank, and crediting the reserve account maintained by the seller's bank or the borrowing bank at its regional Federal Reserve Bank. Such transactions are instantaneous and can be effected in a matter of seconds in practice. On the contrary, conventional payments by way of checks, entail the role of a clearinghouse, which means that same-day credit is usually infeasible. This is not acceptable for money market participants because, as we mentioned earlier, money is a perishable asset.

Banks and other depository institutions must hold in a special reserve account liquid assets equal to a fraction of the funds deposited with them. Only vault cash held within the bank and reserve balances kept with the local Federal Reserve Bank count in meeting a U.S. bank's requirement to hold legal reserves. An increase in deposits consequently leads to an increase in the availability of federal funds, whereas loans made and securities purchased, manifest themselves as a reduction in the availability of such funds. Frequently some, usually smaller, banks hold more legal reserves than what the law requires. These banks tend to keep their surpluses gainfully invested, by lending to the larger banks, which are invariably short of funds. Most lenders tend to make overnight loans of federal funds. This is because the availability of excess reserves tends to vary daily, and in a fairly unpredictable fashion. The lending of such funds is termed as a *sale*, and the borrowing of such funds is referred to as a *purchase*. The 12 member banks of the Federal Reserve System have a share in an Inter-district Settlement Fund that is maintained with the Federal Reserve headquarters in Washington D. C. Consequently, if a member bank wants to transfer funds to another member, all that is required is a debit to the lender's share of the settlement fund and a credit to the borrower's share.

Treasury Bills

Treasury bills (T-bills), are money market instruments issued by the central or federal government of a country. In the United States they are issued by the federal government, and the rates on these securities set the benchmark for the rates on other money market securities with the same tenor. The reasons why T-bills carry the lowest yield for a given tenor are the following. First, they are virtually devoid of credit risk because they are backed by the full faith and credit of the U.S. government. Second, they are highly liquid. Third, income from such securities is exempt from state income tax. In the U.S., unlike in many other countries, state governments are empowered to levy income tax. The governments follow a guideline of mutual reciprocity. That is, federal securities are exempt from state income tax and vice versa.

By law, T-bills in the U.S. must have an original maturity of one year or less. Regular series bills are issued routinely every week or month by way of competitive auctions. Four-week, three-month and six-month bills are auctioned every week, and one-year bills are sold usually once a month. Of the four maturities, the six-month bills provide the largest amount of revenue for the U.S. Treasury. On the other hand, cash management bills are issued only when the Treasury has a special need, on account of low cash balances. Such bills have maturities ranging from as short as a few days to as long as six months. They give the maximum flexibility to the Treasury because they can be issued as and when required. The money raised through these issues is used by the Treasury to meet any temporary shortfalls.

T-bills are sold by an auction process. The Treasury entertains both competitive and non-competitive bids. Large investors submit competitive bids, wherein they indicate not only the quantity sought, but also the minimum yield that they are prepared to accept. The yield in this case refers to the discount yield for the bill being auctioned. Non-competitive tenders, on the other hand, are submitted by small investors who agree to accept the yield at which the securities are auctioned off, whatever that yield may be. Thus, such bidders have to indicate only the quantities sought. Generally the Treasury fills all non-competitive bids.

Besides being traded in the U.S., T-bills issued by the U.S. Treasury are actively traded in other major financial centers like London and Tokyo. Thus the market for such securities operates virtually around the clock. The globalization of the market is characterized by the presence of non-U.S. dealers in the U.S. market, as well as by the activities of American dealers in markets outside the country.

Re-openings of T-bills

Every T-bill issue is identified with a unique CUSIP number. Some issues, however, are a reopening of an existing issue. That is, the new issue is identical in all respects to an issue that is already trading in the secondary market. For instance, the three-month bill issued three months after the issue of a six-month bill is considered a re-opening of the six-month bill. The new issue in this case is given the same CUSIP number. For a given maturity, the most recently issued securities are referred to as *on the run*, whereas those issued earlier are referred to as *off-the-run*. On-the-run securities generally trade at slightly lower yields because they are more liquid. The reason is that, for some time after the issue of such bills, there tends to be active trading in the secondary market. Thereafter most securities pass into the hands of investors who choose to hold them until maturity. Consequently, off-the-run securities are less liquid, which explains the higher yield.

Cash management bills are issued via a standard auction process. However, they are irregular with respect to their term to maturity and auction schedule. If a cash management bill matures on the same day as a regular bill, which is usually a Thursday, then it is said to be *on-cycle*. In this case, the issue is considered to be a reopening, and is consequently allotted the same CUSIP. However, if it matures on a different day, it is said to be *off-cycle*, and obviously carries a different CUSIP number.

Discount Rates and T-bill Prices

The quoted yield on a T-bill is a discount rate, which is used to determine the difference between the price of a T-bill and its face value. For the purpose of calculation in the U.S. market, the year is treated as if it has 360 days.

If d is the quoted yield for a T-bill, with a face value of $\$V$ and having T_m days to maturity, the dollar discount D is given by

$$D = V \times \frac{d}{100} \times \frac{T_m}{360}$$

Given the discount, the price may be calculated as $P = V - D$

We illustrate these concepts with the help of Example 6.6.

Example 6.6. A T-bill with 90 days to maturity and a face value of $1 million, has a quoted yield of 4.8%. What is the price in dollars?

The discount is $1{,}000{,}000 \times 0.048 \times \frac{90}{360} = \$12{,}000$.

The price is given by

$$P = V - D = 1{,}000{,}000 - 12{,}000 = \$988{,}000$$

Example 6.7. A one-year bill (364 days) has just been issued at a quoted yield of 5.4%. What is the corresponding price in dollars?

The discount is $1{,}000{,}000 \times 0.054 \times \frac{364}{360} = \$54{,}600$.

The price is given by

$$P = V - D = 1{,}000{,}000 - 54{,}600 = \$945{,}400.$$

The Money Market Yield of a T-bill

The money market yield is defined as

$$\frac{V - P}{P} \times \frac{360}{T_m}$$

The quoted yield is defined as

$$\frac{V-P}{V} \times \frac{360}{T_m}$$

For a discount security, the price is always lower than its face value. Consequently, the money market yield for such a security is always higher than the quoted yield.

Example 6.8. Consider the T-bill with 90 days to maturity and a face value of $1 million. The quoted yield is 4.8%. We have already computed the price as $988,000. The money market yield is

$$\frac{12{,}000}{988{,}000} \times \frac{360}{90} = 0.048583 \equiv 4.8583\%$$

The Bond Equivalent Yield of a T-bill

The objective of calculating the *bond equivalent yield*, also known as the *coupon equivalent yield*, is to compute a yield measure that facilitates comparisons between the rate of return on discount securities like T-bills and capital market debt instruments like coupon-paying bonds. The procedure that is adopted to compute the BEY depends on whether the discount instrument under consideration has less than six months left to maturity or more.

Case A: T_m < 182 days

The bond equivalent yield for a T-bill with less than 182 days to maturity is just the equivalent rate of return on a simple interest basis, computed under the assumption that the year has 365 days. As we saw in the case of the money market yield, the bond equivalent yield for a T-bill with a given discount rate is always greater than the stated discount rate. The reason once again is that the bond equivalent yield, as is the case for the money market yield, is based on the market price, whereas the quoted yield is based on the face value. Since the price is always less, the quoted yield is always lower.

The BEY in this case is defined as

$$\frac{V-P}{P} \times \frac{365}{T_m}$$

It can be directly computed given the quoted yield, using the following equation:

$$\text{BEY} = \left(\frac{V}{P} - 1\right) \times \frac{365}{T_m} \tag{6.3}$$

$$P = V \times \left[1 - \frac{d \times T_m}{360}\right] \tag{6.4}$$

Substituting we get

$$\text{BEY} = \frac{d \times 365}{(360 - d \times T_m)} \tag{6.5}$$

Example 6.9 gives an illustration for computing the BEY.

Example 6.9. A T-bill with a face value of $1 million and 90 days to maturity, has a quoted yield of 6%. What is the bond equivalent yield?

The price is given by

$$P = 1{,}000{,}000 - 1{,}000{,}000 \times 0.06 \times \frac{90}{360} = \$985{,}000$$

The bond equivalent yield is given by

$$\text{BEY} = \frac{0.06 \times 365}{(360 - 0.06 \times 90)} = 6.1760\%$$

In the case of a bill with fewer than 182 days to maturity, the money market yield can be transformed into the bond equivalent yield by simply multiplying the former by 365 and dividing by 360.

Example 6.10. Take the case of the bill in Example 6.8. The money market yield was computed to be 4.8583%. The BEY can be computed as

$$4.8583 \times \frac{365}{360} = 4.9258\%$$

Case B: T_m > 182 days

A T-bill with fewer than 182 days to maturity can be directly compared with a bond with fewer than 182 days to maturity, for the latter is also a zero coupon security and hence is comparable. However, a conventional coupon paying bond with a time to maturity that is greater than 182 days (half a year) will make a coupon payment before it matures. It is inappropriate to compare the simple yield on a discount security with the YTM of a bond, because although the bond yields an interest payment before maturity, the discount security does not. To facilitate a comparison between the BEY for a discount instrument, like a T-bill, with more than 182 days to maturity and the yield to maturity (YTM) for the bond, the T-bill must be treated as if it too would pay interest after six months, and that interest is paid on this intermediate interest for the remaining period left to maturity.

If we denote the BEY as y, we can state that it is the solution to

$$P\left[\left(1+\frac{y}{2}\right)\left\{1+\frac{y}{2}\left(\frac{T_m - \frac{365}{2}}{\frac{365}{2}}\right)\right\}\right] = V \tag{6.6}$$

The logic is as follows. The future value of an investment equal to P, at the end of six months, is

$$P\left(1+\frac{y}{2}\right)$$

The future value of this expression, as calculated on the date of maturity must equal the face value. The compounding factor for the remaining period, on a simple interest basis, is

$$\left[1+\frac{y}{2}\left(\frac{T_m-\frac{365}{2}}{\frac{365}{2}}\right)\right]$$

The end result is that we have a quadratic equation in y. This has two roots, and we discard the negative root and retain the positive. The positive root for y is given by

$$\frac{\frac{-2T_m}{365}+2\sqrt{\left(\frac{T_m}{365}\right)^2-\left(\frac{2T_m}{365}-1\right)\left(1-\frac{V}{P}\right)}}{\frac{2T_m}{365}-1}$$

Holding Period Return for an Investor

Take the case of an investor who buys a bill at a quoted yield of d_1, when there are T_{m1} days left to maturity, and sells it at a discount rate of d_2, when there are T_{m2} days left to maturity. Let's denote the purchase price by P_1 and the sale price by P_2. The holding period return is given by

$$\frac{P_2-P_1}{P_1}\times\frac{365}{T_{m1}-T_{m2}}$$

$P_2 - P_1$ represents the capital gain or loss. The number of days for which the bill has been held is $T_{m1} - T_{m2}$.

Concept of a Tail in a T-bill Transaction

What is a tail? Trading-glossary.com defines a tail as follows: *Calculating the yield at which a future money market security (one available some period hence) is purchased when that future security is created by buying an existing instrument and financing the initial portion of its life with a term repo.* We have not dealt with repos yet. For the moment let's just interpret it as a collateralized loan.

We can illustrate it with the help of an example.

Example 6.11. Marc Anthony & Co., a brokerage house, is acquiring a 144-day bill. It plans to hold it for 36 days and then sell it. The issue is, what should be the quoted yield at the time of sale if the firm is to break even on the transaction. Assume the face value of the bill is $1 million and the quoted yield at the outset is 6%. The purchase price is

$$1{,}000{,}000 \times \left(1 - 0.06 \times \frac{144}{360}\right) = \$976{,}000$$

The funding cost for 36 days, which is either an actual cost or an opportunity cost, assuming a borrowing rate of 6.40% is

$$976{,}000 \times 0.064 \times \frac{36}{360} = \$6{,}246.40$$

Thus the effective cost of the bill is 976,000+6,246.40 = 982,246.40. To break even on the transaction, the bill, which will have 108 days to maturity at the time of the sale, must be sold for this amount. The corresponding discount rate can be obtained from the following equation:

$$982{,}246.40 = 1{,}000{,}000 \times \left(1 - d \times \frac{108}{360}\right)$$
$$\Rightarrow d = 5.9179\%$$

If the discount rate at the time of sale were to be lower, there would be a profit for the brokerage house. However, if it were to be higher, there would be a loss.

T-bill Related Computations Using Excel

To compute the price of a T-bill, we use the TBILLPRICE function.

The parameters are:

- Settlement
- Maturity
- Discount

Example 6.12. Consider a 126-day T-bill with a quoted yield of 6% per annum. What is the price? If we knew the actual settlement and maturity dates, we could enter them using the DATE function in a YYYY,MM,DD format. In this case, all we know is that the bill has 126 days to maturity. Consequently, we can specify any two numbers so that the difference is 126. The easiest approach is to specify a value of 0 for settlement and 126 for maturity. Note we could have specified 100 and 226 had we so desired. The discount is 0.06. Excel computes the price per $100 of face value. Consequently, if we have a bill with a face value of $1 million, we multiply the answer by 10,000.

In our case: The price = TBILLPRICE(0,126,0.06) = $97.90.

We can verify it:

$$P = 100 \times \left(1 - 0.06 \times \frac{126}{360}\right) = \$97.90$$

To compute the money market yield, we use the TBILLYIELD function.

The parameters are
- Settlement
- Maturity
- Price

Settlement and maturity are defined as for the TBILLPRICE function. Price is the price per $100 of face value.

Example 6.13. Consider the bill with 126 days to maturity and a quoted yield of 6%. The price is $97.90. So we compute the yield as:

Money market yield = TBILLYIELD(0,126,97.90) = 6.1287%.

We can verify it:

$$\text{Money Market Yield} = \frac{(100 - 97.9)}{97.90} \times \frac{360}{126} = 6.1287\%$$

To compute the bond equivalent yield, we need the TBILLEQ function.

The parameters are
- Settlement
- Maturity
- Discount

The parameters are specified as for the TBILLPRICE function. There are two formulas for the bond equivalent yield, depending on the time to maturity of the bill, and Excel automatically uses the appropriate method. If we use the TBILLEQ function with values such that the difference between maturity and settlement is 182 or less, it uses the first method. However, if the difference is more than 182, it automatically switches to the second method.

Example 6.14. Let's reconsider the bill with 126 days to maturity and a quoted yield of 6%. Bond equivalent yield = TBILLEQ(0,126,0.06) = 6.2138%.

We can verify it:

$$\text{Bond Equivalent Yield} = \frac{(100 - 97.9)}{97.90} \times \frac{365}{126} = 6.2138\%.$$

Finally if we know the maturity of the bill and its price, we can compute the corresponding discount rate. This can be done using a function called DISC.

The parameters are:
- Settlement
- Maturity
- Price
- Redemption
- Basis

Settlement and maturity have the same meaning as in the case of the Excel functions invoked earlier. Price is per $100 of face value. Redemption is invariably 100. Basis is the day-count convention. In the U.S. we use the Actual/360 convention.

Table 6.3: Basis values for day-count conventions.

Basis Value	Day-Count Convention
0	30/360 NASD
1	Actual/Actual
2	Actual/360
3	Actual/365
4	30/360 European

Example 6.15. Once again, let's take the bill with 126 days. We can compute the discount rate as d = DISC(0,126,97.90,100,2) = 0.06 ≡ 6%.

We can verify it:

$$\text{Quoted Yield} = \left[1 - \frac{97.90}{100}\right] \times \frac{360}{126} \equiv 6\%$$

Repurchase Agreements

A repurchase agreement, or repo, is a money market transaction with two legs. In the first leg, a party agrees to sell securities at a specified price. At the same time, the same party agrees to buy back the security subsequently at the original price plus interest, in what constitutes the second leg of the transaction. Thus, a repo is essentially a collateralized loan. Because if the party selling the securities does not buy them back, the lender has access to the securities to recover what is owed. Such a transaction has two perspectives. From the borrower's side, it is termed as a repo. From the lender's side, it is known as a reverse repo. Thus every repo transaction is accompanied by a reverse repo. Most of these transactions are overnight. That is, the money is repaid and the securities reacquired on the following day. However, there are transactions of longer duration known as *term repos*. In some markets, a repo is known as a *ready-forward* contract. This is because, although the first leg is immediate, the second is a forward contract.

The motive for these transactions is as follows. Dealers in financial markets carry large quantities of securities as a part of their inventory. Their own capital is usually inadequate to fund these purchases, and the bulk of the securities held are funded with borrowed money. A securities dealer may buy a security hoping to sell it soon.

However, if the sale does not materialize, the dealer has securities coming and an urgent need for cash. An obvious way to raise money is by doing a repo. The motive for a reverse repo is the converse. A dealer may have sold a security thinking that he will acquire and deliver. But he may be unable to do so. In this case, he has cash coming his way and needs securities. An obvious solution is a reverse repo. Thus dealers in search of cash do repos, and those in search of securities do reverse repos.

Repos were first introduced by the Federal Reserve as a tool for regulating the supply of money in the economy. Although securities dealers undertake such transactions to fund their positions, the FED uses them as a monetary policy tool. Today repos are a major constituent of money market operations worldwide, in both developed capital markets and markets in the emerging economies. The securities used in repo transactions are typically government securities such as T-bills and T-bonds. However, highly rated corporate debt securities may also be pledged as collateral in some markets.

If the bond, which is pledged as collateral, pays a coupon during the life of the repo, the lender collects and hands over the coupon to the borrower. In other words, although a repo constitutes a transfer of ownership, the borrower continues to enjoy the benefits of the bond in terms of the coupon payments. That is, the borrower continues to remain the beneficial owner of the security.

Example 6.16. A dealer wants to borrow by pledging government securities with a face value of \$5 million. The current market price is 100-24, and the accrued interest is \$3.75 per \$100 of face value. Thus the dirty price of the bond is:

$$5{,}000{,}000 \times \frac{100 + \frac{24}{32} + 3.75}{100} = \$5{,}225{,}000$$

The loan carries an interest of 3.6% per annum and is repayable after 27 days. Thus the amount payable at maturity, when the collateral is taken back, is

$$5{,}225{,}000 \times \left(1 + 0.036 \times \frac{27}{360}\right) = \$5{,}239{,}107.50$$

Repo Rates

Most securities in the repo trade are close substitutes for each other. Thus there is a common interest rate known as the *general collateral rate*. However, at times a dealer may require a security very urgently and find that it is in short supply. On such an occasion, he can agree to lend money at a lower rate of interest if this particular security is offered as collateral. Such securities are said to be on *"special."*

Margins in Repo Transactions

In principle both the parties to a repo face credit risk. If the collateral declines in value, the lender is at risk because the borrower may refuse to return the cash, and the market value of the securities may be inadequate to recover the loan. On the contrary, if the collateral appreciates in value, the borrower is at risk, for the lender may decide to retain the security which by assumption is worth more than what was lent initially. There is no strategy that can simultaneously protect both parties, and more protection for one side means greater risk for the other.

Lenders can protect themselves by applying what is termed in market parlance as a *"haircut."* For instance, if the current market price is \$100, a lender who applies a haircut of 4%, will lend only \$96. A borrower can protect himself by insisting on a reverse haircut. That is, he can offer a security priced at \$100 for a loan of say \$104. In practice, we cannot have a situation where the lender applies a haircut and the borrower applies a reverse haircut. In the market we have haircuts. The rationale is that the lender is giving cash that is more liquid than the security that is being offered in return. Consequently the right to collect a margin is given to the lender and not to the borrower.

The size of the haircut depends on the following factors:

- The credit quality of the collateral
- The time to maturity of the collateral
- The term to maturity of the repo

The collateral is periodically valued at the prevailing market rate, a procedure that is known as *"marking to market."* In practice the lender sets a threshold level for the value of the collateral termed as the *maintenance margin level.* If the securities fall in value and a situation arises in which their current market value is lower than the maintenance level, the borrower must provide additional securities with a market value that is sufficient to make up the deficit. On the other hand, if the securities rise in value, the borrower can ask for extra cash or a partial return of collateral.

Example 6.17 shows the two ways in which the haircut can be applied.

Example 6.17. A dealer that is prepared to offer bonds with a face value of \$40 million, enters into a six-day repurchase agreement with a bank. The collateral is T-bonds with a coupon of 6% and a market price of \$95 per \$100 of face value. The haircut is 1.25%. Accrued interest is \$2.50 per \$100 of face value. The repo rate is 6.00% per annum.

The loan amount can be calculated in either of two ways:

Method I: The loan amount is

$$40{,}000{,}000 \times \frac{95 + 2.50}{100} \times (1 - 0.0125) = \$38{,}512{,}500$$

The amount repayable at maturity is

$$38{,}512{,}500 \times \left(1 + 0.06 \times \frac{6}{360}\right) = \$38{,}551{,}012$$

Method II: The loan amount is

$$40{,}000{,}000 \times \frac{95 + 2.50}{100} \times \frac{1}{(1 + 0.0125)} = \$38{,}518{,}518.50$$

The amount repayable at maturity is

$$38{,}518{,}518.50 \times \left(1 + 0.06 \times \frac{6}{360}\right) = \$38{,}557{,}037$$

Thus a haircut of $x\%$ may be applied by either multiplying the dirty price by $(1 - x)$, or else, by dividing it by $(1 + x)$. We do not get the same loan amount in both cases. However, both are legitimate methods for applying a haircut.

The Federal Reserve and Repos

The central bank undertakes repos and reverse repos with primary dealers. A primary dealer is defined as a dealer who is authorized to deal directly with the central bank of a country. In the U.S. a primary dealer is authorized to deal with the New York Fed. The Federal Reserve Bank of New York (FRBNY) is first among equals in the central banking structure of the United States. This is because all decisions pertaining to open market operations, are implemented by the FRBNY, as New York is the largest money market in the world.

Although the mechanics of a repo are standard, the motives of security dealers differ from those of the central bank. Dealers use repos and reverse repos to manage their inventories. For the central bank, these transactions constitute an important component of the monetary policy instruments available to it. A repo represents a collateralized loan made by the Fed to primary dealers. Thus repos are used by dealers to borrow funds from the Fed. On the other hand, a reverse repo transaction entails borrowing funds by the Fed from the primary dealers. From a monetary policy standpoint, a repo temporarily adds reserve balances to the banking system, whereas a reverse repo transaction temporarily drains such balances from the system. These transactions are undertaken by the trading desk at the New York Fed, which in turn implements monetary policy decisions taken by the Federal Open Market Committee (FOMC). When the Fed does a repo, funds are credited to the dealer's commercial bank. This enhances the level of reserves in the banking system. At maturity, in return for the amount lent plus interest, the Fed transfers the collateral back to the dealer concerned. This automatically neutralizes the extra reserves that were created by the original transaction. Thus, such operations undertaken by the Fed have a short-term, self-reversing effect on bank reserves. Reverse repos are similar from the standpoint of their impact on reserves. In such transactions, the Fed sends collateral to the dealer's clearing bank in return for the funds. This action reduces the availability of reserves in the banking system. At the time of maturity of the contract, the dealer returns the collateral to the Fed, which in turn returns with interest the funds that were initially borrowed. This automatically restores the reserves that were reduced by the original transaction.

Negotiable Certificates of Deposit (CDs)

A certificate of deposit, or CD, is an interest-bearing receipt for funds left with a depository institution for short periods of time. CDs are usually issued at par and pay interest explicitly, although banks also issue discount CDs that are similar to T-bills in structure. Payment is made in federal funds on the day of maturity. Banks and other institutions issue many types of CDs, but true money market CDs are negotiable instruments that can be resold before maturity and are typically issued with a face value of $1 million. CDs issued to retail investors are non-negotiable and consequently not classified as money market instruments. CDs issued in the U.S. and eurodollar CDs usually have an original maturity that is less than or equal to one year and pay interest at maturity. The day-count convention is Actual/360, and the rate of interest is referred to as the coupon rate. The interest rate on a money market CD is slightly less than that on a standard time deposit of the same tenor, because the instrument is negotiable.

Required Symbols

We will now derive the expression for determining the price of a CD, given its yield, and vice versa.

- N is the OTM, that is, the number of days from the time of issue until the time of maturity.
- T_m is the ATM, that is, the number of days from the settlement date until the maturity date.
- c is the coupon rate.
- y is quoted yield.
- V is the face value or principal amount of the CD.
- P is the dirty price of the CD.

The amount payable at maturity is given by:

$$V \times \left[1 + c \times \frac{N}{360}\right]$$

If the quoted yield is y, the dirty price is given by:

$$P = \frac{V \times \left[1 + c \times \frac{N}{360}\right]}{\left[1 + y \times \frac{T_m}{360}\right]} \qquad (6.7)$$

The accrued interest may be computed as:

$$\text{AI} = V \times c \times \frac{(N - T_m)}{360} \qquad (6.8)$$

Given the dirty price, the yield is given by the following equation:

$$y = \left\{ \frac{V \times \left[1 + c \times \frac{N}{360}\right] - P}{P} \right\} \times \frac{360}{T_m} \tag{6.9}$$

Example 6.18. Consider a CD with 144 days to maturity that has just been issued with a face value of $1 million and a coupon rate of 3.60%. The amount that the holder receives at maturity is equal to

$$1{,}000{,}000 \times \left[1 + 0.036 \times \frac{144}{360}\right] = \$1{,}014{,}400$$

If the quoted yield is 4.80%, and there are 108 days until maturity, the dirty price is given by

$$P = \frac{1{,}014{,}400}{\left(1 + 0.048 \times \frac{108}{360}\right)} = \$1{,}000{,}000$$

The accrued interest is:

$$\text{AI} = 1{,}000{,}000 \times 0.036 \times \frac{(144 - 108)}{360} = \$3{,}600$$

Thus the clean price is 1,000,000 − 3,600 = $996,400.

Example 6.19. Consider the CD with a coupon of 3.60%, an OTM of 144 days, and 108 days until maturity. The dirty price is $995,200. What is the yield?

$$y = \frac{1{,}000{,}000 \times \left[1 + 0.036 \times \frac{144}{360}\right] - 995{,}200}{995{,}200} \times \frac{360}{108} = 6.4309\%$$

Term Certificates of Deposit

Term CDs have a maturity in excess of one year at the time of issue, and usually pay coupons on a semiannual basis. The price of the instrument is the present value of all the cash flows to be received from it as of the settlement date, where the discounting is done using the quoted yield. The procedure is analogous to the valuation of a bond, where the coupons and the face value are discounted at the YTM, with certain critical differences.

1. In the case of a bond, the coupon interest for a full coupon period is $\frac{C}{2}$ irrespective of the actual number of days in the coupon period. In the case of a term CD, the coupon for a full period depends on the actual number of days in the period. That is, the interest in this case is given by $V \times c \times \frac{N_i}{360}$ where N_i is the number of days in the ith coupon period. Thus the coupon will vary from period to period.
2. The second difference is that for a bond the discount factor for a full coupon period is $(1 + \frac{y}{2})^t$. In the case of a term CD, the discounting is based on the actual number of days in the coupon period.

3. The third crucial difference is that for bonds, cash flows are discounted using compound interest, whereas for a term CD we use simple interest for discounting.

We can illustrate the valuation of a term CD with the help of an example.

Example 6.20. A CD with a coupon rate of 3.6% was issued on 1 July 2019. It is scheduled to mature on 30 June 2021. On 15 November 2019, the quoted yield is 4.8%. What should be its market price?

The first step is to calculate the number of days in each coupon period, as well as the number of days from the date of settlement to the first coupon. The length of each period is given in Table 6.4.

Table 6.4: Number of days in each period.

Start Date	End Date	No. of Days
1 July 2019	1 January 2020	184
1 January 2020	1 July 2020	182
1 July 2020	1 January 2021	184
1 January 2021	30 June 2021	180
15 November 2019	1 January 2020	47

To value the security, we start with the cash flow at maturity. This is discounted back to the penultimate coupon date. The coupon payment at this point of time is added to the present value obtained in the previous step. The sum is then discounted back to the previous coupon date. This procedure is repeated until we reach the settlement date.

In our example, the cash flow at maturity is

$$1{,}000{,}000 \times \left(1 + 0.036 \times \frac{180}{360}\right) = \$1{,}018{,}000$$

The present value of this on 1 January 2021 is

$$\frac{1{,}018{,}000}{\left(1 + 0.048 \times \frac{180}{360}\right)} = \$994{,}140.62$$

The coupon due on 1 January 2021 is

$$1{,}000{,}000 \times 0.036 \times \frac{184}{360} = \$18{,}400$$

The amount to be discounted to the previous coupon date is

$$994{,}140.62 + 18{,}400 = \$1{,}012{,}540.60$$

The present value on 1 July 2020 is

$$\frac{1{,}012{,}540.60}{\left(1 + 0.048 \times \frac{184}{360}\right)} = \$988{,}294.47$$

The coupon due on 1 July 2020 is

$$1{,}000{,}000 \times 0.036 \times \frac{182}{360} = \$18{,}200$$

The amount to be discounted to the previous coupon date is

$$988{,}294.47 + 18{,}200 = \$1{,}006{,}494.40$$

The present value on 1 January 2020 is

$$\frac{1{,}006{,}494.40}{\left(1 + 0.048 \times \frac{182}{360}\right)} = \$982{,}648.85$$

The coupon due on 1 January 2020 is

$$1{,}000{,}000 \times 0.036 \times \frac{184}{360} = \$18{,}400$$

The amount to be discounted to the settlement date is

$$982{,}648.85 + 18{,}400 = \$1{,}001{,}048.80$$

The present value on 15 November 2019 is

$$\frac{1{,}001{,}048.80}{\left(1 + 0.048 \times \frac{47}{360}\right)} = \$994{,}814.69$$

This is the dirty price of the CD as of 15 November 2019. The accrued interest as of this day is

$$1{,}000{,}000 \times 0.036 \times \frac{184 - 47}{360} = \$13{,}700$$

Thus the clean price is

$$994{,}814.69 - 13{,}700 = \$981{,}114.69$$

NCDs vs. Money Market Time Deposits

In the case of a conventional time deposit, an investor deposits a sum of money with a bank for a stated period of time. The bank pays interest at a specified rate. At the end of the deposit period, the investor can withdraw the original sum deposited plus the interest. In the case of an NCD, however, the depositor is typically issued a bearer security. Although entitled to claim the deposit with interest at the end of the deposit period, the depositor can always sell the security prior to maturity in the secondary market. In the process, ownership of the underlying deposit transfers from the seller to the buyer. Thus NCDs have one major advantage over a conventional money market deposit, namely liquidity. A money market deposit cannot be easily terminated until it matures. If the investor wants to withdraw the funds prior to maturity, he may have to pay a penalty in terms of a lower rate of interest. However, with increasing competition in many markets, banks are finding it difficult to levy a penalty. In contrast, NCDs can be liquidated at any time at the prevailing market rate. Thus these instruments are attractive for investors who seek the high interest rates offered by time deposits but who are reluctant to commit their money for the full term of the deposit.

The Effective Cost of a CD

For the issuing bank, the effective cost of the CD is greater than the quoted rate of interest. This is because, first, the bank has to keep a certain percentage of the deposit as a reserve with the central bank, which may or may not earn interest. Even if the central bank does pay interest, it is below the market rate. The second reason is that in most countries the deposits are insured up to a certain limit. Example 6.21 illustrates what we have just described.

Example 6.21. A bank has issued a CD carrying interest at the rate of 4.50% per annum. It is required to maintain a reserve of 10% with the central bank, on which it earns nil interest. The deposits have to be insured and the cost is 10 bp. Thus if a deposit of $100 is made, the bank is paying $4.50 of interest on $90 of usable money. Thus the effective cost is 5%. If we factor in the insurance premium, the cost is 5.10%.

Commercial Paper

Commercial paper is a term used for short-term unsecured promissory notes issued by corporations, primarily for funding their working capital requirements. The term "unsecured" means that no assets are being pledged as collateral. The issuers are generally financially strong with high credit ratings, which is a prerequisite for successful issue of such an instrument. The funds raised in this manner are normally used for current account transactions such as, purchase of raw materials, payment of accrued taxes, meeting of wage and salary obligations, and other short-term expenditures, rather than for capital account transactions or in other words long-term investments. Although most issuers of paper enjoy a high credit rating, they invariably secure a line of credit at a commercial bank to provide a greater degree of assurance to investors. But, the line of credit cannot be used to directly guarantee payment if the company goes bankrupt, and the lender may renege on the credit line if in its perception the credit quality of the borrower has significantly deteriorated. Consequently, an irrevocable letter of credit opened by a commercial bank offers a greater degree of reassurance to buyers. Such a letter of credit (LC) makes a bank unconditionally responsible for repayment if the corporation defaults on its paper.[1]

There are two major types of commercial paper, namely *direct paper* and *dealer paper*.[2] As the name suggests, direct paper refers to securities issued directly by the borrower and does not involve a dealer as an intermediary. The main issuers of direct paper are large finance companies and bank holding companies that deal directly with the investors rather than using securities dealers as intermediaries. Such borrowers have an ongoing need for huge amounts of short-term money, possess top credit rat-

1 We discuss LCs in more detail shortly.

2 See Stigum and Crescenzi [60].

ings, and have established working relationships with major institutional investors in order to place new issues regularly. Direct issues involve substantial distribution and marketing costs, and consequently need to be issued in large volumes. Issuers need a dedicated in-house marketing division to maintain sustained contact with potential investors.

The alternative to direct paper is what is termed as dealer paper. Such paper, as the name suggests, is issued by security dealers on behalf of their corporate customers. Dealer paper is issued mainly by firms that borrow less frequently than companies that issue direct paper. The dealer may underwrite the issue, or may agree to sell on a best efforts basis. In the case of the former, a dealer or syndicate of dealers, buys the entire issue from the company at a discount and then tries to resell it at the best available price in the market. If anything remains unsold, then it falls on the dealer's lap. In the case of a best efforts deal, the dealer promises to make a best effort to market the issue. However, if something remains unsold, the dealer is not required to acquire it. Companies prefer underwritten issues to best efforts issues because in the former, there is a risk of devolvement. The term *"devolvement,"* refers to the risk that the issue may flop and a portion may devolve on the underwriter, who will be required to buy it. The specter of this makes a dealer market the issue aggressively. In the case of a best efforts deal, there is no way of verifying whether the dealer has done his best.

Letters of Credit (LCs)

A letter of credit (LC) is a document issued by a bank, called the issuer or opener, at the behest of a client, referred to as the applicant. The document is drawn in favor of a stated beneficiary, stating that the opening bank will effect payment of a stated sum of money for certain specified good or services, against presentation of a predefined set of documents. LC based transactions are very common in international trade transactions, although they may be occasionally used for domestic deals, as well.

A letter of credit is a bank's direct undertaking to the beneficiary. That is, when the shipment of goods occurs under a letter of credit, the issuing bank does not wait for the buyer to default, or in other words, for the seller to invoke the undertaking, before making the payment to the beneficiary. Therefore, in the case of an LC, the principal liability is that of the issuing bank. It must first pay, on submission of the predefined set of documents, and then collect the amount from its client. Thus an LC substitutes the bank's credit-worthiness for that of its client.

Yankee Paper

Paper that is issued in the U.S. by foreign firms is called Yankee paper. Foreign issuers find that they can often issue Yankee paper at a cheaper rate than what it would cost them to borrow outside the U.S. However, foreign borrowers must generally pay higher interest costs than U.S. companies with comparable credit ratings. That is, Yankee paper generally carries a higher yield than U.S. paper of the same credit quality. This is because an American investor can demand higher returns due to the difficulty of gathering information on a foreign firm. Samurai paper refers to yen-denominated paper issued by foreign issuers in Japan. Both Yankee and Samurai paper are examples of foreign debt securities. That is, although these securities are denominated in the domestic currency, the issuers are foreign entities.

Credit Rating

Short-term debt securities are rated by the three major rating agencies. Their scales, with the interpretation, are as follows.

Moody's Rating Scale

Moody's uses the following rating scale for short-term taxable instruments:
- Prime-1: Superior ability to repay short-term debt obligations.
- Prime-2: Strong ability to repay short-term debt obligations.
- Prime-3: Acceptable ability to repay short-term debt obligations.
- Not Prime: These do not fall within any of the prime rating categories.

Prime-1, Prime-2, and Prime-3 are all investment-grade ratings.

S&P's Rating Scale

Standard & Poor's rates issues on a scale from A-1 to D. Within the A-1 category, an issue can be designated with a plus sign. This indicates that the issuer's ability to meet its obligation is extremely strong. Country risk and currency of repayment of the obligor are factored into the credit analysis and are reflected in the issue rating.
- A-1: Issuer's capacity to meet its financial commitment on the obligation is strong.
- A-2: The issuer is susceptible to adverse economic conditions. However, the issuer's capacity to meet its financial commitment is satisfactory.
- A-3: Adverse economic conditions are likely to weaken the issuer's capacity to meet its financial commitment on the obligation.
- B: The issue has significant speculative characteristics. The issuer currently has the capacity to meet its financial obligation but faces major ongoing uncertainties that could impact its financial commitment.

- C: The issue is currently vulnerable to nonpayment and is dependent upon favorable business, financial and economic conditions for the obligor to meet its financial commitment.
- D: The issue is in payment default. The rating is also used upon the filing of a bankruptcy petition.

A-1, A-2, and A-3 are all investment-grade ratings.

Fitch's Rating Scale

Fitch's short-term ratings indicate the potential level of default within a 12-month period. A plus or minus sign, may be appended to the F1 rating to denote relative status within the category.
- F1: Best quality grade. Indicates strong capacity of obligor to meet its financial commitment.
- F2: Good quality grade. Indicates satisfactory capacity of obligor to meet its financial commitment.
- F3: Fair quality grade. Adequate capacity of obligor to meet its financial commitment, but near term adverse conditions could impact the obligor's commitments.
- B: Of speculative nature. Obligor has minimal capacity to meet its commitment and is vulnerable to short-term adverse changes in financial and economic conditions.
- C: Possibility of default is high. Financial commitment of the obligor is dependent upon sustained, favorable business and economic conditions.
- D: The obligor is in default as it has failed on its financial commitments.

Short-term debt issues given a top-grade credit rating by both S&P and Moody's are referred to as A1/P1 debt. A1/P1 paper sells at the finest rates.

Bills of Exchange

A bill is an unconditional order addressed by the party that is to be paid, to the counterparty that is required to make the payment. The party that makes out the bill is termed the *drawer*. The party that is required or directed to pay is termed the *drawee*. Thus the bill is drawn by the drawer on the drawee. The latter is required to make the payment to the former, as per the terms of the document.

There are three categories of bills of exchange: Treasury bills, bank bills, and trade bills. A trade bill is drawn by one non-bank company on another, typically demanding payment for a trade debt. A bank bill, on the other hand, is a bill that is drawn on and payable by a commercial bank. A bank bill is generally considered safer than a trade bill. Treasury bills are issued by the federal government. They are considered to be the safest of the bills in the market for a given maturity. Trade bills can be classified as sight bills, and time, term or usance bills. A sight bill has to be honored on demand, that is, the drawee is expected to pay on sight. In the case of a term bill, however, the specified amount is payable on a future date that is mentioned in the bill. For a bill with a future payment date, the drawee signs its acceptance across the face of the bill and returns it either to the drawer or to its bank. When such a bill is accepted by the debtor, it becomes a promise to pay or an IOU. Because a term bill represents an undertaking to pay a stated amount at a future date, it is a form of short-term finance for the debtor. The holder of the bill therefore effectively gives credit to the debtor.

When the drawee stamps its acceptance on a term trade bill, it becomes what is called a *trade acceptance*. The drawer can hold the accepted bill until maturity and present it to the drawee for payment, or sell it in the money market at any time prior to its maturity date. A bill of exchange can thus be transferred by a simple endorsement. An accepted bill is essentially a zero coupon security. The last holder, at maturity, receives the stated value from the drawee. Thus a bill can be repeatedly traded in the secondary market, at a price that is determined by the prevailing yield for such securities. The ability of a holder of a bill to sell it at a reasonable price depends on the credit quality of the drawee and on the existence of a liquid secondary market.

In most commercial transactions, one or more banks enter the picture. For instance, if a U.S. company imports goods from Scania, a Swedish company, the foreign company will require the American firm to have a letter of credit opened in its favor. When the goods have been shipped, Scania has the bills sent to the U.S. importer's bank. If it is a sight bill, the U.S. bank makes the payment immediately. If it is a time draft, the bank signs its acceptance on the bill. A bill that is accepted by a commercial bank is termed a *bankers' acceptance* or BA. BAs are obviously more marketable than trade acceptances. The transactions are usually with recourse. That is, assume Scania sends the bill to Citibank which accepts it. Subsequently the bill is sold by Scania to Siemens. On the maturity date, Siemens presents the bill to Citibank. If Citibank is not in a position to pay, the holder, Siemens in this case, can demand that the drawer, Scania, make the payment.

Example 6.22. Scania has drawn a bill on Midland Bank for \$10 million, with a maturity of 180 days. The bank has accepted it, and the drawer has sold it to HSBC at a discount of 3.60%. Now, 60 days hence, HSBC has sold the bill to First National Bank at a discount of 2.70%. The rate of return for HSBC may be computed as follows.

The purchase price is given by

$$10{,}000{,}000 \times \left[1 - 0.036 \times \frac{180}{360}\right] = \$9{,}820{,}000$$

The sale price is given by

$$10{,}000{,}000 \times \left[1 - 0.027 \times \frac{120}{360}\right] = \$9{,}910{,}000$$

The profit is

$$9{,}910{,}000 - 9{,}820{,}000 = \$90{,}000$$

The return on investment on a 365-day year basis is

$$\text{ROI} = \frac{90{,}000}{9{,}820{,}000} \times \frac{365}{60} = 5.5753\%$$

The yield on bankers' acceptances is usually only slightly higher than the rate on T-bills because banks that issue such acceptances are normally large and have a good reputation from the standpoint of credit risk. The discount rate on an acceptance is also comparable with the rate on an NCD, because both instruments are unconditional obligations of the issuing bank.

Chapter Summary

In this chapter, we examined various money market or short-term debt instruments. We defined the key dates in such transactions and looked at market conventions in the event of the maturity dates being market holidays. We began by looking at transactions in the interbank market. In this context, we introduced the concepts of LIBOR and LIBID. In Chapter 4, we looked at the term structure of interest rates, and in this chapter we extended it to money markets. Treasury bills, which are one of the most important constituents of the money market, were studied in detail. We looked at concepts such as the money market yield, the bond equivalent yield, the holding period return, and the tail. We then demonstrated the use of Excel functions to compute these yield/return measures. Repurchase agreements and reverse repurchase agreements were the next topic of discussion. We looked at repos from the perspective of a securities dealer, as well as a central bank. Negotiable certificates of deposit and term CDs were studied next, followed by commercial paper. The chapter concluded with a look at bills of exchange, trade acceptances, and bankers' acceptances. In the following chapter, we examine issues pertaining to floating rate bonds.

Chapter 7
Floating Rate Bonds

Unlike plain vanilla bonds, whose coupons remain fixed from issue until maturity, floating rate notes and bonds, also referred to as *floaters*, are debt securities whose coupons are reset periodically based on a reference or benchmark rate. Typically the coupon on such a security is defined as Benchmark Rate + Quoted Margin.

If the benchmark rate is a short-term rate, say 6-M LIBOR, we refer to the bond as a floating rate bond.[1] However, if the benchmark is a long-term rate, the bond is referred to as a *variable* or *adjustable rate bond*. For instance, consider a security whose coupon is specified as five-year T-note rate + 75 basis points.

In this case, the reference or benchmark rate is the yield on a five-year T-note, and consequently, the bond is classified as a variable rate bond. It should be noted that the quoted margin need not always be positive. For instance, a floater can have a coupon rate specified as 6-M LIBOR – 25 bp.

Usually the quoted margin remains constant for the life of the floater. However, there are securities, known as *stepped spread floaters*, where the margin is reset at intervals. In the case of such securities, the margin may be increased or decreased.

Call and Put Provisions in Floating Rate Bonds

Floating rate notes often come with call and/or put options. A call option may be invoked by the issuer if the reference rate were to decline. In such a situation, the issuer can recall a floater and issue a fixed rate bond at the prevailing rate, which is lower by assumption. The other situation in which a floater can be recalled is when the currently required margin for the security is lower than what was specified earlier. In such a situation, the floater can be recalled and replaced with a security carrying a lower quoted margin. As we have seen earlier in the case of fixed coupon securities, the call option works against the investors. If they receive the principal prematurely, they have to reinvest it in either a security with a lower coupon, or a security with a smaller quoted margin.

Floaters can come with put options, wherein the holder can surrender the bond prior to maturity. If rates rise in the market, and the floater is putable, the holder can return the bond, recover the principal, and reinvest it in a bond carrying a higher coupon, or in a floater with a higher quoted margin.

1 By short-term, we mean it is for a period less than or equal to one year.

https://doi.org/10.1515/9781547400669-007

Caps and Floors for the Coupon Rate

A floater can come with a cap and/or a floor. A cap puts an upper limit on the coupon and protects issuers against rising rates. A floor on the other hand puts a lower limit and protects investors against falling rates. If we assume that interest rates cannot become negative, a floater has a natural floor equal to the quoted margin because the lowest possible value for the reference rate is zero. Some floaters come with both a cap and a floor, which means that there is a minimum coupon as well as a maximum coupon. Such a feature is referred to as a *collar*.

Symbols: An Important Note of Caution

In some of the mathematical results in this chapter, the symbols for interest rates, both reference rates and yields, represent periodic (semiannual) rates, whereas in others they represent annual rates. This has been done deliberately to avoid cluttering the equations. Wherever required, an explanation has been provided. Apologies to the readers for any confusion.

Valuation of a Floating Rate Bond

In the case of a default risk-free floating rate bond, the price of the security always resets to par on a coupon date, although in between two coupon dates, it may sell at a premium or a discount. For instance, consider a floater with a coupon equal to the 6-M LIBOR. Assume that there are two periods to maturity. The price of the bond at the end of the first coupon period is given by

$$P_{T-1} = \frac{M + M \times \frac{c_{T-1}}{2}}{(1 + \frac{y_{T-1}}{2})} \tag{7.1}$$

In this equation c_{T-1} is the coupon on the penultimate coupon date, and y_{T-1} is the required yield on that day. On the coupon reset date, the yield is equal to the coupon because we have assumed that there is no default risk implicit in the security. Consequently any change in the required yield, also is reflected in the coupon that is set on that day. We know that if the yield is equal to the coupon, then the bond should sell at par. Thus $P_{T-1} = M$. Now let's go to the previous coupon date, which in this case is time 0, because the bond by assumption has only two coupons until maturity.

$$\begin{aligned} P_{T-2} &= \frac{P_{T-1} + M \times \frac{c_{T-2}}{2}}{(1 + \frac{y_{T-2}}{2})} \\ &= \frac{M + M \times \frac{c_{T-2}}{2}}{(1 + \frac{y_{T-2}}{2})} \end{aligned} \tag{7.2}$$

Once again at $T-2$, $c_{T-2} = y_{T-2}$ and consequently $P_{T-2} = M$. This logic can be applied to a bond with any number of coupons remaining to maturity.

In between two coupon dates, however, the price of such a floater may not be equal to par. Consider the valuation of the note at time $T-2+k$. The price is given by[2]

$$P_{T-2+k} = \frac{P_{T-1} + M \times \frac{c_{T-2}}{2}}{\left(1 + \frac{y_{T-2+k}}{2}\right)^{1-k}} \tag{7.3}$$

Although c_{T-2} was set at time $T-2$ and is equal to y_{T-2}, y_{T-2+k} is determined at time $T-2+k$ and reflects the prevailing conditions at that point in time. In general y_{T-2+k} need not equal c_{T-2} and may be higher or lower. Consequently, in between two coupon dates, a floater may sell at a premium or at a discount.

Interestingly, if $y_{T-2+k} = c_{T-2}$, the price is

$$M \times \left(1 + \frac{y_{T-2+k}}{2}\right)^{k} > M$$

Thus, if the yield on a date between coupons is equal to the coupon rate that was set on the preceding coupon date, the bond sells at a premium.

Now let's consider the case of floaters characterized by default risk. In this case, it is not necessary that the risk premium required by the market be constant over time. For instance, assume that when the bond was issued the required return was equal to the five-year T-note rate + 75 bp. The coupon was set equal to this rate, and the bond was sold at par. Six months hence, the issue is perceived to be riskier and the required return in the market is the 5-year T-note rate + 95 bp. However, the coupon resets at the prevailing T-note rate + 75 bp. Hence, this issue does not reset to par at the next coupon date.

Variations on the Floating Rate Feature

Having looked at plain vanilla floating rate notes, we now go on to look at securities with different features. Although these bonds have the floating rate characteristic, they have additional features inherent in them.

Inverse Floating Rate Bonds

Unlike a floating rate bond, whose coupon increases with an increase in the reference rate, for an inverse floater, the higher the reference rate is, the lower the coupon and

2 We denote the time that has elapsed since the previous coupon by k. k is stated in terms of the number of periods. This is different from the convention followed in the earlier discussion on the valuation of a bond between coupon dates, where we had defined k as the time until the next coupon.

vice versa. Thus, the term *inverse floater* arises because the coupon and the reference rate move in opposite directions. The coupon for an inverse floater is specified as

$$\text{Coupon} = K - L \times \text{Reference Rate} \tag{7.4}$$

L is termed as the leverage factor, and an inverse floater with $L > 1$ is termed as a leveraged inverse floater. Assume $K = 4.5\%$ and $L = 1.0$. Assume the reference rate is 3-M LIBOR. Let's also assume that there is a lower bound of zero for LIBOR, although negative interest rates have appeared on the horizon in some markets. In this situation, the maximum coupon on the inverse floater is 4.50%. This is termed as a cap. An alternative method of preventing a negative interest rate, is to specify a floor. For instance, the coupon in Equation (7.4) can be specified as subject to a floor of say 1.50%. Thus the coupon cannot decline below 1.50%, no matter how high the LIBOR. Now let's illustrate the impact of the leverage factor with the help of a numerical example.

Example 7.1. Assume that the coupon is specified as

$$\text{Coupon} = 7.50 - 2.0 \times \text{3-M LIBOR}$$

If on a coupon reset date LIBOR = 2.50%, the coupon is 2.50%. If the leverage factor had been 1.0, the coupon would be 5.00%. If the LIBOR is 3%, the coupon is 1.50%. In the absence of the leveraging effect, it would be 4.50%. Thus a 50-basis point increase in the reference rate reduces the coupon by 100 basis points. This illustrates that the leverage factor is 2.0.

Deleveraged Floating Rate Bonds

In the case of a deleveraged floater, the leverage factor is less than 1.0. For instance, if the coupon is specified as

$$\text{Coupon} = 4.50 - 0.75 \times \text{3-M LIBOR}$$

the leverage factor is 0.75. The impact of a change in the reference rate is illustrated in Example 7.2.

Example 7.2. If on a coupon reset date LIBOR = 2.50%, the coupon is 2.6250%. If the leverage factor had been 1.0, the coupon would be 2.00%. If the LIBOR is 3%, the coupon is 2.25%. In the absence of the leveraging effect, it would be 1.50%. Thus a 50-basis point increase in the reference rate reduces the coupon by 37.50 basis points. This illustrates that the leverage factor is 0.75.

Dual-Indexed Floating Rate Bonds

The coupon for a dual-indexed floating rate security is a function of the difference between two reference rates, denoted as RR1 and RR2, respectively. Thus,

$$\text{Coupon} = K + (\text{RR1} - \text{RR2}) \tag{7.5}$$

Range Notes

In this case, the coupon is equal to the reference rate, as long the reference rate lies in a specified range. If the reference rate goes outside the bound, however, the coupon becomes zero. Here is an example.

Example 7.3. Coupon = 3-M LIBOR, if LIBOR lies between 2.50% and 4.50%. Otherwise, the coupon is zero. So if the LIBOR is 3.25%, the coupon also is 3.25%. If the LIBOR is 2.00%, the coupon is zero. Similarly, if the LIBOR is 5.25%, the coupon again is zero.

Variations on the Principal Repayment Feature

A floater may have a stated time to maturity, like a plain vanilla bond, or else it may be a perpetuity, where the principal is never repaid. There also exist amortized floating rate notes, in which the principal is repaid in installments, starting with a coupon date prior to the maturity date.

Floaters, Inverse Floaters, and Plain Vanilla Bonds

Take the case of a floater that pays LIBOR and an inverse floater, with the same time to maturity, that pays 8% – LIBOR. Assume that LIBOR is lower than 8% during the life of the securities. Let's assume that there are five years to maturity, and the observed values of LIBOR at each coupon reset date are as shown in Table 7.1.

Table 7.1: Observed LIBOR values.

Time	LIBOR
0	3.75%
1	4.50%
2	5.25%
3	6.00%
4	5.75%

Table 7.2: Coupons for the portfolio of a floater and an inverse floater.

Time	Coupon from Floater	Coupon from Inverse Floater	Portfolio Coupon
1	3.75	4.25	8.00
2	4.50	3.50	8.00
3	5.25	2.75	8.00
4	6.00	2.00	8.00
5	5.75	2.25	8.00

Take a portfolio that consists of one floater and one inverse floater. The total coupon on the portfolio is depicted in Table 7.2.

If we assume that both the floater and the inverse floater have a face value of \$1,000, the bond represented by the portfolio has a face value of \$2,000. A cash flow of \$80 per period on a face value of \$2,000 represents a coupon of 4%. Thus the combination of the floater and the inverse floater is equivalent to two plain vanilla bonds with a coupon of 4% each.

Hence, to rule out arbitrage, the price of the floater plus the price of the inverse floater should be equal to twice the price of a plain vanilla bond paying a coupon of 4%.

A More General Relationship for an Inverse Floater

Consider an inverse floater whose coupon rate is $K - L \times r$, where L is the leverage factor and r is the reference rate, such as LIBOR. A floater with the same reference rate has a coupon of r. If we combine one inverse floater with L floaters, we get a bond with a cumulative face value of $(L + 1) \times M$ and a coupon of $M \times K$. This is equivalent to one fixed rate bond with a face value of M and a coupon rate of $\frac{K}{(1+L)}$.

In our illustration, L was equal to 1.0 and K was 8%. Thus the coupon rate of the equivalent fixed rate bond was 4%.

Duration of a Floating Rate Bond

Consider a default risk-free floater. The price of the bond when it is between time $T - N$ and $T - N + 1$ is given by

$$P_{T-N+k} = \frac{M(1 + \frac{c_{T-N}}{2})}{(1 + \frac{y_{T-N+k}}{2})^{1-k}} \tag{7.6}$$

$$\frac{\partial P_{T-N+k}}{\partial \frac{y_{T-N+k}}{2}} = -\frac{(1-k)}{2} \times \frac{M(1 + \frac{c_{T-N}}{2})}{(1 + \frac{y_{T-N+k}}{2})^{2-k}} \tag{7.7}$$

$$\Rightarrow \frac{\partial P_{T-N+k}}{P\partial \frac{y_{T-N+k}}{2}} = -\frac{\frac{(1-k)}{2}}{(1+\frac{y_{T-N+k}}{2})} \tag{7.8}$$

We know that

$$\frac{\partial P_{T-N+k}}{P\partial \frac{y_{T-N+k}}{2}} = -D_M$$

or the modified duration at that point in time. Thus

$$\begin{aligned} \text{Duration} &= \frac{\frac{(1-k)}{2}}{(1+\frac{y_{T-N+k}}{2})} \times \left(1 + \frac{y_{T-N+k}}{2}\right) \\ &= \frac{(1-k)}{2} \end{aligned} \tag{7.9}$$

The duration of the floater is equal to the time left until the next coupon.

Convexity of a Risk-Free Floating Rate Bond

We can differentiate the price of a risk-free bond twice with respect to the yield, in order to derive an expression for its convexity.

$$\frac{\partial^2 P}{P\partial y^2} = \frac{\frac{(1-k)(2-k)}{4}}{(1+\frac{y_{T-N+k}}{2})^{2-k}} \tag{7.10}$$

Comparison with a Zero Coupon Bond

A risk-free floater that is between coupons is equivalent to a zero coupon bond maturing on the next coupon date. The duration of a zero coupon bond with N semiannual periods to maturity is $N/2$ in years, and the convexity is $\frac{N(N+1)}{4(1+\frac{y}{2})^2}$.

If we set $k = 0$, the duration of a risk-free floater is $\frac{1}{2}$ a year and the convexity is $\frac{1\times 2}{4(1+\frac{y_{T-N}}{2})^2}$. This confirms the deduction that a risk-free floater paying semiannual coupons is, on a coupon date, equivalent to a zero coupon bond with one semiannual period to maturity.

Margin Measures for Floaters

A margin measure is essentially a yield spread measure, and such measures are used to evaluate the returns from a floater. There are various types of margins that can be computed in practice. Let's consider each one of them in turn.

- Simple margin
- Modified simple margin
- Adjusted simple margin
- Adjusted total margin
- Discount margin

Simple Margin

If a floater trades at a premium or a discount, then the premium/discount needs to be factored in while computing the return. If the floater trades at a discount, then we need to account for the accretion of the discount over the life of the floater. On the contrary, if the floater trades at a premium, we need to factor in the amortization of the premium over the life of the security. The formula for the simple margin is

$$\text{Simple Margin} = \left[\frac{100 \times (100 - P)}{T_m} + \text{Quoted Margin}\right]$$

P is the market price (clean price) of the floater, as a percentage of par, and T_m is the remaining time until maturity. If it is not an integer, we need to invoke a day-count assumption. The quoted margin must be expressed in basis points and not percentage terms. There is a related metric called *modified simple margin*, which is defined as

$$\text{Modified Simple Margin} = \left[\frac{100 \times (100 - P)}{T_m} + \text{Quoted Margin}\right]\frac{100}{P} \tag{7.11}$$

Example 7.4. A floater is trading at a price of \$98.75. It has one year and nine months to maturity. If we assume a 30/360 day-count convention, the time to maturity is 1.75 years. The quoted margin is 75 basis points.

$$\text{Simple Margin} = \left[\frac{100 \times (100 - 98.75)}{1.75} + 75\right] = 146.43 \text{ basis points}$$

$$\text{Modified Simple Margin} = \left[\frac{100 \times (100 - 98.75)}{1.75} + 75\right] \times \frac{100}{98.75}$$
$$= 148.28 \text{ basis points}$$

Adjusted Simple Margin

Bond dealers fund the bulk of their inventory with borrowed money. The funding transaction usually entails the execution of a repurchase agreement or repo. The funding cost must be incorporated to compute what is termed as the adjusted price. It should be noted that the bond holder earns a return in terms of the coupon and incurs a cost in terms of the repo rate. Let A be the number of days from settlement to the next coupon date, and B the number of days in the coupon period. If we assume a 30/360 day-count convention and that there are 1.75 years to maturity, $A = 90$ and $B = 180$. Thus the bond must be financed for 90 days; the accrued interest is for 90 days; and on the next coupon date, a half-year's coupon is paid out. The adjusted price is defined as

$$P_A = (P + AI) + \frac{(P + AI) \times r \times \frac{90}{360} - c \times 100 \times \frac{180}{360}}{(1 + i \times \frac{90}{360})} \tag{7.12}$$

In this equation, c is the coupon rate, r is the repo rate, and i is the current discount rate.[3] The numerator of the second term represents the net cash flow at the time of the next coupon. We have to discount it to find the present value.

$$\text{Adjusted Simple Margin} = \left[\frac{100 \times (100 - P_A)}{T_m} + \text{Quoted Margin}\right] \frac{100}{P_A} \tag{7.13}$$

Let's illustrate the calculation with the help of an example.

Example 7.5. Let's use the data given in Example 7.4. The clean price is \$98.75. Assume the coupon rate is 6% per annum and the repo rate is 5.40% per annum. Assume that the current 3-M LIBOR is 5.70% per annum. There are 1.75 years until expiration, which means that 90 days of interest has accrued. The accrued interest is

$$100 \times 0.03 \times 0.5 = \$1.50$$

Thus the dirty price is \$100.25. The funding cost is $100.25 \times 0.054 \times 0.25 = \$1.3534$ The coupon for six months is \$3.00. So, the adjusted price is

$$P_A = 98.75 + 1.5 + \frac{1.3534 - 3.00}{(1 + 0.057 \times 0.25)} = \$98.6265$$

The effective margin can be computed by substituting the adjusted price in the formula for the modified simple margin:

$$\begin{aligned}\text{Adjusted Simple Margin} &= \left[\frac{100 \times (100 - 98.6265)}{1.75} + 75\right] \times \frac{100}{98.6265} \\ &= 155.62 \text{ basis points}\end{aligned}$$

Adjusted Total Margin

This margin measure incorporates the interest earned by investing the difference between the bond's face value and the adjusted price as computed in the preceding section. The interest is assumed to be based on the prevailing value of the reference rate. Here is an example.

3 If the benchmark is the 3-M LIBOR, then i is the current value of the 3-M LIBOR.

Example 7.6. Adjusted Total Margin

$$= \left[\frac{100 \times (100 - P_A)}{T_m} + \text{Quoted Margin} + 100 \times (100 - P_A) \times r\right] \frac{100}{P_A}$$

We have assumed the 3-M LIBOR to be 5.70%. Thus the interest

$$= 100 \times (100 - P_A) \times 0.057 = 100 \times (100 - 98.6265) \times 0.057 = 7.8290$$

And the adjusted total margin is

$$= \left[\frac{100 \times (100 - 98.6265)}{1.75} + 75 + 7.8290\right] \times \frac{100}{98.6265}$$
$$= 163.56 \text{ basis points}$$

The Discount Margin

The discount margin is based on a set of assumptions and arrived at by a process of trial and error, although with Excel, it is a fairly easy task. The first assumption is about the evolution of LIBOR, which we can assume is the reference rate, over the life of the security. The common practice is to assume that the current LIBOR will be applicable for all future periods. Based on this assumption, and given the quoted margin, we can project the cash flows over the life of the security. We then need to assume a margin for discounting and add it to the current LIBOR. This rate is used to discount all the remaining cash flows. Typically the present value that we obtain is either lower or higher than the actual price. If it is lower, we need to assume a lower discount margin and repeat the process. On the other hand, if it is higher, we need to repeat the procedure by assuming a higher value. Obviously, if the security is trading at par on a coupon date, the discount margin is equal to the quoted margin.

Let's revisit the data used in Example 7.5.

Example 7.7. The dirty price is $100.25. The 3-M LIBOR is 5.70%, and the quoted margin is 75 bp. There are 1.75 years to maturity. Let's go 0.25 years ahead in time. We will get a cash flow of $3.225. The three remaining cash flows will be 3.225, 3.225, and 103.225. Assume the discount margin is 60 bp. The present value of the cash flows is

$$3.225 + \frac{3.225}{1.0315} + \frac{3.225}{(1.0315)^2} + \frac{103.225}{(1.0315)^3}$$
$$= \$103.4365$$

The value today is

$$\frac{103.4365}{(1.0315)^{0.5}} = \$101.8449$$

The actual price is $100.25. So we need a higher value. Using Goal Seek in Excel, we find the discount rate to be 7.2844% per annum. Given the current LIBOR of 5.70%, the discount margin is 158.44 basis points.

There are obviously certain limitations as far as the discount margin is concerned. It is based on the major assumption that the reference rate, which is 3-M LIBOR in our case, will remain constant for the life of the security. If we relax this assumption, the value changes.

Inflation Indexed Bonds

Many countries issue bonds, whose cash flows are determined by the prevailing inflation rates, such that the cash flow is higher for the holders, when the rate of inflation is high, and lower when the rate is low. The rationale is to ensure that, in real terms, as measured by the purchasing power of the cash flows, the rate of return is reasonably constant. In the U.S., the Treasury issues TIPS, or Treasury Inflation-Protected Securities.

There are two ways in which the cash flows from a bond can be adjusted. One way is by adjusting the coupons, keeping the face value constant. This is similar to the case of a floating rate bond, where if the inflation is high, the coupon is high, and vice versa. Such securities are termed *Coupon-Linkers* or *C-Linkers* for short. The alternative is to keep the coupon rate constant and adjust the principal periodically for inflation to get an adjusted principal. Every period coupons are paid on the adjusted principal. These securities are termed *Principal-Linkers* or *P-Linkers*. In either case, the cash flows per period are variable and related to the rate of inflation.

Although we generally expect cash flows to increase over time on account of inflation, there could be a rare deflationary situation, where inflation rates are actually negative. In such a situation, the adjusted principal, for a P-Linker, may be less than the original par value. In these cases, most governments state at the outset that they will pay back the original par value or the terminal adjusted principal, whichever is higher. Also, in the case of a C-Linker, if there is a sharp decline in the price level, and the inflation adjusted rate is negative, most issuers pay a coupon of zero.

Principal Linkers or P-Linkers

Let's illustrate the cash flows from a P-Linker with the help of an example.

Example 7.8. Consider a P-Linker with a face value of $1,000 and six years to maturity. The coupon is 7.50% per annum, paid annually. The values of the consumer price index (CPI) at various points in time are as depicted in Table 7.3.

The rate of inflation for a year is computed by dividing the index value at the end of the year by the corresponding value at the beginning of the year:

$$\pi_t = \left(\frac{CPI_t}{CPI_{t-1}} - 1 \right) \times 100$$

We can now derive the cash flows and the IRR for a P-Linker.

Table 7.3: Price index values & inflation rates.

Time	CPI	Inflation Rate
0	100.0000	–
1	110.0000	10.00%
2	115.5000	5.00%
3	122.4300	6.00%
4	112.6356	−8.00%
5	123.8992	10.00%
6	139.3866	12.50%

Table 7.4: Cash flows for a P-Linker.

Time	Adjusted Principal	Nominal Cash Flow	Real Cash Flow
0	1,000.00	(1,000)	(1,000)
1	1,100.00	82.5000	75
2	1,155.00	86.6250	75
3	1,224.30	91.8225	75
4	1,126.3560	84.4767	75
5	1,238.9920	92.9244	75
6	1,393.8660	1,498.4060	1,075
IRR		13.5871%	7.50%

Analysis

Let's define the index ratio for the year as I_t/I_0, that is, the ratio of the CPI at the end of the year and the CPI at the very beginning. The adjusted principal at the end of the year is the original principal of $1,000 multiplied by the index ratio. For instance, at the end of the third year, the CPI is 122.43, which means the index ratio is 1.2243. So the adjusted principal is $1{,}000 \times \frac{122.43}{100} = \$1{,}224.30$. The nominal cash flow for this year is $0.075 \times 1{,}224.30 = \$91.8225$. The real cash flow for this period is the nominal cash flow divided by the index ratio. In this case, it is $91.8225 \div [\frac{122.43}{100.00}] = \$75$.

This can be interpreted as follows. The inflation for the third year is 6%. The value of the cash flow in terms of period-2 prices is $\frac{91.8225}{1.06} = \$86.6250$. The value of this in terms of period-1 prices is $\frac{86.6250}{1.05} = \$82.50$. Finally, the value of this in terms of period-0 prices is $\frac{82.50}{1.10} = \$75$. If we denote the inflation for the year i as π_i, we need to discount the cash flow by:

$$\begin{aligned}&(1+\pi_1)\times(1+\pi_2)\times(1+\pi_3)\\&=\frac{I_3}{I_2}\times\frac{I_2}{I_1}\times\frac{I_1}{I_0}=\frac{I_3}{I_0}\end{aligned}$$

The terminal nominal cash flow is the final adjusted principal of $1,393.866 plus that year's coupon, which is 7.50% of this amount. The IRR of the nominal cash flows is 13.5871%. The real cash flows stay constant, and the IRR is equal to the coupon of 7.50% per annum.

Coupon Linkers or C-Linkers

Let's illustrate the cash flows from a C-Linker with the help of an example.

Example 7.9. Now let's consider the case of the C-Linker. The coupon every period is the rate announced at the outset plus the rate of inflation for the year. The coupon is calculated on the original principal of $1,000. That is, the principal stays constant, unlike in the case of the P-Linker, whereas the coupon varies from period to period.

Table 7.5: Cash flows for a C-Linker.

Time	Inflation Rate	Adjusted Coupon	Nominal Cash Flow	Real Cash Flow
0	–	–	(1,000)	(1,000)
1	10.00%	17.50%	175.00	159.0909
2	5.00%	12.50%	125.00	108.2251
3	6.00%	13.50%	135.00	110.2671
4	−8.00%	0.00%	0.00	0.00
5	10.00%	17.50%	175.00	141.2438
6	12.50%	20.00%	1,200.00	860.9149
IRR			13.4434%	7.1793%

Valuing a Risky Floater

In the case of a risk-free floater, the price resets to par on every coupon date because the required margin is always equal to the quoted margin. In the case of a risky floater, however, the required margin is usually different from the quoted margin, which has implications for its valuation.

The general formula for the price of a floating rate bond on a coupon date, when there are N periods until maturity, is[4]

$$P_0 = \frac{M(r_1 + QM)}{(1 + r_1 + DM)} + \frac{M(r_2 + QM)}{(1 + r_1 + DM)(1 + r_2 + DM)} + \text{---------}$$

4 r_i represents the benchmark rate for period i.

$$+\frac{M(r_{N-1}+QM)}{(1+r_1+DM)(1+r_2+DM)\ldots(1+r_{N-2}+DM)(1+r_{N-1}+DM)}$$
$$+\frac{M+M(r_N+QM)}{(1+r_1+DM)(1+r_2+DM)\ldots(1+r_{N-2}+DM)(1+r_{N-1}+DM)(1+r_N+DM)} \tag{7.14}$$

If $QM = DM, P_0 = M$. Both $r+QM$ and $r+DM$ should be interpreted in periodic terms. If the reference rate for a six-monthly period-i is LIBOR$_i$ per annum, $r_i + \text{QM} = \frac{\text{LIBOR}_i+QM}{2}$ and $r_i+\text{DM} = \frac{\text{LIBOR}_i+DM}{2}$. To value a floating rate bond, we have to make an assumption about the one period forward rates for the life of the security. In the case of a risk-free floater, the price on a coupon date is always equal to the par value, irrespective of whether the term structure is flat, upward sloping, or downward sloping, as we shall now demonstrate. Consider the LIBOR rates at a point in time, as depicted in Table 7.6. The first rate is the current one period spot rate, and the rest are one period forward rates for subsequent periods. Assume that the discount margin is equal to the quoted margin and is 50 bp. Assume that all rates are per annum and are reset once per annum.

Table 7.6: Cash flows for a floater trading at par when the yield curve is upward sloping.

Rate	LIBOR Value	Cash Flow	PV of Cash Flow
Spot rate for year 1	2.50%	30	29.1262
Forward rate for year 1–2	3.50%	40	37.3413
Forward rate for year 2–3	4.50%	50	44.4539
Forward rate for year 3–4	5.50%	60	50.3252
Forward rate for year 4–5	7.00%	1,075	838.7534
Bond Price			1,000.00

Pricing Equation

The price of the bond, given the assumed term structure, may be stated as follows.

$$\text{Price} = \frac{30}{(1.03)} + \frac{40}{(1.03)(1.04)} + \frac{50}{(1.03)(1.04)(1.05)} + \frac{60}{(1.03)(1.04)(1.05)(1.06)}$$
$$+\frac{1{,}075}{(1.03)(1.04)(1.05)(1.06)(1.075)} = \$1{,}000.00$$

Now assume a flat term structure where LIBOR is equal to 2.50% per annum for all periods.

Table 7.7: Cash flows for a risk-less floater when the yield curve is flat.

Rate	LIBOR Value	Cash Flow	PV of Cash Flow
Spot rate for year 1	2.50%	30	29.1262
Forward rate for year 1–2	2.50%	30	28.2779
Forward rate for year 2–3	2.50%	30	27.4542
Forward rate for year 3–4	2.50%	30	26.6546
Forward rate for year 4–5	2.50%	1,030	888.4870
Bond Price			1,000.00

Finally let's look at inverted term structure.

Table 7.8: Cash flows for a risk-less floater when the yield curve is downward sloping.

Rate	LIBOR Value	Cash Flow	PV of Cash Flow
Spot rate for year 1	7.00%	75	69.7674
Forward rate for year 1–2	5.50%	60	52.6547
Forward rate for year 2–3	4.50%	50	41.7894
Forward rate for year 3–4	3.50%	40	32.1457
Forward rate for year 4–5	2.50%	1,030	803.6428
Bond Price			1,000.00

Thus when the quoted margin is equal to the discount margin, a floater trades at par on a coupon date, irrespective of the assumed values for the forward rates.

Now let's consider a situation where the quoted margin is different from the discount margin:

$$P_0 = \frac{M(r_1 + QM)}{(1 + r_1 + DM)} + \frac{M(r_2 + QM)}{(1 + r_1 + DM)(1 + r_2 + DM)} + - - - - - - - - \\ + \frac{M(r_{N-1} + QM)}{(1 + r_1 + DM)(1 + r_2 + DM)\ldots(1 + r_{N-2} + DM)(1 + r_{N-1} + DM)} \\ + \frac{M + M(r_N + QM)}{(1 + r_1 + DM)(1 + r_2 + DM)\ldots(1 + r_{N-2} + DM)(1 + r_{N-1} + DM)(1 + r_N + DM)} \tag{7.15}$$

$$\Rightarrow P_0 = \frac{M(r_1 + DM)}{(1 + r_1 + DM)} + \frac{M(r_2 + DM)}{(1 + r_1 + DM)(1 + r_2 + DM)} + - - - - - - - - \\ + \frac{M(r_{N-1} + DM)}{(1 + r_1 + DM)(1 + r_2 + DM)\ldots(1 + r_{N-2} + DM)(1 + r_{N-1} + DM)} \\ + \frac{M + M(r_N + DM)}{(1 + r_1 + DM)(1 + r_2 + DM)\ldots(1 + r_{N-2} + DM)(1 + r_{N-1} + DM)(1 + r_N + DM)}$$

$$+\frac{M(QM-DM)}{(1+r_1+DM)}+\frac{M(QM-DM)}{(1+r_1+DM)(1+r_2+DM)}+-------$$
$$+\frac{M(QM-DM)}{(1+r_1+DM)(1+r_2+DM)\ldots(1+r_{N-2}+DM)(1+r_{N-1}+DM)}$$
$$+\frac{M(QM-DM)}{(1+r_1+DM)(1+r_2+DM)\ldots(1+r_{N-2}+DM)(1+r_{N-1}+DM)(1+r_N+DM)} \tag{7.16}$$

$$=M+\frac{M(QM-DM)}{(1+r_1+DM)}+\frac{M(QM-DM)}{(1+r_1+DM)(1+r_2+DM)}+-------$$
$$+\frac{M(QM-DM)}{(1+r_1+DM)(1+r_2+DM)\ldots(1+r_{N-2}+DM)(1+r_{N-1}+DM)}$$
$$+\frac{M(QM-DM)}{(1+r_1+DM)(1+r_2+DM)\ldots(1+r_{N-2}+DM)(1+r_{N-1}+DM)(1+r_N+DM)} \tag{7.17}$$

In this case, the price will be greater than par if the quoted margin is greater than the discount margin, and less than par if the former is less than the latter. However, the price is a function of the interest rate path that is assumed, as we shall now demonstrate. Let's first consider a flat term structure, such that all one-period rates are 2.50% per annum. Assume the quoted margin is 50 bp., and the discount margin is 75 bp. The details of the price computation are given in Table 7.9.

Table 7.9: Valuation of a floater whose quoted margin is less than its discount margin when the term structure is flat.

Rate	LIBOR Value	Cash Flow	Discount Rate	PV of Cash Flow
Spot rate for year 1	2.50%	30	3.25%	29.0557
Forward rate for year 1–2	2.50%	30	3.25%	28.1411
Forward rate for year 2–3	2.50%	30	3.25%	27.2553
Forward rate for year 3–4	2.50%	30	3.25%	26.3974
Forward rate for year 4–5	2.50%	1,030	3.25%	877.7825
Bond Price				988.6320

The present value of the annuity is:

$$\frac{2.5}{0.0325}\times\left[1-\frac{1}{(1.0325)^5}\right]=11.3680$$

$$1{,}000-11.3680=988.6320$$

Because the term structure by assumption is flat, the yield, as computed by the IRR of the cash flows, is also 3.25%.

Now let's consider an upward sloping term structure, with the same values for the discount margin and the quoted margin.

Table 7.10: Valuation of a floater whose quoted margin is less than its discount margin when the term structure is upward sloping.

Rate	LIBOR Value	Cash Flow	Discount Rate	PV of Cash Flow
Spot rate for year 1	2.50%	30	3.25	29.0557
Forward rate for year 1–2	3.50%	40	4.25	37.1616
Forward rate for year 2–3	4.50%	50	5.25	44.1349
Forward rate for year 3–4	5.50%	60	6.25	49.8464
Forward rate for year 4–5	7.00%	1,075	7.75	828.8463
Bond Price				989.0449

The present value of the annuity is

$$2.50 \times \left[\frac{1}{(1.0325)} + \frac{1}{(1.0325)(1.0425)} + \frac{1}{(1.0325)(1.0425)(1.0525)} + \frac{1}{(1.0325)(1.0425)(1.0525)(1.0625)} + \frac{1}{(1.0325)(1.0425)(1.0525)(1.0625)(1.0775)}\right]$$
$$= 10.9551$$

$$1{,}000 - 10.9551 = 989.0449$$

The yield, using the IRR function, is 5.2427%.

Duration of a Risky Floater

The formula for the duration of a risky floater is

$$D = (1-k) + \left[\frac{(1+y)}{y} - \frac{N-1}{[(1+y)^{(N-1)} - 1]}\right] \times \left[1 - \frac{M(1+r_1)}{P_0(1+y)^{(1-k)}}\right]$$

We have derived a general formula for the duration of a floater between coupon dates, in Appendix 7.1. The price of a risky floater on a coupon date is equal to the price of a risk-free floater plus the present value of an annuity. The face value of the riskless floater is M. The periodic cash flow from the annuity is $\frac{M(QM-DM)}{2}$, which we denote as A. y is the semiannual yield of the bond, which can be computed using the IRR function in Excel; r_1 is the semiannual coupon rate for the first period, which is equal to the benchmark at time 0 plus the quoted margin; and k is the time elapsed since the previous coupon. The market price P (the dirty price) of the floater on the next coupon date is expressed as

$$P_1 = M + \frac{A}{y}\left[1 - \frac{1}{(1+y)^{(N-1)}}\right]$$

If $A = 0$ (that is, the $DM = QM$), or in other words the bond is riskless, then $M \times (1 + r_1) = P_0 \times (1 + y)^{1-k}$. Hence the duration in this case is $(1 - k)$ semiannual periods, which is what we obtained earlier.

$(1-k) \geq 0$ and the second term, $[\frac{(1+y)}{y} - \frac{N-1}{[(1+y)^{(N-1)}-1]}]$, also cannot be negative, since it represents the duration of an $(N-1)$ period annuity. However, $[1 - \frac{M(1+r_1)}{P_0(1+y)^{(1-k)}}]$ may be less than zero if P_0 is very low, or in other words the quoted margin is much lower than the discount margin. Consequently, in such a situation, the duration may be negative.

For a perpetual risky floater, the duration is given by

$$(1 - k) + \frac{A(1 + y)^k}{P_0 y^2}$$

Example 7.10. Consider a floating rate bond with 0.10 half-years to the next coupon. The face value is \$1,000, and the coupon for the first semiannual period is 5.40% per annum. The yield is 9.60% per annum, and there are 10 coupons remaining in the life of the bond. That is, $N = 10$. The current market price is \$915.1262. We have assumed that

$$\frac{M(QM - DM)}{2} = \frac{1{,}000 \times \frac{300}{100 \times 100}}{2} = \$\,15$$

That is, the difference between the quoted margin and the discount margin is 3% or 300 basis points.

$$(1 - k) = 0.10; \quad \frac{1.048}{0.048} - \frac{9}{[(1.048)^9 - 1]} = 4.6884$$

$$\left[1 - \frac{M(1 + r_1)}{P_0(1 + y)^{(1-k)}}\right] = \left[1 - \frac{1{,}000(1.027)}{915.1262(1.048)^{0.10}}\right] = -0.1170$$

Thus the duration is $0.10 + 4.6884 \times -0.1170 = -0.4485$. In this case, the duration is negative, which signifies that as the yield declines, the price will also decline.

Chapter Summary

This chapter examined bonds whose coupons change from period to period, what are termed as floating rate or variable rate bonds. We also studied bonds known as inverse floaters and examined the relationship between floaters, inverse floaters, and plain vanilla bonds. We studied variants of simple floaters, in the form of bonds with call and put provisions, and bonds with caps, floors, and collars. We then derived formulas for the duration and convexity of riskless floaters. The next focus of attention was inflation-indexed bonds, both those for which the principal is linked to inflation, P-Linkers, and those for which the coupon is linked to inflation, C-Linkers. We then derived the valuation equation for risky floating rate bonds. We showed that while the value of a riskless floater is independent of the assumption made about the term structure of interest rates, risky floating rate bonds have a price that is dependent on the assumption about the term structure. The chapter concluded with the derivation of formulas for the duration of risky floating rate bonds, for both bonds with a finite maturity, and for perpetual bonds.

Appendix 7.1: Duration of a Risky Floater

We derive a general formula for the duration of a floater between coupon dates. The price of a risky floater on a coupon date is equal to the price of a risk-free floater plus the present value of an annuity. The face value of the riskless floater is M. The periodic cash flow from the annuity is $\frac{M(QM-DM)}{2}$, which we denote as A. y is the semiannual yield of the bond, which can be computed using the IRR function in Excel; r_1 is the semiannual coupon rate for the first period, which is equal to the benchmark value at the outset plus the quoted margin; and k is the time elapsed since the previous coupon. The market price P (the dirty price) of the floater on the next coupon date is expressed as

$$P_1 = M + \frac{A}{y}\left[1 - \frac{1}{(1+y)^{(N-1)}}\right]$$

The price at time $T - N + k$ is expressed as

$$P_0 = \frac{M(1+r_1) + \frac{A}{y}[1 - \frac{1}{(1+y)^{(N-1)}}]}{(1+y)^{(1-k)}}$$

Let's define $Z = \frac{A}{y}[1 - \frac{1}{(1+y)^{(N-1)}}]$

$$\frac{\partial P}{\partial y} = -(1-k) \times \frac{P_0 \times (1+y)^{(1-k)}}{(1+y)^{(2-k)}} + \frac{\partial Z}{\partial y} \times \frac{1}{(1+y)^{(1-k)}}$$

$$\frac{\partial P}{P\partial y} = -\frac{(1-k)}{(1+y)} + \frac{\partial Z}{P\partial y} \times \frac{1}{(1+y)^{(1-k)}}$$

$$\text{Duration} = -\frac{\partial P}{P\partial y} \times (1+y)$$

Thus in this case, the duration is

$$D = (1-k) - \frac{\partial Z}{P\partial y} \times \frac{1}{(1+y)^{(1-k)}} \times (1+y)$$

Z is an $N - 1$ period annuity. Its duration is given by

$$-\frac{\partial Z}{Z\partial y} \times (1+y) = \frac{(1+y)}{y} - \frac{N-1}{[(1+y)^{(N-1)} - 1]}$$

Thus

$$-\frac{\partial Z}{P\partial y}\times(1+y)=-\frac{\partial Z}{Z\partial y}\times(1+y)\times\frac{Z}{P}=\left[\frac{(1+y)}{y}-\frac{N-1}{[(1+y)^{(N-1)}-1]}\right]\times\frac{Z}{P}$$

And the duration of the risky floater is

$$\begin{aligned}D&=(1-k)+\left[\frac{(1+y)}{y}-\frac{N-1}{[(1+y)^{(N-1)}-1]}\right]\times\frac{Z}{P}\times\frac{1}{(1+y)^{(1-k)}}\\&=(1-k)+\left[\frac{(1+y)}{y}-\frac{N-1}{[(1+y)^{(N-1)}-1]}\right]\\&\quad\times\left[\frac{P_0(1+y)^{(1-k)}-M(1+r_1)}{P_0}\times\frac{1}{(1+y)^{(1-k)}}\right]\\&=(1-k)+\left[\frac{(1+y)}{y}-\frac{N-1}{[(1+y)^{(N-1)}-1]}\right]\times\left[1-\frac{M(1+r_1)}{P_0(1+y)^{(1-k)}}\right]\end{aligned}$$

Appendix 7.2: Duration of a Risky Perpetual Floater

The price of a perpetual floater is expressed as

$$P_0=\frac{M(1+r_1)+\frac{A}{y}}{(1+y)^{1-k}}$$

$$\frac{\partial P}{\partial y}=-\frac{(1-k)}{(1+y)^{2-k}}\times P_0(1+y)^{1-k}-\frac{\frac{A}{y^2}}{(1+y)^{1-k}}$$

$$\frac{\partial P}{P\partial y}=-\frac{(1-k)}{1+y}-\frac{A}{P_0y^2(1+y)^{1-k}}$$

$$\text{Duration}=-\frac{\partial P}{P\partial y}\times(1+y)=(1-k)+\frac{A(1+y)^k}{P_0y^2}$$

Chapter 8
Mortgage Loans

The biggest aspiration of many people in this world is to own a home of their own. And in many countries, particularly in the developed world, the right to own a home is considered to be virtually a fundamental right. However, buying a home is usually a very expensive proposition, and for most people it is probably the largest capital expenditure that they will make in their lifetime. Consequently most of the funds required to buy a home must be borrowed. A loan that is collateralized by real estate is called a *mortgage loan*. The lender is called the *mortgagee*, and the borrower is called the *mortgagor*. Thus, in return for providing the capital, the borrower mortgages the property to the lender. This is termed as a *lien*.

Important Mortgage-Related Terms

We will now discuss some commonly used terms pertaining to mortgage loans.

- Buy-down: This refers to a situation when the seller pays an amount to the lender so that the lender can give a loan at a lower rate and with a lower installment, usually for an initial period in an adjustable rate mortgage (ARM), which is a mortgage loan in which the rate is reset periodically. The seller may increase the price of the home to cover the buy-down.
- Conversion clause: The presence of such a clause in a mortgage loan permits the conversion of the loan from a floating rate to a fixed rate structure. An ARM may have such a provision to facilitate the conversion of the loan to a fixed rate mortgage. This is usually permitted at the end of the first adjustment period. At the time of conversion, the new fixed rate is set at the prevailing rate for fixed rate mortgages.
- Equity: This refers to the difference between the current value of the home and the outstanding balance on the loan.
- Points: A point or a discount point is equal to 1% of the principal. So if the principal is $250,000, two points are $5,000. Points may be charged in the case of both fixed rate and floating rate loans. These are charged to enable the lender to cover loan origination expenses or provide additional compensation. There could be situations where the money required to pay the points can be borrowed. This obviously increases the amount of the loan. Discount points are points that are voluntarily paid by borrowers in return for a reduced interest rate.

Risks in Mortgage Lending

Investors who invest in mortgage loans are exposed to four main risks. These are:

- Default risk

https://doi.org/10.1515/9781547400669-008

- Liquidity risk
- Interest rate risk
- Prepayment risk

Default Risk

Default or credit risk is the risk that the borrower will default. In western countries, for low-income families, government agencies provide the insurance. For such mortgages the risk is minimal because the insuring agencies are government sponsored. For privately insured mortgages, the risk depends on the credit rating of the insurance company. For uninsured mortgages, the risk obviously depends on the credit quality of the borrower.

Liquidity Risk

An asset is said to be liquid if there are plenty of buyers and sellers available. If an asset is actively traded, relatively large transactions can be put through without a significant impact on the price. In the absence of liquidity, large buy orders may send the price shooting up, whereas large sell orders may cause the price to come crashing down. One of the indicators of liquidity is the size of the bid-ask spread. The higher the degree of liquidity, the lower the spread is. Mortgage loans tend to be rather illiquid because they are large and indivisible. That is, one cannot sell a fraction of a loan. Thus, while an active secondary market exists for such loans, bid-ask spreads are large relative to other debt instruments.

Interest Rate Risk

The price of a mortgage loan in the secondary market moves inversely with interest rates, just like any other debt security. The lower the discount rate is, the higher the present value and vice versa. However, among debt securities, mortgages are more vulnerable to interest rate movements. This is because the loans are for long terms to maturity, and consequently the impact of an interest rate change on the price of the mortgage can be significant.

Prepayment Risk

Most homeowners pay off all or a part of their mortgage balance prior to the maturity date. As we have seen in the case of amortized loans, every monthly payment consists partly of a principal repayment, with the difference being the interest payment on the outstanding balance at the end of the previous month. This principal component is referred to as the scheduled principal for the month. However, at times the homeowner may pay more than what is scheduled. Payments made in excess of the scheduled principal repayments are called prepayments. Prepayments may occur for one of several reasons. First, borrowers tend to prepay the entire mortgage when they sell their home. The sale of the house may be due to

- A change of employment that necessitates moving
- The purchase of a more expensive home
- A divorce in which the settlement requires sale of the marital residence

Second, if market interest rates decline below the loan rate, the borrower may prepay the loan and refinance at a lower rate. Third, in the case of homeowners who cannot meet their mortgage obligations, the property will be repossessed and sold. The proceeds from the sale are used to pay off the mortgage in the case of uninsured mortgages. For an insured mortgage the insurance company pays off the balance. Finally, if the property is destroyed by an act of God, such as natural calamities, the insurance proceeds are used to pay off the mortgage. The effect of prepayments, irrespective of the reason, is that the cash flows from the mortgage become unpredictable. This is because the amount of principal received at the end of a month, depends on how much the borrower chooses to prepay in that month, which depends on both economic and non-economic factors.

Example 8.1. Carol Saunders has taken a mortgage loan for \$800,000. It is an eight-year mortgage with an interest rate of 8.40% per annum. Installments are due every year. At the end of the second year, that is, just after she has paid the second installment, the interest on housing loans drops to 7.20% per annum. The refinancing fee is 2.75% of the amount being refinanced. Her opportunity cost of funds is 6% per annum. That is, if she were to save a dollar, she could invest it at this rate. Is refinancing an attractive option for Carol? Assume she has enough funds to pay the refinancing fee, and that she therefore need not borrow this amount.

The annual installment due at the outset can be computed using the PMT function in Excel:

$$\text{Installment} = \text{PMT}(0.084, 8, -800000) = \$141{,}332.19$$

The principal outstanding after two installments can be computed using the PV function in Excel:

$$\text{Principal} = \text{PV}(0.084, 6, -141332.19) = \$645{,}508.52$$

If this is reamortized over six years using the new rate of 7.20% per annum, the new annual payment is

$$\text{Installment} = \text{PMT}(0.072, 6, -645508.52) = \$136{,}262.24$$

Thus she will save 141,332.19 – 136,262.24 = \$5,069.95 The present value of the savings can be computed using the PV function:

$$\text{Present Value} = \text{PV}(0.06, 6, -5069.95) = \$24{,}930.59$$

The cost of refinancing is = 0.0275 × 645,508.52 = \$17,751.48.

Because the cost of refinancing is less than the present value of the savings, refinancing is an attractive option. Now let's pose a related question. What is the threshold interest rate, below which refinancing becomes attractive? This may be determined as follows.

To be indifferent to refinancing, the present value of savings should be equal to the cost. Thus the present value of savings ought to be \$17,751.48. The periodic saving is = PMT(0.06, 6, −17751.48) = \$3,610. This implies that the corresponding annual installment on the loan should be \$141,332.19 − \$3,610 = \$137,722.19. The corresponding interest rate is given by

$$\text{Interest Rate} = \text{Rate}(6, -137722.19, 645508.52) = 7.5475\%$$

Thus if the mortgage rate were above 7.5475%, Carol would not refinance. At lower rates, it would be in her interest to refinance.

An alternative perspective is the following. The number of periods required to recover the refinancing cost from the periodic savings is = NPER(0.06, −5069.95, 17751.48) = 4.05 years. Thus if the borrower plans to remain in the home for at least four more periods, then refinancing is a beneficial option.

The Role of the Mortgage Rate in Prepayments

As we have seen, if the prevailing mortgage rate is significantly lower than the rate prescribed in the contract, many homeowners will refinance. The greater the difference between the two rates is, the greater the incentive to refinance. Refinancing is beneficial if the interest saving is greater than the cost of refinancing. The costs include legal expenses, repayment of origination fees, obtaining of fresh title insurance, and the value of the time expended in sourcing a fresh loan. The benefit from refinancing depends on the original loan rate. Assume the contract rate is 4.50% and that the prevailing rate is 3%. If we consider a principal of \$250,000, and 30 years to maturity, the monthly installment declines from \$1,266.71 to \$1,054.01, a change of −16.79%. However if the initial rate were 9.50%, and it declined by 150 bp, the monthly installment would change from \$2,102.14 to \$1,834.41, which represents a reduction of only 12.74%. Interest rates also impact prepayments for the following reason. If the mortgage rate is low, an existing mortgagor may use the opportunity to buy a bigger or more expensive home or move to an up-market locality. Such circumstances also cause borrowers to prepay.

The path taken by mortgage rates also has an impact on prepayment behavior. Let's consider two possible paths for a given value of the mortgage rate. Assume that in path-1, the rate declines from 6% per annum to 3% per annum, increases once again to 5.50%, and then falls to 3%. In path-2, it increases from 6% to 9%, and then falls to 3%. In the case of path-1, many borrowers will refinance when the rate falls from 6% to 3%. When the rate rebounds and falls again to 3% per annum, there are unlikely to be significant prepayments, because most borrowers seeking to benefit from lower rates would have already refinanced. In the case of path-2, however, there are likely to be significant prepayments when the rate declines from 9% to 3%. This phenomenon is termed as *prepayment burnout.*

Negative Amortization

In the case of some mortgage structures, there may be negative amortization. The term refers to a situation where the installment for a period is inadequate to pay the required interest for the period. Consequently the deficit gets added on to the outstanding balance, as a consequence of which the latter increases over time, unlike in the normal case when the outstanding principal steadily decreases. This can be illustrated with the help of an example.

Example 8.2. Consider a mortgage loan with a principal of $100,000 and a tenor of 12 months. The rate is 6% per annum. The monthly installment would have been $8606.64 had it been a plain vanilla mortgage. However, the terms of the loan stipulate that the monthly payment will be $250 for the first three months. The installment will then be revised and remain constant for the remaining life of the loan. The amortization schedule may be depicted as shown in Table 8.1.

Table 8.1: Illustration of negative amortization.

Time	Installment	Interest Component	Principal Component	Outstanding Balance
0				100,000.00
1	250.00	500.00	−250.00	100,250.00
2	250.00	501.25	−251.25	100,501.25
3	250.00	502.51	−252.51	100,753.76
4	11,476.59	503.77	10,972.83	89,780.93
5	11,476.59	448.90	11,027.69	78,753.24
6	11,476.59	393.77	11,082.83	67,670.41
7	11,476.59	338.35	11,138.24	56,532.17
8	11,476.59	282.66	11,193.93	45,338.24
9	11,476.59	226.69	11,249.90	34,088.33
10	11,476.59	170.44	11,306.15	22,782.18
11	11,476.59	113.91	11,362.68	11,419.50
12	11,476.59	57.10	11,419.50	0.00

As can be seen, during the first three months, the installment is inadequate to cover even the interest due. Hence the principal component is negative, and the unpaid principal is added on to the outstanding balance, which as a consequence, increases.

A lender may impose a cap on the negative amortization. For instance, assume that there is cap of 125% of the original loan amount. Thus if the original loan amount is $200,000, the cap on the outstanding balance is $250,000. If because of negative amortization, the balance reaches the limit, the monthly payment resets to fully amortize the loan over the remaining term to maturity. The concept of a payment cap, which puts a limit on the change in the installment from one period to the next, does not apply in such a situation.[1]

Other Mortgage Structures

The level payment mortgage, which entails a constant monthly payment for the life of the mortgage, is the simplest mortgage structure. In practice, other mortgage structures, with more complex features are possible. Let's discuss some of them.

Adjustable Rate Mortgages (ARMs)

In an adjustable rate mortgage, the interest rate is not fixed for the life of the loan, but is reset periodically. Thus the monthly payments rise if the interest rate at the time of resetting is higher than what it was previously and fall if the interest rate declines. The rate on such mortgages is linked to a benchmark such as LIBOR or the rate for Treasury securities. Example 8.3 illustrates such a mortgage loan, assuming that rates are reset at the end of every year.

Example 8.3. Consider a four-year loan with an initial principal of \$800,000. Payments are made annually, and the interest rate is reset every year. Assume that the benchmark is LIBOR, as is the mortgage rate. Assume that the values of LIBOR observed over the next three years are as shown in Table 8.2.

Table 8.2: Observed LIBOR rates.

Time	LIBOR
0	4.80
1	5.40
2	5.10
3	4.50

The installment for the first year is

$$= \text{PMT}(0.048, 4, -800000) = \$224{,}562.25$$

1 We study payment caps in detail later in this chapter.

The outstanding balance at the end of the first year is

$$= \text{PV}(0.048, 3, -224562.25) = \$613{,}837.75$$

The installment for the second year is

$$= \text{PMT}(0.054, 3, -613837.75) = \$227{,}097.96$$

The outstanding balance at the end of the second year is

$$= \text{PV}(0.054, 2, -227097.96) = \$419{,}887.02$$

The installment for the third year is

$$= \text{PMT}(0.051, 2, -419887.02) = \$226{,}137.31$$

The outstanding balance at the end of the third year is

$$= \text{PV}(0.051, 1, -226137.21) = \$215{,}163.95$$

The installment for the fourth year is

$$= \text{PMT}(0.045, 1, -215163.95) = \$224{,}846.33$$

The outstanding balance at the end of the fourth year is obviously zero. The PMT for the final year is the principal outstanding at the end of the third year, plus interest for the fourth year:

$$215{,}163.95 \times 1.045 = \$224{,}846.33$$

Table 8.3: Cash flows of an ARM.

Time	Installment	Interest Component	Principal Component	Outstanding Balance
0				800,000
1	224,562.25	38,400.00	186,162.25	613,837.75
2	227,097.96	33,147.24	193,950.72	419,887.02
3	226,137.31	21,414.24	204,723.07	215,163.95
4	224,846.33	9,682.38	215,163.95	0.00

In practice, the mortgage rate will be higher than the index rate, by a few percentage points, known as the *margin*. For instance, a lender may set the rate as LIBOR + 45 bp. In this case the margin is 45 basis points. Thus if LIBOR is at 3% currently, the rate is 3.45%. This is termed the *fully indexed rate*. The margin can vary depending on the perceived credit quality of the borrower. Thus more credit-worthy borrowers often pay lower rates in practice. Sometimes the initial loan rate can be set lower than what the index level warrants. For instance, if the rate is LIBOR + 45 bp, and the LIBOR is at 2.80%, the loan rate must be 3.25%. However, the lender may set the rate at, say, 2.60%. Such a discounted rate is termed a *teaser rate*, which as the name suggests, is an attempt to induce a potential borrower to take a loan. The teaser rate can be in effect until the first adjustment date, or even longer.

Option to Change the Maturity

In the case of certain adjustable rate mortgages, the borrower may be given the option to keep the monthly installment at the initial level and have the maturity date altered every time the rate is reset. Let's see the implications of this for the mortgage discussed in Example 8.3. In the example, the installment for the first year was $224,562.25. Assume the rate rises from 4.80% per annum to 8.40% per annum. The payment for the second year becomes

$$= \text{PMT}(0.084, 3, -613837.75) = \$239{,}910.70$$

However if we are given an option, we can continue to pay $224,562.25 per annum, and extend the maturity of the loan. The modified time period can be computed using the NPER function in Excel:

$$= \text{NPER}(0.084, -224562.25, 613837.75) = 3.2342 \text{ years}$$

Features of ARMs

Most lenders charge a lower interest rate for an ARM at the outset, as compared to a fixed-rate mortgage. Thus the initial financial burden on the new homeowner is lower. If rates do not change much, or decline sharply, the borrower stands to benefit as compared to a party who has availed of a fixed rate mortgage. However, the flip side is that the interest rates may rise, and the borrower then has to pay higher periodic installments.

The interest rate and consequently the monthly payment of an ARM resets periodically. The rate may change every month, quarter, year, or even longer periods. The time period between rate changes is called the *adjustment period*. For instance, an ARM may have an adjustment period of 12 months. That is, the rate is reset once per annum.

Variations on the ARM Structure

Let's now discuss some alternatives to a simple ARM structure.

Hybrid ARMs: An N/1 ARM is a hybrid of a fixed rate and a variable rate mortgage loan. The rate remains fixed for the first *N* years, after which the loan assumes the feature of an adjustable rate mortgage. For instance, a 5/1 ARM means that the rate is fixed for the first five years. Thereafter the rate adjusts annually until the loan is paid off. A 30 mortgage loan may also be described as an *n*/30-*n* ARM, for instance a 4/26 ARM. This means that the rate remains fixed for the first four years, after which it becomes adjustable. Once the fixed rate period expires, the rate may be adjusted annually or at times even more frequently.

Interest-only or I-O ARMs: In the case of such an ARM, the borrower pays only interest for the first few years. This reduces the cash flow burden on the borrower. At the end of the initial period, the monthly payments increase, even if interest rates do not change, because the entire principal has to be repaid over a truncated period. The interest rate may or may not adjust during the initial (I-O) period. The longer the duration of the I-O period, the higher the periodic payment is after it ends, because the loan has to be repaid during a shorter period. Example 8.4 provides an illustration.

Example 8.4. Consider a 10-year mortgage loan for $800,000. For the first three years, the borrower has to pay interest at the rate of 5% per annum, on an annual basis. There is no scheduled principal repayment during this period. The entire principal will be repaid over the remaining seven years, after the end of the initial 3-year I-O period.

For the first three years, the payment is 800,000 × 0.05 = $40,000. If the interest rate remains constant at 5% per annum, the annual payment after three years becomes = PMT(0.05, 7, −800000) = $138,255.85. Had there been no I-O period, the payment after three years would have been = PMT(0.05, 10, −800000) = $103,603.66. If the I-O period were for five years, the payment after the initial interest-only period would be = PMT(0.05, 5, −800000) = $184,779.84.

ARMs with Payment Options: An ARM with a payment option allows the borrower to choose his payment option every month. There typically is a choice of three options:

- A conventional installment, comprised of principal and interest. This leads to a reducing balance at the end of every month.
- An interest-only option, which requires the payment of interest on the balance outstanding at the start of the month. With this option, the outstanding balance remains constant.
- A reduced installment option, wherein the borrower pays less than under a conventional mortgage. If the total payment is less than the scheduled interest for the period, there is negative amortization.

An ARM with a payment option will have a built-in recalculation period, usually every five years. At the end of the period, the payments are recalculated or recast based on the remaining term of the loan. For instance, assume that you have taken a loan of $250,000 to be repaid over 15 years in monthly installments. At the end of five years, the monthly installments are recalculated for the remaining 10 years. If there has been negative amortization in the first five years, there could be a significant increase in the magnitude of the installment. On each recast date, the new minimum payment becomes a fully amortizing payment over the remaining term of the loan. In such a situation, restrictions like payment caps, which put a limit on the increase in the periodic installment, do not apply.

For instance, consider a loan of $250,000 to be repaid over 15 years in equal monthly installments. Assume that the interest rate is 3% per annum. The installment amount is PMT(0.03/12, 180, −250000) = $1,726.45. If the outstanding balance after five years is $300,000, due to negative amortization, the recast installment becomes PMT(0.03/12, 120, −300000) = $2,896.82, assuming that the mortgage rate remains at 3% per annum. This represents an increase of 68%. It is important to understand that lenders do not allow outstanding balances to increase without limits. In practice, if the outstanding balance reaches a preset limit of say 125% of the original outstanding, the loan is automatically recast, irrespective of whether the scheduled recast period has been reached.

Interest Rate Caps

ARMs may come with interest rate caps. A cap places a limit on the amount that the interest can increase from one coupon reset date to another. There are two possibilities – we can have a periodic adjustment cap or a lifetime cap. A periodic adjustment cap places a limit on the amount that the interest rate can adjust up or down from one adjustment period to another, after the first adjustment. A lifetime cap puts a limit on the maximum interest rate over the life of the loan. In some countries, the law may mandate a lifetime cap.

Example of Interest Rate Caps

Consider a four-year mortgage loan with a principal of $250,000. The rate is equal to LIBOR + 1%. There is a periodic adjustment cap of 1% and a lifetime cap of 5%. The initial mortgage rate is 3%. Assume that the values of LIBOR are as shown in Table 8.4.

Table 8.4: Mortgage rates with and without rate caps.

Time	LIBOR	Rate without Cap	Rate with Cap
0	2.00	3.00	3.00
1	2.50	3.50	3.50
2	3.75	4.75	4.50
3	4.50	5.50	5.00

From period-0 to period-1, the rate increases by 0.50%. This is within the periodic limit of 1%. Also 3.50% is below the maximum permissible limit of 5%. In the absence of a periodic cap, the rate in the third year would have been 4.75%. However, because there is a periodic cap of 1%, it can be only 4.50%, or in other words, the rate for the previous year plus 1%. In the final year, the rate should be 5.50%. This is within the periodic cap of 1%, as compared to the rate for the previous year, which is 4.50%. However, because there is a lifetime cap of 5%, the rate for the last year is 5%.

Carryovers

In certain cases, if the lender cannot increase the rate because of the presence of a rate cap, it can carry over the increase that was not imposed to future periods. This is termed as a *carryover*. For instance, assume that the initial rate is 5%. The LIBOR at the end of the first year is 6.25%. However there is a periodic cap of 0.75%, as a consequence of which the rate for the second year is capped at 5.75%. If the LIBOR for the third year remains unchanged at 5.75%, the rate under normal circumstances ought to remain at 5.75%. However, because there is a *carryover* of 0.50% from the previous year, which is the uncapped rate of 6.25% less the capped rate of 5.75%, the rate for the third year is adjusted to 6.25%.

Payment Caps

A payment cap imposes an upper limit on how much the installment can change from one year to the next. In practice, unlike rate caps, these can lead to negative amortization. Here is an example.

Consider a loan of $250,000 to be repaid in five equal annual installments. Assume that the initial LIBOR is 4%. The payment for the first year is = PMT(0.04, 5, −250000) = $56,156.78. Assume that at the end of the first year, the LIBOR increases to 7.50%. However there is a payment cap of 5%. The outstanding balance at the end of the first year is = PV(0.04, 4, −56156.78) = $203,843.22. The uncapped installment for the second year is = PMT(0.075, 4, −203843.22) = $60,860.96. However, the installment is capped at 56,156.78 × 1.05 = $58,964.62. The interest due for the second year is = 203,843.22 × 0.075 = $15,288.24. Because the capped installment is higher, there is no negative amortization in this illustration.

Graduated Payment Mortgages

Young home buyers may not have the disposable income required to take advantage of a conventional fixed rate mortgage. However, many people in this age bracket have the potential to earn substantially more in the coming years. To encourage such parties to take loans, the graduated payment mortgage was designed. Such a mortgage starts with a level of payment that steadily increases every year up to a point and then remains steady thereafter. We can illustrate it with the help of an example.

Example 8.5. Maureen Toohey is being offered a mortgage loan by Tennessee National Bank with the following terms. She has to repay the loan in eight annual installments. The annual payment increases by 5% for the first three years and remains constant thereafter. The mortgage rate is 7.20% per annum for a loan amount of $800,000. What does the payment schedule look like?

Let's denote the annual payment for the first year by A. The first four payments are A; $1.05A$; $(1.05)^2A$; and $(1.05)^3A$. The next four payments are $(1.05)^3A$, which constitute a four-year annuity. The loan amount is the present value of these eight payments.

$$800{,}000 = \frac{A}{1.072} + \frac{1.05A}{(1.072)^2} + \frac{1.1025A}{(1.072)^3} + \frac{1.157625A}{(1.072)^4} + \frac{\frac{1.157625A}{0.072}\left[1 - \frac{1}{(1.072)^4}\right]}{(1.072)^4}$$

$$\Rightarrow 800{,}000 = 6.5738A$$

$$\Rightarrow A = \$121{,}695.21$$

Thus the payments over the eight-year period are as depicted in Table 8.5.

Table 8.5: Installments for the graduated payment mortgage.

Year	Cash Flow
1	121,695.21
2	127,779.98
3	134,168.97
4	140,877.42
5	140,877.42
6	140,877.42
7	140,877.42
8	140,877.42

Growing Equity Mortgages

There are certain similarities between a graduated payment mortgage, and a growing equity mortgage, although there are key differences. In both cases the monthly payments are scheduled to increase over time. However, in a graduated payment mortgage, there could be negative amortization for an initial period. In contrast, the first period's payment for a growing equity mortgage is the same as that of a traditional fixed rate mortgage. Increases in the periodic payments constitute prepayments, which directly amortize the principal. Thus the term of the mortgage and the total interest payable decreases.

A Comparison of the Three Mortgage Structures

Let's consider the following data to make a comparison between the three mortgage structures. The mortgage rate is 7.20% per annum for a loan amount of $800,000, to be repaid over a period of eight years. Let's assume that the annual payment increases by 5% every year for the graduated payment, as well as the growing equity mortgages.

Table 8.6: Cash flows for a graduated payment mortgage vs. that for a growing equity mortgage.

Yr.	Int. for FRM	Pri. for FRM	Int. for GPM	Pri. for GPM	Int. for GEM	Pri. for GEM
1	57,600.00	77,414.42	57,600.00	57,539.39	57,600.00	77,414.42
2	52,026.16	82,988.26	53,457.16	67,439.19	52,026.16	89,738.98
3	46,051.01	88,963.42	48,601.54	78,339.63	45,564.95	103,288.45
4	39,645.64	95,368.78	42,961.09	90,327.15	38,128.19	118,167.89
5	32,779.09	102,235.33	36,457.53	103,495.11	29,620.10	134,490.78
6	25,418.14	109,596.28	29,005.89	117,944.39	19,936.76	152,379.66
7	17,527.21	117,487.21	20,513.89	133,783.90	8,965.43	124,519.83
8	9,068.13	125,946.29	10,881.45	151,131.23	0.00	0.00
Total	280,115.39		299,478.60		251,841.59	

Yr. stands for year.
Int. stands for the interest payment.
Pri. stands for principal payment.
FRM stands for fixed rate mortgage.
GPM stands for graduated payment mortgage.
GEM stands for growing equity mortgage.

Table 8.7: Outstanding balances for the three mortgage structures.

Time	Outstanding Balance for FRM	Outstanding Balance for GPM	Outstanding Balance for GEM
0	800,000.00	800,000.00	800,000.00
1	722,585.58	742,460.61	722,585.58
2	639,597.31	675,021.42	632,846.59
3	550,633.90	596,681.79	529,558.15
4	455,265.12	506,354.64	411,390.26
5	353,029.78	402,859.53	276,899.49
6	243,433.50	284,915.14	124,519.83
7	125,946.29	151,131.23	0.00
8	0.00	0.00	0.00

FRM stands for fixed rate mortgage.
GPM stands for graduated payment mortgage.
GEM stands for growing equity mortgage.

Let's do a year-by-year analysis to illustrate the concepts.

Year 1

Total outstanding at the beginning of the year for all three mortgages = $800,000
Interest component for all three mortgages = 800,000 × 0.072 = $57,600
Total installment for FRM and GEM = $135,014.42
Total installment for GPM = $115,139.39
Principal component for FRM and GEM = 135,014.42 – 57,600 = $77,414.42
Principal component for GPM = $57,539.39
Total outstanding for FRM and GEM at the end of the year = $722,585.58
Total outstanding for GPM at the end of the year = $742,460.61

Year 2

Interest component for FRM and GEM = $52,026.16
This is because the outstanding balance at the end of the previous period was the same for both.
Interest component for GPM = $53,457.16
Total installment for FRM = $135,014.42, which is obviously a constant for every period.
Total installment for GEM = 135,014.42 × 1.05 = $141,765.14
Total installment for GPM = 115,139,39 × 1.05 = $120,896.36
Principal component for FRM = 135,014.42 – 52,026.16 = $82,988.26
Principal component for GEM == 141,765.14 – 52,026.16 = $89,738.98
Principal component for GPM == 120,896.36 – 53,457.16 = $67,439.20
Total outstanding for FRM at the end of the year = $639,597.31
Total outstanding for GEM at the end of the year = $632,846.59
Total outstanding for GPM at the end of the year = $675,021.42

Year 3

Interest component for FRM = $46,051.01
Interest component for GEM = $45,564.95
Interest component for GPM = $48,601.54
Total installment for FRM = $135,014.42
Total installment for GEM = 141,765.14 × 1.05 = $148,853.40
Total installment for GPM = 120,896.36 × 1.05 = $126,941.18
Principal component for FRM = 135,014.42 – 46,051.01 = $88,963.42
Principal component for GEM == 148,853.40 – 45,564.95 = $103,288.45
Principal component for GPM == 126,941.18 – 48,601.54 = $78,339.63
Total outstanding for FRM at the end of the year = $550,633.90
Total outstanding for GEM at the end of the year = $529,558.15
Total outstanding for GPM at the end of the year = $596,681.79

Year 4

Interest component for FRM = \$39,645.64
Interest component for GEM = \$38,128.19
Interest component for GPM = \$42,961.09
Total installment for FRM = \$135,014.42
Total installment for GEM = 148,853.40 × 1.05 = \$156,296.07
Total installment for GPM = 126,941.18 × 1.05 = \$133,288.23
Principal component for FRM = 135,014.42 – 39,645.64 = \$95,368.78
Principal component for GEM == 156,296.07 – 38,128.19 = \$118,167.89
Principal component for GPM == 133,228.23 – 42,961.09 = \$90,327.15
Total outstanding for FRM at the end of the year = \$455,265.12
Total outstanding for GEM at the end of the year = \$411,390.26
Total outstanding for GPM at the end of the year = \$506,354.64

Year 5

Interest component for FRM = \$32,779.09
Interest component for GEM = \$29,620.10
Interest component for GPM = \$36,457.53
Total installment for FRM = \$135,014.42
Total installment for GEM = 156,296.07 × 1.05 = \$164,110.88
Total installment for GPM = 133,288.23 × 1.05 = \$139,952.65
Principal component for FRM = 135,014.42 – 32,779.09 = \$102,235.33
Principal component for GEM == 164,110.88 – 29,620.10 = \$134,490.78
Principal component for GPM == 139,952.65 – 36,457.53 = \$103,495.11
Total outstanding for FRM at the end of the year = \$353,029.78
Total outstanding for GEM at the end of the year = \$276,899.49
Total outstanding for GPM at the end of the year = \$402,859.53

Year 6

Interest component for FRM = \$25,418.14
Interest component for GEM = \$19,936.76
Interest component for GPM = \$29,005.89
Total installment for FRM = \$135,014.42
Total installment for GEM = 164,110.88 × 1.05 = \$172,316.42
Total installment for GPM = 139,952.65 × 1.05 = \$146,950.28
Principal component for FRM = 135,014.42 – 25,418.14 = \$109,596.28
Principal component for GEM == 172,316.42 – 19,936.76 = \$152,379.66
Principal component for GPM == 146,950.28 – 29,005.89 = \$117,944.39

Total outstanding for FRM at the end of the year = $243,433.50
Total outstanding for GEM at the end of the year = $124,519.83
Total outstanding for GPM at the end of the year = $284,915.14

Year 7

Interest component for FRM = $17,527.21
Interest component for GEM = $8,965.43
Interest component for GPM = $20,513.89
Total installment for FRM = $135,014.42
Total installment for GEM = $133,485.26
This represents the outstanding of $124,519.83 plus $8,965.43 by way of interest.
Total installment for GPM = 146,950.28 × 1.05 = $154,297.79
Principal component for FRM = 135,014.42 – 17,527.21 = $117,487.21
Principal component for GEM == 133,485.26 – 8,965.43 = $124,519.83
Principal component for GPM == 154,297.79 – 20,513.89 = $133,783.90
Total outstanding for FRM at the end of the year = $125,946.29
Total outstanding for GEM at the end of the year = 0.00
Total outstanding for GPM at the end of the year = $151,131.23

Year 8

Interest component for FRM = $9,068.13
Interest component for GPM = $10,881.45
Total installment for FRM = $135,014.42
Total installment for GPM = 154,297.79 × 1.05 = $162,012.68
Principal component for FRM = 135,014.42 – 9,068.13 = $125,946.29
Principal component for GPM == 162,012.68 – 10,881.45 = $151,131.23
Total outstanding for FRM at the end of the year = 0.00
Total outstanding for GPM at the end of the year = 0.00

Mortgage Servicing

A mortgage loan has to be serviced. Servicing a mortgage loan includes the following activities:

- Collection of monthly payments and forwarding the proceeds to the current owner of the loan. Remember, mortgage loans can be sold in the secondary market, and consequently the current owner need not be the original owner.
- Sending payment notices to mortgagors. Mortgage loans are typically paid in monthly installments. Consequently a payment notice has to be sent at monthly intervals.

- Reminding mortgagors whose payments are overdue. If the monthly installment is not paid by the due date, an overdue notice has to be sent.
- Maintaining records of principal balances. Every installment consists of an interest component and a principal component. Consequently, at the time of receipt of each monthly payment, the outstanding principal has to be computed.
- Administering escrow balances for real estate taxes and insurance purposes. An escrow account is a trust account held in the name of the homeowner to pay statutory levies like property taxes and insurance premiums. The maintenance of such an account helps ensure that the payments are made when due, for it becomes the lender's responsibility to do so. Usually, the borrower makes deposits on a monthly basis, along with the loan payment, and the payments accrue at the lender. The amount required to be deposited every month is a function of the cost of insurance and the tax assessment of the property concerned. Consequently, it fluctuates from year to year, because both the insurance premium and the property tax vary over time. The servicer earns interest on such payments.
- Initiating foreclosure proceedings if necessary. If the borrower defaults on the payment obligation, the lender can seize the property in order to recover what is due. This is termed as the *right of foreclosure*.
- Furnishing tax information to mortgagors when applicable. In most countries the interest payments on the mortgage loan during the course of a financial year, as well as a percentage of the principal that is repaid during the year, are eligible for an income tax benefit. Consequently it is a common practice to provide the borrower with an annual statement that includes the total interest payment made during the year and the total principal repaid in that year.

Income for the Servicer

The primary source of income is the servicing fee, which is a fixed percentage of the outstanding mortgage balance. Because the mortgage loan is an amortized loan, where the outstanding principal declines with each payment, the revenue from servicing, declines over time. The typical servicing fee could be in the range of 25 to 50 basis points per annum. The servicer also earns interest on the escrow balances. Servicing rights can be traded in the market.

Because the servicer gets a servicing fee, the lender in a mortgage loan gets only a reduced percentage of the interest payment on the mortgage loan. This is termed *net interest.*

Example 8.6. Consider a mortgage loan of $100,000 to be repaid in four equal annual installments. The interest rate is 6% per annum, and the servicing fee is 0.50% per annum. The amortization schedule is depicted in Table 8.8.

Table 8.8: Amortization schedule with a servicing fee.

Time	Inst.	Int.	Ser.	Net.	Prin.	Outst.
0						100,000.00
1	28,859.15	6,000.00	500.00	5,500.00	22,859.15	77,140.85
2	28,859.15	4,628.45	385.70	4,242.75	24,230.70	52,910.15
3	28,859.15	3,174.61	264.55	2,910.06	25,684.54	27,225.61
4	28,859.15	1,633.54	136.13	1,497.41	27,225.61	0.00

Inst. stands for installment.
Int. stands for interest component.
Ser. stands for servicing fee.
Net. stands for net interest.
Prin. stands for principal component.
Outst. stands for outstanding balance.

Computing the Servicing Fee and the Net Interest Using the IPMT Function

The scheduled outstanding at the beginning of "period t" is

$$\frac{A}{r}\left[1 - \frac{1}{(1+r)^{N-t}}\right]$$

The interest component is

$$A \times \left[1 - \frac{1}{(1+r)^{N-t}}\right]$$

Let's denote the servicing fee percentage by s and the net interest percentage by i. Therefore, $r = s + i$. If we multiply the outstanding balance at the beginning of the period by s, we get the servicing fee as $\frac{As}{r}[1 - \frac{1}{(1+r)^{N-t}}]$ and the net interest as $\frac{Ai}{r}[1 - \frac{1}{(1+r)^{N-t}}]$. The sum of the two is equal to

$$\frac{A(s+i)}{r}\left[1 - \frac{1}{(1+r)^{N-t}}\right] = A \times \left[1 - \frac{1}{(1+r)^{N-t}}\right]$$

Thus the gross interest for a period is equal to the sum of the servicing fee and the net interest.

Now let's consider the data in Example 8.6. If we compute the servicing fee for the first period as = IPMT(0.005, 1, 4 − 0, −100000), we get $500.00, and similarly if we compute the net interest as = IPMT(0.055, 1, 4 − 0, −100000), we get $5,500. The total of the two is the gross interest of $6,000. Similarly, for the second month the servicing fee = IPMT(0.005, 1, 4−1, −77140.85) = $385.70, and the net interest = PMT(0.055, 1, 4−1, −77140.85) = $4,242.75. The sum of the two is equal to the gross interest of $4,628.45.

Consequently if we use the IPMT function to compute the servicing fee and net interest, we have to specify PER as 1, NPER as the remaining number of periods, and the PV as the outstanding balance at the end of the previous period.

Mortgage Insurance

There are two types of mortgage-related insurance. The first type, required by the lender to insure against default by the borrower, is called mortgage insurance or private mortgage insurance. It is usually required by lenders on loans with a *loan-to-value* (LTV) ratio that is greater than a specified limit. The amount insured is some percentage of the loan and may decline as the LTV declines. The loan to value ratio can be understood as follows. Every borrower has to make a down payment, which is the difference between the price of the property and the loan amount. That is, the percentage of the property value that is funded with borrowed money is less than 100%. The LTV ratio is obtained by dividing the loan amount by the market value of the property. The lower the LTV ratio, the greater is the protection for the lender in the event of default by the borrower.

The second type of mortgage-related insurance is acquired by the borrower, usually through a life insurance company, and is typically called *credit life*. This is not required by the lender. Such policies provide for the continuation of mortgage payments after the death of the insured person so that survivors can continue to live in the house.

Sale of Mortgage Loans

There are agencies that buy and pool mortgage loans and issue securities that are backed by the underlying pool. This phenomenon is termed as *securitization* and is examined in detail in the next chapter. Such agencies buy what they call *conforming mortgages*. A conforming mortgage is one that meets the underwriting criteria established by the agency, from the standpoint of being eligible to be included in a pool for the purpose of being securitized. A conforming mortgage must satisfy three criteria.

- A maximum *payment to income* (PTI) ratio. The PTI ratio is the ratio of monthly payments (the loan payment plus any real estate tax payments) to the borrower's monthly income. Obviously, the lower the ratio, the greater is the likelihood of the borrower being able to pay as scheduled. For the purpose of computing the PTI ratio, the normal practice is to take the income as the borrower's take-home salary. This gives a more conservative estimate, for the cost of the employee to the company is typically much higher.
- A maximum loan-to-value or LTV ratio.
- A maximum loan amount. Mortgages that are non-conforming because they are for amounts in excess of the purchasing limit set by these agencies are termed *jumbo* mortgages.

Certain mortgages may not meet the underwriting guidelines from the standpoint of credit quality or loan-to-value ratio. These are termed as *subprime* mortgages and have now become world famous for the wrong reasons.

The Average Life of a Mortgage Loan

Unlike a plain vanilla bond, which returns the entire principal as a bullet payment at the end, a mortgage loan pays back a portion of the principal as a part of every monthly installment. Thus the average life of a mortgage loan is less than its stated life. The average life is defined as

$$\sum_{t=1}^{N}(t \times PCF_t)/L$$

In this expression, PCF_t is the principal component of the cash flows at time t, and L is the loan amount. In the case of a mortgage loan that is repaid strictly as per schedule, that is, without any prepayments, the PCF is the principal component of the installment, or what is termed as the *scheduled principal*. However, if in a period there is a prepayment, the PCF is the sum of the scheduled principal and the prepayment. Quite obviously, the larger the prepayments, the shorter the average life becomes.

Let's illustrate the computation of average life with the help of an example.

Example 8.7. Consider a 15-month mortgage loan for an amount of $250,000. The interest rate is 7.20% per annum, and payments are made in 15 equal monthly installments. The payment schedule is presented in Table 8.9.

Table 8.9: Average life of a mortgage loan in the absence of pre-payments.

Time	Installment	Interest Component	Principal Component	Outstanding Balance
0				250,000.00
1	17,477.83	1,500.00	15,977.83	234,022.17
2	17,477.83	1,404.13	16,073.70	217,948.47
3	17,477.83	1,307.69	16,170.14	201,778.33
4	17,477.83	1,210.67	16,267.16	185,511.17
5	17,477.83	1,113.07	16,364.76	169,146.40
6	17,477.83	1,014.88	16,462.95	152,683.45
7	17,477.83	916.10	16,561.73	136,121.72
8	17,477.83	816.73	16,661.10	119,460.62
9	17,477.83	716.76	16,761.07	102,699.55
10	17,477.83	616.20	16,861.63	85,837.91
11	17,477.83	515.03	16,962.80	68,875.11
12	17,477.83	413.25	17,064.58	51,810.53
13	17,477.83	310.86	17,166.97	34,643.56
14	17,477.83	207.86	17,269.97	17,373.59
15	17,477.83	104.24	17,373.59	0.00

Assume the data for column 1 of the table is in cells A2 to A17 of the Excel sheet, and the data for the principal component of an installment is in cells D3 to D17. The average life can be computed using the SUMPRODUCT function in Excel.

Average life = SUMPRODUCT(A3:A17,D3:D17) = 8.11.

Thus this loan has an average life of 8.11 months.

The various functions need to be invoked as follows:

- Payment = PMT(.072/12, 15, −250000)
- Interest = IPMT(.072/12, A3, 15, −250000)
- Principal = PPMT(.072/12, A3, 15, −250000)

PER will have a value of 1 when we compute IPMT and PPMT for the first month, 2 when we compute for the second month, and so on.

Prepayments of Principal

In practice, the cash flows from a mortgage loan are unpredictable, because most homeowners prepay at one or more stages during the life of the loan. Prepayments reduce the average life, and the higher the prepayment speed is, the shorter the average life. Thus, without making an assumption about prepayments, we cannot project the cash flows from a mortgage loan.

Single Month Mortality (SMM)

The single month mortality can be defined as:

$$\text{SMM}_t = \frac{(SP_t - L_t)}{SP_t}$$

SP_t is the scheduled outstanding principal at the end of month t. This is what the outstanding principal will be if there is no prepayment at the end of the month. L_t is the actual outstanding at the end of the month. The actual outstanding is less than the scheduled outstanding if there is a prepayment. The difference between the two constitutes the prepayment. We can rewrite the equation as

$$L_t = SP_t(1 - \text{SMM}_t)$$

Example 8.8. Consider a 15-month mortgage loan for an amount of $250,000. The interest rate is 7.20% per annum, and payments are made in 15 monthly installments. Assume that the SMM is 2.50% for all months. The payment schedule is presented in Table 8.10.

Table 8.10: Average life of a mortgage loan with prepayments.

Time	Inst.	Int.	Sch. Pr.	Sch. Out.	Prep.	Act. Out.
0				250,000		250,000
1	17,477.83	1,500.00	15,977.83	234,022.17	5,850.55	228,171.61
2	17,040.89	1,369.03	15,671.86	212,499.76	5,312.49	207,187.26
3	16,614.86	1,243.12	15,371.74	191,815.52	4,795.39	187,020.14
4	16,199.49	1,122.12	15,077.37	171,942.76	4,298.57	167,644.20
5	15,794.50	1,005.87	14,788.64	152,855.56	3,821.39	149,034.17
6	15,399.64	894.20	14,505.44	134,528.73	3,363.22	131,165.51
7	15,014.65	786.99	14,227.66	116,937.85	2,923.45	114,014.41
8	14,639.28	684.09	13,955.20	100,059.21	2,501.48	97,557.73
9	14,273.30	585.35	13,687.96	83,869.77	2,096.74	81,773.03
10	13,916.47	490.64	13,425.83	68,347.20	1,708.68	66,638.52
11	13,568.56	399.83	13,168.73	53,469.79	1,336.74	52,133.04
12	13,229.34	312.80	12,916.55	39,216.50	980.41	38,236.08
13	12,898.61	229.42	12,669.19	25,566.89	639.17	24,927.72
14	12,576.15	149.57	12,426.58	12,501.14	312.53	12,188.61
15	12,261.74	73.13	12,188.61	0.00	0.00	0.00

Inst. stands for installment.
Int. stands for interest component.
Sch. Pr. stands for scheduled principal.
Sch. Out. stands for scheduled outstanding.
Prep. stands for prepayment.
Act. Out. stands for actual outstanding.

Analysis of a Loan with Prepayments

Let's analyze the cash flows for the first two periods in Table 8.10. At the outset, the outstanding principal was \$250,000. The first installment is= PMT(0.072/12, 15, −250000), which is \$17,477.83. The interest is = IPMT(0.072/12, 1, 15, −250000) = \$1,500. The scheduled principal is = PPMT(0.072/12, 1, 15, −250000) = \$15,977.83. The scheduled outstanding is the previous actual outstanding minus the scheduled principal payment. In this case, it is \$250,000 − \$15,977.83 = \$234,022.17. The prepayment for the month is the scheduled outstanding times the SMM. In our example it is 234,022.17 × 0.025 = \$5,850.55. The actual outstanding at the end of the first month is the scheduled outstanding minus the prepayment. In our case it is \$234,022.17 − \$5,850.55 = \$228,171.61.

Now let's consider the second period. The actual outstanding at the end of the first period is \$228,171.61. The installment for the period is = PMT(0.072/12, 14, −228171.61), which is \$17,040.89. The interest is = IPMT(0.072/12, 1, 14, −228171.61) = \$1,369.03. The scheduled principal is = PPMT(0.072/12, 1, 14, −228171.61) = \$15,671.86. The scheduled outstanding is the previous actual outstanding minus the scheduled principal payment. In this case it is \$228,171.61 – \$15,671.86 = \$212,499.76. The prepayment for the month is the scheduled outstanding times the SMM. In our example it is \$212,499.76 × 0.025 = \$5,312.49. The actual outstanding at the end of the second period is the scheduled outstanding minus the prepayment. In our case it is \$212,499.76 – \$5,312.49 = \$207,187.26.

It can be seen that the three functions, PMT, IPMT, and PPMT, are invoked using the actual outstanding balance at the start of the period as the parameter PV. The scheduled outstanding balance is computed purely to facilitate the calculation of the pre-payment amount.

To compute the average life, we first need to compute the total principal repaid in a month. This is the sum of the scheduled principal for the month and the pre-payment for the month. Table 8.11 has the data.

Table 8.11: Total monthly principal with prepayments.

Time	Total Principal
1	21,828.39
2	20,984.35
3	20,167.13
4	19,375.94
5	18,610.03
6	17,868.66
7	17,151.10
8	16,456.68
9	15,784.70
10	15,134.51
11	14,505.47
12	13,896.96
13	13,308.37
14	12,739.11
15	12,188.61

Assume that the time period is in columns A2 to A16, and the total principal is in B2 to B16. Average life = SUMPRODUCT(A2:A16,B2:B16) = 7.23. In this illustration, the average life has come down from 8.11 months to 7.23 months.

Relationship between Cash Flows with and without Prepayments

Let's define the following variables:

- A is the constant periodic installment in the absence of prepayments.
- A_t is the installment payment in "period t" in the presence of prepayments.

- I^*_t is the interest payment in month t in the absence of prepayments.
- I_t is the interest payment in month t in the presence of prepayments.
- P^*_t is the principal payment in month t in the absence of prepayments.
- P_t is the scheduled principal payment in month t in the presence of prepayments.
- SP^*_t is the outstanding balance at the end of month t in the absence of prepayments.
- SP_t is the outstanding balance at the end of month t in the presence of prepayments.
- L_t is the actual outstanding at the end of month t in the event of prepayments.

The relationship between these variables are as follows. Additional details are given in Appendix 8.1.

$$A_t = A\prod_{i=1}^{t-1}[1 - \text{SMM}_i]$$
$$= A \times [1 - \text{SMM}]^{t-1} \text{ if } \text{SMM}_i = \text{SMM } \forall i$$

$$I_t = I_t^* \prod_{i=1}^{t-1}[1 - \text{SMM}_i]$$

$$P_t = P_t^* \prod_{i=1}^{t-1}[1 - \text{SMM}_i]$$

$$SP_t = SP_t^* \prod_{i=1}^{t-1}[1 - \text{SMM}_i]$$

$$L_t = SP_t \times [1 - \text{SMM}_t] = SP_t^* \prod_{i=1}^{t}[1 - \text{SMM}_i]$$

Example 8.9. Consider the data in Table 8.9 and Table 8.10. The former depicts the amortization schedule in the absence of prepayments, while the latter presents the cash flows in the presence of prepayments. The SMM is 2.50% for all months.

Let's consider the data for the sixth month to illustrate our arguments:

$A = \$17{,}477.83$; $A_6 = \$15{,}399.64$

$$A_6 = 17{,}477.83 \times (1 - 0.025)^5 = \$15{,}399.64$$

$I^*_6 = \$1{,}014.88$; $I_6 = \$894.20$

$$I_6 = 1{,}014.88 \times (1 - 0.025)^5 = \$894.20$$

$P^*_6 = \$16{,}462.95$; $P_6 = \$14{,}505.44$

$$P_6 = 16{,}462.95 \times (1 - 0.025)^5 = \$14{,}505.44$$

$SP^*_6 = \$152{,}683.45$; $SP_6 = \$134{,}528.73$

$$SP_6 = 152{,}683.45 \times (1 - 0.025)^5 = \$134{,}528.73$$
$$L_6 = 152{,}683.45 \times (1 - 0.025)^6 = \$131{,}165.50$$

Conditional Prepayment Rate (CPR)

Whereas the SMM is a monthly rate, the prepayment rate is often expressed in annual terms, as what is termed the *conditional prepayment rate* or the CPR. The mathematical relationship between the two is given by

$$CPR = 1 - [1 - SMM]^{12}$$

Example 8.10. The projected CPR for a mortgage loan is 7.20%. What is the corresponding SMM?

$$SMM = 1 - (1 - 0.072)^{\frac{1}{12}} = 0.006208 \equiv 0.6208\%$$

When we assume a CPR of $x\%$ per annum, it amounts to the assumption of a constant prepayment rate for the life of the mortgage. However, this is contrary to what is observed in reality. Borrowers usually do not sell their homes or refinance their mortgage loan when the loan is fairly new. With the passage of time, the propensity to sell or refinance increases, and so does the CPR, in a fairly linear fashion. After a certain period, the prepayment speeds flatten out and remain fairly constant. This is termed as *seasoning*.

The Public Securities Association, which is known today as SIFMA, created a PSA model for mortgage loans. The PSA divided the life of a mortgage loan into two distinct periods. The initial period of 30 months is referred to as the *ramp*. During this period, the CPR grows linearly at the rate of 0.2% per month, starting from a value of zero, until it attains a value of 6% at the end of the 30th month. After the 30th month, the mortgage is considered to be off the ramp, and the CPR is assumed to remain constant at 6%. This can be summarized as follows:

Let t be the number of months after the mortgage was originated. If $t \leq 30$, CPR = $6 \times \frac{t}{30}\%$. If $t > 30$, CPR = 6%. This is termed as 100 PSA.

So for the 12th month, the CPR = 2.40%. The SMM is $1 - (1 - 0.024)^{\frac{1}{12}} = 0.002022 \equiv$ 0.2022%. For months 31-360, the CPR is 6%, and the SMM is 0.5143%.

Faster and slower speeds can be assumed. For a particular month, 75 PSA, means that the CPR is 75% of what it would have been had the prepayment speed been 100 PSA. Similarly, 125 PSA means that the CPR is 125% of what it would have been under the assumption of 100 PSA.

So if we assume 75 PSA, the CPR in the 12th month is 1.80%, and for months 31-360, it is 4.50%. Similarly, if we assume 125 PSA, the CPR in the 12th month is 3%, and that in months 31-360 is 7.50%.

Note that if we assume a speed of X PSA, it means that the CPR for a month is X times what it would have been under 100 PSA. It does not mean that the SMM would be X times the SMM under 100 PSA.

An Equal Principal Repayment Loan

Sometimes a loan is structured in such a way that the principal is repaid in equal installments. This is an alternative to an amortized loan. Thus, the principal component of each installment remains constant. However, like in the case of the amortized loan, the interest component of each payment declines steadily, on account of the diminishing loan balance. Therefore, the total magnitude of each payment also declines.

Let's illustrate the payment stream for a four year loan of $100,000, assuming that the interest rate is 6% per annum.

Table 8.12: Payment schedule for an equal principal repayment loan.

Time	Interest	Principal	Total Payment	Outstanding Balance
0				100,000
1	6,000	25,000	31,000	75,000
2	4,500	25,000	29,500	50,000
3	3,000	25,000	28,000	25,000
4	1,500	25,000	26,500	0.00

If we denote the number of installments by N, the periodic principal amount is L/N. The interest for "period t" is

$$r \times \left[L - \frac{(t-1)L}{N}\right] = r \times \frac{L(N-t+1)}{N}$$

The outstanding principal at the end of "period t" is $L - \frac{LT}{N}$.

Weighted Average Coupon (WAC) and Weighted Average Maturity (WAM)

Although mortgage loans are extremely illiquid, they can be pooled in order to issue securities backed by the underlying pool. These are termed *mortgage-backed securities* MBS and can be extremely liquid. However, all the mortgages that constitute the pool do not have the same mortgage rate or time to maturity. Thus it is a common practice in the market for mortgage-backed securities to account for the weighted average coupon rate and the weighted average time to maturity. The weighted average coupon (WAC) of a mortgage pool is determined by weighting the mortgage rate of each loan in the pool by the principal amount outstanding. That is, the weight for each mortgage rate is the outstanding amount of that mortgage divided by the cumulative outstanding amount of all the mortgages in the pool. Similarly, the weighted average maturity (WAM) is found by weighting the remaining number of months to maturity of each of the loans in the pool by the principal amount outstanding. Let's illustrate the calculations, for a hypothetical pool.

Assume that four mortgages are being pooled. Mortgage-A has a life of 350 months and a coupon of 6.40%; mortgage-B has a life of 320 months and a coupon of 4.80%; mortgage-C has a life of 280 months and a coupon of 5.40%; and mortgage-D has a life of 300 months and a coupon of 5.70%. The current outstanding for loan-A is 100,000; loan-B is 200,000; loan-C is 300,000; and loan-D is 400,000. Thus the weights are 10%, 20%, 30%, and 40%.

$$\text{WAM} = 350 \times 0.10 + 320 \times 0.20 + 280 \times 0.30 + 300 \times 0.40 = 303 \text{ months}$$

$$\text{WAC} = 6.40 \times 0.10 + 4.80 \times 0.20 + 5.40 \times 0.30 + 5.70 \times 0.40 = 5.50\%$$

Chapter Summary

This chapter addressed the issue of mortgage loans. We started with a discussion on the risks inherent in such loans and the concept of loan refinancing. We studied alternatives to plain vanilla mortgages, such as adjustable rate mortgages (ARMs), graduated payment mortgages (GPM), and growing equity mortgages (GEM). In the context of ARMs, we introduced the concepts of rate and payment caps. The concept of the average life of a mortgage loan was explained. We then brought in the issue of prepayments, and introduced the concepts of single month mortality (SMM) and the conditional prepayment rate (CPR). The chapter concluded with a brief introduction to equal principal repayment loans.

Appendix 8.1

The single month mortality rate for a given month t, SMM_t is defined as:

$$\text{SMM}_t = \frac{SP_t - L_t}{SP_t}$$

where SP_t is the scheduled principal outstanding at the end of month t, and L_t is the actual principal outstanding at the end of month t.

Thus the actual principal at the end of month t is given by

$$L_t = SP_t[1 - \text{SMM}_t]$$

Consider a mortgage with N months to maturity, and a monthly interest rate of r. The original loan balance is given by

$$L_0 = \frac{A_1}{r} \times \left[1 - \frac{1}{(1+r)^N}\right]$$

where A_1 is the scheduled monthly installment for month 1. The scheduled principal at the end of the first month is given by

$$\begin{aligned} SP_1 &= L_0 - [A_1 - r \times L_0] \\ &= L_0 \times (1+r) - A_1 \\ &= \frac{A_1}{r}\left[1 - \frac{1}{(1+r)^{(N-1)}}\right] \end{aligned}$$

The actual balance at time 1 is given by

$$L_1 = SP_1[1 - \text{SMM}_1]$$
$$L_1 = \frac{A_2}{r} \times \left[1 - \frac{1}{(1+r)^{(N-1)}}\right]$$

where A_2 is the scheduled monthly installment for month 2.

$$\Rightarrow SP_1[1 - \text{SMM}_1] = \frac{A_2}{r} \times \left[1 - \frac{1}{(1+r)^{(N-1)}}\right]$$
$$\Rightarrow \frac{A_1}{r}\left[1 - \frac{1}{(1+r)^{(N-1)}}\right][1 - \text{SMM}_1] = \frac{A_2}{r} \times \left[1 - \frac{1}{(1+r)^{(N-1)}}\right]$$
$$\Rightarrow A_2 = A_1 \times [1 - \text{SMM}_1]$$

Similarly, it can be shown that

$$\begin{aligned} A_3 &= A_2 \times [1 - \text{SMM}_2] \\ &= A_1 \times [1 - \text{SMM}_1] \times [1 - \text{SMM}_2] \end{aligned}$$

In general, the scheduled monthly installment in month t is given by

$$A_t = A_1 \prod_{i=1}^{t-1}[1 - \text{SMM}_i]$$

If $\text{SMM}_i = \text{SMM} \forall i$, then

$$A_t = A_1 \times [1 - \text{SMM}]^{t-1}$$

Let's denote the monthly payment on the original principal in the absence of prepayments by A. Then we can state

$$\begin{aligned} A_t &= A \prod_{i=1}^{t-1}[1 - \text{SMM}_i] \\ &= A \times [1 - \text{SMM}]^{t-1} \text{ if } \text{SMM}_i = \text{SMM } \forall i \end{aligned}$$

In the absence of prepayments, the interest and principal components of "payment t" and the outstanding principal at the end of *t* periods are given by

$$I_t^* = A \times \left[1 - \frac{1}{(1+r)^{N-t+1}}\right]$$

$$P_t^* = \frac{A}{(1+r)^{N-t+1}}$$

$$SP_t^* = \frac{A}{r}\left[1 - \frac{1}{(1+r)^{N-t}}\right]$$

In the presence of prepayments, the actual principal outstanding at the end of $t-1$ is given by

$$L_{t-1} = \frac{A_t}{r} \times \left[1 - \frac{1}{(1+r)^{N-t+1}}\right]$$

Thus, in the presence of prepayments, the interest and principal components of the t th payment are given by

$$I_t = A_t \times \left[1 - \frac{1}{(1+r)^{N-t+1}}\right]$$

and

$$P_t = \frac{A_t}{(1+r)^{N-t+1}}$$

The scheduled principal at the end of the "period t" is given by

$$SP_t = \frac{A_t}{r}\left[1 - \frac{1}{(1+r)^{N-t}}\right]$$

We know that

$$A_t = \mathrm{A}\prod_{i=1}^{t-1}[1 - \mathrm{SMM}_i]$$

Thus

$$I_t = I_t^* \prod_{i=1}^{t-1}[1 - \mathrm{SMM}_i]$$

$$P_t = P_t^* \prod_{i=1}^{t-1}[1 - \mathrm{SMM}_i]$$

and

$$SP_t = SP_t^* \prod_{i=1}^{t-1}[1 - \mathrm{SMM}_i]$$

The actual principal at the end of t periods is given by

$$L_t = SP_t \times [1 - \text{SMM}_t]$$

$$\Rightarrow L_t = SP_t{}^{*} \prod_{i=1}^{t} [1 - \text{SMM}_i]$$

Chapter 9
Mortgage-Backed Securities

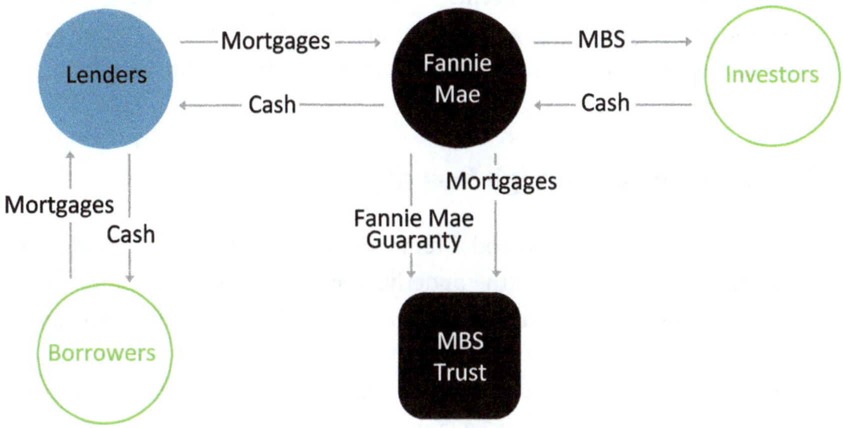

Figure 9.1: The process of securitization.

Mortgage loans are extremely illiquid. Besides, the lender faces significant exposure to credit risk as well as prepayment risk. Thus making a secondary market for whole loans is an extremely difficult proposition. However, it is possible to issue liquid debt securities that are backed by underlying pools of mortgage loans, known as *mortgage-backed securities* (MBS). That is, the cash flows stemming from the underlying loans are passed through to the holders of these debt securities, and hence the name pass-through. Each holder of a pass-through security is entitled to a prorata undivided share of each cash flow that emanates from the underlying pools, as and when the homeowners make monthly payments. Each monthly payment consists of an interest component, a principal component, and potentially an additional amount on account of prepayment. Any amount that constitutes a prepayment is termed an unscheduled principal, as opposed to the scheduled or expected principal repayment. Such pooling of multiple loans makes the issuance of a large quantity of mortgage-backed securities feasible, and consequently improves their liquidity. Also it facilitates the diversification of credit risk, and other risks such as geographic risks.

In the U.S. the Government National Mortgage Association (GNMA), which is a federal government entity, and quasi-government agencies such as the Federal National Mortgage Association (FNMA) and the Federal Home Loan Mortgage Corporation (Freddie Mac), issue mortgage-backed securities. These are termed as Ginnie Maes, Fannie Maes, and Freddie Macs in the market. There are also non-agency securities termed as *private label* securities. Agency passthroughs are a unique feature of the U.S. market, and equivalent examples may not be available in other markets.

https://doi.org/10.1515/9781547400669-009

GNMA guarantees the timely payment of principal and interest on securities that are issued by lenders approved by it. This guarantee enables the corresponding securities to be priced higher. It must be understood the GNMA does not acquire mortgage loans, and nor does it issue securities. In practice, private institutions, approved by GNMA, originate and pool loans and issue securities backed by them. The resulting securities are guaranteed by GNMA. FNMA purchases mortgage loans from big commercial banks, whereas Freddie Mac purchases loans from smaller banks and lenders.

Cash Flows for a Pass-Through Security

In practice, the cash flow that is passed through to investors in a given period is not equal to the payment received from the underlying pool. The monthly cash flow for a pass-through is less than the monthly cash flow from the underlying loans by an amount equal to the servicing and guaranteeing fees. Thus, the coupon rate on the pass-through is less than the mortgage rate of the underlying pool by an amount equal to the servicing and guaranteeing fees. Let's assume a servicing fee of 0.6% per annum and a guaranteeing fee of 0.6% per annum. If the mortgage rate is 9% per annum, the coupon rate of the pass-through is 7.80%. The examples in this chapter are generic in nature, and are not intended to illustrate the structure of an agency pass-through in the U.S.

The monthly cash flow consists of the net interest, which is the gross interest less the servicing and guaranteeing fees, the scheduled principal payment, and the prepayment.

The cash flow for the month is different from the total principal for the month, for the latter is the sum of the scheduled principal payment and the prepayment for the month. It does not include the net interest. The average life of a security is based on the total principal received. However, the price of a pass-through and its bond equivalent yield, which we define in the next section, are based on the cash flow stream. The mechanics of a pass-through are illustrated in Example 9.1.

Example 9.1. Consider a home loan with a principal of $500,000 and 15 months to maturity. The mortgage rate is 9% per annum. 500 securities backed by these loans have been created. These securities have been distributed as follows: 200 to Michael, 200 to Scott, and 100 to Maureen. These securities are identical in all respects, and the holder of a security is entitled to 0.2% of any cash flow that arises from the underlying loans.

As we mentioned in the chapter introduction, each holder is entitled to a pro rata undivided share of any cash flow. *Undivided* may be understood as follows. Michael owns 40% of the securities which are equivalent to 40% of the underlying collateral that is tantamount to one loan of $200,000. However, by virtue of the fact that he has 40% of the securities, it cannot be construed that Michael owns one underlying loan in its entirety. All that we can say is that Michael is entitled to 40% of each cash flow that emanates from the underlying pool.

The total cash flow for the first month, as shown in Table 9.1, is:

$$3{,}250 + 31{,}618.2 + 11{,}709.6 = \$46{,}577.80$$

Because 500 securities have been issued, the first month's cash flow is $93.16 per security. This consists of $6.50 of interest, $63.24 of scheduled principal, and $23.42 of unscheduled principal or pre-payment. Because Michael and Scott own 200 securities each, they each receive

$$200 \times 93.16 = \$18{,}632$$

Maureen has 100 securities, so she receives $9,316.

Now assume that at the end of the first month there is an additional pre-payment of $15,000. Each security is entitled to $30 extra. As Michael and Scott have 200 securities each, they receive an additional payment of $6,000, whereas Maureen receives an additional payment of $3,000.

Table 9.1: Cash flows for a pass-through security.

Time	Inst.	SFee	GFee	NINT	SPR	SOUT	PREP	AOUT
0						500,000		500,000
1	35,368.2	250.0	250.0	3,250.0	31,618.2	468,381.8	11,709.6	456,672.3
2	34,484.0	228.3	228.3	2,968.4	31,059.0	425,613.3	10,640.3	414,973
3	33,621.9	207.5	207.5	2,697.3	30,509.6	384,463.4	9,611.6	374,851.8
4	32,781.3	187.4	187.4	2,436.5	29,970.0	344,881.9	8.622.0	336,259.8
5	31,961.8	168.1	168.1	2,185.7	29,439.9	306,819.9	7,670.5	299,149.4
6	31,162.8	149.6	149.6	1,944.5	28,919.1	270,230.3	6,755.8	263,474.5
7	30,383.7	131.7	131.7	1,712.6	28,407.6	235,066.9	5,876.7	229,190.2
8	29,624.1	114.6	114.6	1,489.7	27,905.2	201,285.1	5,032.1	196,252.9
9	28,883.5	98.1	98.1	1,275.6	27,411.6	168,841.3	4,221.0	164,620.3
10	28,161.4	82.3	82.3	1,070.0	26,926.8	137,693.5	3,442.3	134,251.2
11	27,457.4	67.1	67.1	872.6	26,450.5	107,800.7	2,695.0	105,105.7
12	26,770.9	52.6	52.6	683.2	25,982.7	79,123.0	1,978.1	77,145.0
13	26,101.7	38.6	38.6	501.4	25,523.1	51,621.9	1,290.6	50,331.3
14	25,499.1	25.2	25.2	327.2	25,071.6	25,259.7	631.5	24,628.2
15	24,812.9	12.3	12.3	160.1	24,628.2	0	0	0

Inst. is the periodic installment.
SFee is the servicing fee.
GFee is the guaranteeing fee.
NINT is the net interest.
SPR is the scheduled principal repayment.
SOUT is the scheduled outstanding at the end of the month.
PREP is the prepayment for the month.
AOUT is the actual outstanding at the end of the month.

The average life is 7.25 months, assuming the SMM is 2.50%. The monthly IRR of a security under three different price assumptions is given is Table 9.2.

Table 9.3 depicts the cash flows and the IRR for each of the three cases, assuming the SMM increases from 2.50% to 5.00%.

Table 9.2: Total principal and cash flow for the pass-through security.

Time	Total Principal	Cash Flow Per Security		
		Case-A	Case-B	Case-C
0	0	(975)	(1,000)	(1,025)
1	43,327.74	93.16	93.16	93.16
2	41,699.28	89.34	89.34	89.34
3	40,121.18	85.64	85.64	85.64
4	38,592.00	82.06	82.06	82.06
5	37,110.36	78.59	78.59	78.59
6	35,674.90	75.24	75.24	75.24
7	34,284.31	71.99	71.99	71.99
8	32,937.30	68.85	68.85	68.85
9	31,632.64	65.82	65.82	65.82
10	30,369.10	62.88	62.88	62.88
11	29,145.51	60.04	60.04	60.04
12	27,960.73	57.29	57.29	57.29
13	26,813.63	54.63	54.63	54.63
14	25,703.14	52.06	52.06	52.06
15	24,628.19	49.58	49.58	49.58
IRR		1.0137%	0.65%	0.30%

Table 9.3: The case of a 5% SMM and cash flows from a pass-through security.

Time	Cash Flow Per Security		
	Case-A	Case-B	Case-C
0	(975)	(1,000)	(1,025)
1	116.57	116.57	116.57
2	107.78	107.78	107.78
3	99.55	99.55	99.55
4	91.86	91.86	91.86
5	84.66	84.66	84.66
6	77.94	77.94	77.94
7	71.66	71.66	71.66
8	65.80	65.80	65.80
9	60.33	60.33	60.33
10	55.22	55.22	55.22
11	50.46	50.46	50.46
12	46.02	46.02	46.02
13	41.89	41.89	41.89
14	38.04	38.04	38.04
15	34.46	34.46	34.46
IRR	1.0554%	0.65%	0.2603%

The average life declines to 6.50 months. As should be obvious, the higher the SMM, the lower is the average life.

Cash Flow Yield of a Pass-Through Security

The cash flow yield for a pass-through is the IRR computed using the projected cash flow stream. The result is a monthly rate, which is usually converted to a *bond equivalent yield* to facilitate comparisons with conventional debt securities. If we denote the IRR as i_m, where i_m denotes a monthly rate, then the bond equivalent yield may be expressed as

$$2[(1+i_m)^6 - 1]$$

As you can see from Tables 9.2 and 9.3, the IRR, and consequently the BEY, for a pass-through is inversely related to the price of the security, as is the case for a conventional debt security. If the security is priced at par, the cash flow yield is equal to the coupon rate, irrespective of the rate that is assumed for prepayment.

This can be demonstrated as follows. Let's assume for ease of exposition that the SMM is the same for all months. This is a convenient but not essential assumption. Let's also assume that there are no servicing or guaranteeing fees.

Symbols Required for the Exposition

We use the following symbols:

- $CF_t \equiv$ cash flow from the pass-through in month t.
- $I_t \equiv$ the interest component of the cash flow in month t.
- $P_t \equiv$ the scheduled principal component of the cash flow in month t.
- $S_t \equiv$ the prepayment rate in month t.
- $A \equiv$ the monthly installment in the absence of prepayments.
- $I_t^* \equiv$ the interest component of the cash flow in month t in the absence of prepayments.
- $P_t^* \equiv$ the principal component of the cash flow in month t in the absence of prepayments.
- $y \equiv$ the IRR of the pass-through.
- $r \equiv$ the coupon rate of the underlying mortgage loan.
- $SP_t \equiv$ the scheduled outstanding balance at the end of month t.

The cash flow in month t is

$$\begin{aligned} CF_t &= [I_t + P_t + S_t \times SP_t] \\ &= I_t^* \prod_{i=1}^{t-1}[1-S_i] + P_t^* \prod_{i=1}^{t-1}[1-S_i] + S_t \times SP_t^* \prod_{i=1}^{t-1}[1-S_i] \\ &= A\prod_{i=1}^{t-1}[1-S_i] + \frac{A \times S_t}{r} \times \prod_{i=1}^{t-1}[1-S_i] \times \left[1 - \frac{1}{(1+r)^{(N-t)}}\right] \end{aligned}$$

$$= A\left[\prod_{i=1}^{t-1}[1-S_i] + \frac{S_t}{r}\prod_{i=1}^{t-1}[1-S_i] - \frac{\frac{S_t}{r}}{(1+r)^{(N-t)}}\prod_{i=1}^{t-1}[1-S_i]\right]$$

Now assume that $S_i = S \; \forall \; i$:

$$\sum_{i=1}^{N}\frac{CF_t}{(1+y)^t} = \left[1 - \frac{(1-S)^N}{(1+y)^N}\right] \times \frac{A(r+S)}{r(y+S)}$$

$$- \frac{A \times S(1+r)}{r[(y-r)+S(1+r)]}\left[\frac{1}{(1+r)^N} - \frac{(1-S)^N}{(1+y)^N}\right]$$

$$A = \frac{Lr(1+r)^N}{(1+r)^N - 1}$$

If $r = y$ then

$$\sum_{i=1}^{N}\frac{CF_t}{(1+y)^t} = L$$

Thus irrespective of the prepayment speed, if the pass-through is trading at par, the IRR is equal to the coupon rate.

Collateralized Mortgage Obligations

In the case of a pass-through, there is only one class of security that is issued, and every security is entitled to the same undivided share of the cash flows from the underlying pool. The feature of such securities is that prepayments have the same implications for all the security holders.

In real life, however, investors differ with respect to the prepayment exposure and the average security life sought by them. The securitization process can take these preferences into account by creating multiple classes of securities, or what are referred to in MBS parlance as *tranches*. There are clearly specified rules as to how the cash flows from the underlying pool are to be directed to the holders of the various tranches. Such securities, with multiple tranches, are referred to as *collateralized mortgage obligations* or CMOs. Let's introduce the concept by studying a very simple CMO structure known as a sequential pay CMO.

Example 9.2. Consider the mortgage loan with a size of \$500,000. The time to maturity is 15 months, and the SMM is 2.50% for all months. Instead of issuing 500 securities with a face value of \$1,000 each, we issue 250 tranche A securities, with a face value of \$1,000, 150 tranche B securities with a face value of \$1,000, and 100 tranche C securities with a face value of \$1,000.

The cash flows from the underlying mortgage loan are directed as follows. All principal payments from the underlying loan, both scheduled and unscheduled, first go to tranche A. During this time, the remaining tranches continue to earn interest on the outstanding principal. Once tranche A is fully paid off, all subsequent principal payments, scheduled and unscheduled, are directed to the holders of tranche B. Once again, while tranche B is being paid off, holders of tranche C get interest on their outstanding principal. Extending the logic, the redemption of tranche B results in further principal payments being directed to tranche C.

Let's do an analysis month by month to illustrate the concepts.

Month-1
Total principal = \$43,327.74
Net interest = \$3,250
Tranche B and C holders receive a total interest of (0.078/12) × 250,000 = \$1,625.
Tranche A receives the entire principal and 3,250 – 1,625 = \$1,625 by way of interest.

$$\$ 1{,}625 = (0.078/12) \times 250{,}000$$

The outstanding balance for tranche A is 250,000 – 43,327.74 = \$206,672.26.

Month-2
Total principal = \$41,699.28
Net interest = \$2,968.40
Tranche B and C holders receive a total interest of \$1,625.
Tranche A receives the entire principal and \$1,343.40 by way of interest.

$$\$ 1{,}343.40 = (0.078/12) \times 206{,}672.26$$

The outstanding balance for tranche A is 206,672.26 – 41,699.28 = \$164,973.00.

Month-3
Total principal = \$40,121.18
Net interest = \$2,697.30
Tranche B and C holders receive a total interest of \$1,625.
Tranche A receives the entire principal and \$1,072.30 by way of interest.

$$\$ 1{,}072.30 = (0.078/12) \times 164{,}973.00$$

The outstanding balance for tranche A is 164,972.98 – 40,121.18 = \$124,851.80.

Month-4
Total principal = \$38,592.00
Net interest = \$2,436.50
Tranche B and C holders receive a total interest of \$1,625.
Tranche A receives the entire principal and \$811.50 by way of interest.

$$\$ 811.50 = (0.078/12) \times 124{,}851.80$$

The outstanding balance for tranche A is 124,851.80 – 38,592.00 = \$86,259.80.

Month-5
Total principal = \$37,110.36
Net interest = \$2,185.70
Tranche B and C holders receive a total interest of \$1,625.
Tranche A receives the entire principal and \$560.70 by way of interest.

$$\$ 560.70 = (0.078/12) \times 86{,}259.80$$

The outstanding balance for tranche A is 86,259.80 – 37,110.36 = \$49,149.44.

Month-6
Total principal = \$35,674.90
Net interest = \$1,944.50
Tranche B and C holders receive a total interest of \$1,625.
Tranche A receives the entire principal and \$319.50 by way of interest.

$$\$\ 319.50 = (0.078/12) \times 49{,}149.44$$

The outstanding balance for tranche A is 49,149.44 – 35,674.90 = \$13,474.54.

Month-7
Total principal = \$34,284.31
Net interest = \$1,712.60
Tranche B and C holders receive a total interest of \$1,625.
Tranche A receives \$13,474.54 by way of principal and \$87.60 by way of interest.

$$\$1{,}625.00 + \$87.60 = \$1{,}712.60$$

$$\$\ 87.60 = (0.078/12) \times 13{,}474.54$$

The outstanding balance for tranche A is zero.
Tranche B gets 34,284.31 – 13,474.54 = \$20,809.77 by way of principal.
The outstanding balance for tranche B is 150,000 – 20,809.77 = \$129.190.23.

Month-8
Total principal = \$32,937.30
Net interest = \$1,489.70
Tranche C receives (0.078/12) × 100,000 = \$650 by way of interest.
Tranche B receives the entire principal and \$839.70 by way of interest.

$$\$\ 839.70 = (0.078/12) \times 129{,}190.23$$

The outstanding balance for tranche B is 129,190.23 – 32,937.30 = \$96,252.93.

Month-9
Total principal = \$31,632.64
Net interest = \$1,275.60
Tranche C receives \$650 by way of interest.
Tranche B receives the entire principal and \$625.60 by way of interest.

$$\$\ 625.60 = (0.078/12) \times 96{,}252.93$$

The outstanding balance for tranche B is 96,252.93 – 31,632.64 = \$64,620.29.

Month-10
Total principal = \$30,369.10
Net interest = \$1,070.00
Tranche C receives \$650 by way of interest.
Tranche B receives the entire principal and \$420.00 by way of interest.

$$\$\ 420.00 = (0.078/12) \times 64{,}620.29$$

The outstanding balance for tranche B is 64,620.29 – 30,369.10 = \$34,251.19.

Month-11
Total principal = \$29,145.51
Net interest = \$872.60
Tranche C receives \$650 by way of interest.
Tranche B receives the entire principal and \$222.60 by way of interest.

$$\$\ 222.60 = (0.078/12) \times 34{,}251.19$$

The outstanding balance for tranche B is 34,251.19 – 29,145.51 = \$5,105.68.

Month-12
Total principal = \$27,960.73
Net interest = \$683.20
Tranche C receives \$650 by way of interest.
Tranche B receives \$5,105.68 by way of principal and \$33.20 by way of interest.

$$\$\ 33.20 = (0.078/12) \times 5{,}105.68$$

Tranche C receives 27,960.73 – 5,105.68 = \$22,855.05 by way of principal.
The outstanding balance for tranche C is 100,000 – 22,855.05 = \$77,144.95.

Month-13
Total principal = \$26,813.63
Net interest = \$501.40
The entire principal as well as the interest goes to tranche C.

$$\$\ 501.40 = (0.078/12) \times 77{,}144.95$$

The outstanding balance for tranche C is 77,144.95 – 26,813.63 = \$50,331.32.

Month-14
Total principal = \$25,703.14
Net interest = \$327.20
The entire principal as well as the interest goes to tranche C.

$$\$\ 327.20 = (0.078/12) \times 50{,}331.32$$

The outstanding balance for tranche C is 50,331.32 – 25,703.14 = \$24,628.18.

Month-15
Total principal = \$24,628.19
Net interest = \$160.10
The entire principal as well as the interest goes to tranche C.

$$\$\ 160.10 = (0.078/12) \times 24{,}628.18$$

The outstanding balance for tranche C is zero.

Tranche A has an average life of 3.5815 months; tranche B has an average life of 9.1961 months; and tranche C has an average life of 13.5210 months. The mother loan has an average life of 7.2538 months.

$$7.2538 = 0.50 \times 3.5815 + 0.30 \times 9.1961 + 0.20 \times 13.5210$$

Thus the average life of the mother loan is a weighted average of the average lives of the tranches.

Table 9.4: Summary of a Sequential Pay CMO.

T	Tranche A			Tranche B			Tranche C		
	Int.	Prin.	Out.	Int.	Prin.	Out.	Int.	Prin.	Out.
0			250,000.0			150,000.0			100,000.0
1	1,625.0	43,327.7	206,672.3	975.0	0	150,000.0	650.0	0	100,000.0
2	1,343.4	41,699.3	164,973.0	975.0	0	150,000.0	650.0	0	100,000.0
3	1,072.3	40,121.2	124,851.8	975.0	0	150,000.0	650.0	0	100,000.0
4	811.5	38,592.0	86,259.8	975.0	0	150,000.0	650.0	0	100,000.0
5	560.7	37,110.4	49,149.4	975.0	0	150,000.0	650.0	0	100,000.0
6	319.5	35,674.9	13,474.5	975.0	0	150,000.0	650.0	0	100,000.0
7	87.6	13,474.5	0	975.0	20,809.8	129,190.2	650.0	0	100,000.0
8	0	0	0	839.7	32,937.3	96,252.9	650.0	0	100,000.0
9	0	0	0	625.6	31,632.6	64,620.3	650.0	0	100,000.0
10	0	0	0	420.0	30,369.1	34,251.2	650.0	0	100,000.0
11	0	0	0	222.6	29,145.5	5,105.7	650.0	0	100,000.0
12	0	0	0	33.2	5,105.7	0	650.0	22,855.1	77,144.9
13	0	0	0	0	0	0	501.4	26,813.6	50,331.3
14	0	0	0	0	0	0	327.2	25,703.1	24,628.2
15	0	0	0	0	0	0	160.1	24,628.2	0

T is the time.
Int. is the interest received in the month.
Prin. is the principal payment received in the month.
Out. is the outstanding balance at the end of the month.

Extension Risk and Contraction Risk for Mortgage-backed Securities

Pass-through securities and CMOs expose investors to prepayment risk. In a declining interest rate environment, prepayments impact security holders in two ways. As they are debt securities, we would expect the price of such securities to rise in a scenario where rates are declining. However, in the case of mortgage-backed securities, holders of underlying bonds are likely to prepay and refinance at a lower rate when market rates go down. The overall result is price compression; that is, the rise in price is not as large as in the case of plain vanilla bonds. The second adverse consequence for holders of such securities is, of course, reinvestment risk, as is the case for all debt holders. That is, cash flows that are received in a declining interest rate environment obviously have to be reinvested at lower rates of interest. The risk due to these two adverse consequences is termed as *contraction risk.*

Now let's consider a rising interest rate environment. We would obviously expect the prices of mortgage-backed securities to fall. However, unlike the case of plain vanilla bonds, principal payments are likely to slow down because holders of underlying mortgage loans are less likely to refinance when mortgage rates are rising. This exacerbates the anticipated price decline. In such a situation, the security holders want prepayments to be high to afford them an opportunity to reinvest larger amounts at high rates of interest. The adverse impact for mortgage-backed securities in a rising interest rate environment is termed *extension risk.*

Accrual Bonds

In the case of the sequential pay CMO that we just studied, every tranche receives interest every month, based on the principal outstanding for that particular tranche at the beginning of the month. However, many sequential pay CMO structures do not require that every tranche be paid interest every month based on the outstanding principal. In the case of a sequential pay CMO with an accrual bond, also termed as a Z-bond, the Z bond does not receive any monthly interest until the previous tranches are fully retired. Therefore, the interest for the Z-bond accrues and is added to its original principal, leading to negative amortization, until the other classes of the CMO have been paid off. In the months prior to the retirement of the penultimate tranche, the interest that would otherwise have been paid to the Z-bond is directed to the tranche that is receiving principal at that point in time and thus helps to speed up the repayment of principal.

Let's consider a CMO in which tranches A and B are as specified in Example 9.2. However, the last tranche is an accrual bond. Quite obviously, the inclusion of the Z-bond reduces the maturity as well as the average life of each of the two other tranches.

Example 9.3. Let's do an analysis month by month to illustrate the concepts.

Month-1
Total principal = \$43,327.74
Net interest = \$3,250
Tranche B holders receive a total interest of (0.078/12) × 150,000 = \$975.
Tranche A holders receive an interest of (0.078/12) × 250,000 = \$1,625.
Tranche A holders receive a total principal of 43,327.74 + (3,250 − 975 − 1,625) = \$43,977.74.
The unpaid interest on the Z-bond is (0.078/12) × 100,000 = \$650.
The outstanding balance for tranche A is 250,000 − 43,977.74 = \$206,022.26.
The outstanding balance for tranche B is \$150,000.
The outstanding balance for the Z-bond is 100,000 + 650 = \$100,650.

Month-2
Total principal = \$41,699.28
Net interest = \$2,968.40
Tranche B holders receive a total interest of (0.078/12) × 150,000 = \$975.
Tranche A holders receive an interest of (0.078/12) × 206,022.26 = \$1,339.14.
Tranche A holders receive a total principal of 41,699.28 + (2,968.4 − 975 − 1,339.14) = \$42,353.54.
The unpaid interest on the Z-bond is (0.078/12) × 100,650 = \$654.23.
The outstanding balance for tranche A is 206,022.26 − 42,353.54 = \$163,668.72.
The outstanding balance for tranche B is \$150,000.
The outstanding balance for the Z-bond is 100,650 + 654.23 = \$101,304.23.

Month-3
Total principal = \$40,121.18

Net interest = \$2,697.30
Tranche B holders receive a total interest of (0.078/12) × 150,000 = \$975.
Tranche A holders receive an interest of (0.078/12) × 163,668.72 = \$1,063.85.
Tranche A holders receive a total principal of 40,121.18 + (2,697.3 – 975 – 1,063.85) = \$40,779.63.
The unpaid interest on the Z-bond is (0.078/12) × 101,304.23 = \$658.48.
The outstanding balance for tranche A is 163,668.72 – 40,779.634 = \$122,889.09.
The outstanding balance for tranche B is \$150,000.
The outstanding balance for the Z-bond is 101,304.23 + 658.48 = \$101,962.71.

Month-4
Total principal = \$38,592.00
Net interest = \$2,436.50
Tranche B holders receive a total interest of (0.078/12) × 150,000 = \$975.
Tranche A holders receive an interest of (0.078/12) × 122,889.09 = \$798.78.
Tranche A holders receive a total principal of 38,592 + (2,436.50 – 975 – 798.78) = \$39,254.72.
The unpaid interest on the Z-bond is (0.078/12) × 101,962.71 = \$662.76.
The outstanding balance for tranche A is 122,889.09 – 39,254.72 = \$83,634.37.
The outstanding balance for tranche B is \$150,000.
The outstanding balance for the Z-bond is 101,962.71 + 662.76 = \$102,625.57.

Month-5
Total principal = \$37,110.36
Net interest = \$2,185.70
Tranche B holders receive a total interest of (0.078/12) × 150,000 = \$975.
Tranche A holders receive an interest of (0.078/12) × 83,634.37 = \$543.62.
Tranche A holders receive a total principal of 37,110.36 + (2,185.70 – 975 – 543.62) = \$37,777.44.
The unpaid interest on the Z-bond is (0.078/12) × 102,625.57 = \$667.07.
The outstanding balance for tranche A is 83,634.37 – 37,777.44 = \$45,856.93.
The outstanding balance for tranche B is \$150,000.
The outstanding balance for the Z-bond is 102,625.57 + 667.07 = \$103,292.64.

Month-6
Total principal = \$35,674.90
Net interest = \$1,944.50
Tranche B holders receive a total interest of (0.078/12) × 150,000 = \$975.
Tranche A holders receive an interest of (0.078/12) × 45,856.93 = \$298.07.
Tranche A holders receive a total principal of 35,674.90 + (1,944.50 – 975 – 298.07) = \$36,346.33.
The unpaid interest on the Z-bond is (0.078/12) × 103,292.64 = \$671.40.
The outstanding balance for tranche A is 45,856.93 – 36,346.33 = \$9,510.60.
The outstanding balance for tranche B is \$150,000.
The outstanding balance for the Z-bond is 103,292.64 + 671.40 = \$103,964.04.

Month-7
Total principal = \$34,284.31
Net interest = \$1,712.60
Tranche B holders receive a total interest of (0.078/12) × 150,000 = \$975.
Tranche A holders receive an interest of (0.078/12) × 9,510.60 = \$61.82.
Tranche A holders receive a total principal of \$9,510.60.
The unpaid interest on the Z-bond is (0.078/12) × 103,964.04 = \$675.77.
Tranche B holders receive a principal payment of (34,284.31 – 9,510.60) + (1,712.60 – 975 – 61.82) = \$25,449.50.

The outstanding balance for tranche A is zero.
The outstanding balance for tranche B is 150,000 – 25,449.50 = $124,550.50.
The outstanding balance for the Z-bond is 103,964.04 + 675.77 = $104,639.81.

Month-8
Total principal = $32,937.30
Net interest = $1,489.70
The unpaid interest on the Z-bond is (0.078/12) × 104,639.81 = $680.16.
Tranche B holders receive an interest of (0.078/12) × 124,550.50 = $809.58.
Tranche B holders receive a principal payment of (32,937.30 + 1,489.70 – 809.58) = $33,617.42.
The outstanding balance for tranche B is 124,550.50 – 33,617.42 = $90,933.08.
The outstanding balance for the Z-bond is 104,639.81 + 680.16 = $105,319.97.

Month-9
Total principal = $31,632.64
Net interest = $1,275.60
The unpaid interest on the Z-bond is (0.078/12) × 105,319.97 = $684.58.
Tranche B holders receive an interest of (0.078/12) × 90,933.08 = $ 591.07.
Tranche B holders receive a principal payment of (31,632.64 + 1,275.60 – 591.07) = $32,317.17.
The outstanding balance for tranche B is 90,933.08 – 32,317.17 = $58,615.91.
The outstanding balance for the Z-bond is 105,319.97 + 684.58 = $106,004.55.

Month-10
Total principal = $30,369.10
Net interest = $1,070.00
The unpaid interest on the Z-bond is (0.078/12) × 106,004.55 = $689.03.
Tranche B holders receive (0.078/12) × 58,615.91 = $381 by way of interest.
Tranche B holders receive a principal payment of (30369.1 + 1,070 – 381) = $31,058.10.
The outstanding balance for tranche B is (58,615.91 – 31,058.10) = $27,557.81.
The outstanding balance for the Z-bond is 106,004.55 + 689.03 = $106,693.58.

Month-11
Total principal = $29,145.51
Net interest = $872.60
Tranche B holders receive (0.078/12) × 27,557.81 = $179.13 by way of interest.
Tranche B holders receive a principal payment of $27,557.81.
The outstanding balance for tranche B is zero.
The interest for the Z-bond is (0.078/12) × 106,693.58 = $693.51.
The Z-bond holders receive a principal payment of (29,145.51 + 872.60 – 179.13 – 27,557.81 – 693.51) = $1,587.66.
The outstanding balance on the Z-bonds is (106,693.58 – 1,587.66) = $105,105.90.

Month-12
Total principal = $27,960.73
Net interest = $683.20
Principal for the Z-bond is $27,960.73.
Interest for the Z-bond is $683.20. $\frac{0.078}{12} \times 105{,}105.90 = \$683.20$.
The outstanding balance on the Z-bonds is (105,105.90 – 27,960.73) = $77,145.20.

Month-13
Total principal = $26,813.63
Net interest = $501.40

Principal for the Z-bond is $26,813.63.
Interest for the Z-bond is $501.40.
The interest for the Z-bond is $(0.078/12) \times 77{,}145.20 = \$501.40$.
The outstanding balance on the Z-bonds is $(77{,}145.20 - 26{,}813.63) = \$50{,}331.60$.

Month-14
Total principal = $25,703.14
Net interest = $327.20
Principal for the Z-bond is $25,703.14.
Interest for the Z-bond is $327.20.
The interest for the Z-bond is $(0.078/12) \times 50{,}331.608 = \$327.20$.
The outstanding balance on the Z-bonds is $(50{,}331.60 - 25{,}703.14) = \$24{,}628.45$.

Month-15
Total principal = $24,628.19
Net interest = $160.10
Principal for the Z-bond is $24,628.19.
Interest for the Z-bond is $160.10.
The interest for the Z-bond is $(0.078/12) \times 24{,}628.45 = \$160.10$.
The outstanding balance on the Z-bonds is zero.

Table 9.5: Summary of a CMO with an accrual bond.

T	Tranche A			Tranche B			Z-Bond		
	Int.	Prin.	Out.	Int.	Prin.	Out.	Int.	Prin.	Out.
0			250,000.0			150,000.0			100,000.0
1	1,625.0	43,977.7	206,022.3	975.0	0	150,000.0	0	0	100,650.0
2	1,339.1	42,353.5	163,668.8	975.0	0	150,000.0	0	0	101,304.2
3	1,063.8	40,779.7	122,889.1	975.0	0	150,000.0	0	0	101,962.7
4	798.8	39,254.8	83,634.3	975.0	0	150,000.0	0	0	102,625.5
5	543.6	37,777.4	45,856.9	975.0	0	150,000.0	0	0	103,292.5
6	298.1	36,346.3	9,510.6	975.0	0	150,000.0	0	0	103,963.9
7	61.8	9,510.6	0	975.0	25,449.5	124,550.5	0	0	104,639.7
8	0	0	0	809.6	33,617.5	90,933.1	0	0	105,319.9
9	0	0	0	591.1	32,317.2	58,615.9	0	0	106,004.4
10	0	0	0	381.0	31,058.1	27,557.7	0	0	106,693.5
11	0	0	0	179.1	27,557.7	0.0	693.5	1,587.80	105,105.7
12	0	0	0	0	0	0	683.2	27,960.7	77,145.0
13	0	0	0	0	0	0	501.4	26,813.6	50,331.3
14	0	0	0	0	0	0	327.2	25,703.1	24,628.2
15	0	0	0	0	0	0	160.1	24,628.2	0

T is the time.
Int. is the interest received in the month.
Prin. is the principal payment received in the month.
Out. is the outstanding balance at the end of the month.

The average life of tranche A is 3.5263 months, and that of tranche B is 9.0110. As we can see, the average life of each of the tranches has reduced due to the presence of the

Z-bond. Z-bonds have appeal to investors who are primarily concerned with the specter of reinvestment risk. Because such bonds do not entail the receipt of any cash flows until all the other classes are fully retired, reinvestment risk is totally eliminated until the Z-bond starts receiving its first cash flow. Accrual bonds are popular with pension funds and life insurance companies, since they are securities with high durations, but which offer higher yields than other high duration securities such as long-term Treasuries.

Creating Floating Rate Tranches

Floating rate bonds can be created from a fixed rate tranche. Let's illustrate this using tranche A of the sequential pay CMO, which has a par value of $250,000 and a 7.80% coupon. In practice, to create a floater, we have to simultaneously create an inverse floater. The cumulative principal of the two tranches in this case is $250,000. There is no rule as to what the principal values of the respective tranches should be as long as their combined par value is $250,000.

Let's assume that the benchmark for the two tranches is the 3-month LIBOR and that we want to create a floater with a par value of $150,000 and an inverse floater with a par value of $100,000. The coupon on the floater is LIBOR + m basis points, and that for the inverse floater is $C - L \times$ LIBOR.

It is a common practice to specify the coupon for an inverse floater as $C - L\times$ Benchmark. C is the cap or maximum interest on the inverse floater, whereas L is the coupon leverage. The concept of a cap is easily understood as the maximum possible coupon. The lower limit for LIBOR is zero. Consequently the upper limit for the coupon on the inverse floater is C. The coupon leverage measures the rate of change of the coupon of the inverse floater with respect to the benchmark. We know that the total annual interest available is 7.80% of $250,000, which is $19,500. This is also the maximum interest available for the floating tranche. Thus the cap on the floater is 19,500÷150,000 = 13%. The ratio of floaters to inverses is 3:2, which implies that the coupon leverage for the inverse floater is 1.50. If we assume that the coupon on the floater is LIBOR + 125 bp, the minimum coupon on the floater is 1.25%, which is the case if LIBOR is zero. Hence, the minimum interest on the floater is 150,000 × 0.0125 = $1,875. Thus the maximum interest for the inverse floater is 19,500 − 1,875 = $17,625. The cap on the inverse is therefore 17,625 ÷ 100,000 = 0.17625 or 17.625%. We can express the coupons of the two tranches as

Floater Coupon: LIBOR + 1.25%

Inverse Floater Coupon: 17.625% − 1.50× LIBOR

The weighted average coupon is:

$$0.60 \times (\text{LIBOR} + 1.25) + 0.40 \times (17.625 - 1.50 \times \text{LIBOR}) = 7.80\%$$

Notional Interest-Only Tranches

Let's go back to the sequential pay CMO that we studied earlier. We assumed that the underlying mortgage had a coupon rate of 7.80% and that each of the three tranches that we created also had a coupon of 7.80%. In practice, each tranche of a CMO has a different coupon rate, and there is an excess representing the difference between the interest on the underlying collateral and the coupons on the various tranches. Therefore, it is a common practice to create a tranche that is entitled to receive only the excess coupon interest. Such tranches are referred to as *notional interest-only securities*.

Let's now assume that the underlying collateral has a coupon of 7.8%, and the three tranches created from it have coupon rates as shown in Table 9.6.

Table 9.6: Coupon rates for a sequential pay CMO.

Tranche	Initial Principal	Coupon Rate
A	250,000	6.60%
B	150,000	7.20%
C	100,000	7.50%

Consider tranche A. It pays a coupon of 6.60%, and the coupon on the underlying loan is 7.80%. Thus there is excess interest of 1.20%. Let's assume that we want to create a notional interest-only security with a coupon of 8.0%. To find the notional amount on which the interest payable to this security is calculated, we proceed as follows. An excess interest of 1.20% on $250,000 worth of principal can be used to pay an interest of 8.0% on a principal amount of $37,500. Similarly, in the case of tranche B, an excess interest of 0.60% on a principal amount of $150,000 can be used to pay an interest of 8.0% on a principal of $11,250. Tranche C, using the same logic, generates excess interest to support $3,750 worth of principal. Thus the excess interest generated can service a bond with a principal of 37,500 + 11,250 + 3,750 = $52,500. This is the notional principal for the tranche that is scheduled to receive the excess interest. The term *notional* connotes that this principal amount is used merely to compute the interest payable to this class for the month, and that the principal per se is not repaid.

The contribution of a tranche to the notional principal is in general given by the following formula:

$$\text{Notional amount for an x\% interest only (IO) class} = \frac{\text{Par Value of the Tranche} \times \text{Excess Interest}}{\frac{x}{100}}$$

Interest-Only and Principal-Only Strips

Stripped mortgage-backed securities can be created by either directing all the principal or all the interest to a particular class. The security that is scheduled to receive only the principal is referred to as the principal-only or PO class. The other security is obviously termed the interest-only or IO class.

Let's first consider the PO class. The yield obtained by the security holder depends on the speed with which the underlying pool generates prepayments. The faster the speed with which prepayments are received, the greater the rate of return for holders of such securities is. In the case of the IO class holders, however, the desire is to have slow prepayments. Such securities do not receive any principal payments, and the income, which is exclusively by way of interest payments will be higher, the larger the outstanding balance on the underlying pool. This corresponds to a slower prepayment rate on the underlying pool. In the case of a PO security, we know the amount of cash to be received but not the timing of the cash flows. However, in the case of IO securities we know neither the magnitude of the cash flows nor the timing.

Planned Amortization Class (PAC) Bonds

In the case of planned amortization class (PAC) bonds, if the prepayment pattern falls within a prespecified range, then the cash flows received by the security are known. PAC bonds are not created in isolation. They are accompanied by a category of bonds called *support bonds*. It is this category that absorbs the pre-payment risk, thereby protecting the PAC bonds against both extension risk and contraction risk. To create a PAC bond, we need to specify a range of prepayment speeds. These are referred to as the PAC *collars*. The PAC schedule lists the principal amount payable to the PAC bondholders if the prepayment speed is within the range provided by the lower PAC collar and the upper PAC collar. The schedule is obtained by taking the lower of the principal cash flows generated by the lower collar and the upper collar.

Example 9.4. Consider a home loan with a principal of \$250,000 and 15 months to maturity. The mortgage rate is 7.2% per annum. There are no servicing or guaranteeing fees. A PAC bond and a support bond are created, where the lower PAC collar is an SMM of 2.50% and the upper collar is an SMM of 12.50%. Table 9.7 lists the principal payments from the underlying loan assuming three different prepayment speeds between the lower and upper collars, namely 2.50%, 7.50%, and 12.50%. As before, let's do a month-by-month analysis.

The scheduled principal for month t is

$$P_t = P_t^* \prod_{i=1}^{t-1}[1 - \text{SMM}_i] = \frac{A}{(1+r)^{N-t+1}} \prod_{i=1}^{t-1}[1 - \text{SMM}_i]$$

The prepayment for the month is

$$SP_t \times \text{SMM}_i = \frac{A}{r} \times \left[1 - \frac{1}{(1+r)^{N-t}}\right] \prod_{i=1}^{t-1}[1 - \text{SMM}_i] \times \text{SMM}_i$$

The total principal that is received in a month is

$$PCF_t = \frac{A}{(1+r)^{N-t+1}} \prod_{i=1}^{t-1} [1 - SMM_i] + \frac{A}{r} \times \left[1 - \frac{1}{(1+r)^{N-t}}\right] \prod_{i=1}^{t-1} [1 - SMM_i] \times SMM_i$$

If we assume a constant SMM for all months,

$$PCF_t = \frac{A}{(1+r)^{N-t+1}} [1 - SMM]^{t-1} + \frac{A}{r} \times \left[1 - \frac{1}{(1+r)^{N-t}}\right] [1 - SMM]^{t-1} \times SMM$$

Table 9.7: Scheduled principal payments and prepayments under various prepayment speeds.

Time	SMM = 2.50%		SMM = 7.50%		SMM = 12.50%	
	Sch. Pr	Prep.	Sch. Pr	Prep.	Sch. Pr	Prep.
1	15,977.83	5,850.55	15,977.83	17,551.66	15,977.83	29,252.77
2	15,671.86	5,312.49	14,868.17	15,120.18	14,064.49	23,838.11
3	15,371.74	4,795.39	13,835.58	12,948.49	12,380.26	19,310.82
4	15,077.37	4,298.57	12,874.70	11,011.75	10,897.73	15,534.75
5	14,788.64	3,821.39	11,980.55	9,287.33	9,592.73	12,393.81
6	14,505.44	3,363.22	11,148.50	7,754.64	8,444.00	9,789.09
7	14,227.66	2,923.45	10,374.24	6,394.98	7,432.83	7,636.35
8	13,955.20	2,501.48	9,653.75	5,191.32	6,542.75	5,863.96
9	13,687.96	2,096.74	8,983.29	4,128.23	5,759.25	4,411.06
10	13,425.83	1,708.68	8,359.40	3,191.66	5,069.58	3,225.98
11	13,168.73	1,336.75	7,778.84	2,368.87	4,462.50	2,264.92
12	12,916.55	980.41	7,238.60	1,648.31	3,928.12	1,490.79
13	12,669.19	639.17	6,735.88	1,019.49	3,457.72	872.23
14	12,426.58	312.53	6,268.07	472.93	3043.66	382.74
15	12,188.61	0	5,832.76	0	2,679.18	0

Sch. Pr stands for scheduled principal.
Prep. stands for prepayment.

The maximum total principal for the PAC bond can be \$187,358.11, as can be seen from Table 9.8. Let's round down to \$187,000. The principal for the last month is 2,679.18 – (187,358.11 – 187,000) = \$2,321.08. The support bond has a principal of 250,000 – 187,000 = \$63,000.

The average life for the PAC bond is 5.67 months, and that for the support bond is 11.88 months, when the SMM is 2.50%.

However, when the SMM is 12.50%, the average life for the PAC bond is 5.67 months, and that for the support bond is 2.29 months. We can see that, although the average life of the PAC bond stays the same as in the case of an SMM of 2.50%, the average life of the support bond reduces drastically from 11.88 months to 2.29 months. Thus the stability accorded to the PAC bond is at the cost of the support bond.

Table 9.8: Total principal under various pre-payment speeds and the total principal for a PAC bond.

Time	SMM = 2.50% Tot. Pr	SMM = 7.50% Tot. Pr	SMM = 12.50% Tot. Pr	Minimum Tot. Pr.
1	21,828.39	33,529.49	45,230.60	21,828.39
2	20,984.35	29,988.35	37,902.60	20,984.35
3	20,167.13	26,784.07	31,691.08	20,167.13
4	19,375.94	23,886.45	26,432.48	19,375.94
5	18,610.03	21,267.88	21,986.54	18,610.03
6	17,868.66	18,903.14	18,233.08	17,868.66
7	17,151.10	16,769.21	15,069.18	15,069.18
8	16,456.68	14,845.07	12,406.71	12,406.71
9	15,784.70	13,111.52	10,170.31	10,170.31
10	15,134.51	11,551.06	8,295.56	8,295.56
11	14,505.47	10,147.71	6,727.42	6,727.42
12	13,896.96	8,886.91	5,418.91	5,418.91
13	13,308.37	7,755.38	4,329.95	4,329.95
14	12,739.11	6,741.00	3,426.40	3,426.40
15	12,188.61	5,832.76	2,679.18	2,679.18
Total	250,000	250,000	250,000	187,358.11

Tot. Pr. stands for total principal.

Table 9.9: Total principal and principal for the PAC bond and the support bond under 2.50% SMM.

Time	SMM = 2.50%		
	Tot. Pr	Prin. for PAC Bond	Prin. for Support Bond
1	21,828.39	21,828.39	0.00
2	20,984.35	20,984.35	0.00
3	20,167.13	20,167.13	0.00
4	19,375.94	19,375.94	0.00
5	18,610.03	18,610.03	0.00
6	17,868.66	17,868.66	0.00
7	17,151.10	15,069.18	2,081.93
8	16,456.68	12,406.71	4,049.97
9	15,784.70	10,170.31	5,614.39
10	15,134.51	8,295.56	6,838.95
11	14,505.47	6,727.42	7,778.05
12	13,896.96	5,418.91	8,478.05
13	13,308.37	4,329.95	8,978.42
14	12,739.11	3,426.40	9,312.71
15	12,188.61	2,321.08	9,867.53
Total	250,000	187,000	63,000

Prin. stands for principal.
Tot. Pr. stands for total principal.

Table 9.10: Total principal and principal for the PAC bond and the support bond under 12.50% SMM.

Time	SMM = 12.50%		
	Tot. Pr	Prin. for PAC Bond	Prin. for Support Bond
1	45,230.60	21,828.39	23,402.22
2	37,902.60	20,984.35	16,918.25
3	31,691.08	20,167.13	11,523.95
4	26,432.48	19,375.94	7,056.54
5	21,986.54	18,610.03	3,376.51
6	18,233.08	17,868.66	364.43
7	15,069.18	15,069.18	0.00
8	12,406.71	12,406.71	0.00
9	10,170.31	10,170.31	0.00
10	8,295.56	8,295.56	0.00
11	6,727.42	6,727.42	0.00
12	5,418.91	5,418.91	0.00
13	4,329.95	4,329.95	0.00
14	3,426.40	3,426.40	0.00
15	2,679.18	2,321.08	358.11
Total	250,000	187,000	63,000

Prin. stands for principal.
Tot. Pr. stands for total principal.

Table 9.11: Total principal and principal for the PAC bond and the support bond under an SMM of zero.

Time	SMM = 0.00%			
	Tot. Pr	Prin. for PAC Bond	Out. Bal. for PAC Bond	Prin. for Sup. Bond
1	15,977.83	15,977.83	171,022.17	0.00
2	16,073.70	16,073.70	154,948.47	0.00
3	16,170.14	16,170.14	138,778.33	0.00
4	16,267.16	16,267.16	122,511.17	0.00
5	16,364.76	16,364.76	106,146.40	0.00
6	16,462.95	16,462.95	89,683.45	0.00
7	16,561.73	16,561.73	73,121.72	0.00
8	16,661.10	16,661.10	56,460.62	0.00
9	16,761.07	16,761.07	39,699.55	0.00
10	16,861.63	16,861.63	22,837.91	0.00
11	16,962.80	16,962.80	5,875.11	0.00
12	17,064.58	5,875.11	0.00	11,189.47
13	17,166.97	0.00	0.00	17,166.97
14	17,269.97	0.00	0.00	17,269.97
15	17,373.59	0.00	0.00	17,373.59
Total	250,000	187,000		63,000.00

Tot. Pr. stands for total principal.
Prin. stands for principal.
Out. Bal. stands for outstanding balance.
Sup. stands for support.

When the SMM is zero, for months 1–6, the total principal received is less than what is due for the PAC bond. Hence the entire principal is directed to the PAC bond. For months 7–11, the entire principal received is directed to the PAC bond. In these months, the cash flow directed to the PAC bond is more than the payment required as per the PAC schedule. However, because there is a deficit in the earlier months, the entire principal is directed to the PAC bond. At the end of the 11th month, the outstanding principal is $5,875.11. The total principal that is received in the 12th month is $17,064.58. Thus $5,875.11 is directed to the PAC bond, which as a consequence is fully paid off, and $11,189.47 is directed to the support bond. For months 13–15, the entire principal is directed to the support bond.

The average life for the PAC bond is 6.25 months, and that for the support bond is 13.65 months.

Table 9.12: Total principal and principal for the PAC bond and the support bond under 15.00% SMM.

Time	SMM = 15.00%			
	Tot. Pr	Prin. for PAC Bond	Out. Bal. for PAC Bond	Prin. for Sup. Bond
1	51,081.16	21,828.39	165,171.61	29,252.77
2	41,451.07	20,984.35	144,187.26	20,466.72
3	33,550.65	20,270.15	123,917.12	13,280.50
4	27,079.13	27,079.13	96,837.99	0.00
5	21,786.83	21,786.83	75,051.16	0.00
6	17,466.67	17,466.67	57,584.49	0.00
7	13,946.98	13,946.98	43,637.50	0.00
8	11,085.62	11,085.62	32,551.89	0.00
9	8,764.93	8,764.93	23,786.96	0.00
10	6,887.67	6,887.67	16,899.29	0.00
11	5,373.50	5,373.50	11,525.78	0.00
12	4,156.16	4,156.16	7,369.62	0.00
13	3,181.02	3,181.02	4,188.60	0.00
14	2,403.12	2,403.12	1,785.48	0.00
15	1,785.48	1,785.48	0.00	0.00
Total	250,000	187,000		63,000.00

Tot. Pr. stands for total principal.
Prin. stands for principal.
Out. Bal. stands for outstanding balance.
Sup. stands for support.

Analysis of the SMM = 15% Scenario

In the first month, the amount due for the PAC bond is $21,828.39, whereas the total principal received is $51,081.16. The difference of $29,252.77 is paid to the support bond. The outstanding for the support bond is 63,000 – 29,252.77 = $33,747.23.

In the second month, the amount due for the PAC bond is \$20,984.35, whereas the total principal received is \$41,451.07. The difference of \$20,466.72 is paid to the support bond. The outstanding for the support bond is 33,747.23 – 20,466.72 = \$13,280.51.

In the third month, the total principal received is \$33,550.65. The amount paid to the support bond is \$13,280.51. The outstanding for the support bond is zero. The balance of \$20,270.15 is paid to the PAC bond.

Because the support bond has been fully paid off at the end of the third month, the entire principal received for the remaining months is directed to the PAC bond, which is fully paid off at the end of the 15th month.

The average life of the PAC bond is 5.30 months, and the average life of the support bond is 1.75 months.

Chapter Summary

The chapter looked at mortgage-backed securities. We first analyzed the cash flows to a pass-through security and examined the concept of a cash flow yield. We then considered two types of collateralized mortgage obligations in detail, namely sequential pay CMOs, and CMOs with an accrual bond. The issues of extension risk and contraction risk in the context of mortgage-backed securities was studied. We examined how to create a floating rate tranche from a sequential pay CMO and also looked at notional interest-only tranches, as well as interest-only (IO) and principal-only (PO) strips. Finally, we examined in detail a class of securities known as planned amortization class (PAC) bonds.

The chapter contains an appendix, in which the relationship between the SMM and the coupon rate for the scheduled principal component is studied. We also look at the relationship between the pre-payment for a month and the time of receipt, for a given value of the SMM. The appendix concludes with a study of the relationship between scheduled principal payments and prepayments, and the SMM for a given value of the time period.

Appendix 9.1

We now derive a relationship between the SMM and the coupon rate, and the scheduled principal component. The scheduled principal for month t is

$$\begin{aligned} P_t &= P_t^* \prod_{i=1}^{t-1} [1 - \text{SMM}_i] = \frac{A}{(1+r)^{N-t+1}} \prod_{i=1}^{t-1} [1 - \text{SMM}_i] \\ &= \frac{Lr}{\left[1 - \frac{1}{(1+r)^N}\right]} \times \frac{(1-s)^{t-1}}{(1+r)^{N-t+1}} \end{aligned}$$

$$= \frac{Lr}{(1+r)^N - 1} \times (1+r)^{t-1} \times (1-s)^{t-1}$$

Let's call this expression Z.

$$\frac{\partial Z}{\partial t} = \frac{Lr}{(1+r)^N - 1} \times (1+r)^{t-1} \times (1-s)^{t-1} [\ln(1+r) + \ln(1-s)]$$

$$= Z [\ln(1+r)(1-s)]$$

$$\text{If } (1+r)(1-s) = 1 \text{ then } \frac{\partial Z}{\partial t} = 0$$

and the scheduled principal for the month is a constant.

$$\text{Thus if } r = \frac{s}{1-s} \text{ then } \frac{\partial Z}{\partial t} = 0$$

$$\text{However, if } r > \frac{s}{1-s} \text{ then } \frac{\partial Z}{\partial t} > 0 \text{ and if } r < \frac{s}{1-s} \text{ then } \frac{\partial Z}{\partial t} < 0$$

Let's analyze this result using some data. Assume $s = 0.01$. Thus $\frac{s}{1-s} = 0.010101$. Consider three values for r, namely 1.0101% per month, 1.125% per month, and 0.875% per month. The results are summarized in Table 9.13.

Table 9.13: Scheduled principal and the relationship between the interest rate and the SMM.

Time	r = 1.0101%	r = 0.8750%	r = 1.25%
1	15,519.79	15,669.54	15,256.62
2	15,519.79	15,648.58	15,292.85
3	15,519.79	15,627.65	15,329.17
4	15,519.79	15,606.75	15,365.58
5	15,519.79	15,585.88	15,402.07
6	15,519.79	15,565.03	15,438.65
7	15,519.79	15,544.21	15,475.32
8	15,519.79	15,523.42	15,512.07
9	15,519.79	15,502.66	15,548.91
10	15,519.79	15,481.93	15,585.84
11	15,519.79	15,461.22	15,622.86
12	15,519.79	15,440.54	15,659.96
13	15,519.79	15,419.89	15,697.15
14	15,519.79	15,399.26	15,734.43
15	15,519.79	15,378.67	15,771.80

Now let's study the relationship between the prepayment and time. Given a constant SMM, we expect the prepayment to steadily decline with time because the scheduled outstanding balance steadily declines. The prepayment for the month is

$$SP_t \times \text{SMM}_i = \frac{A}{r} \times \left[1 - \frac{1}{(1+r)^{N-t}}\right] \prod_{i=1}^{t-1} [1 - \text{SMM}_i] \times \text{SMM}_i$$

$$
\begin{aligned}
&= SP_t \times s = \frac{A}{r} \times \left[1 - \frac{1}{(1+r)^{N-t}}\right](1-s)^{t-1} \times s \\
&= \frac{L}{[(1+r)^N - 1]} \times [(1+r)^N - (1+r)^t] \times s \times (1-s)^{t-1} \\
&= \frac{L}{[(1+r)^N - 1]} \times s \times (1+r)^N \times (1-s)^{t-1} - \frac{L}{[(1+r)^N - 1]} \\
&\times s \times (1+r)^t (1-s)^{t-1}
\end{aligned}
$$

Let's call this Z.

$$
\begin{aligned}
\frac{\partial Z}{\partial t} &= \frac{L}{[(1+r)^N - 1]} \times s \times (1+r)^N \times (1-s)^{t-1} \times \ln(1-s) \\
&- \frac{L}{[(1+r)^N - 1]} \times s \times (1+r)^t (1-s)^{t-1} \times \ln(1-s) \\
&- \frac{L}{[(1+r)^N - 1]} \times s \times (1+r)^t (1-s)^{t-1} \times \ln(1+r) \\
&= \frac{L}{[(1+r)^N - 1]} \times s \times (1-s)^{t-1} \left[(1+r)^N \ln(1-s) - (1+r)^t \{\ln(1-s) + \ln(1+r)\}\right] \\
&= \frac{L}{[(1+r)^N - 1]} \times s \times (1-s)^{t-1} \left[(1+r)^N \ln(1-s) - (1+r)^t \{\ln(1-s)(1+r)\}\right] \\
&\frac{L}{[(1+r)^N - 1]} \times s \times (1-s)^{t-1} > 0
\end{aligned}
$$

Consider

$$\left[(1+r)^N \ln(1-s) - (1+r)^t \{\ln(1-s)(1+r)\}\right]$$

If it has to be positive

$$
\begin{aligned}
&(1+r)^N \ln(1-s) > (1+r)^t \{\ln(1-s)(1+r)\} \Rightarrow (1+r)^{N-t} \ln(1-s) > \ln(1-s)(1+r) \\
&\Rightarrow \ln(1-s)\left[(1+r)^{N-t} - 1\right] > \ln(1+r)
\end{aligned}
$$

This cannot be true, because

$$\ln(1-s) < 0; \ln(1+r) > 0 \quad \text{and} \quad \left[(1+r)^{N-t} - 1\right] > 0$$

Thus

$$\frac{\partial Z}{\partial t} < 0$$

which implies that pre-payments will steadily decline over time.

Now let's study the relationship between the scheduled principal and the SMM for a given value of t.

$$P_t = \frac{Lr}{(1+r)^N - 1} \times (1+r)^{t-1} \times (1-s)^{t-1}$$

$$\frac{\partial P_t}{\partial s} = -\frac{Lr(t-1)}{(1+r)^N - 1} \times (1+r)^{t-1} \times (1-s)^{t-2} < 0$$

Thus, as the SMM increases, the scheduled principal payment declines.

Then, let's consider the relationship between the pre-payment and the SMM. The pre-payment for a given value of t is

$$SP_t \times s = \frac{L}{[(1+r)^N - 1]} \times s \times (1+r)^N \times (1-s)^{t-1} - \frac{L}{[(1+r)^N - 1]} \times s \times (1+r)^t (1-s)^{t-1}$$

Let's call this Z.

$$\begin{aligned}
\frac{\partial Z}{\partial s} &= \frac{L}{[(1+r)^N - 1]} \times (1+r)^N \times (1-s)^{t-1} - \frac{L(t-1)}{[(1+r)^N - 1]} \times s \times (1+r)^N \times (1-s)^{t-2} \\
&\quad - \frac{L}{[(1+r)^N - 1]} \times (1+r)^t (1-s)^{t-1} + \frac{L(t-1)}{[(1+r)^N - 1]} \times s \times (1+r)^t (1-s)^{t-2} \\
&= \frac{L}{[(1+r)^N - 1]} \times (1+r)^N \times (1-s)^{t-1} \left[1 - \frac{s(t-1)}{1-s}\right] \\
&\quad - \frac{L}{[(1+r)^N - 1]} \times (1+r)^t (1-s)^{t-1} \left[1 - \frac{s(t-1)}{1-s}\right] \\
&= \frac{L}{[(1+r)^N - 1]} \times (1-s)^{t-1} \left[1 - \frac{s(t-1)}{1-s}\right] \times \left[(1+r)^N - (1+r)^t\right]
\end{aligned}$$

$$\frac{L}{[(1+r)^N - 1]} \times (1-s)^{t-1} \geq 0$$

$$\left[(1+r)^N - (1+r)^t\right] \geq 0$$

However, $[1 - \frac{s(t-1)}{1-s}]$ may be positive or negative. Thus the pre-payment may increase or decrease with an increase in the SMM. Because the total principal is the sum of the scheduled principal and the pre-payment, the total principal may increase or decrease with an increase in the SMM.

Chapter 10
A Primer on Derivatives

To understand the nature of derivatives, we first need to consider the nature of a typical cash or spot transaction. In a cash or a spot transaction, as soon as a deal is struck between the buyer and the seller, the buyer has to hand over the payment for the asset to the seller, who in turn has to transfer the rights to the asset to the buyer.

In the case of a forward or a futures contract, however, the actual transaction does not take place when an agreement is reached between a buyer and a seller. In such cases, at the time of negotiating the deal, the two parties merely agree on the terms at which they will transact at a future point in time, including the price to be paid per unit of the underlying asset. Thus, the actual transaction per se occurs only at a future date that is decided at the outset. Consequently, unlike the case of a cash transaction, no money changes hands when two parties enter into a forward or futures contract. But both of them have an obligation to go ahead with the transaction on the scheduled date. Failure to perform by either party is construed as default. Consequently, forward and futures contracts are termed *commitment* contracts.

Example 10.1. Mitosa Inc. has entered into a forward contract with Hudson Bank to acquire £250,000 after 120 days at an exchange rate of $1.60 per pound. Four months hence, the company is required to pay $400,000 to the bank and accept the pounds in lieu. The bank, as per the contract, has to accept the dollars, and deliver the British currency.

In the case of both forward and futures contracts, there obviously has to be a buyer and a seller. The party that agrees to buy the underlying asset in such contracts is known as the *long* and is said to assume a *long position*. That party is also termed the buyer. On the other hand, the counter party that agrees to sell the underlying asset as per the contract is known as the *short* and is said to assume a *short position*. That party is also termed as the seller. Thus the long agrees to take delivery of the underlying asset on a future date, and the short agrees to make delivery on that date. In Example 10.1, Mitosa is the long, and Hudson Bank is the short.

Futures and Forwards: Comparisons and Contrasts

Although both forward and futures contracts contain certain essential similarities, they differ in certain crucial respects. Forward contracts and futures contracts are similar in the sense that both require the long to acquire the asset on a future date and the short to deliver the asset on that date. Both types of contracts impose an obligation on the long as well as the short. However, there is one major difference between the two types of contracts. Futures contracts are *standardized*, whereas forward contracts are *customized*.

https://doi.org/10.1515/9781547400669-010

Let's clarify the meaning of "standardization" and "customization." In any contract of this nature, certain terms and conditions need to be clearly defined. The major terms that should be made explicit are the following:

- How many units of the underlying asset is the long required to acquire, or put differently, how many units of the asset does the short have to deliver?
- What is the acceptable grade, or in certain cases, what are the acceptable grades of the underlying asset that are allowable for delivery?
- Where should delivery be made? Can delivery be made only at a particular location, or do one or both parties have a choice of locations?
- When can delivery be made? Is it possible only on a particular day, or is there a specified period during which it can occur?

In a customized contract, the preceding terms and conditions have to be negotiated between the buyer and the seller of the contract. Consequently, the two parties are free to incorporate any features that they can mutually agree upon. However, in a standardized contract, there is a third party that specifies the allowable terms and conditions. The long and the short have the freedom to design a contract within the boundaries specified by such a party. However, they cannot incorporate features other than those that are specifically allowed. The third party in the case of futures contracts is the *futures exchange*. A futures exchange is similar to a stock exchange and is an arena where trading in futures contracts takes place. We can illustrate the difference between customization and standardization with the help of an example.

Example 10.2. Consider the wheat futures contract that is listed for trading on the Kansas City Board of Trade. According to the terms specified by the exchange, each futures contract requires the delivery of 5,000 bushels of wheat. A bushel is a unit of measure for agricultural commodities. A bushel of wheat is equivalent to 60 pounds or 27.216 kilograms. The allowable grades are No. 1, No. 2, and No. 3. The allowable locations for delivery are Kansas City and Hutchinson. The specifications state that delivery can be made at any time during the expiration month. Both the allowable grades and the permissible delivery locations, are specified by the futures exchange.

Now take the case of Ronald Peters, a wholesale dealer, who wants to acquire 5,000 bushels of No. 1 wheat in Kansas City during the last week of the month. Assume that there is another party, Mike Smith, a farmer, who is interested in delivering 5,000 bushels of No. 1 wheat in Kansas City during the last week of the month. In this case, the futures contracts that are listed on the exchange are obviously suitable for both the parties. Consequently, if they were to meet on the floor of the exchange at the same time, a trade could be executed for one futures contract, at a price of say $2.75 per bushel. Notice that the price that is agreed upon for the underlying asset is one feature that is not specified by the exchange. This has to be negotiated between the two parties who are entering into the contract and is a function of demand and supply conditions.

Let's now consider a slightly different scenario. Assume that Ronald wants to acquire 4,750 bushels of No. 1 quality wheat in Topeka during the last week of the month and that Mike is looking to sell the same quantity of wheat in Topeka during that period. The terms of the contract that are being sought by the two parties are not within the framework that has been specified by the futures exchange in Kansas City. There are two reasons for this. First, 4,750 represents a quantity that is less than the size of one contract, and fractional contracts cannot be bought or sold. Second, Topeka is not a permissible location for delivery. Consequently, neither party can enter into a futures contract to fulfill its objectives. However, nothing prevents the two men from getting together to negotiate an agreement that incorporates the features that they desire. Such an agreement would be a customized agreement that is tailor made to their needs. This kind of an agreement is called a *forward contract*. Thus futures contracts are exchange-traded products just like common stocks and bonds, and forward contracts are private contracts.

One of the key issues in the case of futures contracts that permit delivery of more than one specified grade or at multiple locations is who gets to decide where and what to deliver. Traditionally, the right to choose the location and the grade has always been given to the short. Also, the right to initiate the process of delivery has traditionally been given to the short. A person with a long position, therefore, cannot demand delivery. What this also means is that, in practice, investors with a long position and no desire to take delivery exit the market prior to the commencement of the delivery period by taking an opposite or offsetting position. For, after the delivery period commences, they can always be called upon to take delivery without having the right to refuse.

The Role of the Clearinghouse in a Futures Trade

A clearinghouse is an entity that is associated with a futures exchange. The clearinghouse essentially guarantees that neither the long nor the short, needs to worry about the possibility of the other party defaulting. It does so by positioning itself as the effective counter-party for each of the two original parties to the trade when a futures deal is struck. That is, the clearinghouse becomes the effective buyer for every seller, and the effective seller for every buyer. Thus, each party to a transaction needs to worry only about the financial strength and integrity of the clearinghouse, and not of the other party with which it has traded. It must be remembered that neither the long nor the short trades with the clearinghouse. The clearinghouse enters the picture only after an agreement is reached between the two parties.

What happens in practice is the following. Assume that Ronald goes long in one futures contract and that Mike goes short. The moment this trade is executed, it is replaced by two equivalent trades. The first equivalent trade has Ronald going long and the clearinghouse going short, and the second has the clearinghouse going long and Mike going short. The clearinghouse is hence termed the *central counter-party* (CCP), and this process is termed *novation*.

The need for a clearinghouse arises for the following reason. A futures contract imposes an obligation on both the parties. On the expiration date of the contract, depending on the movement of prices in the interim, it is in the interest of one of the two parties to the agreement, either the long or the short, to go through with the transaction. However, a price move in favor of one party would clearly translate into a loss for the other. Consequently, given an opportunity, one of the two parties would like to default on the expiration date. Let's illustrate this with the help of an example.

Example 10.3. Consider two people, Peter and Keith. Assume that Peter has gone long in a futures contract to buy an asset five days hence at a price of $40 and that Keith has taken the opposite side of the transaction. Let's first take the case where the spot price of the asset five days later is $42.50. If Keith already has the asset, he is obliged to deliver it for $40, thereby foregoing an opportunity to sell it in the spot market at $42.50. Otherwise, if he does not have the asset, he is required to acquire it by paying $42.50, and then subsequently deliver it to Peter for $40. Quite obviously, Keith will choose to default unless he has an impeccable conscience and character.

Now let's consider a second situation where the price of the asset five days hence is $37.50. If Keith already has the asset, he would be delighted to deliver it for $40, for the alternative is to sell it in the spot market for $37.50. Even if he were not to have the asset, he is more than happy to acquire it for $37.50 in the spot market and deliver it to Peter. The problem here is that Peter will refuse to pay $40 for the asset if he can get away with it. There are two ways of looking at it. If he does not want the asset, taking delivery at $40 would entail a subsequent sale at $37.50 and therefore a loss of $2.50. On the other hand, even if he were to require the asset, he would be better off buying it in the spot market for $37.50.

The purpose of having a clearinghouse is to ensure that defaults do not occur. A clearinghouse ensures protection for both the parties to the trade by requiring them to post a performance bond or collateral called a margin. The amount of collateral is adjusted daily to reflect any profit or loss for each party, as compared to the previous day, based on the price movement during the day. By doing so, the clearinghouse effectively takes away the incentive for a party to default as you shall shortly see.

Margins for Futures Trades

As we have just seen, whenever two parties enter into an agreement to trade at a future date, there is always an element of default risk. In other words, there is always a possibility that one of the parties does not carry out its part of the deal as required by the contract.

In the case of futures contracts, compliance is ensured, by requiring both the long and the short to deposit collateral with their broker, in an account known as the *margin account*. This margin deposit is therefore a performance guarantee.

The amount of collateral is related to the potential loss that each party is likely to incur. In the case of a futures contract, because both the parties have an obligation, it is necessary to collect collateral from both of them. After such potential losses are collected, the incentive to default is effectively taken away. For even if the party that ends up on the losing side were to fail to perform its obligation, the collateral collected from it would be adequate to take care of the interests of the other party.

Marking to Market of Futures Contracts

The reason for collecting margins is to protect both the parties against default by the other. The potential for default, to reiterate once again, arises because a position once opened can and will invariably lead to a loss for one of the two parties if it complies with the terms of the contract.

This loss, however, does not arise all of a sudden at the time of expiration of the futures contract. As the futures price fluctuates in the market from trade to trade, one of the two parties to an existing futures position experiences a gain, and the other experiences a loss. Thus, the total loss or gain from the time of getting into a futures position until the time the contract expires or is offset by taking a counter-position, whichever happens first, is the sum of these small losses and profits corresponding to each observed price in the interim.

The term *marking to market* refers to the process of calculating the loss for one party, or equivalently the corresponding gain for the other, at specified points in time, with reference to the futures price that prevailed at the time the contract was previously marked to market. In practice, when a futures contract is entered into, it is marked to market for the first time at the end of the day. Subsequently, it is marked to market every day until the position is either offset or the contract itself expires. The party that has incurred a profit has the amount credited to its margin account, and the other party, which has incurred an identical loss, has its margin account debited.

Let's illustrate how profits and losses arise in the process of marking to market and highlight the corresponding changes to the margin accounts of the respective parties. Let's take the case of Peter who has gone long in a futures contract, expiring five days hence, with Keith at a futures price of $40. Assume that the price at the end of five days is $42.50 and the prices at the end of each day prior to expiration are as depicted in Table 10.1.

Table 10.1: End of the day futures prices.

Day	Futures Price
0	40.00
1	40.50
2	39.50
3	38.00
4	40.50
5	42.50

Day 0 denotes the time the contract was entered into, and the corresponding price is the futures price at which the deal was struck.
Day t represents the end of that particular day, and the corresponding price is the prevailing futures price at that instant.

Let's assume that per the contract, Peter is committed to buying 100 units of the asset, and that at the time of entering into the contract, both the parties had to deposit $500 as collateral in their margin accounts. The amount of collateral that is deposited when a contract is first entered into is called the *initial margin*.

At the end of the first day the futures price is $40.50. This means that the price per unit of the underlying asset for a futures contract being entered into at the end of the day is $40.50. If Peter were to offset the position that he had entered into in the morning, he would have to do so by agreeing to sell 100 units at $40.50 per unit. If so, he would earn a profit of $0.50 per unit, or $50 in all. While marking Peter's position to market, the broker behaves as though it were offsetting. That is, the broker calculates Peter's profit as $50 and credits it to his margin account. However, because Peter has not expressed a desire to actually offset, the broker acts as if it were reentering into a long position at the prevailing futures price of $40.50.

At the end of the second day, the prevailing futures price is $39.50. When the contract is marked to market, Peter takes a loss of $100. Remember that his contract was reestablished the previous evening at a price of $40.50, and if the broker now behaves as if it were offsetting at $39.50, the loss is $1 per unit, or $100 in all. Once again a new long position is automatically established, this time at a price of $39.50.

This process continues either until the delivery date, when Peter actually takes possession of the asset, or until the day that he chooses to offset his position if that happens earlier. As you can see from this illustration, rising futures prices lead to profits for the long, whereas falling futures prices lead to losses.

Now let's consider the situation from Keith's perspective. At the end of the first day, when the futures price is $40.50, marking to market means a loss of $50 for him. That is, his earlier contract to sell at $40 is effectively offset by making him buy at $40.50, and a new short position is established for him at $40.50. By the same logic, at the end of the second day, his margin account is credited with a profit of $100. As you can see, shorts lose when futures prices rise and gain when the prices fall.

Thus, the profit or loss for the long is identical to the loss or profit for the short. It is for this reason that futures contracts are called *zero sum games*. One man's gain is another man's loss.

As you can see, by the time the contract expires, the loss incurred by one of the two parties, in this case the short, has been totally recovered. In our illustration, Peter's account has been credited with $250 by the time the contract expires. This amount represents the difference between the terminal futures price and the initial futures price, multiplied by the number of units of the underlying asset. These funds come from Keith's account which is debited. Now, if Keith were to refuse to deliver the asset at expiration, Peter would not be at a disadvantage. For, because he has already realized a profit of $250, he can take delivery in the spot market at the terminal spot price of $42.50 per unit in lieu of taking delivery under the futures contract. Effectively, he gets the asset at a price of $40 per unit, which is what he contracted for in the first place.

Forward contracts, unlike futures contracts, are not marked to market. Consequently, both the parties to the contract are exposed to credit risk, which is the risk that the other party may default. Thus, in practice, the parties to a forward contract tend to be large and well known, such as banks, financial institutions, corporate houses, and brokerage firms. Such parties find it easier to enter into forward contracts, compared to individuals, because their credit worthiness is easier to appraise.

Both longs and shorts in the case of futures contracts therefore have to deposit a performance bond, known as the initial margin, with their brokers as soon as they enter into a futures contract. If the markets subsequently move in favor of a party to the contract, the balance in the margin account increases, or if the market moves against the party, the balance is depleted.

Now, the broker has to ensure that a client always has adequate funds in its margin account. Otherwise the entire purpose of requiring clients to maintain margins is defeated. Consequently, the broker specifies a threshold balance called the *maintenance margin*, which is less than the initial margin. If the balance in the margin account declines below the level of the maintenance margin, due to adverse price movements the client is immediately asked to deposit additional funds to take the account balance back to the level of the initial margin. In futures market parlance, we say that the broker has issued a *margin call* to the client. A margin call is always bad news, for it is an indication, that a client has suffered major losses since opening the margin account. The additional funds deposited by a client when a margin call is complied with are referred to as a *variation margin*.

The Settlement Price for Futures Contracts

The price that is used to compute the daily gains and losses for the longs and the shorts, when the futures contracts are marked to market at the end of each day, is called the *settlement price*. In many cases, futures exchanges adopt the practice of setting the settlement price equal to the observed closing price for the day. Some exchanges believe that there is often heavy trading towards the close of the day and consequently set the settlement price equal to a volume-weighted average of the observed futures prices, in the last half hour or hour of trading. At the other extreme, if there are no trades at the end of the day, the exchange may set the settlement price equal to the average of the observed bid and ask quotes.

Movements in the Margin Account

Let's now look at a detailed example to illustrate the concepts that we have just discussed. Let's consider the case of Patty, who went long in a contract for 100 units of the asset at a price of $60 per unit, and deposited $2,000 as collateral for the same. Let's assume that the broker fixes a maintenance margin of $1,250 for the contract, the contract lasts for a period of five days, and the futures prices on the subsequent days are as shown in the second column of Table 10.2. The effect on the margin account is summarized in the same table.

Table 10.2: Changes in the margin account over the course of time.

Day	Futures Price	Daily Gain/Loss	Cumulative Gain/Loss	Account Balance	Margin Call
0	60.00			2,000	
1	62.50	250	250	2,250	
2	56.50	(600)	(350)	1,650	
3	50.00	(650)	(1,000)	1,000	1,000
4	58.50	850	(150)	2,850	
5	62.50	400	250	3,250	

Numbers in parentheses denote losses.

Let's analyze in detail a few of the entries in Table 10.2 to illustrate the concepts. Consider the second row. As compared to the time the contract was entered into, the price has increased by $2.50 per unit or $250 for 100 units. Thus, Patty, who entered into a long position, has gained $250, which is required to be credited to her margin account. After this amount is credited, the margin account, which had an opening balance of $2,000, has an end-of-the day balance of $2,250.

The settlement price at the end of the second day is $56.50. Thus, as compared to the position at the end of the previous day, Patty has suffered a loss of $6 per unit or $600 for 100 units. When this loss is debited to her margin account, the balance in the account falls to $1,650. Since this is above the maintenance level of $1,250, there is no margin call. The settlement price at the end of the next day is $50, which implies that Patty has suffered a further loss of $650. When this loss is factored into the margin account by debiting it with $650, the balance in the account falls to $1,000, which is less than the maintenance margin requirement of $1,250. Therefore, at this point in time, a margin call will be issued for $1,000, which is the amount required to take the balance back to the initial margin level of $2,000. In response to the call, Patty is expected to pay a variation margin of $1,000. The accuracy of the computation may be viewed as follows. She initially deposits $2,000 and then subsequently deposits another $1,000. Her cumulative gain/loss is $250. Hence the terminal balance in the account is 2,000 + 1,000 + 250 = $3,250, which is what we observe.

Offsetting of Futures Contracts

Futures contracts are easier to offset than forward contracts. Offsetting essentially means taking a counterposition. It means that if a party has originally gone long, it should subsequently go short and vice versa. The effect of offsetting is to cancel an existing long or short position in a contract. Remember, that a forward contract is a customized private contract between two parties. Thus, if a party to a forward contract wants to cancel the original agreement, it must seek out the counterparty with which it had entered into a deal and have the agreement canceled.

However, canceling a futures contract is a lot simpler. For example, a futures contract between two parties, say Jacob and Victor, to transact in wheat at the end of a particular month, will be identical to a similar contract between two other parties, say Kimberly and Patricia. This is because both the contracts would have been designed according to the features specified by the exchange. So if Jacob, who entered into a long position, wants to get out of his position, he need not seek out Victor, the party with whom he had originally traded. All he has to do is to go back to the floor of the exchange and offer to take a short position in a similar contract. This time the opposite position may be taken by a new party, say Robert. Thus, by taking a long position initially with Victor, and a short position subsequently with Robert, Jacob can ensure that he is effectively out of the market and has no further obligations. This is the meaning of offsetting.

The profit or loss for an investor who takes a position in a futures contract and subsequently offsets it is equal to the difference between the futures price that prevailed at the time the original position was taken and the price at the time the position is offset. For a long, the profit is $F_T - F_0$, where F_0 is the initial futures price and F_T is the terminal futures price. Thus, if the futures price increases, the long has a profit; otherwise, he has a loss. For the short, the profit is $F_0 - F_T$. Hence a price decline leads to a profit, whereas a price rise amounts to a loss.

Spot-Futures Convergence of Prices

At the time of expiration of the futures contract, the futures price must be the same as the cash or *spot* market price. For, after all, what is a futures contract? It is a contract to transact at a future point in time. At the expiration date of the contract, any futures contract must lead to an immediate transaction because the contract is scheduled to expire immediately and hence is valid only for an instant. Thus a person who enters into a futures contract at the time of expiration is effectively entering into a spot market transaction. Consequently, if the futures price at expiration is different from the spot price, there will be arbitrage opportunities.

Let's denote the futures price at expiration by F_T and the spot price at that point in time by S_T. It must be the case that $F_T = S_T$. Let's examine the consequences of F_T being greater than S_T, or F_T being less than S_T.

- $F_T > S_T$

  This situation can be exploited by an arbitrageur as follows. The investor can acquire the asset in the spot market at a price of S_T and simultaneously go short in a futures contract. Because the contract is scheduled to expire immediately, the investor can at once deliver for a price of F_T. Thus $F_T - S_T$, which by assumption is positive, represents an arbitrage profit for such an individual.

Example 10.4. Assume that the futures price of an asset at the time of expiration is $425, whereas the spot price is $422. An arbitrageur immediately acquires 100,000 units of the underlying asset in the spot market at $422 per unit and simultaneously goes short in a futures contract. Because the contract is expiring he immediately delivers at $425, thereby making a costless riskless profit of $300,000.

- $F_T < S_T$
  An arbitrageur exploits this condition by going long in a futures contract. Because it is about to expire, the investor can take immediate delivery by paying F_T and then sell the asset in the spot market for S_T. In this case, $S_T - F_T$, which by assumption is positive, represents an arbitrage profit.

Example 10.5. Assume that the futures price of an asset at the time of expiration is $422, whereas the spot price is $425. An arbitrageur takes a long position in a futures contract, which entails taking immediate delivery at $422 per unit. The asset can then be immediately sold in the spot market for $425 per unit. Thus, once again, the arbitrageur is able to lock in a costless, riskless profit of $300,000 for a transaction involving 100,000 units.

Delivery in the Case of Futures Contracts

Although both forward and futures contracts call for delivery at the time of expiration, there are fundamental differences between them in this context. First, in practice, most forward contracts are settled by delivery. However, only a small fraction of the futures contracts that are entered into (in some markets the figure is as low as 2%), result in actual delivery. The remainder are offset prior to expiration by taking a counterposition.

Second, a forward contract is a customized agreement between two parties, so unless it is canceled, it usually results in the short delivering to the original party who had gone long. In the case of futures, however, the link between the long and the short is broken by the clearinghouse, once a contract is entered into. In a futures trade, one or both parties may offset and exit the market. Hence, when a short expresses the desire to deliver, it is not necessarily the original long that takes delivery of the asset, for that party may no longer have an open long position. Thus, in the case of futures contracts, the exchange decides to whom the short should deliver. In practice, the person with the oldest outstanding long position is usually called upon to take delivery.

An OTC derivative such as a forward contract can also be assigned to another party. The process can be tricky and can vary. Usually the non-broker party finds a Wall Street firm to "step in" as it steps out. Brokers are generally happy to face each other so they would not generally see this as increasing counterparty risk. All parties typically need to agree on terms and price, the new broker who is stepping in and the original non-broker party. The original broker and the incoming Wall Street firm now face each other with respect to counterparty credit risk.

Finally, under a forward contract, the price that is paid by the long at the time of delivery, is different from the amount paid to take delivery under a futures contract with the same features and on the same underlying asset. A forward contract, it must be remembered, is not marked to market at intermediate points in time. Consequently, at expiration, the long has to pay the price that was agreed upon at the outset, to take delivery. However, in the case of a futures contract, the contract is marked to market on every business day during its lifetime. Hence, in order to ensure that the long gets to acquire the asset at the price that is agreed upon at the outset, he is asked to pay the prevailing futures price at expiration, which as you have seen earlier, is the same as the prevailing spot price at expiration. We can illustrate the above arguments using symbols, and with the help of a numerical example.

Consider a futures contract that was entered into on day 0 at a price F_0 and expires on day T. We denote the price at expiration by F_T. Such a contract is marked to market on days 1, 2, 3... up to day T. The cumulative profit for the long due to marking to market is

$$(F_T - F_{T-1}) + (F_{T-1} - F_{T-2}) + (F_{T-2} - F_{T-3}) + ... + (F_2 - F_1) + (F_1 - F_0) = (F_T - F_0)$$

To acquire the asset at the original price of F_0, the long must be asked to pay a price P at the time of delivery, such that

$$P - (F_T - F_0) = F_0$$
$$\Rightarrow P = F_T = S_T$$

Thus the price paid by the long at the time of delivery must equal the prevailing futures price at expiration, or equivalently, the prevailing spot price at expiration. In the case of a forward contract, however, is no marking to market and, hence, no intermediate cash flows. Consequently, at the time of delivery, the price P paid by the long, must be the same as the price that was agreed upon originally. That is

$$P = F_0$$

Example 10.6. Let's now illustrate these arguments using a numerical example. Consider a futures contract on wheat that was entered into at a price of $2.50 per bushel. Assume that the contract lasts for a period of 5 days and the movement in the futures price on subsequent days is as depicted in Table 10.3.

In this case, $F_0 = 2.5$ and $F_T = 3.5$. A person who went long in a futures contract at a time when the futures price was $3.50 at the time of delivery. Taking into account the profit of $1.00 due to marking to market, the long effectively gets the asset for $2.50, which is nothing but the initial futures price. On the other hand, a person who went long in a forward contract at a price of $2.50, has to pay $2.50 at the time of taking delivery.

Table 10.3: Marking a contract to market.

Day	Futures Price	Profit from Marking to Market
0	2.5	
1	2.4	(0.10)
2	2.2	(0.20)
3	2.5	0.30
4	2.8	0.30
5	3.5	0.70
	Total	1.00

Cash Settlement of Futures Contracts

There are certain futures contracts that do not allow for physical delivery of the underlying asset. In such cases, the contract is marked to market until the last day, and subsequently all positions are declared closed. Under such circumstances, both the long and the short exit the market, with their cumulative profit (which could also be a loss) since the inception of the contract. However, the short does not deliver the underlying asset at the end.

Valuation of Futures and Forwards

A forward contract entails an obligation on the part of the short to make delivery of the asset on a future date, and an equivalent obligation on the part of the long to take delivery.

From the perspective of the short, if the difference between the forward price and the prevailing spot price exceeds the cost of carrying the asset until delivery, then clearly there is an arbitrage opportunity. For instance, in the case of an asset that pays no income before the maturity of the forward contract, the cost of carrying the asset is rS_t, where r is the riskless rate of interest and S_t is the prevailing spot price. Consequently, if

$$F_t - S_t > rS_t$$

then a person could exploit the situation by borrowing and buying the asset, and simultaneously going short in a forward contract to deliver on a future date.

Such an arbitrage strategy is called *cash-and-carry arbitrage*. Hence, to rule it out, we require that

$$F_t - S_t \leq rS_t \Rightarrow F_t \leq S_t(1 + r)$$

Example 10.7. Cash-and-carry arbitrage can be illustrated with the help of an example.

Assume that IBM is currently selling for $100 per share, and is not expected to pay any dividends for the next six months. The price of a forward contract for one share of IBM to be delivered after six months is $106.

Consider the case of an investor who can borrow funds at the rate of 5% per six-month period. Such an individual can borrow $100 and acquire one share of IBM, and simultaneously go short in a forward contract to deliver the share after six months for $106. Thus the rate of return on the investment is

$$\frac{(106-100)}{100} = 0.06 \equiv 6\%$$

whereas the borrowing cost is only 5%.

Consequently, cash-and-carry arbitrage is a profitable proposition under such circumstances. This is because

$$F_t > S_t(1+r)$$

or, in other words, the forward contract is overpriced.

The rate of return obtained from a cash-and-carry strategy is called the *implied repo rate*. Thus, a cash-and-carry strategy is profitable if the implied repo rate exceeds the borrowing rate. The two statements mean the same. That is, if cash-and-carry arbitrage is possible, the futures contract is overpriced and the implied repo rate is higher than the borrowing rate. Conversely, if the implied repo rate is higher than the borrowing rate, then cash-and-carry arbitrage is profitable, for the contract is overpriced.

By engaging in a cash-and-carry strategy, the investor has ensured a payoff of $106 after six months for an initial investment of $100. It is as if the investor has bought a zero coupon debt instrument with a face value of $106 for a price of $100. Hence, a combination of a long position in the stock and a short position in a forward contract is equivalent to a long position in a zero coupon bond. Such a deep discount instrument is referred to as a *synthetic T-bill*. Hence we can express the relationship as

$$\text{Spot-Forward} = \text{Synthetic T-bill.}$$

The implication is that, while a long spot position, as well as a short forward position, are risky in isolation, their combination is risk-less.

A negative sign indicates a short position in that particular asset. Thus, if we own any two of the three assets, we can artificially create the third.

Cash and carry arbitrage requires a short position in a forward contract and arises if the contract is overpriced. However, if F_t were to be less than $S_t(1+r)$, then such a situation too would represent an arbitrage opportunity, this time for the long. Under such circumstances, an investor could short sell the asset and invest the proceeds at the risk-less rate, and simultaneously go long in a forward contract to reacquire the asset at a future date.

This kind of an arbitrage strategy is called *reverse cash-and-carry arbitrage*. In order to rule out such profit opportunities, we require that

$$F_t \geq S_t(1+r)$$

Example 10.8. We can illustrate reverse cash-and-carry arbitrage with the help of a numerical example.

Assume once again that IBM is selling for $100 per share and the company is not expected to pay any dividends for the next six months. Let the price of a forward contract for one share of IBM to be delivered after six months be $104.

Consider the case of an arbitrageur who can lend money at the rate of 5% per six monthly period. Such an individual can short sell a share of IBM and invest the proceeds at 5% interest for six months, and simultaneously go long in a forward contract to acquire the share after six months for $104. We are assuming that the arbitrageur can lend the proceeds from the short sale. In practice, the amount has to be deposited with the broker, who, of course, can invest it to earn interest. In a competitive market, brokers may pass on a part of the interest income to the client who is short selling. This is called a *short interest rebate*. However, the effective rate of return earned by the short-seller is lower than the prevailing market rate. In practice, although institutional traders have the clout to demand a short interest rebate, individual traders do not.

The effective borrowing cost is

$$\frac{(104-100)}{100} = 0.04 \equiv 4\%$$

which is less than the lending rate of 5%.

Consequently there is a profit to be made by employing a reverse cash-and-carry strategy under such circumstances. This is because

$$F_t < S_t(1+r)$$

or, in other words, the forward contract is underpriced.

The cost of borrowing funds under a reverse cash-and-carry strategy is called the *implied reverse repo rate*. Thus reverse cash-and-carry arbitrage is profitable only if the implied reverse repo rate is less than the lending rate. Once again, if the implied reverse repo rate is less than the lending rate, then reverse cash-and-carry arbitrage is profitable, for the contract is underpriced. Equivalently, if the futures contract is underpriced, it means that the implied repo rate is less than the lending rate, and consequently, reverse cash-and-carry arbitrage is profitable.

Cash-and-carry arbitrage is ruled out if $F_t \leq S_t(1+r)$, whereas reverse cash-and-carry arbitrage is ruled out if $F_t \geq S_t(1+r)$. Thus, in order to rule out both forms of arbitrage, we require that

$$F_t = S_t(1+r) \tag{10.1}$$

This is termed the *cost of carry* relationship.

The Case of Assets Making Payouts

If a person who is holding an asset receives income from it, then such an inflow obviously reduces the carrying cost. The carrying cost can now be defined as $rS_t - I$ where I is the future value of the income as calculated at the time of expiration of the forward contract.[1] Consequently, in order to rule out cash-and-carry arbitrage, we require that

$$F_t - S_t \leq rS_t - I \Rightarrow F_t \leq S_t(1 + r) - I$$

Similarly, from a short-seller's perspective, the effective income obtained by investing the proceeds from the short sale are reduced by the amount of payouts from the asset because the short-seller is required to compensate the lender of the asset for the payouts.

Thus to rule out reverse cash-and-carry arbitrage, we require that

$$F_t - S_t \geq rS_t - I \Rightarrow F_t \geq S_t(1 + r) - I$$

Therefore, to preclude both forms of arbitrage, it must be the case that

$$F_t = S_t(1 + r) - I \tag{10.2}$$

Now let's illustrate cash-and-carry arbitrage in the case of assets making payouts with the help of a numerical example. The extension to reverse cash-and-carry arbitrage is straightforward.

Example 10.9. Let's go back to the case of the IBM share. Assume that the share is selling for $100 and the stock is expected to pay a dividend of $5 after three months and another $5 after six months. Forward contracts with a time to expiration of six months are available at a price of $96 per share. Let's assume that the second dividend payment will occur just an instant before the forward contract matures.

Consider the case of an investor who can borrow at the rate of 10% per annum. Such an individual can borrow $100, buy a share of IBM, and simultaneously go short in a forward contract to sell the share after six months for $96. After three months, the investor gets a dividend of $5 which can be invested for the remaining three months at a rate of 10% per annum. And finally, just prior to delivering the share under the forward contract, the individual receives a second dividend of $5.

Thus, at the time of delivery of the share, the total cash inflow for the investor is

$$96 + 5 \times \left[1 + \frac{0.10}{4}\right] + 5 = \$106.125$$

Hence the rate of return on the synthetic T-bill is

$$\frac{(106.125 - 100)}{100} = 0.06125 \equiv 6.125\%$$

which is greater than the borrowing rate of 5% for six months.

---

1 The reason why we take the future value of income, is because the interest cost is computed at the point of expiration of the futures contract. So in order to be consistent with the principles of the time value of money, the income too should be computed at the same point in time.

Consequently, cash-and-carry arbitrage is profitable. This is because

$$F_t + I > S_t(1 + r)$$

where I is the future value of the payouts from the asset as calculated at the point of expiration of the forward contract.

Conversion Factors When There Are Multiple Deliverable Grades

Certain futures contracts give the short the flexibility to deliver more than one grade of the underlying asset. Thus the short can choose the grade to deliver. The exchange in such cases designates one grade as the *par* grade. If the short delivers the par grade, he will receive the prevailing futures price at expiration, F_T, for reasons that we have already explained. However, delivering a more valuable grade results in a premium, and when delivering a less valuable grade, the short does so at a discount. There are two ways of incorporating the premium or discount for grades other than the par grade: *multiplicative adjustment* and *additive adjustment*. Let's examine each of these techniques.

Multiplicative Adjustment of the Futures Price

In the case of contracts that permit more than one grade of the underlying asset to be delivered and specify a multiplicative system of price adjustment, the short receives an amount equal to $a_i F_T$ at the time of delivery of grade i. For premium grades, a_i is greater than 1.0, whereas for discount grades, it is less than 1.0.

We denote the spot price of grade i at expiration by $S_{i,T}$. Hence, the profit for the short when delivering grade i is

$$a_i F_T - S_{i,T} \tag{10.3}$$

Grade i is preferred to another grade j if

$$a_i F_T - S_{i,T} > a_j F_T - S_{j,T} \tag{10.4}$$

At expiration, in order to preclude arbitrage, the profit from delivering the most preferred grade must be zero. If we denote this grade as grade i, it must be the case that

$$\begin{aligned} a_i F_T - S_{i,T} &= 0 \\ \Rightarrow F_T &= \frac{S_{i,T}}{a_i} \end{aligned} \tag{10.5}$$

In the case of all other grades, it must be the case that

$$a_j F_T - S_{j,T} < 0$$
$$\Rightarrow F_T < \frac{S_{j,T}}{a_j} \forall j \tag{10.6}$$

Thus, the grade chosen for delivery obviously will be the one for which $\frac{S}{a}$ is the lowest. Such a grade is called the *cheapest to deliver grade*, and $\frac{S}{a}$ is called the *delivery adjusted spot price*. Thus, the cheapest to deliver grade, is the one with the lowest delivery adjusted spot price. At expiration therefore, the futures price must converge to the delivery-adjusted spot price of the cheapest to deliver grade.

Gold futures contracts allow for the delivery of gold within a certain weight range and with varying degrees of fineness.[2] The price received by the short = weight × fineness × futures price. Thus, per ounce of gold delivered, the short receives fineness $\times F$. The conversion factor in this case is the fineness, and the par grade is 100% fine.

Assume that gold is available with either 99% fineness or with 100% fineness. Let the spot price of 99% fine gold be \$495 per ounce and that of 100% fine gold be \$505 per ounce. The delivery adjusted spot prices are $\frac{495}{0.99} = 500$, and $\frac{505}{1} = 505$ respectively. Thus the 99% fine gold is the cheapest to deliver grade.

Additive Adjustment of the Futures Price

Now let's consider the case of contracts that permit more than one grade to be delivered but use an additive system of price adjustment. In the case of such contracts, the short receives $F_T + a_i$ for the delivery of grade i. For a premium grade, a_i is positive, whereas for a discount grade, it is negative.

The profit from delivering grade i is

$$F_T + a_i - S_{i,T} \tag{10.7}$$

and grade i is preferred to another grade j if

$$F_T + a_i - S_{i,T} > F_T + a_j - S_{j,T}$$
$$\Rightarrow S_{i,T} - a_i < S_{j,T} - a_j \tag{10.8}$$

Hence, the cheapest to deliver grade is the one for which $S - a$ is the lowest. That is, grade i is the cheapest to deliver grade if

$$S_{i,T} - a_i < S_{j,T} - a_j \forall j \tag{10.9}$$

2 See Siegel and Siegel [55].

To rule out arbitrage, the profit from delivering the cheapest to deliver grade must be zero. That is

$$F_T + a_i - S_{i,T} = 0$$
$$\Rightarrow F_T = S_{i,T} - a_i \tag{10.10}$$

In this case $S - a$ is the delivery-adjusted spot price, and once again, the futures price converges to the delivery-adjusted spot price of the cheapest to deliver grade.

It must be noted that irrespective of whether the multiplicative or the additive system is used, the cheapest to deliver grade need not be the one with the lowest spot price. For example, consider the following data for corn.

Table 10.4: An illustration of additive price adjustment.

Grade	Spot Price	Conversion Factor	Delivery-Adjusted Spot Price
No. 1	6.51	0.015	6.495
No. 2	6.50	0	6.500
No. 3	6.49	−0.015	6.505

The par grade is obviously No. 2. But the cheapest to deliver grade is No. 1, which incidentally has the highest spot price.

Hedging Using Futures Contracts

A *hedger*, by definition, is a person who wants to protect himself against an unfavorable movement in the price of the underlying asset. Quite obviously, a person who seeks to hedge has already assumed a position in the underlying asset. If the hedger already owns the asset, or in other words has a long position, the worry is that the price of the asset may fall subsequently. On the other hand, if the hedger has made a commitment to buy, or in other words has taken a short position, the worry is that the price of the asset may rise subsequently. In either case, the reason to hedge is to avoid risk.

Notice that we have defined a short position in a broader sense then in the case of a short sale involving an asset. In the case of a short sale, the short-seller borrows an asset from a broker in order to sell and therefore has a commitment to buy it back at a future date and return it. Now take the case of a German company that has imported goods from the U.S and been given 90 days credit by the American supplier. The company therefore has a commitment to buy dollars after 90 days. Just like in the case of the short-seller, this company also worries that the price of the asset, in this case the U.S. dollar, may go up by the time it is procured. Thus in a more general sense, a short position connotes a commitment to buy an asset at a future date. An example in the case of physical commodities would be the case of a wheat mill that knows it will have to procure wheat after the harvest, which we can assume is one month away. Its worry consequently would be that the harvest may be less plentiful than anticipated, and therefore the price of the wheat in the spot market may turn out to be higher than what is currently expected. Such an entity also may exhibit a desire to hedge.

Futures contracts can help people to hedge, irrespective of whether they have a long or a short position in the underlying asset. Consider a person who owns an asset. Such a person can hedge by taking a short position in a futures contract. If the price of the underlying asset falls subsequently, that person can still sell at the original futures price because the other party is under an obligation to buy at this price. We can illustrate this with the help of an example.

Example 10.10. Greg owns 50,000 shares of IBM. His worry is that the spot price of the shares may decline substantially during the next three months.

Futures contracts on IBM are available with a time to maturity of three months, and each contract is for 100 shares. If the current futures price is $75 per share, then by going short in 500 futures contracts, Greg can ensure that he can sell the shares three months hence for $3,750,000.

This amount of $3,750,000 is guaranteed irrespective of what the actual spot price at the end of three months turns out to be. Thus, by locking in this amount, Greg can protect himself against a decline in the price below the contracted value of $75 per share. However, the flip side is that he is unable to benefit if the spot price at expiration turns out to be greater than $75, for he is obliged to deliver at this price.

Now consider the issue from the perspective of a person, Tom, who has a short position in the underlying asset. His worry is that the price may rise by the time he acquires it in the cash market. He can hedge by taking a long position in the futures market. For, if the spot price rises subsequently, he can still buy at the original futures price because the other party is under an obligation to sell at this price.

Example 10.11. Vincent has imported goods worth £312,500 from London, and is required to pay after one month. He is worried the dollar may depreciate by then, or in other words, that the dollar price of the pound may go up. A futures contract expiring after one month is available, and the contract size is 62,500 pounds. Let the futures price be $1.75 per pound.

So if Vincent takes a long position in five futures contracts, he can lock in a dollar value of $546,875 for the pounds. Once again this is true irrespective of the spot exchange rate one month later. So although Vincent can protect himself against a depreciating dollar, or in other words an exchange rate greater than $1.75 per pound, he is precluded from taking advantage of an appreciating dollar, which would manifest itself as an exchange rate below $1.75 per pound.

Hedging and Ex-Post Regret

A hedger who uses futures contracts may end up regretting a decision ex-post because the result would have been better without the hedge. Take the case of Vincent who went long in futures to acquire £312,500 at $1.75 per pound. If the spot exchange rate at the end turns out to be greater than $1.75 per pound, or in other words, if the dollar depreciates, then his decision to hedge would certainly be perceived as wise and sound.

But, if the spot exchange rate at expiration were to be less than $1.75 per pound, or in other words if the dollar appreciates, Vincent would end up looking a little foolish. For he could have bought the pounds at a lower cost in terms of dollars had he decided not to hedge.

The problem is that, a priori, Vincent cannot be expected to be certain as to whether the dollar would depreciate or appreciate. So if he is a risk-averse individual, then he may very well decide to hedge his risk, notwithstanding the possibility that he may end up looking silly ex-post.

Thus, an investor will hedge when uncomfortable leaving open exposure to price risk, where price risk refers to the risk that the spot price of the asset may end up moving in an adverse direction from the investor's perspective. There is no guarantee that ex-post the decision will be vindicated. Hindsight as they say is a *perfect science.* A normal individual cannot be expected to be prescient, and a prescient investor certainly would not need derivatives in order to hedge.[3]

Hedging and the Case of Cash-Settled Contracts

The effective price at which to sell if a hedger takes a short futures position, or buy in the case of a long futures position, is equal to the futures price prevailing at the time of initiation of the futures position, irrespective of whether the contract is delivery settled or cash settled.

Let's first take the case of a hedger who goes short in futures contracts. If the contract is cash settled, the total profit from marking to market is $F_0 - F_T$. The hedger has to sell the asset in the spot market at a price of S_T, and the overall cash inflow will be

$$S_T + (F_0 - F_T) = F_0$$

because by the no-arbitrage condition, $F_T = S_T$. Notice that the profit from the futures position has to be added to determine the effective inflow. If it is a positive number, that is, it actually is a profit, then it leads to a higher effective inflow. If it is a negative number, that is, it is a loss, then it leads to a lower effective inflow.

Example 10.12. Let's take the case of Greg who went short in 500 futures contracts at a price of $75 per share, where each contract is for 100 shares. Assume that the futures price or equivalently the spot price at expiration is $78.50 per share.

3 See Parameswaran and Hegde [36].

Greg's cumulative profit from marking to market is

$$500 \times 100 \times (75.00 - 78.50) = -\$175{,}000$$

He can sell the shares in the spot market for $78.50 per share or $3,925,000 in all. The effective amount received for 50,000 of shares is

$$\$\,3{,}925{,}000 - \$175{,}000 = \$3{,}750{,}000$$

which amounts to $75 per share.

The same is true for a hedger who goes long in futures. If the contract is cash settled, the cumulative profit from marking to market is $F_T - F_0$. The hedger then has to buy the asset in the spot market by paying S_T. The overall cash outflow is[4]

$$-S_T + (F_T - F_0) = -F_0$$

Notice that the profit from the futures position is added to the outflow in the spot market to determine the effective outflow. Thus a profit, or inflow from the futures market, reduces the effective outflow, whereas a loss, or outflow from the futures market, increases the effective outflow.

Example 10.13. Take the case of Vincent who went long in a futures contract at a price of $1.75 per pound. Assume that the terminal spot or equivalently futures price is $1.72 per dollar. His cumulative profit from marking to market is

$$312{,}500 \times (1.72 - 1.75) = -\$9{,}375$$

He can acquire £312,500 in the spot market by paying $537,500. His effective outflow is therefore $546,875 which translates into an exchange rate of $1.75 per pound, which is the initial futures price.

Perfect Hedges Using Futures Contracts

A hedge using futures contracts that can lock in, with absolute certainty, a selling price for an investor with a long position in the spot market, or a buying price for an investor with a short position in the spot market, is called a *perfect hedge*. Both the examples given earlier are illustrations of a perfect hedge. In the first case, Greg was assured of a selling price of $75 per share, and in the second case, Vincent was assured of a buying price of $1.75 per pound.

If we are to ensure that the hedge is perfect, then the following conditions must necessarily hold:

4 The negative sign denotes an outflow.

1. Futures contracts must be available on the commodity that the hedger is seeking to buy or to sell. If this is not the case, then one has to use a contract on a related commodity. This is termed *cross-hedging*. The criterion for a close relationship, is that the prices of the two should be highly positively correlated.
2. The date on which the hedger wishes to buy or sell the underlying asset must coincide with the date on which the futures contract being used is scheduled to expire.
3. The number of units of the underlying asset, which is sought to be bought or sold by the hedger, must be an integer multiple of the size of the futures contract.

The Importance of Terminating the Hedge on the Expiration Date

It important that the date on which the asset is bought or sold be the same as the expiration date of the futures contract, to ensure that the hedge is perfect.

Take the case of a hedger who has gone short in futures contracts. We can denote the initial futures price by F_0 and the terminal spot and futures prices by S_T and F_T, respectively. Now assume that the hedger wishes to sell the goods in his possession on day t^*, where $0 < t^* < T$. That is, the hedger wishes to sell the goods prior to the date of expiration of the futures contract. Doing so requires offsetting the futures position on that day by taking a counterposition.

The cumulative profit from the futures market due to marking to market is $F_0 - F_{t^*}$. The proceeds from the sale of the good in the spot market are S_{t^*}. Thus the effective sale proceeds are

$$S_{t^*} + (F_0 - F_{t^*}) = F_0 + (S_{t^*} - F_{t^*})$$

Now if t^* were the same as T, then S_{t^*} would be equal to F_{t^*} and the effective price received would be F_0. In other words, the hedge would be perfect, for the initial futures price would have been locked in. But, in general, when t^* is a date prior to the expiration of the futures contract, F_{t^*} will not be equal to S_{t^*}. Thus, the effective price received ultimately depends on both F_{t^*} and S_{t^*}. Because these are unknown variables until the end, there is always uncertainty regarding the effective price that will ultimately be received by the hedger.

A similar argument can be advanced for the case where the hedger takes a long position in a futures contract. If the asset is bought on day t^* and the futures position taken earlier is offset, the effective outflow on account of the asset is

$$-S_{t^*} + (F_{t^*} - F_0) = -F_0 - (S_{t^*} - F_{t^*}) \tag{10.11}$$

Once again there will be uncertainty about the effective price at which the asset will be bought.

Thus, because spot-futures convergence is assured only at the time of expiration of the futures contract, it is necessary that the date on which the transaction in the underlying asset takes place be the same as the expiration date of the futures contract, if we are to ensure that the hedge is perfect.

The Importance of Hedging an Integer Multiple of the Contract Size

It is essential that the number of units that the hedger is seeking to buy or sell be an integer multiple of the size of the futures contract, if we are to ensure that the hedge is perfect.

Assume that a farmer has 1,050 units of a commodity that he wishes to sell after one month. Futures contracts on the commodity expiring after one month are available, and each contract is for 100 units. So this farmer theoretically needs to go short in 10.5 futures contracts, but in practice, must go short in 10 contracts or in 11. In either case, the effective price received per unit is uncertain.

Case-A: The farmer uses 10 contracts
The profit from marking to market is

$$10 \times 100 \times (F_0 - F_T)$$

The proceeds when the goods are sold in the spot market are $1{,}050S_T$. The effective price received per unit of the good is

$$\frac{1{,}050S_T + 1{,}000(F_0 - F_T)}{1{,}050}$$
$$= \frac{50S_T + 1{,}000F_0}{1{,}050}$$

Since S_T is a random variable whose value is known only at the end, the effective price that will be received per unit is uncertain.

Case-B: The farmer uses 11 contracts
The profit from marking to market is

$$11 \times 100 \times (F_0 - F_T)$$

The proceeds from the sale of goods are $1{,}050S_T$. The effective price received per unit of the good is

$$\frac{1{,}050S_T + 1{,}100(F_0 - F_T)}{1{,}050}$$
$$= \frac{1{,}100F_0 - 50S_T}{1{,}050}$$

Once again there is uncertainty regarding the effective price that will be received.

Choosing an Expiration Month for Hedging

Let's assume that futures contracts are available on the commodity whose price we want to hedge and that the transaction size is an integer multiple of the size of the futures contract. However, the scheduled transaction date rarely coincides with the expiration date of the futures contract. The only option under such circumstances is to choose a futures contract that expires after the date on which we want to transact. For, if we use a futures contract that expires earlier, then subsequently we will have an open or uncovered position, which means that we will not be hedged or protected until the transaction date.

If we use a contract that expires after the transaction date, then such a contract has to be offset on the transaction date. For a short hedger, the effective price received under such circumstances is

$$F_0 + (S_{t^*} - F_{t^*})$$

The uncertainty in this case arises because S_{t^*} need not equal F_{t^*}. The same holds true for a hedger who takes a long position in futures contracts.

At any point in time t, $S_t - F_t$ is called the basis and is denoted by b_t. At the time of expiration of the futures contract, S_T is guaranteed to equal F_T, and we can be sure that the basis will be zero. However, prior to expiration we cannot make such an assertion. Consequently, a hedger who is forced to offset the futures contract prior to expiration faces uncertainty regarding the basis, or what is called *basis risk*.

We have defined the basis as $S_t - F_t$.[5] For a short hedger, the effective price received is $F_0 + b_t$. Thus the higher the value of the basis the better it is for the hedger, who benefits from a rising basis. However, for a long hedger, the effective outflow is $F_0 + b_t$. Thus the lower the value of the basis, the smaller the outflow is. We know that a person with a long futures position benefits from a rising futures price, whereas an investor with a short futures position benefits from a declining futures price. The basis is a synthetic price, for it is the difference of two prices. We have seen that a rising basis benefits the shorts, and a falling basis benefits the longs. Consequently we can say that *a short hedger is long the basis, and a long hedger is short the basis.*

Speculation Using Futures Contracts

Unlike a hedger, whose objective is to avoid risk, a speculator is a person who consciously seeks to take risk, hoping to profit from subsequent price movements. Such a person is either betting that the price will rise, and he is said to be bullish, or is hoping that it will fall, and he is said to be bearish.

5 Some authors prefer to define it as the futures price minus the spot price.

From the standpoint of finance theory, speculation and gambling are two different phenomena. A speculator is a person who evaluates the risk of an investment and the anticipated return from it prior to committing. Such a trader therefore takes a position only if he feels that the anticipated return is adequate considering the risk being taken. In other words, the trader may be said to be taking a calculated risk.

A gambler on the other hand is someone who takes a risk purely for the thrill of taking it. The expected return from the strategy is of no consequence for such a person when taking a decision to gamble.

Active speculation adds depth to a market and makes it more liquid. A market characterized solely by hedgers does not have the kind of volumes required to make it efficient. In practice, when a hedger seeks to take a position, very often the opposite side of the transaction is taken by a speculator, although this need not always be the case. There could be situations where both traders are speculators and the long is a bull who is anticipating a price rise, and the short is a bear who believes that prices are likely to decline. It is also possible that both traders are hedgers. The long may be a consumer who is worried about rising prices, and the short may be a producer, who is perturbed by the specter of declining prices. Divergence of views, and a desire to take positions based on those views is a sin qua non for making the free market system a success. Thus speculators, along with hedgers and arbitrageurs, play a pivotal role in financial markets.

Consider an investor who is of the view that the price of an asset is going to rise. One way that a person can take a speculative position is by buying the asset in the spot market and holding on to it, in the hope of offloading it subsequently at a higher price.

However, buying the asset in the spot market entails incurring substantial costs. In addition, in the case of a physical asset, the investor has to face the hassle of storing and insuring it.

All this can be avoided if futures contracts are used for speculation. When taking a long futures position, the investor can lock in a price at which to acquire the asset subsequently. If the hunch is true and the spot price at the time of expiration of the futures contract is higher, then the investor can take delivery at the initial futures price as per the contract and sell it at the prevailing spot price, thereby making a profit.

The advantage of using futures is that the entire value of the asset need not be paid at the outset. All that is required is a small margin. In other words, futures contracts provide leverage.

Example 10.14. Futures contracts on IBM with three months to expiration are available at a price of $75 per share. Alex is of the opinion that the spot price of IBM three months hence will be at least $78 per share. Therefore, he chooses to speculate by going long in 100 futures contracts, each of which is for 100 shares.

If his hunch is right and the spot price after three months is $80 per share, then Alex makes a profit of

$$100 \times 100 \times (80 - 75) = \$50{,}000$$

However, there is always a possibility that Alex is wrong. Let's assume that he read the market incorrectly and the price at expiration turns out to be $72 per share. If so, he would have to acquire the shares at $75 per share and sell them in the spot market at $72 per share, thereby making a loss of

$$100 \times 100 \times (72 - 75) = -\$30{,}000$$

Thus speculation using futures can give rise to substantial gains if one is right, but can lead to significant losses if one misjudges the market.

Now let's take the case of a bear, who is of the opinion that the market is going to fall. He too can speculate, but by going short in a futures contract. If his hunch turns out to be right, and the market price at the time of expiration of the futures contract is indeed lower than what the futures price was at the outset, he can buy at the prevailing market price and sell it at the contract price, thereby making a profit.

Example 10.15. Nina, like Alex, observes that the futures price for a three-month contract on IBM is $75 per share. However, unlike Alex, she is of the opinion that in three months time, IBM will be selling for $72 or less per share in the spot market. Assume that she takes a short position in 100 futures contracts.

If her hunch is right and the price of IBM after three months is $70 per share, Nina makes a profit of

$$100 \times 100 \times (75 - 70) = \$50{,}000$$

However, if the market rises to $78 after three months, Nina incurs a loss of

$$100 \times 100 \times (75 - 78) = -\$30{,}000$$

So, like bulls, bears can use futures to speculate, but in their quest for substantial gains, there is always a risk of substantial losses.

Introduction to Options

We have covered two types of derivative securities, namely futures and forward contracts, in detail. In a futures contract no money changes hands when the contract is negotiated, nor does the title to the goods. The important point to note is that once a futures contract is negotiated, both the long and the short have an obligation at a future date. Because both parties have an obligation, there is always a possibility that the party with a loss at the expiration of the contract may default. As discussed previously, compliance is ensured by requiring both the parties to deposit good faith money or collateral called *margins* and by adjusting the profits and losses on a daily basis by a procedure known as *marking to market*.

Options contracts, which are the focus now, are derivative contracts, but by design are different from futures contracts. In an options contract, the buyer of the contract, also called the *holder* or the *long*, has a right, and the seller, also known as the *writer* or the *short*, has an obligation. Thus, in the case of an options contract, the long has the freedom to decide whether to go through with the transaction, whereas the short has no choice but to carry out the seller's part of the agreement if and when the holder chooses to exercise his right. Therefore, unlike in the case of futures contracts, both the parties need not deposit collateral. For, if a person has a right, there is no fear of noncompliance because he will exercise his right if it is in his interest and need not otherwise. Consequently, in the case of options contracts, only the shorts have to deposit margins.

The buyer of an option has either the right to buy the underlying asset or the right to sell it, depending on the terms of the agreement. Therefore, there are two types of options contracts, *calls* and *puts*. A call option gives the long the right to acquire the underlying asset, whereas a put option gives the long the right to sell the underlying asset. An option may give the long the right to transact only at a future point in time, namely the expiration date of the option, or else it may give the flexibility of exercising the option at any point in time, up to and including the expiration date. Consequently, both calls and puts can be of two types, *European* and *American*. A European option gives the holder the freedom to exercise the right only at the time of expiration of the contract, whereas an American option can be exercised by the long at any point in time on or before expiration. It must be noted that the terms European and American have nothing to do with geographical locations and that in practice most exchange traded contracts are American. Most textbooks, however, begin with an analysis of European options because they are easier to value, as we have to take into account the possibility of exercise at only a single point in time. Given the same features in all other respects, an American option is more valuable than the corresponding European option. This is because the holder of an American option has the flexibility to exercise early, whereas the holder of a European option does not have the freedom to exercise prior to expiration.

Common Terms Associated with Options

Let's define the various terms that are used in connection with options contracts.

Exercise Price

This is the price the holder of a call option has to pay to the writer, per unit of the underlying asset, if exercising the option. In the case of puts, it is the price the holder of a put option receives per unit of the underlying asset, if the option is exercised. The exercise price is also known as the *strike price*.

The exercise price enters the picture only if the holder chooses to exercise the option. The holder has a right and not an obligation, and may or may not decide to transact, which means that the exercise price may or may not be paid/received.

Expiration Date

This is the point in time after which the contract becomes void. It is the only point in time at which a European option can be exercised and the last point in time at which an American option can be exercised. The expiration date is also known as the *exercise date*, *strike date* or *maturity date*.

Option Premium

This is the price that the holder has to pay to the writer at the outset, in order to acquire the right to exercise. The option premium is a *sunk cost*. If the holder were not to exercise prior to expiration, the premium cannot be recovered.

Why does the buyer of an option have to pay a premium at the outset? Options contracts entail the payment of a premium at the outset, because the buyer is acquiring a right from the writer, who is taking on an obligation to perform if the buyer exercises the right. Rights, it must be understood, are never free, and one always has to pay a price to acquire them.

Futures and forward contracts, in contrast, do not entail the payment of a premium by the long. Such contracts impose an equivalent obligation on both the long and the short. The futures price, which is the price at which the long will acquire the asset at the time of expiration, is set in such a way that from the standpoints of both the long and the short, the value of the contract at inception is zero. In other words, the two equivalent and opposite obligations ensure that neither party has to pay the other at the outset.

Another way of appreciating the difference between a commitment contract, such a futures contract, and a contingent contract, such as an options contract, is as follows. When a futures contract is sealed, either the long or the short may have to countenance a loss. However, after a party buys an option from a writer, thereafter he will not have to witness the specter of a cash outflow. If he exercises he will get a positive cash flow, or else if he does not there will be no consequence. On the contrary, the writer may have to face a cash outflow subsequently.

Notation

We use the following symbols to depict the various variables:

- $t \equiv$ today, a point in time before the expiration of the options contract.
- $T \equiv$ the point of expiration of the options contract.
- $S_t \equiv$ the stock price at time t.
- $S_T \equiv$ the stock price at the point of expiration of the options contract.
- $X \equiv$ the exercise price of the option.
- $C_t \equiv$ a general symbol for the premium of a call option at time t, when we do not wish to make a distinction between European and American options.
- $P_t \equiv$ a general symbol for the premium of a put option at time t, when we do not wish to make a distinction between European and American options.
- $C_{E,t} \equiv$ the premium of a European call option at time t.
- $P_{E,t} \equiv$ the premium of a European put option at time t.
- $C_{A,t} \equiv$ the premium of an American call option at time t.
- $P_{A,t} \equiv$ the premium of an American put option at time t.
- $r \equiv$ the riskless rate of interest per annum.

Exercising Call and Put Options

Let's now take a look at the cash flows involved when an option is exercised. To keep matters simple, we focus on European options, although the underlying logic is the same in the case of American options. We use stock options, that is contracts based on the common stock of a company, for the purpose of illustration. In principle, however, an options contract can be written on any asset.

Example 10.16. Consider a person who buys a call option on IBM that expires in December 2019 and has an exercise price of \$125. Let's assume that the option premium is \$7.50 per unit of the underlying asset, which in this case is a share of IBM. Option premia are always quoted on a per share basis. The contract size for stock options, or in other words, the number of shares that the option holder can buy or sell per contract, is kept fixed at 100 in the U.S. So, in this case, as soon as the deal is struck, the buyer has to pay \$7.50 × 100 = \$750 to the writer. In exchange, the buyer gets the right to buy 100 shares of IBM on the expiration date at a price of \$125 per share.

When will the holder choose to exercise his right? Quite obviously, if the stock price at the time of expiration of the option is greater than \$125, then it makes sense to exercise the option and buy the shares at \$125 each. Otherwise, it is best to let the option expire worthless. Readers encountering options for the first time may feel that it makes sense to exercise only if the stock price at expiration is greater than (125 + 7.50) or \$132.50. This viewpoint is erroneous. Assume that the terminal stock price is \$127.50. If the option is exercised, the holder can buy 100 shares for \$125 each and immediately sell them for \$127.50 each. We use the symbol π to denote profits and indicate losses by putting the numbers in parentheses after the corresponding currency symbol. After taking into account the option premium that was paid at the outset, the total profit is

$$\pi = (127.50 - 125) \times 100 - 750 = \$(500)$$

Thus, the holder who exercises the option, suffers a loss of $500, but allowing the contract to expire worthless means losing the entire initial premium of $750. This argument is an illustration of the maxim that *sunk costs are irrelevant* when taking investment decisions.

Example 10.17. Let's reconsider the previous example, but assume that the options under consideration are put options. The question is, when will the holder choose to exercise his right? Exercise is a profitable proposition if the terminal stock price is less than $125. Otherwise, it is best to let the option expire worthless. Assume that the terminal stock price is $115 and the premium paid for the option is $3.00 per share. The profit is

$$\pi = (125 - 115) \times 100 - 300 = \$700$$

Notice, that in either case, when it is in the interest of the option holder to exercise, the circumstances are not in favor of the option writer. You should now be able to appreciate why an options contract is a right for the holder, but an obligation for the writer. If both parties were to have rights, then the writer would refuse to transact when conditions are in favor of the holder and vice versa. Thus, we can impose obligations on both the parties like in the case of forward and futures contracts, or else give one party a right and impose an obligation on the other like in the case of options contracts.

Payoffs and Profits: A Symbolic Representation

The payoff for a call holder at expiration is equal to $S_T - X$, if $S_T > X$, or 0 if $S_T \leq X$. The payoff can therefore be represented as $\text{Max}(0, S_T - X)$.

The profit can be represented as $\text{Max}(0, S_T - X) - C_t$, where C_t is the premium paid for the call when it was acquired.

The payoff for the call writer is $-\text{Max}(0, S_T - X) = \text{Min}(0, X - S_T)$, and the profit is $\text{Min}(0, X - S_T) + C_t$.

In the case of call options, therefore, the maximum profit for the holder is unlimited because the stock price at the time of exercise has no theoretical upper limit. The maximum loss, however, is restricted to the initial premium that is paid. From the standpoint of the call writer, the situation is just the reverse. The maximum loss is unlimited, whereas the maximum profit is the option premium that the writer receives at the outset.

Similarly, the payoff for a put holder is equal to $X - S_T$, if $S_T < X$, or 0 if $S_T \geq X$. The payoff can therefore be represented as $\text{Max}(0, X - S_T)$.

The profit can be represented as $\text{Max}(0, X - S_T) - P_t$, where P_t is the premium paid for the put when it was acquired.

The payoff for the put writer is $-\text{Max}(0, X - S_T) = \text{Min}(0, S_T - X)$, and the profit is $\text{Min}(0, S_T - X) + P_t$.

For a put holder, therefore, the maximum profit is equal to the exercise price less the option premium. Because, stocks have limited liability, the price cannot go below zero. The holder's maximum loss is once again the option premium. For the put writer, the maximum profit is equal to the premium received, whereas the maximum loss is equal to the exercise price minus the premium. Thus, irrespective of whether it is a call or a put, an option is a *zero sum game*. The holder's profit is equal to the writer's loss and vice versa.

As can be seen, an option holder can never lose more than the premium, whereas the profit for an option writer can never exceed the premium. Call option buyers face the possibility of finite losses and theoretically infinite profits. However, both the profits and losses are capped for put holders. For call writers, profits are finite, but losses are theoretically infinite. Put writers, however, face finite profits as well as losses.

Moneyness of the Option

The moneyness of an option refers to the relationship between the prevailing spot price of the underlying asset, and the exercise price of the option.

Call Options

- If $S_t > X$, the call option is said to be *in-the-money*.
- If $S_t = X$, the call option is said to be *at-the-money*.
- If $S_t < X$, the call option is said to be *out-of-the-money*.

Example 10.18. Consider a stock that is currently trading at $500. A call option with an exercise price of $500 is said to be at the money. A call with a lower exercise price, say $450, is said to be in the money, whereas one with a higher exercise price, say $550, is considered to be out of the money. Obviously, a call option is exercised only if it happens to be in the money.

Put Options

- If $S_t > X$, the put option is said to be *out-of-the-money*.
- If $S_t = X$, the put option is said to be *at-the-money*.
- If $S_t < X$, the put option is said to be *in-the-money*.

Example 10.19. Consider a stock that is currently trading at $500. A put option with an exercise price of $500 is said to be at the money. A put with a lower exercise price, say $450, is considered to be out of the money, whereas one with a higher exercise price, say $550, is said to be in the money. Obviously, a put option, too is exercised only if it happens to be in the money.

Intrinsic Value and Time Value of Options

The intrinsic value of an option is equal to the amount by which it is in the money, if it is in the money; otherwise, it is equal to zero. Therefore, the intrinsic value of a call option is

$$\text{I.V.} = \text{Max}[(S_t - X), 0] \tag{10.12}$$

and that of a put option is

$$\text{I.V.} = \text{Max}[(X - S_t), 0] \tag{10.13}$$

The difference between an option's price and its intrinsic value is called the time value or the speculative value of the option. By definition, no option, European or American, call or put, can have a negative intrinsic value. However, some options may have a negative time value.

Example 10.20. Assume that the price of a stock is $100 and the exercise price of a call option is $97.50. If the call premium is $3.50, then

$$100.00 - 97.50 = \$2.50$$

is the intrinsic value of the call option, and

$$3.50 - 2.50 = \$1.00$$

is its time value.

Example 10.21. Assume that the price of a stock is $100 and the exercise price of a put option is $97.50. The put premium is $1.25. In this case, the intrinsic value is zero because the put is out of the money. Therefore, the entire premium of $1.25 is the time value of the option.

The Absence of Arbitrage and Its Implications for Option Prices

Let's now state certain results pertaining to option prices. All option prices must satisfy these properties, or else there will be arbitrage opportunities. What do we mean by an arbitrage opportunity? *Arbitrage refers to the ability of a trader to make cost-less and risk-less profits.* The phrase of significance here is *cost less* and *risk-less*. A costly but risky investment should yield a risk-adjusted expected rate of return. A strategy that entails an investment, but is devoid of risk, should yield the risk-less rate of return. The ability of an individual to earn a return without making an investment, in an environment devoid of risk, is referred to as arbitrage. In other words, a strategy that yields a cash inflow at certain points in time and a zero cash flow at other points in time can be termed an arbitrage strategy. This is because it leads to non-negative returns for the investor without requiring an investment (which would have manifested itself as a cash outflow) at any point in time. As should be obvious, an arbitrage opportunity will be exploited by anyone who perceives it to the maximum possible extent until it is eliminated.

These conditions must hold if arbitrage is to be ruled out. They are, however, independent of the way the option prices are determined. In other words, these conditions are not specific to a particular option valuation model.

Non-Negative Option Premia

An option cannot have a negative price. The existence of a negative price would mean that the writer is prepared to pay the holder to buy the option. If so, the holder can acquire the option, pocket the payment, and simply forget about the contract. The reason why the holder need not worry about further adverse consequences, or in other words, subsequent negative cash flows, is because the option is a right and not an obligation. Obviously, the presence of negative option premia would be a classic example of an arbitrage opportunity.

Non-Negative Time Value of American Options

Consider American calls. We use the symbol $C_{A,t}$ to denote the price of an American call option at time t. $C_{A,t}$, should be greater than or equal to $\text{Max}[(S_t - X),0]$.

Proof

If $S_t - X$ is less than zero, we can say that $C_{A,t} \geq 0$ because an option cannot have a negative premium. However, if $S_t - X > 0$, $C_{A,t}$ must be worth at least $S_t - X$. The proof can be demonstrated as follows. Consider a case where $S_t - X > 0$ and $C_{A,t} < S_t - X$. If so, you can buy the option by paying $C_{A,t}$ and immediately exercise it. The profit of $S_t - X - C_{A,t}$ that you get is clearly an arbitrage profit. Therefore, to preclude arbitrage, we require that

$$C_{A,t} \geq \text{Max}[(S_t - X), 0]$$

In other words, an American call must be worth at least its intrinsic value. That is, an American call cannot have a negative time value.

Example 10.22. Let S_t = \$105 and X = \$100. Assume that $C_{A,t}$ = \$4.50. An arbitrageur can buy the call and immediately exercise it. This yields an arbitrage profit of

$$(105 - 100) - 4.50 = \$0.50$$

per share.

A similar argument demonstrates that the put premium for an American option, $P_{A,t}$, should be greater than or equal to Max$[(X - S_t),0]$. That is, an American put, too, is worth at least the intrinsic value and cannot have a negative time value.

Lower Bound for Call Options

$$C_t \geq \text{Max}\left[0, S_t - \frac{X}{(1+r)^{T-t}}\right]$$

If $S_t - \frac{X}{(1+r)^{T-t}} > 0$, the call premium will be greater. This automatically implies that $C_t > S_t - X$. This result is common for European as well as American calls. The implication is that an American call will never be exercised early, because its price is always greater than its intrinsic value. A party who seeks to encash, will rather offset than exercise. Consequently both European and American calls on a non-dividend paying stock will have the same premium.

The rationale is the following. Keeping other variables constant, which obviously implies a constant intrinsic value, the longer the time to expiration is, the greater the interest earned on the exercise price by the call holder. Thus the longer the time to expiration, the greater the time value is. Thus European and American calls on a non-dividend paying stock, always have a non-negative time value except at the point of expiration, at which time all options must have a premium equal to the intrinsic value, as we shall shortly see.

Lower Bound for Put Options

$$P_{E,t} \geq \text{Max}\left[0, \frac{X}{(1+r)^{T-t}} - S_t\right]$$

If $\frac{X}{(1+r)^{T-t}} - S_t > 0$, the put premium will be greater for European options. However, this result does not necessarily imply that $P_{E,t} > X - S_t$. Thus a European put on a non-dividend paying stock may have a negative time value.

Keeping other variables constant, which obviously implies a constant intrinsic value, the longer the time to expiration is, the greater the interest lost on the exercise price by the put holder. Thus there could be a situation where the time value is negative. For instance, if the stock price is zero, the put holder will want to exercise immediately. However, because the option is European, the holder is compelled to wait, which explains the possible negative time value. In such a situation, an American put may be exercised. Consequently, unlike American calls, American puts on non-dividend paying stocks may be exercised early.

Put-Call Parity for European Options

The put-call parity theorem states that

$$C_{E,t} - P_{E,t} = S_t - \frac{X}{(1+r)^{T-t}} \tag{10.14}$$

where $C_{E,t}$ represents the price of a European call with an exercise price of X and time to expiration equal to $T - t$ periods, and $P_{E,t}$ represents the price of a European put with the same exercise price and expiration date.

Now let's extend the result to a stock that pays a known dividend D at time t^*, which is a point in time before the expiration of the contract.

$$C_{E,t} - P_{E,t} = S_t - \frac{X}{(1+r)^{T-t}} - \frac{D}{(1+r)^{t^*-t}} \tag{10.15}$$

Option Premia at Expiration

American options and European calls on non-dividend paying stocks have a non-negative time value, as we have seen earlier, whereas European puts on non-dividend paying stocks may have either a positive or a negative time value depending on the extent to which the option is in the money. At the time of expiration, the time value of an option must be zero, that is, the option premium must be equal to the intrinsic value. This is because, the holder does not have the freedom of waiting any further, and consequently will not pay for the option to wait.

Proof

Consider a call option that is in the money at expiration. Assume that the time value is positive, that is, C_T is greater than $S_T - X$. If so, an arbitrageur will immediately sell the call. If it is exercised, the net cash flow is $C_T - (S_T - X)$, which by assumption is positive. The same holds true if the option is out of the money and the time value is positive, because in this case the writer need not worry about exercise. On the other hand, if the time value is negative, that is, C_T is less than $(S_T - X)$, an arbitrageur will buy the option and immediately exercise it. The net cash flow is $S_T - X - C_T$, which is guaranteed to be positive. Thus, to preclude arbitrage, an option must sell for its intrinsic value at expiration. The same rationale holds for put options, whether European or American.

Variables of Interest for Option Valuation

The values of call and put options, depend on the following variables.

The Current Stock Price

The prevailing stock price is obviously a major factor in determining the value of an option. Everything else remaining constant, the higher the current stock price is, the greater the value of a call option and the lower the value of a put option.

The Exercise Price

As one would expect, the higher the exercise price is for a given set of values for the other variables, the lower the value of a call option and the higher the value of a put option.

Dividends

A dividend payout leads to a drop in the stock price as the stock goes ex-dividend. Consequently, dividends paid out during the life of the option lead to a reduction in call values and an increase in put values. *Exchange traded options are usually not payout protected from the standpoint of cash dividends*. That is, the terms of the original option contract are not modified if the underlying stock pays a dividend subsequently.[6] The terms of the agreement, however, do change in the event of stock splits or stock dividends.

Volatility

Modern finance theory is based on the assumption that all investors are risk averse. Consequently, increases in the volatility, as measured by the variance of the rate of return of the stock, are perceived negatively and therefore lead to a higher risk premium being demanded.

In the case of an options contract, however, the holder is protected on one side, because the maximum loss is limited to the initial premium paid by the holder. Therefore, an increase in the volatility is perceived positively, although it signals a greater

6 Some exchanges make an adjustment if the dividend is perceived to be *extraordinary*. In such cases, the exchange has to define the meaning of what it terms as extraordinary.

probability of higher stock prices as well as lower stock prices. Hence an increase in the volatility of the rate of return on the underlying asset leads to an increase in the value of both call as well as put options.

Time to Maturity

American options and European calls on non-dividend paying stocks have a non-negative time value, whereas European puts on such stocks may have either a positive or a negative time value depending on the extent to which the option is in the money.

As we have seen, the time value of an option must be zero at the time of expiration; that is, the option premium must be equal to the intrinsic value. Therefore, everything else remaining constant, the value of an option generally declines with the passage of time. We use the word *"generally,"* because certain European puts that are deep in the money may have a negative time value that approaches zero at expiration. Hence, options are also known as *wasting assets*, because they experience a decline in value with the passage of time.

Riskless Rate of Interest

Let's take the case of an investor who is contemplating the purchase of a stock. One alternative is to buy a call instead, which can be subsequently exercised. The price of a call must be less than the prevailing stock price. This is because if a stock is desirable, it would make sense to acquire it at the current stock price, rather than pay a premium that, by assumption, is greater and subsequently pay the exercise price in the event of exercise.

So a person who has an amount equal to the value of the stock with him, can decide to buy the call instead of the stock and then invest the difference at the riskless rate of interest. Everything else being the same, the higher the rate of interest, the more attractive the strategy is of buying the call and investing the surplus. Therefore, it follows that the higher the interest rate is, the higher the price of the call.

What about puts? Consider the case of a person who already owns the stock and is contemplating selling it. One alternative is to buy a put, which ensures that the buyer will receive a minimum price of $X for it subsequently. The higher the interest rate is, the more attractive the alternative of selling immediately in the spot market rather than buying a put. Consequently, everything else being the same, the higher the interest rate, the less attractive the put option is. Hence, put prices decline as interest rates rise.

The Binomial Model of Option Valuation

Let's now go on to study a theoretical pricing model for call and put options called the *binomial option pricing model* (BOPM).

The binomial model assumes that given the current stock price, during the next period the price can either change by $X\%$ or $Y\%$, where X and Y are specified. Because the stock price can take on only two possible values at the end of the period, the model is called *binomial.* A realistic portrayal of the behavior of a stock requires the specification of Y as a negative number.

The One Period Binomial Model

In the one period case, we consider only two points in time. These are, the present time (T-1) and the expiration time of the option T.

Let the current stock price be S_t. The stock price at the end of the period can take on only the following values:

$$S_T = S_t\left(1 + \frac{X}{100}\right) = uS_t \tag{10.16}$$

where $u = (1 + \frac{X}{100})$ and stands for the *up state*, or

$$S_T = S_t\left(1 + \frac{Y}{100}\right) = dS_t \tag{10.17}$$

where $d = (1 + \frac{Y}{100})$ and stands for the *down state*. Y, in this case, is a negative number.

The price tree may be depicted as shown in Figure 10.1.

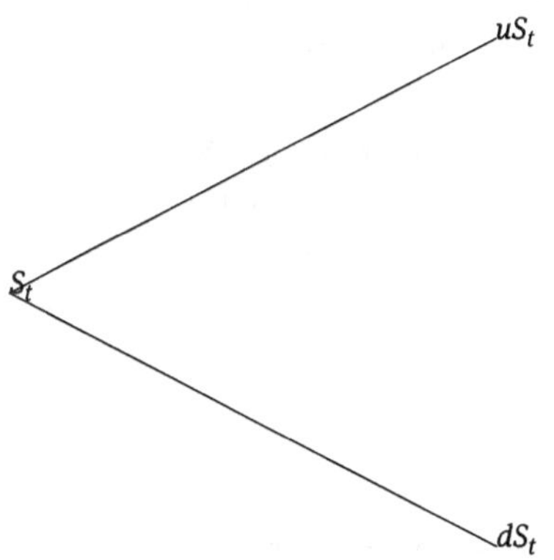

Figure 10.1: Stock price tree for the one period case.

Now, the call value at expiration will be $\text{Max}[0, uS_t - E]$ if the up state is reached, or $\text{Max}[0, dS_t - E]$ if the down state is reached. We are going to use the symbol E to denote the exercise price because the symbol X has already been used to denote the extent of an up movement.

Let $C_u = \text{Max}[0, uS_t - E]$ and $C_d = \text{Max}[0, dS_t - E]$.

C_u is the call value at expiration if the up state is reached, and C_d is the call value at expiration if the down state is reached.

Our objective is to find the value of the call today, that is C_t.

Consider the following strategy. Let's buy α shares of stock and write one call option. The current value of this portfolio is $\alpha S_t - C_t$.

If the up state is reached, the portfolio will have a value $= \alpha uS_t - C_u$, whereas if the down state is reached, it will have a value $= \alpha dS_t - C_d$.

Now let's make this portfolio riskless by choosing α, such that

$$\begin{aligned} \alpha uS_t - C_u &= \alpha dS_t - C_d \\ \Rightarrow \alpha S_t(u - d) &= C_u - C_d \\ \Rightarrow \alpha &= \frac{C_u - C_d}{S_t(u - d)} \end{aligned} \tag{10.18}$$

α is known as the hedge ratio.

This portfolio is riskless because the payoff is independent of the state of nature at time T. Since our portfolio by design is riskless, it must earn the riskless rate of return to preclude arbitrage. Therefore,

$$\alpha uS_t - C_u = \alpha dS_t - C_d = (\alpha S_t - C_t)r$$

where $r = 1+$ *riskless rate of interest*. The symbol r is often used to denote the riskless rate of interest per period. In the binomial model, r represents one plus the riskless rate per period, and is defined as one plus the periodic interest rate.

We typically assume that the parameters u and d, as well as the riskless rate of return r, are constant. However, although this is done in order to simplify the calculations, this is not a necessary condition. The model merely requires that these variables be deterministic, that is they are known with certainty to all investors. It can also be shown that u should be greater than r, which in turn should be greater than d, to preclude arbitrage. Thus,

$$\begin{aligned} &\alpha uS_t - C_u = (\alpha S_t - C_t)r \\ \Rightarrow &\left[\frac{C_u - C_d}{S_t(u - d)}\right] \times uS_t - C_u = \left(\frac{C_u - C_d}{S_t(u - d)}\right) \times rS_t - C_t r \\ \Rightarrow &\left(\frac{C_u - C_d}{u - d}\right) \times (u - r) - C_u = -C_t r \\ \Rightarrow &C_t = \left(\frac{C_u\left(\frac{r-d}{u-d}\right) + C_d\left(\frac{u-r}{u-d}\right)}{r}\right) \end{aligned} \tag{10.19}$$

Let $\frac{r-d}{u-d} = p$. Therefore,

$$\frac{u-r}{u-d} = 1-p$$

$$\Rightarrow C_t = \left(\frac{pC_u + (1-p)C_d}{r}\right) \tag{10.20}$$

This is the one-period binomial call option pricing formula. p and $(1-p)$ are referred to as risk-neutral probabilities.

Example 10.23. Let $S_t = 100$, and $X = 100$. $u = 1.2$, $d = 0.80$, $r = 1.05$

$$C_u = \text{Max}[0, 1.2 \times 100 - 100] = 20$$

$$C_d = \text{Max}[0, 0.8 \times 100 - 100] = 0$$

$$p = \frac{r-d}{u-d} = \frac{1.05 - 0.80}{1.2 - 0.80} = 0.625$$

$$1 - p = 0.375$$

The hedge ratio = $\frac{C_u - C_d}{S_t(u-d)} = \frac{20-0}{100(1.2-0.80)} = 0.5$
That is, we have to buy 0.5 shares for every call that we write, in order to form a riskless portfolio.

$$C_t = \frac{0.625 \times 20 + 0.375 \times 0}{1.05} = \$11.9048$$

The Two-Period Case

Thus far, we have assumed that the option has only one period left to expiration. In general, the stock price will move many times between the date of valuation and the expiration date. In the multi-period case also, the same arguments hold.

Let the stock price two periods before the expiration date be S_t. The stock price tree can then be depicted as shown in Figure 10.2.

At T-1, there is only one period left to expiration, and so we an apply the one-period model to get C_u and C_d at $T-1$:

$$C_u = \frac{pC_{uu} + (1-p)C_{ud}}{r}$$

$$C_d = \frac{pC_{ud} + (1-p)C_{dd}}{r}$$

We know C_{uu}, C_{ud}, and C_{dd} because they represent terminal values of the option.

C_{uu} is the option price at T if there are two upticks in the stock price. C_{ud} is the option price at T if there is an uptick followed by a downtick or vice versa. C_{dd} is the option price at T if there are two downticks in the stock price.

After we find C_u and C_d, we can work backwards to find C_t:

$$C_t = \frac{pC_u + (1-p)C_d}{r}$$

$$= \frac{p^2C_{uu} + 2p(1-p)C_{ud} + (1-p)^2C_{dd}}{r^2} \tag{10.21}$$

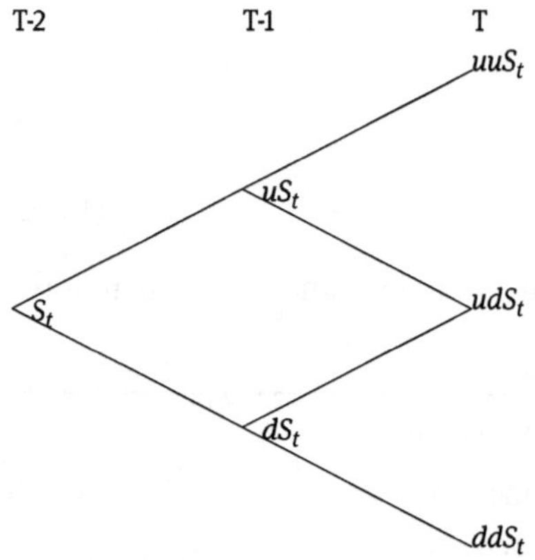

Figure 10.2: Stock price tree for the two-period case.

Using the same iterative process we can work backwards, moving one period at a time, to solve the N-period case.

Example 10.24. Let's use the same data as in the earlier example. $S_t = X = 100$, $u = 1.2$, $d = 0.8$, $r = 1.05$.

First, let's draw the price tree.

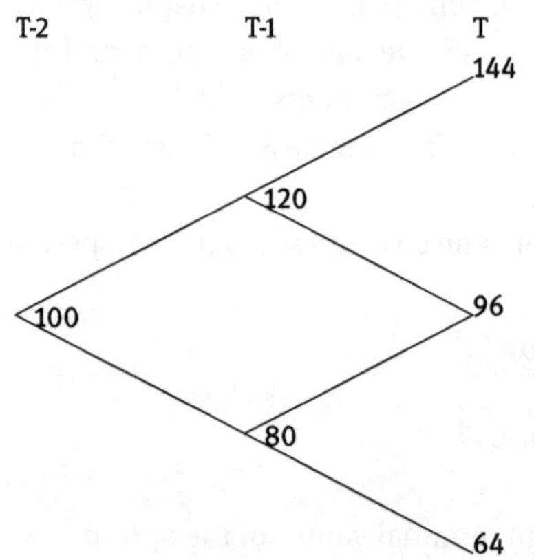

Figure 10.3: Stock price tree for the two-period example.

$$p = 0.625, (1 - p) = 0.375$$
$$C_{uu} = \text{Max}[0, 144 - 100] = 44$$
$$C_{ud} = \text{Max}[0, 96 - 100] = 0$$
$$C_{dd} = \text{Max}[0, 64 - 100] = 0$$

$$C_u = \frac{0.625 \times 44 + 0.375 \times 0}{1.05} = \$26.1905$$

$$C_d = \frac{0.625 \times 0 + 0.375 \times 0}{1.05} = 0$$

$$C_t = \frac{0.625 \times 26.1905 + 0.375 \times 0}{1.05} = \$15.5896$$

Thus the two-period call is priced higher than the one-period call. This is to be expected because European calls on a non-dividend paying stock will have a positive time value.

The Binomial Model for European Puts

Consider the one-period case. The put value at expiration is $\text{Max}[0, E - uS_t]$ if the up state is reached, or $\text{Max}[0, E - dS_t]$ if the down state is reached. Therefore,

$$P_u = \text{Max}[0, E - uS_t]$$

$$\text{and} \quad P_d = \text{Max}[0, E - dS_t]$$

Using arguments similar to what we used for the call, it can be shown that

$$P_t = \frac{pP_u + (1 - p)P_d}{r} \tag{10.22}$$

where, p and $(1 - p)$ are as defined before.

Example 10.25. Let's use the same data that we used for the call. That is, $S_t = X = 100$, $u = 1.2$, $d = 0.8$, $r = 1.05$.

$$P_u = \text{Max}[0, 100 - 120] = 0$$

$$P_d = \text{Max}[0, 100 - 80] = 20$$

$$P_t = \frac{0.625 \times 0 + 0.375 \times 20}{1.05} = \$7.1429$$

Using the Binomial Model: The Case of European vs. American Puts

Consider the data used in the earlier examples. Now, assume that the stock pays no dividends. If so, American and European calls have the same premium. However, an American put may be priced higher than a European put. Let's look at a put option with three periods to expiration. The stock price tree can be depicted as shown in Figure 10.4.

Valuing a European Put Using the Binomial Model

To value the option, we proceed backwards as follows:

$$P_{uu} = \frac{0.625 \times 0 + 0.375 \times 0}{1.05} = 0$$

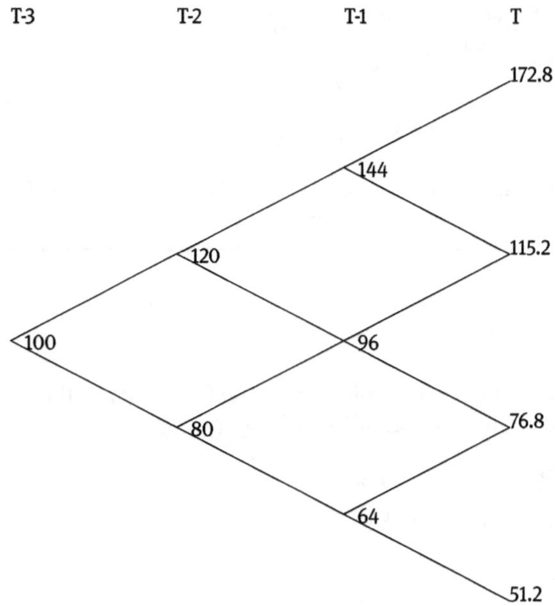

Figure 10.4: Stock price tree for the three-period case.

$$P_{ud} = \frac{0.625 \times 0 + 0.375 \times 23.20}{1.05} = \$8.2857$$

$$P_{dd} = \frac{0.625 \times 23.2 + 0.375 \times 48.8}{1.05} = \$31.2381$$

$$P_u = \frac{0.625 \times 0 + 0.375 \times 8.2857}{1.05} = \$2.9592$$

$$P_d = \frac{0.625 \times 8.2857 + 0.375 \times 31.2381}{1.05} = \$16.0884$$

$$P_t = \frac{0.625 \times 2.9592 + 0.375 \times 16.0884}{1.05} = \$7.5073$$

Valuing an American Put Using the Binomial Model

For American puts, we have to, compare, at each node, the value obtained from the model with the intrinsic value. If the intrinsic value is greater, we have to use it for subsequent calculations. The rationale is the following. If the intrinsic value is higher than the model value, a trader who wants to exercise will obviously do so. A trader who wants to wait would rather exercise, collect the intrinsic value, and recreate the option at the model value. Thus if the intrinsic value at a node is greater than the model value, early exercise takes place.

At uuS_t, the value according to our previous calculations is 0. The intrinsic value is also 0.

At udS_t, the model price is \$8.2857, and the intrinsic value is 4, which is less. Thus P_u has the same value for an American put.

But at ddS_t, the model price is \$31.2381, and the intrinsic value is 36. So we calculate P_d as follows:

$$P_d = \frac{0.625 \times 8.2857 + 0.375 \times 36}{1.05} = \$17.7891$$

The intrinsic value at the node corresponding to a stock price of dS_t is 20, which is greater than \$17.7891.

So we calculate P_t as follows:

$$P_t = \frac{0.625 \times 2.9592 + 0.375 \times 20}{1.05} = \$8.9043$$

This is not the final step, however. You must compare \$8.9043 with the intrinsic value at T-3 which in this case is 0. Thus the option will sell for \$8.9043.

As you can see, the American put is priced higher than the European put. This is because early exercise is optimal at an intermediate stage.

The Black-Scholes Formula for Valuing Options

Black and Scholes obtained exact formulae for valuing call and put options on non-dividend paying stocks, by assuming that stock prices follow a lognormal process. This assumption implies that logs of prices are normally distributed. The formulae obtained by them are:

$$C_{E,t} = S_t N(d_1) - Xe^{-r(T-t)} N(d_2) \tag{10.23}$$

and

$$P_{E,t} = Xe^{-r(T-t)} N(-d_2) - S_t N(-d_1) \tag{10.24}$$

where

$$d_1 = \frac{\ln\left(\frac{S_t}{X}\right) + \left(r + \frac{\sigma^2}{2}\right)(T-t)}{\sigma\sqrt{(T-t)}} \tag{10.25}$$

and

$$d_2 = d_1 - \sigma\sqrt{(T-t)} \tag{10.26}$$

$N(X)$ is the cumulative probability distribution function for a standard normal variable, and σ is the standard deviation of the rate of return on the stock. $N(X)$ may be computed in Excel by using the NORMSDIST function.

Example 10.26. Consider a stock which is currently selling for \$100. Call and put options are available with $X = 100$ and time to expiration = 6 months.

The riskless rate of interest = 10% per annum, and the volatility is 30% per annum. So, $S_t = X = 100$; $T - t = 0.5$ years; $r = 10\% \equiv 0.10$; $\sigma = 30\% \equiv 0.30$.

Let's consider the call first:

$$\begin{aligned} d_1 &= \frac{\ln\left(\frac{100}{100}\right) + \left[0.10 + \frac{(0.30)^2}{2}\right]0.5}{0.3\sqrt{0.5}} \\ &= \frac{0.0725}{0.2121} = 0.3418 \\ d_2 &= 0.3418 - 0.2121 = 0.1296 \end{aligned}$$

$N(0.3418) = 0.6337$ and $N(0.1296) = 0.5516$.

$$\begin{aligned} C_{E,t} &= 100 \times 0.6337 - 100e^{-0.10\times 0.5} \times 0.5516 \\ &= 10.9065 \\ P_{E,t} &= 100e^{-0.10\times 0.5}N(-0.1296) - 100N(-0.3418) \end{aligned}$$

Now, $N(-X) = 1 - N(X)$. This is because the normal distribution is symmetrical. So, $N(-0.1296) = 1 - 0.5516 = 0.4484$, and $N(-0.3418) = 0.3663$. Thus, $P_{E,t} = \$6.0294$.

Put-Call Parity and Option Pricing Models

Put-call parity is a more general result than either the binomial or the Black-Scholes models. This is because put-call parity merely requires the absence of arbitrage, whereas option pricing models require an additional assumption about the evolution of stock prices. In the following section, we show that the Black-Scholes formula satisfies put-call parity.

$$\begin{aligned} C_{E,t} &= S_tN(d_1) - Xe^{-r(T-t)}N(d_2) \\ &= S_t[1 - N(-d_1)] - Xe^{-r(T-t)}[1 - N(-d_2)] \\ &= Xe^{-r(T-t)}N(-d_2) - S_tN(-d_1) + S_t - Xe^{-r(T-t)} \\ &= P_{E,t} + S_t - Xe^{-r(T-t)} \end{aligned}$$

Consider the data given earlier when we illustrated the one-period binomial model. The one period call was priced at \$11.9048, while the one period put was priced at \$7.1429. The difference is \$4.7619. The stock price and the exercise price were both \$100 and the risk-less rate per period was 5%. Thus

$$S_t - \frac{X}{(1 + r)} = 100 - \frac{100}{1.05} = \$4.7619$$

Hence put-call parity is satisfied as expected.

Interpretation of $N(d_1)$ and $N(d_2)$

The Black-Scholes formula for call options states that

$$C_{E,t} = S_t N(d_1) - Xe^{-r(T-t)} N(d_2)$$

The option premium is invariant to the risk preferences of investors and is consequently valid in a world characterized by risk neutrality. A risk-neutral investor would value the option as the discounted value of its expected payoff. Consequently, because

$$C_{E,t} = e^{-r(T-t)} [S_t e^{r(T-t)} N(d_1) - XN(d_2)]$$

it is obvious that

$$[S_t e^{r(T-t)} N(d_1) - XN(d_2)]$$

is the expected payoff from the option from the perspective of a risk-neutral investor.

$S_t e^{r(T-t)} N(d_1)$ is the expected value of a variable in a risk-neutral world, that is equal to S_T if the option is exercised, and is equal to zero otherwise. $N(d_2)$ is the probability that the option will be exercised in a risk-neutral world. If the option is exercised, there is an outflow of X, otherwise the outflow is zero. Consequently, $XN(d_2)$ is the expected outflow on account of the exercise price.

The formula for puts states that

$$\begin{aligned} P_{E,t} &= Xe^{-r(T-t)} N(-d_2) - S_t N(-d_1) \\ \Rightarrow &= e^{-r(T-t)} [XN(-d_2) - S_t e^{r(T-t)} N(-d_1)] \end{aligned}$$

If $N(d_2)$ is the probability that a call option with an exercise price of X is exercised in a risk-neutral world, then $1 - N(d_2)$ or $N(-d_2)$ is the probability that a put with the same exercise price will be exercised. Thus $XN(-d_2)$ is the expected inflow on account of the exercise price. $S_t e^{r(T-t)} N(-d_1)$ is the expected value of a variable that is equal to S_T if the option is exercised or equal to zero otherwise.

$N(d_1)$ is known as *delta*, which is the partial derivative of the call price with respect to the stock price. For put options, the delta is $-N(-d_1)$. For calls delta is between zero and one. That is, an option that is deep out-of-the-money has a delta close to zero, whereas a deep in-the-money call option has a delta close to one. For puts, delta is between −1 and zero. Deep out-of-the-money options have a delta close to zero, whereas deep-in-the-money options have a delta equal to minus one.

Chapter Summary

The chapter provided an introduction to forward and futures contracts, as well as options contracts. We go on to study interest rate forwards, futures, and options, for which this chapter should prove to be an adequate introduction to readers who are not well-acquainted with financial derivatives. The chapter commenced with a study of forward contracts and futures contracts, and presented their similarities and differences. In this context, key issues such as margining, and marking to market, were introduced. We then presented no-arbitrage arguments to value forward contracts. The concept of the cheapest to deliver grade, when multiple grades are allowed for delivery, was examined. The use of futures contracts for hedging and speculation was studied in detail. The focus then turned to options contracts. Properties of European and American options, both calls and puts, were studied. The binomial model, which is used later to study forward rate agreements, and bond options, was examined in detail. The chapter concluded with a study of the Black-Scholes model. The use of this model from a pricing standpoint was illustrated, and the key terms of the formula were interpreted.

Chapter 11
The Valuation of Interest Rate Options

In this chapter we study models for the evolution of interest rates over time, and their use in the valuation of options on interest rates. We briefly discuss equilibrium models of the term structure, although the bulk of the discussion is on no-arbitrage models. The primary focus is on the Ho-Lee model and the Black-Derman-Toy (BDT) models.

Short Rates

A short rate of interest is a future spot rate of interest that might rise over time. Usually it is denoted as a single-period rate of interest and defined as the rate for the shortest period of time considered by a model. In a fixed income context, we take the shortest period of time as six months, as most bonds generate cash flows on a semiannual basis.

At any point in time, if we consider a series of spot rates corresponding to different lengths of time, we can derive a unique vector of forward rates. However, for any future point in time, there are an infinite number of short rates that may arise. Each possible value has a varying probability of occurrence. At the initial point in time, the one-period spot rate is equal to the one-period forward rate, which is equal to the one-period short rate. However, if we look at a time horizon beyond the first period, these interest rate measures in general are not equal to each other.

Issues in the Valuation of Interest Rate Derivatives

A Black-Scholes approach or a standard binomial model, which works well in the case of stock options, is inappropriate for interest rate dependent financial claims and their derivatives. For instance, let us take the case of a bond maturing after N years. Although the price before maturity is expected to evolve in a random fashion, as the time to expiration approaches zero, the price of the underlying security should tend towards its par value. Consequently, option pricing models based on lognormal or binomial outcomes for the price of the underlying asset are unsuitable for valuing a derivative like an option on an interest rate dependent asset such as a bond.

There is no standard model for pricing options on debt securities. However, almost all of the models that have been postulated are based on the following three-step approach:[1]

1. The random character of interest rate movements is first modeled.

1 See Rendleman [53].

https://doi.org/10.1515/9781547400669-011

2. The interest rate process is used to infer the distribution of prices of the underlying debt securities.
3. The distribution of prices of the underlying asset is used to value the option.

Thus, the difference between competing models lies in the way they model the interest rate process.

Equilibrium Models of the Term Structure

Such models derive a stochastic process for the evolution of the short rate by making a set of assumptions about economic variables. In a one-factor model, the stochastic process for the short rate is the only source of uncertainty. In general, short rates are assumed to follow an Ito process of the form:[2]

$$dr = \mu(r)dt + \sigma(r)dZ$$

That is, the drift μ, and the variance rate σ^2 are assumed to be functions of the short rate, but are considered to be independent of time. There is, however, a critical problem with this approach to the pricing of interest rate derivatives. In practice, it is usually the case that the prices of the underlying debt securities, which are inferred from the postulated interest rate process, are not equal to their observed market prices. It is obvious that if we are unable to correctly price the underlying security, it is impossible for us to have faith in the derivative prices that are obtained from the same.

Arbitrage-Free Term Structure Models

This class of option pricing models takes the observed term structure of interest rates as an input, unlike the earlier class of models that generate the term structure as an output. The stochastic process for the short rate that is implied by the observed term structure is deduced, and from it the values of the underlying debt securities are inferred. Finally, the price of the derivative security is obtained. The appealing feature of this approach is that the prices of the debt securities that are derived in this fashion are entirely consistent with the observed term structure.

Let's now look at alternative models of the term structure.

---

2 $dZ = \epsilon\sqrt{\Delta t}$, where $\epsilon \sim N(0,1)$; that is, it is drawn from a standard normal distribution, which has a mean of zero and a variance of 1.

The Ho-Lee Model

Per the Ho-Lee model, the evolution of the short rate may be specified as

$$dr_t = \mu_t dt + \sigma dZ \tag{11.1}$$

In this model, the drift varies over time, and the variance remains constant. A shortcoming of this model is that interest rates can become negative, although this is not as outrageous today as it was a decade ago. The other drawback of this model is that it does not incorporate *mean reversion*, which refers to the tendency of a variable to return to its long-term average, after moving up and down in the short-run. Interest rates and security prices are obvious candidates. In practice mean reversion can be self-fulfilling. If a variable moves to an abnormally low or high value, it can attract players who do not subscribe to the herd mentality and take a counter-approach. If a sufficient segment of the market were to think along the lines of the heretics, the market could move back to a long-term average.

The Hull-White Model

The Hull-White model specifies the evolution of the short rate as

$$dr_t = [\mu_t - \alpha r_t]dt + \sigma dZ \tag{11.2}$$

This model builds in mean reversion. Like in the case of the Ho-Lee model, interest rates can become negative.

The Black-Derman-Toy Model

The Black-Derman-Toy (BDT) model may be stated as

$$d\ln r_t = \mu_t dt + \sigma_t dZ \tag{11.3}$$

The BDT model, like the other two, is a single-factor model. That is, it assumes that there is a single stochastic factor. The model was the first to combine the lognormal distribution with mean reversion. Unlike the Ho-Lee and Hull-White models, the volatility is not a constant. Thus, in order to use the model, we need to take cognizance of both the term structure of interest rates and the term structure of volatility.

The Binomial Tree Approach to the Term Structure

Now let's illustrate no-arbitrage models of the term structure using a discrete time framework. Before we proceed we need to define certain variables.

We denote the length of a time period in the binomial tree as $\triangle t$, where time is measured in years. Interest rates consequently are specified as annual rates. s_n is the n-period spot rate at time 0, quoted as a percentage per annum, but compounded at an interval equal to $\triangle t$. Thus if a dollar is invested at time 0 for n periods, the future value is

$$\text{F.V.} = (1 + s_n \triangle t)^n$$

We define r_n as the short rate that will prevail n periods later. r_0 is obviously equal to the one-period spot rate s_1. The time step in the binomial tree is taken as six months for the purpose of illustration. Consequently, $\triangle t = 0.50$.

Consider a bond that pays $1 after two periods. Its present value is

$$\frac{1}{(1 + \frac{s_2}{2})^2}$$

The short rate after one period is either r_u or r_d. Thus the value of the bond after one period is either

$$P_u = \frac{1}{(1 + \frac{r_u}{2})}$$

or

$$P_d = \frac{1}{(1 + \frac{r_d}{2})}$$

The present value of the one-period bond is therefore

$$\frac{P_u}{(1 + \frac{s_1}{2})}$$

or

$$\frac{P_d}{(1 + \frac{s_1}{2})}$$

Let q be the probability of an up move and $(1 - q)$ be the probability of a down move. Thus

$$\frac{1}{(1 + \frac{s_2}{2})^2} = \frac{q \times P_u}{(1 + \frac{s_1}{2})} + \frac{(1 - q) \times P_d}{(1 + \frac{s_1}{2})}$$

$$\Rightarrow \frac{1}{(1 + \frac{s_2}{2})^2} = \frac{q}{(1 + \frac{s_1}{2})(1 + \frac{r_u}{2})} + \frac{1 - q}{(1 + \frac{s_1}{2})(1 + \frac{r_d}{2})}$$

$$\Rightarrow \frac{(1 + \frac{r_u}{2})(1 + \frac{r_d}{2})(1 + \frac{s_1}{2})}{(1 + \frac{s_2}{2})^2} = q\left(1 + \frac{r_d}{2}\right) + (1 - q)\left(1 + \frac{r_u}{2}\right)$$

$$\Rightarrow \frac{(1+\frac{r_u}{2})(1+\frac{r_d}{2})(1+\frac{s_1}{2})}{(1+\frac{s_2}{2})^2} - q\left(1+\frac{r_d}{2}\right) - (1-q)\left(1+\frac{r_u}{2}\right) = 0 \qquad (11.4)$$

This is the fundamental equation that is used in no-arbitrage models to determine the short rates. To apply these models in practice, one has to model r_u and r_d. The models differ in their approaches to modeling these parameters.

Some Insights into the Ho-Lee Model

Let's depict a four-period interest rate tree. Each node is denoted as $r_{k,j}$, where k represents the point in time that we are at and j represents the state. The tree can be modeled as shown in Figure 11.1.

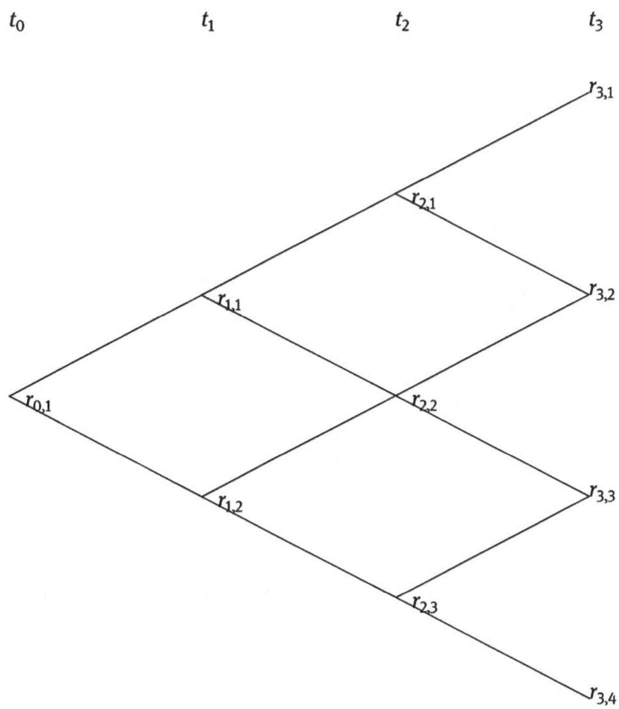

Figure 11.1: Interest rate tree.

Thus an up move from node $r_{k,j}$ is a move to node $r_{k+1,j}$, while a down move is a move to node $r_{k+1,j+1}$. Notice that the tree in Figure 11.1 is recombining; that is, r_{ud} is the same as r_{du}. The recombination condition not only reduces the number of nodes at each point in time and consequently makes computation relatively easier, it also has implications for σ, as we demonstrate shortly.

Interest rates span time whereas prices do not. Consequently the interest rate tree can be used to price bonds with up to four periods to maturity. That is, if we have a bond that pays $1,000 at time t_4, the price tree corresponding to the preceding interest rate tree can be depicted as shown in Figure 11.2.

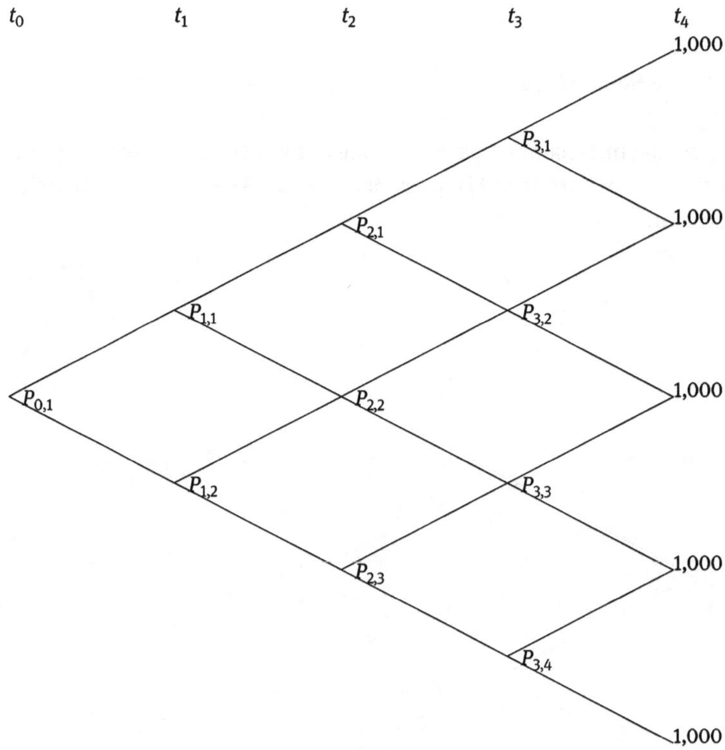

Figure 11.2: Price tree.

Consider time point t_k, where $t_k = k \triangle t$, and let r_k be the short rate at this point in time. For the process

$$dr = \mu_t dt + \sigma_t dZ$$

we can approximate dr as $r_{k+1,j} - r_{k,j}$ or as $r_{k+1,j+1} - r_{k,j}$, and write

$$r_{k+1,j} = r_{k,j} + \mu_k \triangle t + \sigma_k \sqrt{\triangle t}, \quad \text{that is } \epsilon = +1,$$

and

$$r_{k+1,j+1} = r_{k,j} + \mu_k \triangle t - \sigma_k \sqrt{\triangle t}, \quad \text{that is } \epsilon = -1$$

Thus

$$r_{1,1} = r_{0,1} + \mu_0 \triangle t + \sigma_0 \sqrt{\triangle t}$$

and

$$r_{1,2} = r_{0,1} + \mu_0 \triangle t - \sigma_0 \sqrt{\triangle t}$$
$$\Rightarrow r_{1,1} - r_{1,2} = 2\sigma_0 \sqrt{\triangle t}$$

Hence the spread between the upstate and the down state is a function of the volatility parameter. Similarly

$$r_{2,1} = r_{1,1} + \mu_1 \triangle t + \sigma_1 \sqrt{\triangle t}$$
$$r_{2,2} = r_{1,1} + \mu_1 \triangle t - \sigma_1 \sqrt{\triangle t} = r_{1,2} + \mu_1 \triangle t + \sigma_1 \sqrt{\triangle t}$$
$$r_{2,3} = r_{1,2} + \mu_1 \triangle t - \sigma_1 \sqrt{\triangle t}$$

Notice that $r_{2,2}$ can be expressed as a down move from $r_{1,1}$ or as an up move from $r_{1,2}$ because of the recombination requirement. Thus

$$r_{1,1} + \mu_1 \triangle t - \sigma_1 \sqrt{\triangle t} = r_{1,2} + \mu_1 \triangle t + \sigma_1 \sqrt{\triangle t}$$
$$\Rightarrow 2\sigma_1 \sqrt{\triangle t} = r_{1,1} - r_{1,2}$$
$$\Rightarrow \sigma_1 = \frac{r_{1,1} - r_{1,2}}{2\sqrt{\triangle t}} = \frac{2\sigma_0 \sqrt{\triangle t}}{2\sqrt{\triangle t}} = \sigma_0$$

Therefore if the interest rate tree is to recombine, then it must be the case that σ is a constant for all points in time. In other words, $\sigma_k = \sigma \forall k$.

Calibrating the Ho-Lee Model

Let's now illustrate how the Ho-Lee model can be fitted to the observed term structure using the binomial tree approach. The parameters of the model are chosen in a way such that the branches of the tree recombine. This, as you have already seen, implies that the standard deviation, σ, is constant for all points in time. In practice the value of σ is chosen arbitrarily. It is also assumed that given a state of nature, there is a 50% probability of an up move and, therefore, obviously a 50% probability of a down move.

The movements in the short rate are expressed as follows:

$$r_{t+1} = r_t + \mu_t \triangle t + \sigma \epsilon_{t+1} \sqrt{\triangle t}$$

where $\epsilon_{t+1} = +1$ with a probability of 0.50 and is equal to –1 with a probability of 0.50. Thus

$$r_{k+1,j} = r_{k,j} + \mu_k \triangle t + \sigma \sqrt{\triangle t}$$

and

$$r_{k+1,j+1} = r_{k,j} + \mu_k \triangle t - \sigma\sqrt{\triangle t}$$

The values of μ are determined to generate the term structure that is observed in practice. Before we proceed to illustrate the calibration technique, let's first introduce the concept of an Arrow-Debreu security, a concept that we use subsequently to value interest rate dependent securities.

Arrow-Debreu Securities

Arrow-Debreu securities, also known as *pure securities* pay \$1 if a particular state of nature occurs. However, in all other states of nature, the payoff is zero. Obviously each node of a binomial tree represents a particular state of nature. The value at time t_0 of a pure security that pays off \$1 in state (k, j) is denoted by $q_{k,j}$.

Let's first consider a one-period binomial tree, shown in Figure 11.3. We assume that the one-period interest rate is 8% per annum. Each period represents a time interval of six months.

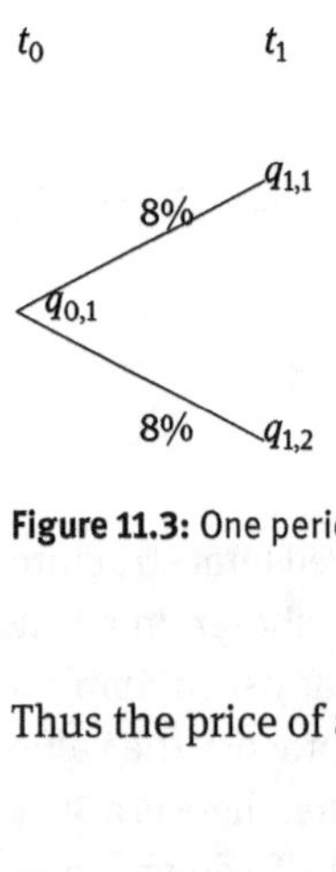

Figure 11.3: One period interest rate and state price tree.

Thus the price of a security that pays off \$1 in the up state is given by

$$q_{1,1} = 0.50 \times \frac{1}{(1 + 0.08 \times 0.5)} = \frac{0.50}{1.04} = \$0.4808$$

$q_{1,2}$ or the price of a security that pays \$1 in the down state, is obviously the same. The values of q that are calculated in this fashion are referred to as *state prices*.

A riskless security in such an environment is obviously one that pays off \$1 irrespective of the state of nature after one period. Its price is obviously given by

$$q_{1,1} + q_{1,2} = 0.4808 + 0.4808 = \$0.9616$$

The riskless rate of interest is therefore

$$\frac{1-0.9616}{0.9616} \equiv 4\%$$

per half-yearly period, or 8% per annum, which is what we expect.

Now let's extend the model by a period, as shown in Figure 11.4. Assume that if the up state is reached after a period, the rate of interest will be 8.75% per annum, whereas if the down state is reached, it will be 7.25% per annum.

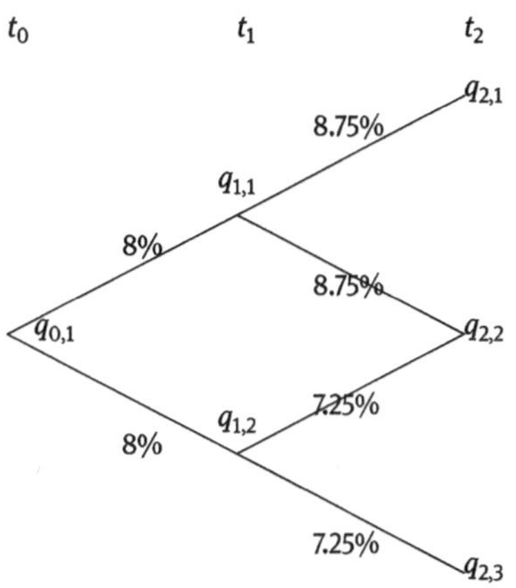

Figure 11.4: Two-period interest rate and state price tree.

At the end of two periods, there obviously are three states of nature. We can calculate the prices of the Arrow-Debreu securities as follows:

$$q_{2,1} = \frac{0.5 \times 0.5}{(1.04) \times (1 + \frac{0.0875}{2})}$$
$$= q_{1,1} \times \frac{0.5}{1.04375} = 0.4808 \times \frac{0.5}{1.04375} = \$0.2303$$

Let's analyze this expression. The value of an Arrow-Debreu security that pays off \$1 at state (2,1) is $\frac{0.5}{1.04375}$ at state (1,1). We know that the value of a pure security that pays off \$1 in state (1,1) is \$0.4808 as calculated at state (0,1). Consequently, the value of a pure security that pays off \$1 in state (2,1), as calculated at state (0,1), is

$$0.4808 \times \frac{0.5}{1.04375} = \$0.2303$$

Now let's consider a pure security that pays off \$1 if state (2,2) occurs. This state can be attained via two paths. Hence, using the same logic

$$q_{2,2} = q_{1,1} \times \frac{0.5}{(1 + \frac{0.0875}{2})} + q_{1,2} \times \frac{0.5}{(1 + \frac{0.0725}{2})}$$

$$= 0.4808 \times \frac{0.5}{1.04375} + 0.4808 \times \frac{0.5}{1.03625} = \$0.4623$$

Similarly,

$$q_{2,3} = q_{1,2} \times \frac{0.5}{1.03625} = \$0.2320$$

Thus this approach enables us to price pure securities at various states of nature by working our way forward through the tree.

Now consider the term structure in Table 11.1.

Table 11.1: Vector of spot rates.

Period	Spot Rate
0	7.50%
1	7.00%
2	6.25%
3	6.75%

Assume that $\sigma = \frac{1}{\sqrt{\Delta t}}$. Thus $\sigma \times \sqrt{\Delta t} = 1.0$. $r_{0,1}$ is obviously 7.50%. $q_{0,1} = 1$

We know that

$$r_{1,1} = r_{0,1} + \mu_0 \, \triangle t + 1.00 = 8.50\% + \mu_0 \times 0.50$$

and

$$r_{1,2} = r_{0,1} + \mu_0 \times 0.50 - 1.00 = 6.50\% + \mu_0 \times 0.50$$

$$q_{1,1} = q_{1,2} = \frac{0.50}{\left(1 + \frac{0.075}{2}\right)} = \$0.481928$$

The prices of the pure securities for the next period may be computed as follows:

$$q_{2,1} = q_{1,1} \times \frac{0.50}{\left(1 + \frac{0.085 + \mu_0 \times 0.50}{2}\right)} = \frac{0.481928}{2.085 + \mu_0 \times 0.50}$$

$$q_{2,2} = q_{1,1} \times \frac{0.50}{\left(1 + \frac{0.085 + \mu_0 \times 0.50}{2}\right)} + q_{1,2} \times \frac{0.50}{\left(1 + \frac{0.065 + \mu_0 \times 0.50}{2}\right)}$$

$$= \frac{0.481928}{2.085 + \mu_0 \times 0.50} + \frac{0.481928}{2.065 + \mu_0 \times 0.50}$$

$$q_{2,3} = q_{1,2} \times \frac{0.50}{\left(1 + \frac{0.065 + \mu_0 \times 0.50}{2}\right)} = \frac{0.481928}{2.065 + \mu_0 \times 0.50}$$

Obviously,

$$q_{2,1} + q_{2,2} + q_{2,3} = \frac{1}{(1 + 0.5 \times s_2)^2} = \frac{1}{(1.035)^2} = \$0.933511$$

Thus,

$$\frac{2}{2.085+\mu_0\times 0.50}+\frac{2}{2.065+\mu_0\times 0.50}=\frac{0.933511}{0.481928}=1.937034$$
$$\Rightarrow \mu_0=-1.9874\%$$

Thus $r_{1,1}=0.085-0.019874\times 0.50=0.075063\equiv 7.5063\%$ and $r_{1,2}=0.065-0.019874\times 0.50=0.055063\equiv 5.5063\%$ The prices of the pure securities are

$$q_{2,1}=\$0.232247$$
$$q_{2,2}=\$0.466755$$
$$q_{2,3}=\$0.234508$$

Now let's proceed to the next point in time:

$$r_{2,1}=r_{1,1}+\mu_1\times 0.50+1.0=7.5063+1.0+\mu_1\times 0.50=8.5063+\mu_1\times 0.50$$
$$r_{2,2}=r_{1,1}+\mu_1\times 0.50-1.0=7.5063-1.0+\mu_1\times 0.50=6.5063+\mu_1\times 0.50$$
$$r_{2,3}=r_{1,2}+\mu_1\times 0.50-1.0=5.5063-1.0+\mu_1\times 0.50=4.5063+\mu_1\times 0.50$$

The prices of the pure securities for the next point in time can be expressed as follows:

$$q_{3,1}=q_{2,1}\times\frac{0.50}{\left(1+\frac{0.085063+\mu_1\times 0.50}{2}\right)}=\frac{0.232247}{2.085063+\mu_1\times 0.50}$$
$$q_{3,2}=q_{2,1}\times\frac{0.50}{\left(1+\frac{0.085063+\mu_1\times 0.50}{2}\right)}+q_{2,2}\times\frac{0.50}{\left(1+\frac{0.065063+\mu_1\times 0.50}{2}\right)}$$
$$=\frac{0.232247}{2.085063+\mu_1\times 0.50}+\frac{0.466755}{2.065063+\mu_1\times 0.50}$$
$$q_{3,3}=q_{2,2}\times\frac{0.50}{\left(1+\frac{0.065063+\mu_1\times 0.50}{2}\right)}+q_{2,3}\times\frac{0.50}{\left(1+\frac{0.045063+\mu_1\times 0.50}{2}\right)}$$
$$=\frac{0.466755}{2.065063+\mu_1\times 0.50}+\frac{0.234508}{2.045063+\mu_1\times 0.50}$$
$$q_{3,4}=q_{2,3}\times\frac{0.50}{\left(1+\frac{0.045063+\mu_1\times 0.50}{2}\right)}=\frac{0.234508}{2.045063+\mu_1\times 0.50}$$

Obviously,

$$q_{3,1}+q_{3,2}+q_{3,3}+q_{3,4}=\frac{1}{(1+0.5\times s_3)^3}=\frac{1}{(1.03125)^3}=\$0.911818$$

Thus,

$$2\times\frac{0.232247}{2.085063+\mu_1\times 0.50}+2\times\frac{0.466755}{2.065063+\mu_1\times 0.50}+2\times\frac{0.234508}{2.045063+\mu_1\times 0.50}$$
$$=0.911818\Rightarrow \mu_1=-0.034677=-3.4677\%$$

Therefore,

$$r_{2,1} = 8.5063 - 3.4677 \times 0.50 = 6.7725\%$$
$$r_{2,2} = 6.5063 - 3.4677 \times 0.50 = 4.7725\%$$
$$r_{2,3} = 4.5063 - 3.4677 \times 0.50 = 2.7725\%$$

The prices of the pure securities are

$$q_{3,1} = \$0.112320$$
$$q_{3,2} = \$0.340258$$
$$q_{3,3} = \$0.343589$$
$$q_{3,4} = \$0.115651$$

Finally, let's proceed to the penultimate point in time:

$$r_{3,1} = r_{2,1} + \mu_2 \times 0.50 + 1 = 6.7725 + 1 + \mu_2 \times 0.50 = 7.7725 + \mu_2 \times 0.50$$
$$r_{3,2} = r_{2,1} + \mu_2 \times 0.50 - 1 = 6.7725 - 1 + \mu_2 \times 0.50 = 5.7725 + \mu_2 \times 0.50$$
$$r_{3,3} = r_{2,2} + \mu_2 \times 0.50 - 1 = 4.7725 - 1 + \mu_2 \times 0.50 = 3.7725 + \mu_2 \times 0.50$$
$$r_{3,4} = r_{2,3} + \mu_2 \times 0.50 - 1 = 2.7725 - 1 + \mu_2 \times 0.50 = 1.7725 + \mu_2 \times 0.50$$

The prices of the pure securities at this point in time can be expressed as

$$q_{4,1} = q_{3,1} \times \frac{0.50}{\left(1 + \frac{0.077725 + \mu_2 \times 0.50}{2}\right)} = \frac{0.112320}{2.077725 + \mu_2 \times 0.50}$$

$$q_{4,2} = q_{3,1} \times \frac{0.50}{\left(1 + \frac{0.077725 + \mu_2 \times 0.50}{2}\right)} + q_{3,2} \times \frac{0.50}{\left(1 + \frac{0.057725 + \mu_2 \times 0.50}{2}\right)}$$
$$= \frac{0.112320}{2.077725 + \mu_2 \times 0.50} + \frac{0.340258}{2.057725 + \mu_2 \times 0.50}$$

$$q_{4,3} = q_{3,2} \times \frac{0.50}{\left(1 + \frac{0.057725 + \mu_2 \times 0.50}{2}\right)} + q_{3,3} \times \frac{0.50}{\left(1 + \frac{0.037725 + \mu_2 \times 0.50}{2}\right)}$$
$$= \frac{0.340258}{2.057725 + \mu_2 \times 0.50} + \frac{0.343589}{2.037725 + \mu_2 \times 0.50}$$

$$q_{4,4} = q_{3,3} \times \frac{0.50}{\left(1 + \frac{0.037725 + \mu_2 \times 0.50}{2}\right)} + q_{3,4} \times \frac{0.50}{\left(1 + \frac{0.017725 + \mu_2 \times 0.50}{2}\right)}$$
$$= \frac{0.343589}{2.037725 + \mu_2 \times 0.50} + \frac{0.115651}{2.017725 + \mu_2 \times 0.50}$$

$$q_{4,5} = q_{3,4} \times \frac{0.50}{\left(1 + \frac{0.017725 + \mu_2 \times 0.50}{2}\right)} = \frac{0.115651}{2.017725 + \mu_2 \times 0.50}$$

Obviously,

$$q_{4,1} + q_{4,2} + q_{4,3} + q_{4,4} + q_{4,5} = \frac{1}{(1 + 0.5 \times s_4)^4} = \frac{1}{(1.03375)^4} = \$0.875665$$

Thus,

$$2 \times \frac{0.112320}{2.077725 + \mu_2 \times 0.50} + 2 \times \frac{0.340258}{2.057725 + \mu_2 \times 0.50} + 2 \times \frac{0.343589}{2.037725 + \mu_2 \times 0.50} + 2 \times \frac{0.115651}{2.017725 + \mu_2 \times 0.50} = 0.875665$$

$$\Rightarrow \mu_2 = 0.070277 = 7.0277\%$$

Therefore,

$$r_{3,1} = 7.7725 + \frac{7.0277}{2} = 11.2863\%$$
$$r_{3,2} = 5.7725 + \frac{7.0277}{2} = 9.2863\%$$
$$r_{3,3} = 3.7725 + \frac{7.0277}{2} = 7.2863\%$$
$$r_{3,4} = 1.7725 + \frac{7.0277}{2} = 5.2863\%$$

The prices of the pure securities are

$$q_{4,1} = \$0.053160$$
$$q_{4,2} = \$0.215741$$
$$q_{4,3} = \$0.328336$$
$$q_{4,4} = \$0.222092$$
$$q_{4,5} = \$0.056336$$

Table 11.2: Summary of the Ho-Lee model-based interest rates.

Period	Node	Interest Rate
1	$r_{1,1}$	7.5063%
1	$r_{1,2}$	5.5063%
2	$r_{2,1}$	6.7725%
2	$r_{2,2}$	4.7725%
2	$r_{2,3}$	2.7725%
3	$r_{3,1}$	11.2863%
3	$r_{3,2}$	9.2863%
3	$r_{3,3}$	7.2863%
3	$r_{3,4}$	5.2863%

The no-arbitrage interest rate tree we derived is shown in Figure 11.5.

The state price tree is shown in Figure 11.6.

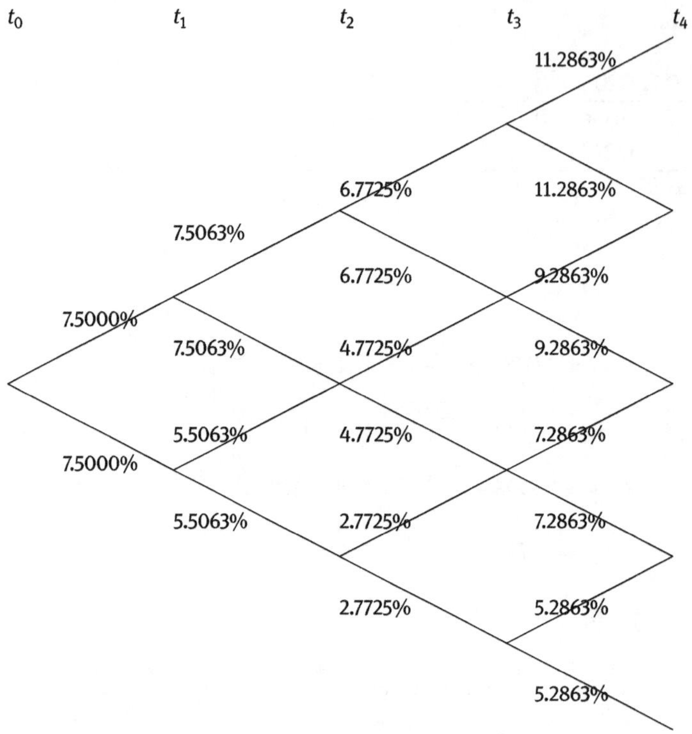

Figure 11.5: No-arbitrage interest rate tree.

Note: Readers will observe that in the figures depicting the short rates, the nodes are linked by straight lines. This is because interest rates span a period of time. However, in the figures depicting the state prices, that follow, there are no links between the nodes. This is because state prices represent a point in time. This mode of depiction is intentional and should not be construed as an error.

t_0	t_1	t_2	t_3	t_4
				0.053160
			0.112320	
		0.232247		0.215741
	0.481928		0.340258	
1.0		0.466755		0.328336
	0.481928		0.343589	
		0.234508		0.222092
			0.115651	
				0.056336

Figure 11.6: State price tree.

Calibrating the Black-Derman-Toy Model

Let's now illustrate how the BDT model can be fitted to the observed term structure using the binomial tree approach. Table 11.3 gives the term structure of interest rates and also the local volatility, or the volatility of short rates at each point in time.

Table 11.3: Vector of spot rates and local volatilities.

Period	Spot Rate	$\sigma\sqrt{\Delta t}$
0	7.50%	
1	7.00%	6.00%
2	6.25%	4.50%
3	6.75%	3.00%

The stochastic process for the BDT model is

$$d\ln r = \mu_t dt + \sigma_t dZ$$

Consider time point t_k, where $t_k = k \triangle t$, and let r_k be the short rate at this point in time. For the process

$$d\ln r = \mu_t dt + \sigma_t dZ$$

define $z(r) = \ln(r)$ We can approximate $d\ln(r)$ as $\ln(r_{k+1,j}) - \ln(r_{k,j})$ or as $\ln(r_{k+1,j+1}) - \ln(r_{k,j})$, and write

$$\begin{aligned}
&\ln(r_{k+1,j}) - \ln(r_{k,j}) = \mu_k \triangle t + \sigma_{k+1}\sqrt{\triangle t} \quad \text{and}\\
&\ln(r_{k+1,j+1}) - \ln(r_{k,j}) = \mu_k \triangle t - \sigma_{k+1}\sqrt{\triangle t}\\
&\Rightarrow z_{1,1} = z_{0,1} + \mu_0 \triangle t + \sigma_1\sqrt{\triangle t} \quad \text{and}\\
&\Rightarrow z_{1,2} = z_{0,1} + \mu_0 \triangle t - \sigma_1\sqrt{\triangle t} \quad \text{and}\\
&\Rightarrow z_{1,2} = z_{1,1} - 2\sigma_1\sqrt{\triangle t}
\end{aligned}$$

Similarly,

$$\begin{aligned}
&z_{2,1} = z_{1,1} + \mu_1 \triangle t + \sigma_2\sqrt{\triangle t} \quad \text{and}\\
&z_{2,2} = z_{1,1} + \mu_1 \triangle t - \sigma_2\sqrt{\triangle t} = z_{1,2} + \mu_1 \triangle t + \sigma_2\sqrt{\triangle t}\\
&\Rightarrow z_{2,2} = z_{2,1} - 2\sigma_2\sqrt{\triangle t}
\end{aligned}$$

Similarly,

$$z_{2,3} = z_{1,2} + \mu_1 \triangle t - \sigma_2\sqrt{\triangle t}$$

$$\Rightarrow z_{2,3} = z_{2,2} - 2\sigma_2\sqrt{\triangle t}$$
$$= z_{2,1} - 4\sigma_2\sqrt{\triangle t}$$

Similarly,

$$z_{3,1} = z_{2,1} + \mu_2 \triangle t + \sigma_3\sqrt{\triangle t} \quad \text{and}$$
$$z_{3,2} = z_{2,1} + \mu_2 \triangle t - \sigma_3\sqrt{\triangle t} = z_{2,2} + \mu_2 \triangle t + \sigma_3\sqrt{\triangle t}$$
$$\Rightarrow z_{3,2} = z_{3,1} - 2\sigma_3\sqrt{\triangle t}$$

Similarly,

$$z_{3,3} = z_{2,2} + \mu_2 \triangle t - \sigma_3\sqrt{\triangle t} = z_{2,3} + \mu_2 \triangle t + \sigma_3\sqrt{\triangle t}$$
$$\Rightarrow z_{3,3} = z_{3,2} - 2\sigma_3\sqrt{\triangle t}$$
$$\Rightarrow z_{3,3} = z_{3,1} - 4\sigma_3\sqrt{\triangle t}$$
$$z_{3,4} = z_{2,3} + \mu_2 \triangle t - \sigma_3\sqrt{\triangle t}$$
$$\Rightarrow z_{3,4} = z_{3,3} - 2\sigma_3\sqrt{\triangle t}$$
$$z_{3,4} = z_{3,1} - 6\sigma_3\sqrt{\triangle t}$$

In general,

$$z_{k+1,j+1} = z_{k+1,1} - 2 \times j\sigma_{k+1}\sqrt{\triangle t}$$
$$\Rightarrow \ln\left(\frac{r_{k+1,j}}{r_{k,j}}\right) = \mu_k \triangle t + \sigma_{k+1}\sqrt{\triangle t} \quad \text{and}$$
$$\ln\left(\frac{r_{k+1,j+1}}{r_{k,j}}\right) = \mu_k \triangle t - \sigma_{k+1}\sqrt{\triangle t}$$
$$\Rightarrow \left(\frac{r_{k+1,j}}{r_{k,j}}\right) = \exp[\mu_k \triangle t + \sigma_{k+1}\sqrt{\triangle t}]$$
$$\Rightarrow r_{k+1,j} = r_{k,j} \times \exp[\mu_k \triangle t + \sigma_{k+1}\sqrt{\triangle t}] \quad \text{and}$$
$$\Rightarrow r_{k+1,j+1} = r_{k,j} \times \exp[\mu_k \triangle t - \sigma_{k+1}\sqrt{\triangle t}]$$

An Issue with Recombination

Consider state (2,2). There are two paths, namely an up move from (0,1), followed by a down move from (1,1). Or a down move from (0,1), followed by an up move from (1,2).

$$z_{1,1} = z_{0,1} + \mu_0 \triangle t + \sigma_1\sqrt{\triangle t}$$
$$z_{2,2} = z_{1,1} + \mu_1 \triangle t - \sigma_2\sqrt{\triangle t}$$
$$\Rightarrow z_{2,2} = z_{0,1} + [\mu_0 + \mu_1] \triangle t + [\sigma_1 - \sigma_2]\sqrt{\triangle t}$$

$$z_{1,2} = z_{0,1} + \mu_0 \triangle t - \sigma_1 \sqrt{\triangle t}$$
$$z_{2,2} = z_{1,2} + \mu_1 \triangle t + \sigma_2 \sqrt{\triangle t}$$
$$\Rightarrow z_{2,2} = z_{0,1} + [\mu_0 + \mu_1] \triangle t - [\sigma_1 - \sigma_2] \sqrt{\triangle t}$$

For the tree to recombine, we require that

$$z_{0,1} + [\mu_0 + \mu_1] \triangle t + [\sigma_1 - \sigma_2] \sqrt{\triangle t} = z_{0,1} + [\mu_0 + \mu_1] \triangle t - [\sigma_1 - \sigma_2] \sqrt{\triangle t}$$
$$\Rightarrow \sigma_1 = \sigma_2$$

This is inconsistent with our assumption of time varying volatility. The issue can be resolved by noticing that

$$z_{k+1,j+1} = z_{k+1,1} - 2 \times j\sigma_{k+1} \sqrt{\triangle t}$$

Thus all we need to do is estimate $z_{k+1,1}$, and we can derive all the other rates at time $(k + 1)$ using the given value of sigma. Thus instead of estimating the μs as we did in the case of the Ho-Lee model, we estimate $z_{k+1,1}$, or equivalently $r_{k+1,1}$, and derive the rates at the other nodes at that point in time from the estimate.

The one-period spot rate is 7.50%. The corresponding volatility at time one is $6/\triangle t\%$. The variable to be estimated is $r_{1,1}$.

$$r_{1,2} = r_{1,1} \times \exp[-2\sigma_1 \sqrt{\triangle t}]$$
$$= r_{1,1} \times \exp(-2 \times 0.06) = r_{1,1} \times \exp(-0.12)$$
$$q_{1,1} = q_{1,2} = \frac{0.50}{(1 + \frac{0.075}{2})} = 0.481928$$

The prices of the pure securities for the next period are computed as follows:

$$q_{2,1} = q_{1,1} \times \frac{0.50}{(1 + \frac{r_{1,1}}{2})} = \frac{0.481928}{(2 + r_{1,1})}$$
$$q_{2,2} = q_{1,1} \times \frac{0.50}{(1 + \frac{r_{1,1}}{2})} + q_{1,2} \times \frac{0.50}{(1 + \frac{r_{1,2}}{2})}$$
$$= \frac{0.481928}{(2 + r_{1,1})} + \frac{0.481928}{[2 + r_{1,1} \times \exp(-0.12)]}$$
$$q_{2,3} = q_{1,2} \times \frac{0.50}{(1 + \frac{r_{1,2}}{2})}$$
$$= 0.481928 \times \frac{1}{[2 + r_{1,1} \times \exp(-0.12)]}$$

Obviously,

$$q_{2,1} + q_{2,2} + q_{2,3} = 0.933511 = \frac{0.481928}{(2 + r_{1,1})} + \frac{0.481928}{(2 + r_{1,1})}$$

$$+\frac{0.481928}{[2+r_{1,1}\times\exp(-0.12)]}+\frac{0.481928}{[2+r_{1,1}\times\exp(-0.12)]}$$
$$=\frac{2\times0.481928}{(2+r_{1,1})}+\frac{2\times0.481928}{[2+r_{1,1}\times\exp(-.12)]}$$

The solution is $r_{1,1}=6.8915\%$.
Thus,

$$r_{1,2}=6.8915\times\exp(-0.12)=6.1122\%$$

The state prices are

$$q_{2,1}=\$0.232938$$
$$q_{2,2}=\$0.466756$$
$$q_{2,3}=\$0.233818$$

In the next period, the variable to be estimated is $r_{2,1}$:

$$\begin{aligned}r_{2,2}&=r_{2,1}\times\exp[-2\sigma_2\sqrt{\Delta t}]\\&=r_{2,1}\times\exp(-2\times0.045)=r_{2,1}\times\exp(-0.09)\\r_{2,3}&=r_{2,1}\times\exp[-4\sigma_2\sqrt{\Delta t}]\\&=r_{2,1}\times\exp(-4\times0.045)=r_{2,1}\times\exp(-0.18)\end{aligned}$$

The prices of pure securities for the next point in time may be expressed as follows:

$$\begin{aligned}q_{3,1}&=q_{2,1}\times\frac{0.50}{(1+\frac{r_{2,1}}{2})}=\frac{0.232938}{(2+r_{2,1})}\\q_{3,2}&=q_{2,1}\times\frac{0.50}{(1+\frac{r_{2,1}}{2})}+q_{2,2}\times\frac{0.50}{(1+\frac{r_{2,2}}{2})}\\&=\frac{0.232938}{(2+r_{2,1})}+\frac{0.466756}{[2+r_{2,1}\times\exp(-0.09)]}\\q_{3,3}&=q_{2,2}\times\frac{0.50}{(1+\frac{r_{2,2}}{2})}+q_{2,3}\times\frac{0.50}{(1+\frac{r_{2,3}}{2})}\\&=\frac{0.466756}{[2+r_{2,1}\times\exp(-0.09)]}+\frac{0.233818}{[2+r_{2,1}\times\exp(-0.18)]}\\q_{3,4}&=q_{2,3}\times\frac{0.50}{(1+\frac{r_{2,3}}{2})}=\frac{0.233818}{[2+r_{2,1}\times\exp(-0.18)]}\end{aligned}$$

Obviously,

$$q_{3,1}+q_{3,2}+q_{3,3}+q_{3,4}=\frac{1}{(1+0.5\times s_3)^3}=\frac{1}{(1.03125)^3}==\$0.911818$$

Thus,

$$2 \times \frac{0.232938}{(2 + r_{2,1})} + 2 \times \frac{0.466756}{[2 + r_{2,1} \times \exp(-0.09)]} + 2 \times \frac{0.233818}{[2 + r_{2,1} \times \exp(-0.18)]} = 0.911818$$

$$\Rightarrow r_{2,1} = 5.1969\%$$

Therefore,

$$r_{2,2} = 4.7497\%$$
$$r_{2,3} = 4.3409\%$$

The prices of the pure securities are

$$q_{3,1} = \$0.113519$$
$$q_{3,2} = \$0.341483$$
$$q_{3,3} = \$0.342390$$
$$q_{3,4} = \$0.114425$$

Finally, let's proceed to the penultimate point in time. The variable to be estimated is $r_{3,1}$:

$$\begin{aligned}
r_{3,2} &= r_{3,1} \times \exp[-2\sigma_3 \sqrt{\triangle t}] \\
&= r_{3,1} \times \exp(-2 \times 0.03) = r_{3,1} \times \exp(-0.06) \\
r_{3,3} &= r_{3,1} \times \exp[-4\sigma_3 \sqrt{\triangle t}] \\
&= r_{3,1} \times \exp(-4 \times 0.03) = r_{3,1} \times \exp(-0.12) \\
r_{3,4} &= r_{3,1} \times \exp[-6\sigma_3 \sqrt{\triangle t}] \\
&= r_{3,1} \times \exp(-6 \times 0.03) = r_{3,1} \times \exp(-0.18)
\end{aligned}$$

The prices of pure securities for the next point in time may be expressed as follows:

$$\begin{aligned}
q_{4,1} &= q_{3,1} \times \frac{0.50}{(1 + \frac{r_{3,1}}{2})} = \frac{0.113519}{(2 + r_{3,1})} \\
q_{4,2} &= q_{3,1} \times \frac{0.50}{(1 + \frac{r_{3,1}}{2})} + q_{3,2} \times \frac{0.50}{(1 + \frac{r_{3,2}}{2})} \\
&= \frac{0.113519}{(2 + r_{3,1})} + \frac{0.341483}{[2 + r_{3,1} \times \exp(-0.06)]} \\
q_{4,3} &= q_{3,2} \times \frac{0.50}{(1 + \frac{r_{3,2}}{2})} + q_{3,3} \times \frac{0.50}{(1 + \frac{r_{3,3}}{2})} \\
&= \frac{0.341483}{[2 + r_{3,1} \times \exp(-0.06)]} + \frac{0.342390}{[2 + r_{3,1} \times \exp(-0.12)]} \\
q_{4,4} &= q_{3,3} \times \frac{0.50}{(1 + \frac{r_{3,3}}{2})} + q_{3,4} \times \frac{0.50}{(1 + \frac{r_{3,4}}{2})}
\end{aligned}$$

$$= \frac{0.342390}{[2 + r_{3,1} \times \exp(-0.12)]} + \frac{0.114425}{[2 + r_{3,1} \times \exp(-0.18)]}$$

$$q_{4,5} = \frac{0.114425}{[2 + r_{3,1} \times \exp(-0.18)]}$$

Obviously,

$$q_{4,1} + q_{4,2} + q_{4,3} + q_{4,4} + q_{4,5} = \frac{1}{(1 + 0.5 \times s_4)^4} = \frac{1}{(1.03375)^4} = \$0.875665$$

Thus,

$$2 \times \frac{0.113519}{(2 + r_{3,1})} + 2 \times \frac{0.341483}{(2 + r_{3,1} \times \exp(-0.06))}$$
$$+ 2 \times \frac{0.342390}{(2 + r_{3,1} \times \exp(-0.12))} + 2 \times \frac{0.114425}{(2 + r_{3,1} \times \exp(-0.18))} = 0.875665$$
$$\Rightarrow r_{3,1} = 9.0245\%$$

Therefore,

$$r_{3,2} = 8.4990\%$$
$$r_{3,3} = 8.0040\%$$
$$r_{3,4} = 7.5379\%$$

The prices of the pure securities are

$$q_{4,1} = \$0.054309$$
$$q_{4,2} = \$0.218091$$
$$q_{4,3} = \$0.328389$$
$$q_{4,4} = \$0.219742$$
$$q_{4,5} = \$0.055135$$

The no-arbitrage interest rate tree we derive is shown in Figure 11.7.
The state price tree is shown in Figure 11.8.

An Issue with Calibration

If we assume that the local volatilities are given in order to calibrate the model, it is necessary that all the forward rates be positive to ensure that the short rates are not negative. In our case, all the forward rates are positive, and consequently there is no issue on this score.

At time zero, the forward rates are 6.5012% for a one-period loan after one period; 5.6278% for a two-period loan after one period; and 6.5006% for a three-period loan

Table 11.4: Summary of BDT model-based interest rates.

Period	Node	Interest Rate
1	$r_{1,1}$	6.8915%
1	$r_{1,2}$	6.1122%
2	$r_{2,1}$	5.1969%
2	$r_{2,2}$	4.7497%
2	$r_{2,3}$	4.3409%
3	$r_{3,1}$	9.0245%
3	$r_{3,2}$	8.4990%
3	$r_{3,3}$	8.0040%
3	$r_{3,4}$	7.5379%

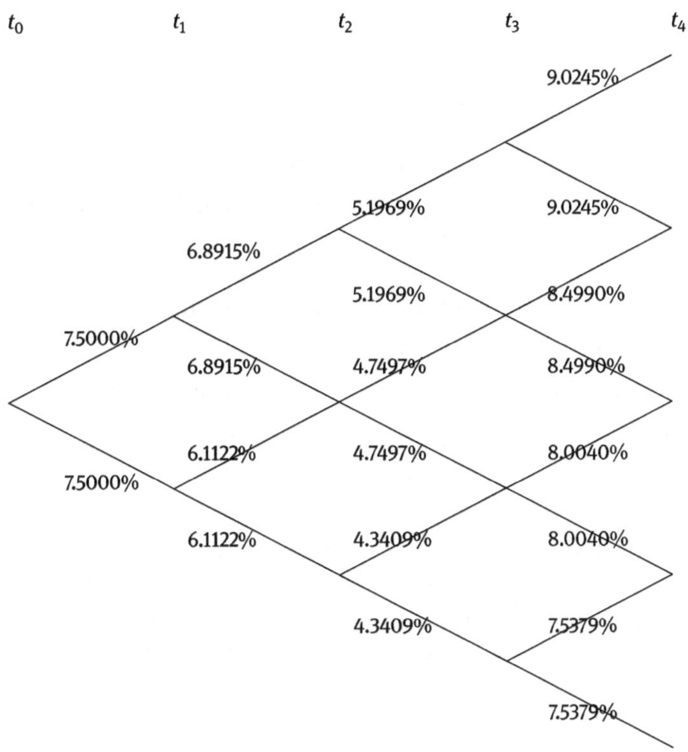

Figure 11.7: No-arbitrage interest rate tree for the BDT model.

after one period, where all the rates are annualized. The forward rate for a one-period loan after two periods is 4.7581% and 6.5003% for a two-period loan after two periods. Finally, the rate for a one-period loan after three periods is 8.2573% per annum. Thus, it is not surprising that all the short rates that we have generated are positive.

t_0	t_1	t_2	t_3	t_4
				0.054309
			0.113519	
		0.232938		0.218091
	0.481928		0.341483	
1.0		0.466756		0.328389
	0.481928		0.342390	
		0.233818		0.219742
			0.114425	
				0.055135

Figure 11.8: State price tree for the BDT model.

Valuation of a Plain Vanilla Bond

Consider a four-period bond with a face value of \$1,000 that pays a coupon of \$40 every period. Using the state price tree obtained by calibrating the Ho-Lee model, we can compute the value of this bond as follows:

$$\begin{aligned}
&1,040 \times (0.053160 + 0.215741 + 0.328336 + 0.222092 + 0.056336)\\
&\quad + 40 \times (0.112320 + 0.340258 + 0.343589 + 0.115651)\\
&\quad + 40 \times (0.232247 + 0.466755 + 0.234508) + 40 \times (0.481928 + 0.481928)\\
&= 1,040 \times 0.875665 + 40 \times 0.911818 + 40 \times 0.933511 + 40 \times 0.963856\\
&= \$1,023.0589
\end{aligned}$$

The value will be the same if we use the state prices obtained from the Black-Derman-Toy model. This is because at a point in time, the sum of the state prices is the same irrespective of the model being used, as the computation is based on the same vector of spot rates. Another way to understand this is as follows. The bond price is given by

$$\begin{aligned}
&\frac{40}{(1+\frac{s_1}{2})} + \frac{40}{(1+\frac{s_2}{2})^2}\\
&\quad + \frac{40}{(1+\frac{s_3}{2})^3} + \frac{1,040}{(1+\frac{s_4}{2})^4}\\
&= 38.5542 + 37.3404 + 36.4727 + 910.6914 = \$1,023.0587
\end{aligned}$$

Because both the models have been calibrated using the same vector of spot rates, they give the same bond price.

Valuation of a Zero Coupon Bond

Consider a zero coupon bond that pays $1,000 at time t_4. Its value at various nodes of the tree can be computed by working backwards. Let's first consider the Ho-Lee-based tree.

At t_3, its value at node (3,1) is given by

$$\frac{1{,}000}{\left(1+\frac{0.112863}{2}\right)} = \$946.5829$$

At node (3,2), the value is given by

$$\frac{1{,}000}{\left(1+\frac{0.092863}{2}\right)} = \$955.6287$$

Similarly at node (3,3), the value is

$$\frac{1{,}000}{\left(1+\frac{0.072863}{2}\right)} = \$964.8491$$

Finally at node (3,4), the value is

$$\frac{1{,}000}{\left(1+\frac{0.052863}{2}\right)} = \$974.2491$$

Working backwards we can calculate the prices at time t_2 as follows. At node (2,1) the value is

$$0.5 \times \frac{946.5829}{\left(1+\frac{0.067725}{2}\right)} + 0.5 \times \frac{955.6287}{\left(1+\frac{0.067725}{2}\right)} = \$919.9539$$

Similarly at node (2,2), the value is

$$0.5 \times \frac{955.6287}{\left(1+\frac{0.047725}{2}\right)} + 0.5 \times \frac{964.8491}{\left(1+\frac{0.047725}{2}\right)} = \$937.8592$$

Finally at node (2,3), the value is

$$0.5 \times \frac{964.8491}{\left(1+\frac{0.027725}{2}\right)} + 0.5 \times \frac{974.2491}{\left(1+\frac{0.027725}{2}\right)} = \$956.2925$$

Using the same logic, the value at (1,1) is

$$0.5 \times \frac{919.9539}{\left(1+\frac{0.075063}{2}\right)} + 0.5 \times \frac{937.8592}{\left(1+\frac{0.075063}{2}\right)} = \$895.3044$$

and the value at (1,2) is

$$0.5 \times \frac{937.8592}{\left(1+\frac{0.055063}{2}\right)} + 0.5 \times \frac{956.2925}{\left(1+\frac{0.055063}{2}\right)} = \$921.7001$$

At the starting node, the value is therefore

$$0.5 \times \frac{895.3044}{(1+\frac{0.075}{2})} + 0.5 \times \frac{921.7001}{(1+\frac{0.075}{2})} = \$875.6648$$

The bond prices may be depicted in a tree format as in Figure 11.9.

t_0	t_1	t_2	t_3
			946.5829
		919.9539	
	895.3044		955.6287
875.6648		937.8592	
	921.7001		964.8491
		956.2925	
			974.2491

Figure 11.9: Evolution of the price of a zero coupon bond: The Ho-Lee tree.

Now reconsider a zero coupon bond that pays \$1,000 at time t_4, and consider the BDT tree. At t_3, its value at node (3,1) is given by

$$\frac{1{,}000}{(1+\frac{0.090245}{2})} = \$956.8256$$

At node (3,2) the value is given by

$$\frac{1{,}000}{(1+\frac{0.084990}{2})} = \$959.2372$$

Similarly at node (3,3), the value is

$$\frac{1{,}000}{(1+\frac{0.08004}{2})} = \$961.5200$$

Finally at node (3,4), the value is

$$\frac{1{,}000}{(1+\frac{0.075379}{2})} = \$963.6794$$

Working backwards we can calculate the prices at time t_2 as follows. At node (2,1) the value is

$$0.5 \times \frac{956.8256}{\left(1 + \frac{0.051969}{2}\right)} + 0.5 \times \frac{959.2372}{\left(1 + \frac{0.051969}{2}\right)} = \$933.7679$$

Similarly at node (2,2), the value is

$$0.5 \times \frac{959.2372}{\left(1 + \frac{0.047497}{2}\right)} + 0.5 \times \frac{961.5200}{\left(1 + \frac{0.047497}{2}\right)} = \$938.1001$$

Finally at node (2,3), the value is

$$0.5 \times \frac{961.5200}{\left(1 + \frac{0.043409}{2}\right)} + 0.5 \times \frac{963.6794}{\left(1 + \frac{0.043409}{2}\right)} = \$942.1508$$

Using the same logic, the value at (1,1) is

$$0.5 \times \frac{933.7679}{\left(1 + \frac{0.068915}{2}\right)} + 0.5 \times \frac{938.1001}{\left(1 + \frac{0.068915}{2}\right)} = \$904.7583$$

while the value at (1,2) is

$$0.5 \times \frac{938.1001}{\left(1 + \frac{0.061122}{2}\right)} + 0.5 \times \frac{942.1508}{\left(1 + \frac{0.061122}{2}\right)} = \$912.2463$$

At the starting node, the value is therefore

$$0.5 \times \frac{904.7583}{\left(1 + \frac{0.075}{2}\right)} + 0.5 \times \frac{912.2463}{\left(1 + \frac{0.075}{2}\right)} = \$875.6649$$

The bond prices may be depicted in a tree format as in Figure 11.10.

t_0	t_1	t_2	t_3
			956.8256
		933.7679	
	904.7583		959.2372
875.6649		938.1001	
	912.2463		961.5200
		942.1508	
			963.6794

Figure 11.10: Evolution of the price of a zero coupon bond: The BDT tree.

The price of the bond is the same at time t_0, although it differs from model to model at subsequent nodes. This is because the price at t_0 is

$$\frac{1{,}000}{(1+\frac{s_4}{2})^4} = \frac{1{,}000}{(1.03375)^4} = \$875.6649$$

Valuing a European Call

Consider a two-period European call on the zero coupon bond with an exercise price of $925. Let's first value it using the Ho-Lee model. The payoff is zero in node (2,1), $12.8592 at node (2,2), and $31.2925 at node (2,3). The value of the option at t_0 is

$$0.466755 \times 12.8592 + 0.234508 \times 31.2925 = \$13.3404$$

Now let's value it using the BDT model. The payoff is 8.7679 in node (2,1), $13.1001 at node (2,2), and $17.1508 at node (2,3). The value of the option at t_0 is

$$0.232938 \times 8.7679 + 0.466756 \times 13.1001 + 0.233818 \times 17.1508 = \$12.1671$$

Valuing an American Put

Valuing an American option is more complex because we have to check for the possibility of early exercise at every node. Consider a two-period put on the zero coupon bond with an exercise price of $930. Let's look at the Ho-Lee model first. The payoffs from the option at time t_2 are $10.0461 at node (2,1) and zero at nodes (2,2) and (2,3).

The model value at (1,1) is

$$.5 \times \frac{10.0461}{\left(1+\frac{0.075063}{2}\right)} = \$4.8413$$

The payoff from early exercise is $34.6956. Thus the option will be exercised early.

The model value at node (1,2) is zero. The payoff from early exercise is $8.2999. Thus the option will be exercised early.

The model value at (0,1) is

$$.5 \times \frac{34.6956}{(1+\frac{0.075}{2})} + .5 \times \frac{8.2999}{(1+\frac{0.075}{2})} = \$20.7207$$

The payoff from early exercise is $54.3352. So the option will be exercised right at the outset, that is, at time t_0.

Now let's turn to the BDT model. The payoffs from the option at time t_2 is zero at all three nodes.

The model value at (1,1) is zero. The payoff from early exercise is \$25.2417. Thus the option will be exercised early.

The model value at node (1,2) is zero. The payoff from early exercise is \$17.7537. Thus the option will be exercised early.

The model value at (0,1) is

$$.5 \times \frac{25.2417}{(1+\frac{0.075}{2})} + .5 \times \frac{17.7537}{(1+\frac{0.075}{2})} = \$20.7207$$

The payoff from early exercise is \$54.3351. So the option will be exercised right at the outset, that is, at time t_0.

Let us take a closer look at this result. In the case of both the models, the zero coupon bond price at each node is less than the prices of the two nodes at the next point in time, from which it is derived. Thus the intrinsic value at every node is greater than or equal to the model value that is obtained from the subsequent point in time. Thus the American put will always be exercised at time zero if it is in the money, that is, the exercise price is higher than the price at that time. If however the exercise price is lower than the price at time zero, then the intrinsic and the model values at all points in time are zero, and consequently the option has a zero premium at the outset.

Caps, Floors, and Collars

Before we go on to analyze caps and floors, let's first define *caplets* and *floorlets*. A caplet is a call option on an interest rate, whereas a floorlet is a put option on an interest rate. To evaluate these options, we first reproduce a segment of the no-arbitrage interest rate tree that we derived earlier.

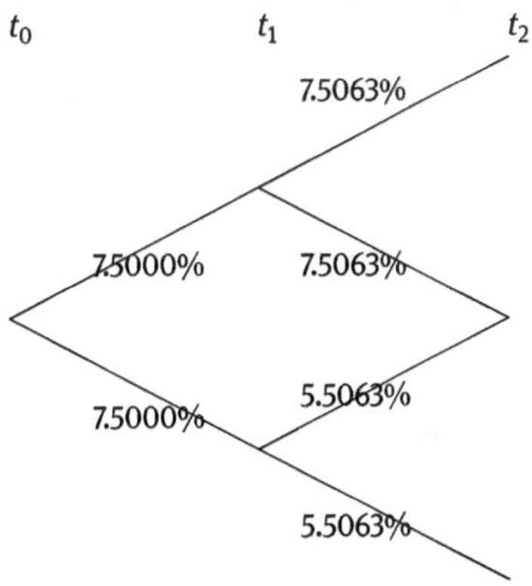

Figure 11.11: Segment of the Ho-Lee no-arbitrage interest rate tree.

Consider a one-period caplet with an exercise price of 5%. Let the underlying principal be $1,000. Each time period is assumed to be of six months duration, and we take it as 0.5 years in order to avoid issues regarding day-count conventions.[3]

At time t_1 if the node (1,1) is attained, the call is in the money because the interest rate of 7.5063% is greater than the exercise price of 5%. The payoff is

$$1{,}000 \times (0.075063 - 0.05) \times 0.5 = \$12.5315$$

In the case of interest rate options, the payoff occurs not when the option expires, but at a point in time when the next interest payment is due. In the preceding case, the rate as determined at t_1 is applicable for computing the interest due at t_2. Consequently the caplet pays off at t_2. Thus the value at t_1 is the present value of the payoff. In this case, the value is

$$\frac{12.5315}{\left(1 + \frac{0.075063}{2}\right)} = \$12.0782$$

If we attain node (1,2) at time t_1, the caplet once again is in the money. The payoff is

$$1{,}000 \times (0.055063 - 0.05) \times 0.5 = \$2.5315$$

The value at t_1 is the present value of the payoff. In this case, the value is

$$\frac{2.5315}{\left(1 + \frac{0.055063}{2}\right)} = \$2.4637$$

Thus the value of the caplet at time t_0 is computed as

$$\begin{aligned} &0.5 \times \frac{12.5315}{(1.0375)\left(1 + \frac{0.075063}{2}\right)} + 0.5 \times \frac{2.5315}{(1.0375)\left(1 + \frac{0.055063}{2}\right)} \\ &= 5.8208 + 1.1873 = \$7.0081 \end{aligned}$$

Now consider a one-period floorlet with an exercise price of 7% and a principal of $1,000. At node (1,1), the option is out of the money because the interest rate is greater than the exercise price. However, at node (1,2), the option is in the money. The payoff is

$$1{,}000 \times (0.07 - 0.055063) \times 0.5 = \$7.4685$$

Thus the value of the floorlet at t_0 is computed as

$$0.5 \times \frac{7.4685}{(1.0375)\left(1 + \frac{0.055063}{2}\right)} = \$3.5028$$

3 In practice, the length of the time period has to be calculated per the day-count convention that is applicable in the market in question.

Caps and Floors: A Detailed Perspective

A cap is a portfolio of caplets that can be acquired by a borrower who has taken advantage of a floating rate loan, to protect against an increase in interest rates. Similarly, a floor is a portfolio of floorlets that can be acquired by a lender who has made a loan on a floating rate basis to protect against a decline in interest rates. Caps and floors are cash settled. If a caplet or floorlet is in the money, the writer makes a payment to the holder. The principal that is used to compute the payoff is termed as a *notional principal*, for it is specified purely to facilitate the computation of the payoff and is not intended to be paid or received.

Required Symbols

- $P \equiv$ notional principal.
- $K \equiv$ contract rate or the exercise price.
- $R \equiv$ reference rate used to compute the payoff, like the LIBOR.
- $N_i \equiv$ the number of days in the time period from the exercise date until the payment date.
- $N \equiv$ the number of days in the calendar year. In the US and the EU, it is taken as 360, whereas in the UK, it is taken as 365.

The payment, if the caplet or floorlet is in the money, is usually made in arrears. Thus with reference to Figure 11.9, if the caplet or floorlet is in the money at a node at time t_1, the payment will occur at time t_2, which we assume, is six months hence. Consequently, there is no need to discount the payoff, as would be required if the payment were made at time t_1 itself.

Example 11.1. Consider a notional principal of $1,000,000. The reference rate is the 6-M LIBOR, and the contract rate is 5%. The day-count convention is Actual/360. Assume that the number of days in the next semiannual period is 184. If the reference rate is 6.50%, the payoff after six months is

$$\begin{aligned} &1{,}000{,}000 \times \frac{(6.50 - 5.00)}{100} \times \frac{184}{360} \\ &= \$7{,}666.67 \end{aligned}$$

Example 11.2. Consider the same data as in the previous example. Consider a floor with a contract rate of 7.50%. If reference rate is 5%, the payoff after six months is

$$\begin{aligned} &1{,}000{,}000 \times \frac{(7.50 - 5.00)}{100} \times \frac{184}{360} \\ &= \$12{,}777.78 \end{aligned}$$

Using the interest rate tree that we derived earlier (Figure 11.5), let's price a three-period cap and a three-period floor. The cap consists of three caplets, expiring after one, two, and three periods respectively. The value of the one-period caplet is \$7.0081. The value of the two-period caplet is calculated as follows.

The payoff if state (2,1) is attained is

$$1{,}000 \times [0.067725 - 0.05] \times 0.5 = \$8.8625$$

The payoff in states (2,2) and (2,3) is zero. The value at time t_0 of the payoff is

$$0.5 \times 0.5 \times \frac{1}{1.0375} \times \frac{1}{\left(1 + \frac{0.075063}{2}\right)} \times \frac{8.8625}{\left(1 + \frac{0.067725}{2}\right)}$$
$$= \$1.9909$$

Thus the value of the caplet = \$1.9909.

Similarly, the value of a three-period caplet is given by

$$\begin{aligned}
&0.5 \times 0.5 \times 0.5 \times \frac{1}{1.0375} \times \frac{1}{\left(1 + \frac{0.075063}{2}\right)} \\
&\quad \times \frac{1}{\left(1 + \frac{0.067725}{2}\right)} \times \frac{1}{\left(1 + \frac{0.112863}{2}\right)} \times 1{,}000 \times [0.112863 - 0.05] \times 0.5 \\
&\quad + 0.5 \times 0.5 \times 0.5 \times \frac{1}{1.0375} \times \frac{1}{\left(1 + \frac{0.075063}{2}\right)} \\
&\quad \times \frac{1}{\left(1 + \frac{0.067725}{2}\right)} \times \frac{1}{\left(1 + \frac{0.092863}{2}\right)} \times 1{,}000 \times [0.092863 - 0.05] \times 0.5 \\
&\quad + 0.5 \times 0.5 \times 0.5 \times \frac{1}{1.0375} \times \frac{1}{\left(1 + \frac{0.075063}{2}\right)} \\
&\quad \times \frac{1}{\left(1 + \frac{0.047725}{2}\right)} \times \frac{1}{\left(1 + \frac{0.092863}{2}\right)} \times 1{,}000 \times [0.092863 - 0.05] \times 0.5 \\
&\quad + 0.5 \times 0.5 \times 0.5 \times \frac{1}{1.0375} \times \frac{1}{\left(1 + \frac{0.055063}{2}\right)} \\
&\quad \times \frac{1}{\left(1 + \frac{0.047725}{2}\right)} \times \frac{1}{\left(1 + \frac{0.092863}{2}\right)} \times 1{,}000 \times [0.092863 - 0.05] \times 0.5 \\
&\quad + 0.5 \times 0.5 \times 0.5 \times \frac{1}{1.0375} \times \frac{1}{\left(1 + \frac{0.075063}{2}\right)} \\
&\quad \times \frac{1}{\left(1 + \frac{0.047725}{2}\right)} \times \frac{1}{\left(1 + \frac{0.072863}{2}\right)} \times 1{,}000 \times [0.072863 - 0.05] \times 0.5 \\
&\quad + 0.5 \times 0.5 \times 0.5 \times \frac{1}{1.0375} \times \frac{1}{\left(1 + \frac{0.055063}{2}\right)} \\
&\quad \times \frac{1}{\left(1 + \frac{0.047725}{2}\right)} \times \frac{1}{\left(1 + \frac{0.072863}{2}\right)} \times 1{,}000 \times [0.072863 - 0.05] \times 0.5 \\
&\quad + 0.5 \times 0.5 \times 0.5 \times \frac{1}{1.0375} \times \frac{1}{\left(1 + \frac{0.055063}{2}\right)}
\end{aligned}$$

$$\times \frac{1}{\left(1+\frac{0.027725}{2}\right)} \times \frac{1}{\left(1+\frac{0.072863}{2}\right)} \times 1{,}000 \times [0.072863 - 0.05] \times 0.5$$
$$+ 0.5 \times 0.5 \times 0.5 \times \frac{1}{1.0375} \times \frac{1}{\left(1+\frac{0.055063}{2}\right)}$$
$$\times \frac{1}{\left(1+\frac{0.027725}{2}\right)} \times \frac{1}{\left(1+\frac{0.052863}{2}\right)} \times 1{,}000 \times [0.052863 - 0.05] \times 0.5$$
$$= 3.3418 + 2.3004 + 2.3228 + 2.3455 + 1.2510 + 1.2631 + 1.2756 + 0.1613 = \$14.2615$$

Thus the value of a three-period cap is

$$\$7.0081 + \$1.9909 + \$14.2615 = \$23.2605$$

The value of a three-period floor is computed in a similar fashion. Let's consider a one-period floorlet with an exercise price of 6.4620% and an underlying principal of $1,000. The payoff is zero in state (1,1). However, there is a positive payoff at state (1,2), that is given by

$$1{,}000 \times [0.06462 - 0.055063] \times 0.5 = \$4.7785$$

This payoff obviously occurs at time t_2. Consequently, the value of the floorlet at t_0 is

$$0.5 \times \frac{4.7785}{(1.0375)\left(1+\frac{0.055063}{2}\right)} = \$2.2412$$

The value of the two-period floorlet is computed as follows. The payoff in state (2,1) is zero. The payoff in state (2,2) is

$$1{,}000 \times [0.06462 - 0.047725] \times 0.5 = \$8.4475$$

and the payoff in state (2,3) is

$$1{,}000 \times [0.06462 - 0.027725] \times 0.5 = \$18.4475$$

The floorlet is valued as

$$0.5 \times 0.5 \times \frac{1}{1.0375} \times \frac{1}{\left(1+\frac{0.075063}{2}\right)}$$
$$\times \frac{1}{\left(1+\frac{0.047725}{2}\right)} \times 1{,}000 \times [0.06462 - 0.047725] \times 0.5$$
$$+ 0.5 \times 0.5 \times \frac{1}{1.0375} \times \frac{1}{\left(1+\frac{0.055063}{2}\right)}$$
$$\times \frac{1}{\left(1+\frac{0.047725}{2}\right)} \times 1{,}000 \times [0.06462 - 0.047725] \times 0.5$$

$$+0.5 \times 0.5 \times \frac{1}{1.0375} \times \frac{1}{\left(1 + \frac{0.055063}{2}\right)}$$
$$\times \frac{1}{\left(1 + \frac{0.027725}{2}\right)} \times 1{,}000 \times [0.06462 - 0.027725] \times 0.5$$
$$= 1.9162 + 1.9348 + 4.2669 = \$8.1179$$

Similarly, the value of a three-period floorlet is given by

$$0.5 \times 0.5 \times 0.5 \times \frac{1}{1.0375} \times \frac{1}{\left(1 + \frac{0.055063}{2}\right)}$$
$$\times \frac{1}{\left(1 + \frac{0.027725}{2}\right)} \times \frac{1}{\left(1 + \frac{0.052863}{2}\right)} \times 1{,}000 \times [0.06462 - 0.052863] \times 0.5$$
$$= \$0.6623$$

Thus the value of a three-period floor is

$$\$2.2412 + \$8.1179 + \$0.6623 = \$11.0215$$

Interest Rate Collars

An interest rate collar is a combination of a cap and a floor. It requires the investor to take a long position in a cap and a short position in a floor, or vice versa. A borrower takes a long position in the collar by buying the cap and selling the floor. This puts a maximum and a minimum on the borrowing rate. A lender takes a short position in a collar by selling the cap and buying the floor. This too puts a maximum and a minimum on the lending rate.

Let us first consider the case of a borrower. If the rates rise, the borrower exercises the cap and the counterparty does not exercise the floor. Thus there is an upper limit on the borrowing rate. However, if rates decline, the borrower does not exercise the cap, and the counterparty exercises the floor. Hence, although the rates have moved in the borrower's favor, he still has to pay a minimum rate that is equivalent to the contract rate of the floor.

Now consider the case of a lender. If rates rise, the lender does not exercise the floor, whereas the counterparty does exercise the cap. This puts an upper limit on the lending rate, equivalent to the contract rate of the cap, which means that the lender cannot take full benefit of the higher rate. However, if rates decline, the lender exercises the floor, and the counterparty does not exercise the cap. Consequently there is a lower limit on the lending rate.

Example 11.3. Consider a long collar with a notional principal of \$1,000,000. The contract rate is 6% for the cap and 4.50% for the floor. The number of days in the semiannual period is 184, and the day-count convention is Actual/360.

If the LIBOR on the exercise date is 7.50%, the holder of the collar exercises the cap. The writer of the collar, who is the holder of the floor, does not exercise. The payoff is

$$1{,}000{,}000 \times \frac{(7.50 - 6.00)}{100} \times \frac{184}{360} = \$7{,}666.67$$

The actual interest paid is

$$1{,}000{,}000 \times 0.075 \times \frac{184}{360} = \$38{,}333.33$$

The effective interest paid is 38,333.33 – 7,666.67 = $30,666.67. This translates to a rate of

$$\frac{30{,}666.67}{1{,}000{,}000} \times \frac{360}{184} \times 100 = 6.00\%$$

If the LIBOR on the exercise date is 3%, the counterparty exercises the floor. The holder of the cap obviously does not exercise it. The payoff is

$$-1{,}000{,}000 \times \frac{(4.50 - 3.00)}{100} \times \frac{184}{360} = -\$7{,}666.67$$

The actual interest paid is

$$1{,}000{,}000 \times 0.03 \times \frac{184}{360} = \$15{,}333.33$$

The effective interest paid is 15,333.33 + 7,666.67 = $23,000.00. This translates to a rate of

$$\frac{23{,}000.00}{1{,}000{,}000} \times \frac{360}{184} \times 100 = 4.50\%$$

Thus the maximum interest payable is 6%, which is the exercise price of the cap, and the minimum interest payable is 4.50%, which is the exercise price of the floor. Thus, although protected if rates rise above 6%, the holder of the collar cannot take advantage of the situation if the rate declines below 4.50%.

If the rate is between 6% and 4.5%, neither the cap nor the floor are exercised, and the borrower pays the prevailing market rate. For instance, if the rate is 5.25% per annum, the interest paid is

$$1{,}000{,}000 \times 0.0525 \times \frac{184}{360} = \$26{,}833.33$$

which is between the upper bound of $30,666.67 and the lower bound of $23,000.00.

Valuation of a Zero Cost Collar

A zero cost collar is a position where the premium of the cap is equal to that of the floor, and as a consequence the premium paid for the collar is zero and hence the name.

Using the interest rate tree that we derived previously (Figure 11.5), let's price a three-period cap and a three-period floor. The cap consists of three caplets, expiring after one, two, and three periods, respectively, and the floor consists of three floorlets. Assume the exercise price for the caplets is 6.50% per annum and the underlying principal is $1,000.

At time t_1, if the node (1,1) is attained, the call is in the money, and the payoff is

$$1{,}000 \times (0.075063 - 0.065) \times 0.5 = \$5.0315$$

If we attain node (1,2) at time t_1, the caplet is out of the money. Thus the value of the caplet at time t_0 is computed as

$$0.5 \times \frac{5.0315}{(1.0375)\left(1 + \frac{0.075063}{2}\right)} = \$\,2.3371$$

The value of the two-period caplet is calculated as follows. The payoff if state (2,1) is attained is

$$1{,}000 \times [0.067725 - 0.065] \times 0.5 = \$1.3625$$

The payoff in states (2,2) and (2,3) is zero. The value at time t_0 of the payoff is

$$0.5 \times 0.5 \times \frac{1}{1.0375} \times \frac{1}{\left(1 + \frac{0.075063}{2}\right)} \times \frac{1.3625}{\left(1 + \frac{0.067725}{2}\right)}$$
$$= \$0.3061$$

Similarly, the value of a three-period caplet is given by

$$\begin{aligned}
&0.5 \times 0.5 \times 0.5 \times \frac{1}{1.0375} \times \frac{1}{\left(1 + \frac{0.075063}{2}\right)} \\
&\times \frac{1}{\left(1 + \frac{0.067725}{2}\right)} \times \frac{1}{\left(1 + \frac{0.112863}{2}\right)} \times 1{,}000 \times [0.112863 - 0.065] \times 0.5 \\
&+ 0.5 \times 0.5 \times 0.5 \times \frac{1}{1.0375} \times \frac{1}{\left(1 + \frac{0.075063}{2}\right)} \\
&\times \frac{1}{\left(1 + \frac{0.067725}{2}\right)} \times \frac{1}{\left(1 + \frac{0.092863}{2}\right)} \times 1{,}000 \times [0.092863 - 0.065] \times 0.5 \\
&+ 0.5 \times 0.5 \times 0.5 \times \frac{1}{1.0375} \times \frac{1}{\left(1 + \frac{0.075063}{2}\right)} \\
&\times \frac{1}{\left(1 + \frac{0.047725}{2}\right)} \times \frac{1}{\left(1 + \frac{0.092863}{2}\right)} \times 1{,}000 \times [0.092863 - 0.065] \times 0.5 \\
&+ 0.5 \times 0.5 \times 0.5 \times \frac{1}{1.0375} \times \frac{1}{\left(1 + \frac{0.055063}{2}\right)} \\
&\times \frac{1}{\left(1 + \frac{0.047725}{2}\right)} \times \frac{1}{\left(1 + \frac{0.092863}{2}\right)} \times 1{,}000 \times [0.092863 - 0.065] \times 0.5 \\
&+ 0.5 \times 0.5 \times 0.5 \times \frac{1}{1.0375} \times \frac{1}{\left(1 + \frac{0.075063}{2}\right)}
\end{aligned}$$

$$\times \frac{1}{\left(1+\frac{0.047725}{2}\right)} \times \frac{1}{\left(1+\frac{0.072863}{2}\right)} \times 1{,}000 \times [0.072863 - 0.065] \times 0.5$$
$$+ 0.5 \times 0.5 \times 0.5 \times \frac{1}{1.0375} \times \frac{1}{\left(1+\frac{0.055063}{2}\right)}$$
$$\times \frac{1}{\left(1+\frac{0.047725}{2}\right)} \times \frac{1}{\left(1+\frac{0.072863}{2}\right)} \times 1{,}000 \times [0.072863 - 0.065] \times 0.5$$
$$+ 0.5 \times 0.5 \times 0.5 \times \frac{1}{1.0375} \times \frac{1}{\left(1+\frac{0.055063}{2}\right)}$$
$$\times \frac{1}{\left(1+\frac{0.027725}{2}\right)} \times \frac{1}{\left(1+\frac{0.072863}{2}\right)} \times 1{,}000 \times [0.072863 - 0.065] \times 0.5$$
$$= 2.5444 + 1.4954 + 1.5100 + 1.5247 + 0.4302 + 0.4344 + 0.4387 = \$8.3777$$

Thus the value of a three-period cap is

$$\$2.3371 + \$0.3061 + \$8.3777 = \$11.0209$$

The premium of the three-period floor with a contract rate of 6.4620% and a principal of $1,000 is $11.0215. If this collar is bought, the investor has to pay a maximum rate of 6.50% per annum and a minimum rate of 6.4620% per annum, which virtually amounts to a fixed rate loan because the difference is only 3.8 basis points. The cost of the strategy is 11.0215 – 11.0209 = $0.0006, which is essentially a cost of zero.

Captions and Floortions

A caption is a financial instrument that gives the holder the right to buy a cap at a future point in time. Take the case of a firm that may borrow funds at a later date. If it decides to avail itself of the loan, it becomes concerned about the prospect of a rising interest rate and consequently may decide to acquire the cap. However, if it decides not to avail of the loan, there is no need to acquire the cap. The caption permits it to set the contract rate in advance for the cap, while giving it the freedom to refrain from exercise if the cap is not required. If the contract rate in the option is X and prevailing contract rate in the future is K, the caption is exercised if $K > X$. Otherwise, the buyer can allow the caption to expire and acquire a cap at the prevailing contract rate if required.

Similarly, a floortion gives the holder the right to buy a floor at a future point in time. An investor who may make a loan at a later date would be interested in such an instrument. If a party decides to extend the loan, it will be perturbed about the prospect of declining interest rates and consequently may exercise the floortion. However, if the party decides not to extend the loan, the option can be allowed to expire. If the contract rate in the option is X, and prevailing contract rate in the future is K, the floortion is exercised if $X > K$. Otherwise, the buyer can allow the floortion to expire and acquire a floor at the prevailing contract rate if required.

Chapter Summary

In this chapter we looked at interest rate options. The issues involved in building models of the term structure were briefly discussed and the focus then shifted to no-arbitrage models. We examined in detail both the Ho-Lee model and the Black-Derman-Toy model. In this context, the concept of Arrow-Debreu securities was explained. We calibrated both the models and derived the short-rate tree. The trees were used to value coupon paying bonds, zero coupon bonds, and options such as caps, floors, and collars. The chapter concludes with a very brief introduction to captions and floortions. In the next chapter, we look at interest rate forward and futures contracts.

Chapter 12
Interest Rate Forwards and Futures

In this chapter we first discuss forward contracts on interest rates, known as *forward rate agreements* or FRAs. Subsequently we go on to look at short-term interest rate (*STIR*) or money market futures, primarily Eurodollar futures, and long-term interest rate futures, namely T-bond and T-note futures.

Forward Rate Agreements (FRAs)

Forward rate agreements are over-the-counter (OTC) derivatives, based on a short-term interest rate such as LIBOR. They represent an agreement between two counter-parties to fix a future interest rate. There is no physical delivery of cash. The contract specifies a notional principal on the basis of which interest is computed, and the profit/loss is settled at the end of the contract period.

On the contract settlement date, if the contract rate specified in the FRA differs from the reference rate such as LIBOR, which is usually the case, one party makes a cash payment to the other. For a potential borrower the FRA locks in a borrowing rate, whereas for a potential lender it locks in a lending rate. It should be noted that there is no obligation to borrow or lend at a subsequent date, and such a contract may be used purely as a speculative tool.

The fixed interest rate in the contract, or what is termed the *contract rate*, is the rate that is compared subsequently with the prevailing reference rate. The party who agrees to pay the contract rate is termed the buyer, and the party who agrees to receive the contract rate is termed the seller. As we mentioned, FRAs are used for hedging or for speculation. Traders who are bullish about interest rates buy FRAs. If the reference rate on the settlement date is higher than the contract rate, then they receive a cash inflow. However, if the reference rate is lower, then they have to make a cash payment. On the other hand, traders who are bearish about interest rates sell FRAs. If the reference rate on the settlement date is lower than the contract rate, then they receive a cash inflow. However, if the reference rate is higher, then they have to make a cash payment. Here is an example.

Example 12.1. Consider an FRA with a contract rate of 6% per annum. Assume that the reference rate is 6-M LIBOR. If on the settlement date the prevailing LIBOR is 4.50%, the buyer makes a payment to the seller. However if it is 7.50%, the seller makes a payment to the buyer.

Assume that the notional principal is \$10,000,000 and that the day-count is 30/360. Thus six months is 180 days. If LIBOR is 4.50%, the buyer of the FRA pays

$$10{,}000{,}000 \times \frac{180}{360} \times \frac{6.00 - 4.50}{100} = \$75{,}000$$

https://doi.org/10.1515/9781547400669-012

to the seller of the FRA. On the other hand if the LIBOR is 7.50%, the seller of the FRA pays

$$10{,}000{,}000 \times \frac{180}{360} \times \frac{7.50 - 6.00}{100} = \$75{,}000$$

to the buyer.

Example 12.2. Now let's consider a situation where a FRA is used as a hedge.

Metro Rail has borrowed on a floating rate basis and is consequently worried about the possibility of rising interest rates. The interest payable is LIBOR + 50 bp, and interest is determined in advance and paid in arrears. To lock in a borrowing rate, the firm buys a FRA with a contract rate of 4.75%. Assume that the LIBOR on the settlement date is 5.50%. The firm borrows at 6.00% in the market. However, because the reference rate is higher than the contract rate, the counter-party pays the cash equivalent of the difference in rates, namely 5.50 − 4.75 = 0.75%, based on the specified principal amount and the prescribed day-count convention. Thus the effective borrowing cost for the firm is 6.00 − 0.75 = 5.25%, which is the contract rate of 4.75% plus the spread of 50 bp.

However, what if the LIBOR on the settlement rate is 3.50%. The firm borrows at 4.00% in the market. In this case, because the contract rate is higher than the reference rate, it has to pay the cash equivalent of the difference in rates, namely 4.75−3.50 = 1.25% to the counter-party. Thus the effective borrowing cost for the firm is 4.00 + 1.25 = 5.25%, which once again is the contract rate of 4.75% plus the spread of 50 bp. Thus this is a perfect hedge, for it locks in a borrowing rate will absolute certainty. In the next example, we will consider a situation where a party wants to hedge a lending rate.

Example 12.3. Jyske Bank in Copenhagen plans to lend at LIBOR + 50 bp after six months. However, it is worried about a declining interest rate. It therefore sells a FRA with a contract rate of 6.50%. If the LIBOR on the settlement date is 4%, the bank lends at 4.50%. However, because the reference rate is less than the contract rate, the counter-party, who in this case is the buyer of the FRA, pays the cash equivalent of 6.50 − 4.00 = 2.50%. Thus the effective lending rate for the bank is 2.50 + 4.50 = 7.00%, which is the contract rate plus the spread. On the other hand, if the LIBOR on the settlement date is 7.50%, the bank lends at 8%. In this case, it has to pay the equivalent of 7.50 − 6.50 = 1.00% to the counter-party. The effective rate of interest is once again 7%, which is the contract rate plus the spread.

Thus borrowers can lock in a borrowing rate using an FRA, whereas lenders can lock in a lending rate. Because an FRA is a commitment contract, the hedgers cannot take advantage of the situation if the market moves in their favor. In Example 12.2, if the rate falls to 3.50%, in the absence of the FRA Metro Rail could have borrowed at 4% per annum. However, because it has an obligation under the FRA, it is committed to borrow at 5.25%. Similarly, if the LIBOR were to rise to 7.50%, Jyske Bank could have lent at 8% in the absence of the FRA. However, because of its prior obligation, it is committed to lend at 7%. Thus FRAs lock in borrowing and lending rates with absolute certainty. However, there is no assurance that the outcome with hedging will be superior to the outcome without hedging. In other words, there is always a risk of ex-post regret. Hedgers use FRAs to eliminate risk, despite the fact that their decision may have to be regretted subsequently.

An FRA is quoted using two numbers. An $A \times B$ FRA implies that settlement is A months from today for a loan or deposit of $B - A$ months. The first date is referred to as the settlement date, and the second is termed the final maturity date. Standard FRAs have maturities of 3, 6, or 12 months. However, because they are OTC products, contracts with nonstandard maturities, can also be bought and sold. Standard specifications are like 1×4, 3×6, 6×9, 1×7, 3×9, and 6×12.

Let's consider a 6×12 FRA. If today is the transaction date, the spot settlement date is $T + 2$. The settlement date is six months from $T + 2$. The reference rate is fixed two days before the settlement date, or six months from the trade date. The maturity date is six months from the settlement date. There are two possibilities; that is, the cash payment may be made on the settlement date, which is termed an in arrears FRA, or the payment may occur on the maturity date, which is termed a delayed settlement FRA.[1] We will now give a detailed example of both types of FRAs. In the market, in arrears contracts are more common than delayed settlement contracts.

Let's consider a 3×9 FRA with a contract rate of 6%. Assume that the LIBOR on the reference fixing date is 7.50%. Also assume that the notional principal is $18 million, and that the day-count convention is Actual/360. In our case, we assume that six months corresponds to 184 days.[2] Because the reference rate is higher than the contract rate, the seller has to pay the buyer.

The cash amount is

$$18{,}000{,}000 \times (0.075 - 0.06) \times \frac{184}{360} = \$138{,}000$$

Had the FRA been a delayed settlement contract, the cash flow would occur six months from the settlement date, and the value on the settlement date would be the present value of this amount, determined by discounting at the LIBOR prevailing on the reference fixing date. In our case, the present value would be

$$\frac{138{,}000}{(1 + 0.075 \times \frac{184}{360})} = \$132{,}905.30$$

Determining the Contract Rate

If we are given rates for money market deposits, we can easily determine the contract rate. Consider a 3×9 FRA. Assume the three-month LIBOR is s_1% per annum and the nine-month LIBOR is s_2% per annum. Investing for nine months at the 9-M LIBOR is equivalent to investing for three months at the 3-M LIBOR and rolling over for six months using the FRA. To keep the mathematics simple, let's assume a 30/360 day-count convention, which implies that three months consist of 90 days and nine months consist of 270 days. Let $s_1 = 6\%$ and $s_2 = 7.50\%$. To rule out arbitrage[3]

$$\left[1 + s_1 \times \frac{90}{360}\right] \times \left[1 + k \times \frac{180}{360}\right] = \left[1 + s_2 \times \frac{270}{360}\right]$$

1 See Chance [8].

2 For contracts in USD and EUR, the day-count convention is Actual/360, as is the practice in the money market. For transactions in GBP, AUD, CAD, or JPY, the convention is Actual/365.

3 We are using k as a symbol for the FRA rate.

$$\Rightarrow \left[1 + 0.06 \times \frac{90}{360}\right] \times \left[1 + k \times \frac{180}{360}\right] = \left[1 + 0.075 \times \frac{270}{360}\right]$$
$$\Rightarrow k = 8.1281\%$$

If we are given the borrowing/lending rates in the money market, we can determine an upper as well as a lower bound for the contract rate. Consider the following quote in the market:

3-M: 0.05000 – 0.05125 and 9-M: 0.0600 – 0.0625.

That is, the dealer is prepared to borrow at 5% for three months and lend at 5.125% for the same period. In the case of a nine-month transaction, the same dealer is prepared to borrow at 6% and lend at 6.25%. Assume a 30/360 day-count convention. A dealer can borrow for three months, roll over the loan using a FRA, and lend for nine months. Quite obviously a dealer does so only if there is a profit to be made. Thus we require that

$$\Rightarrow \left[1 + 0.05 \times \frac{90}{360}\right] \times \left[1 + k \times \frac{180}{360}\right] \le \left[1 + 0.0625 \times \frac{270}{360}\right]$$
$$\Rightarrow k \le 6.7901\%$$

Now consider a situation where the dealer borrows for nine months, lends for three months and rolls over using a FRA. In this case, for the transaction to be profitable, we require that

$$\Rightarrow \left[1 + 0.05125 \times \frac{90}{360}\right] \times \left[1 + k \times \frac{180}{360}\right] \ge \left[1 + 0.06 \times \frac{270}{360}\right]$$
$$\Rightarrow k \ge 6.3561\%$$

Thus the bid should be greater than or equal to 6.3561%, and the ask should be less than or equal to 6.7901%. The same result can be obtained using a no-arbitrage argument. First, let's consider the case where the arbitrageur borrows for three months and lends for nine months. He can borrow at the dealer's ask, which is 5.1250%, and lend at the dealer's bid, which is 0.06%. To rule out arbitrage

$$\Rightarrow \left[1 + 0.05125 \times \frac{90}{360}\right] \times \left[1 + k \times \frac{180}{360}\right] \ge \left[1 + 0.06 \times \frac{270}{360}\right]$$
$$\Rightarrow k \ge 6.3561\%$$

Now consider a situation where the arbitrageur borrows for nine months and lends for three months:

$$\Rightarrow \left[1 + 0.05 \times \frac{90}{360}\right] \times \left[1 + k \times \frac{180}{360}\right] \le \left[1 + 0.0625 \times \frac{270}{360}\right]$$
$$\Rightarrow k \le 6.7901\%$$

Using Short Rates to Determine the FRA Rate

We can use the short-rate trees that we obtained in Chapter 11, using the Ho-Lee and BDT models, to compute the FRA rates. Let's first consider the Ho-Lee model-based tree. We will reproduce the short rates and state prices for all the nodes to facilitate the argument.

Table 12.1: Summary of the Ho-Lee model-based interest rates.

Period	Node	Interest Rate
1	$r_{1,1}$	7.5063%
1	$r_{1,2}$	5.5063%
2	$r_{2,1}$	6.7725%
2	$r_{2,2}$	4.7725%
2	$r_{2,3}$	2.7725%
3	$r_{3,1}$	11.2863%
3	$r_{3,2}$	9.2863%
3	$r_{3,3}$	7.2863%
3	$r_{3,4}$	5.2863%

t_0	t_1	t_2	t_3	t_4
				0.053160
			0.112320	
		0.232247		0.215741
	0.481928		0.340258	
1.0		0.466755		0.328336
	0.481928		0.343589	
		0.234508		0.222092
			0.115651	
				0.056336

Figure 12.1: State price tree for the Ho-Lee model.

Consider a one-period in arrears FRA. In six months the short rate can be 7.5063% or 5.5063%. The probability of reaching the respective nodes is 0.50. We know that the value of a forward or a futures contract at the outset must be zero. Thus if the unknown contract rate is k

$$0.481928 \times (7.5063 - k) + 0.481928 \times (5.5063 - k) = 0$$
$$\Rightarrow k = 6.5063\%$$

Now consider a two-period in arrears FRA. There are three nodes respectively. Thus if the unknown contract rate is k

$$0.232247 \times \times(6.7725 - k) + 0.466755 \times (4.7725 - k) + 0.234508 \times (2.7725 - k) = 0$$
$$\Rightarrow k = 4.7677\%$$

Now let's consider a one-period delayed settlement FRA. The payoffs will be received one period hence and thus need to be discounted. Once again if the unknown contract rate is k

$$0.481928 \times \frac{(7.5063 - k)}{\left(1 + \frac{0.075063}{2}\right)} + 0.481928 \times \frac{(5.5063 - k)}{\left(1 + \frac{0.055063}{2}\right)} = 0$$
$$\Rightarrow k = 6.5015\%$$

Now consider a two-period delayed settlement FRA. Using a similar approach,

$$0.232247 \times \times \frac{(6.7725 - k)}{\left(1 + \frac{0.067725}{2}\right)} + 0.466755 \times \frac{(4.7725 - k)}{\left(1 + \frac{0.047725}{2}\right)}$$
$$+ 0.234508 \times \frac{(2.7725 - k)}{\left(1 + \frac{0.027725}{2}\right)} = 0$$
$$\Rightarrow k = 4.7579\%$$

Let's repeat the computations using the BDT tree.

Table 12.2: Summary of BDT model-based interest rates.

Period	Node	Interest Rate
1	$r_{1,1}$	6.8915%
1	$r_{1,2}$	6.1122%
2	$r_{2,1}$	5.1969%
2	$r_{2,2}$	4.7497%
2	$r_{2,3}$	4.3409%
3	$r_{3,1}$	9.0245%
3	$r_{3,2}$	8.4990%
3	$r_{3,3}$	8.0040%
3	$r_{3,4}$	7.5379%

Consider a one-period in arrears FRA. In six months the short rate can be 6.8915% or 6.1122%. Thus if the unknown contract rate is k

$$0.481928 \times (6.8915 - k) + 0.481928 \times (6.1122 - k) = 0$$
$$\Rightarrow k = 6.5019\%$$

t_0	t_1	t_2	t_3	t_4
				0.054309
			0.113519	
		0.232938		0.218091
	0.481928		0.341483	
1.0		0.466756		0.328389
	0.481928		0.342390	
		0.233818		0.219742
			0.114425	
				0.055135

Figure 12.2: State price tree for the BDT model.

Now consider a two-period in arrears FRA:

$$0.232938 \times \times(5.1969 - k) + 0.466756 \times (4.7497 - k) + 0.233818 \times (4.3409 - k) = 0$$
$$\Rightarrow k = 4.7589\%$$

Next let's consider one-period delayed settlement FRA:

$$0.481928 \times \frac{(6.8915 - k)}{\left(1 + \frac{0.068915}{2}\right)} + 0.481928 \times \frac{(6.1122 - k)}{\left(1 + \frac{0.061122}{2}\right)} = 0$$
$$\Rightarrow k = 6.5011\%$$

Finally, consider a two-period delayed settlement FRA. Using a similar approach,

$$0.232938 \times \times \frac{(5.1969 - k)}{\left(1 + \frac{0.051969}{2}\right)} + 0.466756 \times \frac{(4.7497 - k)}{\left(1 + \frac{0.047497}{2}\right)}$$
$$+ 0.233818 \times \frac{(4.3409 - k)}{\left(1 + \frac{0.043409}{2}\right)} = 0$$
$$\Rightarrow k = 4.7584\%$$

The contract rates for the delayed settlement FRAs can be confirmed as follows. The contract rate for the one-period FRA is given by

$$\left[\frac{\left(1 + \frac{s_2}{2}\right)^2}{\left(1 + \frac{s_1}{2}\right)} - 1\right] \times 2 = \left[\frac{(1.035)^2}{(1.0375)} - 1\right] \times 2 = 6.5012\%$$

Similarly, the contract rate for the two-period FRA is given by

$$\left[\frac{\left(1 + \frac{s_3}{2}\right)^3}{\left(1 + \frac{s_2}{2}\right)^2} - 1\right] \times 2 = \left[\frac{(1.03125)^3}{(1.0350)^2} - 1\right] \times 2 = 4.7581\%$$

This is consistent with the results from the Ho-Lee and BDT models. The minor difference is due to rounding errors.

Eurodollar Futures

Eurodollar (ED) futures contracts trade on the CME in Chicago. The underlying interest rate, is the London Inter Bank Offer Rate (LIBOR). Each futures contract is for a time deposit with a principal of $1 million and three months to maturity. The quarterly cycle for Eurodollar contracts is March, June, September, and December. On the CME, a total of 40 quarterly futures contracts spanning 10 years are listed at any point in time. In addition, the four nearest serial months are also listed. Let's assume that we are standing on 30 June 2018. The four available serial months are July, August, October, and November 2018. The remaining available months are September and December 2018; March, June, September, and December 2019–2027; March and June 2028. Eurodollar futures contracts expire at 11:00 a. m. London time, on the second London bank business day before the third Wednesday of the contract month. The contracts are cash settled to the 3-M LIBOR. The futures price is quoted in terms of an index and implies an interest rate.

Quoted ED Futures Price = 100.00 – Implicit Interest Rate

The implicit interest rate in this case is an actual or add-on interest rate and not a discount rate as in the case of T-bills.

Calculating Profits and Losses on ED Futures

Let's suppose that the futures price is 96. This represents a yearly interest rate of 4% or 1% per quarter. Thus the implied quarterly interest payment on a time deposit of $1 million is

$$0.01 \times 1{,}000{,}000 = \$10{,}000$$

If the futures price were to fall to 95 at the end of the day, then it would represent a quarterly interest payment of $12,500 on a deposit of $1 million.

Consider a person who goes long in an ED futures contract at 96. Such a person is agreeing to lend money at the equivalent interest rate, namely 1% per quarter.[4] If interest rates rise subsequently to 5% per annum, that is, the futures price goes down

4 The logic is the same as that for underlying futures in the case of a debt security such as a T-bill. In the case of bills, a long position means that you are willing to buy bills at the expiration of the contract. In the case of ED futures, a long position means that you are willing to make a term deposit of three months. In either case you are a lender.

to 95 and the contract is marked to market, then the long loses $2,500. The logic is that when the contract is marked to market, it is as if the person is offsetting by going short, which in this case, means agreeing to borrow at 1.25% per quarter. Thus when the interest rates rise, the longs lose. The reverse is true for the shorts; that is, when the interest rates fall, they lose.

You should by now be able to see the logic behind quoting futures prices in terms of an index, rather than in terms of interest rates. If futures prices are quoted in terms of interest rates, then the longs gain when the futures prices fall, and the shorts gain when the futures prices rise. But in all the other markets, we observe that the longs gain when futures prices rise, whereas the shorts gain if futures prices fall. Thus to make money market futures consistent with other futures markets, we do not quote futures prices in terms of interest rates, but do so in terms of an index. When the index rises, the longs gain, and when it falls, the shorts gain.

Yet another reason for quoting futures prices in terms of an index rather than in terms of interest rates is to ensure that the bid prices are lower than the ask prices. Remember that as an investor, you typically face borrowing rates that are higher than lending rates. Thus the rates underlying a short position will be greater than the rates underlying a long position. To be consistent with the principle that bid prices are always lower than the ask prices, it is necessary to convert the rates to equivalent index values.

Now consider the case where the ED index changes from F_0 to F_1. The profit for a long is

$$\begin{aligned}&1{,}000{,}000 \times \frac{(100 - F_0)}{100} \times \frac{90}{360} - 1{,}000{,}000 \times \frac{(100 - F_1)}{100} \times \frac{90}{360}\\&= 1{,}000{,}000 \times \frac{(F_1 - F_0)}{100} \times \frac{90}{360}\end{aligned}$$

The cash flow for the short is

$$1{,}000{,}000 \times \frac{(F_0 - F_1)}{100} \times \frac{90}{360}$$

A change of one basis point, corresponds to a price change of

$$\begin{aligned}&1{,}000{,}000 \times \frac{0.01}{100} \times \frac{90}{360}\\&= \$25\end{aligned}$$

Locking in a Borrowing Rate

Let's first illustrate how borrowing and lending rates can be locked in using ED futures before deriving the fair price of a contract using cash-and-carry arbitrage and reverse cash-and-carry arbitrage arguments.

Assume that today is 15 July 2018. Rolodex Inc. is planning to borrow $1 million on 14 September for a period of 90 days. The company is confident that given its rating, it can borrow at LIBOR. It is however worried that interest rates may rise before 14 September, which is the last day of trading for the September futures contract. The current September futures price is 94, and the current LIBOR for a 90 day loan is 5.85%. Because the company is planning to borrow money, it requires a short hedge. The rationale is that a short hedge will yield a profit if rates rise, which is precisely the situation where a borrower needs a positive payoff. Consequently borrowers need to go short in ED futures, whereas lenders need to go long. Assume that Rolodex goes short in one September futures contract, and let's consider two different scenarios on 14 September, one where the LIBOR is higher as compared to the rate implicit in the futures price, and the other where it is lower.

Case A: LIBOR = 4%

The interest payable on the loan of $1 million is

$$0.04 \times 1{,}000{,}000 \times \frac{90}{360}$$
$$= \$10{,}000$$

Gain/loss from the futures market is

$$1{,}000{,}000 \times \frac{(F_0 - F_1)}{100} \times \frac{90}{360}$$
$$= 1{,}000{,}000 \times \frac{(94 - 96)}{100} \times \frac{90}{360}$$
$$= (\$5{,}000)$$

Therefore, the effective interest paid is[5]

$$10{,}000 + 5{,}000 = \$15{,}000$$

Case B: LIBOR = 7%

The interest payable is

$$0.07 \times 1{,}000{,}000 \times \frac{90}{360}$$
$$= \$17{,}500$$

Profit/loss from the futures position is

$$1{,}000{,}000 \times \frac{(94 - 93)}{100} \times \frac{90}{360}$$
$$= \$2{,}500$$

5 The terminal futures price is 100 – 4.00 = 96.

Thus, the effective interest paid is

$$17{,}500 - 2{,}500 = \$15{,}000$$

Thus the company can lock in an interest payable of $15,000, irrespective of the prevailing LIBOR on 14 September. This amount corresponds to a rate of:

$$\frac{15{,}000}{1{,}000{,}000} \times \frac{360}{90} \equiv 6\%$$

which is nothing but the rate implicit in the initial futures price. We should note a couple of points. One, the fact that the 3-M LIBOR at the outset is 5.85% is of no consequence for our analysis. Second, we have assumed that the transaction date is the same as the expiration date of the futures contract. The significance of this is that the expiration date is the point in time at which spot and futures prices will converge, a consequence of which is that the basis risk is zero.

It is also important to take cognizance of the following fact. Because the ED futures contract is cash settled, the profit/loss from the futures contract will be received/paid on 14 September when the contract expires. However, the company is required to pay interest on the loan only 90 days later. Thus, if there is a profit from the futures position, it can be reinvested. On the contrary, a loss from the futures market has to be financed. If adjustments were made for the interest on such profits/losses, the effective interest paid on the loan would be higher than 6% in case A and lower than 6% in case B. In our study of ED futures contracts, we will ignore such interest on profits/losses.

Locking in a Lending Rate

Assume that today is 15 September 2018. Microsoft is planning to lend $1 million on 14 December for a period of 90 days. The company is of the opinion that it can lend at the prevailing LIBOR plus 75 bp and wants to lock in a rate using ED futures. 14 December is the last day of trading for the December contract, and the current futures price is 96. Because the company wishes to lock-in a lending rate, it needs to go long in futures contracts. As before, let's consider two scenarios for the terminal value of LIBOR.

Case A: LIBOR = 5.25%

The interest receivable on the loan is

$$0.06 \times 1{,}000{,}000 \times \frac{90}{360} = \$15{,}000$$

The profit/loss from the futures position is

$$1{,}000{,}000 \times \frac{(94.75 - 96)}{100} \times \frac{90}{360} = (\$3{,}125)$$

Thus the effective interest received is

$$15{,}000 - 3{,}125 = \$11{,}875$$

Case B: LIBOR = 3.25%

The interest receivable on the loan is

$$0.04 \times 1{,}000{,}000 \times \frac{90}{360} = \$10{,}000$$

The profit/loss from the futures position is

$$1{,}000{,}000 \times \frac{(96.75 - 96)}{100} \times \frac{90}{360} = \$1{,}875$$

So the effective interest received is

$$10{,}000 + 1{,}875 = \$11{,}875$$

Thus, irrespective of the scenario at expiration, the company is assured of a receivable of \$11,875. The equivalent interest rate is

$$\frac{11{,}875}{1{,}000{,}000} \times \frac{360}{90} \times 100 = 4.75\%$$

This represents the rate implicit in the initial futures price, plus the assumed spread of 75 bp. Now let's go on to analyze the pricing of ED futures.

Cash-and-Carry Arbitrage

Let's assume that an arbitrageur is confronted with the following situation on 15 August 20XX. Futures contracts expiring on 18 September are priced at 95. The 90-day ED deposit made on 18 September will mature on 17 December. The interest rate for an ED deposit between 15 August and 17 December is 6.12%. The rate for a loan between 15 August and 18 September is 3%.

Consider the following strategy. Borrow \$1 million for 34 days. Simultaneously go short in a futures contract to borrow the maturity amount for another 90 days. Invest the borrowed funds in a 124-day deposit.[6] The amount due after 34 days is $1{,}000{,}000\,(1 + 0.03 \times \frac{34}{360})$. The futures contract locks in a rate of 5% when this amount is rolled over for another 90 days. Thus, the amount payable after 124 days is

$$1{,}000{,}000\left(1 + 0.03 \times \frac{34}{360}\right) \times \left(1 + 0.05 \times \frac{90}{360}\right) = \$1{,}015{,}368.7$$

6 34 is the number of days between 15 August and 18 September, and 124 is the number of days between 15 August and 17 December.

The amount received when the 124-day investment matures is

$$1{,}000{,}000 \times \left(1 + 0.0612 \times \frac{124}{360}\right) = \$1{,}021{,}080$$

Thus there is an arbitrage profit of

$$1{,}021{,}080 - 1{,}015{,}368.70 = \$5{,}711.30$$

Reverse Cash-and-Carry Arbitrage

Let's suppose that all the other variables have the same values as in the preceding section, except for the futures price, which we assume is 91.50. Consider the following strategy. Borrow \$1 million for 124 days. Invest it for 34 days, and go long in a futures contract to roll over the maturity amount for a further period of 90 days. The amount repayable after 124 days is

$$1{,}000{,}000 \times \left(1 + 0.0612 \times \frac{124}{360}\right) = \$1{,}021{,}080$$

The investment in the 34-day deposit yields $1{,}000{,}000\,(1 + 0.03 \times \frac{34}{360})$. The futures contract locks in a rate of 8.50% for this amount. Thus, the amount receivable after 124 days is

$$1{,}000{,}000\left(1 + 0.03 \times \frac{34}{360}\right) \times \left(1 + 0.085 \times \frac{90}{360}\right) = \$1{,}024{,}143.50$$

and there is an arbitrage profit of

$$1{,}024{,}143.50 - 1{,}021{,}080 = \$3{,}063.50$$

The No-Arbitrage Pricing Equation

We now derive an expression for the futures price F, which precludes both cash-and-carry and reverse cash-and-carry arbitrage for a given set of interest rates. We denote the day on which we are standing as day t. The futures contract is assumed to expire at T. We denote the Eurodollar rate for a $T - t$ day loan by s_1 and the borrowing/lending rate for a $T + 90 - t$ day loan by s_2. In order to rule out both forms of arbitrage, we require that

$$\begin{aligned} &1{,}000{,}000 \times \left[1 + \frac{(100 - F)}{100} \times \frac{90}{360}\right] \times \left[1 + \frac{s_1}{100} \times \frac{T - t}{360}\right] \\ &= 1{,}000{,}000 \times \left[1 + \frac{s_2}{100} \times \frac{T + 90 - t}{360}\right] \end{aligned}$$

$$\Rightarrow \left[1+\frac{(100-F)}{100}\times\frac{90}{360}\right]\left[1+\frac{s_1}{100}\times\frac{T-t}{360}\right]=\left[1+\frac{s_2}{100}\times\frac{T+90-t}{360}\right] \tag{12.1}$$

In our case, $s_1 = 3\%$, and $s_2 = 6.12\%$. Therefore

$$\left[1+\frac{(100-F)}{100}\times\frac{90}{360}\right]=1.018195$$

$$\Rightarrow F = 92.7220$$

Thus 95 was too high, which is why cash-and-carry arbitrage was profitable. However, 91.50 was too low, a consequence of which reverse cash-and-carry arbitrage was profitable.

Hedging an *N*-day Loan Using ED Futures

We have illustrated how ED futures can be used to lock in borrowing/lending rates for 90-day loans. These contracts can be used to lock in rates for an N-day loan, where N is close to 90. The necessary condition for such a hedge is that the interest rate for the N-day loan should move closely with the rate for a 90-day loan. Before giving an illustration, let's first derive the required hedge ratio.

Assume that $d_N = \alpha + d_{90} + \epsilon$, where d_N is the annualized rate for an N-day loan and d_{90} is the annualized rate for a 90-day loan. We assume[7] that $\epsilon = 0$. If so

$$\triangle d_N = \triangle d_{90}$$

Take the case of a party that is raising an N-day loan for \$Q million. The change in the interest payable due to a rate change is

$$Q \times 1{,}000{,}000 \times \frac{\triangle d_N}{100}\times\frac{N}{360}$$

The profit/loss per contract from the futures market is

$$1{,}000{,}000 \times \frac{\triangle d_{90}}{100}\times\frac{90}{360}$$

The number of futures contracts, Q_f, ought to be chosen in a way such that:

$$Q \times 1{,}000{,}000 \times \frac{\triangle d_N}{100}\times\frac{N}{360} = Q_f \times 1{,}000{,}000 \times \frac{\triangle d_{90}}{100}\times\frac{90}{360} \tag{12.2}$$

That is, the magnitude of the change in the amount payable/receivable should be equal to the profit/loss from the futures contract. Because we have assumed that $\triangle d_N = \triangle d_{90}$, we get the result that:

$$Q \times N = Q_f \times 90$$

7 The significance of this assumption is that there is no basis risk.

$$\Rightarrow \frac{Q_f}{Q} = \text{the hedge ratio} = \frac{N}{90}$$

Let's illustrate how this hedge will perform in practice, with the help of Example 12.4.

Example 12.4. Once again assume that we are standing on 15 July 20XX and that Rolodex borrows $10 million on 14 September, for a period of 117 days. The current September futures price is 95.75. The firm can borrow at the prevailing LIBOR on 14 September. Because the firm is borrowing, it needs a short position in ED futures. Assume $\alpha = 0$. In other words, the 90-day LIBOR is equal to the 117-day LIBOR.

$$Q_f = 10 \times \frac{117}{90} = 13$$

Let's examine the performance of this hedge. First consider a situation where the LIBOR on 14 September is 4%. The actual interest paid by Rolodex is

$$0.04 \times 10{,}000{,}000 \times \frac{117}{360} = \$130{,}000$$

The profit/loss from the futures position is

$$13 \times 1{,}000{,}000 \times \frac{(95.75 - 96)}{100} \times \frac{90}{360}$$
$$= (\$8{,}125)$$

Thus, the effective interest paid by the company is $138,125.

Now consider a situation where the LIBOR on 14 September is 4.5%. The actual interest paid by Rolodex is

$$0.045 \times 10{,}000{,}000 \times \frac{117}{360} = \$146{,}250$$

Profit/loss from the futures position is

$$13 \times 1{,}000{,}000 \times \frac{(95.75 - 95.50)}{100} \times \frac{90}{360}$$
$$= \$8{,}125$$

The effective interest paid by the company is $138,125.

Hence, irrespective of the prevailing LIBOR on 14 September, the company has locked in an interest expense of $138,125. This amount corresponds to an interest i such that

$$10{,}000{,}000 \left[1 + i \times \frac{117}{360}\right] = \$10{,}138{,}125$$

i is therefore equal to 4.25%, which is nothing but the rate implicit in the initial futures price. Had we assumed a non-zero value for α, we would have locked in the rate implicit in the futures price plus α. For instance, if we had assumed that $\alpha = 0.50\%$, we would have locked in 4.75%.

A More General Argument

Assume that the 90-day LIBOR and the N-day LIBOR are related by the following relationship: $d_N = \alpha + \beta \times d_{90} + \epsilon$. Once again, if we assume $\epsilon = 0$,

$$\triangle d_N = \beta \times \triangle d_{90}$$

Take the case of a party that is raising an N-day loan for \$Q million. The change in the interest payable due to a rate change is

$$Q \times 1{,}000{,}000 \times \frac{\triangle d_N}{100} \times \frac{N}{360}$$

The profit/loss per contract, from the futures market is

$$1{,}000{,}000 \times \frac{\triangle d_{90}}{100} \times \frac{90}{360}$$

The number of futures contracts, Q_f, ought to be chosen in a way such that

$$Q \times 1{,}000{,}000 \times \frac{\triangle d_N}{100} \times \frac{N}{360} = Q_f \times 1{,}000{,}000 \times \frac{\triangle d_{90}}{100} \times \frac{90}{360} \tag{12.3}$$

Because we have assumed that $\triangle d_N = \beta \times \triangle d_{90}$, we get the result

$$Q \times \beta \times N = Q_f \times 90$$
$$\Rightarrow \frac{Q_f}{Q} = \text{the hedge ratio} = \frac{\beta \times N}{90}$$

Now let's illustrate how this hedge will perform in practice, with the help of Example 12.5.

Example 12.5. Once again assume that we are standing on 15 July 20XX and that Rolodex borrows \$10 million on 14 September, for a period of 108 days. The current September futures price is 95.75. The firm can borrow at the prevailing LIBOR plus 50 bp on 14 September. Because the firm is borrowing, it requires a short position in ED futures. Assume $d_{108} = 0.25 + 1.25 \times d_{90} + \epsilon$. Using the same argument

$$Q_f = 10 \times 1.25 \times \frac{108}{90} = 15$$

let's examine the performance of this hedge. Consider a situation where the 90-day LIBOR on 14 September is 4%. Thus the 108-day LIBOR is 0.25 + 1.25 × 4 = 5.25%. The actual interest paid by Rolodex is

$$0.0575 \times 10{,}000{,}000 \times \frac{108}{360} = \$172{,}500$$

The profit/loss from the futures position is

$$15 \times 1{,}000{,}000 \times \frac{(95.75 - 96)}{100} \times \frac{90}{360}$$

$$= (\$9{,}375)$$

Thus, the effective interest paid by the company is 172,500 + 9,375 = $181,875. The corresponding rate is

$$\frac{181{,}875}{10{,}000{,}000} \times \frac{360}{108} \equiv 6.0625\%$$

$$6.0625 = 0.25 + 1.25 \times 4.25 + 0.50 \equiv \alpha + \beta \times 4.25 + 50 \text{ bp}$$

Using ED Futures to Create a Fixed Rate Loan

Assume that Jyske Bank is able to borrow money at LIBOR for three monthly periods. Consequently the interest payable on its liability is variable. The bank, however, has a potential client who wishes to borrow at a fixed rate for a period of one year. Thus the interest receivable from the proposed asset is fixed in nature. The bank would like to use futures contracts to mitigate the risk of borrowing at a floating rate, but lending at a fixed rate. It turns out that ED futures contracts can be used to hedge the funding risk and determine a suitable rate that can be quoted by the bank while negotiating a fixed rate loan. We can illustrate the principle involved with the help of Example 12.6.

Example 12.6. IT20, a company based in London, wants a loan for $100 million for a period of one year from 15 September 20XX, at a fixed interest rate. Let's assume that the 90-day LIBOR on 15 September is 4.8% and that December, March, and June contracts are available at 96.1, 95.6, and 96 respectively. For ease of exposition, we assume that the dates on which the bank will roll over its three-month borrowings, namely 15 December, 15 March, and 15 June, are the same as the dates on which the futures contracts for those months are scheduled to expire. Once again, the objective of making such an assumption, is to ensure that there is no basis risk. Each ED futures contract is on $1 million and the bank is borrowing at a floating rate. Consequently, it needs a short position in 100 each of the December, March, and June futures contracts.

For the first quarter, the interest expense for the bank is

$$100{,}000{,}000 \times 0.048 \times \frac{90}{360} = \$1{,}200{,}000$$

There is no uncertainty about this amount because it is based on the current 3M LIBOR. The short position in December contracts, locks in a rate of 3.9% for a period of 90 days from December to March. This corresponds to an interest expense of

$$100{,}000{,}000 \times 0.039 \times \frac{90}{360} = \$975{,}000$$

In a similar fashion, the short position in March contracts, locks in

$$100{,}000{,}000 \times 0.044 \times \frac{90}{360} = \$1{,}100{,}000$$

for the 90-day period from March. The June contracts lock in the following interest amount for the last quarter:

$$100{,}000{,}000 \times 0.04 \times \frac{90}{360} = \$1{,}000{,}000$$

Hence, the total interest payable by the bank for the 12-month period is

$$1{,}200{,}000 + 975{,}000 + 1{,}100{,}000 + 1{,}000{,}000 = \$4{,}275{,}000.$$

This corresponds to an annualized interest rate of

$$\frac{4{,}275{,}000}{100{,}000{,}000} \times 100 = 4.275\%$$

The bank can now quote a fixed rate to the client, based on this effective cost of funding, after factoring in hedging costs and a suitable profit margin.

Stack and Strip Hedges

We assumed in the preceding illustration that the bank would use 100 futures contracts for each of the expiration months. Such a hedge, where the same number of contracts are used for each expiration month right from the outset, is called a *strip hedge*. However, if the maturity of a futures contract is far away, the contract may not be actively traded. Such illiquidity could be a deterrent for a potential hedger, who would seek the ability to enter and exit the market at a price that is close to the true or fair value of the asset. In this case, when the hedge is initiated in September, it is conceivable that the June futures may be illiquid. In such a situation, rather than starting with an equal number of December, March, and June contracts, the bank may initiate the hedge using an unequal number of December and March contracts, without taking a position in the June contract. Subsequently, when the December contracts expire, it will take a position in the June contract. Such a hedge, where the number of contracts for each maturity is not equal at the outset, is known as a *stack hedge*. Let's illustrate the mechanics of such a hedge with the help of Example 12.7.

Example 12.7. Assume that the June futures contracts are perceived to be illiquid when the hedge is initiated. The bank therefore decides to hedge using 100 December contracts and 200 March contracts. The position in December futures is obviously intended to lock in a rate for that month's borrowing. Out of the 200 March contracts, 100 are intended to lock in a rate for March, and the remaining 100 are meant for hedging the June exposure. The inherent assumption is that on 15 December, the bank will partially offset its March position and go short in 100 June contracts, assuming that they have begun to be actively traded by then. The relative performance of a stack hedge vis a vis a strip hedge depends on the movement of interest rates between September and December.

Case A: The Stack Hedge Is Equivalent to the Strip

Assume that the March futures price moves from 95.6 to 95 between September and December, and the June futures price moves from 96 to 95.4 during the same period. When the 100 extra March contracts are liquidated in December, the profit from the position is

$$100{,}000{,}000 \times \left(\frac{95.60 - 95}{100}\right) \times \frac{90}{360}$$

$$= \$150{,}000$$

The 100 June contracts that the bank enters into at 95.4 lock in an interest expense of

$$100{,}000{,}000 \times 0.046 \times \frac{90}{360} = \$1{,}150{,}000$$

for the last quarter. The effective interest expense for this quarter is therefore:

$$1{,}150{,}000 - 150{,}000 = \$1{,}000{,}000$$

which is the same amount that was locked in by the strip hedge.

Thus, if the three-month ED rate, as contained in the March futures price, changes by the same magnitude and direction as the yield contained in the June futures price, then the strip and stack hedges will be equivalent. In interest rate parlance, we would say that there has been a *parallel shift* in the *yield curve*.

Case B: The Strip Outperforms

If the increase in the March yield is less than the increase in the June yield, then the strip hedge will outperform the stack. For instance, assume that the March futures price moves from 95.6 to 95 whereas the June futures price moves from 96 to 95.20. Because the futures price has declined, there is a profit when the extra March contracts are offset, which as before is \$150,000. However, the interest expenses for the last quarter is higher. This expense is

$$100{,}000{,}000 \times 0.048 \times \frac{90}{360} = \$1{,}200{,}000$$

The effective interest is

$$1{,}200{,}000 - 150{,}000 = \$1{,}050{,}000$$

which is greater than the amount of \$1,000,000 that was locked in by the strip hedge.

The same is the case if the decrease in the March yield is more than the decrease in the June yield. In this case, there is a loss when the March contracts are offset. However, the interest expense locked in by the June contracts is lower. For instance, assume that the March futures price moves to 95.9, whereas the June futures price moves to 96.1.

The profit from the March position is

$$100{,}000{,}000 \times \left(\frac{95.6 - 95.9}{100}\right) \times \frac{90}{360}$$
$$= (\$\ 75{,}000)$$

The interest expense for the last quarter, as locked in by the June contracts, is

$$100{,}000{,}000 \times 0.039 \times \frac{90}{360} = \$975{,}000$$

The effective interest paid is

$$975{,}000 + 75{,}000 = \$1{,}050{,}000$$

which is greater than the amount of \$1,000,000 that was locked in by the strip hedge. Clearly the gain on account of the decline in yield implicit in the June contracts is not adequate to compensate for the loss incurred when the March contracts are offset.

Case C: The Stack Outperforms

If the increase in the March yield is more than the increase in the June yield, then the stack hedge will out perform the strip. For instance, assume that the December futures price moves from 95.60 to 95, and the June futures price moves from 96 to 95.60. The effective interest rate for the last quarter in this case is

$$\begin{aligned}&100{,}000{,}000 \times 0.044 \times \frac{90}{360} - 150{,}000\\&= 1{,}100{,}000 - 150{,}000\\&= \$950{,}000\end{aligned}$$

This amount is less than the value of $1,000,000 that was locked in by the strip hedge.

The same is true if the decrease in the March yield is less than the decrease in the June yield. In this case, once again there is a loss when the March contracts are offset. However, this is more than compensated for by the decline in the rate for the last quarter. For instance assume that the March futures price moves from 95.60 to 95.90, whereas the June futures price moves from 96 to 96.50.

The loss from the March position is $75,000. The interest expense for the last quarter is

$$100{,}000{,}000 \times 0.035 \times \frac{90}{360} = \$875{,}000$$

The effective interest is

$$875{,}000 + 75{,}000 = \$950{,}000$$

which is less than the amount of $1,000,000 that was locked in by the strip hedge.

FRAs vs. ED Futures: An Important Point

A bullish speculator who believes that interest rates are going to increase, or a hedger who wants to lock in a borrowing rate, will buy a FRA. Similarly, a bearish speculator who believes that interest rates are going to decline, or a hedger who wants to lock in a lending rate, will sell the FRA. However if such speculators and hedgers use ED futures instead of FRAs, bullish speculators and hedgers seeking to lock in a borrowing rate will go short in ED futures. On the other hand, bearish speculators and hedgers seeking to lock in a lending rate will go long in ED futures. Thus from a hedging/speculation standpoint, long positions in FRAs are equivalent to short positions in ED futures, whereas short positions in FRAs are equivalent to long positions in ED futures.

Federal Funds

Federal funds are perhaps the most important of all money market instruments because they are the primary means of making payments in this market. The term refers to money that is available for immediate payment. Commercial banks use this instrument as the principal way to adjust their legal reserve account at the Federal Reserve bank in the district where they are located. Federal funds are same-day money. In contrast, the normal payments that are made by check take at least 24 hours for the payee to receive the funds. As can be appreciated, such transactions, called *clearinghouse funds*, are far too slow for money market participants. Banks and other depository institutions must hold in a reserve account assets equal to a fraction of the funds deposited with them. Legal reserve requirements are met by holding vault cash and reserve balances with the local Federal Reserve bank. Because these reserves earn little or no income, banks whose reserve balances exceed statutory requirements lend the excess reserves in their possession to financial institutions with a deficit. Here is an illustration.

Example 12.8. Consider the following balance sheets for two commercial banks.

Liabilities	Assets
Deposit from Alice $5,000	Reserves at the Fed $2,000
	Vault Cash $500
	Loan to Maureen $2,500

Figure 12.3: Balance Sheet of Bank One.

Liabilities	Assets
Deposit from Paula $2,000	Reserves at the Fed $500
	Loan to Rita $1,500

Figure 12.4: Balance Sheet of Bank Two.

Assume that banks are required to maintain 10% of their liabilities as reserves. Bank One therefore is required to keep \$500 as reserves. However, it has \$2,000. Consequently it has excess reserves of \$1,500. Bank Two on the other hand is required to keep a reserve of \$200. Thus it has an excess of \$300. Now assume that a customer called Rachel approaches Bank Two seeking a loan of \$840. Because it has excess reserves of \$300, the bank needs to borrow an additional \$$X$, to meet the request. The amount borrowed should be such that

$$0.9X + 300 = 840 \Rightarrow X = \$600$$

Bank One is obviously in a position to lend this amount to Bank Two. If it does, the positions of the two banks are as depicted in Figures 12.5 and 12.6.

Liabilities	Assets
Deposit from Alice \$5,000	Reserves at the Fed \$1,400
	Loan to Maureen \$2,500
	Loan to Bank Two \$600
	Vault Cash \$500

Figure 12.5: Balance sheet of Bank One following the transaction.

Liabilities	Assets
Deposit from Paula \$2,000	Reserves at the Fed \$260
Loan from Bank One \$600	Loan to Rita \$1,500
	Loan to Rachel \$840

Figure 12.6: Balance sheet of Bank Two following the transaction.

Bank Two has total reserves of \$260 which is exactly 10% of its total liability of \$2,600.

The legal reserve requirement of banks is calculated on a daily average basis over a period known as the *reserve computation period*. The Federal Reserve calculates the daily average of transaction deposits held by each depository institution over this period and then multiplies that average by the required reserve percentage to determine the amount of legal reserves that must be held by each institution. These legal reserves must on average be equal to the required amount over a period known as the *reserve maintenance period.*

Once the borrower and the lender agree on the terms of the loan, the lending institution contacts the district Federal Reserve bank requesting a wire transfer of federal funds. The Fed then transfers reserves through its wire network, FEDWIRE, to the Federal Reserve bank serving the region where the borrowing institution is located. The transaction is reversed when the loan is repaid. Most federal funds loans are overnight transactions or continuing contracts that have no specific maturity date and can be terminated without advance notice by either party. Longer maturity loans are referred to as *term federal funds.* Most of the transactions are overnight, because the reserve position can fluctuate substantially from day to day, a consequence of which banks with excess reserves prefer to lend on an overnight basis.

Fed Funds Futures

The underlying asset is a 30-day federal funds loan, with a principal value of $5 million. Prices are quoted as 100.00 minus the average daily fed funds overnight rate. At any point, in time contracts for the next 36 consecutive months are available. Contracts expire on the last business day of the delivery month and are cash settled.

A change of one basis point in the quoted futures price is equivalent to

$$5{,}000{,}000 \times \frac{0.01}{100} \times \frac{30}{360} = \$41.67$$

T-Note and T-Bond Futures

Futures contracts in the US are available on 2-year, 5-year, and 10-year T-notes. In the case of the 2-year T-note contract, the underlying asset is a T-note with a face value of $200,000. Multiple grades are allowable for delivery. The deliverable grade must have an original maturity of not more than 5 years and 3 months, and an actual maturity of not less than 1 year and 9 months from the first day of the delivery month, and not more than 2 years from the last day of the delivery month. The actual futures price is subject to a multiplicative adjustment factor called the *conversion factor* (CF).[8]

In the case of futures contracts on 5-year T-notes, the underlying asset is a T-note with a face value of $100,000. The deliverable grade must have an original maturity

8 The conversion factor is a multiplicative adjustment factor. In the "Conversion Factors" section, we describe in detail the procedure for its computation.

of not more than 5 years and 3 months, and an actual maturity of not less than 4 years and 2 months from the first day of the delivery month.

The underlying asset for contracts on 10-year notes is a T-note with a face value of $100,000. The deliverable grade must have an actual term to maturity of not less than 6 years and 6 months from the first day of the delivery month and not more than 10 years from that date. There is also a futures contract called an ultra 10-year T-note futures contract. The underlying asset is a T-note with a face value of $100,000 and an actual term to maturity of not less than 9 years and 5 months and not greater than 10 years from the first day of the delivery month.

T-Bond Contracts

The underlying asset is a T-bond with a face value of $100,000. Multiple grades are allowable for delivery. The deliverable grades must have a maturity of at least 15 years from the first day of the delivery month and less than 25 years from that date. There is also a futures contract termed as an ultra T-bond futures contract. The underlying asset is a T-bond with a face value of $100,000 and an actual term to maturity of at least 25 years as of the first day of the delivery month.

All the preceding contracts, on T-notes and T-bonds, are subject to delivery settlement.

Conversion Factors

As one can see from the contract specifications, a wide variety of notes and bonds with different coupons and maturity dates are eligible for delivery under any particular futures contract. The choice as to which bond to deliver is made by the short, and obviously the price received depends on the bond that it chooses to deliver. If the short delivers a more valuable bond, it should receive more than what it would, were it to deliver a less valuable bond. Thus, in order to facilitate comparisons between bonds, the exchange specifies a conversion factor for each bond that is eligible for delivery. This is a multiplicative price adjustment system to facilitate comparisons between different bonds that are eligible for delivery.

The conversion factor, for a bond is the value of the bond per $1 of face value, as calculated on the first day of the delivery month, using an annual YTM of 6% with semiannual compounding. For the purpose of calculation, the life of the bond is rounded down to the nearest multiple of three months. If after rounding off, the bond has a life that is an integer multiple of semiannual periods, then the first coupon is assumed to be paid after six months. However, after rounding off, if the life of the bond is not equal to an integer multiple of half-yearly periods, then the first coupon is assumed to be paid after three months and the accrued interest is subtracted. The following examples illustrate these principles.

The invoice price, which is the price received by the short, is calculated as follows:

$$\begin{aligned}\text{Invoice Price} &= \text{Invoice Principal Amount} + \text{Accrued Interest}\\ &= CF_i \times F \times 100{,}000 + AI_i \qquad (12.4)\end{aligned}$$

where CF_i is the conversion factor of bond i, F is the quoted futures price per dollar of face value,[9] and AI_i is the accrued interest.

Example 12.9. Let's assume that we are short in a September futures contract and that today is 1 September 2018. Consider a 5% T-Bond that matures on 15 May 2047. This bond is obviously eligible for delivery under the futures contract. On September 1, this bond has 28 years and $8\frac{1}{2}$ months to maturity. When we round down to the nearest multiple of 3 months, we get a figure of 28 years and 6 months.

The first coupon is assumed to be paid after six months. The conversion factor may therefore be calculated as follows

$$\begin{aligned}CF &= \frac{\frac{5}{2}\text{PVIFA}(3,57) + 100\text{PVIF}(3,57)}{100}\\ &= \frac{67.8773 + 18.5472}{100}\\ &= 0.8642\end{aligned}$$

PVIFA stands for *present value interest factor annuity* and PVIF stands for *present value interest factor.*

$$\text{PVIFA}(3,57) = \frac{1}{0.03} \times [1 - \frac{1}{(1.03)^{57}}]$$

$$\text{PVIF}(3,57) = \frac{1}{(1.03)^{57}}$$

Example 12.10. Instead of the May 2047 bond, consider another bond that is maturing on 15 February 2047, with a coupon of 4.75%. This bond, too, is suitable for delivery. On 1 September 2018, this bond has 28 years and $5\frac{1}{2}$ months to maturity. The life of the bond when we round down to the nearest multiple of 3 months is 28 years and 3 months.

In this case, we assume that the first coupon is paid after three months. The conversion factor *CF*, can be calculated in three steps as shown here:

1. First, find the price of the bond three months from today, using a yield of 6% per annum.

$$\begin{aligned}P &= \frac{4.75}{2} + \frac{4.75}{2}\text{PVIFA}(3,56) + 100\text{PVIF}(3,56)\\ &= 2.375 + 64.0430 + 19.1036\\ &= \$85.5216\end{aligned}$$

2. Discount the price gotten in the preceding step for another three months:

$$\frac{85.5216}{(1.03)^{\frac{1}{2}}} = \$84.2669$$

9 T-Bond futures prices are quoted in the same way as the cash market prices, that is, they are clean prices.

3. Subtract the accrued interest for three months from the price obtained in the second step:

$$AI = \frac{4.75}{2} \times \frac{1}{2} = 1.1875$$

$$CF = \frac{84.2669 - 1.1875}{100} = 0.8308$$

Why do we adopt two different procedures for calculating the CF? The CF is used to multiply the quoted futures price, which is a clean price. Hence the CF should not include any accrued interest. In the first example, the bond has a life that is an integer multiple of semiannual periods after rounding off. Consequently, we need not be concerned with accrued interest.[10] However, in the second example, accrued interest for a quarter is present in the value we get in the second step. Hence, in this case, we need to subtract this interest in order to arrive at the conversion factor.

Calculating the Invoice Price for a T-Bond

Assume that on 15 September 2018 the short declares a decision to deliver the 5% bond maturing on 15 May 2047 under the September futures contract. The actual delivery will obviously take place two business days later, that is, on 17 September.

The invoice price may be computed as follows. The first step is obviously to calculate the accrued interest. The last coupon would have been paid on 15 May 2018, and the next is due on 15 November 2018. Between the two coupon dates there are 184 days. Between the last coupon date and the delivery date, there are 125 days. The accrued interest for a T-bond with a face value of $100,000 is

$$AI = \frac{0.05}{2} \times \frac{125}{184} \times 100{,}000 = \$1{,}698.3696$$

The futures settlement price[11] on 15 September is assumed to be 95-12. This corresponds to a decimal futures price per dollar of face value of

$$\frac{95 + \frac{12}{32}}{100} = \$0.9538$$

The conversion factor has already been calculated to be 0.8642.

$$\text{Invoice Price} = 0.9538 \times 0.8642 \times 100000 + 1{,}698.3696 = \$84{,}125.77$$

---

10 On a coupon date, the accrued interest is zero.

11 Note that the settlement price is based on the day the intention to deliver is declared, whereas accrued interest is computed as of the delivery day. The reason for this is that after the intention to deliver is declared, marking to market ceases and hence the futures price payable by the long is the settlement price as of that day. However, because the long receives the bond only on the delivery day, accrued interest must be computed until that day.

The Cheapest-to-Deliver (CTD) Bond

The conversion factor is an example of a multiplicative adjustment, when more than one grade of the underlying asset is specified for delivery. As we have seen, under such circumstances the short will choose to deliver the bond that is the cheapest to deliver. To illustrate this, as well as other concepts that follow, let's depict a hypothetical situation.

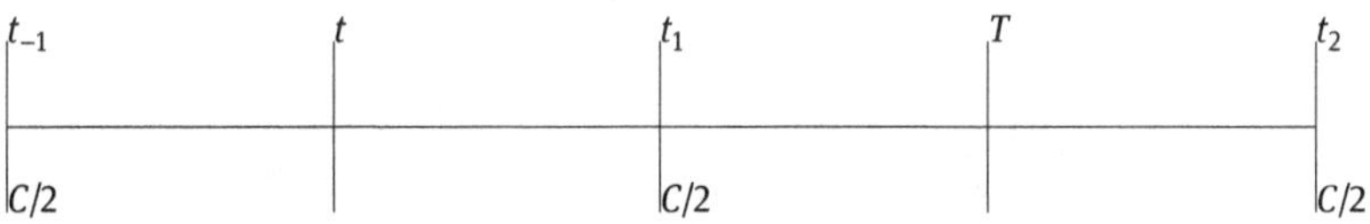

Figure 12.7: Time line for the CTD bond at expiration.

t represents today. The last coupon of $\$C/2$ was paid at t_{-1} and the next coupon is due at time t_1. There is a T-bond futures contract expiring at time T, which is followed by a coupon at time t_2. When the short delivers a particular bond, bond i, at time T, it will receive[12]

$$(F_T \times CF_i + AI_{i,t_1,T}) \times 100{,}000$$

The cost of acquisition of the bond in the spot market at time T is $(P_{i,T} + AI_{i,t_1,T}) \times$ 100,000. Thus the profit for the short is

$$\begin{aligned}&(F_T \times CF_i + AI_{i,t_1,T}) \times 100{,}000 - (P_{i,T} + AI_{i,t_1,T}) \times 100{,}000\\ &\quad = (F_T \times CF_i - P_{i,T}) \times 100{,}000 \end{aligned} \tag{12.5}$$

If $F_T \times CF_i - P_{i,T}$ is to be maximized, or equivalently, $CF_i(F_T - \frac{P_{i,T}}{CF_i})$ is to be maximized, we require that $\frac{P_{i,T}}{CF_i}$ be minimized. $\frac{P_{i,T}}{CF_i}$ is the *delivery adjusted spot price* in this case. Thus, as we have seen, the cheapest-to-deliver bond is the one with the lowest delivery-adjusted spot price. The delivery date spot-futures convergence ensures that $F_T \times CF_i - P_{i,T} = 0$; that is, the quoted futures price at expiration equals the delivery-adjusted spot price of the cheapest-to-deliver bond.

In practice, T-bond futures contracts give the short a number of delivery options. Consequently, the quoted futures price at expiration is usually less than the delivery-adjusted spot price of the cheapest-to-deliver bond.

12 From now on, we denote the clean price per dollar of face value by P, and the futures price per dollar of face value by F. AI is used to denote the accrued interest per dollar of face value.

The Cheapest-to-Deliver Bond Prior to Expiration

Consider the following cash-and-carry arbitrage strategy. Buy bond i at time t by borrowing at the rate r. Simultaneously go short in CF_i futures contracts expiring at time T, where CF_i is the conversion factor of the bond.

Let $P_{i,t}$ be the clean spot price of the T-bond at time t and $P_{i,T}$ be the clean spot price at time T. We denote the corresponding quoted futures prices by F_t and F_T, respectively. The payoff at the time of expiration is given by

$$\begin{aligned}&(F_T \times CF_i + AI_{i,t_1,T}) \times 100{,}000 + CF_i(F_t - F_T) \times 100{,}000 \\ &\quad = (F_t \times CF_i + AI_{i,t_1,T}) \times 100{,}000\end{aligned} \tag{12.6}$$

The arbitrageur receives a coupon of $C/2$ at time t_1. This can be reinvested until time T to yield an amount I_i, which is the future value of the payout per dollar of face value. Hence the implied repo rate is

$$\text{IRR} = \frac{F_t \times CF_i + AI_{i,t_1,T} + I_i - (P_{i,t} + AI_{i,t_{-1},t})}{(P_{i,t} + AI_{i,t_{-1},t})} \tag{12.7}$$

To preclude cash-and-carry arbitrage, the IRR should be less than the borrowing rate. But in the case of T-bonds, as in the case of other futures contracts that allow for multiple deliverable grades, more than one bond is eligible for delivery, and each one has its own IRR. If the IRR is greater than the borrowing rate, then arbitrage is possible. Such arbitrage continues, until there is no profit to be made from any of the bonds that are eligible for delivery. At this point in time, the cheapest-to-deliver bond is the one that maximizes the IRR, which in an arbitrage free setting just equals the borrowing rate. If we call this bond i, then

$$\begin{aligned}&F_t \times CF_i + AI_{i,t_1,T} = (P_{i,t} + AI_{i,t_{-1},t}) \times (1 + r) - I_i \\ &\Rightarrow F_t = \frac{[(P_{i,t} + AI_{i,t_{-1},t}) \times (1 + r) - I_i - AI_{i,t_1,T}]}{CF_i}\end{aligned} \tag{12.8}$$

We define

$$[(P_{i,t} + AI_{i,t_{-1},t}) \times (1 + r) - I_i - AI_{i,t_1,T}]$$

as the no-arbitrage futures price for bond i less accrued interest, F_i^*, or the *no-arbitrage quoted futures price*. Therefore,

$$F_t = \frac{F_i^*}{CF_i} \tag{12.9}$$

Prior to expiration, the actual futures price is equal to the delivery-adjusted no-arbitrage quoted futures price for the cheapest-to-deliver bond. For any other bond j,[13]

$$\frac{F_t \times CF_j + AI_{j,t_1^*,T} + I_j - (P_{j,t} + AI_{j,t_{-1}^*,t})}{(P_{j,t} + AI_{j,t_{-1}^*,t})} < r$$

$$\Rightarrow F_t < \frac{[(P_{j,t} + AI_{j,t_{-1}^*,t}) \times (1 + r) - I_j - AI_{j,t_1^*,T}]}{CF_j}$$

$$\Rightarrow F_t = \frac{F_i^*}{CF_i} < \frac{F_j^*}{CF_j} \forall j \tag{12.10}$$

Example 12.11. Let's illustrate the preceding concepts in detail using a numerical example. Assume that today is 14 August 2018. September futures contracts expire on 30 September. There are two bonds that are eligible for delivery. One is a 5% coupon bond maturing on 15 May 2047, and the other is a 6.5% coupon bond expiring on 15 November 2047. For ease of exposition, we have chosen bonds that do not pay any coupons between time t, which represents the day on which we are standing, and time T, which is the expiration date of the futures contract. Hence we do not have to worry about the future value of payouts I. The conversion factor for the first bond, which we call bond A, is 0.8642, whereas that for the second, which we call bond B, is 1.0683.

The quoted spot price for bond A is 108-00 and that for bond B is 132-11. These prices correspond to a YTM of 4.5% per annum.The borrowing rate is 7% per annum. Now if a bond is traded on 14 August, the actual settlement takes place on 15 August, which is the next business day and therefore the relevant day for our calculations.

The market price of bond A can be calculated as follows. The number of days from the last coupon date, which is 15 May 2018, until 15 August 2018 is 92. The number of days from 15 May 2018 until 15 November 2018, which is the next coupon date, is 184. Hence the accrued interest per \$100 of face value is

$$\frac{5}{2} \times \frac{92}{184} = \$1.25$$

The dirty price per \$100 of face value is therefore

$$108 + 1.25 = \$109.25$$

Similarly in the case of bond B, the accrued interest is

$$\frac{6.5}{2} \times \frac{92}{184} = \$1.6250$$

and the total market price is

$$\left(132 + \frac{11}{32}\right) + 1.6250 = \$133.9688$$

---

13 t_{-1}^* denotes the last coupon date of bond j, and t_1^* denotes the coupon date corresponding to t_1 for bond i.

The next step is to calculate the delivery-adjusted no-arbitrage quoted futures prices for the two bonds. The number of days between 15 August and 30 September is 46. Hence, for bond A,

$$P_d(1+r) = 109.25 \times \left[1 + 0.07 \times \frac{46}{360}\right] = \$110.2272$$

The accrued interest from the last coupon date until the expiration date of the futures contract is

$$\frac{5}{2} \times \frac{138}{184} = \$1.8750$$

Hence the no-arbitrage futures price of bond A less accrued interest is

$$110.2272 - 1.8750 = \$108.3522$$

The delivery-adjusted no-arbitrage quoted futures price for bond A is therefore

$$\frac{108.3522}{0.8642} = 125.3786 \equiv 125 - 12$$

Similarly, the no-arbitrage futures price for bond B less accrued interest is

$$133.9688 \times \left[1 + 0.07 \times \frac{46}{360}\right] - \frac{6.5}{2} \times \frac{138}{184} = 135.1671 - 2.4375$$
$$= 132.7295 \equiv 132 - 23$$

Hence, the delivery-adjusted no-arbitrage quoted futures price for bond B is

$$\frac{132.7295}{1.0683} = 124.2437 \equiv 124 - 08$$

Thus bond B is cheaper to deliver as of 14 August 2018.

Risk in an Arbitrage Strategy Due to Multiple Deliverable Grades

Financing risk and payout risk are inherent in arbitrage strategies. The first refers to the fact that the arbitrageur may be unable to borrow or lend at a fixed rate for the entire time horizon, and in practice may have to do so for short periods and repeatedly roll forward. Each time the arbitrageur rolls forward in practice, there is a risk that interest rates may have increased or declined. Payout risk refers to the fact that the underlying asset may not make payouts as forecasted. This is very important for an asset such as an equity share, where the actual dividend could be substantially different from the forecasted value. However, for federal government securities such as T-notes and T-bonds, that is not an issue. However, there is a third element of risk as well, which is confronted by arbitrageurs who take long positions in contracts that specify multiple grades of the underlying asset as suitable for delivery. As we have seen in the case of such contracts, the option of which grade to deliver is always given to the short. The short will obviously opt to deliver the grade that is the cheapest at the time of delivery. The issue is that this grade need not correspond to the grade that has been sold short by an arbitrageur at an earlier point in time, as part of a reverse cash-and-carry arbitrage strategy. If the grade that is delivered by the short is different from what the long requires, then the arbitrageur has to acquire the grade that he originally short sold. The grade received from the short as a part of the futures contract has to be disposed of in the spot market. The net result is that the ex-post implied reverse repo rate for the arbitrageur could be higher than the ex-ante implied reverse repo rate and may at times be even higher than the lending rate. If so, the realized profit may be less than anticipated, or in a worse situation, the arbitrageur may end up with a net loss. Hence, reverse cash-and-carry arbitrage, under such circumstances is fraught with danger and more appropriately termed as *risk arbitrage*.

Before we go on to analyze the additional risk in the case of a reverse cash-and-carry transaction, let's first reconsider a cash-and-carry transaction. Normally we assume that the arbitrageur will take a spot-futures position in the ratio of 1:1. That is, if the futures contract is for 100 units of the underlying asset, the arbtrageur goes long in 100 units for every contract in which he has a short position. However, although this is appropriate in the case of contracts that specify only one deliverable grade, the situation is different for cases where multiple deliverable grades have been specified and a multiplicative price adjustment method is in use. Assume that the arbitrageur goes long in one unit of grade i of the asset. We assume that multiple grades have been specified for delivery, and that a multiplicative price adjustment system is in operation. Let's denote the required short position as h futures contracts. When delivering the asset at expiration, the arbitrageur receives a_iF_T. The profit from marking to market is $h(F_t - F_T)$. For the strategy to be riskless, we require that

$$\begin{aligned} a_iF_T + h(F_t - F_T) &= a_iF_t \\ \Rightarrow h &= a_i \end{aligned} \tag{12.11}$$

Thus the appropriate number of futures contracts is equal to the price adjustment factor of the grade in which the arbitrageur has taken a long position. It should be noted that if an additive system of price adjustment is used, then the arbitrageur still needs a spot futures position of 1:1. This can be demonstrated as follows:

$$F_T + a_i + h(F_t - F_T) = F_t + a_i \Rightarrow h = 1$$

The very fact that a cash-and-carry arbitrage strategy is initiated signifies that the ex-ante implied repo rate is greater than the borrowing rate. That is,

$$\frac{a_iF_t - S_{i,t}}{S_{i,t}} > r \tag{12.12}$$

At the point of expiration of the futures contract, there are two possibilities. It may be the case that grade i is the cheapest-to-deliver grade. If so, the arbitrageur will deliver it and have a realized implied repo rate equal to what has been anticipated from the very outset. However, what if some other grade, j, has become the cheapest to deliver? If this is the case, the arbitrageur can sell the unit of grade i in his possession at its prevailing spot price and acquire a_i units of grade j to deliver under the futures contract.

The cash inflow is

$$S_{i,T} + a_i \times (a_j F_T) + a_i(F_t - F_T)$$

This represents the inflow from three sources, namely, the cash flow from the sale of grade i in the spot market, the proceeds from the delivery of grade j under the futures contract, and the cumulative profit from marking to market. The cash outflow, on account of the acquisition of grade j, is

$$a_i S_{j,T}$$

The net inflow therefore is

$$\begin{aligned} &S_{i,T} + a_i \times (a_j F_T) + a_i(F_t - F_T) - a_i S_{j,T} \\ &= S_{i,T} + a_i S_{j,T} + a_i(F_t - F_T) - a_i S_{j,T} \\ &= a_i F_t + a_i \left[\frac{S_{i,T}}{a_i} - \frac{S_{j,T}}{a_j} \right] \\ &> a_i F_t \end{aligned} \tag{12.13}$$

because if grade j is the cheapest-to-deliver by assumption, then its delivery adjusted spot price $\frac{S_{j,T}}{a_j}$ will be lower than that of grade i and equal to the futures price, F_T. Thus we conclude that if a cash-and-carry arbitrage strategy is initiated because it looks profitable at the outset, it can only lead to a greater profit, if not the anticipated profit, at the time of expiration. In other words, the ex-post implied repo rate is greater than or equal to the ex-ante implied repo rate, which by assumption is greater than the borrowing rate. Hence, there is no risk as such.

Now let's turn our attention to a reverse cash-and-carry strategy. The very fact that such a strategy is being initiated, implies that

$$\frac{a_i F_t - S_{i,t}}{S_{i,t}} < r \tag{12.14}$$

If the short delivers grade i, the grade that has been short sold by the arbitrageur, at the end, then the anticipated arbitrage profit is realized. However, what if the arbitrageur is forced to take delivery of another grade, j, because the short finds that it is the cheapest to deliver? If so, the arbitrageur has to sell this grade in the spot market and acquire grade i at its prevailing spot price to cover the short position.

The outflow is

$$a_i(a_jF_T) + S_{i,T}$$

This represents the outflow on account of taking delivery under the futures contract and the cost on account of the covering of the initial short position. The inflow is

$$a_iS_{j,T} + a_i(F_T - F_t)$$

This represents the cash flow on account of the sale of grade j, as well as the cumulative cash flow due to marking to market.

The net outflow is

$$\begin{aligned} &a_i(a_jF_T) + S_{i,T} - a_iS_{j,T} - a_i(F_T - F_t) \\ &\quad = a_iS_{j,T} + S_{i,T} - a_iS_{j,T} - a_i(F_T - F_t) \\ &\quad = a_iF_t + a_i\left[\frac{S_{i,T}}{a_i} - \frac{S_{j,T}}{a_j}\right] \\ &\quad > a_iF_t \end{aligned} \tag{12.15}$$

Consequently, the ex-post implied reverse repo rate can be greater than the ex-ante implied reverse repo rate and perhaps even greater than the lending rate. Therefore, to reiterate, what looked like a profitable arbitrage opportunity may end up as a reduced arbitrage profit or perhaps even a loss. Thus arbitrage, under such circumstances, is accompanied by an additional element of risk.

Seller's Options

A person who takes a short position in a T-bond futures contract has a number of options at the time of delivery. These options are referred to as *quality* options and *timing* options. A quality option in one under which the short has the right to select which bond to deliver. With a timing option, the short can choose the time of delivery. Before we go on to analyze the options in detail, let's take a look at the delivery procedure.

The Delivery Process

Delivery in the case of T-bond and T-note futures contracts is a three-day process. The three-day period begins with what is called the *intention day*, which is the day on which the short notifies the clearing corporation of an intention to deliver. The intention day can be any day from two business days prior to the first business day of the delivery month until two business days before the last business day of the delivery month. On the next day, which is called the *notice day*, the clearing corporation informs both parties of the other's intention to make or take delivery. The short has to then prepare an invoice for the long that gives details about the security being delivered and the amount of payment for delivery. Finally, on the next day, which is the *delivery day*, the short has to deliver the bonds to the long in exchange for the amount mentioned in the invoice.

Although delivery continues until the end of the delivery month, trading in the futures contracts ceases on the seventh business day prior to the last business day of the delivery month.

The Wild Card Option

Before we examine it in detail, let's first define the wild card option. It is an option that gives the right to the short to decide whether to deliver, even after trading has ceased for the day. The futures market closes at 2:00 p. m. However, the short has until 8:00 p. m. on a given day to declare an intention to deliver. Thus the option allows the short the right to profit from a favorable price movement in the six-hour interval between 2:00 p. m. and 8:00 p. m.

The settlement price used to calculate the invoice price is the price that is determined at 2:00 p.m.on the intention day.[14] However, the short has until 8:00 p. m. on that day to notify the exchange of a decision to deliver. Thus the short has an option to lock in the 2:00 p. m. price by announcing an intention to deliver any time before 8:00 p. m. This means that if interest rates change after 2:00 p. m. then the short can profit by delivering a bond that is now cheaper to deliver.

In actual practice the short has a bouquet of wild card options, that is, one for every potential intention day. On the first intention day,[15] the short has the wild card option described in the preceding paragraph. However, if there is no change in prices between 2:00 p. m. and 8:00 p. m., then the short can simply wait for the next day hoping that something will happen between 2:00 p. m. and 8 p. m. on that day. This can go on until the last intention day which is the third to last business day of the expiration month.

In practice there are the end-of-day wild card options that we just described and also an end-of-month wild card option. The end-of-month option works as follows. The final settlement price is determined seven days before the end of the contract month. However, the short can wait until the end of the contract month to make a call on whether to deliver.

The wild card option has a timing component as well as a quality component. Let's first illustrate the timing option component of the wild card option.

14 This price changes from day to day during the delivery period until the last day of trading. For all subsequent deliveries, the settlement price is the price as of the last trading day.

15 This is the second to last business day of the month preceding expiration.

The Timing Option

Consider the following time line.

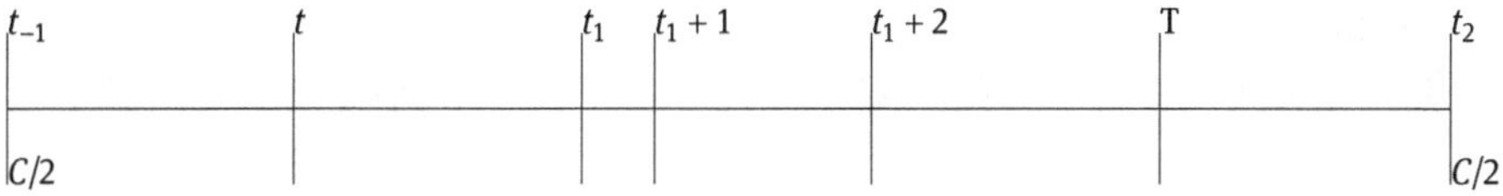

Figure 12.8: The delivery process.

t_{-1} denotes the time when the last coupon was paid, and t_2 denotes the next coupon date. The contract expires at T.

Let's consider the case of an investor who gets into a cash-and-carry strategy at time t, by buying 1 unit of bond i and going short in CF_i futures contracts, where CF_i is the conversion factor of the bond that has been bought.

Assume that the investor decides to deliver at time $t_1 + 2$ by declaring an intention to deliver at time t_1. We assume that bond i, the bond in question, is the cheapest to deliver at that point in time. Therefore, the futures settlement price at time t_1, F_{t_1}, is such that

$$F_{t_1} = \frac{P_{i,t_1}}{CF_i}$$

where P_{i,t_1} is the quoted price of bond i at time t_1.

If there is no timing option, then bond i indeed is delivered, and the proceeds from delivery under the futures contract are

$$CF_i \times (F_{t_1} \times CF_i + AI_{i,t_{-1},t_1+2}) \times 100{,}000$$

The proceeds from the sale of the surplus bonds[16] are

$$(1 - CF_i)(P_{i,t_1} + AI_{i,t_{-1},t_1+1}) \times 100{,}000$$

The total proceeds are[17]

$$\begin{aligned} &CF_i \times (F_{t_1} \times CF_i + AI_{i,t_{-1},t_1+2}) \times 100{,}000 + (1 - CF_i)(P_{i,t_1} + AI_{i,t_{-1},t_1+1}) \times 100{,}000 \\ &\quad = CF_i \times (P_{i,t_1} + AI_{i,t_{-1},t_1+2}) \times 100{,}000 + (1 - CF_i)(P_{i,t_1} + AI_{i,t_{-1},t_1+1}) \times 100{,}000 \\ &\quad = (P_{i,t_1} + AI_{i,t_{-1},t_1+1}) \times 100{,}000 \end{aligned} \tag{12.16}$$

16 If $CF_i > 1$, additional bonds have to be purchased if the short decides to deliver, which means that there will be an outflow.

17 $AI_{i,t_{-1},t_1+2} \cong AI_{i,t_{-1},t_1+1}$.

Now assume that between 2:00 p. m. and 8:00 p. m. on day t_1, the YTM changes. Let the corresponding spot price of bond i be P^*_{i,t_1}. We assume that bond i continues to be the cheapest-to-deliver bond, in order for us to be able to focus exclusively on the timing option.

The proceeds from delivery under the futures contract are the same, namely

$$CF_i \times (P_{i,t_1} + AI_{i,t_{-1},t_1+2}) \times 100{,}000$$

But the proceeds from the sale of the surplus bonds are

$$(1 - CF_i)(P^*_{i,t_1} + AI_{i,t_{-1},t_1+1}) \times 100{,}000$$

The total proceeds therefore are

$$CF_i \times (P_{i,t_1} + AI_{i,t_{-1},t_1+2}) \times 100{,}000 + (1 - CF_i)(P^*_{i,t_1} + AI_{i,t_{-1},t_1+1}) \times 100{,}000$$

The incremental profit from the yield change is

$$\begin{aligned} &CF_i \times (P_{i,t_1} + AI_{i,t_{-1},t_1+2}) \times 100{,}000 + (1 - CF_i)(P^*_{i,t_1} + AI_{i,t_{-1},t_1+1}) \times 100{,}000 \\ &\quad - (P_{i,t_1} + AI_{i,t_{-1},t_1+1}) \times 100{,}000 \\ &= (1 - CF_i)(P^*_{i,t_1} - P_{i,t_1}) \times 100{,}000 \end{aligned} \tag{12.17}$$

If $CF_i > 1$, the incremental profit will be positive if $P^*_{i,t_1} < P_{i,t_1}$, that is, if yields rise. Thus, in the case of a bond whose conversion factor is greater than one, the timing option is beneficial if yields rise. Conversely, if the conversion factor is less than one, then the yield has to fall in order to enable the investor to profit from the timing option. We can illustrate this principle with the help of Example 12.12.

Example 12.12. Assume that there are two bonds that are eligible for delivery on 7 September 2018. Bond A carries a 5% coupon and matures on 15 May 2047. Bond B carries a 11% coupon and matures on 15 November 2038. The conversion factor for bond A is 0.8642, and that for bond B is 1.5777. If we assume that the YTM for both the bonds is 6%, then the quoted spot price for bond A is 86-12, and that for bond B is 158-02. The delivery-adjusted spot price of bond A is 99-30, and that of bond B is 100-06. Bond A is cheaper to deliver and the futures price at 2:00 p. m. is equal to its delivery-adjusted spot price of 99-30.

Let's assume that an investor has initiated a cash-and-carry strategy on 7 August 2018 with bond A and suddenly announces an intention to deliver on 7 September 2018. In the absence of a timing option, the investor would lock in

$$\begin{aligned} &\frac{99 + \frac{30}{32}}{100} \times 0.8642 \times 100{,}000 + \frac{\frac{5}{2}}{100} \times \frac{117}{184} \times 100{,}000 \\ &= \$87{,}955.65 \end{aligned}$$

Let's assume that after 2:00 p. m., the YTM suddenly falls to 4.50%. The quoted price of bond A is now \$108. Now, if bond A is delivered, the proceeds are

$$0.8642 \times \left(\frac{99 + \frac{30}{32}}{100} \times 0.8642 + \frac{\frac{5}{2}}{100} \times \frac{117}{184} \right) \times 100{,}000$$

$$+ (1 - 0.8642)\left(\frac{108}{100} + \frac{\frac{5}{2}}{100} \times \frac{116}{184}\right) \times 100{,}000$$

$$= 76{,}011.2720 + 14{,}880.4310$$

$$= \$90{,}891.7030$$

Thus the timing option has clearly paid off.

The Quality Option

Let's examine the wild card option again. Assume that after 2:00 p. m. on 7 September, the interest rate suddenly rises to 7.50%. The new spot price of bond A becomes 70-22, whereas that of bond B is 136-03. The timing option has no value in this case as one can verify. But let's consider what happens if we deliver bond B instead of bond A. If bond A is delivered in the absence of the wild card option, then the payoff is $87,955.65. However, if bond A is sold at the new price and CF_a units of bond B are purchased for delivery under the futures contract, the proceeds are as follows.

Payoff from delivery under the futures contract:

$$= 0.8642 \times \left(\frac{99 + \frac{30}{32}}{100} \times 1.5777 + \frac{5.5}{100} \times \frac{117}{184}\right) \times 100{,}000$$

$$= \$139{,}281.95$$

Proceeds from the sale of bond A:

$$= \left(\frac{70 + \frac{22}{32}}{100} + \frac{2.5}{100} \times \frac{116}{184}\right) \times 100{,}000$$

$$= \$72{,}263.59$$

Cost of acquisition of bond B:

$$= 0.8642\left(\frac{136 + \frac{03}{32}}{100} + \frac{5.5}{100} \times \frac{116}{184}\right) \times 100{,}000$$

$$= \$120{,}608.70$$

The net proceeds = 139,281.95 + 72,263.59 − 120,608.70 = $90,936.82, which is greater than $87,955.65, the amount that would have been received in the absence of the wild card option. The quality option is clearly valuable in this case.

The End-of-Month Option

We have already examined the wild card option inherent in the end-of-month option. There is, however, another dimension to this option. Let's assume that interest rates are stable for the days after the last day of trading. Under these conditions, for every additional day while holding the bond, the short earns accrued interest, but must finance it for every day it is held. If the coupon rate of the bond exceeds the financing rate, then the short should deliver on the last day, or else immediately. This timing option is known as the *accrued interest* option.

The Pure Quality Option

We have seen that there is an end-of-day wild card option as well as an end-of-month wild card option, both of which have a quality option component. But even in the absence of these options, the short can decide which bond to deliver, which itself is a quality option. This is because the party who has the right to choose the grade stands to benefit if another grade is cheaper to deliver subsequently. Thus, even in the absence of the wild card or the end-of-month options, a cash-and-carry strategy gives a quality option to the short.

Hedging

Let's first illustrate our arguments using the cheapest-to-deliver bond and then discuss the case where other bond portfolios have to be hedged.

Hedging the Cheapest-to-Deliver Bond: A Naive Approach

A naive approach for hedging Q bonds is to use Q futures contracts, or in other words, a hedge ratio of 1:1. This strategy is not satisfactory, as the following example illustrates.

Example 12.13. Let's go back to our earlier illustration in Example 12.11 regarding a cash-and-carry strategy initiated on 14 August. We found that the bond that carried a coupon of 6.5% was the cheapest-to-deliver bond. The quoted spot price was 132-11, and the corresponding futures price was 124-08. The conversion factor was 1.0683. Assume that on 15 September, the settlement price is 82-19. The corresponding quoted spot price is 88-07. We are assuming that this bond continues to be the cheapest-to-deliver bond.

The bond can be sold in the spot market to yield

$$\frac{88 + \frac{7}{32}}{100} \times 100{,}000 + \frac{3.25}{100} \times \frac{123}{184} \times 100{,}000$$
$$= \$90{,}391.30$$

The profit from the short futures position is

$$\frac{(124 + \frac{8}{32}) - (82 + \frac{19}{32})}{100} \times 100{,}000$$
$$= \$41{,}656.25$$

The total payoff is \$132,047.55. A perfect hedge would lock in the original futures price of 124-08 to yield

$$\frac{124 + \frac{8}{32}}{100} \times 1.0683 \times 100{,}000 + \frac{3.25}{100} \times \frac{123}{184} \times 100{,}000$$
$$= \$134{,}908.82$$

In this case we are clearly under-hedged.

The Conversion Factor Approach

Let's assume that the hedge is initiated at time t_0 and lifted at time t_1, after delivery has commenced:

$$\begin{aligned}
F_{t_0} &= \frac{(P_{t_0} + AI_{t_{-1},t_0})(1+r) - AI_{t_{-1},t_1}}{CF_i} \\
F_{t_1} &= \frac{P_{t_1}}{CF_i} \\
\Rightarrow F_{t_1} - F_{t_0} &= \frac{P_{t_1} - (P_{t_0} + AI_{t_{-1},t_0})(1+r) + AI_{t_{-1},t_1}}{CF_i} \\
\Rightarrow F_{t_1} - F_{t_0} &\cong \frac{P_{t_1} - P_{t_0}}{CF_i} \\
\Rightarrow \triangle F &\cong \frac{\triangle P}{CF_i}
\end{aligned} \tag{12.18}$$

if we ignore the cost of carry.

Now a perfect hedge should be such that

$$\triangle P = h^* \triangle F$$

where $h^* = \frac{Q_f}{Q}$ is the optimal hedge ratio.[18] Therefore,

$$h^* = \frac{\triangle P}{\triangle F} = CF_i \tag{12.19}$$

Let's examine the efficiency of this hedge using the same data as for the example on the naive hedging strategy.

Example 12.14. The proceeds from the spot market when the cheapest-to-deliver bond is sold are \$90,391.30.

Profit from the futures market = 1.0683 × 41,656.25 = \$44,501.37.

The total proceeds = \$134,892.67, which is very close to the value of \$134,908.82 that is implied by the original futures price.

---

18 Q is the exposure in the spot market and Q_f is the number of futures contracts.

Hedging a Portfolio Other Than the CTD Bond

The naive hedging strategy has been discredited even for hedging the price of the CTD bond. Hence we will not pursue it further. Let's instead analyze how to extend the conversion factor approach to hedge a bond other than the CTD bond.

Our hedge ratio h should be such that $\triangle P = h \triangle F$. We know that

$$\triangle F \cong \frac{\triangle P_{CTD}}{CF_{CTD}}$$

Therefore

$$\triangle P = h \frac{\triangle P_{CTD}}{CF_{CTD}} \Rightarrow h = CF_{CTD} \frac{\triangle P}{\triangle P_{CTD}}. \tag{12.20}$$

Such hedge ratios are called *perturbation hedge ratios.*[19] To use these ratios, for a given change in yield, we have to calculate the ratio of the change in the price of the bond being hedged to the change in the price of the CTD bond. In practice, the problem is that this ratio depends on the change in the yield, which cannot be predicted exactly. Hence for hedging a portfolio of bonds other than the CTD bond, the preferred hedging technique involves the use of the duration of the bond.

The hedge ratio, which is derived in Appendix 12.1, is given by

$$CF_{CTD} \times \frac{D_h \times P_h \times (1 + \frac{y_{CTD}}{2})}{D_{CTD} \times P_{CTD} \times (1 + \frac{y_h}{2})}$$

The number of futures contracts required is

$$\frac{\text{Face Value of Spot Exposure}}{\text{Face Value of the Bond Underlying the Futures Contract}} \times h$$

We next illustrate this hedging technique with the help of Example 12.15.

Example 12.15. Assume that today is 14 August 2018. September futures contracts expire on 30 September. The cheapest-to-deliver bond, as we saw earlier, is a 6.5% coupon bond maturing on 15 November 2047. Its quoted price is 132-11, which corresponds to a YTM of 4.5% per annum, and the conversion factor is 1.0683. The quoted futures price, as calculated before, is 124-08.

Consider a portfolio manager who is holding 10,000 IBM bonds maturing on 15 August 2047. The face value is \$100, the coupon rate is 7.50% per annum, and the YTM is 8.50% per annum. The manager plans to sell the bonds on 30 September and wants to protect against an increase in the yield using T-bond futures contracts. The duration of the CTD bond on 14 August is 15.1947 years. The dirty price is \$133.9688. The price of the IBM bonds is \$89.2877, and the corresponding duration is 11.3778 years.

19 See Blake [4].

The hedge ratio is therefore

$$1.0683 \times \frac{(11.3778 \times 89.2877 \times 1.0225)}{(15.1947 \times 133.9688 \times 1.0425)} = 0.5229$$

Let's assume that the YTM of the IBM bonds on 30 September is 10% per annum and that the YTM of the CTD bond is 6%. The price of the IBM bond therefore is $77.4141, and the futures price is $100.0045. If the yield remains at 8.50%, the dirty price of IBM is $90.2216.

The loss from the spot market is

$$10{,}000 \times (90.2216 - 77.4141) = (\$128{,}075.00)$$

The profit from the futures market is

$$10{,}000 \times 0.5229 \times (124.25 - 100.0045) = \$126{,}779.70$$

The net loss = 126,779.70 – 128,075.00 = ($1,295.28).

The tracking error = $\frac{1{,}295.28}{128{,}075.00} \equiv 1.01\%$.

One issue that arises in the context of the duration-based hedging approach is whether we should use input values as calculated at the inception of the hedge or as determined at the point of termination. Most authors argue that we should use the expected values of the variables as of the termination date of the hedge. However, in practice, forecasting these variables is not always easy, and consequently, the current values are often used as inputs. The two approaches do not yield substantially different results unless the instrument being hedged and the CTD bond are significantly different.[20]

Changing the Duration of a Portfolio of Bonds

Consider a portfolio of bonds that currently has a duration of D_h. Let's assume that we want to change its duration to D_T, which denotes the target duration, by going long in futures contracts. The question is, what is the appropriate number of futures contracts to use? Let's denote the required hedge ratio by h, the current value per unit of the bond being hedged by P_h, and the value of the overall portfolio consisting of the bonds and the futures contracts by V. It can be shown that[21]

$$\Rightarrow h = \frac{(D_T - D_h) \times P_h \times (1 + \frac{y_{CTD}}{2})}{D_{CTD} \times P_{CTD} \times (1 + \frac{y_h}{2})} \times CF_{CTD} \tag{12.21}$$

The required number of futures contracts is

$$\frac{\text{Face Value of Spot Exposure}}{\text{Face Value of the Bond Underlying the Futures Contract}} \times h$$

---

20 See Daigler [18].

21 See Appendix 12.2.

Here is a numerical illustration.

Example 12.16. Assume that we are on 14 August 2018 and want to increase the duration of the IBM bonds from 11.3778 to 15. If we are holding IBM bonds with a face value of \$100 million we need to go long in

$$1.0683 \times \frac{(15.0 - 11.3778) \times 89.2877 \times 1.0225}{15.1947 \times 133.9688 \times 1.0425} \times \frac{100{,}000{,}000}{100{,}000}$$
$$= 0.1665 \times 1{,}000 \simeq 167 \text{ contracts}$$

If we want to reduce the duration, we have to go short in futures contracts.

Chapter Summary

In this chapter we looked at interest rate forward and futures contracts. We began by considering forward rate agreements, and their use in hedging and speculation. The focus then shifted to Eurodollar futures and their uses from the standpoints of locking in borrowing and lending rates. We also briefly looked at federal funds and futures on them. The chapter concluded with a detailed study of Treasury bond and Treasury note futures. We examined issues pertaining to their valuation, the issue of conversion factors, and the concept of the cheapest-to-deliver (CTD) bond. We looked at the various options given to the sellers of T-note and T-bond futures. Finally we studied the use of T-bond futures to hedge corporate bonds and their usefulness in changing the duration of a bond.

Appendix 12.1: Duration-Based Hedge Ratio

For any bond, we know that

$$\frac{dP}{P} = \frac{-D}{(1 + \frac{y}{2})} \times dy$$

where D is the duration of the bond in annual terms.[22] Therefore

$$\frac{\Delta P}{P} \cong \frac{-D}{(1 + \frac{y}{2})} \times \Delta y$$

If we denote the bond being hedged as bond h, then the optimal hedge ratio is

$$CF_{CTD}\frac{\Delta P_h}{\Delta P_{CTD}} = CF_{CTD} \times \frac{\frac{-D_h}{(1+\frac{y_h}{2})} \times P_h \times \Delta y_h}{\frac{-D_{CTD}}{(1+\frac{y_{CTD}}{2})} \times P_{CTD} \times \Delta y_{CTD}}$$

---

22 We are assuming that the bond pays semiannual coupons.

$$= CF_{CTD} \times \frac{D_h \times P_h \times (1 + \frac{y_{CTD}}{2}) \times \Delta y_h}{D_{CTD} \times P_{CTD} \times (1 + \frac{y_h}{2}) \times \Delta y_{CTD}} \quad (12.22)$$

If we assume that yield curve movements are parallel, that is $\Delta y_{CTD} = \Delta y_h$, then the hedge ratio is[23]

$$CF_{CTD} \times \frac{D_h \times P_h \times (1 + \frac{y_{CTD}}{2})}{D_{CTD} \times P_{CTD} \times (1 + \frac{y_h}{2})}$$

which simplifies further to

$$CF_{CTD} \times \frac{D_h \times P_h}{D_{CTD} \times P_{CTD}}$$

if we assume that percentage yield curve movements are parallel.[24] The number of futures contracts required is

$$\frac{\text{Face Value of Spot Exposure}}{\text{Face Value of the Bond Underlying the Futures Contract}} \times h$$

Appendix 12.2: Required Number of Contracts to Change the Duration

We know that

$$\Delta V = \Delta P + h \Delta F$$

$$\Rightarrow \frac{-D_V}{(1 + \frac{y_V}{2})} \times V \times \Delta y_V$$

$$= \frac{-D_h}{(1 + \frac{y_h}{2})} \times P_h \times \Delta y_h \; - \; h \times \frac{\frac{D_{CTD}}{(1+\frac{y_{CTD}}{2})} \times P_{CTD} \times \Delta y_{CTD}}{CF_{CTD}}$$

Let's assume that $\Delta y_v = \Delta y_h = \Delta y_{CTD}$. Therefore

$$\frac{-D_V}{(1 + \frac{y_V}{2})} \times V = \frac{-D_h}{(1 + \frac{y_h}{2})} \times P_h \; - \; h \times \frac{\frac{D_{CTD}}{(1+\frac{y_{CTD}}{2})} \times P_{CTD}}{CF_{CTD}}$$

At the inception of the hedge, $V = P_h$ because the value of the futures contracts is zero. Thus the preceding expression can be written as

$$\frac{-(D_V - D_h)}{(1 + \frac{y_h}{2})} \times P_h = -h \times \frac{\frac{D_{CTD}}{(1+\frac{y_{CTD}}{2})} \times P_{CTD}}{CF_{CTD}}.$$

23 The per unit face value of the bond being hedged should be taken to be equal to the face value of the bond underlying the futures contract.

24 This implies that $\frac{\Delta y_{CTD}}{(1+y_{CTD})} = \frac{\Delta y_h}{(1+y_h)}$.

If our target duration for the overall portfolio is D_T, then we should choose h such that

$$h = \frac{\frac{(D_T - D_h)}{\left(1+\frac{y_h}{2}\right)} \times P_h}{\frac{D_{CTD}}{\left(1+\frac{y_{CTD}}{2}\right)} \times P_{CTD}} \times CF_{CTD}$$

$$\Rightarrow h = \frac{(D_T - D_h) \times P_h \times \left(1 + \frac{y_{CTD}}{2}\right)}{D_{CTD} \times P_{CTD} \times \left(1 + \frac{y_h}{2}\right)} \times CF_{CTD} \tag{12.23}$$

The required number of futures contracts is

$$\frac{\text{Face Value of Spot Exposure}}{\text{Face Value of the Bond Underlying the Futures Contract}} \times h$$

Chapter 13
Bonds with Embedded Options

In this chapter we take a detailed look at bonds with built-in options. More specifically, we examine the intricacies of bonds with built-in call and put options and bonds that give the holders the option to convert them into shares of stock. Callable bonds, which have a built-in call option, give the issuer the right to call back the bond prior to the maturity date. If the interest rates have declined, the issuer can exercise this option, retire the existing bonds, and issue new bonds with a lower coupon, in accordance with the prevailing low-interest environment. Putable bonds, which have a built-in put option, enable the holders to prematurely surrender the bonds in return for the face value. Quite obviously, if interest rates have increased, the holders can exercise this option to recover their principal, and re-invest the money in bonds with a higher coupon, which are likely to be available in the prevailing high-interest environment. Convertible bonds can be converted into shares of common stock of the entity that issued the bonds. Exchangeable bonds are similar, except that they facilitate conversion into shares of another company and not the issuing company, although in practice the two may be related.

Callable Bonds

In the case of a callable bond, the issuer has the option to call back the bond prior to the scheduled maturity date. As the holder of the option, the issuer has to pay a premium for it. This shows up in the form of a lower price compared to a plain vanilla bond, which is identical in all other respects except for the call feature. In practice, a party who is planning a bond issue has to offer a higher coupon on the callable bond, as compared to an otherwise similar plain vanilla bond. Subsequently if we compare a plain vanilla bond and a callable bond that are identical in all respects including the coupon, the callable will have a lower price or a higher yield to maturity.

Why does the callable bond have a higher yield to maturity? The call option enables the issuer to call the bond back when interest rate are declining. If the holder gets his money back in such circumstances, he has to re-invest at a lower rate of interest. Thus the call option works in favor of the issuer and against the investor. From the investors' perspective, they are perfectly happy receiving a higher coupon, and will not appreciate being compelled to invest in lower return instruments. Thus the holder of a callable bond faces uncertainty about the number of coupons he or she is going to get, and the time when the principal will be repaid. This is referred to as *timing risk*. In practice, to compensate for this, the issuer states in advance that it will pay a call premium, over and above the face value, if the bond is recalled. The premium may be equal to six month's coupon, or at times may even be one year's coupon.

https://doi.org/10.1515/9781547400669-013

A bond may be discretely callable or continuously callable. The former is callable only on specific dates, typically coupon dates. Thus if today is a coupon date, and the bond is not called, it cannot be called for another six months, assuming semiannual coupons. Continuously callable bonds on the other hand, can be called at any point in time. In options parlance, discretely callable bonds embody a Bermudan option and are characterized by a finite number of call dates, whereas continuously callable bonds have a built-in American option, which permits the issuer to call back at any date. In practice, if we issue a 20-year bond and say that it can be recalled right away, it is unlikely to have many takers. Consequently a callable bond may have a *call protection period*, during which it cannot be called, no matter how low the prevailing interest rates may be. Such bonds are referred to as *deferred callable bonds*. Once the call protection period expires, the bonds become freely callable.

If we denote the dirty price of the callable bond by P_{cal}, the dirty price of the corresponding plain vanilla bond by P_{pv}, and the premium for the call option by C, we can state that:

$$P_{cal} = P_{pv} - C \tag{13.1}$$

Yield to Call

Consider a bond with a face value of M, N semiannual coupon periods until maturity, and a coupon rate of c% per annum, which translates to $\$C/2$ every six months. Assume that the bond can be called at $M*$ where $M* = M + C$ or $M + \frac{C}{2}$. Let's denote a call date by $N*$, where $N* < N$. We denote the dirty price by P_d. The yield to call is the value of the discount rate that satisfies the following equation:

$$P_d = \sum_{t=1}^{N*} \left[\frac{\frac{C}{2}}{(1 + \frac{y_c}{2})^t} \right] + \frac{M*}{(1 + \frac{y_c}{2})^t} \tag{13.2}$$

Let's illustrate the computation of the yield to call using Excel.

Example 13.1. Consider a bond with a face value of \$1,000 and eight years to maturity. It pays a coupon of 8% per annum on a semiannual basis. It is callable after five years, just after the tenth coupon is paid, and if called, one year's coupon is paid as a call premium. If the yield to maturity is 10% per annum, what is the yield to call? The first step is to compute the dirty price using the PV function in Excel. The parameters are RATE, NPER, PMT, and FV. RATE is the semiannual YTM, which is 5%; NPER is the number of semiannual periods until maturity, which is 16; PMT is the periodic coupon, which is \$40; and FV is the terminal cash flow, which is \$1,000:

The price = PV(0.05, 16, −40, −1000) = \$891.62

Given this information we can use the RATE function to determine the yield to call. The parameters are NPER, PMT, PV, and FV. The call price is 1,000 + 80 = \$1,080. Thus FV = (1,080). PV is the dirty price, which is $891.62. PMT is −40, and NPER is equal to 10, since the bond is callable after five years. Note that PMT and FV should have the same sign, whereas PV should have the opposite sign. This is because the first two are inflows for the bond holder, and the third is an outflow. Thus we need to invoke the RATE function as follows:

$$= \text{RATE}(10, -40, 891.62, -1080) * 2 = 12.1658\%$$

We need to multiply the answer by two because the RATE function gives the semiannual yield to call. This is because time is being measured in semiannual periods.

For a bond with multiple call dates, there is a yield to call for each such date. In Excel we can easily compute the yields to call for multiple call dates.

Relationship between the Yield to Call and the Yield to Maturity

Let's first consider a callable bond without a call premium. If the bond is trading at a discount, and we use a discount rate equal to the YTM, the price increases as we reduce the number of periods. As we saw in Chapter 2, this is because of the pull to par effect. For the price to remain the same, we need to use a higher discount rate. Thus the YTC will be higher than the YTM. If a call premium is applicable, the YTC will be even higher.

Now consider a bond trading at par. If there is no call premium, the yield to call is equal to the yield to maturity. If there is a call premium, however, the yield to call becomes greater than the YTM because of a larger terminal cash flow.

Finally let's consider a bond that is trading at a premium. First assume that there is no call premium. If we use a discount rate equal to the YTM, the price decreases as we reduce the number of periods. For the price to remain the same, we need to use a lower discount rate. Thus the YTC will be less than the YTM. However, if we build in a call premium, the result is ambiguous, for the YTC may be less than or greater than the YTM because the terminal cash flow used for computing the former is greater than that for the latter. Let's illustrate these concepts using Example 13.2.

Example 13.2. Consider a bond with eight years to maturity, a coupon of 8% per annum, paid semi-annually, and a YTM of 10% per annum. The face value is $1,000. The dirty price as obtained earlier is $891.62. If the bond is called after five years, and there is no call premium, the YTC is given by

$$= \text{RATE}(10, -40, 891.62, -1000) * 2 = 10.8664\%$$

If a call premium equal to one year's coupon is built in, the YTC is given by

$$= \text{RATE}(10, -40, 891.62, -1080) * 2 = 12.1658\%$$

Thus in both the cases the YTC is greater than the YTM.

Now assume the YTM is 8% per annum. The price is obviously $1,000. If the bond is called after five years, and there is no call premium:

$$= \text{RATE}(10, -40, 1000, -1000) * 2 = 8\%$$

Thus the YTC is equal to the YTM.

If a call premium equal to one year's coupon is built in, the YTC is given by

$$= \text{RATE}(10, -40, 1000, -1080) * 2 = 9.2932\%.$$

As is to be expected the YTC is greater than the YTM.

Finally assume the YTM is 6% per annum. The dirty price is $1,125.61. If the bond is called after five years, and there is no call premium, the YTC is given by:

$$= \text{RATE}(10, -40, 1125.61, -1000) * 2 = 5.1206\%.$$

Thus as expected the YTC is less than the YTM.

If a call premium equal to one year's coupon is built in, the rate is given by:

$$= \text{RATE}(10, -40, 1125.61, -1080) * 2 = 6.4069\%.$$

The YTC is higher than the YTM.

However what if the bond is called after three years.

$$= \text{RATE}(6, -40, 1125.61, -1080) * 2 = 5.8520\%.$$

Hence the YTC for premium bonds may be greater than or less than the YTM, if a call premium is built in, depending on the call date.

The Approximate Yield to Call Approach

The approximate yield to call may be defined as[1]

$$\text{AYC} = \frac{C + \frac{(M^* - P)}{N^*/2}}{(M^* + P)/2} \tag{13.3}$$

Example 13.3. Let's reconsider the data used in Example 13.1. That is, the time to maturity is eight years, the face value is $1,000, and the coupon is 8% per annum. The price as we demonstrated earlier is $891.62.

$$\text{AYC} = \frac{80 + (1{,}080 - 891.62)/5}{(1{,}080 + 891.62)/2} = 11.9370\%$$

Let's consider a higher value, namely 12.50%, and a lower value, 11.50%:

The price using a rate of 11.50% is = PV(0.0575, 10, −40, −1080) = $915.40.

The price using a rate of 12.50% is = PV(0.0625, 10, −40, −1080) = $879.97.

Now let's interpolate:

$$0.1150 - 0.1250 \equiv 915.40 - 879.97 \quad \text{and} \quad 0.1150 - X \equiv 915.40 - 891.62$$

$$\text{Thus } X = 0.1150 + 0.01 \times \frac{23.78}{35.43} = 12.1712\%$$

The exact value from the RATE function in Excel is 12.1658%. Thus the approximation is excellent.

---

1 M^* is the call price; N^* is the call date; C is the annual coupon, and P is the dirty price.

Reinvestment Assumption

The yield to maturity calculation is based on the assumption that the bond is held until maturity and all intermediate cash flows are reinvested at the yield to maturity. Similarly the yield to call is calculated based on the assumption that the bond is held until the call date and all the intermediate cash flows are reinvested at the yield to call. Example 13.4 demonstrates this.

Example 13.4. Consider the data used in Example 13.1. The dirty price is $891.62, the call price is $1,080, the periodic coupon is $40, and the call date is 10 semiannual periods away. Assume all intermediate cash flows can be reinvested at 12.1658% per annum. The future value of 10 coupons is given by:

$$= \mathrm{FV}(0.121658/2, 10, -40) = \$529.29$$

Thus the terminal cash flow is 529.29 + 1,080 = $1,609.29. As the initial investment is 891.62, the rate of return is given by

$$891.62 \times (1 + i)^{10} = 1{,}609.29 \Rightarrow i = 6.0829\%$$

which corresponds to an annual rate of 12.1658%. Thus in order to earn the yield to call corresponding to a particular call date, we need to hold the bond until the call date and reinvest all the intermediate cash flows at the yield to call.

Concept of the Yield to Worst

If a bond has a number of call dates, we can compute the yield to call for each call date, as well as the yield to maturity. The lowest of these values is termed the *Yield to Worst* (YTW). The problem with this measure is that it is a function of the bond price.

Consider a five-year bond that pays annual coupons at the rate of 6% per annum. The face value is $1,000. We assume that the bond is callable at the end of the first, second, third, or fourth year. If called after one year, $80 is paid as a call premium. Every subsequent call date the call premium is assumed to decline by $20. Let's consider three different price scenarios: a par bond, a discount bond with a dirty price of $880, and a premium bond with a dirty price of $1,120. The results are summarized in Table 13.1. All the results have been obtained using the RATE function in Excel.

As we can see, if the bond is trading at a discount, the yield to worst is 9.9025%, which corresponds to the YTM. The same is the case if the bond is trading at par. However if the bond is trading at a premium, the yield to worst is 1.7857%, which is the yield to call corresponding to the first call date.

Table 13.1: The yields for different price scenarios.

Time to Redemption	Redemption Price	Dirty Price 880 Yield	1,000 Yield	1,120 Yield
5	1,000	9.0925%	6.0000%	3.3533%
4	1,020	10.2343%	6.4541%	3.2303%
3	1,040	12.1962%	7.2413%	3.0473%
2	1,060	16.2758%	8.8726%	2.7144%
1	1,080	29.5455%	14.0000%	1.7857%

Valuation of a Callable Bond

Let's value a callable bond using the Ho-Lee and BDT interest rate trees that we obtained in Chapter 11. Let's first reproduce the Ho-Lee tree, and the corresponding state prices.

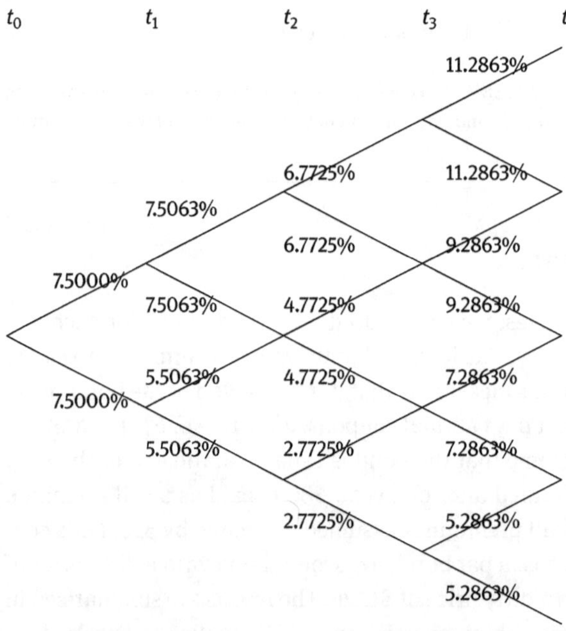

Figure 13.1: The Ho-Lee no-arbitrage interest rate tree.

The state price tree is shown in Figure 13.2.

Consider a four-period bond with a face value of $1,000 that pays a coupon of $40 every period. Using the state price tree obtained by calibrating the Ho-Lee model, we can compute the value of this bond as follows:

$$1{,}040 \times (0.053160 + 0.215741 + 0.328336 + 0.222092 + 0.056336)$$

t_0	t_1	t_2	t_3	t_4
				0.053160
			0.112320	
		0.232247		0.215741
	0.481928		0.340258	
1.0		0.466755		0.328336
	0.481928		0.343589	
		0.234508		0.222092
			0.115651	
				0.056336

Figure 13.2: State price tree.

$$+\ 40 \times (0.112320 + 0.340258 + 0.343589 + 0.115651)$$
$$+\ 40 \times (0.232247 + 0.466755 + 0.234508) + 40 \times (0.481928 + 0.481928)$$
$$= 1{,}040 \times 0.875665 + 40 \times 0.911818 + 40 \times 0.933511 + 40 \times 0.963856$$
$$= \$1{,}023.0589$$

Now assume that this bond is callable, and if called, a call premium of $40 is paid. At time t_4, the cash flow is 1,000 + 40 = $1,040. The value at t_3 node-1 is

$$\frac{1{,}040}{\left(1+\frac{0.112863}{2}\right)} + 40 = 984.4462 + 40 = \$1{,}024.4462$$

If the bond is called, the issuer has to pay 40 + 40 + 1,000 = $1,080. Thus the bond will not be recalled.

The value at node-2 is

$$\frac{1{,}040}{\left(1+\frac{0.092863}{2}\right)} + 40 = 993.8539 + 40 = \$1{,}033.8539$$

If the bond is called, the issuer has to pay $1,080. Thus the bond will not be recalled.

The value at node-3 is

$$\frac{1{,}040}{\left(1+\frac{0.072863}{2}\right)} + 40 = 1{,}003.4430 + 40 = \$1{,}043.4430$$

If the bond is called, the issuer has to pay $1,080. Thus the bond will not be recalled.

The value at node-4 is

$$\frac{1{,}040}{\left(1+\frac{0.052863}{2}\right)} + 40 = 1{,}013.2190 + 40 = \$1{,}053.2190$$

If the bond is called, the issuer has to pay $1,080. Thus the bond will not be recalled.

Now let's move to time t_2. The value at node-1 is

$$0.5 \times \frac{1{,}024.4462}{\left(1+\frac{0.067725}{2}\right)} + 0.5 \times \frac{1{,}033.8539}{\left(1+\frac{0.067725}{2}\right)} + 40 = 495.4461 + 499.9958 + 40$$

$$= \$1{,}035.4419$$

If the bond is called, the issuer has to pay \$1,080. Thus the bond will not be recalled.

The value at node-2 is

$$0.5 \times \frac{1{,}033.8539}{\left(1+\frac{0.047725}{2}\right)} + 0.5 \times \frac{1{,}043.4430}{\left(1+\frac{0.047725}{2}\right)} + 40 = 504.8793 + 509.5621 + 40$$

$$= \$1{,}054.4414$$

If the bond is called, the issuer has to pay \$1,080. Thus the bond will not be recalled.

The value at node-3 is

$$0.5 \times \frac{1{,}043.4430}{\left(1+\frac{0.027725}{2}\right)} + 0.5 \times \frac{1{,}053.2190}{\left(1+\frac{0.027725}{2}\right)} + 40 = 514.5880 + 519.4092 + 40$$

$$= \$1{,}073.9972$$

If the bond is called, the issuer has to pay \$1,080. Thus the bond will not be recalled.

Now let's move to time t_1. The value at node-1 is

$$0.5 \times \frac{1{,}035.4419}{\left(1+\frac{0.075063}{2}\right)} + 0.5 \times \frac{1{,}054.4414}{\left(1+\frac{0.075063}{2}\right)} + 40 = 498.9930 + 508.1491 + 40$$

$$= \$1{,}047.1421$$

If the bond is called, the issuer has to pay \$1,080. Thus the bond will not be recalled.

The value at node-2 is

$$0.5 \times \frac{1{,}054.4414}{\left(1+\frac{0.055063}{2}\right)} + 0.5 \times \frac{1{,}073.9972}{\left(1+\frac{0.055063}{2}\right)} + 40 = 513.0944 + 522.6104 + 40$$

$$= \$1{,}075.7048$$

If the bond is called, the issuer has to pay \$1,080. Thus the bond will not be recalled.

The value at time t_0 is

$$0.5 \times \frac{1{,}047.1421}{\left(1+\frac{0.075}{2}\right)} + 0.5 \times \frac{1{,}075.7048}{\left(1+\frac{0.075}{2}\right)} = 504.6468 + 518.4120$$

$$= \$1{,}023.0587$$

Since the bond is not recalled at any of the subsequent nodes, the value of the callable bond is equal to that of the plain vanilla bond. In other words, the call option has a value of zero.

Now let's increase the coupon to 10% per annum. The value of the plain vanilla bond is

$$\begin{aligned}&1{,}050 \times (0.053160 + 0.215741 + 0.328336 + 0.222092 + 0.056336)\\&\quad + 50 \times (0.112320 + 0.340258 + 0.343589 + 0.115651)\\&\quad + 50 \times (0.232247 + 0.466755 + 0.234508) + 50 \times (0.481928 + 0.481928)\\&= 1{,}050 \times 0.875665 + 50 \times 0.911818 + 50 \times 0.933511 + 50 \times 0.963856\\&= \$1{,}059.9075\end{aligned}$$

Now consider the callable bond. At time t_4, the cash flow is $1{,}000 + 50 = \$1{,}050$. The value at t_3 node-1 is

$$\frac{1{,}050}{\left(1 + \frac{0.112863}{2}\right)} + 50 = 993.9121 + 50 = \$1{,}043.9121$$

If the bond is called, the issuer has to pay $50 + 50 + 1{,}000 = \$1{,}100$. Thus the bond will not be recalled.

The value at node-2 is

$$\frac{1{,}050}{\left(1 + \frac{0.092863}{2}\right)} + 50 = 1{,}003.4101 + 50 = \$1{,}053.4101$$

If the bond is called, the issuer has to pay \$1,100. Thus the bond will not be recalled.

The value at node-3 is

$$\frac{1{,}050}{\left(1 + \frac{0.072863}{2}\right)} + 50 = 1{,}013.0915 + 50 = \$1{,}063.0915$$

If the bond is called, the issuer has to pay \$1,100. Thus the bond will not be recalled.

The value at node-4 is

$$\frac{1{,}050}{\left(1 + \frac{0.052863}{2}\right)} + 50 = 1{,}022.9615 + 50 = \$1{,}072.9615$$

If the bond is called, the issuer has to pay \$1,100. Thus the bond will not be recalled.

Now let's move to time t_2. The value at node-1 is

$$\begin{aligned}0.5 \times \frac{1{,}043.9121}{\left(1 + \frac{0.067725}{2}\right)} + 0.5 \times \frac{1{,}053.4101}{\left(1 + \frac{0.067725}{2}\right)} + 50 &= 504.8602 + 509.4538 + 50\\&= \$1{,}064.3140\end{aligned}$$

If the bond is called, the issuer has to pay \$1,100. Thus the bond will not be recalled.

The value at node-2 is

$$\begin{aligned}0.5 \times \frac{1{,}053.4101}{(1 + \frac{0.047725}{2})} + 0.5 \times \frac{1{,}063.0915}{(1 + \frac{0.047725}{2})} + 50 &= 514.4295 + 519.1574 + 50\\&= \$1{,}083.5869\end{aligned}$$

If the bond is called, the issuer will have to pay $1,100. Thus the bond will not be recalled.

The value at node-3 is

$$0.5 \times \frac{1{,}063.0915}{\left(1 + \frac{0.027725}{2}\right)} + 0.5 \times \frac{1{,}072.9615}{\left(1 + \frac{0.027725}{2}\right)} + 50 = 524.2779 + 529.1455 + 50$$

$$= \$1{,}103.4234$$

If the bond is called, the issuer has to pay $1,100. Thus the bond will be recalled, and the value will be $1,100.

Now let's move to time t_1. The value at node-1 is

$$0.5 \times \frac{1{,}064.3140}{\left(1 + \frac{0.075063}{2}\right)} + 0.5 \times \frac{1{,}083.5869}{\left(1 + \frac{0.075063}{2}\right)} + 50 = 512.9068 + 522.1947 + 50$$

$$= \$1{,}085.1015$$

If the bond is called, the issuer has to pay $1,100. Thus the bond will not be recalled.

The value at node-2 is

$$0.5 \times \frac{1{,}083.5869}{\left(1 + \frac{0.055063}{2}\right)} + 0.5 \times \frac{1{,}100.0000}{\left(1 + \frac{0.055063}{2}\right)} + 50 = 527.2767 + 535.2634 + 50$$

$$= \$1{,}112.5401$$

If the bond is called, the issuer will have to pay $1,100. Thus the bond will be recalled.

The value at time t_0 is

$$0.5 \times \frac{1{,}085.1015}{\left(1 + \frac{0.075}{2}\right)} + 0.5 \times \frac{1{,}100.0000}{\left(1 + \frac{0.075}{2}\right)} = 522.9405 + 530.1205$$

$$= \$1{,}053.0610$$

Because the value of the plain vanilla bond is $1,059.9075, the value of the call option inherent in the callable bond is

$$1{,}059.9075 - 1{,}053.0610 = \$6.8465$$

Putable Bonds

In the case of a putable bond, the holder has the option to turn in the bond prior to the scheduled maturity date. Being in possession of the option, the holder has to pay a premium for it. This shows up in the form of a higher price, compared to a plain vanilla bond, which is identical in all other respects except for the put feature. In practice, a party that is planning a bond issue can offer a lower coupon on the putable bond, as compared to an otherwise similar plain vanilla bond. If we compare a plain vanilla and a putable bond that are identical in all respects including the coupon, the putable will have a higher price or a lower yield to maturity.

Why does the putable bond have a higher price? The put option enables the holder to turn in the bond in a rising interest rate environment. If the issuer gets the bond back in such circumstances, it has to reissue new bonds with a higher coupon, as the market rates have increased. Thus the put option works in favor of the investor and against the issuer. Issuers are perfectly happy paying a lower coupon and do not want to reissue bonds with a higher coupon rate, which is a consequence of the investors exercising their put options. Thus issuers of putable bonds face uncertainty about the number of coupons they have to pay and the time when the principal has to be repaid. This too is a manifestation of *timing risk*.

If we denote the dirty price of the putable bond by P_{put}, the dirty price of the corresponding plain vanilla bond by P_{pv}, and the premium for the put option by P, we can state that

$$P_{put} = P_{pv} + P \tag{13.4}$$

Valuation of a Putable Bond

Consider a four-period bond with a face value of $1,000 that pays a coupon of $40 every period, and let's use the Ho-Lee tree to price it. The price of a plain vanilla bond, as shown earlier, is $1,023.0589. Now consider a bond that allows the holder to put back at par. Obviously a put option is exercised at a node only if the model value is lower than the price at which it can be put back.

At time t_4, the cash flow is 1,000 + 40 = $1,040. The value at t_3 node-1 is

$$\frac{1{,}040}{\left(1+\frac{0.112863}{2}\right)} + 40 = 984.4462 + 40 = \$1{,}024.4462$$

If the bond is put back, the issuer has to pay $1,040. Thus the bond will be put back by the investor.

The value at node-2 is

$$\frac{1{,}040}{\left(1+\frac{0.092863}{2}\right)} + 40 = 993.8539 + 40 = \$1{,}033.8539$$

If the bond is put back, the issuer has to pay $1,040. Thus the bond will be put back by the investor.

The value at node-3 is

$$\frac{1{,}040}{\left(1+\frac{0.072863}{2}\right)} + 40 = 1{,}003.4430 + 40 = \$1{,}043.4430$$

If the bond is put back, the issuer has to pay \$1,040. Thus the bond will not be put back by the investor.

The value at node-4 is

$$\frac{1{,}040}{\left(1+\frac{0.052863}{2}\right)}+40=1{,}013.2190+40=\$1{,}053.2190$$

If the bond is put back, the issuer has to pay \$1,040. Thus the bond will not be put back by the investor.

Now let's move to time t_2. The value at node-1 is

$$0.5\times\frac{1{,}040.0000}{\left(1+\frac{0.067725}{2}\right)}+0.5\times\frac{1{,}040.0000}{\left(1+\frac{0.067725}{2}\right)}+40=502.9682+502.9682+40$$
$$=\$1{,}045.9364$$

If the bond is put back, the issuer has to pay \$1,040. Thus the bond will not be put back.

The value at node-2 is

$$0.5\times\frac{1{,}040.0000}{\left(1+\frac{0.047725}{2}\right)}+0.5\times\frac{1{,}043.4430}{\left(1+\frac{0.047725}{2}\right)}+40=507.8807+509.5621+40$$
$$=\$1{,}057.4428$$

If the bond is put back, the issuer has to pay \$1,040. Thus the bond will not be put back.

The value at node-3 is

$$0.5\times\frac{1{,}043.443}{\left(1+\frac{0.027725}{2}\right)}+0.5\times\frac{1{,}053.2190}{\left(1+\frac{0.027725}{2}\right)}+40=514.5880+519.4092+40$$
$$=\$1{,}073.9972$$

If the bond is put back, the issuer has to pay \$1,040. Thus the bond will not be put back.

Now let's move to time t_1. The value at node-1 is

$$0.5\times\frac{1{,}045.9364}{\left(1+\frac{0.075063}{2}\right)}+0.5\times\frac{1{,}057.4428}{\left(1+\frac{0.075063}{2}\right)}+40=504.0504+509.5955+40$$
$$=\$1{,}053.6459$$

If the bond is put back, the issuer has to pay \$1,040. Thus the bond will not be put back.

The value at node-2 is

$$0.5\times\frac{1{,}057.4428}{\left(1+\frac{0.055063}{2}\right)}+0.5\times\frac{1{,}073.9972}{\left(1+\frac{0.055063}{2}\right)}+40=514.5549+522.6104+40$$
$$=\$1{,}077.1653$$

If the bond is put back, the issuer has have to pay \$1,040. Thus the bond will not be put back.

The value at time t_0 is

$$0.5 \times \frac{1{,}053.6459}{(1 + \frac{0.075}{2})} + 0.5 \times \frac{1{,}077.1653}{(1 + \frac{0.075}{2})} = 507.7812 + 519.1158 = \$1{,}026.8970$$

The price of the plain vanilla bond is \$1,023.0589. Thus the value of the put option is

$$P = 1{,}026.8970 - 1{,}023.0589 = \$3.8381$$

Pricing the Callable and Putable Bonds Using the BDT Model

Let's first reproduce the BDT interest rate tree.

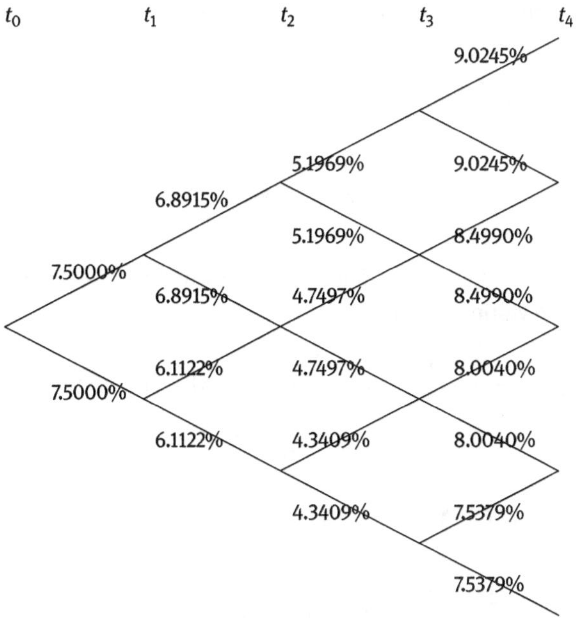

Figure 13.3: No-arbitrage interest rate tree for the BDT model.

Because both the Ho-Lee and BDT models have been calibrated using the same vector of spot rates, there is no difference in the prices of the plain vanilla bonds. However, the prices of the callable and putable bonds differ because the option premium is path dependent.

Let's first value the callable bond using the BDT tree. We once again consider the bond paying an annual coupon of 10%.

The Callable Bond and the BDT Model

At time t_4, the cash flow is 1,000 + 50 = \$1,050. The value at t_3 node-1 is

$$\frac{1{,}050}{(1+\frac{0.090245}{2})} + 50 = 1{,}004.6669 + 50 = \$1{,}054.6669$$

If the bond is called, the issuer has to pay 50 + 50 + 1,000 = \$1,100. Thus the bond will not be recalled.

The value at node-2 is

$$\frac{1{,}050}{(1+\frac{0.084990}{2})} + 50 = 1{,}007.1990 + 50 = \$1{,}057.1990$$

If the bond is called, the issuer has to pay \$1,100. Thus the bond will not be recalled.

The value at node-3 is

$$\frac{1{,}050}{(1+\frac{0.080040}{2})} + 50 = 1{,}009.5959 + 50 = \$1{,}059.5959$$

If the bond is called, the issuer has to pay \$1,100. Thus the bond will not be recalled.

The value at node-4 is

$$\frac{1{,}050}{(1+\frac{0.075379}{2})} + 50 = 1{,}011.8633 + 50 = \$1{,}061.8633$$

If the bond is called, the issuer has to pay \$1,100. Thus the bond will not be recalled.

Now let's move to time t_2. The value at node-1 is

$$0.5 \times \frac{1{,}054.6669}{\left(1+\frac{0.051969}{2}\right)} + 0.5 \times \frac{1{,}057.1990}{\left(1+\frac{0.051969}{2}\right)} + 50 = 513.9780 + 515.2120 + 50$$
$$= \$1{,}079.1900$$

If the bond is called, the issuer has to pay \$1,100. Thus the bond will not be recalled.

The value at node-2 is

$$0.5 \times \frac{1{,}057.1990}{(1+\frac{0.047497}{2})} + 0.5 \times \frac{1{,}059.5959}{(1+\frac{0.047497}{2})} + 50 = 516.3373 + 517.5079 + 50$$
$$= \$1{,}083.8452$$

If the bond is called, the issuer has to pay \$1,100. Thus the bond will not be recalled.

The value at node-3 is

$$0.5 \times \frac{1{,}059.5959}{(1+\frac{0.043409}{2})} + 0.5 \times \frac{1{,}061.8633}{(1+\frac{0.043409}{2})} + 50 = 518.5432 + 519.6528 + 50$$
$$= \$1{,}088.1960$$

If the bond is called, the issuer has to pay \$1,100. Thus the bond will not be recalled.

Now let's move to time t_1. The value at node-1 is

$$0.5 \times \frac{1{,}079.1900}{\left(1 + \frac{0.068915}{2}\right)} + 0.5 \times \frac{1{,}083.8452}{\left(1 + \frac{0.068915}{2}\right)} + 50 = 521.6212 + 523.8713 + 50$$
$$= \$1{,}095.4926$$

If the bond is called, the issuer has to pay \$1,100. Thus the bond will not be recalled.

The value at node-2 is

$$0.5 \times \frac{1{,}083.8452}{\left(1 + \frac{0.061122}{2}\right)} + 0.5 \times \frac{1{,}088.1960}{\left(1 + \frac{0.061122}{2}\right)} + 50 = 525.8520 + 527.9629 + 50$$
$$= \$1{,}103.8149$$

If the bond is called, the issuer has to pay \$1,100. Thus the bond will be recalled.

The value at time t_0 is:

$$0.5 \times \frac{1{,}095.4926}{\left(1 + \frac{0.075}{2}\right)} + 0.5 \times \frac{1{,}100.0000}{\left(1 + \frac{0.075}{2}\right)} = 527.9484 + 530.1205 = \$1{,}058.0689$$

Because the value of the plain vanilla bond is \$1,059.9075, the value of the call option inherent in the callable bond is

$$1{,}059.9075 - 1{,}058.0689 = \$1.8386$$

Valuation of the Putable Bond

Consider a four-period bond with a face value of \$1,000 that pays a coupon of \$40 every period, and let's use the BDT tree to price it. The price of a plain vanilla bond, as shown earlier, is \$1,023.0589.

At time t_4, the cash flow is 1,000 + 40 = \$1,040. The value at t_3 node-1 is

$$\frac{1{,}040}{\left(1 + \frac{0.090245}{2}\right)} + 40 = 995.0987 + 40 = \$1{,}035.0987$$

If the bond is put, the issuer has to pay \$1,040. Thus the bond will be put back by the investor.

The value at node-2 is

$$\frac{1{,}040}{\left(1 + \frac{0.084990}{2}\right)} + 40 = 997.6067 + 40 = \$1{,}037.6067$$

If the bond is put, the issuer has to pay \$1,040. Thus the bond will be put back by the investor.

The value at node-3 is

$$\frac{1{,}040}{\left(1+\frac{0.080040}{2}\right)}+40=999.9808+40=\$1{,}039.9808$$

If the bond is put, the issuer has to pay $1,040. Thus the bond will be put back by the investor.

The value at node-4 is

$$\frac{1{,}040}{\left(1+\frac{0.075379}{2}\right)}+40=1{,}002.2265+40=\$1{,}042.2265$$

If the bond is put, the issuer has to pay $1,040. Thus the bond will not be put back by the investor.

Now let's move to time t_2. The value at node-1 is

$$0.5\times\frac{1{,}040.0000}{\left(1+\frac{0.051969}{2}\right)}+0.5\times\frac{1{,}040.0000}{\left(1+\frac{0.051969}{2}\right)}+40=506.8303+506.8303+40$$
$$=\$1{,}053.6606$$

If the bond is put, the issuer has to pay $1,040. Thus the bond will not be put back.

The value at node-2 is

$$0.5\times\frac{1{,}040.0000}{\left(1+\frac{0.047497}{2}\right)}+0.5\times\frac{1{,}040.0000}{\left(1+\frac{0.047497}{2}\right)}+40=507.9373+507.9373+40$$
$$=\$1{,}055.8746$$

If the bond is put, the issuer has to pay $1,040. Thus the bond will not be put back.

The value at node-3 is

$$0.5\times\frac{1{,}040.0000}{\left(1+\frac{0.043409}{2}\right)}+0.5\times\frac{1{,}042.2265}{\left(1+\frac{0.043409}{2}\right)}+40=508.9534+510.0430+40$$
$$=\$1{,}058.9964$$

If the bond is put, the issuer has to pay $1,040. Thus the bond will not be put back.

Now let's move to time t_1. The value at node-1 is

$$0.5\times\frac{1{,}053.6606}{\left(1+\frac{0.068915}{2}\right)}+0.5\times\frac{1{,}055.8746}{\left(1+\frac{0.068915}{2}\right)}+40=509.2817+510.3519+40$$
$$=\$1{,}059.6336$$

If the bond is put, the issuer has to pay $1,040. Thus the bond will not be put back.

The value at node-2 is

$$0.5\times\frac{1{,}055.8746}{\left(1+\frac{0.061122}{2}\right)}+0.5\times\frac{1{,}058.9964}{\left(1+\frac{0.061122}{2}\right)}+40=512.2815+513.7961+40$$
$$=\$1{,}066.0776$$

If the bond is put, the issuer has to pay \$1,040. Thus the bond will not be put back.

The value at time t_0 is

$$0.5 \times \frac{1{,}059.6336}{(1+\frac{0.075}{2})} + 0.5 \times \frac{1{,}066.0776}{(1+\frac{0.075}{2})} = 510.6668 + 513.7723 = \$1{,}024.4391$$

The price of the plain vanilla bond is \$1,023.0589. Thus the value of the put option is

$$P = 1{,}024.4391 - 1{,}023.0589 = \$1.3802$$

Yield Spreads for Callable Bonds

There are different ways in which the yield of a callable bond can be compared with that of an equivalent plain vanilla bond. We study three such approaches in this section.

The Traditional Yield Spread

In this approach we compare the YTM of a plain vanilla bond, with that of the callable bond. Let's use the prices obtained using the Ho-Lee model. The price of the plain vanilla bond is \$1,059.9075, and that of the callable is \$1,053.0610. The periodic cash flow is \$50, and the face value is \$1,000. There are four periods until maturity. We use the RATE function in Excel to compute the YTMs.

$$= \text{RATE}(4, -50, 1059.9075, -1000) = 6.7478\%$$
$$= \text{RATE}(4, -50, 1053.0610, -1000) = 7.1071\%$$

Thus the yield spread is 7.1071 – 6.7478 = 0.3593%.

Similarly, we can find the yield spread for the putable bond, which has a coupon of \$40 per period. The YTM of the equivalent plain vanilla bond is

$$= \text{RATE}(4, -40, 1023.0589, -1000) = 6.7482\%$$

The YTM of the putable is given by

$$= \text{RATE}(4, -40, 1026.8970, -1000) = 6.5434\%$$

Thus the yield spread is 6.5434 – 6.7482 = –0.2048%.

The Static Spread

We saw earlier that the YTM of a plain vanilla bond is a complex average of the spot rates. Consequently, it is vulnerable to the coupon effect. In other words, two bonds with the same maturity, but different coupons, will have different YTMs, although the cash flows in both cases have been discounted using the same vector of spot rates.

The static spread on the other hand is based on the spot rates. It is obtained by adding a constant spread s to each element of the spot-rate vector. For a plain vanilla bond, the static spread is zero. Now let's compute the static spread for the callable bond with a periodic coupon of $50.

$$\frac{50}{\left(1+\frac{0.0750+s}{2}\right)}+\frac{50}{\left(1+\frac{0.0700+s}{2}\right)^2}+\frac{50}{\left(1+\frac{0.0625+s}{2}\right)^3}+\frac{1{,}050}{\left(1+\frac{0.0675+s}{2}\right)^4}=1{,}053.0610$$

Using Solver in Excel, $s = 0.3592\%$, which is exactly what we got for the yield spread.

Now let's consider the four-period putable bond with a price of $1,026.8970.

$$\frac{40}{\left(1+\frac{0.0750+s}{2}\right)}+\frac{40}{\left(1+\frac{0.0700+s}{2}\right)^2}+\frac{40}{\left(1+\frac{0.0625+s}{2}\right)^3}+\frac{1{,}040}{\left(1+\frac{0.0675+s}{2}\right)^4}=1{,}026.8970$$

Using Solver in Excel, $s = -0.2048\%$, which is again equal to the yield spread.

As we can see, for both the callable and the putable bond, the yield spread is the same as the static spread. This is not surprising because the respective YTMs for the two bonds are obtained from the same vector of spot rates.

The Option-Adjusted Spread

In this approach, we add a constant spread to each interest rate along the various paths. The spread is adjusted using a trial-and-error process, until the price obtained is equal to the market price of the bond. Let's illustrate this approach for the plain vanilla and the callable bond.

The Plain Vanilla Bond

Consider the bond with four periods to maturity, a face value of $1,000, and a coupon of 10% per annum. Let's use the Ho-Lee tree to illustrate our arguments and denote the unknown spread by s.

At time t_4, the cash flow is 1,000 + 50 = $1,050. The value at t_3 node-1 is

$$\frac{1{,}050}{\left(1+\frac{0.112863+s}{2}\right)}+50$$

The value at node-2 is

$$\frac{1{,}050}{\left(1+\frac{0.092863+s}{2}\right)}+50$$

The value at node-3 is

$$\frac{1{,}050}{\left(1+\frac{0.072863+s}{2}\right)}+50$$

The value at node-4 is

$$\frac{1{,}050}{\left(1+\frac{0.052863+s}{2}\right)}+50$$

Now let's move to time t_2. The value at node-1 is

$$0.5\times\left[\frac{\frac{1{,}050}{\left(1+\frac{0.112863+s}{2}\right)}+50}{\left(1+\frac{0.067725+s}{2}\right)}\right]+0.5\times\left[\frac{\frac{1{,}050}{\left(1+\frac{0.092863+s}{2}\right)}+50}{\left(1+\frac{0.067725+s}{2}\right)}\right]+50$$

The value at node-2 is

$$0.5\times\left[\frac{\frac{1{,}050}{\left(1+\frac{0.092863+s}{2}\right)}+50}{\left(1+\frac{0.047725+s}{2}\right)}\right]+0.5\times\left[\frac{\frac{1{,}050}{\left(1+\frac{0.072863+s}{2}\right)}+50}{\left(1+\frac{0.047725+s}{2}\right)}\right]+50$$

The value at node-3 is

$$0.5\times\left[\frac{\frac{1{,}050}{\left(1+\frac{0.072863+s}{2}\right)}+50}{\left(1+\frac{0.027725+s}{2}\right)}\right]+0.5\times\left[\frac{\frac{1{,}050}{\left(1+\frac{0.052863+s}{2}\right)}+50}{\left(1+\frac{0.027725+s}{2}\right)}\right]+50$$

Now let's move to time t_1. The value at node-1 is

$$\frac{0.5\times\left[0.5\times\left\{\frac{\frac{1{,}050}{\left(1+\frac{0.112863+s}{2}\right)}+50}{\left(1+\frac{0.067725+s}{2}\right)}\right\}+0.5\times\left\{\frac{\frac{1{,}050}{\left(1+\frac{0.092863+s}{2}\right)}+50}{\left(1+\frac{0.067725+s}{2}\right)}\right\}+50\right]}{\left(1+\frac{0.075063+s}{2}\right)}$$

$$+\frac{0.5\times\left[0.5\times\left\{\frac{\frac{1{,}050}{\left(1+\frac{0.092863+s}{2}\right)}+50}{\left(1+\frac{0.047725+s}{2}\right)}\right\}+0.5\times\left\{\frac{\frac{1{,}050}{\left(1+\frac{0.072863+s}{2}\right)}+50}{\left(1+\frac{0.047725+s}{2}\right)}\right\}+50\right]}{\left(1+\frac{0.075063+s}{2}\right)}+50$$

The value at node-2 is

$$\frac{0.5\times\left[0.5\times\left\{\frac{\frac{1{,}050}{\left(1+\frac{0.092863+s}{2}\right)}+50}{\left(1+\frac{0.047725+s}{2}\right)}\right\}+0.5\times\left\{\frac{\frac{1{,}050}{\left(1+\frac{0.072863+s}{2}\right)}+50}{\left(1+\frac{0.047725+s}{2}\right)}\right\}+50\right]}{\left(1+\frac{0.055063+s}{2}\right)}$$

$$+\frac{0.5\times\left[0.5\times\left\{\frac{\frac{1{,}050}{\left(1+\frac{0.072863+s}{2}\right)}+50}{\left(1+\frac{0.027725+s}{2}\right)}\right\}+0.5\times\left\{\frac{\frac{1{,}050}{\left(1+\frac{0.052863+s}{2}\right)}+50}{\left(1+\frac{0.027725+s}{2}\right)}\right\}+50\right]}{\left(1+\frac{0.055063+s}{2}\right)}+50$$

The value at time t_0 is

$$\frac{0.5\times 0.5\times\left[0.5\times\left\{\frac{\frac{1{,}050}{\left(1+\frac{0.112863+s}{2}\right)}+50}{\left(1+\frac{0.067725+s}{2}\right)}\right\}+0.5\times\left\{\frac{\frac{1{,}050}{\left(1+\frac{0.092863+s}{2}\right)}+50}{\left(1+\frac{0.067725+s}{2}\right)}\right\}+50\right]}{\left(1+\frac{0.075063+s}{2}\right)\times\left(1+\frac{0.075+s}{2}\right)}$$

$$+\frac{0.5\times 0.5\times\left[0.5\times\left\{\frac{\frac{1{,}050}{\left(1+\frac{0.092863+s}{2}\right)}+50}{\left(1+\frac{0.047725+s}{2}\right)}\right\}+0.5\times\left\{\frac{\frac{1{,}050}{\left(1+\frac{0.072863+s}{2}\right)}+50}{\left(1+\frac{0.047725+s}{2}\right)}\right\}+50\right]}{\left(1+\frac{0.075063+s}{2}\right)\times\left(1+\frac{0.075+s}{2}\right)}$$

$$+\frac{0.5\times 0.5\times\left[0.5\times\left\{\frac{\frac{1{,}050}{\left(1+\frac{0.092863+s}{2}\right)}+50}{\left(1+\frac{0.047725+s}{2}\right)}\right\}+0.5\times\left\{\frac{\frac{1{,}050}{\left(1+\frac{0.072863+s}{2}\right)}+50}{\left(1+\frac{0.047725+s}{2}\right)}\right\}+50\right]}{\left(1+\frac{0.055063+s}{2}\right)\times\left(1+\frac{0.075+s}{2}\right)}$$

$$+\frac{0.5\times 0.5\times\left[0.5\times\left\{\frac{\frac{1{,}050}{\left(1+\frac{0.072863+s}{2}\right)}+50}{\left(1+\frac{0.027725+s}{2}\right)}\right\}+0.5\times\left\{\frac{\frac{1{,}050}{\left(1+\frac{0.052863+s}{2}\right)}+50}{\left(1+\frac{0.027725+s}{2}\right)}\right\}+50\right]}{\left(1+\frac{0.055063+s}{2}\right)\times\left(1+\frac{0.075+s}{2}\right)}$$

$$+\frac{0.5\times 50}{\left(1+\frac{0.075+s}{2}\right)}+\frac{0.5\times 50}{\left(1+\frac{0.075+s}{2}\right)}=\$1{,}059.9075$$

Using Solver in Excel, we get a value of zero for s, the option-adjusted spread (OAS).

Now let's turn to the callable bond.

$$\frac{0.5\times 0.5\times\left[0.5\times\left\{\frac{\frac{1{,}050}{\left(1+\frac{0.112863+s}{2}\right)}+50}{\left(1+\frac{0.067725+s}{2}\right)}\right\}+0.5\times\left\{\frac{\frac{1{,}050}{\left(1+\frac{0.092863+s}{2}\right)}+50}{\left(1+\frac{0.067725+s}{2}\right)}\right\}+50\right]}{\left(1+\frac{0.075063+s}{2}\right)\times\left(1+\frac{0.075+s}{2}\right)}$$

$$+\frac{0.5\times 0.5\times\left[0.5\times\left\{\frac{\frac{1{,}050}{\left(1+\frac{0.092863+s}{2}\right)}+50}{\left(1+\frac{0.047725+s}{2}\right)}\right\}+0.5\times\left\{\frac{\frac{1{,}050}{\left(1+\frac{0.072863+s}{2}\right)}+50}{\left(1+\frac{0.047725+s}{2}\right)}\right\}+50\right]}{\left(1+\frac{0.075063+s}{2}\right)\times\left(1+\frac{0.075+s}{2}\right)}$$

$$+0.5\times\frac{1{,}100}{\left(1+\frac{0.075+s}{2}\right)}+0.5\times\frac{50}{\left(1+\frac{0.075+s}{2}\right)}=\$1{,}053.0610$$

Using Solver in Excel, we get a value of zero for s, the OAS.

Analysis of the Option-Adjusted Spread (OAS)

For both the plain vanilla bond and the callable bond, we find that the OAS is zero if the bonds are fairly priced. The OAS is used to measure the extent to which a bond is mispriced. A positive OAS indicates that the security is under-priced whereas a negative OAS indicates that it is overvalued. However, the issue in practice is that the spread may be non-zero due to mispricing, as well as due to misspecification of the valuation model. For instance, assume that the callable bond has been valued using the BDT model and the price has been determined to be $1,058.0689. If an analyst computes the OAS using this price and the BDT model, the result is a value of zero for it. However, what if the analyst chooses to use the Ho-Lee model? The result is a value of −0.5221%. In this case, the conclusion of a non-zero spread is because of model misspecification and not due to the mispricing of the bond.

Convertible Bonds

Convertible bonds, or convertibles, can be converted to equity shares at a prespecified conversion rate. Exchangeable bonds are structurally identical, but the identity of the bond issuer and that of the company whose shares are offered on conversion is not the same. Convertibles offer a lower coupon than plain vanilla debt with similar investment characteristics. The reduced coupon reflects the value of the inherent option to convert to shares of equity. A convertible bond may contain an event-risk clause. If such a covenant is present, the bond holders can demand immediate redemption in the event the issuing entity is taken over by another entity or merged with it. Such bonds also contain call and put options in practice, which can be used to enforce conversion.

The right to convert is an option given to the holder. It may be exercisable only on a particular date, which is akin to a European option; on one of several exercise dates, which is similar to a Bermudan option; or at any time in a specified interval, which is equivalent to an American option. The number of shares into which the bond can be converted is termed as the *conversion ratio* (CR). The ratio may be constant for the life of the bond, or else may vary over time. For instance, if the issuing company feels that its stock price will increase over time, it may issue a bond with a declining conversion ratio. In this case, the later the conversion option is exercised, the greater is the price paid per share. For instance, in the case of a bond with a face value of $1,000, the issuer may state that the bond can be converted into 40 shares if the option is exercised within three years, into 32 shares if exercise takes place between three and five years, and 25 shares if the exercise occurs after five years. The price per share at which the bond can be converted into equity is termed the *conversion price* (CP). In most cases the conversion price is higher than the prevailing stock price at the time of issue. Subsequently, the market price must at least reach this threshold before holders will contemplate conversion. The relationship between the conversion ratio and the conversion price may be stated as:

$$\text{Conversion Price} = \frac{\text{Redemption Value}}{\text{Conversion Ratio}}$$

Issuers first set the required conversion price and then determine the corresponding conversion ratio. For instance, in the case of a bond with a face value of $1,000, the issuer may fix the conversion price at \$25. This means that the conversion ratio is $\frac{1,000}{25} = 40$.

The current market value of the shares if the bond is converted is known as the *conversion value* or the *parity value*. For instance, if the conversion ratio is 40, and the prevailing share price is \$21.50, the parity value is $40 \times 21.50 = \$860$. The market price of a plain vanilla bond that is equivalent in all respects except for the conversion feature is termed the *straight value* of the bond. At any point in time, the price of the convertible bond must be greater than or equal to the higher of the parity value and the straight value to preclude arbitrage. Here is an illustration.

Example 13.5. Consider a convertible bond with a face value of \$1,000 and 10 years to maturity. The coupon is 8% per annum, payable semiannually. The bond is convertible into 40 shares of equity, which are currently priced at \$21.50 each. The YTM of a comparable plain vanilla bond is 10% per annum. The parity value is \$860. The straight value using Excel is = PV(0.05, 20, −40, −1000) = \$875.38. Because the straight value is higher than the parity value, the bond must trade for at least \$875.38 to preclude arbitrage. Thus if the price of the convertible is \$890, there is no arbitrage opportunity. Let's examine the consequences if this condition is violated.

Assume the market price of the convertible bond is below the parity value of \$860, for instance, \$845. An arbitrageur would buy 1,000 bonds by paying \$845,000 and immediately convert them into 40,000 shares, which can be sold at a price of \$21.50 each, to yield \$860,000. The difference of \$15,000 is clearly an arbitrage profit.

Now consider the situation where the price of the convertible is between the parity value and the straight value. Let's assume it is \$870. An arbitrageur would buy 1,000 convertible bonds and short 1,000 plain vanilla bonds. The initial cash flow is 875,380 − 870,000 = \$5,380. Every six months the convertible pays a coupon of \$40 per bond, which can be used to pay the coupon due on the bond that has been shorted. At the end, the face value that is received on redemption of the convertible bonds can be used to fulfill the payment obligation on account of the plain vanilla bonds that were shorted at the outset. Consequently the initial cash flow of \$5,380 does indeed represent an arbitrage profit.

Bonds are usually issued at their face value. At the time of issue, the difference between the face value of the convertible bond and the parity value is termed the *conversion premium* (CP). The premium is usually expressed as a percentage of the parity value. If the conversion value is \$860, the premium is 1,000 − 860 = \$140. This is usually expressed as

$$CP = \frac{140}{860} \times 100 \equiv 16.2790\%$$

The premium may also be stated as the difference between the conversion price and the current market price per share, divided by the current share price. In this case the conversion price is $\frac{1,000}{40} = 25$ and the share price is 21.50. Thus the premium is \$3.50. The premium in percentage terms is:

$$\frac{3.5}{21.50} \times 100 = 16.2790\%$$

Subsequently the premium is computed as the difference between the prevailing price of the convertible and the conversion value. This, too, is expressed as a percentage of the conversion value. For instance, assume that weeks after the issue, the convertible is trading at $1,040. The premium is

$$1{,}040 - 860 = \$180 \equiv \frac{180}{860} \times 100 = 20.93\%$$

Changes in the Conversion Ratio

The conversion ratio is changed if the underlying stock undergoes a split or a reverse split, or the issuer declares a stock dividend. A stock dividend is a dividend that is paid to the shareholders in the form of shares. That is, the company offers additional shares to the shareholders without requiring them to pay any money. The issue of such shares without any monetary consideration entails the transfer of funds from the reserves and surplus account on the balance sheet to the share capital account. Such a fund transfer is known as the *capitalization of reserves*.[2] From a theoretical standpoint, stock dividends do not create any value for the shareholders. The issue of additional shares, per se, does not lead to an increase in the asset base of the issuing entity, nor does it have any implications for the earnings capacity of the firm. Consequently, following a stock dividend the share price should theoretically decline. For instance, assume that a firm has issued 250,000 shares and the share price prior to the dividend announcement is $42 per share. If the firm announces a 20% stock dividend, there is an issue of an additional 50,000 shares, and there will be 300,000 shares outstanding after the dividends are paid. Considering that there is no change in the value of the firm, the ex-dividend price, P, should be such that

$$42 \times 250{,}000 = P \times 300{,}000$$
$$\Rightarrow P = \$35$$

Unlike stock dividends, which entail the capitalization of reserves, stock splits lead to a decrease in the par value of the shares, accompanied by a simultaneous increase in the number of shares outstanding. An n:1 stock split means that n new shares are issued to the existing shareholders in lieu of one existing share. Take the case of an 8:5 split. What this means is that the holder of five shares will have eight shares after the split. This is exactly analogous to a 60% stock dividend. Thus splits and stock dividends are mathematically equivalent. However, they are operationally different. Take the case of a company that has issued 250,000 shares with a par value of $100

2 In some markets, a stock dividend is termed as a *bonus share*, where the word "bonus" connotes that shareholders are being offered additional shares without having to make a monetary investment.

each. If it announces an 8:5 split, the number of shares issued increases to 400,000. However the par value declines to $62.50. The issued capital remains at $25,000,000. Because a split is equivalent to a stock dividend, the share price after a split behaves in the same way as it would after an equivalent stock dividend. Assume that an investor is holding 10,000 shares worth $42 each. The market value of the shares is $420,000. If the firm announces an 8:5 split, then the investor will have 16,000 shares after the split. Because the split is value neutral in theory, the post-split share price ought to be

$$\frac{420{,}000}{16{,}000} = \$26.25$$

A reverse split or a consolidation is similar to a split, with the difference being the following. In the case of an $n : m$ reverse split, n will be less than m. Take the case of an investor who is holding 10,000 shares with a market price of $42 per share. If the firm were to announce a 5:8 reverse split, the post-reverse split price ought to be

$$\frac{420{,}000}{6{,}250} = \$67.20$$

Now let's illustrate how the conversion price and the conversion ratio are adjusted for corporate actions such as splits/reverse splits and stock dividends.

Example 13.6. Consider a bond with a face value of $1,000 and a conversion ratio of 40. The conversion price is obviously $25. In the case of an $n : m$ split, the conversion ratio is multiplied by n/m, which implies that the conversion price is multiplied by m/n. For instance, if there is an 8:5 split, the conversion ratio becomes $(40 \times 8) \div 5 = 64$, and the corresponding conversion price is $(25 \times 5) \div 8 = \$15.625$. On the other hand, if there is a 5:8 reverse split, the conversion ratio becomes $(40 \times 5) \div 8 = 25$, and the corresponding conversion price is $(25 \times 8) \div 5 = \$40$. In the case of an $n : m$ stock dividend, the adjustment factor is $(n + m) \div m$. For instance, if there is a 3:2 stock dividend, the adjustment factor is $5/2 = 2.5$. The conversion ratio is multiplied by the factor, and the conversion price is divided by the factor. In our case the new ratio is $40 \times 2.5 = 100$, and the corresponding conversion price is $25 \div 2.5 = \$10$.

Convertible bonds often come with built-in call options. If the issuer invokes the option, it gives the holders some time to decide if they wish to convert. If they do not, the bonds are redeemed. The call option may be provisional or absolute. In the case of the former, there is a threshold price level for the share price. If this trigger is hit, then the call option can be invoked. However, if the call option is absolute, then there is no attached precondition.

These bonds also may have built-in put options. One such option is a *rolling premium put* option. Bonds with such an option, provide a bouquet of put options that enable the holder to redeem at a premium over the par value at dates spread out over time. The redemption price increases at each successive option exercise date. The presence of a call option in a convertible bond warrants a higher coupon. On the other hand, a rolling premium put, if incorporated, results in a bond with a lower coupon than a plain convertible. The rationale for an increasing premium is as follows. If the share price is not increasing at an attractive rate, the holder of a put may choose to redeem. However, the increasing premium in a rolling put acts as an incentive to stay invested. A consequence of an increasing premium is that, as each exercise date elapses, the share price has to rise even more to make conversion an attractive proposition. Assume for instance that the bond is issued at par with a conversion ratio of 40. Thus the original conversion price is $25. Assume that after *N* years the price at which it can be put is $1,200. The new conversion price is $30. If after another few years the price at which it can be put is $1,325, the corresponding conversion price becomes even higher at $33.1250.

Pros and Cons of a Convertible Issue: The Issuer's Perspective

Take the case of a company that is seeking to raise capital. If it is already listed, one alternative is a follow-on public offering (FPO). However, the issuer may or may not be able to command an attractive premium to the prevailing share price. Another alternative is a rights issue to existing shareholders. But such an issue has to be made at a discount to the prevailing market price. The issue of a convertible bond offers a third alternative. The conversion option enables the issue of an instrument with a lower coupon. And if the conversion price is set above the prevailing share price, the issuer can expect an attractive price per issued share if the conversion happens subsequently. The third option allows the issuer to take advantage of the tax deductible feature of interest on debt. Also, if the issuer resorts to a follow-on public offering or a rights issue, there is a dividend implication almost immediately, for the new shareholders would expect compensation by way of dividends. In contrast, if convertible bonds are issued, there would be a dividend implication only if the bonds are converted at a later date, by which time the issuer may be in a more comfortable financial position.

The negative feature of a convertible is that typically such bonds come with a put feature. If the share price does not appreciate adequately, holders may choose to exercise the put option rather than convert. And as can be appreciated, put options are exercised in a rising interest rate environment. As is the case with all putable bonds, the exercise of the inherent put option means that the issuer has to reissue fresh debt at a higher coupon rate.

Concept of Break-Even

The current yield of a convertible bond is usually higher than the dividend yield for investors who are holding the equity shares of the bond issuer. The *break-even period* of the bond is defined as the number of years it would take for the bond holder to recover the conversion premium out of the differential between the current yield and the dividend yield. Here is an example.

Example 13.7. Consider a convertible bond with a face value of $1,000 and a coupon of 8.16% per annum payable semiannually. The market price of the bond is $1,088. The current yield is

$$\frac{81.60}{1{,}088} = 7.50\%$$

The conversion ratio is 40. The current share price is $25. The dividend per share is $1.25. Thus the dividend yield is

$$\frac{1.25}{25} = 5.00\%$$

The conversion value of the bond is $40 \times 25 =$ $1,000. Thus the conversion premium is $88 or 8.8% of the conversion value. The break even is therefore:

$$\frac{0.088}{(0.075 - 0.0500)} = 3.52 \text{ years}$$

Liquid Yield Option Notes (LYONs)

These are essentially zero coupon bonds with a conversion feature. Consequently they can be redeemed at face value at maturity, assuming of course that they have not been converted earlier. The terms of conversion are usually set in such a way that there must be a significant appreciation in the share price to make conversion attractive. Thus in practice, redemption at maturity is more probable than conversion prior to it, and hence such bonds offer high yields to induce investors to invest. We can illustrate the mechanics of such a bond with the help of Example 13.8.

Example 13.8. Consider a zero coupon bond with a face value of $1,000 and eight years to maturity. Assume the YTM is 6% per annum. The price at the outset is given by

$$\frac{1{,}000}{(1.03)^{16}} = \$623.1669$$

The bond gives the holder the right to put after five years, at a price corresponding to an annual return of 6%. The corresponding price is therefore

$$623.1669 \times (1.03)^{10} = \$837.4842$$

Assume the current share price is $25 and the conversion price is $40. Thus the conversion ratio is

$$\frac{623.1669}{40} = 15.5792$$

At the end of five years the choices available to the holder are the following: surrender it for \$837.4842 or convert it into 15.5792 shares. For the conversion option to be attractive, the share price at the end of five years must be greater than

$$\frac{837.4842}{15.5792} = \$53.7566$$

Because the current share price is \$25, the required compounded average growth rate is

$$\left[\left(\frac{53.7566}{25}\right)^{1/10} - 1\right] \times 2 = 15.9132\%$$

Exchangeable Bonds

Exchangeable bonds are convertible bonds with a difference. In the case of a convertible bond, if the bonds have been issued by a company ABC, then the bond holders get shares of ABC if they choose to convert. However, if the bonds are exchangeable in nature, then the holders get the shares of another company XYZ. One possibility is that XYZ is a subsidiary of ABC. The other possibility is that ABC has taken a stake in XYZ at some stage and, instead of offloading the shares in the stock market at a future point in time, has chosen to link them with a bond issue in the form of an exchangeable bond. The provision of the conversion option allows the bonds to be issued with a lower coupon. Also, if the issuer has a significant stake in the other company, a stake sale at a subsequent date may lead to a depression in the share price, unless the market is buoyant enough to absorb the sale. The reduction in the stake by inducing the bond holders to convert can achieve the same objective without the specter of a significant share price decline. It must be noted that if a convertible bond is converted to a share of stock, there is a dilution of holding for the shareholders of the company that issued the bonds. However, if an exchangeable bond is converted, there is no dilution for shareholders of the firm that has chosen to issue these bonds.

Valuing a Convertible Bond with Built-in Call and Put Options

Consider a three-period convertible bond with a face value of \$1,000 and a coupon of 7% per annum. The bond can be called back by the issuer at the end of one period, or after two periods by paying six month's coupon as a call premium. We assume that each period is equivalent to six months. The bond also has a put option with a rolling premium. If put back after one period, the issuer pays \$20 as premium, whereas if it is put after two periods, it pays \$40 as premium. The conversion ratio is 25. The current stock price is \$40, and every period the stock may increase by 20% or decline by 20%. The riskless rate is 5% per period.

From our discussion on the binomial model of option pricing in Chapter 10, we know that the probability of an up move is[3]

$$\frac{(r-d)}{(u-d)} = \frac{(1.05-0.80)}{(1.20-0.80)} = 0.625$$

Thus the probability of a down move is 0.375.

The stock price tree is shown in Figure 13.4.

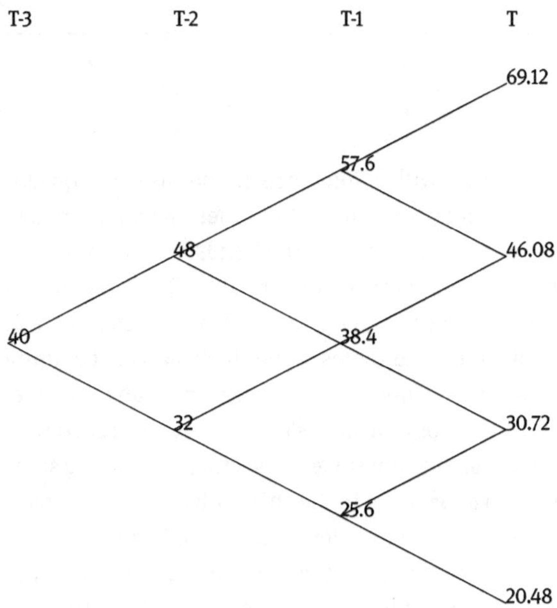

Figure 13.4: Stock price tree for the three-period case.

Let's examine the bond node-wise, starting with the point of maturity.

Consider node-1 at time T.

If the bond is converted, the shares are worth 25 × 69.12 = \$1,728. The cash flow including the coupon is \$1,763. The face value plus the coupon is \$1,035. Thus the bond will be converted, and the value will be \$1,763.

Now consider node-2 at time T.

If the bond is converted, the shares are worth 25 × 46.08 = \$1,152. The cash flow including the coupon is \$1,187. The face value plus the coupon is \$1,035. Thus the bond will be converted, and the value will be \$1,187.

3 u represents the magnitude of an up move, and d is the magnitude of a down move. r is one plus the periodic riskless rate.

Now consider node-3 at time T.

If the bond is converted, the shares are worth $25 \times 30.72 = \$768$. The cash flow including the coupon is \$803. The face value plus the coupon is \$1,035. Thus the value of the bond is \$1,035.

Finally consider node-4 at time T.

If the bond is converted, the shares are worth $25 \times 20.48 = \$512$. The cash flow including the coupon is \$547. The face value plus the coupon is \$1,035. Thus the value of the bond is \$1,035.

Now consider node-1 at time $T - 1$.

The model value is

$$0.625 \times \frac{1{,}763}{1.05} + 0.375 \times \frac{1{,}187}{1.05} = \$1{,}473.33$$

If we add the coupon, the value is \$1,508.33. If the bond is converted, the shares are worth $25 \times 57.60 = \$1{,}440$. The cash flow including the coupon is \$1,475. The amount payable if called is \$1,070. The amount payable if put is \$1,075. Because the model value is more than the amount payable if called, the issuer will call. In response, the investors will convert since they get more by doing so. The put option has no value in this scenario. Thus the value of the bond is \$1,475.

Now consider node-2 at time $T - 1$.

The model value is

$$0.625 \times \frac{1{,}187}{1.05} + 0.375 \times \frac{1{,}035}{1.05} = \$1{,}076.1904$$

If we add the coupon, the value is \$1,111.1904. If the bond is converted, the shares are worth $25 \times 38.40 = \$960$. The cash flow including the coupon is \$995. The amount payable if called is \$1,070. The amount payable if put is \$1,075. Because the model value is more than the call price, the issuer will exercise the call option. However, as the amount payable if called is more than what can be obtained by conversion, the bonds will not be converted; therefore, if the call option is invoked, the issuer has to pay \$1,070 to the bond holder. However, from the bond holder's perspective, the put option if exercised leads to a higher cash inflow than both the conversion and the call values. Thus the put option is valuable in this scenario, for the alternative is to surrender it for \$1,070, and the bond will therefore be put back. Thus the value of the bond is \$1,075.

Now consider node-3 at time $T - 1$.

The model value is

$$0.625 \times \frac{1{,}035}{1.05} + 0.375 \times \frac{1{,}035}{1.05} = \$985.7143$$

If we add the coupon, the value is \$1,020.7143. If the bond is converted, the shares are worth $25 \times 25.60 = \$640$. The cash flow including the coupon is \$675. The amount payable if called is \$1,070. The amount payable if put is \$1,075. Because the model value is less than the amount payable if called, the issuer will not exercise the call option. And, as the model value is greater than the conversion value, the bond holders will not convert. However, the put option will be exercised in this scenario, and thus the bond will be put back because the amount receivable is \$1,075 which is greater than the model value. Thus the value of the bond is \$1,075.

Now consider node-1 at time $T-2$. The model value is

$$0.625 \times \frac{1{,}475}{1.05} + 0.375 \times \frac{1{,}075}{1.05} = \$1{,}261.9047$$

If we add the coupon, the value is \$1,296.9047. If the bond is converted, the shares are worth $25 \times 48 = \$1{,}200$. The cash flow including the coupon is \$1,235. Because the model value is more than the amount payable if called, which is \$1,070, the issuer will exercise the call option. From the investor's perspective, the value of the shares is higher than the return from surrendering the bond. Thus the investors will convert. The put option has no value in this scenario, for the investors stand to receive only \$1,055. Thus the value of the bond is \$1,235.

Let's now consider node-2 at time $T-2$. The model value is

$$0.625 \times \frac{1{,}075}{1.05} + 0.375 \times \frac{1{,}075}{1.05} = \$1{,}023.8095$$

If we add the coupon, the value is \$1,058.8095. If the bond is converted, the shares are worth $25 \times 32 = \$800$. The cash flow including the coupon is \$835. The amount payable if called is \$1,070, which is more than the model value. Thus, the issuer will not exercise the call option. The put has no value in this case because it results in an inflow of only \$1,055 if exercised, which is less than the model value of \$1,058.8095. Thus the value of the bond is \$1,058.8095.

Finally let's move to time $T-3$. The model value is

$$0.625 \times \frac{1{,}235}{1.05} + 0.375 \times \frac{1{,}058.8095}{1.05} = \$1{,}113.2652$$

Thus this convertible bond, with built-in call and put options, has a price of \$1,113.2652 at the outset based on the assumptions made.

Chapter Summary

In this chapter, we studied bonds with built-in options, such as callable bonds, putable bonds, and convertible bonds. We examined the yield to call and its relationship with the yield to maturity, for callable bonds. We used the short rates obtained by the Ho-Lee model, as well as the BDT model, to value these bonds. In this context we studied the yield differences between plain vanilla bonds and bonds with call or put options, using the concepts of the yield spread, the static spread, and the option-adjusted spread (OAS). Although the static spread is equal to the yield spread, the option-adjusted spread of a bond is zero if the bond is fairly priced. However, the presence of a non-zero spread need not imply that the bond is mispriced. For model misspecification could lead to a similar conclusion. The chapter concludes with a detailed study of convertible bonds. We examined the valuation of a convertible bond using the binomial model for the evolution of the underlying stock price and incorporated call and put options to make the analysis more realistic.

Chapter 14
Interest Rate Swaps and Credit Default Swaps

Swaps are a popular form of OTC derivative instruments. What is a swap? As the name connotes, it is a contract to exchange or swap two cash flows. It is an exchange between two parties of two payment streams that are different from each other. In the case of an *interest rate swap* (IRS), the contract requires the specification of a principal amount termed the *notional principal*, for it is not meant to be exchanged, but has been specified purely to facilitate the computation of interest. Each of the two counterparties use a different benchmark for computing the interest on the specified notional principal. For instance, one party may use a fixed rate of interest, whereas another may use a variable rate such as the three-month LIBOR. This is referred to as a *coupon swap*. The alternative is a contract, where both the parties use variable rates to compute their respective obligations. This is referred to as a *basis swap*. After the obligations have been determined, the party owing the higher amount pays the difference between the two computed amounts to the counterparty. This is termed as *netting*. Netting is feasible because both cash flow streams are denominated in the same currency. Had they been in two different currencies, this kind of netting would not be feasible. In this chapter, we do not consider currency swaps, which entail the exchange of cash flows in different currencies.

Although coupon and basis swaps are possible, a contract which requires both the parties to pay a fixed rate is not feasible. This is because the party that is required to pay the higher rate would be paying constantly, and the counterparty would be receiving constantly. This is clearly a manifestation of arbitrage, and consequently the party that is required to pay a higher rate will never accept such an arrangement. In an interest rate swap, whether it is a coupon swap or a basis swap, we do not know a priori, which of the two counterparties will have to make a payment, and correspondingly the identity of the receiver is unknown at the outset.

Interest Rate Swaps

We will now define briefly the various terms that need to be incorporated into a swap contract.

Contract Terms

The following terms must be explicitly stated while designing an interest rate swap contract:
- The identities of the two counterparties.

https://doi.org/10.1515/9781547400669-014

- The maturity of the swap. This is the date on which the last exchange of cash flows takes place between the two parties.
- The interest rate used by the first party to calculate its payments. It may be fixed or floating.
- The interest rate used by the second party to calculate its payments. It must be floating if the first party is making payments based on a fixed rate of interest.
- The day-count convention for the computation of interest.
- The frequency of payment
- The notional principal

Example 14.1. Consider a four-year fixed-floating swap between Scotia Bank and Dominion Bank. Scotia will make payments based on an annual rate of 5%. Dominion will compute its liability based on the six-month LIBOR. We assume that every month consists of 30 days and that the year as a whole consists of 360 days. The implication is that every semiannual period consists of 180 days, and consequently the interest rate per semiannual period is one half of the annual rate. Other day-count conventions such as Actual/Actual or Actual/360 are possible. In such cases, the amount payable by the fixed rate payer varies from period to period, even though the interest rate remains constant, because the number of days per semiannual period varies. The exchange of payments takes place on a semiannual basis. The notional principal amount is $8 million.

Assume that the six-month LIBOR, as observed at semiannual intervals over the next four years, is as shown in Table 14.1.

Table 14.1: Observed values of LIBOR.

Time	LIBOR
0	5.25%
After 6 Months	5.40%
After 12 Months	5.10%
After 18 Months	4.75%
After 24 Months	4.30%
After 30 Months	4.00%
After 36 Months	4.80%
After 42 Months	5.20%

Using this data, let's compute the payments to be made by the two parties every six months. Let's analyze the cash flows to be exchanged after six months. Scotia has to pay $200,000 every six months. This may be calculated as follows:

$$0.5 \times 0.05 \times 8{,}000{,}000 = \$200{,}000$$

This amount remains constant every period. If, however, we assume an Actual/360 day-count convention and that the actual number of days in the period is 184 days, the amount payable becomes

$$\frac{184}{360} \times 0.05 \times 8{,}000{,}000 = \$204{,}444.44$$

In the following period, if the number of days is assumed to be 181, the amount payable is

$$\frac{181}{360} \times 0.05 \times 8{,}000{,}000 = \$201{,}111.11$$

At the end of six months, Dominion has to pay

$$0.5 \times 0.0525 \times 8{,}000{,}000 = \$210{,}000$$

Because Scotia owes $200,000 and Dominion owes $210,000, Dominion pays the difference of $10,000 to Scotia. In the following period, Scotia once again owes $200,000. But the amount owed by Dominion is

$$0.5 \times 0.0540 \times 8{,}000{,}000 = \$216{,}000$$

Consequently Dominion has to pay $16,000 to Scotia.

The cash flows made by the two counterparties and the net cash flow are shown in Table 14.2.

Table 14.2: Cash flows in an interest rate swap.

Time	Payment by Scotia	LIBOR	Payment by Dominion	Net Payment
Zero	–	5.25%	–	–
6 Month	$200,000	5.40%	$210,000	$(10,000)
12 Month	$200,000	5.10%	$216,000	$(16,000)
18 Month	$200,000	4.75%	$204,000	$(4,000)
24 Month	$200,000	4.30%	$190,000	$10,000
30 Month	$200,000	4.00%	$172,000	$28,000
36 Month	$200,000	4.80%	$160,000	$40,000
42 Month	$200,000	5.20%	$192,000	$8,000
48 Month	$200,000		$208,000	$(8,000)
TOTAL	$1,600,000		$1,552,000	$48,000

The payments that are made by Dominion are based on the LIBOR that is observed at the start of the period concerned. However, the interest itself is payable at the end of the period. For instance, the payment made by Dominion at the end of the first period is based on a interest rate of 5.25%, which corresponds to the LIBOR at the start of the period. This system of computation is known as *determined in advance and paid in arrears* and is the most commonly used system in practice.

The last column of Table 14.2 shows the net payment. Positive entries connote that Scotia has to pay the counterparty, whereas negative amounts indicate that the counterparty has to pay Scotia. The advantage of netting is that it reduces delivery risk. For instance, if Scotia pays the gross amount it owes to Dominion at the end of the first six months, it is exposed to the risk that the payment of $210,000 owed by Dominion may never arrive. On the contrary, because of netting, the risk for Scotia in this case is only the sum of $10,000 that would not be received if Dominion were to renege.

In a swap contract, certain terms and conditions need to be specified at the very outset to avoid ambiguities and potential future conflicts. Every swap contract must clearly spell out the identities of the two counterparties to the deal. In our example, the two counterparties are Scotia Bank and Dominion Bank.

Second, the tenor of the swap must be clearly stated. The tenor or maturity of the swap refers to the length of time at the end of which the last exchange of cash flows between the two parties takes place. In our example, the tenor is four years. Unlike exchange-traded products like futures contracts, where the exchange specifies a maximum maturity for contracts on an asset, swaps are OTC products that can have any maturity that is agreed upon by bilateral discussions.

Third, the interest rates on the basis of which the two parties have to make payments should be clearly spelled out. To avoid ambiguities, the basis on which the cash inflow and cash outflow are arrived at for both the counterparties should be explicitly stated. In our example, Scotia Bank is a fixed rate payer with the rate of interest being fixed at 5.00% per annum, whereas Dominion Bank is a floating rate payer with the amount payable being based on the six-month LIBOR prevalent at the start of the interest computation period.

Fourth, the frequency with which the cash flows are to be exchanged has to be clearly defined. In our example, we have assumed that cash flow exchanges will take place at six-monthly intervals. In the market such swaps are referred to as *semi-semi swaps*. Other contracts may entail payments on a quarterly basis or on an annual basis. The benchmark that is chosen for the floating rate payment is usually based on the frequency of the exchange. For instance a swap entailing the exchange of cash flows at six-monthly intervals will specify six-month LIBOR as the benchmark, whereas a swap entailing the exchange of payments at three-monthly intervals will specify the three-month LIBOR as the benchmark. The most popular benchmark in the market is the six-month LIBOR.

Fifth, the day-count convention that is used to compute the interest must be explicitly stated. In our illustration we have assumed that every six-month period amounts to exactly one-half of a year. The underlying convention is referred to as 30/360. That is every month is assumed to consist of 30 days while the year as a whole is assumed to consist of 360 days.

Finally, the principal amounts on the basis on which each party has to figure out the payment to the counterparty have to be clearly stated. In the case of interest rate swaps, there is obviously only one currency that is involved. However, the magnitude of the principal has to be specified to facilitate the computation of interest. In our example, the principal is $8 million.

In a coupon swap, the party that agrees to make payments based on a fixed rate is referred to as the *payer*. The counterparty, which is committed to making payments on a floating rate basis, is referred to as the *receiver*. Quite obviously these terms cannot be used in the case of basis swaps because both the cash flow streams are determined based on floating rates. Consequently, in order to be explicit and avoid ambiguities, it is a good practice to describe for each of the two parties, the rates at which they are scheduled to make and receive payments. Thus in the preceding example, we would state that Scotia is scheduled to pay a fixed rate of 5% and receive the six-month LIBOR, whereas Dominion is scheduled to pay the six-month LIBOR and receive a payment based on an interest rate of 5% in return. In the case of coupon swaps, some markets refer to the fixed rate payer as the *buyer* and the fixed rate receiver as the *receiver*.

The payments in a swap may be settled either on a money-market basis or on a bond-market basis, the difference being that the first convention is based on a 360-day year and an Actual/360 day-count convention, and the second is based on a 365-day year and an Actual/365 day-count convention. In practice, the fixed rates payable are quoted on a bond basis, and floating rates are quoted on a money-market basis. To convert from a bond basis to a money-market basis, we have to multiply the quote by 360/365; whereas to do the reverse, we multiply by 365/360.

Key Dates in a Swap Contract

There are four important dates that have to be specified in a swap contract. Consider the four-year swap between Scotia Bank and Dominion Bank. Assume that the swap was negotiated on 15 June 20XX with a specification that the first payments are for a six-month period commencing on 1 July 20XX. 15 June is referred to as the *transaction date*. The date from which the interest counter payments start to accrue is termed the *effective date*. In our example, the effective date is 1 July.

Our swap, by assumption, has a tenor of four years and consequently the last exchange of payments take place on 30 June 20XX+4. This date consequently is referred to as the *maturity date* of the swap. We assume that the eight cash-flow exchanges will occur on 31 December and 30 June of every year. The first seven dates, on which the floating rate will be reset for the next six-monthly period, are referred to as *reset* or *re-fixing dates*.

The Swap Rate

The fixed rate of interest that has been agreed upon in a coupon swap is referred to as the *swap rate*. If the swap rate is quoted as a percentage, it is referred to as an *all-in price*. However, in certain interbank markets, the fixed rate is not quoted as a percentage. Instead, what is quoted is the difference, in basis points, between the agreed upon fixed rate and a benchmark interest rate. The benchmark chosen to compute this differential is usually the government security whose remaining term to maturity is closest to the life of the swap in question. For instance, in the case of the Scotia-Dominion swap, the fixed rate is 5% per annum. If the swap rate were quoted as an all-in price, it would obviously be reported as such. However, in the second convention, the rate would be quoted as follows. Assume that a four-year T-note has a yield to maturity of 4.80%. The swap price is then quoted as 5% minus 4.80% or as 20 basis points.

Risk

Whether it is a coupon swap or a basis swap, an interest rate swap exposes both the parties to interest rate risk. In the case of Scotia, which is the fixed rate payer in this case, the risk is that the LIBOR may decline during the life of the swap. If so, the payments due to Scotia may stand reduced, whereas the payments to be made by it are invariant to interest rate changes. On the other hand, the risk for Dominion, the floating rate payer, is that the LIBOR may increase over the life of the swap. If so, Dominion's payment amounts will increase, whereas the payments it is due to receive will be invariant to rate changes. The same is true in the case of a basis swap. Assume one party pays Rate-1 and the other pays Rate-2, where both the rates are variable. The risk scenarios for the party paying Rate-1 are that the increase in Rate-1 is more than the increase in Rate-2, the decline in Rate-1 less than the decline in Rate-2, or Rate-1 increases and Rate-2 declines. For the counterparty, the situation is just the opposite. That is, the increase in Rate-2 is more than the increase in Rate-1, the decrease in Rate-2 is less than the decrease in Rate-1, or Rate-2 increases and Rate-1 declines. Also, in every swap, both the counterparties are exposed to default risk.

Quoted Swap Rates

A swap dealer quotes two rates for a coupon swap, a *bid* and an *ask*. The bid is the fixed rate at which the dealer is willing to do a swap that requires it to pay the fixed rate, and the ask represents the rate at which the dealer will do a swap that requires it to receive the fixed rate. The bid will be lower than the ask.

Consider the hypothetical quotes for US dollar-denominated interest rate swaps on a given day, shown in Table 14.3. Assume that the corresponding floating rate is the six-month LIBOR.

We have assumed a spread of 5 bp for all tenors, to make matters simple. Let's consider the rates for a 1-year swap. The bid is 3.70%, and the ask is 3.75%. Thus if the dealer does a swap where it has to make a fixed rate payment in return for a cash flow based on a floating rate, it agrees to pay 3.70% per annum. However, if the dealer is asked to do a swap wherein it receives the fixed rate in exchange for a floating rate, it asks for a rate of 3.75% per annum. Equivalently, if the dealer pays the fixed rate in a coupon swap, it pays 20 bp over the prevailing rate on a one-year Treasury security,

Table 14.3: All-in prices and spreads for swaps.

Tenor	All-in Prices		Spread over Treasury	
	Bid	Ask	Bid	Ask
1-Year	3.70%	3.75%	20 bp	25 bp
2-Year	3.90%	3.95%	15 bp	20 bp
3-Year	3.25%	3.30%	25 bp	30 bp
5-Year	2.90%	2.95%	15 bp	20 bp
10-Year	3.45%	3.50%	20 bp	25 bp

whereas if it receives the fixed rate, it demands a spread of 25 bp over the yield on a comparable Treasury security.

Comparative Advantage and Credit Arbitrage

There could be situations where a party has a disadvantage from the standpoint of borrowing rates with respect to another party in the markets for fixed rate as well as for variable rate loans. However, despite this, the former may have a comparative advantage in one of the two markets, as the following example illustrates.

Example 14.2. A company called Mount Holly, can borrow at a fixed rate of 5.25% and a variable rate of LIBOR + 1% in the US debt market. On the other hand, another company, Checkmate, can borrow at 4.90% in the fixed rate market and LIBOR + 25 bp in the variable rate market. Thus Mount Holly has to pay 35 bp more than Checkmate does if it borrows in the fixed rate market. However, it has to pay 75 basis points more if it borrows on a floating rate basis. Because Checkmate can get funds at a lower rate in both the markets, we say that it enjoys an absolute advantage in both markets compared to Mount Holly. However, because the spread for Mount Holly is lower in the fixed rate market, compared to the floating rate market, we say that Mount Holly enjoys a comparative advantage in the fixed rate market.

Assume that Mount Holly wants to borrow at a floating rate, whereas Checkmate would like to borrow at a fixed rate. However, if Mount Holly borrows in the fixed rate market, an arena where it has a comparative advantage, and then swaps the interest payments with Checkmate, it could be a win-win situation for both the entities. In other words, as a consequence of the swap, both the parties can borrow at a reduced rate of interest compared to what they would have had to pay in the absence of it.

Let's assume that Mount Holly borrows $10 million at a fixed rate of 5.25% per annum, and Checkmate borrows the same amount at LIBOR + 25 bp. The two parties can then enter into a swap wherein the former agrees to pay interest on a notional principal of $10 million at the rate of LIBOR + 40 bp per annum in exchange for a fixed rate payment based on a rate of 4.90% from the latter. The effective interest rate for the two parties may be computed as follows:

Mount Holly: 5.25% + LIBOR + 40 bp – 4.90% = LIBOR + 75 bp

Checkmate: LIBOR + 25 bp + 4.90% – LIBOR – 40 bp = 4.75%

Mount Holly has a saving of 25 basis points on the floating rate debt, and Checkmate has a saving of 15 bp on the fixed rate debt. Checkmate has an advantage of 75 bp in the market for floating rate debt and 35 bp in the market for fixed rate debt. The difference of 40 bp manifests itself as the savings for both parties considered together. In our illustration, Mount Holly has saved 25 bp, and the counterparty has saved 15 bp, which adds up to 40 basis points. In practice, we can have any pair of numbers, as long as the sum total is 40 bp.

In practice, a swap dealer such as a commercial bank plays a role in the transaction. Assume that Mount Holly borrows at 5.25% per annum and enters into a swap with Scotia Bank wherein it has to pay LIBOR + 55 bp in return for a fixed-rate payment based on a rate of 5.00%. Checkmate on the other hand borrows at LIBOR + 25 bp and enters into a swap with the same bank wherein in receives LIBOR + 20 bp in return for payment of 4.80%.

The net result of the transaction may be summarized as follows:

Mount Holly: Effective interest paid = 5.25% + LIBOR + 55 bp − 5.00 = LIBOR + 80 bp

Checkmate: Effective interest paid = LIBOR + 25 bp + 4.80% − LIBOR − 20 bp = 4.85%

Scotia Bank: Profit from the transaction = LIBOR + 55 bp − 5.00 − LIBOR − 20 bp + 4.80 = 15 bp

The difference in this case is that the comparative advantage of 40 basis points has been split three ways. Mount Holly saves 20 basis points; Checkmate saves 5 basis points; and the bank makes a profit of 15 basis points.

The Role of Banks in the Swap Market

When the swap market was at its nascent stage the normal practice was for investment banks to play the role of an intermediary. These banks would arrange the transaction by bringing together two counterparties and in return would be paid an arrangement fee. Over a period of time, the role of an intermediary evolved from that of an agent that facilitated a swap to that of a principal. One of the main reasons for this was that parties to swaps did not want their identities to be revealed to the counterparty. Second, as we have seen, swaps expose both counterparties to default risk. For this reason, parties to a swap were more comfortable dealing with a bank, whose creditworthiness was easier to appraise. As the market has evolved, such arrangement fees have become extremely rare except perhaps for contracts that are very exotic or unusual.

In the days when the market was at its infancy, banks would primarily do *reversals*. A reversal entails the offsetting of a swap with a counter agreement with another client. For instance, they would do a fixed-floating deal with a party only if they were hopeful of immediately concluding a floating-fixed deal for the same tenor with a third party. Parties that carry equal and offsetting swaps in their books are said to be running a *matched book*. These days banks are less finicky about maintaining such a matched position, and in most cases are willing to take on the inherent exposure until they eventually locate a party for an offsetting transaction. It must be understood that a dealer that maintains a matched book is exposed to default risk from both the parties with which it has entered into swaps.

Valuing an Interest Rate Swap

In our illustration of a swap between Scotia Bank and Dominion Bank, we arbitrarily assumed that the fixed rate or swap rate was 5% per annum. We now demonstrate how this rate is determined in practice.

Consider a two-year swap between Bank Alpha and Bank Beta. Bank Alpha has to pay a fixed rate of $k\%$ per annum on a semiannual basis, whereas the counterparty has to pay the six-month LIBOR every six months. As an alternative, assume that instead of entering into a swap, Bank Alpha has issued a two-year fixed rate note with a principal of \$8 million on which it has to make semiannual interest payments at the rate of $k\%$ per annum. This money has been used to acquire a two-year floating rate note with the same principal, and which pays coupons semiannually based on the LIBOR observed at the start of the six-monthly period.

If we look at the cash flows of this alternate arrangement, the result is equivalent to that on a two-year fixed-floating swap. At the outset there is an inflow of \$8 million for Bank Alpha when the fixed rate note is issued. But this amount is just adequate to purchase the floating-rate loan. Thus the net cash flow is zero. Similarly, at the point of termination, that is after two years, Bank Alpha receives \$8 million when the floating rate note matures, and this amount also is just adequate to retire the fixed rate note. The net result is that there is no exchange of principal, either at the outset or at the end, which is consistent with what we have seen for interest rate swaps.

Every six months, the floating rate note pays a coupon based on the LIBOR at the start of the period. Bank Alpha receives this amount and is required to pay interest at the rate of $k\%$ per annum to service the fixed rate note that it has issued. Consequently the cash flows every six months are identical to that of the swap. Thus a long position in a floating rate note coupled with a short position in a fixed rate note is equivalent to a swap that requires fixed-rate payments in return for payments based on a floating rate. Now let's demonstrate as to how the fixed rate of a coupon swap can be determined.

Let's use the same vector of spot rates that we used to calibrate the Ho-Lee and BDT models in Chapter 11.

Table 14.4: Vector of spot rates.

Period	Spot Rate
0	7.50%
1	7.00%
2	6.25%
3	6.75%

Because, by assumption, the current point in time is the start of the next six-monthly period, the price of the two-year floating rate note is equal to its face value of \$8 million. For, on a coupon reset date, the price of a default risk-free floating rate bond reverts to its face value. The question to be answered is what the coupon rate should be for the fixed rate note so that it too has a current price of \$8 million. Let's first determine the discount factors corresponding to the observed LIBOR rates.

The discount factor for a given maturity is the present value of a dollar to be received at the end of the stated period. The convention in the LIBOR market is that if the number of days for which the rate is quoted is N, then the corresponding discount factor is given by $\frac{1}{(1+i\times\frac{N}{360})}$. For instance, the discount factor for an investment of 18 months is $\frac{1}{(1+i\times\frac{540}{360})}$ where i is obviously the quoted 18-month LIBOR. Table 14.5 shows the vector of discount factors for our example.

Table 14.5: Discount factors.

Time to Maturity	Discount Factor
6M	0.9639
12M	0.9346
18M	0.9143
24M	0.8811

If we denote the semiannual coupon by $\frac{C}{2}$, it must be that

$$\frac{C}{2}\times 0.9639+\frac{C}{2}\times 0.9346+\frac{C}{2}\times 0.9143+\left[\frac{C}{2}+8{,}000{,}000\right]\times 0.8811$$
$$=8{,}000{,}000 \Rightarrow 3.6939\times\frac{C}{2}=951{,}200 \Rightarrow \frac{C}{2}=257{,}505.61 \Rightarrow C=515{,}011.22$$

Thus the swap rate is:

$$\frac{515{,}011.22}{8{,}000{,}000}\times 100=6.4376\%$$

Valuing a Swap at an Intermediate Stage

Assume that three months have elapsed since the preceding swap was initiated. Consider the term structure in Table 14.6.

Table 14.6: Spot rates and discount factors after three months.

Time to Maturity	Rate	Discount Factor
3M	7.75%	0.9810
9M	7.25%	0.9484
15M	6.50%	0.9249
21M	6.80%	0.8937

The value of the fixed rate note is computed as follows:

$$\frac{C}{2} \times [0.9810 + 0.9484 + 0.9249 + 0.8937] + 8{,}000{,}000 \times 0.8937$$
$$= 257{,}505.61 \times 3.748 + 8{,}000{,}000 \times 0.8937 = 965{,}131.10 + 7{,}149{,}600$$
$$= \$8{,}114{,}731$$

The value of the floating rate bond is computed as follows. Three months hence it pays a coupon based on the original six-month rate which is 7.50%. The amount of this coupon is

$$0.5 \times 0.0750 \times 8{,}000{,}000 = \$300{,}000$$

When this coupon is paid, the value of the bond reverts to its face value of $8 million. Consequently, its value today is

$$8{,}300{,}000 \times 0.9810$$
$$= \$8{,}142{,}300$$

From the standpoint of the fixed-rate payer, the swap is tantamount to a long position in a floating rate note that is combined with a short position in a fixed rate note. Thus the value of the swap is

$$8{,}142{,}300 - 8{,}114{,}731 = \$27{,}568.95$$

For the counterparty, the value is obviously –$27,568.95, for a swap is also a *zero sum game*. A negative value indicates that the position holder has to pay to assign the swap to someone else, whereas a positive value indicates that the holder receives the value if it chooses to assign the swap to another party.

Terminating a Swap

Let's suppose that after three months have elapsed, the fixed-rate payer in the preceding swap decides that it no longer wants to be a party to the swap. It can get out of the current situation in a variety of ways. One way is by way of a reversal. That is, it can enter into a swap with 21 months to maturity, wherein it is required to pay floating and receive fixed. The index for the floating-rate payments must obviously be the same. In this case two swaps exist. So the party is exposed to credit risk in both swaps. The second way to exit the swap is by selling it to a new party. In this case, Scotia Bank has to be paid $27,568.95 by the acquirer because the swap has a positive value. In this case, the original counterparty to the swap, that is Dominion Bank, has to agree to the deal. Finally, Dominion itself may buy out the swap from Scotia by paying the value. This is known as *buy-back* or *close-out*.

Motives for the Swap

A party to a swap may enter into the contract with a speculative motive, or else with an incentive to hedge. In addition such transactions may also be used to undertake credit arbitrage arising due to the comparative advantage enjoyed by the participating institutions, as we learned earlier. Let's analyze each of these potential uses.

Speculation

Scotia Bank and Dominion Bank are both players in the Canadian financial market. However they have very different perspectives about the direction in which interest rates are headed. Scotia believes the domestic interest rates are likely to increase steadily over the next decade. On the contrary, Dominion is of the opinion that domestic interest rates will decline steadily over the next 10 years. A coupon swap with 10 years to maturity is a suitable speculative tool for both parties. Scotia, which is bullish about interest rates, can enter the contract as the fixed-rate payer, and Dominion, which is bearish about interest rates, can be the counterparty as the fixed-rate receiver. Obviously both the speculators cannot earn a profit, for one of them will be proved wrong subsequently. If interest rates rise, Scotia, the fixed-rate payer, stands to benefit. On the contrary, if yields decline, Dominion Bank, the floating-rate payer, gets positive cash inflows.

Hedging a Liability

Swaps can be used as a hedge against anticipated interest rate movements. Parties may choose to hedge an asset or a liability, depending on their prior position. Carpenters Inc., a company based in Kansas City, has taken a floating-rate loan on which it has to pay an interest rate equal to the six-month LIBOR + 1%. Its apprehension is that rates may increase, and consequently it would have to pay more. It can use an interest rate swap to convert its existing liability into an effective fixed-rate loan. One alternative way to do so in practice is to renegotiate the loan and have it converted to a loan carrying a fixed rate of interest. This may not be easy in real life, for there are a lot of administrative and legal issues and related costs. However, it is relatively easier to enter into a swap with a bank, wherein the company has to pay a fixed rate in return for a LIBOR-based payment.

Assume that Prudential Bank agrees to enter into a swap with Carpenters wherein it pays LIBOR in return for a fixed interest stream based on a rate of 4.25% per annum. One possibility is that the bank is bearish about interest rates and wants to speculate. The other possibility is that the bank has an asset on which it is earning a floating rate of interest. Being bearish, it seeks to hedge by entering into a coupon swap as a fixed-rate receiver.

The net result from the standpoint of Carpenters may be analyzed as follows:

- Outflow-1(interest on the original loan): LIBOR + 1%
- Inflow-1(receipt from Prudential Bank): LIBOR
- Outflow-2 (payment to Prudential Bank): 4.25%
- Net Outflow: 4.25% + LIBOR + 1% – LIBOR = 5.25% per annum

Thus the company has converted its variable rate liability, to an effective fixed-rate liability carrying interest at the rate of 5.25% per annum.

Yet another reason for using swaps is to change the mix of fixed-rate and floating-rate debt on a company's balance sheet. Riviera Corporation has a liability profile consisting of $50 million in fixed-rate debt and another $50 million in floating-rate debt. It is now taking over Rodeo Corporation, and after the amalgamation it will have $100 million of fixed-rate debt and $70 million of floating-rate debt. The firm is eager to maintain the 50:50 ratio between fixed and floating debt after the merger. The total debt post-merger will be $170 million, and a 50:50 ratio implies a fixed-rate debt of $85 million and a floating-rate debt of an equivalent amount. One way of restructuring is to borrow another $15 million at a floating rate and repay $15 million worth of fixed-rate debt. Another alternative is the use of an interest rate swap.

Riviera can enter into a swap wherein it receives interest at a fixed rate on a notional principal of $15 million and pays interest on a floating rate basis on the same amount. The portfolio of the existing liabilities plus the swap is effectively a fixed-rate liability of $85 million and a floating-rate liability of $85 million.

Yet another reason for using a swap is the inability of a party to obtain loans at a fixed rate of interest. In practice a small company, a new company, or even an existing company that is large but has a weak credit rating, may be unable to borrow at a fixed rate of interest. Such a company has to raise capital in the bond market, and the bond markets are very particular about the credit rating of the potential borrower. One possibility is to issue junk bonds carrying high coupons. An alternative is to borrow at a floating rate of interest and then do a coupon swap, wherein the entity pays a fixed rate and receives a floating rate. The net result is the conversion of a floating-rate liability to a fixed-rate liability.

Hedging an Asset

A swap can be used by a borrower to convert its liability from a fixed-rate loan to a floating-rate loan or vice versa. Such contracts, however, may also be used by entities that seek to transform the income from their assets from a fixed rate cash inflow to a floating rate cash inflow or vice versa. For instance, a company that has invested in fixed rate bonds may use an interest rate swap to convert it into a synthetic floating-rate asset.

Assume that a company has bought 100,000 bonds with a face value of $1,000 and a coupon of 6% per annum paid semiannually. Let's assume that we are on the issue date and that the value of the bonds is equal to the par value. On the issue date, or any coupon date, the accrued interest will be zero. A conventional coupon swap, wherein the company pays fixed and receives LIBOR, is appropriate under these circumstances.

However, consider a situation where we are three months into the coupon period. The bond has 21 months to maturity. Table 14.7 shows the prevailing LIBOR values.

Table 14.7: Spot rates and discount factors after three months.

Time to Maturity	Rate	Discount Factor
3M	7.75%	0.9810
9M	7.25%	0.9484
15M	6.50%	0.9249
21M	6.80%	0.8937

In this case there is accrued interest for three months. In practice, investors prefer an arrangement where the assets do not have any accrued interest, and where the swap rate is equal to the coupon rate on the bonds. If we assume that the bonds are quoting at 97-08, the clean price of the bond is

$$1{,}000 \times \frac{97 + \frac{8}{32}}{100} = \$972.50$$

The accrued interest, assuming a 30/360 day-count convention, is

$$1{,}000 \times \frac{30}{2} = \$15$$

and consequently the dirty price is \$987.50. In practice, investors entering into asset swaps prefer contracts where the notional principal is equal to the par value of the bonds. In our case the difference between the par value and the dirty price per bond is \$12.50, and for 100,000 bonds, it is \$1,250,000. This amount is payable by the bond holder to the counterparty. Thus the cash flows over the next 21 months are those in Table 14.8.

Table 14.8: Cash flows from the asset holder's perspective.

Time	Amount
0	1,250,000
3M	3,000,000
9M	3,000,000
15M	3,000,000
21M	3,000,000

Each of the subsequent cash flows are \$3 million, because the semiannual coupon payment is \$30 per bond.

The value of these cash flows given the LIBOR rates and using the market method for computing the discount factors is

$$1{,}250{,}000 + \frac{3{,}000{,}000}{\left(1 + \frac{0.0775}{4}\right)} + \frac{3{,}000{,}000}{\left(1 + \frac{0.0725\times3}{4}\right)}$$
$$\frac{3{,}000{,}000}{\left(1 + \frac{0.0650\times5}{4}\right)} + \frac{3{,}000{,}000}{\left(1 + \frac{0.0680\times7}{4}\right)}$$
$$= \$12{,}493{,}800$$

The corresponding fixed rate is given by

$$12{,}493{,}800 = \frac{k}{4} \times 0.9810 \times 100{,}000{,}000$$
$$+ \frac{k}{2}[0.9484 + 0.9249 + 0.8937] \times 100{,}000{,}000$$
$$\Rightarrow k = 7.6709\%$$

Had the price of the bond been equal to par, and the counterparty had paid LIBOR, the value of the cash flows would have been

$$\frac{100{,}000{,}000 \times 0.0775 \times 0.25}{\left(1 + \frac{0.0775}{4}\right)} + \frac{100{,}000{,}000 \times 0.0725 \times 0.50}{\left(1 + \frac{0.0725\times3}{4}\right)}$$
$$\frac{100{,}000{,}000 \times 0.065 \times 0.5}{\left(1 + \frac{0.0650\times5}{4}\right)} + \frac{100{,}000{,}000 \times 0.068 \times 0.5}{\left(1 + \frac{0.0680\times7}{4}\right)}$$
$$= \$11{,}382{,}938$$

The corresponding fixed rate is given by

$$11{,}382{,}938 = \frac{k}{4} \times 0.9810 \times 100{,}000{,}000$$
$$+ \frac{k}{2}[0.9484 + 0.9249 + 0.8937] \times 100{,}000{,}000$$
$$\Rightarrow k = 6.9889\%$$

Thus the fixed rate is higher by 68.20 basis points because the bond is trading at a discount. Consequently the counterparty pays LIBOR + 68.20 basis points.

Had the bond been at a premium, the analysis would be as follows. Assuming that the bonds are quoting at 100-24, the clean price of the bond is

$$1{,}000 \times \frac{100 + \frac{24}{32}}{100} = \$1{,}007.50$$

The accrued interest is \$15, and consequently the dirty price is \$1,022.50. Thus the difference between the par value and the dirty price per bond is \$22.50, and for 100,000 bonds, it is \$2,250,000. This amount is payable by the counterparty to the bond holder.

Each of the subsequent cash flows are \$3 million, because the semiannual coupon payment is \$30 per bond. The value of these cash flows given the LIBOR rates and using the market method for computing the discount factors is

$$
\begin{aligned}
&-2{,}250{,}000+\frac{3{,}000{,}000}{\left(1+\frac{0.0775}{4}\right)}+\frac{3{,}000{,}000}{\left(1+\frac{0.0725\times 3}{4}\right)}\\
&\frac{3{,}000{,}000}{\left(1+\frac{0.0650\times 5}{4}\right)}+\frac{3{,}000{,}000}{\left(1+\frac{0.0680\times 7}{4}\right)}\\
&=\$8{,}993{,}800
\end{aligned}
$$

The corresponding fixed rate is given by

$$
\begin{aligned}
8{,}993{,}800 &= \frac{k}{4}\times 0.9810\times 100{,}000{,}000\\
&+\frac{k}{2}[0.9484+0.9249+0.8937]\times 100{,}000{,}000\\
\Rightarrow k &= 5.5220\%
\end{aligned}
$$

Had the bond been at trading at par, the corresponding fixed rate would have been 6.9889%. Thus the fixed rate is lower by 1.4669%, and the counterparty pays LIBOR – 1.4669%.

Equivalence with FRAs

We now show that a position in an interest rate swap is equivalent to a series of *forward rate agreements* (FRAs). Consider a portfolio of one-period FRAs paying after one, two, three, and four periods. Consider the case of an investor who has taken a long position in the portfolio with a notional principal of \$8 million. Let's assume that the FRAs are delayed settlement agreements that pay six months after the LIBOR is determined. This is to be consistent with the payment convention of an interest rate swap. Figures 14.1 and 14.2 show the interest rate, and state price trees, for the Ho-Lee model that we derived in Chapter 11.

Determining the Fixed Rate

Let's denote the unknown fixed rate by k. The value of the cash flow at time 1 is

$$
\frac{8{,}000{,}000\times 0.5\times(0.075-k)}{\left(1+\frac{0.075}{2}\right)}
$$

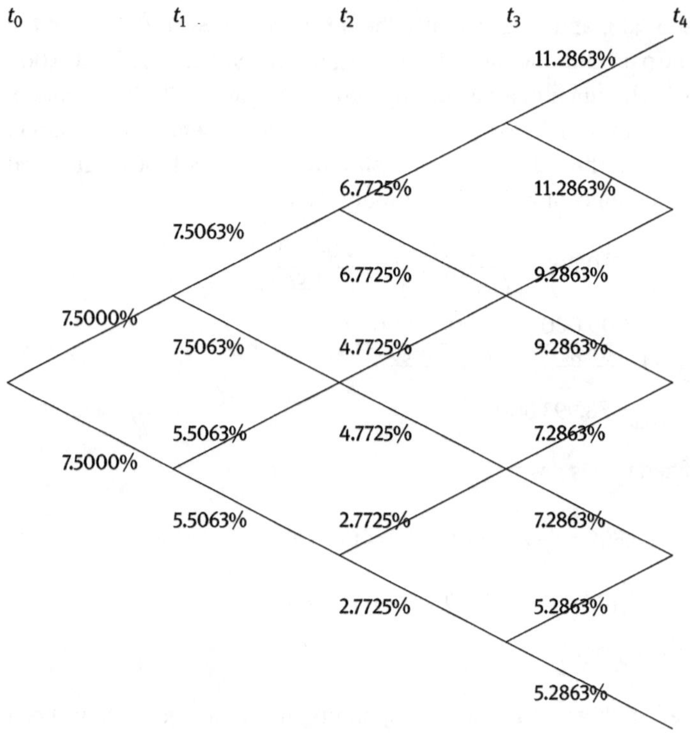

Figure 14.1: No-arbitrage interest rate tree.

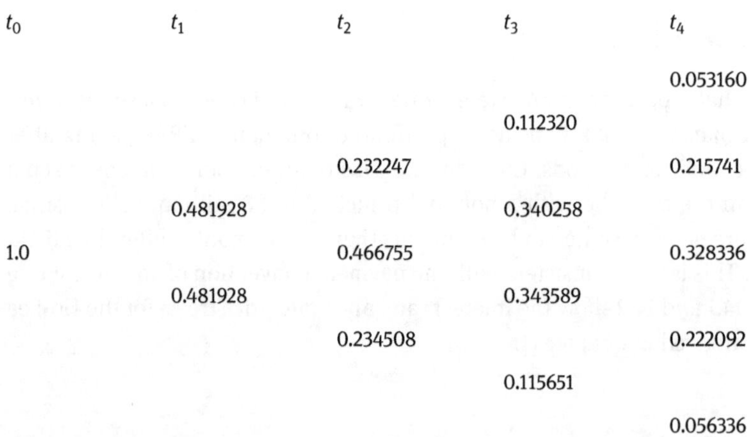

Figure 14.2: State price tree.

The value of the payoff from the FRA at time 2 is

$$0.481928 \times \frac{8{,}000{,}000 \times 0.5 \times (0.075063 - k)}{\left(1 + \frac{0.075063}{2}\right)} + 0.481928 \times \frac{8{,}000{,}000 \times 0.5 \times (0.055063 - k)}{\left(1 + \frac{0.055063}{2}\right)}$$

The value of the payoff from the FRA at time 3 is

$$0.232247 \times \frac{8{,}000{,}000 \times 0.5 \times (0.067725 - k)}{\left(1 + \frac{0.067725}{2}\right)} + 0.466755 \times \frac{8{,}000{,}000 \times 0.5 \times (0.047725 - k)}{\left(1 + \frac{0.047725}{2}\right)} + 0.234508 \times \frac{8{,}000{,}000 \times 0.5 \times (0.027725 - k)}{\left(1 + \frac{0.027725}{2}\right)}$$

Finally, the value of the payoff at time 4 is

$$0.112320 \times \frac{8{,}000{,}000 \times 0.5 \times (0.112863 - k)}{\left(1 + \frac{0.112863}{2}\right)} + 0.340258 \times \frac{8{,}000{,}000 \times 0.5 \times (0.092863 - k)}{\left(1 + \frac{0.092863}{2}\right)} + 0.343589 \times \frac{8{,}000{,}000 \times 0.5 \times (0.072863 - k)}{\left(1 + \frac{0.072863}{2}\right)} + 0.115651 \times \frac{8{,}000{,}000 \times 0.5 \times (0.052863 - k)}{\left(1 + \frac{0.052863}{2}\right)}$$

The unknown fixed rate k should be set such that the value of the portfolio is zero. Using SOLVER in Excel, we get a value of 6.7485% per annum.

An identical solution can be obtained by computing the coupon rate corresponding to a par bond:

$$1{,}000 = \frac{1{,}000 \times 0.5 \times k}{\left(1 + \frac{0.075}{2}\right)} + \frac{1{,}000 \times 0.5 \times k}{\left(1 + \frac{0.07}{2}\right)^2} + \frac{1{,}000 \times 0.5 \times k}{\left(1 + \frac{0.0625}{2}\right)^3} + \frac{[1{,}000 + 1{,}000 \times 0.5 \times k]}{\left(1 + \frac{0.0675}{2}\right)^4}$$

$$k = 6.7485\%$$

The equivalence of swaps and FRAs may be demonstrated as follows. The first payment due to Scotia Bank is known at the very outset because the applicable LIBOR is determined at the start of the period. Hence the first transaction may be viewed as a spot transaction in which Scotia Bank receives \$300,600 from Dominion six months hence. This may be computed as

$$8{,}000{,}000 \times 0.5 \times (0.075 - 0.067485) = \$300{,}600$$

The remaining three transactions are FRAs in which Scotia Bank agrees to make payments based on a rate of 6.7485% per annum and receive payments based on the LIBOR that prevails at the start of the corresponding period.

The par bond can also be valued as the present value of a series of cash flows based on the implied one-period forward rates. These are

$$\frac{(1.035)^2}{1.0375} = 1.032506 \equiv 3.2506\%$$
$$\frac{(1.03125)^3}{(1.035)^2} = 1.023791 \equiv 2.3791\,\%$$
$$\frac{(1.03375)^4}{(1.03125)^3} = 1.041286 \equiv 4.1286\%$$

The forward rate for the first period is equal to the spot rate, which is equal to 7.50% per annum. If we assume a face value of 1,000, the cash flows are \$37.50 after six months, \$32.506 after 12 months, \$23.791 after 18 months, and \$41.286 after 24 months. If we denote the unknown fixed rate by k

$$\begin{aligned}
&\frac{1{,}000 \times 0.5 \times k}{\left(1 + \frac{0.075}{2}\right)} + \frac{1{,}000 \times 0.5 \times k}{\left(1 + \frac{0.07}{2}\right)^2} \\
&\quad + \frac{1{,}000 \times 0.5 \times k}{\left(1 + \frac{0.0625}{2}\right)^3} + \frac{[1{,}000 + 1{,}000 \times 0.5 \times k]}{\left(1 + \frac{0.0675}{2}\right)^4} \\
&= \frac{37.50}{\left(1 + \frac{0.075}{2}\right)} + \frac{32.506}{\left(1 + \frac{0.07}{2}\right)^2} \\
&\quad + \frac{23.791}{\left(1 + \frac{0.0625}{2}\right)^3} + \frac{[1{,}000 + 41.286]}{\left(1 + \frac{0.0675}{2}\right)^4} = 1{,}000 \\
&\Rightarrow k = 6.7485\%
\end{aligned}$$

Forward-Start Swaps

A plain vanilla interest rate swap starts at time zero. That is, the first cash flows arise one period after inception. However, we can design contracts that are scheduled to start at a later date. Such contracts are termed *forward-start swaps*. The contract rate for such a swap will obviously be different from that for a corresponding plain vanilla swap. However, it can be determined using the same vector of spot rates.

For instance, let's consider a three-period (18 months) swap that is scheduled to come into existence six months from now. The cash flows based on the one-period forward rates are \$32.506 after 12 months, \$23.791 after 18 months, and \$41.286 after 24 months. If we denote the unknown contract rate by k

$$\frac{1{,}000 \times 0.5 \times k}{\left(1+\frac{0.07}{2}\right)^2} + \frac{1{,}000 \times 0.5 \times k}{\left(1+\frac{0.0625}{2}\right)^3} + \frac{[1{,}000 + 1{,}000 \times 0.5 \times k]}{\left(1+\frac{0.0675}{2}\right)^4}$$
$$= \frac{32.506}{\left(1+\frac{0.07}{2}\right)^2} + \frac{23.791}{\left(1+\frac{0.0625}{2}\right)^3} + \frac{[1{,}000 + 41.286]}{\left(1+\frac{0.0675}{2}\right)^4} \Rightarrow k = 6.4822\%$$

The same answer can be derived by computing the coupon rate corresponding to a par bond. For this we need to compute the one-period, two-period, and three-period forward rates one period from now.

The one-period forward rate, per annum, for a loan after one period is

$$3.2506 \times 2 = 6.5012\%$$

The two-period forward rate, per annum, for a loan after one period is

$$\left\{\left[\frac{(1.03125)^3}{(1.0375)}\right]^{1/2} - 1\right\} \times 2$$
$$= 5.6278\%$$

The three-period forward rate, per annum, for a loan after one period is

$$\left\{\left[\frac{(1.03375)^4}{(1.0375)}\right]^{1/3} - 1\right\} \times 2$$
$$= 6.5006\%$$

The coupon rate of the par bond may be calculated as

$$1{,}000 = \frac{1{,}000 \times 0.5 \times c}{(1.032506)} + \frac{1{,}000 \times 0.5 \times c}{(1.028139)^2} + \frac{[1{,}000 + 1{,}000 \times 0.5 \times c]}{(1.032503)^3}$$
$$\Rightarrow c = 6.4823\%$$

Amortizing Swaps

In an amortizing swap, the notional principal declines steadily over the life of the swap. Let's reconsider the swap between Scotia Bank and Dominion Bank. Assume that the initial notional principal is \$8 million, and that it declines by \$2 million at the end of every six-monthly period. The fixed rate may be determined as follows

$$1{,}000 = \frac{[250 + 1{,}000 \times 0.5 \times k]}{\left(1+\frac{0.075}{2}\right)} + \frac{[250 + 750 \times 0.5 \times k]}{\left(1+\frac{0.07}{2}\right)^2}$$

$$+\frac{[250+500\times 0.5\times k]}{\left(1+\frac{0.0625}{2}\right)^3}+\frac{[250+250\times 0.5\times k]}{\left(1+\frac{0.0675}{2}\right)^4}$$

$$k = 6.7375\%$$

In-Arrears Swaps

In the case of an in-arrears swap, as soon as the LIBOR is determined at the end of every period, the interest is paid out immediately. We can determine the fixed rate for such a swap by viewing it as a portfolio of in-arrears FRAs.

Let's denote the unknown fixed rate by k. The cash flow at time 1 is

$$\begin{aligned}&0.481928\times[8{,}000{,}000\times 0.5\times(0.075063-k)]\\&\quad+0.481928\times[8{,}000{,}000\times 0.5\times(0.055063-k)]\end{aligned}$$

The payoff from the FRA at time 2 is

$$\begin{aligned}&0.232247\times[8{,}000{,}000\times 0.5\times(0.067725-k)]\\&\quad+0.466755\times[8{,}000{,}000\times 0.5\times(0.047725-k)]\\&\quad+0.234508\times[8{,}000{,}000\times 0.5\times(0.027725-k)]\end{aligned}$$

Finally, the payoff at time 3 is

$$\begin{aligned}&0.112320\times[8{,}000{,}000\times 0.5\times(0.112863-k)]\\&\quad+0.340258\times[8{,}000{,}000\times 0.5\times(0.092863-k)]\\&\quad+0.343589\times[8{,}000{,}000\times 0.5\times(0.072863-k)]\\&\quad+0.115651\times[8{,}000{,}000\times 0.5\times(0.052863-k)]\end{aligned}$$

The unknown fixed rate k should be set such that the value of the portfolio is zero. Using SOLVER in Excel, we get a value of 6.5016% per annum.

Extendable and Cancelable Swaps

An *extendable swap* gives one of the counterparties, usually the fixed-rate payer, the option to extend the maturity date beyond the scheduled date. From the perspective of a fixed-rate payer, the option to extend is likely to be invoked in an economic environment in which interest rates are increasing, in which the cash inflows due to floating-rate payments are likely to be higher than the counter payments based on the fixed rate. The extension option needs to be priced and has a higher fixed rate compared to a plain vanilla interest rate swap.

A *cancelable swap* gives one of the counterparties the option to terminate the swap prior to the scheduled maturity date. From the perspective of a fixed-rate payer, the option to cancel is likely to be invoked in an economic environment in which interest rates are declining, in which the cash inflows due to floating-rate payments are likely to be lower than the counter payments based on the fixed rate. A swap with this option has a higher fixed rate compared to a plain vanilla swap. A swap that is cancelable by the fixed-rate payer swap is also termed a *callable swap*.

Another type of a cancelable swap is a *putable swap*. This gives the floating-rate payer the right to terminate the swap prior to the original maturity date. Obviously a payer chooses to do so when interest rates are rising. Consequently the fixed rate for a swap with a put option is lower than that of a plain vanilla swap.

Swaptions

A *swaption* is an option on a swap. Such an option requires the buyer to pay an up-front premium, for the right to enter into a coupon swap. There are two types of swaptions. The holder of the option may enter into a coupon swap as a fixed-rate payer or as a fixed-rate receiver. In the case of a *payer swaption*, the option holder can exercise it to enter into the swap as a fixed-rate payer. On the other hand, a *receiver swaption* gives the holder the right to enter into a swap as a fixed-rate receiver.

The exercise price specified in the swaption is an interest rate. The underlying asset is a swap with a specified term to maturity. A payer swaption is exercised only if the prevailing rate for a swap with the specified maturity is higher than the exercise price of the swaption. Quite obviously, a receiver swaption is exercised only if the prevailing swap rate is lower than the exercise price. Swaptions may be European or American in nature.

Swaptions may be useful for entities that are not sure whether they will face interest rate exposure in the future. Consider the case of a corporation that decides to borrow in the future. It obviously worries about the specter of a rising interest rate. It can protect itself by buying a payer swaption. If rates go up, it borrows at the market rate and exercises the option, which results in receipt of a series of positive cash flows because the market rates are higher than the swap rate. However, if rates decline, it refrains from exercising the option and borrows at the market rate, which by assumption has declined and consequently is favorable to it.

An asset holder, such as a bank that holds a portfolio of mortgages, will be perturbed about falling interest rates, which are likely to lead to substantial prepayments. Such an entity can protect itself by buying a receiver option. If rates go up, the protection is not required, and the option is allowed to expire. However, if rates decline, the bank exercises the swaption and receives a series of positive cash flows that help mitigate the effect of prepayments from the mortgage holders.

Issuers of callable bonds can also use swaptions. Assume that a company has issued 10-year deferred callable bonds with a 5-year call protection period. Let's assume that the coupon rate is 7.50% per annum. At the end of two years, rates decline substantially, to say 4% per annum. Given a choice, the issuer wants to call back the bonds. However, it is constrained by the call protection feature. In such circumstances, it can sell a receiver option with a strike price of 7.50%, for which it obviously receives a premium. Three years hence if interest rates are more than 7.50%, the swaption is not exercised, and the bonds are not recalled. However, if the rate falls to say 5%, the counterparty does exercise the option. The issuer of callables receives LIBOR in return for a fixed-rate payment of 7.50%. It can then call back the bonds and issue fresh floating rate bonds carrying an interest of LIBOR. The funds required to pay the coupon come from the counterparty to the swaption. Thus the consequence of the transaction is that the company continues to pay 7.50% for the remaining life of the bond. At the outset, however, it receives a premium due to the sale of the option. It is as if it has sold the call option inherent in the callable bond, although the inherent option per se is not a tradable asset. Consequently, this strategy is termed *call monetization.*

It is not necessary that the company sell a swaption with an exercise price equal to the coupon of 7.50%. It can choose to sell a swaption with a lower or a higher exercise price. If it chooses a lower exercise price of, say, 6.00%, and the rate after two years is 4%, the counterparty will exercise. The effective rate on its debt is 6%. The premium received for the receiver swaption is lower in this case because the exercise price of 6% is lower than the exercise price of 7.50% that was assumed earlier. If the company sells a swaption with a higher exercise price of, say, 9%, it has to pay a higher rate on its debt, but receives a higher premium at the outset.

In practice, the swap rate and the bond rate need not be perfectly correlated. Assume that the company has sold a receiver swaption with an exercise price of 7.50%. The LIBOR is assumed to be 4%. The holder pays the LIBOR in return for a fixed rate of 7.50%. However, the credit quality of the bond issuer may have deteriorated, and as a consequence, it has to pay LIBOR plus 1.50% if it issues floating rate bonds to refinance its debt. The net result is that the rate for the issuer is 9% per annum.

Credit Default Swaps

A *credit default swap* (CDS) is a contract between two parties, known as the protection buyer and the protection seller, respectively. At the outset, the buyer of protection has to pay a premium to the counterparty. In return it gets protection against credit risk or default risk pertaining to an issuing entity, or to a specific security that has been issued by an entity. The security or entity for which protection has been sought, is known as the *reference asset*. In practice it may be a standalone asset, or a basket or portfolio of assets. The protection seller is required to make a payment if a specified credit event occurs. If the event does not happen, the seller makes no payment. In the case of the credit event happening, the seller pays the loss due to the event to the buyer. The contract then terminates. The purpose of a CDS is to transfer the credit risk pertaining to an asset without transferring its ownership.

The specified credit event may be one of the following:

- Bankruptcy or insolvency
- Default on a payment
- Decline in the price of a specified asset by more than a certain prespecified amount
- Credit downgrade of a security or an issuing entity

If a credit event occurs, it leads to one of the following situations. The protection seller determines the post-default value, or in other words, the percentage of the distressed asset's value that can be recovered. The par value minus this post-default value is then paid to the protection buyer. There also is something called a *digital swap*. In this case, the post-default price or recovery value is a prespecified amount. This mode of settlement is termed *cash settlement*. Finally, the seller may pay the entire par value to the buyer and take over the security in return. This is referred to as *delivery settlement*. Here is an example of cash settlement.

Example 14.3. Arizona Bank has bought a CDS from Xylo Bank. The notional principal is \$25 million. Every year the buyer has to pay a premium of 80 basis points to the seller. Thus the premium in this case is

$$25{,}000{,}000 \times 0.008 = \$200{,}000$$

If there is a credit event, and assuming that the recovery rate is 60% of par, the seller pays

$$25{,}000{,}000 \times \frac{(100 - 60)}{100} = \$10{,}000{,}000$$

In the absence of the event, nothing is payable, and the seller retains the premiums.

In practice the premiums are paid quarterly or semiannually in arrears, and it is not always necessary that the credit event conveniently occurs at the beginning of a period. If a credit event occurs in the middle of a period, the accrued premium has to be paid. A CDS is a tool that facilitates the trading of credit risk, just the way other tools facilitate the trading of market risk. It should be noted that the maturity of the swap contract does not need to match the maturity of the reference asset, and in practice, it does not in most cases.

If the contract is on an issuing entity and not on a specific issue, the buyer may have a choice of deliverable assets or what are termed deliverable obligations. In such a situation, the buyer delivers the cheapest of the assets that are eligible for delivery. In principle, there is no difference between cash settlement and delivery settlement from the standpoint of protection against a credit event. However, in practice, delivery settlement offers a benefit to the seller. If the status of the issuer or the security improves after the seller has taken possession of the underlying asset, it may be able to derive a higher recovery value than what was anticipated at the time of default. In the market, buyers prefer cash settlement. This is because, if they are not in prior possession of the underlying asset, they have to acquire it in the market. In this case, if there are liquidity issues, the price of acquisition of the asset may be higher than what the recovery rate warrants. In practice, physical settlement is commonly used because it facilitates the determination of the security's market value. In practice, if there is a credit event, a cooling period such as a fortnight is provided so that the market stabilizes, before the post default value is determined. The contracts usually stipulate that if the value cannot be ascertained after a credit event, the value of a similar asset in terms of maturity and credit quality can be used.

In the case of a basket CDS, which is based on a portfolio of assets, one possibility is a *first to default swap*. As the name suggests, the swap terminates the moment one of the constituent assets suffers a credit event, unless of course the CDS itself terminates before any of the component securities experience a credit event. In the case of such swaps, if the buyer seeks protection for the remaining constituents of the portfolio, it has to enter into a fresh contract, for the original contract becomes void the moment a credit event occurs. An alternative is an *all to default swap*, which terminates when all the assets in the basket have defaulted, unless of course the contract itself terminates prior to that. In this case, the buyer receives compensation for all the defaulting securities.

Valuation of a CDS

A combination of a long position in a risky bond and a long position in a CDS is equivalent to a long position in a synthetic T-bill. Thus the premium for the CDS should be approximately equal to the default risk premium inherent in the bond's yield. Take the case of a party that short sells a riskless bond with a coupon of $r\%$ and buys a risky bond with a coupon of $c\%$, where $c = r + p$, where p is the default risk premium. To keep the issue simple, let's assume that p is a constant. If we assume that both bonds are trading at par, the proceeds from the short sale are adequate to buy the risky bond, and consequently there is neither a net inflow nor a net outflow. Assume that the investor goes long in a CDS and has to pay a premium of $s\%$ every period. At the end of every coupon period, there is an inflow of $c = r + p$ from the risky bond and a outflow of r. There also is an outflow on account of the swap premium. The net cash flow is $c - (r + s)$.

On the coupon date, if the risky bond does not default, the holder can sell it and retire the short position in the riskless bond. However, if the risky bond defaults, the holder can deliver it under the swap in return for the par value if it is delivery settled, or sell it at the prevailing price, receive the deficit under the swap, and use the proceeds to retire the short position. In either case the net cash flow is zero. Because the cash flows at the outset and at the end are zero, all intermediate cash flows should be zero to rule out arbitrage. Thus

$$c - (r + s) = 0 \Rightarrow c = r + s = r + p \Rightarrow s = p$$

This confirms our claim that the swap premium should be equal to the default risk premium. There are some inherent assumptions in this argument. First, the credit spread p is a constant. Second, the bonds are floating rate issues, which reset to par on every coupon date. And as usual, we assume that there are no market imperfections such as transaction costs, and if an asset is short-sold, the full proceeds are immediately available for use.

Using Default Probabilities to Determine the Swap Rate

Consider an eight-year swap. Every period has a 2.50% probability of default, assuming that there is no earlier default. We assume that the swap premium is paid in arrears at the end of each year. If a default occurs, it happens at the middle of the period. The recovery rate is assumed to be 60%. We denote the unknown swap premium by s per dollar of notional principal. The survival probabilities are given in Table 14.9.

Table 14.9: Default and survival probabilities.

Time	Default Probability	Survival Probability
1	0.025000	0.975000
2	0.024375	0.950625
3	0.023766	0.926859
4	0.023171	0.903688
5	0.022592	0.881096
6	0.022027	0.859069
7	0.021477	0.837592
8	0.020940	0.816652

The survival probability at the end of the first year is one minus the default probability, which is 1.00 – 0.025 = 0.975. The default probability for the second year is 0.025 × 0.975000 = 0.024375. Thus the probability of survival after two years is 0.975000 – 0.024375 = 0.950625. In general the survival probability at the end of period t is $(1.000 - 0.025)^t$. The default probability for period t is the survival probability at the end of the previous period multiplied by the default intensity of 2.50%.

Assume that the discount rate is 6% per annum. Thus the discount factor for a cash flow occurring at time t is

$$\frac{1}{(1.06)^t}$$

At the end of every period, if there has been no prior default, a premium of s is payable per dollar. Hence, the expected payoff at the end of the year is the corresponding survival probability multiplied by s.

Table 14.10: Expected premium payments and their present values.

Time	Survival Probability	Expected Premium Pmt.	Discount Factor	PV of Expected Premium Pmt.
1	0.975000	0.975000s	0.943396	0.919811s
2	0.950625	0.950625s	0.889996	0.846052s
3	0.926859	0.926859s	0.839619	0.778208s
4	0.903688	0.903688s	0.792093	0.715805s
5	0.881096	0.881096s	0.747258	0.658406s
6	0.859069	0.859069s	0.704960	0.605609s
7	0.837592	0.837592s	0.665057	0.557046s
8	0.816652	0.816652s	0.627412	0.512377s
			Total	5.593314s

Pmt. stands for Payment.

Table 14.11: Expected accrued premium payments and expected payoffs and their present values.

Time	Default Probability	Expected Payoff Payment	Discount Factor	PV of Expected Payoff	Expected Accrual Payment	PV of Exp. Accrual Payment
0.5	0.025000	0.010000	0.971286	0.009713	0.012500s	0.012141s
1.5	0.024375	0.009750	0.916307	0.008934	0.012188s	0.011168s
2.5	0.023766	0.009506	0.864441	0.008217	0.011883s	0.010272s
3.5	0.023171	0.009268	0.815510	0.007558	0.011586s	0.009448s
4.5	0.022592	0.009037	0.769349	0.006953	0.011296s	0.008691s
5.5	0.022027	0.008811	0.725801	0.006395	0.011014s	0.007994s
6.5	0.021477	0.008591	0.684718	0.005882	0.010739s	0.007353s
7.5	0.020940	0.008376	0.645960	0.005411	0.010470s	0.006763s
			Total	0.059063		0.073830s

Exp. stands for Expected.

The present value of the expected swap payment is 5.593314s + 0.073830s = 5.667144s. The break-even CDS spread is given by

$$5.667144s = 0.059063 \Rightarrow s = 0.010422 \equiv 104 \text{ basis points}$$

The expected accrual premium at time t is the default probability multiplied by half the premium, as default is assumed to occur in the middle of the year. The expected payoff from the swap is the default probability multiplied by 0.40 because the recovery rate is assumed to be 60%.

Chapter Summary

This chapter looked at two important OTC derivatives, namely interest rate swaps and credit default swaps. We demonstrated the valuation of an interest rate swap given a vector of spot rates. We showed that it is equivalent to a combination of a fixed rate bond and a floating rate bond. We also illustrated that an interest rate swap is equivalent to a portfolio of FRAs and showed how to compute the swap rate given a model for determining the short rates such as the Ho-Lee model. The alternatives to a plain vanilla interest rate swap, such as a forward-start swap, an amortizing swap, and an in-arrears swap, were also discussed. It was shown that swaps could be used for both hedging and speculation, in conjunction with both assets and liabilities. While discussing the possible motives for a swap, the concept of credit arbitrage was discussed in detail. The chapter concluded with a study of credit default swaps. We showed how to determine the swap premium for such contracts by assuming survival probabilities and a recovery rate.

With this final chapter, the book is concluded. This book seeks to provide a comprehensive treatment of bonds, bond valuation, and yield computation. Derivatives based on interest rate products are also extensively covered. To facilitate the comprehension, two detailed chapters, on time value of money, and derivatives, are presented. At every appropriate step, the use of Excel for solving problems is demonstrated in adequate detail.

Appendix A

Goal Seek

Goal Seek is a tool in Excel, which can be used to determine the value that needs to be input in a cell so that the target value is achieved in a formula cell. It is called Goal Seek because the objective is to achieve a computational goal, by using Excel to determine the appropriate value of the input cell. We will use Goal Seek to determine the target present value of a series of cash flows, by varying the discount rate. Consider the following Excel sheet.

Table A.1: Goal Seek example.

Row	Time	Cash Flow	Present Value	Input Value
Number	Column A	Column B	Column C	Column D
1	1	2,000	= PV(D1, A1,, −B1)	0.10
2	2	3,000	= PV(D1, A2,, −B2)	
3	3	4,000	= PV(D1, A3,, −B3)	
4	4	6,000	= PV(D1, A4,, −B4)	
5	Total Present Value		= SUM(C1 : C4)	

The objective is to determine the value in cell D1 that will make the sum of the present values equal to $12,500. We have chosen to use an initial input of 10% per period, which will obviously be entered as 0.10. Notice that to compute the present value of a cash flow we need to always use the value in cell D1. Consequently we enter the rate parameter in the PV function as D1. The formula for PV need not be input four times. We can simply enter the function in cell C1, and drag and use the control D option in Excel.

If we invoke Goal Seek it asks for the following:

- Set cell
- To value
- By changing cell

We give C5, 12,500, and D1 as the inputs. Then we need to click on OK. The answer is 6.4948%. The result is shown in the table below.

Table A.2: The result from Goal Seek.

Row	Time	Cash Flow	Present Value	Input Value
Number	Column A	Column B	Column C	Column D
1	1	2,000	1,878.03	0.064948
2	2	3,000	2,645.24	
3	3	4,000	3,311.88	
4	4	6,000	4,664.85	
5	Total Present Value		12,500	

https://doi.org/10.1515/9781547400669-015

Solver

Solver also enables us to achieve a target value for a formula cell. However it allows us to change the values of multiple cells to achieve our goal. In our illustration, however, we need to change the value of only a single input cell.

If we use Solver to achieve a goal it asks for the following:

- Set objective:
- To: (there are three options: Max; Min; and Value Of)
- By changing variable cells:
- Subject to the constraints:
- Option to Make Unconstrained Variables Non Negative:
- Select a Solving Method:

We give C5, 12,500 (by choosing the *value of* option), and D1 as the inputs. We do not input any constraints and do not choose the option to make unconstrained variables non negative. The default solving method is GRG Nonlinear, and that is adequate for most problems. We then need to click on Solve. The solution once again is 6.4948%.

Bibliography

[1] Annaert, J., Claes, A. G. P., de Ceuster, M. J. K., and Zhang H. *Estimating the Yield Curve Using the Nelson Siegel Model: A Ridge Regression Approach.* International Review of Economics and Finance, 2012.

[2] Babbel, D. F. and Merrill, C. B. *Valuation of Interest-Sensitive Financial Instruments.* Schaumburg, IL: Society of Actuaries, 1996.

[3] Bierwag, G. O. *Duration Analysis.* Cambridge, MA: Ballinger Publishing, 1987.

[4] Blake, D. *Financial Market Analysis.* New York, NY: John Wiley, 1999.

[5] Bodie, Z., Kane, A., Marcus, J. A., and Mohanty P. *Investments.* Chennai, McGraw Hill Education, 2018.

[6] Brown, P. J. *Bond Markets.* Chicago: Glenlake Publishing, 1998.

[7] Chance, D. M. *An Introduction to Options and Futures.* New York: The Dryden Press, 1991.

[8] Chance, D. M. *An Introduction to Derivatives and Risk Management.* Mason, OH: South-Western, 2004.

[9] Choudhry, M. *An Introduction to Repo Markets.* London: Securities Institute, 2001.

[10] Choudhry, M. *An Introduction to Bond Markets.* London: Securities Institute, 2001.

[11] Choudhry, M. *Analyzing and Interpreting the Yield Curve.* New York: John Wiley, 2004.

[12] Comotto, R. *The Money Market.* London: Euromoney Publications, 1998.

[13] Coyle, B. *Corporate Bonds & Commercial Paper.* Canterbury U.K.: Financial World Publishing, 2002.

[14] Coyle, B. *Government Bonds.* Canterbury U.K.: Financial World Publishing, 2002.

[15] Coyle, B. *Interest-Rate Options.* London: Financial World Publishing, 2001.

[16] Coyle, B. *Interest-Rate Swaps.* London: Financial World Publishing, 2001.

[17] Coyle, B. *Money Markets.* London: Financial World Publishing, 2001.

[18] Daigler, R. T. *Financial Futures and Options Markets: Concepts and Strategies.* Harper Collins, 1994.

[19] Davidson, A. S., and Herskovitz, M. D. *The Mortgage-Backed Securities Workbook.* New York: Irwin McGraw Hill, 1996.

[20] Davidson, A., Sanders, A., Wolff, L., and Ching, A. *Securitization.* New York: John Wiley, 2003.

[21] Dodd, R. *Primer on Repurchase Agreements Market.* Online at www.financialpolicy.org.

[22] Douglas, L. G. *Bond Risk Analysis.* New York: New York Institute of Finance, 1990.

[23] Dubofsky, D. A. *Options and Financial Futures: Valuation and Uses.* New York: McGraw-Hill, 1992.

[24] Dym, S. I. *The Complete Practitioner's Guide to the Bond Market.* New York: McGraw Hill, 2010.

[25] Edwards, F. R., and Ma, C. W. *Futures and Options.* New York: McGraw-Hill, 1992.

[26] Fabozzi, F. J. *Bond Markets: Analysis and Strategies.* Englewood Cliffs, NJ: Prentice Hall, 2015.

[27] Fabozzi, F. J. *Fixed Income Mathematics.* New York: McGraw Hill, 2006.

[28] Fabozzi, F. J. *Handbook of Fixed Income Securities.* New York: McGraw Hill, 2012.

[29] Fabozzi, F. J., Bhattacharya, A. K., and Berliner, W. S. *Mortgage-Backed Securities.* New York: John Wiley, 2007.

[30] Fabozzi, F. J., and Mann, S. V. *Introduction to Fixed Income Analytics.* New Hope, PA: Frank J Fabozzi Associates, 2001.

[31] Fabozzi, F. J., and Modigliani, F. *Mortgage and Mortgage-Backed Securities Markets.* Cambridge, MA: Harvard Business School Press, 1992.

[32] Figlewski, S., Silber, W. L., and Subrahmanyam, M. G. *Financial Options: From Theory to Practice.* New York: Irwin, 1990.

[33] Garbade, K. D. *Fixed Income Analytics.* Cambridge: MIT Press, 1996.

[34] Geroulanos P. *An Introduction to Swaps.* London: The Securities Institute, 1998.

https://doi.org/10.1515/9781547400669-016

[35] Gray, S. *Repo of Government Securities*: Handbooks in Central Banking, No. 16. London: Bank of England, 1998.
[36] Hegde, S. P., and Parameswaran, S. K. *Futures Markets: 200 Questions and Answers*. New York: John Wiley, 2007.
[37] Hull, J. *Fundamentals of Futures and Options Markets*. Englewood Cliffs, NJ: Prentice Hall, 2004.
[38] Hull, J. *Options, Futures, and Other Derivatives*. Upper Saddle River, NJ: Prentice Hall, 2006.
[39] James, T. *Interest Rate Derivatives*. London: Risk Books, 2006.
[40] Kellison, S. G. *The Theory of Interest*. New York: Irwin McGraw-Hill, 1991.
[41] Kolb, R. W. *Futures, Options, and Swaps*. New York: Blackwell, 2003.
[42] Kolev, I. *Mortgage-Backed Securities*. Washington, DC: Financial Policy Forum, 2004.
[43] Liaw, K. T. *Capital Markets*. Mason, OH: Thomson/South-Western, 2004.
[44] Liaw, K. T. and Moy, R. L. *Stocks, Bonds, Futures, and Options*. New York: McGraw Hill, 2001.
[45] Livingston, M. *Bonds and Bond Derivatives*. New York: Blackwell Publishing, 2004.
[46] Logue, D. E. *The WG&L Handbook of International Finance*. Mason, OH: South-Western, 1995.
[47] McDonald, R. L. *Derivatives Markets*. New York: Pearson Education, 2006.
[48] Mclnish, T. H. *Capital Markets: A Global Perspective*. New York: Blackwell, 2000.
[49] Mobius, M. *Bonds*. Singapore: John Wiley, 2012.
[50] Needles, B. E. and Powers, M. *Principles of Financial Accounting*. Boston: Houghton Mifflin, 2008.
[51] Parameswaran, S. K. *Fundamentals of Financial Instruments*. Singapore: John Wiley, 2011.
[52] Parameswaran, S. K. *Futures and Options: Concepts and Applications*. Singapore: McGraw Hill, 2011.
[53] Rendleman, R. J. *Applied Derivatives*. Oxford, U.K.: Wiley-Blackwell, 2002.
[54] Saunders, A., and Cornett, M. M. *Financial Institutions Management*. New York: McGraw-Hill, 2003.
[55] Siegel, D. R., and Siegel, D. F. *Futures Markets*. New York: The Dryden Press, 1990.
[56] Smith, D. J. *Bond Math*. New Jersey: John Wiley, 2011.
[57] Steiner, B. *Foreign Exchange and Money Markets*. Oxford, UK: Butterworth-Heinemann, 2002.
[58] Steiner, R. *Mastering Financial Calculations*. London: Financial Times Prentice Hall, 1998.
[59] Stigum, M., and Robinson, F. L. *Money Market and Bond Calculations*. New York: Irwin, 1996.
[60] Stigum, M., and Crescenzi, A. *Stigum's Money Market*. New York: McGraw-Hill, 2007.
[61] Strumeyer, G. *Investing in Fixed Income Securities*. New York: John Wiley, 2005.
[62] Sundaresan, S. *Fixed Income Markets and Their Derivatives*. San Diego: Academic Press, 2009.
[63] Taff, L. G. *Investing in Mortgage Securities*. St. Lucie Press, 2003.
[64] Taggart, R. A. *Quantitative Analysis for Investment Management*. Englewood Cliffs: Prentice Hall, 2002.
[65] Veronesi, P. *Fixed Income Securities*. New Delhi: Wiley India, 2012.
[66] Windas, T., and Miller, T. *Introduction to Option Adjusted Spread Analysis*. Chennai: Viva Books, 2009.

Index

https://doi.org/10.1515/9781547400669-017

www.ingramcontent.com/pod-product-compliance
Lightning Source LLC
LaVergne TN
LVHW060017210926
848481LV00013B/3729
9781547416738